JOINT AVIATION AUTHORITIES

Theoretical Training Manuals

Revised Edition

AIRCRAFT GENERAL KNOWLEDGE 4

INSTRUMENTATION

This learning material has been approved as JAA compliant by the United Kingdom Civil Aviation Authority

CIVIL AVIATION AUTHORITY

OXFORD
Aviation Training
Succeed through our experience™

This text book has been written and published as a reference work to assist students enrolled on an approved JAA Air Transport Pilot Licence (ATPL) course to prepare themselves for the JAA ATPL theoretical knowledge examinations. Nothing in the content of this book is to be interpreted as constituting instruction or advice relating to practical flying.

Whilst every effort has been made to ensure the accuracy of the information contained within this book, neither Oxford Aviation Services Limited nor the publisher gives any warranty as to its accuracy or otherwise. Students preparing for the JAA ATPL theoretical knowledge examinations should not regard this book as a substitute for the JAA ATPL theoretical knowledge training syllabus published in the current edition of 'JAR-FCL 1 Flight Crew Licensing (Aeroplanes)' (the Syllabus). The Syllabus constitutes the sole authoritative definition of the subject matter to be studied in a JAA ATPL theoretical knowledge training programme. No student should prepare for, or is currently entitled to enter himself/herself for the JAA ATPL theoretical knowledge examinations without first being enrolled in a training school which has been granted approval by a JAA-authorised national aviation authority to deliver JAA ATPL training.

Oxford Aviation Services Limited excludes all liability for any loss or damage incurred or suffered as a result of any reliance on all or part of this book except for any liability for death or personal injury resulting from Oxford Aviation Services Limited's negligence or any other liability which may not legally be excluded.

Cover photo by Chris Sheldon e-mail: fwog@mindless.com

First published by Jeppesen GmbH, Frankfurt, Germany: 2001
Second edition: Jeppesen GmbH, Frankfurt, Germany: 2002
This edition published by Transair (UK) Ltd, Shoreham, England: 2005
Printed in Singapore by KHL Printing Co. Pte Ltd

Contact Details:

Ground Training Department
Oxford Aviation Services Ltd
Oxford Airport
Kidlington
Oxford OX5 1RA
England

Tel: +44 (0)1865 844299
E-mail: ddd@oxfordaviation.net

Transair Pilot Shop
Transair (UK) Limited
Shoreham Airport
Shoreham-by-Sea
West Sussex BN43 5PA
England

Tel: +44 (0)1273 466000
E-mail: info@transair.co.uk

For further information on products and services from Oxford Aviation Training and Transair visit our websites at: www.oxfordaviation.net and www.transair.co.uk

FOREWORD

Joint Aviation Authorities (JAA) pilot licences were first introduced in 1999, and have now been adopted by nearly all member states. A steadily increasing number of non-European countries have also expressed the intention of aligning their training with JAA requirements, and some have already begun this process. The syllabi and the regulations governing the award and the renewal of licences are currently defined by the JAA's licensing agency, known as "Joint Aviation Requirements-Flight Crew Licensing", or JAR-FCL. Over the next few years, JAA responsibilities, including licensing, will gradually be transferred to the new European Aviation Safety Agency (EASA).

The JAR-FCL ATPL theoretical training requirements and associated ground examinations, although possibly similar in scope to those previously used by many national authorities, are inevitably different in a number of respects from the syllabi and examinations previously used under national schemes. Consequently, students who wish to train for the JAA ATPL licence need access to study material which has been specifically designed to meet the requirements of the new licensing system. This series of text books, prepared by Oxford Aviation Training (OAT) and published exclusively by Transair Pilot Shop, covers all JAR-FCL requirements and is specifically designed to help student pilots prepare for the ATPL theoretical knowledge examinations.

OAT is one of the world's leading professional pilot schools. Established for 40 years, Oxford has trained more than 14,000 professional pilots for over 80 airlines, world-wide. OAT was the first pilot school in the United Kingdom to be granted approval to train for the JAA ATPL and has been the leading contributor within Europe to the process of defining and improving the training syllabus. OAT led and coordinated the joint-European effort to produce the ATPL Learning Objectives which are now published by the JAA as the definitive guide to the theoretical knowledge requirements of ATPL training.

Since JAA ATPL training started in 1999, OAT has achieved an unsurpassed success rate in the JAA ATPL examinations. At the start of this year, OAT students had successfully passed more than 25,000 individual JAR-FCL examinations and currently more than 300 students a year graduate from Oxford's theoretical training programmes. The text books, together with an increasing range of Computer Based Training (CBT) products, are also now used by other Flight Training Organizations both in Europe and increasingly, throughout the world. Recognized by leading National Aviation Authorities as being fully compliant with JAR-FCL training requirements, the series has now effectively become the de-facto standard for JAR-FCL ATPL theoretical training. This achievement is the result of OAT's continued commitment to the development of the JAA licensing system. OAT's unrivalled experience and expertise make these books the best learning material available to any student who aspires to hold a JAA ATPL. The series is continually updated, with this year's edition incorporating specimen examination papers and "feedback" information, all specifically intended to help candidates prepare fully for their ATPL theoretical examinations

For those aspirant airline pilots who are not yet able to begin training but hope to do so in the future, these text books provide high-quality study material to help them prepare thoroughly for their formal training. The books also make excellent reading for general aviation pilots or for aviation enthusiasts who simply wish to further their knowledge of aeronautical subjects. We trust that your study of these books will not only be enjoyable but, for those of you currently undergoing ATPL training, will also lead to success in the JAA ATPL ground examinations.

Whatever your aviation ambitions, we wish you every success and above all, happy landings.

Mike Langley
Commercial Director

Oxford Aviation Training
March 2005

Textbook Series

Book	Title	JAR Ref. No.	Subject
1	010 Air Law	010	
2	020 Aircraft General Knowledge 1	021 01	Airframes & Systems
		021 01 01/04	Fuselage, Wings & Stabilising Surfaces
		021 01 07	Hydraulics
		021 01 05	Landing Gear
		021 01 06	Flight Controls
		021 01 08/09	Air Systems & Air Conditioning
		021 01 09/10	Anti-icing & De-icing
		021 04 00	Emergency Equipment
		021 01 11	Fuel Systems
3	020 Aircraft General Knowledge 2	021 02	Electrics – Electronics
		021 02 01	Direct Current
		021 02 02	Alternating Current
		021 02 05	Basic Radio Propagation.
4	020 Aircraft General Knowledge 3	021 00	Powerplant
		021 03 01	Piston Engines
		021 03 02	Gas Turbines
5	020 Aircraft General Knowledge 4	022	Instrumentation
		022 01	Flight Instruments
		022 03	Warning & Recording
		022 02	Automatic Flight Control
		022 04	Power Plant & System Monitoring Instruments
6	030 Flight Performance & Planning 1	031	Mass & Balance
		032	Performance
7	030 Flight Performance & Planning 2	033	Flight Planning & Monitoring
8	040 Human Performance & Limitations	040	
9	050 Meteorology	050	
10	060 Navigation 1	061	General Navigation
11	060 Navigation 2	062	Radio Navigation
12	070 Operational Procedures	070	
13	080 Principles of Flight	080	
14	090 Communications	091	VFR Communications
		092	IFR Communications
15	Reference Material		CAP 696, CAP 697, CAP 698
			Aerodrome Information
			JAR FCL 1 Subpart J

INSTRUMENTATION

TABLE OF CONTENTS

Subject Number	Title
1	**FLIGHT INSTRUMENTS**

Chapter 1	Aircraft Instrument Displays
Chapter 2	Pressure Heads
Chapter 3	Air Temperature Measurement
Chapter 4	The Airspeed Indicator
Chapter 5	The Pressure Altimeter
Chapter 6	The Vertical Speed Indicator
Chapter 7	The Machmeter
Chapter 8	Magnetism
Chapter 9	The Direct Indicating Compass
Chapter 10	Gyroscopes
Chapter 11	Directional Gyro Indicator
Chapter 12	The Artificial Horizon & Vertical Gyro Unit
Chapter 13	The Turn and Slip Indicator
Chapter 14	Turn Co-ordinator
Chapter 15	Aircraft Magnetism
Chapter 16	Remote Indicating Compass - The Slaved Gyro Compass
Chapter 17	Inertial Navigation System
Chapter 18	Inertial Reference System
Chapter 19	Air Data Computer
Chapter 20	The Radio Altimeter
Chapter 21	Flight Management System (FMS)
Chapter 22	The Electronic Flight Instrument System (EFIS)
Chapter 23	Objective Revision Questions

Subject Number	Title
2	**AUTOMATIC FLIGHT CONTROL SYSTEMS**

Chapter 1	Flight Director Systems (FDS)
Chapter 2	Auto Pilot and Auto Land Systems
Chapter 3	Autoland
Chapter 4	Autothrottle
Chapter 5	Yaw Dampers
Chapter 6	Fly by Wire
Chapter 7	Question Papers

3 **WARNING AND RECORDING**

Chapter 1   Flight Warning System
Chapter 2   Aerodynamic Warnings
Chapter 3   Ground Proximity Warning System (GPWS)
Chapter 4   Collision Avoidance System
Chapter 5   Flight Data Recorder
Chapter 6   Cockpit Voice Recorder
Chapter 7   Question Papers

4 **POWER PLANT & SYSTEMS MONITORING INSTRUMENTS**

Chapter 1   Engine Instrumentation
Chapter 2   Electronic Instrumentation

5 **SPECIMEN QUESTIONS**

PRACTICE EXAMINATION PAPER

JAAatpl
JOINT AVIATION AUTHORITIES

Revised Edition

AIRCRAFT GENERAL KNOWLEDGE 4

INSTRUMENTATION
FLIGHT INSTRUMENTS

CIVIL AVIATION AUTHORITY

OXFORD
Aviation Training
Succeed through our experience™

CHAPTER ONE - AIRCRAFT INSTRUMENT DISPLAYS

Contents

		Page
1.1	INTRODUCTION	1 - 1
1.2	THE INSTRUMENT LAYOUT	1 - 1
1.3	THE THREE DIFFERENT TYPES OF DISPLAY	1 - 2
1.4	QUANTITATIVE DISPLAYS	1 - 3
1.5	STRAIGHT SCALE DISPLAYS	1 - 5
1.6	QUALITATIVE DISPLAYS	1- 5
1.7	DIRECTOR DISPLAYS	1 - 6

1.1   INTRODUCTION.

Since the early days of flying there has been an ever increasing requirement for information about the progress of the flight to be available to the pilot.

Once the aeroplane became capable of moving out of the field from which the collection of bits of wood, metal and fabric had staggered into the air, it became necessary to know the state of the internal combustion engine driving the propellers, the direction in which the aeroplane was pointing, and the speed at which it was travelling.

Instruments giving information about the state of the engine had been in use for some time on motor cars and trucks and, of course, magnetic compasses had been used on ships for an even longer time.

An instrument to indicate the speed of the aircraft through the air presented a new problem, but within a few years of the first successful manned flight, quite sophisticated instruments had been produced.

1.2   THE INSTRUMENT LAYOUT.

The rapid advances in aeronautics meant that aeroplanes were now capable of flying for hours instead of minutes and flying for miles instead of yards. Inevitably this meant that aeroplanes might find themselves in cloud, without a visible horizon, and this posed more problems.

The cockpit was being filled with more and more dials and indicators and it was necessary to create some order out of chaos, to decide which instruments should have prominence and to achieve some standardisation.

The 'flying' instruments which covered the handling of the aircraft were arranged in the layout of the **'basic six'**. Other instruments tended to be scattered around the cockpit in positions most convenient to the designer and manufacturer, seldom to suit the needs of the pilot.

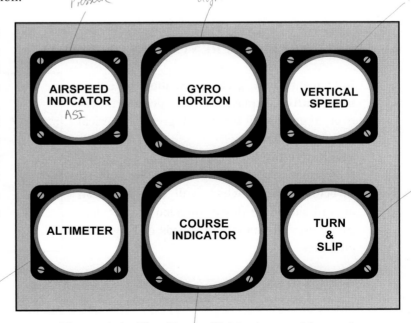

Figure 1.1. The 'Basic Six' Instrument Layout.

© Oxford Aviation Services Limited

Since the introduction of the 'basic six' developments in aircraft instruments and operations led to the introduction of the **'basic T'**. These layouts are shown in Figures 1.1 and 1.2.

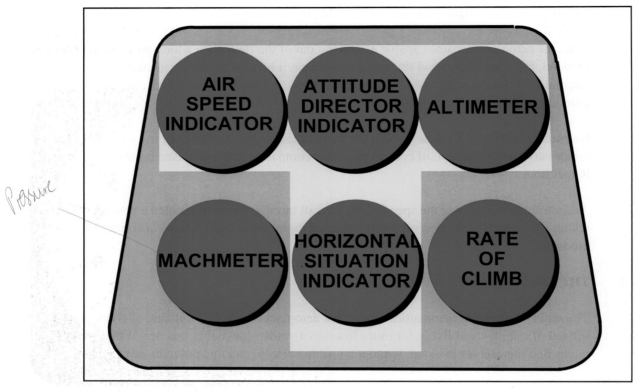

Pressure

Figure 1.2 The 'Basic T' Instrument Layout.

1.3   THE THREE DIFFERENT TYPES OF DISPLAY.

Instruments may give information in either: **quantitative** display, where a pointer moves over a graduated scale and gives numerical values of parameters; **qualitative** display, in the form of a pictorial representation of the change of these parameters; **director** display, which will show how an aircraft should be flown (directed), rather than supplying information on speeds or heights or pressures.

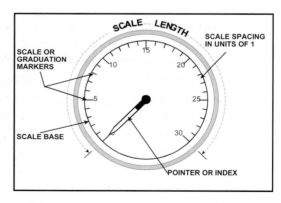

Figure 1.3 A Circular (Linear) Scale.

1.4   QUANTITATIVE DISPLAYS.

Circular Scale (Linear).

A simple indicator showing the change of value of the parameter to be measured over a range of 0 to 30 units is shown in Figure 1.3. The accuracy with which these values need to be measured will govern the spacing of the graduation.

Circular Scale (Non-Linear).

Some instruments are required to show changes of parameters more accurately at certain parts of the scale. The example in Figure 1.4 shows a rate of climb indicator where low rates of climb are more easily read than high rates. This is a **logarithmic** scale.

Figure 1.4. Circular (Non-Linear) Scales.

High Range Long Scale Displays.

Where the instrument needs to show changes over a high range of values and these changes need to be read with a fair degree of accuracy, 360° of movement of the pointer may not be sufficient. The pointer may make more than one revolution to cover the required range, as on the **air speed indicator** shown in Figure 1.5., though this type of display may lead to some confusion.

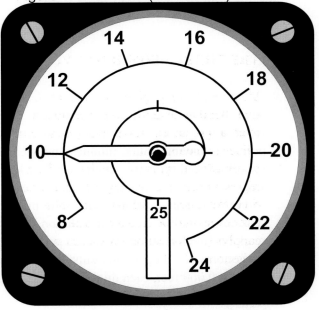

Figure 1.5. A Single Pointer Air Speed Indicator.

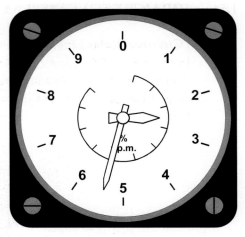

Figure 1.6. A Revolution Counter.

A less confusing display uses two concentric pointers moving over two separate scales, as shown on the revolution counter in Figure 1.6.

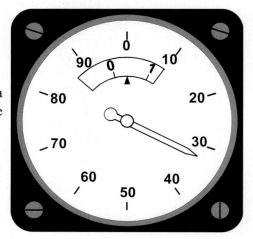

Figure 1.7. An Air Speed Indicator.

Another solution is to have a pointer moving over a fixed scale (e.g. tens of knots) with a moving scale indicating larger units (hundreds of knots).

A further solution, shown in Figure 1.8, is to display information in a similar fashion to a clock, with pointers showing hours, minutes and seconds. This system is used on many altimeters. The long pointer will cover 1000 feet in one revolution, so each division of the scale represents 100 feet. The middle pointer will cover 10,000 feet per revolution, each division marking 1000 feet and the smallest pointer (sometimes in the form of a 'bug' on the outside of the scale) will cover 100,000 feet, each division representing 10,000 feet.

Figure 1.8. A Three Pointer Altimeter.

1.5   STRAIGHT SCALE DISPLAYS.

Until recently most instruments displayed information on a circular scale, but with the introduction of Electronic Flight Information Systems (EFIS) increasing use of **straight scale** displays has been made. In the example below, airspeed, altitude and vertical speed are shown on an Electronic Attitude Director Indicator (EADI) otherwise known as Primary Flight Display (PFD).

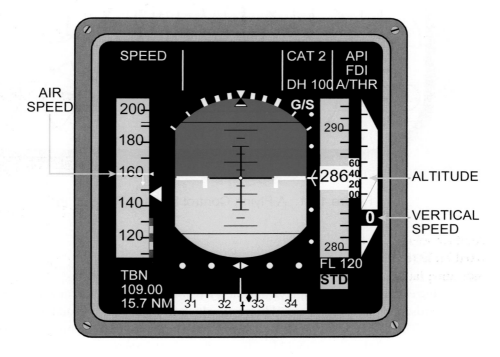

Figure 1.9. An Electronic Attitude Director Indicator (EADI).

1.6   QUALITATIVE DISPLAYS

Qualitative displays are used to show, for instance, relative speeds of engines or the position of flying control surfaces as shown in Figures 1.10 and 1.11.

Figure 1.10. Engine Relative Speed Indicator.

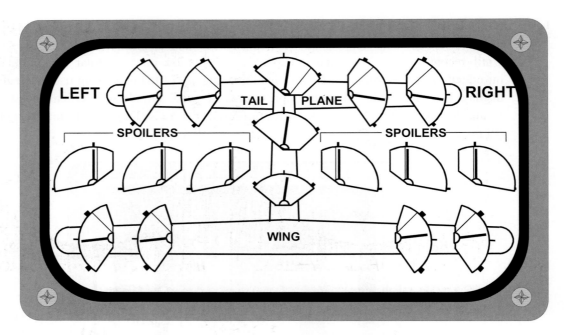

Figure 1.11. A Flying Control Surface Position Indicator.

1.7 DIRECTOR DISPLAYS.

One of the earliest director displays was the gyro horizon. In this instrument the natural rigidity of the gyroscope defines the natural horizon, which to an aircraft in cloud, or on a dark night, is invisible. The displays in Figure 1.12. show, in diagram (a) that the horizon is below the nose of the aircraft and the nose should be 'directed' down to resume level flight. In display (b), the nose is on the horizon, but the aircraft is flying left wing below the horizon and the left wing should be brought up to resume level flight.

A more recent instrument, the Director Horizon, combines the artificial horizon with radio and navigation information or a Flight Management System (FMS) to indicate **Commands**. The situations shown by the artificial horizons above are now shown as commands, the object being to fly the aircraft (the flat diamond) to align with the **Command Bars**.

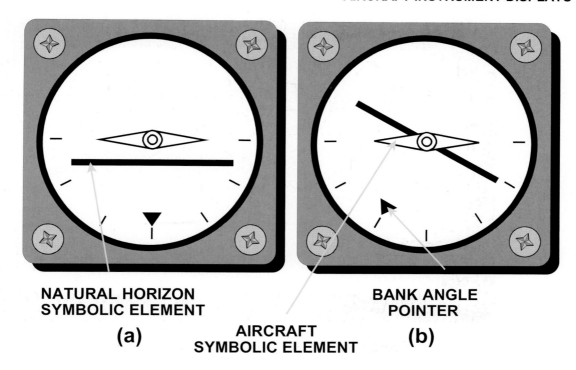

NATURAL HORIZON
SYMBOLIC ELEMENT   BANK ANGLE
                                                         POINTER
        (a)   AIRCRAFT   **(b)**
                    SYMBOLIC ELEMENT

Figure 1.12. The Gyro Horizon.

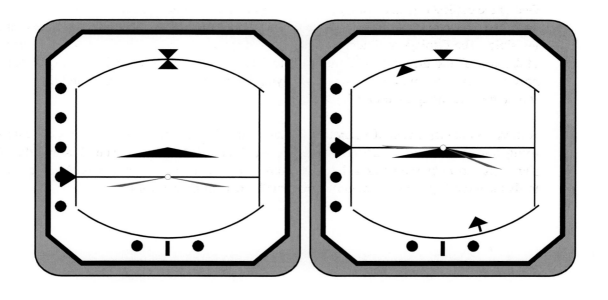

(a) FLY DOWN   **(b) BANK RIGHT**

Figure 1.13. The Director Horizon.

CHAPTER TWO - PRESSURE HEADS

Contents

Page

2.1   INTRODUCTION. . . . . 2 - 1

2.2   PITOT/STATIC HEADS. . . . . 2 - 1

2.3   POSITION ERROR . . . . 2 - 2

2.4   MANOEUVRE-INDUCED ERROR . . . . 2 - 3

2.5   EMERGENCY STATIC SOURCE. . . . . 2 - 4

2.6   ADVANTAGES OF THE STATIC VENT. . . . . 2 - 5

2.7   PRE FLIGHT CHECKS OF THE PITOT/STATIC SYSTEM. . . . . 2 - 5

PRESSURE HEADS QUESTIONS . . . . 2 - 7

CRP-5 (see 5-20)

- Indicated = Inner
- True = Outer

- If TAS = CAS (ie at Sea Level) & Air Temp = 15°C @ 0ft

- Density Error corrections = ASI window
- Temp Error corrections = ALT window

Density/Speed Problems & MN:
- Find TAS from CAS with given altitude & temp deviation. If TAS is >er than 300kts we have to correct for compressibility error.
To find MN, go to Mach indicator on Airspeed window & point to temp. read off Mn against TAS.

- Find Altitude with given TAS & Mach No & temp dev".
  ⇒ Line up MN & TAS & read off temp(SAT) against MN index ↑.
  If we are given the dev" from ISA we can work out what the height is by calculating altitude from +15°C @ 0ft and dividing temp by 2.

- Find LSS from given temperature. → line up Mn ↑ with temp.
Read off LSS @ Mach 1.
- LSS @ MSL is 661 kts

Temperature / Altitude problem
- Find true altitude from given indicated Alt & temperature.
  → Using altitude window line up Alt & Actual temp in 'Alt' window.
  - Read off 'True' altitude on outer scale against Indicated Altitude on 'Inner' scale

✱ Low temp = Alt overread, decrease is low.

✱ JAA Q - A/C at 3,000ft QNH over airfield elevation 2000ft and SAT = -20°C How high above airfield are we

2.1   INTRODUCTION.

An aircraft at rest on the ground in still air is subject to normal atmospheric pressure, which bears equally on all parts of the aircraft. This ambient pressure is known as **Static** pressure. An aircraft in flight, while still subject to the static pressure at its flight level, experiences an additional pressure on the leading edges due to the resistance of the air to the aircraft's movement.

This additional pressure is **Dynamic** pressure, and its value depends on the speed of the aircraft through the air and on the density of the air. The leading edges, therefore, encounter a total pressure consisting of static plus dynamic pressures. This total pressure is also known as **Pitot** pressure.   *or total*

Two of the pressure-dependent flight instruments, the altimeter and vertical speed indicator, operate solely on static pressure, whereas the airspeed indicator and machmeter utilise both static and pitot pressures.

Inside an aircraft, pressure and temperature are seldom the same as outside the aircraft so pitot and static pressures must be sensed by devices mounted on the outside of the aircraft.

2.2   PITOT/STATIC HEADS.

An open-ended tube parallel to the longitudinal axis of the aircraft is used to sense the total pressure (static plus dynamic). This device is a 'pitot tube' mounted in a 'pitot head'.

The open end of the tube faces into the moving airstream, the other end leading to the airspeed capsules in the ASI and **machmeter.**

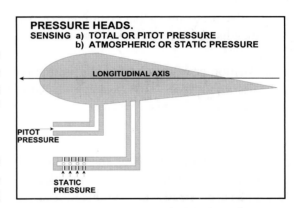

Figure 2.1. Pitot and Static Heads.

The moving airstream is thus brought to rest in the tube, so generating the extra (dynamic) pressure which together with the static pressure already in the tube provides the required total (pitot) pressure.

A 'static head' consists of a tube with its forward end sealed but with holes or slots cut in the sides. These slots do not face into the airflow and therefore they sense only the static pressure. This pressure supplies the static 'line' to the pressure instruments. A pressure sensing system consisting of separate pitot and static heads is shown in Figure 2.1.

The static and pitot sources may be combined in one 'pressure head', the static tube surrounding the pitot tube, with separate pressure lines leading to the pressure instruments. An electric anti-icing heater coil is usually incorporated. Figure 2.2 illustrates an example of this type. Any errors due to the heating effect may be reduced by design, and calibration.

© Oxford Aviation Services Limited

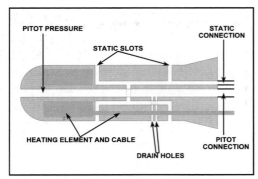

Figure 2.2. A Combined Pitot/Static
Pressure Head.

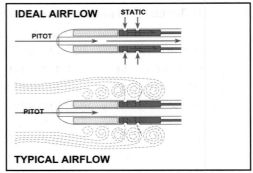

Figure 2.3. How Turbulence Affects
the Value of Static Pressure

2.3   POSITION ERROR

It will be appreciated that if, due to turbulent airflow in the region of the pitot/static heads, the pressures sensed are not truly representative of the pitot and static pressures, the pressure-dependent instruments will not read correctly. The error involved is called **Position Error** (or alternatively 'pressure' error). At large angles of attack the pressure head is inclined at an angle to the airstream so that position error is usually biggest at the lower airspeeds. Flight manuals may list different values of position error for different flap settings.

Position error depends mainly on the positioning of the pressure head, the airspeed, and the aircraft attitude. Turbulence produced in the airstream by the pressure head itself affects the value of static pressure sensed rather than the pitot pressure. This is shown diagrammatically in Figure 2.3.

Approximately 95% of the position error associated with a combined pressure head is produced by turbulence about the static head.

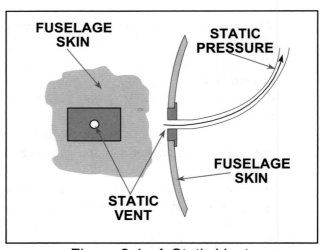

Because of this, the **Static Vent**, was introduced as a source of static pressure instead of the static head, pitot pressure then being sensed by a simple pitot head. About 90% of the combined pressure head position error is eliminated by use of a separate pitot head and static vent as shown in Figure 2.4.

Figure 2.4. A Static Vent.

There is usually some place on the airframe, usually on the side of the fuselage, where true (or nearly true) static pressure obtains over the whole speed range of the aircraft.

2 - 2

A flat metal plate is fitted at this position, the static line from the pressure instruments terminating at a small circular hole - the static vent - in this plate. A similar vent may be positioned on the opposite side of the fuselage and the two interconnected for transmission of static pressure to the instruments so that errors produced by yawing are largely eliminated.

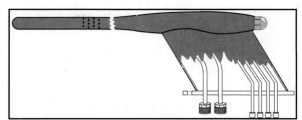

Figure 2.5. A High Speed Pitot Static Probe.

The shock waves associated with flight at high mach numbers can produce significant errors in pressure sensed by a static vent. Modern high speed aircraft may accordingly be fitted with a more sophisticated combined pitot/static pressure head in order to keep position error within acceptable limits. The choice of location for a probe, or vent, is dependant upon the aerodynamics of the aircraft. Typical locations are: ahead of a wing tip, under a wing, ahead of the vertical stabiliser tip, at the side of the fuselage nose section, and ahead of the fuselage nose section.

2.4   MANOEUVRE-INDUCED ERROR

Manoeuvre-induced errors are caused by short-term fluctuations of pressure at the static vents and delays in the associated pipelines transmitting pressure changes to the instruments.

Even servo-altimeters and Air Data Computer systems suffer from this type of error as they utilise the same static vents as the simple pressure instruments. Change in angle of attack, and turbulence due to lowering (or raising) flaps and landing gear are the prime causes of the error-producing changes in airflow over the static vents.

Most commonly, manoeuvre-induced error appears as a marked lag in pressure instrument indications.

The errors are usually more significant during changes of pitch attitude than during yawing or rolling movements so that the worst effects are at the start of the climb or descent and on levelling out.

Overshooting and flight in rough air are particularly vulnerable.

The errors are unpredictable both in size and in sense so that pressure instruments cannot be relied upon to indicate accurate instantaneous values or accurate rates of change.

This particularly applies to vertical speed indicators. In-flight manoeuvres should therefore be carried out using gyroscopic instruments as the primary reference. A manoeuvre-induced error may be present for some time after movement of the control surfaces has ceased, values of three seconds at low altitude increasing to 10 seconds at 30,000 feet (longer for VSIs) being quite common.

2.5   EMERGENCY STATIC SOURCE.

An emergency static source is normally provided in the event of the static head/vents becoming blocked.

The emergency static source may be to the outside of the aircraft or from inside the cabin(in unpressurised aircraft only).

On those aircraft which sense emergency static pressure from outside the hull of the aircraft, the source will be **less accurate** than the primary (blocked) static vent/head, since that would have been in the optimum position. ✳

When an emergency static source is fed from within the cabin, the static pressure sensed is likely to be **lower** than ambient due to aerodynamic suction.

Note: When alternate (standby) pressure systems are used, correction values for the instruments concerned may be found in the Operating Data Manual for the aircraft.

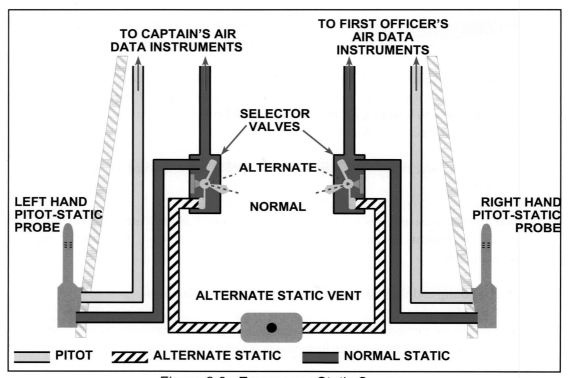

Figure 2.6. Emergency Static Source.

2.6   ADVANTAGES OF THE STATIC VENT.

a)   The airflow in the region of the vents is less turbulent and the static pressure measured is more accurate.

b)   Errors produced when side slipping or yawing are reduced.

c)   Duplication of vents either side of fuselage reduces blockage errors.

2.7   PRE FLIGHT CHECKS OF THE PITOT/STATIC SYSTEM.

a)   All covers and plugs removed and stowed.

b)   All tubes, holes, slots free of obstructions.

c)   Pitot head heater operating.

* In the event of use of alternate static source
a lower static pressure will enter the system
causing Pressure Instruments to 'over read'

* If there's no alternate static source :-
   break glass to VSI so it is open to static pressure

PRESSURE HEADS

1.   A pitot head is used to measure:

        a)   dynamic minus static pressure.
        b)   static plus dynamic pressure.
        c)   static pressure.
        d)   dynamic pressure.

2.   A static vent is used to measure:

        a)   dynamic pressure minus pitot excess.
        b)   dynamic pressure plus pitot excess.
        c)   atmospheric pressure.
        d)   pitot excess pressure.

3.   A pressure head is subject to the following errors: To revise

        a)   position, manoeuvre induced, temperature.
        b)   position, manoeuvre induced.
        c)   position, manoeuvre induced, density.
        d)   position, manoeuvre induced, instrument.

4.   Turbulent flow around a pressure head will cause:

        a)   density error.
        b)   95% increase in manoeuvre induced error.
        c)   an increase in the dynamic pressure.
        d)   95% of pressure error.

5.   Manoeuvre induced error:

        a)   is caused by transient pressure changes at static vents.
        b)   is likely to be greatest when yawing after engine failure.
        c)   is combined with instrument and position error on a correction card.
        d)   lasts for only a short time at high altitude.

6.   Position error:

        a)   may be reduced by the fitting of static vents.
        b)   will usually decrease with an increase in altitude.
        c)   will depend solely on the attitude of the aircraft.
        d)   will usually decrease as the aircraft approaches the speed of sound.

7.   Pressure heads supply data to the following instruments:

      a)   air data computers, compasses, altimeters, and ASI's.
      b)   standby instruments only, when air data computers fitted.
      c)   altimeters, ASI's, VSI's, machmeters, air data computers.
      d)   all the above plus air driven gyros.

8.   Static vents are usually fitted to both sides of the aircraft fuselage. This will:

      a)   reduce the position error.
      b)   balance out errors caused by side slipping or yawing.
      c)   require a calibration card for each static vent.
      d)   enable a greater number of instruments to be fitted.

9.   Which of the following instruments require inputs of both pitot and static pressure:

      a)   airspeed indicator, machmeter and vertical speed indicator.
      b)   airspeed indicator, vertical speed indicator, altimeter.
      c)   airspeed indicator only.
      d)   airspeed indicator and machmeter.

10.   Where an alternate static source is fitted, use of this source usually leads to:

      a)   a temporary increase in lag error.
      b)   a lower pressure error than with normal sources.
      c)   an increase in position error.
      d)   no change in position error.

CHAPTER THREE - AIR TEMPERATURE MANAGEMENT

Contents

Page

3.1 INTRODUCTION. . . . . 3 - 1

3.2 THE EFFECT OF COMPRESSIBILITY. . . . . 3 - 1

3.3 AIR TEMPERATURE THERMOMETERS. . . . . 3 - 2

3.4 TOTAL AIR TEMPERATURE PROBE . . . . 3 - 3

3.5 ERRORS. . . . . 3 - 4

3.6 BOEING 737 TEMPERATURE CORRECTIONS. . . . . 3 - 7

AIR TEMPERATURE MEASUREMENT QUESTIONS . . . . 3 - 9

3.1   INTRODUCTION.

The measurement of air temperature is of importance to a pilot, not just to establish the likelihood of engine or airframe icing, but also in connection with many other aspects of aircraft performance. Increasing air traffic, higher operating costs, and greater performance demands have made precision air data measurements necessary for safety, economy and maximum performance. Thus, accurate and reliable air temperature measurement is essential to the safe, efficient operation of aircraft.

3.2   THE EFFECT OF COMPRESSIBILITY.

The measurement of air temperature outside the aircraft appears a simple task, a thermometer which protrudes into the air stream should apparently be sufficient to do the job. However this is not the case, because as aircraft speed increases, the air close up to the aircraft becomes compressed, and because of this compression that air is heated. This means that the temperature sensed will too warm and not representative of the actual air temperature.

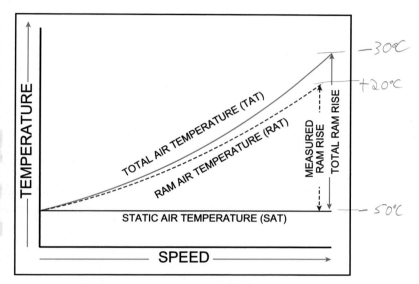

Figure 3.1. Temperature Relationships in Level Flight.

Static Air Temperature (SAT) is the temperature of the undisturbed air through which the aircraft is about to fly.

Total Air Temperature (TAT) is the maximum temperature attainable by the air when brought to rest, adiabatically.

The increase of air temperature at higher speeds as a result of compression and the effects of friction is known as the **'ram rise'**.

The percentage of the 'ram rise' (RAT) sensed and recovered by a TAT probe is termed the Recovery Factor (k).

Thus a TAT probe having a factor of 0.90 would measure SAT plus 90% of the ram rise. A recovery factor of 1.0 would produce a reading of SAT plus 100% ram rise = TAT.
Modern air temperature probes have recovery factors approaching 1.0.

3.3   AIR TEMPERATURE THERMOMETERS.

Air Temperature Thermometers may be divided into two basic types:

a)   **Direct Reading**. A commonly used direct reading thermometer used in low speed aircraft uses a bimetallic strip consisting of two metals, such as Invar and Brass, bonded together as shown in Figure 3.2.a)

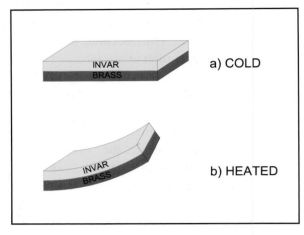

When this strip is heated, the brass, having a higher coefficient of expansion than the Invar, will expand much more than the Invar with the result that the strip will curl as shown in Figure 3.2. b).

Figure 3.2. A Bi-Metallic Strip.

How much the strip curls depends on the temperature rise to which the strip is subjected, and is therefore a measure of the temperature.

The principle of the bimetallic strip is used to provide a direct indication of temperature, and a thermometer using this principle is shown in Figure 3.3.

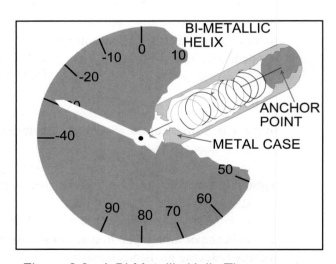

The thermometer is mounted on the windscreen or fuselage with the tube protruding into the air stream and the dial is made visible to the pilot.

Figure 3.3. A Bi-Metallic Helix Thermometer.

b)   **Remote Reading**. The probe element forms one part of a resistance bridge circuit. As the temperature changes the resistance of this element changes, and the bridge is unbalanced causing current to flow through the moving coil of the indicator.

3.4   TOTAL AIR TEMPERATURE PROBE

The layout of a TAT probe in very common use is shown in Figure 3.4.

The probe is in the form of a small strut and air intake made of nickel-plated beryllium copper which provides good thermal conductivity and strength. It is secured at a pre-determined location in the front fuselage section of an aircraft outside of any boundary layer.

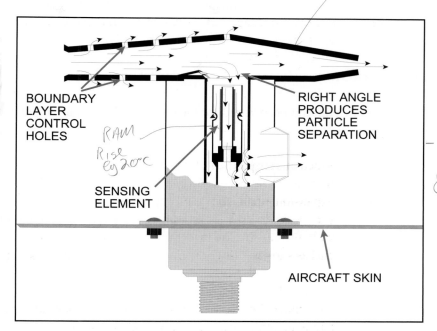

"ROSEMOUNT PROBE"

BOUNDARY LAYER CONTROL HOLES

RAM Rise eg 20°C

RIGHT ANGLE PRODUCES PARTICLE SEPARATION

Recovery (k) factor of 1

SENSING ELEMENT

AIRCRAFT SKIN

Figure 3.4. A Total Air Temperature Probe.

In flight, the air flows through the probe in the manner indicated; separation of any water particles from the air is effected by the airflow being caused to turn through a right angle before passing round the sensing element.

The bleed holes in the intake casing permit boundary layer air to be drawn off under the influence of the higher pressure that is created within the intake and casing of the probe.

A pure platinum wire resistance-type sensing element is used. The probe has an almost negligible time-lag, and a high recovery factor of approximately 1.00.

A heating element is mounted integral with the probe to prevent the formation of ice, and is of the self-compensating type in that as the temperature rises so does the element resistance rise, thereby reducing the heater current.

The heater dissipates a nominal 260 Watts under in-flight icing conditions, and can have an effect on indicated air temperature readings. The errors involved, however, are small, some typical values obtained experimentally being 0.9°C at 0.1 Mach, decreasing to 0.15° at Mach 1.0.

※ Cannot have Recovery (k) factor > 1.

In order to measure air temperature on the ground an air to air ejector (aspirator) may be fitted to the probe. Engine bleed air creates a negative differential pressure within the casing so that outside air is drawn through it at a rate sufficient to provide a reliable indication of temperature. This device is used with turbine engine take off setting and auto throttle systems; it eliminates temperature soaking inaccuracies caused by bright sunshine heating the probe, or hot ramp heat radiation.

3.5   ERRORS.

Aircraft thermometers used for the measurement of air temperature are subject to the following errors:

a)   Instrument errors   -   imperfections in manufacture.

b)   Environmental error   -   solar heating of the sensor.
                            -    Ice accretion on the probe.

c)   Heating error   -   adiabatic and kinetic (friction) heating

The relationship between heating error, SAT and TAT is shown:-

$$SAT = TAT - k\left(\frac{V}{100}\right)^2 \quad \text{OR} \quad SAT = TAT - RAM\ RISE$$

Where:
              V is the true airspeed in knots

              SAT is the Static Air Temperature

              TAT is the Total Air Temperature

              TAT = SAT + Ram Rise

Note: Calculations of RAM Rise can be achieved on the CRP5 series of computers using the Blue Segment on the reverse with regard to TAS in knots.

Errors due to adiabatic or frictional heating can be calculated and allowed for by use of the following correction formula.

$$SAT^{(°K)} = \frac{TAT^{(°K)}}{1 + 0.2kM^2}$$

✱ Temp are in °Kelvin

where: SAT   = Correct outside air temperature
            TAT   = Indicated outside air temperature
            M   = Mach number
            k   = Recovery factor of the temperature bulb

Temperatures are in A. 'k' is determined by flight testing, and its value is to be found in the operating instructions for the aircraft.

$Mn = 0.8$

$TAT = -35°C$ $238°K$

$K = 1$

$$\frac{238}{1 + 0.2 \; 0.8^2} = \underline{\underline{-62°C}}$$

✱ Computer: ✱

Blue scale on CRP-5 shows RAM rise for
a given TAS

Temperature Rise Scale - CRP5 Navigation Computer.

Except at very low speeds Indicated Outside Air Temperature(IOAT) is always warmer than Corrected Outside Air Temperature(COAT) and this is due to a combination of kinetic and adiabatic heating. The heating that creates this difference is a function of speed and the "Temp Rise" scale(in blue) of the CRP5 gives the amount of "over-indication" of temperature at different True Air Speeds.

If COAT is not available but IOAT is, it is possible to find the correct value of TAS and Temperature but in two stages.

Firstly an approximate Ram Rise value may be found using IOAT to assess TAS, this is then subtracted from the original IOAT to obtain COAT and then used to find a more accurate TAS.

Method:

1.   Compute TAS from CAS using IOAT and altitude to give an approximate TAS value.
2.   On the "Temp Rise" scale use the approximate TAS value to determine the value of temperature rise.
3.   Subtract the temperature rise from IOAT to find COAT.
4.   Recompute TAS using COAT and altitude.

Calculation:

IOAT -30C   Altitude 25,000ft   CAS 200kts

1.   Airspeed window (-30 / 25,000ft) gives <u>Outer Scale approx' TAS 297</u>
                                                  Inner Scale CAS 200
2.   Temp Rise scale gives rise of 9°C for TAS 297kts.
3.   Subtract 9°C from IOAT to find COAT .... -30 - 9 = -39°C
4.   Recompute TAS using new COAT and original CAS / Alt = TAS 292kts.

Caution - if TAS initially computed is greater than 300kts allowance must also be made for compressibility as indicated below:

IOAT -30C   Altitude 25,000ft   CAS 250kts

1.   Determine approx' TAS as before = 372kts.
2.   Correct for compressibility 372/100 - 3 = 0.72units = revised TAS 369kts.
3.   Use this value to determine Temperature Rise = 14°C.
4.   Apply temperature rise to IOAT to obtain COAT (-30 -14) = -44°C.
5.   Using COAT and altitude calculate updated TAS = 362kts
6.   Correct for compressibility again 362/100 - 3 = 0.62units = final TAS 358kts.

3.6   BOEING 737 TEMPERATURE CORRECTIONS.

Most jet transport aircraft are provided with a table giving corrected TAT and the B737 table follows.

	INDICATED MACH NUMBER										
	.30	.40	.50	.60	.70	.73	.76	.78	.80	.82	.84
TAT - °C	STATIC AIR TEMPERATURE -°C										
70				47	39	37	35	33	31	29	27
65			49	42	35	33	30	28	26	25	23
60		49	44	37	30	28	25	24	22	21	19
55	49	45	40	33	26	24	21	19	18	16	14
50	45	40	35	28	21	19	17	15	13	11	10
45	40	35	30	23	17	15	12	11	9	7	5
40	35	30	25	19	12	10	8	6	4	3	1
35	30	26	20	14	8	6	3	1	0	-2	-3
30	25	21	16	10	3	1	-1	-3	-5	-5	-7
25	20	16	11	5	-2	-3	-6	-7	-9	-11	-12
20	15	11	6	0	-6	-8	-10	-12	-13	-15	-16
15	10	6	2	-5	-11	-13	-15	-16	-18	-19	-21
10	5	1	-3	-9	-15	-17	-19	-21	-22	-24	-25
5	0	-3	-8	-14	-20	-21	-24	-25	-27	-28	-29
0	-5	-8	-13	-18	-24	-26	-28	-30	-31	-33	-34
-5	-10	-13	-18	-23	-29	-31	-33	-34	-35	-37	-38
-10	-15	-18	-22	-28	-33	-35	-37	-39	-40	-41	-43
-15	-20	-23	-27	-32	-38	-39	-42	-43	-44	-46	-47
-20	-24	-27	-32	-37	-42	-44	-46	-47	-49	-50	-51
-25	-29	-32	-36	-42	-47	-49	-51	-52	-53	-55	-56
-30	-34	-37	-41	-46	-51	-53	-55	-57	-58	-59	-60
-35	-39	-42	-46	-51	-56	-58	-60	-61	-62	-63	-65
-40	-44	-47	-51	-56	-61	-62	-64	-65	-66	-68	-69

TAT will always be WARMER than the SAT

- Probe has a heater

- Radiation shield protects sensors from heater

- Aspirated Airflow from engine:
  - prevents thermometer suffering from a hot soak.
  - Instrument is able to measure 'oat' on ramp - on ground

✻ Computer ✻ Correcting for Density Error ~ finding RAS from TAS

- Use 'Airspeed' window
- line up FL & temp.
- Correct for Compressibility error $\left(\dfrac{TAS}{100} - 3\right)$
- Move left in Comp window then read RAS from TAS (on outside)

AIR TEMPERATURE MEASUREMENT

1.   Converted into degrees Celsius - 40°F is:

        a)   -56.5°C
        b)   -4°C
        c)   -20°C
        d)   -108°C

2.   In an aircraft thermometer with an electrical resistance sensor to measure the air temperature, the resistance wire element is probably:

        a)   plutonium
        b)   platinum
        c)   potassium
        d)   beryllium copper

3.   Flying at high speed at high altitude, the difference between ram air temperature and static air temperature is:

        a)   likely to be less than when flying low and slow.
        b)   due to adiabatic cooling.
        c)   due to adiabatic warming.
        d)   proportional to the square of the absolute temperature.

4.   Aircraft air temperature thermometers are shielded to protect them from:

        a)   solar radiation.
        b)   accidental physical damage on the ground or hailstones in flight.
        c)   airframe icing.
        d)   kinetic heating.

5.   At a true airspeed of 500 knots, a ram rise of air temperature can be expected of:

        a)   50 degrees Celsius
        b)   25 degrees Celsius
        c)   5 degrees Celsius
        d)   16 degrees Celsius

$$SAT = \frac{TAT}{1 \times 0.2 k (}$$

$$SAT = TAT - \left(\frac{V}{100}\right)^2$$

$$100 - \left(\frac{500}{100}\right)^2 = 25$$

6.   An air temperature probe may be aspirated in order to:

    a)   prevent icing.
    b)   measure air temperature on the ground.
    c)   compensate for thermal soaking at the ramp position.
    d)   reduce the effect of solar radiation.

7.   Total Air Temperature is:

    a)   the maximum temperature attainable by the air when brought to rest, adiabatically.
    b)   the temperature indicated on the air temperature thermometer plus the ram rise.
    c)   the static air temperature minus the recovery factor.
    d)   the recovery factor plus the ram rise.

8.   The difference between static air temperature and total air temperature is known as:

    a)   corrected outside air temperature.
    b)   the ram rise.
    c)   the recovery factor.
    d)   hot ramp radiation.

9.   A direct reading aircraft thermometer usually consists of a bimetallic helix protruding into the airstream. Movement of the pointer over the temperature scale will depend upon:

    a)   difference in electrical resistance of the two metals.
    b)   increase in pressure as airspeed increases.
    c)   increase in adiabatic cooling as airspeed increases.
    d)   different coefficients of expansion of the two metals.

10.   A remote reading thermometer depends upon .... to indicate changes in temperature:

    a)   change of electrical resistance of the two metals.
    b)   change of electrical resistance with temperature.
    c)   change of electrical resistance with change in pressure.
    d)   change of electrical capacitance with change in temperature.

CHAPTER FOUR - THE AIRSPEED INDICATOR

Contents

		Page
4.1	PRINCIPLE OF OPERATION	4 - 1
4.2	CONSTRUCTION.	4 - 1
4.3	CALIBRATION	4 - 2
4.4	A.S.I. ERRORS	4 - 2
4.5	BLOCKAGES AND LEAKS	4 - 6
4.6	SERVICEABILITY CHECKS	4 - 7
AIRSPEED INDICATORS QUESTIONS		4 - 9

4.1 PRINCIPLE OF OPERATION

The notes on pressure heads explain that whereas an aircraft on the ground in still air is subject only to atmospheric (static) pressure (S), the leading edges of an aircraft in forward flight are subject to an additional (dynamic) pressure. This results in a total (pitot) pressure (P) on the leading edges of dynamic pressure plus static pressure.

$$\textbf{Pitot = Dynamic + Static}$$
$$\textbf{or P = Dy + S}$$

Total'' [handwritten]

The dynamic pressure is often called 'pitot excess' pressure (PE) so we have:-

$$\textbf{P = PE + S}$$

The pitot head senses pitot pressure and the static/vent senses static pressure. These two pressures are fed to the airspeed indicator, a differential pressure gauge, which measures their difference PE (the dynamic pressure). Now dynamic pressure is a measure of airspeed, because:-

TAS is airspeed with all errors removed [handwritten, left margin]

$$\text{Dynamic Pressure} = \tfrac{1}{2}\rho V^2$$

Calibrated Air Speed $CAS = \dfrac{\rho \times TAS^2}{2}$ [handwritten, right]

where V is true airspeed and ρ is density of the surrounding air.

Thus the ASI measures airspeed by measuring dynamic pressure, displaying the result (usually in knots) on a suitably calibrated scale.

4.2 CONSTRUCTION.

In principle, the simple ASI can be considered as an airtight box divided by a flexible diaphragm, with pitot pressure fed to one side and static pressure to the other side. Figure 4.1 illustrates such a system. The pressure difference across the diaphragm is (Dy + S) - S, which is Dy, the dynamic pressure. Accordingly, the diaphragm deflects by an amount proportional solely to this dynamic pressure, its movement being transmitted by a system of levers to the indicating needle on the face of the ASI. Note that static pressure is common to both sides of the diaphragm, and so does not influence diaphragm movement.

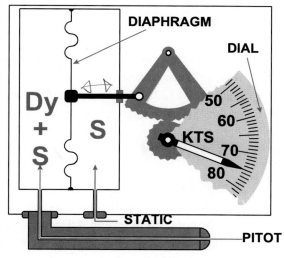

Figure 4.1. The Simple Air Speed Indicator.

ie movement is solely due to Dynamic Pressure [handwritten]

☆ ASI does not suffer from Compressibility error at low airspeeds & altitudes as it is calibrated out [handwritten, bottom]

In practice, the static pressure is fed into the hermetically-sealed instrument case, the pitot pressure being piped to a thin metal capsule capable of expansion and contraction. The layout is shown in Figure 4.2.

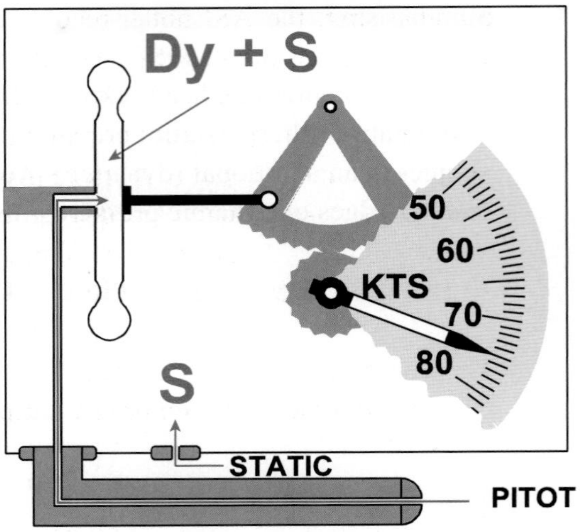

Note that the pressure differential between the inside and outside of the capsule is (Dy + S) - S which is Dy, as with the diaphragm. Expansion or contraction on the capsule will therefore be proportional to the changes in dynamic pressure produced by changes of airspeed.

When capsule expands Readings Increase

The capsule movements are transmitted by a temperature-compensated magnifying linkage to the pointer indicating airspeed on the face of the ASI.

Figure 4.2. A Functional Diagram of an Air Speed Indicator.

4.3   CALIBRATION

From the formula in paragraph 4.1 it can be seen that dynamic pressure depends not only on the speed of the aircraft but also on the air density.

This density varies with temperature and pressure and so with **altitude**. *ie ISA density* The ASI is calibrated to read true airspeed for the air density of 1225 grammes per cubic metre which would be produced by the ISA MSL pressure of 1013.25 mb and temperature + 15°C (dry air conditions). No allowance is made in the calibration for the change in density which occurs with change of altitude.

It follows that even if there were no other errors, the ASI could only indicate TAS when ISA MSL air density existed at the flight level, that is to say when the aircraft was flying in air having a density of 1225 grammes per cubic metre. This density value can only be found at or close to sea level (depending on how much the actual conditions deviate from standard).

4.4   A.S.I. ERRORS

Density Error. Unless the air round the aircraft is at the calibration density of 1225 grammes per cubic metre, which can only occur near sea level, the ASI cannot correctly indicate TAS. The formula in Paragraph 4.1. shows that dynamic pressure is proportional to density, so at altitude, where density is less, the dynamic pressure generated by a given TAS will be less than for the same TAS in flight at sea level. ASI capsule expansion will be proportionately less and the speed indicated will be less than the true speed.

Summarising, the ASI under-reads the true speed at altitude, the discrepancy being called 'density error'. If below MSL, the ASI will over read the true speed.

The navigational computer is commonly used to correct for density error, computing true airspeed from CAS (the 'Calibrated' Air Speed obtained by applying corrections for instrument and position errors to the reading of the ASI). In the Airspeed window, set pressure altitude against Corrected Outside Air Temperature (COAT); then read off TAS on the outer scale against CAS on the inner scale.

This computation allows for the height of the aircraft above the calibration 1013.25 mb pressure level (which should be set on the altimeter subscale) and also for temperature deviation from standard conditions.

Summarising, CAS ± correction for density error (nearly always +) = TAS

Problem

If the temperature at FL 100 is ISA minus 15°C (about - 20°C), will the TAS for a given CAS be greater or smaller than in standard conditions?

Solution

TAS will be smaller in the lower temperature conditions. If the CAS is kept the same as in standard conditions, the dynamic pressure must be the same.

So $\frac{1}{2} \rho V^2$ is unchanged and since a lower temperature must increase the air density, then V, the TAS, must be less to preserve the balance of the equation ($Dy = \frac{1}{2} \rho V^2$).

Instrument Error. Manufacturing imperfections and usage result in small errors which are determined on the ground under laboratory conditions by reference to a datum instrument.

A correction card can be produced for the speed range of the instrument.

Position Error. Alternatively known as 'pressure' error, this arises mainly from the sensing of incorrect static pressure, and is described more fully in the section entitled Pressure Heads.

Position errors throughout the speed range are determined by the aircraft manufacturer during the test flying programme for a particular aircraft type.

It is not unusual to compile a joint correction card for position and instrument errors and place it in the aircraft near the ASI concerned.

Summarising:-

IAS (indicated air speed) ± P and I correction = CAS

Manoeuvre-Induced Errors. These are associated chiefly with manoeuvres involving change in angle of attack, giving transient errors and a lag in the indication of changes in airspeed.

Chapter 2 (Pressure Heads) covers this subject in greater detail.

Compressibility Error. Air is compressible and except at true airspeeds below about 150 knots where the effect is negligible, the pressure produced in the pitot tube is higher than it would be for an ideal incompressible fluid, for which the dynamic pressure is ½ ρV^2.

The ASI is calibrated to this ideal incompressible flow formula instead of to a more complex compressible flow formula.

Because of this, the instrument will over-read, IAS and CAS will be too high, and a subtractive compressibility correction will have to be applied preferably before correcting for density error, i.e. to CAS giving what is known as **EAS** (equivalent airspeed).

The correction, which exceeds 20 knots if TAS is near the speed of sound, can be obtained from graphs or tables, or it can be applied by most high speed navigation computers.

With true airspeeds of less than 300 knots the error is small enough to be ignored in the calculation of TAS from IAS.

With most ASIs, compressibility error appropriate to IAS mean sea level conditions is allowed for in the calibration of the instrument.

Order of Correction.

a)   Apply P and I correction to IAS, giving CAS.

b)   At high speeds, apply the subtractive compressibility correction to CAS to give EAS.

c)   From CAS or EAS, obtain TAS by use of the computer (or a special chart) to correct for density error.

Air Speed Definitions. ✻ *Need to know all details of this table*

IAS(Indicated Air Speed)   =   indicated reading on instrument
    ↓ Corrected for Inst & Pressure Error

CAS(Calibrated Air Speed)   =   IAS ± correction for instrument & position error
    AKA(Rectified Air Speed)

    ↓ Corrected for Compressibility Error ✻ (with TAS >300kt)

due to factory imperfections   *posn of pitot & static vents*

4 - 4

" Compressibility Error is Caused by a False __INCREASE__ in __DYNAMIC__ Pressure and requires a __NEGATIVE__ Correction on the Nav "Computer"

occurs when TAS > 300 kts at high alt where Air is Thinner

EAS(Equivalent Air Speed) = CAS ± compressibility corrections *

↳ Corrected for Density Error

TAS(True Air Speed) = CAS ± density error ± compressibility error

or EAS ± density error

More ASI Definitions:

V_{so} = The stall speed or the minimum steady flight speed in the landing configuration.

V_{s1} = The stall speed or the minimum steady flight speed in a specified configuration.

V_{FE} = The maximum Flap Extension speed

V_{NO} = The maximum normal operating limit speed. *(aka V_{RA} = Velocity Rough Air Speed)*

V_{NE} = The Never Exceed speed

V_{LO} = The maximum Landing Gear Operation speed (up or down).

V_{LE} = The maximum speed Landing Gear Extended speed

V_{YSE} = Best rate of climb when Single Engine (2 eng a/c)

V_{MCA} = Minimum Control speed in the Air   *V_{MCG} = Minimum Control Speed on Ground*

Some ASI's incorporate coloured markings on the dial - these 'range markings' consist of coloured arcs and radial lines.

The White Arc denotes the flap operating range, from stall at maximum AUW in the landing configuration (full flap, landing gear down, wings level, power-off) up to V_{FE} (maximum flaps extended speed).   *V_{SO} ↔ V_{FE}*

The Green Arc denotes the normal operating speed range, from stall speed at maximum all-up weight (flaps up, wings level) up to V_{NO} ('normal operating limit speed' or 'maximum structural cruising speed') which should not be exceeded except in smooth air. Operations at IASs in the green arc should be safe in all conditions, including turbulence.   *V_{S1} ↔ V_{NO}*

Only allowed to enter Yellow Arc in Smooth Air Conditions (non turbulent)

Upper Speed

The Yellow Arc denotes the caution range, which extends from V_{NO} (normal operating limit speed) up to V_{NE} (the never exceed speed). The aircraft should be operated at IASs in the caution range only in smooth air.   *V_{NO} ↔ V_{NE}*   *(always commences at V_{NO} ie where Green ends)*

A Red Radial Line denotes V_{NE}, the never exceed speed. Some ASIs have blue radial lines to denote certain important speeds, (e.g. best single-engines speed for a light twin-engined aeroplane).

4 - 5

* Pressure Altitude is set at 1013.25mb

Optionally for piston engined light twins:

A blue radial line denotes the best rate of climb speed for one engine out, maximum weight, at mean sea level (V_{YSE}).

A red radial line denotes the minimum control speed at maximum weight (V_{MCA}).

A useful formula for estimating TAS is: TAS = CAS + (1.75% of CAS per 1,000 ft of Altitude).

e.g. for a CAS of 100 kt at 10,000 ft: TAS = CAS + (1.75 x 100 x 10) = 117.5 kt

TOLERANCE - (JAR 25) - $\pm$ 3% or **5 Kts** whichever is the greater.

4.5   BLOCKAGES AND LEAKS

Pitot Head. If the pitot head becomes blocked, the ASI reading will, in general, remain unchanged.

In level cruise, a blockage (probably ice) will lock in the previous pitot pressure and any change in actual airspeed will not be registered. However, a slow leakage in the pitot pipeline is likely, so that the IAS gradually decreases.

If altitude is changed with a blocked pitot head and clear static source, the IAS will increase during a climb because the pressure locked inside the capsule remains constant while the static pressure of the air surrounding the capsule decreases. Conversely the IAS decreases during a descent with blocked head.

Static Head. A static head is more exposed to icing conditions and is therefore more likely to become obstructed than is a static vent.

A blocked static source during descent will mean that the 'old' (higher altitude) static pressure surrounding the capsule will be lower than it should be, so that if the pitot supply is normal the ASI will over-read. This could be dangerous in that the aircraft is nearer the stall than the ASI is indicating.

Note that a climb with blocked static source and normal pitot air will result in the ASI under-reading.

If the alternative static source is selected an error may occur. This error will be due to position error. Any dynamic, or turbulence, effects would usually result in a higher static pressure and thus produce an under-reading.

Leaks. Leaks can occur either inside or outside the pressure cabin. A leak in the pitot tube causes the ASI to under read. A leak in the static tube where the outside pressure is lower than static, some unpressurised aircraft, will cause the ASI to over read. Where the outside air is higher than static, in a pressurised cabin the ASI will under read.

4.6   SERVICEABILITY CHECKS

The following checks of the ASI and pressure supply system should be made before flight:-

a)   Pressure head cover(s) and static vent plug(s) removed and stowed aboard the aircraft.

b)   Pitot tube(s), holes/slots in static head(s) and/or static vent(s) should be checked free from obvious obstructions such as insects.

c)   Pitot head heater operative (if fitted).

d)   Dial glass clean and undamaged.

e)   The instrument should indicate airspeed in the correct sense shortly after starting the take-off run.

Exam

✱ ISA deviation ↔ the temp deviations from ISA @ a particular altitude

	ISA	AMB	Dev^n
FC 250	-35	-45	-10°C
FL 350	-55	-47	+8°C

Always give deviation ~ difference from ISA to Ambient.

✱ ISA temp
= Double Height
 then subtract 15
 ie 25,000 ft = 50 - 15 = -35°C

AIRSPEED INDICATORS

1.   If the pitot line to an ASI becomes totally blocked during a climb, the ASI reading will:

   a)   decrease, no matter what the actual airspeed is.
   b)   increase, no matter what the actual airspeed is.
   c)   progressively under indicate the value of the airspeed.
   d)   stick at the airspeed showing at the moment of blockage.

2.   Compressibility error:

   a)   causes overreading of the ASI at all levels whenever TAS exceeds 300 kt.
   b)   causes overreading of the ASI whenever CAS exceeds 300 kt.
   c)   is calibrated out of the ASI at MSL ISA conditions and only causes overreading when air density is decreased and CAS exceeds 300 kt.
   d)   is calibrated out of the ASI at MSL ISA conditions and only causes overreading when air density is decreased and TAS exceeds 300 kt.

3.   If the static line to the ASI becomes blocked during a long descent, a dangerous situation could arise due to the ASI:

   a)   overreading, this indicated speed falsely showing the aircraft to be further from the stalling speed than it actually is.
   b)   underreading, this indicated speed falsely showing the aircraft to be closer to the stalling speed than it actually is.
   c)   underreading, this indicated speed possibly leading to the operation of flaps and/or landing gear at speeds in excess of safety speeds.
   d)   overreading, this indicated speed possibly leading to the operation of flaps and/or landing gear at speeds in excess of safety speeds.

4.   An aircraft maintaining a constant CAS and altitude is flying from a cold airmass into warmer air. The effect of the change of temperature on the speed will be:

   a)   CAS will decrease.
   b)   EAS will increase.
   c)   TAS will increase.
   d)   TAS will decrease.

5.   The airspeed indicator is calibrated to:

   a)   conditions of the International Standard Atmosphere.
   b)   conditions of the International Standard Atmosphere at MSL.
   c)   an air density of 1013.25 gms/m^3.
   d)   indicate correctly in any atmosphere.

6.   Dynamic pressure is equal to:

   a) $\frac{1}{2} v\rho^2$
   b) $\frac{1}{2} \rho v^2$
   c) $(\frac{1}{2} \rho v)^2$
   d) $\frac{1}{2} (\rho v)^2$

7.   Excluding blockages, the full list of errors of the ASI is:

   a)   instrument error, position error, density error, manoeuvre induced error.
   b)   instrument error, position error, temperature error, compressibility error, manoeuvre induced error.
   c)   instrument error, position error, barometric error, temperature error, lag, manoeuvre induced error.
   d)   instrument error, position error, density error, compressibility error, manoeuvre induced error.

8.   Some ASIs have coloured arcs and lines marked on their dials. A yellow arc and a white arc indicate:

   a)   cautionary range and normal operating range.
   b)   flap operating speed range and normal operating range.
   c)   cautionary range and flap operating speed range.
   d)   flap operating speed range and cautionary range.

9.   What will be the TAS if cruising altitude is 39 000 ft, temperature is ISA +5 and CAS 200 kt:

   a)   388 kt
   b)   380 kt
   c)   364 kt
   d)   370 kt

10.   If the static line to the ASI becomes blocked during a climb, the ASI reading will:

   a)   increase, no matter what the actual airspeed is.
   b)   progressively under indicate the value of airspeed.
   c)   progressively over indicate the value of airspeed.
   d)   stick at the airspeed showing at the moment of blockage.

CHAPTER FIVE - THE PRESSURE ALTIMETER

Contents

		Page
5.1	PRINCIPLE OF OPERATION	5 - 1
5.2	CALIBRATION	5 - 1
5.3	CONSTRUCTION	5 - 2
5.4	READING ACCURACY	5 - 4
5.5	SERVO-ASSISTED ALTIMETERS.	5 - 5
5.6	TOLERANCES	5 - 7
5.7	ALTIMETER ERRORS	5 - 7
5.8	BLOCKAGES AND LEAKS.	5 - 8
5.9	SOME DEFINITIONS.	5 - 9
5.10	DENSITY ALTITUDE	5 - 14
5.11	MORE DEFINITIONS	5 - 15
5.12	PRE-FLIGHT ALTIMETER CHECKS.	5 - 16
ALTIMETERS QUESTIONS		5 - 17

5.1   PRINCIPLE OF OPERATION

The pressure altimeter is a simple, reliable, pressure gauge calibrated to indicate height. The pressure at a point depends on the weight of the column of air which extends vertically upwards from the point to the outer limit of the atmosphere.

The higher an aircraft is flying, the shorter is the column of air above it and consequently the lower is the atmospheric pressure at the aircraft.

In other words, the greater the height, the lower the pressure, and by measuring the pressure the altimeter measures height.

Unfortunately, the relationship between pressure and height is not a linear one, so that calibration of the altimeter scale is not a simple matter.

The situation is further complicated by high and low pressure weather systems which produce pressure differences in the horizontal plane. Furthermore, the temperature of the air at the surface and the temperature lapse rate in the air above vary considerably; this affects pressure.

The inter-relationships of these quantities are dealt with more fully in the notes on Meteorology.

5.2   CALIBRATION

With all these variables it becomes necessary to assume certain average or 'standard' conditions, base the calibration formulae on these, and then apply corrections appropriate to the deviations from standard conditions which occur with position and time.
The conditions used for calibration are usually those assumed for the ISA (International Standard Atmosphere). The relevant assumptions are:

a)   **At mean Sea Level**

Pressure 1013.25 millibars   Temperature +15°C   Density 1225gm m³

b)   **From MSL up to 11 km (36,090 feet)**

Temperature falling at 6.5°C per km (1.98°C/1000 feet)

c)   **From 11 km to 20 km (65,617 feet)**

A constant temperature of - 56.5°C

d)   **From 20 km to 32 km (104, 987 feet)**

Temperature rising at 1°C per km (0.3°/1000 feet).

With these assumptions, the pressure corresponding to any given level in the ISA can be calculated from the calibration formulae.

Graphs or tables can be produced showing height in terms of pressure under standard conditions. These tables can be used for the manufacturer's calibration of the altimeter scale.

Basically, the laboratory calibration consists of applying a series of pressures to the altimeter and checking that the instrument indicates the respective levels which correspond to these pressures in the ISA.

Any discrepancies, if within certain agreed tolerances, would be listed over the operating height ranges as instrument errors. (The calibration is carried out with increasing and decreasing readings so that the amount of lag at calibration conditions can be determined).

Note: 1 The Pressure Altimeter is calibrated to give a Linear Presentation of the Non-linear Atmospheric distribution. This is achieved by the use of a variable magnification lever system and the dynamic design of the capsules.

Note:2 Temperature compensation is achieved by the use of a bi-metal compensator connected in the lever/linkage system.

Note: 3 Conversion between "Inches of Mercury (Hg)" and "Hectopascals (Hpa) / Millibars (Mb)" can be achieved by the formula ......Hg x 33.86 = Hpa / Mb and the reverse by the formula .... Hpa / Mb x 0.0295 = Hg. However, it should be noted that the conversion process is normally carried out by the use of conversion tables.

5.3   CONSTRUCTION

Simple Altimeter. Static pressure is fed into the case of the instrument from the static source. As height increases, static pressure decreases and the capsule expands under the control of a leaf spring. A mechanical linkage magnifies the capsule expansion and converts it to a rotational movement of a single pointer over the height scale. The linkage incorporates a temperature-compensating device to minimise errors caused by expansion and contraction of the linkage and changes in spring tension due to fluctuations in the temperature of the mechanism.
Figure 5.1. shows how the linkage works, but the actual arrangements are much more complex.

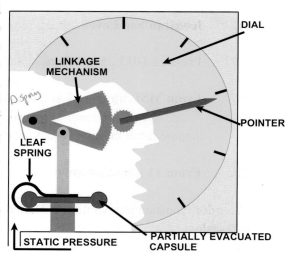

Figure 5.1.   A Simple Altimeter.

The simple altimeter has a setting knob which is geared to the pointer. With this knob the pointer can be set to read zero with the aircraft on the ground so that when airborne the altimeter indicates approximate height above aerodrome level. Alternatively the pointer can be set (before flight) to the aerodrome elevation so that when airborne the instrument shows approximate height above mean sea level.

Sensitive Altimeter. Most aircraft are now equipped with the three-pointer or 'sensitive' type illustrated schematically in Figure 5.2.

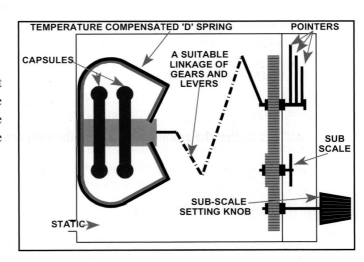

Vibrating or Knocking device vibrate capsules so that inertia is already overcome :: more sensitive

Figure 5.2. A Schematic Diagram of a Sensitive Altimeter.

The principle of operation is similar to that of the simple altimeter but there are the following refinements:-

a)   A bank of two or three capsules gives the increased movement necessary to drive three pointers. These are geared 100:10:1, the smallest indicating 100,000 feet per revolution, the next 10,000 feet per revolution and the largest 1,000 feet per revolution.

b)   Jewelled bearings are fitted, reducing friction and the associated lag in indications.
        Note: Some altimeter systems employ "Knocking / Vibrating" devices to help overcome initial inertia of the internal gear train when transmitting movement from the capsules to the pointers.

c)   A variable datum mechanism is built in. This, with the aid of a setting knob, enables the instrument to be set to indicate height above any desired pressure datum.

The variable datum mechanism is used as follows:-

The pilot turns the knob until the desired pressure level (say, 1005 mb) appears on a pressure sub-scale on the face of the instrument.

As he turns the knob, the height pointers rotate until, when the procedure is completed with the sub-scale showing the desired 1005, the altimeter indicates the aircraft's height above this pressure level.

If for instance the aerodrome level pressure happened to be 1005 mb, the altimeter would be reading height above the aerodrome (and the pilot would have set a 'QFE' of 1005 on the sub-scale). Further details of the procedural uses of the pressure sub-scale are given later in this chapter. The sub-scale setting only changes when the pilot turns the knob. A change in altitude or surface pressure has no direct effect on the reading of the sub-scale. As the pilot alters the sub-scale setting, the altimeter pointers move, but the design of the mechanism is such that the reverse does not apply (for example, during a climb, the pointers rotate but the sub-scale setting remains unchanged). British altimeters have a sub-scale setting range between 800 to 1050 millibars.

5.4   READING ACCURACY

The simple altimeter is not sensitive, recording perhaps 20,000ft for each revolution of its single pointer. The three-pointer instrument gives a much more sensitive indication of height and change of height but suffers from the severe disadvantage that it can be easily misread.

It is not difficult for the pilot to make a reading error of 10,000ft, particularly during a rapid descent under difficult conditions with a high flight-deck work-load.

Accidents have occurred as a result of such misreading. Various modifications to the pointers and warning systems have been tried with the object of preventing this error, including a striped warning sector which appears as the aircraft descends through the 16,000 foot level.

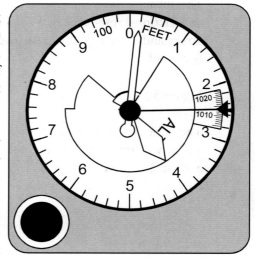

Figure 5.3. A Three Pointer
Indicating 24,020 feet.

The greatest advance has been the introduction of the counter-pointer altimeter, illustrated in Figure 5.4., which gives a much more positive indication than the three-pointer dial drawn in Figure 5.3.

With further reference to Figure 5.4., it will be realised that though the digital counters give an unambiguous indication of the aircraft's height, they give a relatively poor display of the rate of change of height.

For this reason the instrument also has a single pointer which makes one revolution per 1000 feet, giving the clear indication of change of height which is extremely important to the pilot, particularly on the final approach in instrument conditions.

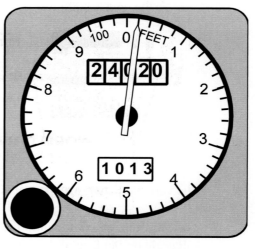

Figure 5.4. A Counter Pointer
Altimeter.

5.5   SERVO-ASSISTED ALTIMETERS.

Though at least one counter-pointer altimeter driven directly by pressure capsules has been produced, most instruments of the type are servo-assisted. This servo-assistance not only gives the altimeter an increased operating range but also improves the instrument accuracy, particularly at high levels.

At high altitude the change in pressure corresponding to a given change in height is much smaller than at low altitude.

This means that for a given height change, capsule movement at high altitude is relatively small, and frictional resistance in the linkage of an unassisted altimeter causes correspondingly greater errors and more lag. With servo-assistance, the requisite power is available to overcome the frictional resistance with consequently enhanced instrument accuracy.

Figure 5.5. shows a schematic diagram of a servo-assisted altimeter.

The principle of the servo-altimeter is that the small movements of the capsules are detected by a very sensitive electro-magnetic pick-off. This produces an electric current which is amplified and used to drive a motor which rotates the counters and pointer.

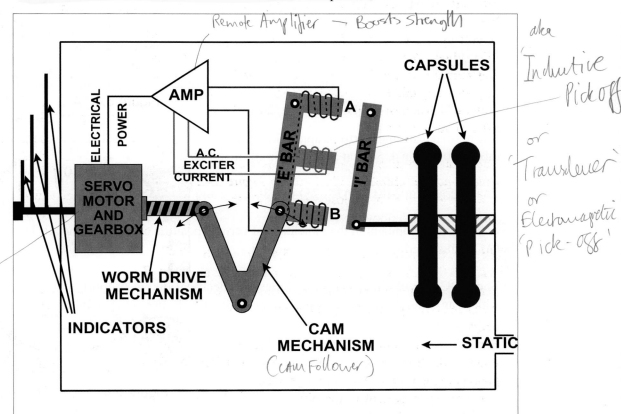

Figure 5.5. A Schematic Diagram of a Servo-Assisted Altimeter.

AC is fed to the middle leg of the E bar, setting up alternating magnetic fields in the outer legs 'A' and 'B'.

The coils on these two legs are wound 180° out of phase. The exciter therefore induces a current in each leg, but since these are 180° out of phase and of equal strength , they cancel each other out when the I bar is equidistant from the legs of the E bar (that is when no pressure change acts on the capsules).

With a change of pressure the capsules expand or contract, moving the I bar on its pivot, closing the gap between the I Bar and E Bar at one end and opening it at the other.

This causes an imbalance of magnetic fields and therefore of the currents induced in the 'A' and 'B' coils . The imbalance causes an error signal which is passed to the amplifier, where it is amplified and rectified, and thence to the servo motor.

The servo motor drives the counter-pointer system of the altimeter and at the same time, via a cam drive, re-aligns the E Bar with the I Bar.

Once re-aligned, the error signal ceases and the altimeter indicates the correct height.
In this system the only work required of the capsules is to move the I Bar, eliminating the effects of friction and manufacturing imperfections in the gearing of a conventional altimeter.

This type of altimeter is sensitive to very small pressure changes and therefore more accurate than the sensitive altimeter, particularly at high altitudes where pressure changes (per unit height increment) are very small. The lag experienced in other types of altimeter with rapid changes of height is greatly reduced.

The normal instrument error is approximately equivalent to the effect of 1 mb change of pressure (about 30 ft at msl, 50 ft at 20,000ft, or 100ft at 40,000 ft).

The tolerance at **MSL (JAR - 25)** is $\pm$ **30ft per 100 kts CAS**

A further development in the indication of vertical position comes with the Air Data Computer (ADC) installed in many transport aircraft.

The ADC provides (among other things) an electrical output proportional to static pressure which can be used to drive a counter-pointer altimeter, the previously required altimeter pressure capsules being dispensed with, unless a standby capability is required.

*Consider
Height of flight deck
above ground
eg) 747 is 20ft above ground.*

5.6   TOLERANCES

Typical Simple Altimeter (range zero to 35,000 feet)

Height (feet)	0	35,000
Tolerance (feet)	±100	± 1,000

Typical Sensitive Altimeter (range zero to 80,000 feet)

Height (feet)	0	40,000	80,000
Tolerance (feet)	±70	± 600	± 1,500

Typical Servo Altimeter (range zero to 100,000 feet)

Height (feet)	0	40,000	60,000	100,000
Tolerance (feet)	±30	± 100	± 300	± 4,000

5.7   ALTIMETER ERRORS

The errors which affect altimeters are many and the extent of some of them varies with altimeter type. Much effort is expended on improving instrument accuracy, and the permissible tolerances of modern altimeters are smaller than with earlier types.

There are other errors caused by deviation of the actual atmosphere from standard conditions, and also the difficulty in sensing correctly the outside air pressure. A list of the main errors follows.

a)   **Time Lag.** With many types of altimeter the response to change of height is not instantaneous. This causes the altimeter to under-read in a climb and over-read in a descent. The lag is most noticeable when the change in altitude is rapid and prolonged. In the laboratory calibration of the sensitive altimeter, the lag between increasing readings and decreasing readings should not exceed 150 feet. With servo-assisted altimeters there is said to be no appreciable lag unless the rate of change of height exceeds 10,000 feet per minute. This is because the servo-altimeter does not suffer from the linkage friction which causes a much larger error in the sensitive altimeter.

b)   **Instrument Error.** Manufacturing imperfections, including friction in the linkage, cause errors throughout the operating range. The errors are kept as small as possible by adjustments within the instrument, and the calibration procedure ensures that they are within permitted tolerances. Residual errors may be listed on a correction card.

Note that with the sensitive altimeter the error increases with altitude as explained in Paragraph 5.5., which also explains why the decrease of accuracy with altitude is less serious with the servo-altimeter.

c)   **Position (or Pressure) Error.** This is largely due to the inability to sense the true static pressure outside the aircraft, as described in the chapter on Pressure Heads. The error is usually small but increases at high mach numbers (and, consequently, at high altitudes usually associated with high mach numbers). Altimeters driven by an Air Data Computer (ADC) may have their accuracy improved by the ADC automatically correcting its static output signal for position error.

d)   **Manoeuvre-Induced Error**. This is caused by transient fluctuations of pressure at the static vent during change of, mainly, pitch attitude and delays in the transmission of pressure changes due to viscous and acoustic effects in the static pipeline. This is discussed more fully in Chapter 2 dealing with Pressure Heads.

e)   **Barometric Error.** Providing the altimeter has a pressure sub-scale, and the local QNH is set on it, the altimeter will indicate height AMSL (though still subject to the other errors). If the local surface pressure has changed since the QNH value was set, a 'barometric' error of roughly 30 feet per millibar will result. If pressure has fallen the altimeter over-reads.

f)   **Temperature Error.** Even with no other errors at all, the pressure altimeter will not indicate true altitude (height AMSL) unless the surface temperature and lapse rate of the column of air are those assumed in the calibration.

When flying in colder air (with an air density greater than ISA at that altitude), the altimeter will over-read.

Where the temperature at cruising level deviates from standard, an approximate correction can be made with most navigational computers. The correction can only be approximate since temperatures in the rest of the column of air are not known. The correction is considered too inaccurate to be worth making at heights above 25,000 feet.

5.8   BLOCKAGES AND LEAKS.

If the static source becomes blocked, the altimeter will not register any change in height - the height at which the blockage occurred will still be indicated regardless of any climb or descent. On many aircraft, an alternative source of static pressure will be available (see Paragraph 2.5.)

Should the static line fracture in a pressurised aircraft, the altimeter will show the (lower) cabin altitude rather than aircraft altitude

A fracture in the static line within an unpressurised aircraft will normally result in the altimeter over-reading, due to the pressure in the cabin being lower than ambient due to aerodynamic suction.

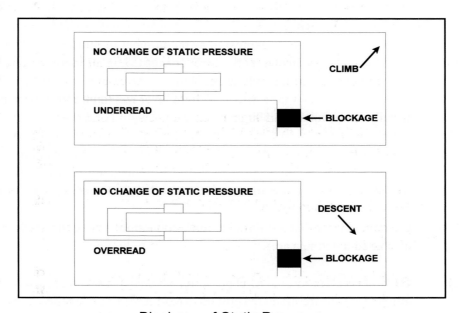

Blockage of Static Pressure.

5.9   SOME DEFINITIONS.

The pilot should be familiar with the following definitions mostly based on those in the UK Air Pilot.

Height

a)   The vertical distance of a level, point or object considered as a point, measured from a specified datum. (Normally associated with QFE and height above aerodrome level).

         or

b)   The vertical dimension (size) of an object.

Altitude.   The vertical distance of a level, point or object considered as a point, measured from MSL. (Normally associated with QNH).

Cruising Level This is a generic term describing vertical position for a significant portion of the flight and can be a height, altitude, or flight level depending on the altimeter setting procedure in force.

Flight Levels   Surfaces of constant pressure related to the standard pressure datum and separated by specified pressure intervals. In the UK these correspond to 500 foot intervals between transition level and FL 245 while from FL 250 they correspond to 1,000 foot intervals. A flight level is expressed as the number of hundreds of feet which would be indicated at the level concerned by an ISA-calibrated altimeter set to 1013.25 mb (29.92 inches). For example, with 1013.25 set and 25 000 feet indicated, the flight level would be 250, (abbreviated to FL 250). With 4,500 feet indicated it would be FL 45.

Absolute Altitude   Alternatively known as Absolute Height, meaning the height of the aircraft above the surface immediately below. Used more often in connection with radio or radar altimeters than with pressure altimeters.

It should be remembered that the altimeter **indicates height above the pressure level** set on the sub-scale. The four settings are:-

a)   **QFE.** This is aerodrome level pressure, which when set on the sub-scale, will cause the altimeter of an aircraft on the ground to read zero, assuming there is no instrument error. In flight, with QFE set, the altimeter will indicate height above the aerodrome QFE reference datum, provided ISA conditions obtain between aerodrome level and the aircraft and there are no other altimeter errors. In practice, QFE is used mainly for circuit-flying and gives a good indication of height above the aerodrome, any errors involved being only small.

b)   **QNH.** This setting is used mainly in flight below transition altitude/level, defined later. It is an equivalent MSL pressure calculated by Air Traffic Control from the aerodrome level pressure assuming ISA conditions prevail between aerodrome level and MSL. With QNH set on the sub-scale, the altimeter of an aircraft on the aerodrome indicates aerodrome elevation, that is, the height AMSL (if there is no instrument error). In flight the altimeter will indicate altitude but this will only be the true altitude if the mean temperature in the column of air beneath the aircraft is the same as in ISA conditions (assuming there are no other altimeter errors). If conditions are different from standard, the indicated altitude, sometimes called QNH altitude, may deviate considerably from true altitude. The navigational computer can be used to make an approximate correction for this temperature error, as mentioned in Paragraph 5.7.f, and as illustrated in Figure 5.7.

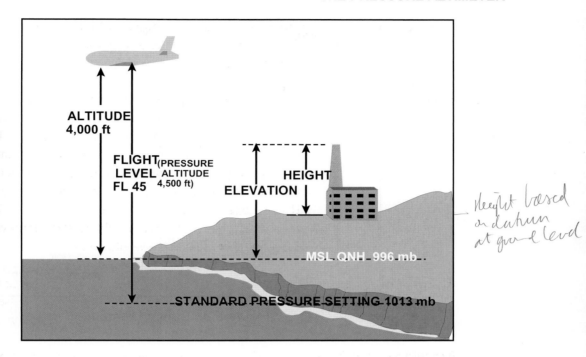

Height based on datum at ground level

Figure 5.7. Terminology.

Problem

An aircraft flies from 'A' to 'B' at a constant indicated altitude of 10,000 feet with the QNH 'A' of 1025 mb set on the sub-scale THROUGHOUT THE FLIGHT. On arrival overhead 'B', where the QNH is 995 mb, what will be the true altitude (assuming that there are no other errors, and assuming that 1 mb corresponds to 30 feet)?

Solution

The altimeter indicates the height above the 1025 mb pressure datum set on the sub-scale. At 'A', 1025 mb is the MSL pressure so the aircraft is actually 10,000 feet above MSL. When it gets to 'B' where MSL pressure is 995 mb, the 1025 mb level will be below sea level, remembering that pressure decreases as height increases. The amount involved is 1025 - 995 = 30 mb, or 30 X 30 = 900 feet. The altimeter is now indicating 10,000 feet above a datum which is 900 feet below MSL. The true altitude (actual height AMSL) of the aircraft must therefore be 10,000 - 900 = 9,100 feet. The altimeter indicates 10,000 feet but the true altitude is 9100 feet. The instrument is over-reading, and the aircraft is closer to the surface than is indicated. This is a potentially dangerous situation, occurring in flight from HIGH TO LOW pressure causing the altimeter to read HIGH. A datum diagram such as that shown in Figure 5.8. helps to sort out this type of problem.

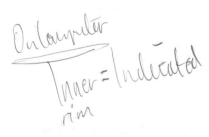

© Oxford Aviation Services Limited

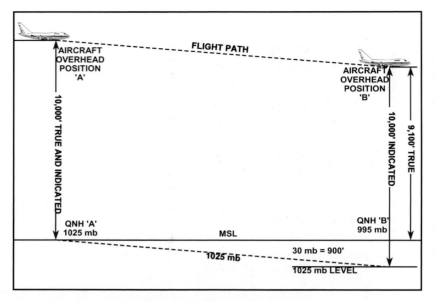

Figure 5.8. Datum Diagram.

Remember:

Pressure always decreases as altitude increases.
The altimeter indicates height above the datum set on the sub-scale.

Problem

The indicated altitude is 10,000 feet with local QNH set and a COAT (corrected outside air temperature) of -25°C. Will the true altitude be more or less than the indicated value?

Solution

The ISA temperature at 10,000 feet would be about -5°C, so the aircraft is flying in colder-than-standard conditions (ISA minus 20°). Pressure decreases more rapidly in cold than in warm air. Therefore, assuming a constant surface pressure, the pressure at a given true altitude in the cold air will be less than at the same altitude in 'standard' air. The altimeter in the cold air will interpret this lower pressure as a higher altitude and will therefore over-read the true altitude. Using the computer set indicated altitude, 10,000 feet, against a COAT of -25°C in the Altitude window. Read off the true altitude, about 9,250 feet, on the outer scale against 10,000 feet on the inner scale.
(An approximation of 4 feet per 1°C away from ISA per 1000 feet above sea level, may be used as a rough guide).

Thus, in **flight from HIGH TO LOW TEMPERATURE the altimeter would read HIGH. This is potentially unsafe**, and is comparable to the case of barometric error illustrated in the previous worked example where with **flight from HIGH TO LOW PRESSURE the altimeter also reads HIGH.**

TEMPERATURE ERROR CORRECTION

Values to be added by the pilot to published altitudes (feet)

Aerodrome Temp °C	Height above the elevation of the altimeter setting source													
	200	300	400	500	600	700	800	900	1,000	1,500	2,000	3,000	4,000	5,000
0	0	20	20	20	20	40	40	40	40	60	80	140	180	220
-10	20	20	40	40	40	60	80	80	80	120	160	260	340	420
-20	20	40	40	60	80	80	100	120	120	180	240	380	500	620
-30	40	40	60	80	100	120	140	140	160	240	320	500	660	820
-40	40	60	**80**	100	120	140	160	180	200	300	400	620	820	1020
-50	40	80	100	120	140	180	200	220	240	360	480	740	980	1220

Note:- The table is based on aerodrome elevation of 2,000 ft; however it can be used operationally at any aerodrome.

Example: Decision height is 400 ft.
Aerodrome temperature is -40 °C.
From table correction = 80 ft.
Revised decision height = 480 ft

c) **Standard Setting.** When 1013.25 mb is set on the sub-scale, the altimeter reading is called 'pressure altitude' or 'pressure height', which when stated in hundreds of feet at one of the specified intervals (mentioned earlier in the definition of flight levels) gives the aircraft's flight level. Thus with 1013.25 set, the altimeter indicates height above the 1013.25 datum (subject to the usual errors). This setting is used in the UK above the transition altitude/level.

d) **Regional QNH.** More correctly called 'lowest forecast QNH', this setting, provided by the Met. Office, is used to ensure safe terrain clearance. It is the value below which QNH is forecast not to fall in a given period and area.

   The value should be lower than the actual QNH anywhere in the area, and if set on the sub-scale, regional QNH will cause the altimeter to under-read (so erring on the safe side - the altimeter showing aircraft to be lower than it actually is).

5.10   DENSITY ALTITUDE

Density altitude can be defined as the altitude in the standard atmosphere at which the prevailing density would occur, or alternatively, as the altitude in the standard atmosphere corresponding to the prevailing pressure and temperature. It is a convenient parameter in respect of engine performance figures.

It can be obtained by use of an airspeed correction chart or by navigational computer. A third (approximate) method is to add to the pressure altitude 118 feet for every degree Celsius that actual temperature exceeds standard. For example, suppose the elevation of an aerodrome is 5,500 feet, with a temperature of ISA plus 30 and a QNH of 1013 mb. Standard temperature at this altitude would be about +4°C, so the actual temperature is +34°C. Higher temperature means lower density and this lower density would be found at a level higher than 5,500 feet in the standard atmosphere, in fact, at a density altitude of 30 X 118 = 3,540 feet higher than pressure altitude. The density altitude(with which the engine performance is associated) would therefore be about 9,000 feet. The answer can be checked on the computer by setting pressure altitude (5,500 feet) against temperature (+34°C) in the Airspeed window and reading off Density Altitude (about 9,000 feet) in its own window.

Note:

a) When calculating errors in Pressure / Density altitude away from ISA conditions always note the Surface Temperature and Pressure prior to attempting the equation.

b) The corrections for altimeter error due to deviations away from ISA under specific conditions may be found in Aircraft Operating Manuals.

Low temp to High temp: Safe (altimeter is underreading)
High temp to Low temp = Unsafe   "High to Low - look out below"
(altimeter overreading)
(Same with pressure)
as Cold air is lower pressure)

5.11   MORE DEFINITIONS

Transition Altitude.   This is the altitude at or below which the vertical position of an aircraft is expressed and controlled in terms of altitude. In the UK its value is commonly 3,000 or 4,000 feet.

Transition Level   This is the lowest flight level available for use above the transition altitude.   At and above transition level, vertical position is expressed as a flight level.

Transition Layer   This is the airspace between transition altitude and transition level. When climbing through it, the aircraft's vertical position is expressed in terms of flight level; when descending through it, in terms of altitude (though in practice the depth of the layer is usually insignificant).

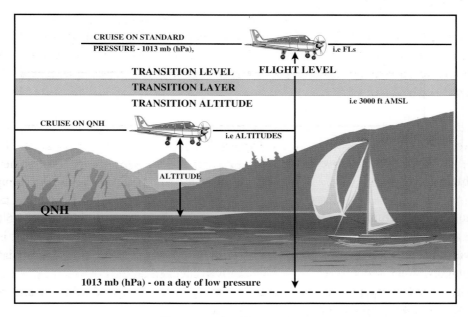

Figure 5.9. Transition.

Per temp is away from ISA the worse it is in terms of payload, take off length, distance / time between V₁ & Rotate on take off.

5.12 PRE-FLIGHT ALTIMETER CHECKS.

In the UK, the apron is the designated location for pre-flight altimeter checks (the apron being the loading and unloading and/or parking area). Apron elevation is displayed in the flight clearance office of the aerodrome concerned and is also published in the AGA section of the UK Air Pilot.

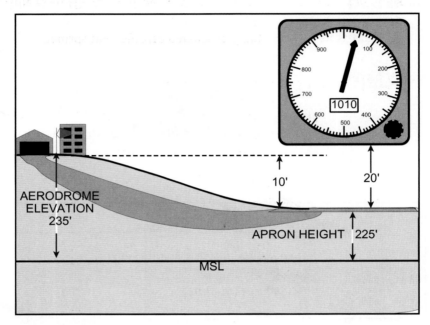

Figure 5.10.

Problem

Calculate the instrument error from the following details of a pre-flight altimeter check:

Aerodrome elevation	235 feet
Apron elevation	225 feet
Height of altimeter above apron	20 feet
Altimeter reading with QFE set	40 feet

Solution

The apron is 10 feet below the stated aerodrome elevation so assuming the QFE to be for the aerodrome level, an altimeter on the apron should read (-10) feet. However, the instrument is positioned in the aircraft 20 feet above the apron so it should show (-10) + 20 = +10 feet. Its actual reading is +40 feet so it is over-reading by 30 feet, an instrument error of +30 feet.

ALTIMETERS

1.   The diagram below shows a simple altimeter. The parts labelled A, B, C and D are:

a)   pitot pressure inlet, linkage mechanism, bellows, quadrant.

b)   air inlet, temperature compensator, leaf spring, linkage mechanism.

c)   static pressure inlet, partially evacuated capsule, linkage mechanism, subscale setting device.

d)   static pressure inlet, partially evacuated capsule, leaf spring, linkage mechanism.

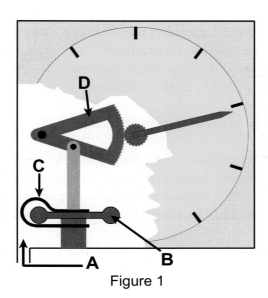

Figure 1

2.   In the International Standard Atmosphere, the mean sea level pressure is ...., the lapse rate of temperature .... between MSL and .... and is isothermal up to .... The numbers missing are:

a)   1225 mb; 2° per 1000 ft; 37 000 ft; 66 000 ft.

b)   1013.25 mb; 1.98°C per 1000 ft; 36 090 ft; 65 617 ft.

c)   1013.25 mb; 1.98°C per 1000 ft; 36 090 ft; 104 987 ft.

d)   1225 mb; 1.98°C per 1000 ft; 36 090 ft; 104 987 ft.

Computer

*Calculating Density Altitude

- Plug airfield altitude & temp into airspeed window

- Read density altitude from density alt window

ie height 5,500'
temp = + 34°
∴ density alt ~ 9,000'

* Temp error
= Use Altitude window.

3.   An aircraft taking off from an airfield with QNH set on the altimeter has both static vents blocked by ice. As the aircraft climbs away the altimeter will:

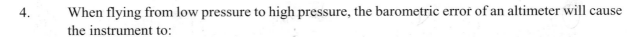

 a)   read the airfield elevation.
 b)   indicate the aircraft height amsl.
 c)   read the height of the aircraft above the airfield.
 d)   show only a very small increase in height.

4.   When flying from low pressure to high pressure, the barometric error of an altimeter will cause the instrument to:

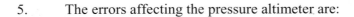

 a)   read the true altitude, providing a correction is made for temperature.
 b)   overread the true altitude of the aircraft.
 c)   indicate a higher altitude than the correct one.
 d)   underread the true altitude of the aircraft.

5.   The errors affecting the pressure altimeter are:

 a)   instrument position, manoeuvre induced, density, temperature, lag.
 b)   instrument, pressure, manoeuvre induced, density, temperature, lag.
 c)   instrument, position, manoeuvre induced, temperature, barometric, lag.
 d)   instrument, pressure, lag, barometric, temperature, compressibility.

6.   An altimeter with .... set on the subscale will indicate ...., but with .... set, the altimeter will show ....

 a)   1013; pressure altitude; QNH; height above mean sea level.
 b)   QNE; pressure altitude; QNH; height above airfield datum.
 c)   QFE; height above the airfield datum; 1013; height amsl.
 d)   QNH; height above touch down; 1013; height amsl.

7.   An aircraft has one altimeter set to QFE and one to aerodrome QNH 1000 mb. If the airfield elevation is 300 ft, immediately before take-off the altimeter with QFE set will read .... and the other .... If the QFE altimeter is set to 1013 when passing through the transition altitude 3000 ft, it will read ...... (Assume 1 mb = 30 ft).

 a)   300 ft; zero; 2610 ft
 b)   zero; 300 ft; 3390 ft
 c)   zero; 300 ft; 3690 ft
 d)   zero; 300 ft; 2610 ft

8.   Which altimeter below is showing FL155:

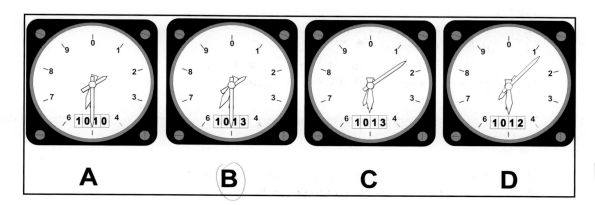

Figure 2

9 .

Below is a schematic diagram of a servo-assisted altimeter. The parts labelled A, B, C and D are:

a)   cam mechanism, amplifier, servo motor, mechanical drive.
b)   mechanical drive, servo motor, amplifier, AC exciter.
c)   cam mechanism, amplifier, E-I bar, mechanical drive.
d)   E-I bar, amplifier, servo motor, AC exciter, mechanical drive.

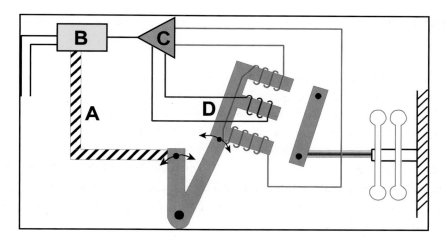

Figure 3

Which Computer Windows for wx?

(ASI)

P.I.M

Comp   C

All speed calculations ≠ Density   D

(ALT)

P.I.M

Barometric

Lag

Temperature   B L T

" altitude corrections

All pressure instruments — Errors

Position

Instrument

Manouvre Induced

ASI = Also
Density
& Compressibility

CHAPTER SIX - THE VERTICAL SPEED INDICATOR

Contents

		Page
6.1	INTRODUCTION.	6 - 1
6.2	PRINCIPLE.	6 - 1
6.3	CONSTRUCTION.	6 - 1
6.4	VSI METERING UNIT	6 - 2
6.5	THE ERRORS OF THE VSI.	6 - 4
6.6	THE INSTANTANEOUS VERTICAL SPEED INDICATOR.	6 - 4
6.7	PRESENTATION.	6 - 5
6.8	SERVICEABILITY CHECKS	6 - 6
	VERTICAL SPEED INDICATOR QUESTIONS	6 - 7

Capillary = Viscosity

Ceilings:

Absolute Ceiling

Service Ceiling
ROC ≠ 100 FPM   " if we can't get more
than this we're at Absolute
Ceiling

6.1 INTRODUCTION.

Rate of change of altitude is indicated to the pilot on the Vertical Speed Indicator (V.S.I.), sometimes referred to as the Rate of Climb Indicator.

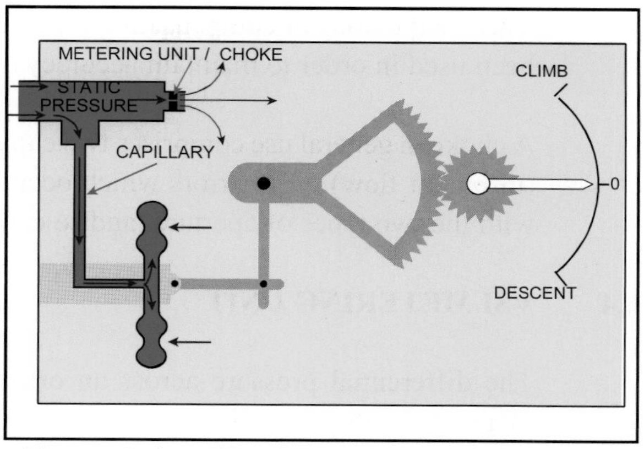

[handwritten note: ✱ Only instrument with Static Pressure in Capsule — Static also goes into Capsule]

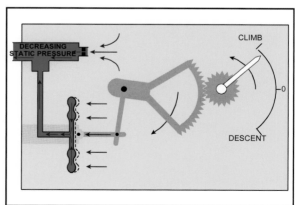

Figure 6.1a. The Principle of Operation of the V.S.I. During Level Flight.

6.2 PRINCIPLE.

[handwritten note: restriction - delays by 4-6 seconds]

When an aircraft departs from level flight, the static pressure will change. The V.S.I. measures the pressure difference between each side of a restricted choke / metering unit.

[handwritten note: ✱ time delay is heart / main principle of VSI indicator]

In level flight the pressures on each side of the choke are the same, during a climb or descent, air fed to the choke immediately responds to the change of atmospheric pressure but the choke transmits this change at a lower rate.

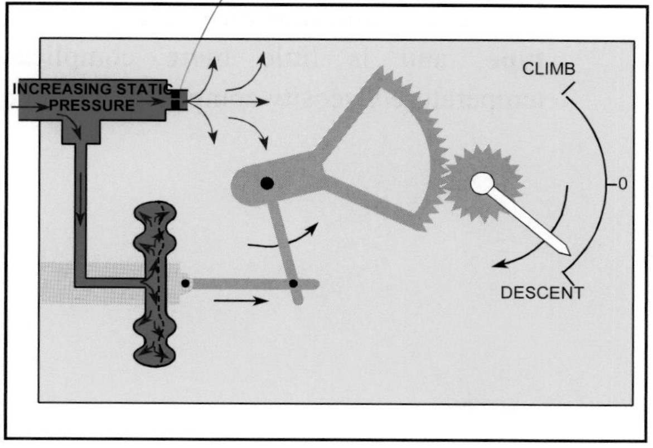

Figure 6.1b. The Principle of Operation of the V.S.I. While Descending.

6.3 CONSTRUCTION.

A capsule in an airtight case is fed with static pressure. The case is also fed with static pressure but through a restricted choke, thus if the static pressure is changed the pressure surrounding the capsule changes at a slower rate than that within the capsule, as shown in Figure 6.1. For example, if the aircraft is climbing, the pressure in the capsule will be less than that in the case, the consequent compression of the capsule is converted by a suitable linkage to a pointer indication of rate of climb.

Figure 6.1c. The Principle of Operation of the V.S.I. While Climbing.

Various methods of compensating for changes in density, temperature, and viscosity of air have been used in order to maintain accuracy over a wide range of operating conditions.

A choke in general use comprises two capillary tubes (laminar flow) and two sharp-edged orifices (turbulent flow). The errors which occur with, mainly, change of altitude are of opposite sign with the two types of aperture, and so cancel out.

6.4   VSI METERING UNIT

The differential pressure across an orifice varies inversely as the temperature, and therefore increases with decreasing temperature. Thus, satisfactory temperature compensation can be obtained by combining the two devices. The size of the orifice and capillary are chosen so that readings of the indicator will be correct over as wide a range of temperature and altitude conditions as possible.

The second unit, illustrated in Figure 6.2a. is known variously as the **ceramic type** and **porous type**, and is little more complicated in its construction, because a mechanical temperature/viscosity compensator is incorporated.

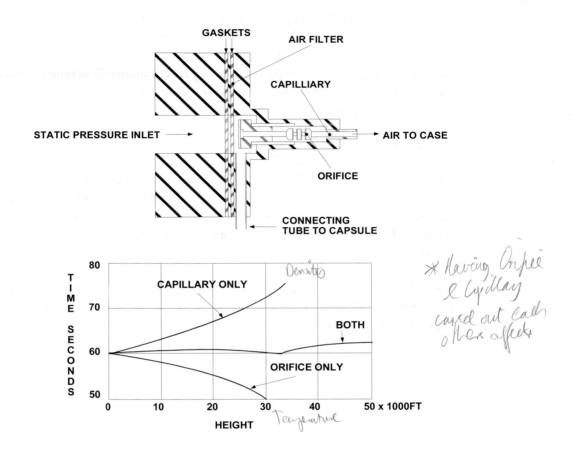

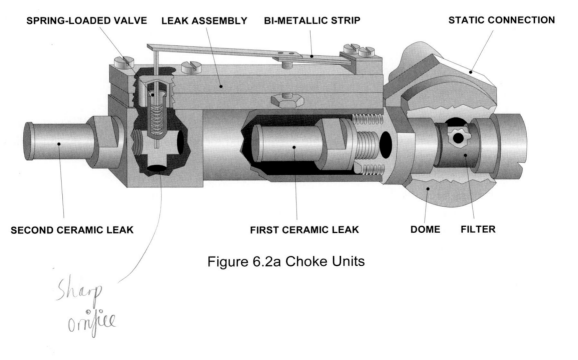

Figure 6.2a Choke Units

6.5   THE ERRORS OF THE VSI.

Instrument Error. Due to manufacturing imperfections.

Position (or Pressure) Error. If the static pressure is subject to position error the V.S.I. will wrongly indicate a climb or descent when speed is suddenly changed, this is most noticeable during take-off acceleration.

Manoeuvre-Induced Error. Any short term fluctuations in pressure at the static vent during attitude changes will cause the instrument to indicate a false rate of climb or descent.

Additionally with most V.S.I.s, the linkage includes a small counterbalance weight, the inertia of which causes delays in the indications of changes in vertical speed during manoeuvres.

Time Lag. The pointer takes a few seconds to steady because of the time taken to build up a steady pressure difference on climb or descent. There will also be a time lag on levelling out because of the time taken for the pressures to equalise. This error is most noticeable after a prolonged climb or descent, especially at a high rate.

Needed but is an error

Any blockages of the static line or vent will cause the needle to **return to zero**. If the supply of air to this instrument is blocked it is probable that the other pressure instruments (A.S.I., altimeter and machmeter) will also be affected.

6.6   THE INSTANTANEOUS VERTICAL SPEED INDICATOR.

To overcome the problem of lag, the Instantaneous Vertical Speed Indicator (I.V.S.I) incorporates an accelerometer unit (dash-pot or vane) which responds quickly to a change of altitude.

Figure 6.2b. shows an IVSI at the beginning of a descent.

The piston in the vertical acceleration pump immediately rises in the cylinder and increases the pressure in the capsule. The capsule expands and the pointer will give an instant indication of descent.

After a few seconds the piston will slowly descend to its original position, but by this time the correct differential pressure between the capsule and the case will have been set up and the correct rate of descent will continue to be shown.

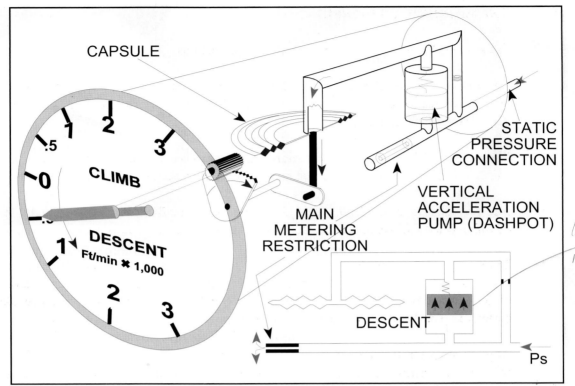

Figure 6.2b. An Instantaneous Vertical Speed indicator Showing a Descent.

Errors Peculiar to the IVSI. Because of the sensitivity of the dash-pot assembly, the instrument tends to overreact to turbulent flying conditions and small fluctuations should be ignored.

If the aircraft should be turning, the piston will tend to sink towards the bottom of the cylinder and there will be an indication of a climb.

6.7   PRESENTATION.

Two types of presentation are available, a linear scale and a logarithmic scale, this latter presentation being more easily read at the lower rates of climb/descent This is easily discerned from Figures 6.3. and 6.4..

It should be noted that diaphragm overload stops may be fitted to prevent damage to the instrument should the rate of climb/descent exceed the maximum to which the instrument is calibrated. On some instruments a zeroing screw is fitted.

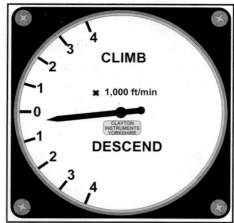

Figure 6.3. A V.S.I. With a Linear Scale Showing a Descent of 250 ft/min.

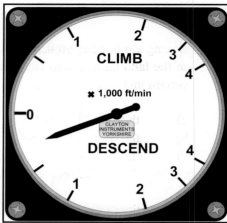

Figure 6.4. A V.S.I. With a Logarithmic Scale Showing a Descent of 250 ft/min.

so slower speeds are easier to read & more accurate

Note: 1) The Vertical Speed Indicator as fitted in Glider Aircraft is sometimes known as a "Variometer" (a simple tube device - Green for upward movement / Red for downward movement).

Note: 2) The device fitted to the IVSI to give an instant indication of vertical movement may be of the Dashpot or Dynamic-Vane type - the indications and errors being the same for both instrument types.

Time lag is overcome

Instant response of piston in Dashpot

When piston moves back when we're in a steady descent the air that comes through from the capillary

6.8   SERVICEABILITY CHECKS

On the Ground.

a)   The instrument should read zero, or the error should be within the permissible limits

    i)   ± 200 feet per minute at temperatures - 20°C + 50°C
    ii)   ± 300 feet per minute outside these temperatures

b)   There should be no apparent damage to the instrument.

In The Air. The accuracy of the instrument may be checked against the altimeter and a stop watch during a steady climb/descent and the instrument should indicate zero climb or descent when in level flight.

Lag is overcome with IVSI - But there is always lag error

VERTICAL SPEED INDICATORS

1.   During a missed approach and go-around procedure the change of aircraft attitude plus raising of the landing gear and changing of flap settings can cause short term unpredictable errors in certain instruments. The instruments most likely to be affected in this case are:

   a)   the altimeter, artificial horizon and vertical speed indicator.
   b)   the airspeed indicator, machmeter and vertical speed indicator.
   c)   the machmeter, airspeed indicator, altimeter and vertical speed indicator.
   d)   the vertical speed indicator, airspeed indicator and altimeter.

2.   The vertical speed indicator indications may be in error for some seconds after starting or finishing a climb or descent. The error is a result of:

   a)   a combination of time lag and manoeuvre induced errors.
   b)   a combination of position error and manoeuvre induced errors.
   c)   manoeuvre induced errors only.
   d)   a combination of time lag and instrument error.

3.   The advantage of having the VSI dial presentation in logarithmic spacing rather than in linear spacing is that:

   a)   at low rates of climb or descent the pointer movement is much larger and so is more easily read.
   b)   readings are instantaneous.
   c)   a greater range of rates of climb and descent is shown.
   d)   the internal mechanism is simplified by deletion of the calibration choke.

4.   In the IVSI, lag error:

   a)   is overcome by feeding a sample of static pressure to the case and delaying it to the capsule.
   b)   is virtually overcome by using a special dashpot accelerometer assembly.
   c)   is overcome by the use of logarithmic presentation.
   d)   is only overcome when initiating a climb or descent.

5.   Because the VSI measures rates of change of static pressure and not actual values of static pressure, position error:

   a)   never affects VSI indications.
   b)   may cause errors in the VSI during the take-off run.
   c)   may cause errors in VSI indications whenever airspeed is changed, if at the same time there is a change in position error.
   d)   may cause errors in VSI indications whenever airspeed is changed, even if there is no change in position error.

© Oxford Aviation Services Limited

6.   When entering a steep turn, an IVSI is likely to show:

    a)   no change in altitude.
    b)   a slight climb.
    c)   a slight descent.
    d)   a slight descent at high airspeed only.

7.   If the static vent becomes blocked during a climb:

    a)   the VSI will stop at the rate of climb of the aircraft at the time of blockage.
    b)   the VSI will indicate a decreasing rate of climb.
    c)   the VSI will return to zero.
    d)   the VSI will indicate an increasing rate of climb.

8.   In conditions of clear air turbulence:

    a)   the standard VSI is more sensitive.
    b)   the IVSI is more sensitive.
    c)   both types will react the same.
    d)   the vertical acceleration pump will not be affected.

9.   Change of temperature as an aircraft climbs or descends:

    a)   will affect VSI readings whenever temperature lapse rate differs from standard conditions.
    b)   is compensated at the metering unit by means of a capillary and orifice.
    c)   has no effect on the VSI as only static pressure is used in this instrument.
    d)   may be allowed for by use of tables or computer.

10.   Permissible limits of accuracy of the VSI are .... when .... within a temperature range of ....
        and .... outside this range.

    a)   ± 250 fpm, on the ground, -20°C to +50°C, ± 300 fpm
    b)   ± 200 fpm, at any height,   -20°C to +30°C, ± 300 fpm
    c)   ± 250 fpm, at any height,   -20°C to +50°C, ± 300 fpm
    d)   ± 200 fpm, on the ground, -20°C to +50°C, ± 300 fpm

CHAPTER SEVEN - THE MACHMETER

Contents

		Page
7.1	HIGH SPEED FLIGHT.	7 - 1
7.2	OPERATING LIMITS.	7 - 1
7.3	SPEED OF SOUND	7 - 1
7.4	MACHMETER. PRINCIPLE OF OPERATION.	7 - 2
7.5	MACHMETER CONSTRUCTION.	7 - 3
7.6	MACHMETER ERRORS.	7 - 3
7.7	BLOCKAGES.	7 - 4
7.8	ABBREVIATIONS.	7 - 4
7.9	MACHMETER SUMMARY.	7 - 4
7.10	CLIMB AT A CONSTANT CAS IN STANDARD (ISA) ATMOSPHERE	7 - 5
7.11	DESCENT AT A CONSTANT MACH NUMBER IN STANDARD CONDITIONS.	7 - 6
7.12	CLIMB AND DESCENT THROUGH AN ISOTHERMAL LAYER.	7 - 6
7.13	CLIMB AND DESCENT THROUGH AN INVERSION	7 - 7
7.14	CLIMB/DESCENT SUMMARY.	7 - 7
7.15	EXAMPLE PROBLEMS ASSOCIATED WITH THE MACHMETER.	7 - 8
7.16	MACH / AIRSPEED INDICATOR - (MASI)	7 - 10
7.17	CONSTRUCTION - (MASI)	7 - 10
	MACHMETERS QUESTIONS	7 - 12

* Only Zerros Mach Meter suffers from
are Instrument
& Pressure Error
(& position & Manauvre)

7.1   HIGH SPEED FLIGHT.

In high speed aircraft the **machmeter is an essential instrument**. As an aircraft approaches the local speed of sound the airflow over some parts of the fuselage or wings may be accelerated up to the speed of sound and a **shock wave** will form. These shock waves cause more drag, less lift, buffeting, and reduction in effectiveness or even a reversal of control reactions.

The speed at which airflow over some part of the aeroplane first reaches the speed of sound, and shock waves form, is called the **critical Mach number,** known as - **Mcrit**.

Mcrit varies with aircraft design, typical values ranging from 0.7 to 0.9 Mach. Only aircraft which are designed for transonic or supersonic flight should closely approach or exceed Mcrit.

The Machmeter therefore displays the present Mach Number so that the pilot can keep his Mach Number well below the particular Mach Crit for his aircraft and avoid the problems associated with high speed flight.

7.2   OPERATING LIMITS.

To limit an aircraft's Mach number to a safe speed below Mcrit operating limits are specified:

M_{no} Maximum permitted Mach number for normal operation

M_{mo} Maximum permitted operating Mach number under any conditions

7.3   SPEED OF SOUND

The **speed of sound** is not constant but **varies with air temperature**. A formula for calculating the local speed of sound (LSS) is:

$$LSS = 38.95\sqrt{T}$$

where,

LSS is given in Knots,
38.95 is a constant, and
T is the **absolute temperature**, (0°C = 273°A = 273° K)

Therefore the higher the air temperature, the higher the speed of sound, and vice versa. Since temperature normally reduces as altitude increases, the speed of sound normally reduces as altitude increases.

In ISA conditions at mean sea level (+15°C) the speed of sound is 661.32 knots, while at 30 000 feet ISA (- 45°C) the speed of sound will have reduced to 589.18 knots.

7 - 1

7.4   MACHMETER. PRINCIPLE OF OPERATION.

The machmeter uses two capsules and linkages to indicate the aircrafts True Air Speed (TAS) as a proportion of the local speed of sound (LSS)

The first capsule is an Airspeed Capsule which will expand and contract as a result of changes in the Dynamic pressure.

$$\text{Mach Number} = \frac{\text{TAS}}{\text{LSS}}$$

The second capsule is a sealed Altimeter Capsule which will expand and contract as the static pressure inside the instrument case changes.

However, MN is proportional to....

$$\frac{\frac{D}{\rho}}{\frac{S}{\rho}}$$

As Density (ρ) cancels out, we can see that:-

MN is proportional to...........

$$\frac{D}{S} = \frac{P - S}{S}$$

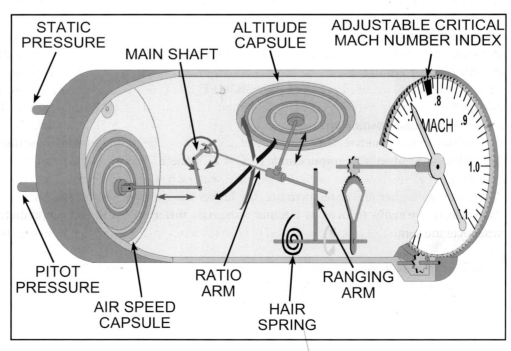

Figure 7.1. The Machmeter.

7.5   MACHMETER CONSTRUCTION.

Figure 7.1. shows the parts of a machmeter (which must be learnt). It consists of a simple aneroid **altitude capsule** and an **airspeed capsule** which are connected at the ratio arm.

Static pressure enters the case of the instrument, while Pitot pressure is fed directly into the airspeed capsule. Expansion or contraction of the airspeed capsule is transmitted via the airspeed link and **main shaft** to the **ratio arm**, but the position of the ratio arm is also governed by expansion or contraction of the altitude capsule.

A spring-loaded **ranging arm** transmits the movement of the ratio arm to the pointer mechanism. Basically, if either or both **capsules expand** (due to an increase in IAS and / or altitude) then the ranging arm will rotate out of the diagram and the indicated **Mach Number will increase**. If airspeed or altitude reduce then the ratio and ranging arms move back into the paper, and a lower Mach Number is displayed.

An **adjustable index** on the instrument scale can be positioned by means of a small knob. This index can be set to the **limiting Mach Number** for the aircraft type (in straight and level flight), to provide a visual warning to the pilot. It may be a wide index, so emphasising the critical Mach number.

7.6   MACHMETER ERRORS.

The machmeter suffers from **instrument, position** and **manoeuvre induced errors only**. It does **not** suffer from temperature or density errors, as these errors cancel out. In addition since compressibility error depends on dynamic / static pressure, and the instrument is calibrated to this ratio, compressibility error is calibrated out.

Position Error. The instrument uses the same sources of Pitot and Static pressure as the ASI and therefore suffers from position error caused by disturbed airflow at the pitot head and / or static vent. At Mach Numbers below M_{mo}, careful design and positioning of the pressure sources ensure that position error on modern jet aircraft is small. However, above M_{mo}, changes in airflow may cause position error to become bigger and possibly change its sign. If the sign of the position error is such that the machmeter under-reads, the error could become dangerous at high Mach numbers. The normal arrangement in modern jet transport aircraft is to allow for instrument and position error such that the machmeter **always over-reads**.

Manoeuvre Induced Error.   The machmeter will suffer an additional, unpredictable error whenever the aeroplane manoeuvres. This is due to the unpredictable changes in the airflow over the static source.

Climbs & Descent checks
→ Same as for ASI
@ 500 PVD

↳ The Rat ran in
ratio arm, ranging arm, indicator

Accuracy → ±0·01 Mach : Start of Scale
to ±0·02 Mach @ Limit of Scale

7.7   BLOCKAGES.

Static Source Blocked. If the static source is blocked the pressure in the Machmeter case will not alter when the aircraft climbs or descends.

If a blockage occurs in a **climb** the altitude capsule will not move. Assuming a constant IAS (and therefore a constant dynamic pressure) the airspeed capsule will contract as the static component of pitot pressure reduces. The Machmeter will therefore **under read.**

If a blockage occurs in a **descent** at a constant IAS, the airspeed capsule will expand due to the increasing static component of pitot pressure. The Machmeter will therefore **over read.**

Pitot Source Blocked. Assuming a climb or descent at a constant IAS (and therefore a constant dynamic pressure) the Machmeter will **over read in the climb** and **under read in the descent.** In the climb the airspeed capsule will expand in error because the static component of pitot in the capsule will be greater than the static in the case. In the descent the static component of pitot will be too small and therefore the airspeed capsule will contract.

NOTE.   It may be noticed that the Machmeter blockage errors are the same as the ASI blockage errors.

7.8   ABBREVIATIONS.

MMR machmeter reading, the uncorrected reading

IMN   indicated Mach number, MMR corrected for instrument error (the values quoted in Flight Manuals are normally IMN)

TMN   true Mach number, IMN corrected for position error $M_{mo.}$ There is much less risk of an over-speed condition arising when this is available.

7.9   MACHMETER SUMMARY.

Mach number = TAS / LSS.

Speed of sound is proportional to the square root of the absolute temperature, and therefore decreases with the decrease in temperature normally encountered with increase in altitude.

While climbing at a constant Mach number, TAS decreases and CAS decreases more rapidly, the LSS also decreases..

While climbing at a constant CAS, TAS and Mach number increase but the LSS decreases.

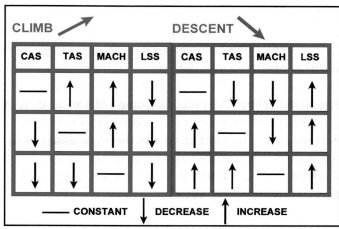

Figures 7.2 & 7.3. Airspeed and Mach N°
Relationship in ISA/JSA.

Remember that in calculations involving the **Jet Standard Atmosphere**, the temperature is assumed to be + 15°C at MSL with a lapse rate of 2° per 1000 with **no** upper limit (ie no tropopause).

7.10   CLIMB AT A CONSTANT CAS IN STANDARD (ISA) ATMOSPHERE.

If we were to climb at 330 kt CAS from sea level to 36,000 ft in the standard atmosphere,

a)   TAS will increase from 330 kt to 593 kt, and

b)   Mach number will increase from 0.5 M to 1.05 M.

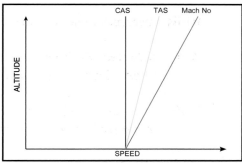

Figure 7.4. Climb / Descent in the
JSA Atmosphere at a Constant CAS.

The rapid rise of Mach number (in this case far exceeding M_{CRIT}) is the reason why high performance aircraft are flown on CAS (or IAS) for the first part of the climb before transferring to a constant Mach number for the rest of the climb. Similarly in the descent at constant CAS, TAS and Mach number reduce, with Mach number reducing at a greater rate.

This is shown diagrammatically in Figure 7.4 For a constant CAS (blue line) as altitude increases, TAS (the yellow line) increases, and Mach number (the red line) increases at a greater rate. The navigation computer can also be used to show the relationship between CAS, TAS and Mach number but also gives us an idea of magnitude.

At MSL under ISA
CAS & TAS are the same

Now consider a descent at 0.8 M from 40,000 ft to sea level in the jet standard atmosphere on the navigation computer.

At 40,000 ft 0.8 M is 450 kt TAS, at sea level it has increased to 528 kt. The CAS has increased more markedly from 242 kt at 40,000 ft to 528 kt at mean sea level. This would exceed V_{NO}. Therefore although Mach number is used at altitude, CAS will be used in the descent.

Note:- You will have probably noticed by now that the relationship of CAS, TAS and Mach number as an aeroplane climbs or descends through the standard atmosphere remains the same. That is Figures 7.4. and 7.5. are the same - just tilted to one side or the other. Therefore when considering the climb/descent through an isothermal layer and an inversion only the constant TAS figure will be shown.

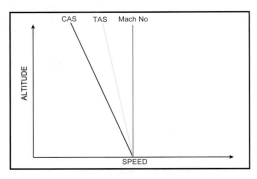

Figure 7.5. Climb / Descent in the JSA Atmosphere at a Constant Mach number.

7.11   DESCENT AT A CONSTANT MACH NUMBER IN STANDARD CONDITIONS.

During a descent in the ISA, the LSS will be increasing (as temperature increases). Therefore if Mach number is being kept constant the TAS must be increasing (Mach number = TAS / LSS) During the descent air density increases and if TAS is also increasing the CAS must also increase at a greater rate (Dynamic Pressure = $\frac{1}{2}\rho V^2$) . This is shown in Figure 7.5. Similarly in a climb at constant Mach number the TAS or CAS both reduce.

7.12   CLIMB AND DESCENT THROUGH AN ISOTHERMAL LAYER.

Constant Mach number

An isothermal layer is a layer of air in which the temperature does not change. Therefore the LSS will not change, and for a constant Mach number the TAS will not alter. The CAS will change however due to density error, reducing during the climb and increasing during a descent.

Constant CAS

Climbing at a constant CAS, the TAS and Mach number will both increase (at the same rate).

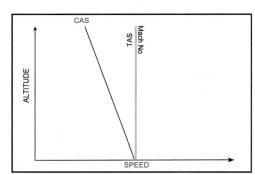

Figure 7.6. Climb / Descent in an Isothermal Layer at a Constant Mach number.

7.13 CLIMB AND DESCENT THROUGH AN INVERSION *(temp increasing)*

Constant Mach number

In an inversion the temperature of the air will increase (get warmer) as altitude increases. Therefore in a climb the LSS will increase, and for a constant Mach number the TAS will increase

(Mach number = TAS/LSS).

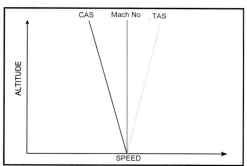

Figure 7.7. Climb / Descent in an Inversion at a Constant Mach number.

CAS will reduce as air density reduces.
Descending at a constant Mach number the TAS will reduce and the CAS will increase.

Constant CAS

Climbing at a constant CAS, the TAS and Mach number will both increase (TAS at a greater rate than Mach number).

7.14 CLIMB/DESCENT SUMMARY.

In summary;

TAS will always increase when an aeroplane climbs at a constant CAS.

Climbing at a constant TAS the CAS will always reduce.

This is because pressure has a greater effect on air density than temperature.

Climbing at a constant CAS the Mach number will always increase.

Climbing at a constant Mach number the CAS will always reduce.

This is because the CAS/TAS density error dominates over the change in LSS due to temperature variation.

✳ Need to know the graphs

✳ Mach Meter only has Instrument & pressure error.

7.15   EXAMPLE PROBLEMS ASSOCIATED WITH THE MACHMETER.

Problem 1.   What is the speed of sound at FL 380 in ISA conditions?

Solution 1.

a)   In the ISA atmosphere FL 380 is above the tropopause and therefore the temperature will be - 56.5°C or 216.5° K

$$LSS = 38.95 \sqrt{T}$$
$$= 38.95 \sqrt{216.5}$$
$$= \textbf{573 knots}$$

b)   These calculations can also be completed on the navigation computer. Place the Mach number index arrow against the temperature (in°C), locate M1.0 (the blue 10 on the CRP5) on the inner Mach number scale and read off the TAS on the outer scale.

Problem 2.   Determine the TAS corresponding to 0.70 M at JSA MSL (+15°C or 288°K).

Solution 2.

a)   Using the computer, set the Mach number index against + 15°C in the Airspeed window. Against 7 (for 0.7 M) on the inner scale, read off the answer (463 knots) on the outer scale.

b)   Alternatively calculate TAS from the formula
$$TAS = Mach\ number \times LSS$$
$$= 0.7 \times 38.95 \sqrt{288}$$
$$= 0.7 \times 661 = 463\ knots$$

Problem 3.   Calculate without using a computer the altitude in the atmosphere at which a TAS of 450 knots corresponds to Mach .80.

Solution 3.

$$Mach\ Number = \frac{TAS}{LSS} \qquad\qquad LSS = \frac{TAS}{MN}$$

$$LSS = \frac{450}{.8} = 562.5\ Kts$$

However, LSS $= 38.95\sqrt{T}$

$$\sqrt{T} = \frac{LSS}{38.95} = \frac{562.5}{38.95} = 14.44$$

$$T = 14.44^2 = 209°$$

T = 209° Absolute which is equal to - 64° C

- 64° C occurs at **FL395** in the JSA which has **no** tropopause.

Problem 4   If a decrease of 0.12 in the Mach Number results in a decrease of 80 Knots in the TAS, what is the local speed of sound.

Solution 4

$$\text{Mach Number} = \frac{TAS}{LSS} \qquad\qquad LSS = \frac{TAS}{MN}$$

$$LSS = \frac{80}{.12} = 667 \text{ Kts}$$

Problem 5   An aircraft is flying at FL360 with a Tas of 467 Knots at Mach No 0.8 when the temperature difference from JSA is +9. What is the Temperature difference at FL320 if Mach 0.8 still gives a TAS of 467 Knots.

Solution 5.

At FL360 in JSA temp would be - 57°C. JSA +9 would be **- 48° C**

However if Mach No and TAS remain the same, then we must be flying in an **Isothermal layer**, so the Temperature of - 48°C and the LSS would remain the **same**.

If the Temperature at FL320 is also - 48°, Temp Deviation from standard must be **+ 1°** as JSA should be - 49°C.

7.16   MACH / AIRSPEED INDICATOR.

Since many commercial aircraft require indications of both IAS and Mach number, it is sensible to combine both instruments. The basic principals of both instruments still apply.

Errors

The combined instrument will have the errors of both the Machmeter and the airspeed indicator, namely; instrument, position, manoeuvre induced, density and compressibility errors.

7.17   CONSTRUCTION

There are two types of Mach/Airspeed Indicator:

a)   A self contained instrument fed from Pitot and Static sources.
b)   A combined instrument fed from the Air Data Computer.

Note that:

i)   The airspeed pointer moves clockwise over a fixed scale.

ii)   From 0.5 M the Mach number is read off the same pointer as it moves over a moving Mach number scale. This scale rotates anti-clockwise beneath the pointer as Mach number increases.

c)   A second striped needle may be present to mark V_{mo}.

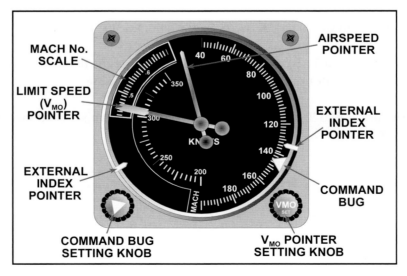

Figure 7.8. A Mach / Airspeed Indicator Fed from Pitot and Static Sources.

If the aircraft is fitted with an Air Data Computer (ADC) it will measure Pitot pressure, Static pressure and Total Air Temperature and then electronically, send the information to any instruments and other computers which require it. The advantages related to the combined Mach / Airspeed instrument are;

a)   The ability to correct for instrument and position errors to give Rectified Airspeed (CAS) instead of ASIR.

b)   The use of a digital displays for both Mach number and CAS.

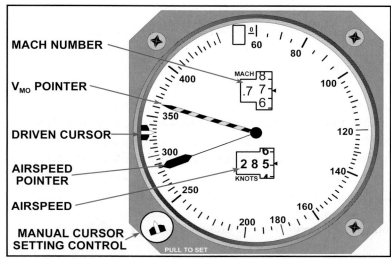

Figure 7.9 A Combined Instrument Fed from the Air Data Computer.

MACHMETERS

1.   The local speed of sound is equal to:

          (K = Constant)
          a)   K $\sqrt{}$ temperature ($^\circ$F) knots
          b)   K $\sqrt{}$ temperature ($^\circ$K) knots
          c)   K $\sqrt{}$ temperature ($^\circ$C) knots
          d)   K $\sqrt{}$ temperature ($^\circ$K) metres per second.

2.   At FL 350 with a JSA deviation of -12, the true airspeed when flying at M 0.78 is:

          a)   460 kt
          b)   436 kt
          c)   447 kt
          d)   490 kt

3.   Below is a schematic diagram of a Machmeter. Parts A, B, C and D are:

          a)   ratio arm, mach no pointer, static pressure inlet, ranging arm.
          b)   ranging arm, critical mach no index, static pressure inlet, ratio arm.
          c)   main shaft, TAS index, pitot pressure inlet, ranging arm.
          d)   ranging arm, critical mach no index, pitot inlet, main shaft.

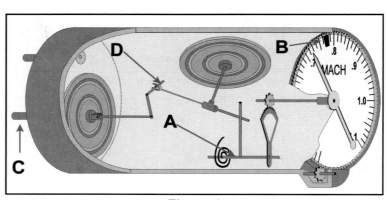

Figure 1

4.   When climbing at a constant mach number below the tropopause through an inversion:

          a)   the CAS and TAS will both increase.
          b)   the CAS and TAS will both decrease.
          c)   the CAS will decrease and the TAS will increase.
          d)   the CAS will increase and the TAS will decrease.

5.   When descending below the tropopause under normal conditions (increasing temperature) at a
        constant CAS:

        a)   both TAS and mach number will decrease.
        b)   both TAS and mach number will increase.
        c)   the TAS will decrease and the mach number will increase.
        d)   the TAS will increase and the mach number will decrease.

6.   Cruising at FL390, M 0.84 is found to give a TAS of 499 kt. The ISA deviation at this level will
        be:

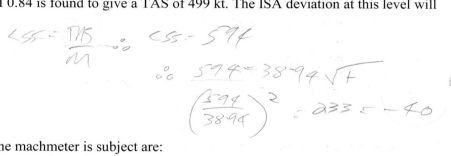

        a)   -17
        b)   +17
        c)   +19
        d)   -19

7.   The errors to which the machmeter is subject are:

        a)   instrument error, position error, compressibility error and manoeuvre induced error.
        b)   instrument error, position error.
        c)   instrument error, position error, barometric error, temperature error and manoeuvre
                induced error.
        d)   instrument error, position error, density error and manoeuvre induced error.

8.   The relationships between TAS, mach number (MNo) and local speed of sound (LSS) is:

        a)   LSS = $\dfrac{MNo}{TAS}$

        b)   MNo = $\dfrac{LSS}{TAS}$

        c)   TAS = MNo x LSS

        d)   MNo = LSS x TAS

9.   The machmeter gives an indication of mach number by measuring the ratio:

      a)   <u>pitot pressure</u>
           static pressure

      b)   <u>static pressure</u>
           dynamic pressure

      c)   <u>dynamic pressure</u>
           pitot pressure

      d)   <u>dynamic pressure</u>
           static pressure

10.   An aircraft is flying at FL350 with a JSA deviation of +8. The mach no is 0.83 and the TAS 485. If the aircraft descends to FL300 and maintains the same mach no and TAS, the JSA deviation will now be:

      a)   +8
      b)   -2
      c)   +2
      d)   -18

$LSS = 38·94 \sqrt{k}$

$\left(\dfrac{584·3}{38·94}\right)^2 = 225$

$- 273$

$- 48°C$

$M = \dfrac{TAS}{LSS}$

$LSS = \dfrac{TAS}{M} = \dfrac{485}{0·83}$

$= 584·3$

CHAPTER EIGHT - MAGNETISM

Contents

		Page
8.1	THE MAGNET	8 - 1
8.2	MAGNETIC FIELD	8 - 1
8.3	POLES OF A MAGNET	8 - 1
8.4	RED AND BLUE POLES	8 - 2
8.5	ATTRACTION AND REPULSION RULES.	8 - 2
8.6	METHODS OF MAGNETISATION	8 - 3
8.7	METHODS OF DEMAGNETISATION	8 - 4
8.8	MAGNETIC AND NON-MAGNETIC MATERIALS	8 - 5
8.9	HARD IRON AND SOFT IRON	8 - 5
8.10	TERRESTRIAL MAGNETISM	8 - 6
8.11	MAGNETIC VARIATION.	8 - 6
8.12	MAGNETIC DIP	8 - 7
8.13	FIELD STRENGTH.	8 - 8
8.14	DIRECTIVE FORCE.	8 - 8
8.16	REGULAR CHANGES IN EARTH MAGNETISM.	8 - 9
8.19	UNPREDICTABLE CHANGES IN EARTH MAGNETISM.	8 - 9
	TERRESTRIAL MAGNETISM QUESTIONS	8 - 10

8.1   THE MAGNET

For thousands of years the oxide of iron called magnetite has been observed to attract small pieces of iron. This property is known as 'magnetism'.

Another property for which magnetite was known was its North-seeking capability; if mounted on wood and floated in water it would swing round and align itself in a roughly North-South direction, so acting as a primitive compass. In more recent history it was found that some metallic elements and alloys (mainly 'ferrous' - iron and steel) could be given these properties, bars of such magnetised material being known as 'magnets'.

8.2   MAGNETIC FIELD

The field of a magnet is the space around it in which its magnetic influence is felt. This may be illustrated by placing a piece of card over a bar magnet and scattering iron filings on it. When the card is shaken or tapped the filings will take up the field pattern as shown in Figure 8.1.

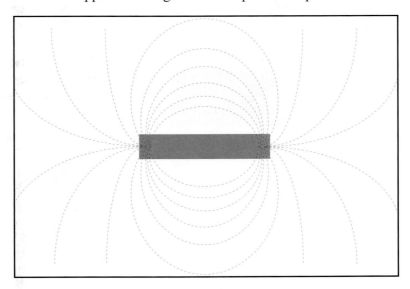

Figure 8.1. The Pattern of the Magnetic Field.

8.3   POLES OF A MAGNET

From Figure 8.1. it can be seen that the 'lines of force' traced by the iron filings converge towards small areas near the ends of the magnet.

These two areas are called the 'poles' of the magnet and are where the properties of magnetism are most strongly displayed. Magnets are made in various shapes but each magnet always has two poles.

A unit pole cannot exist. If a magnet is cut into two pieces, each piece will have two poles.

8.4   RED AND BLUE POLES

A freely suspended bar magnet (or compass needle) in the earth's magnetic field will align itself roughly North-South.

The end which points North is known as a North-seeking or **red** pole. The other end is a South-seeking or **blue** pole.

By convention, magnetic lines of force are directed out from the red pole and back in to the blue pole as shown in Figure 8.2.

— Lines of Force are unbroken   — Lines never cross

Again referring to Figure 8.2, for convenience the magnet has been divided into two halves, one half containing the red pole, the other half containing the blue pole.

The position of the poles of a magnet is determined by the ratio of the length to the width (poles are never at end of magnet)

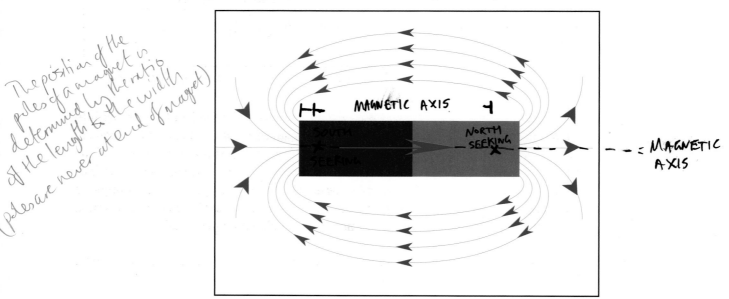

Figure 8.2. The Red and Blue Poles.

8.5   ATTRACTION AND REPULSION RULES.

If two bar magnets are placed in a line, end to end, so that the blue pole of one faces the blue pole of the other, a repulsion can be felt. If both magnets are turned around, so that red pole is close to red pole, then again the ends try to move apart. If, on the other hand, the blue pole of one magnet is placed close to the red pole of the other, an attraction is felt.
The rule is:

Like poles repel each other.

Unlike poles attract each other.

✱ Impossible to have a unit pole (single pole) magnet.

8.6 METHODS OF MAGNETISATION

Magnetism may be induced in an unmagnetised bar of iron by one of the following methods:-

a) By stroking the bar repeatedly in the same direction with one end of a magnet, a process in which the end of the bar last touched by the red end of the magnet is left as a blue pole. Figure 8.3. depicts the process and shows the resulting polarity of the iron bar.

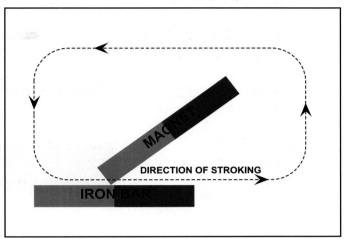

Figure 8.3. Making a Magnet by Stroking.

b) By aligning the iron bar with the lines of force of a magnetic field and subjecting it to vibration or hammering. Such agitation during manufacture (in the earth's magnetic field) is the main cause of aircraft magnetism. Figure 8.4. shows the polarity of the induced magnetism in the iron bar; it is such that there is continuity in the pattern of lines of force, as usual directed **in** to a blue pole, **out** from a red pole. The example is analogous to an aircraft being manufactured on a Northerly heading in the earth's field and acquiring a permanent red pole in the nose and blue pole in the tail.

c) In the case of soft iron (see Paragraph 8.11) simply by subjecting to a magnetic field. The induced polarity is shown in Figure 8.4.

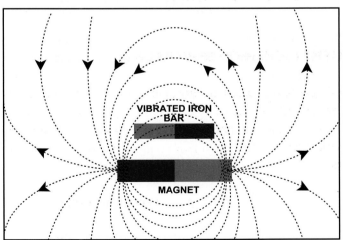

Figure 8.4. Making a Magnet by Vibrating or Hammering.

d)   By placing the specimen within a solenoid (a cylindrical coil of wire) carrying a Direct
        Current. This is the most satisfactory method as the current flowing in the coil produces
        a concentrated magnetic field along the axis of the coil so that a high degree of
        magnetism can be induced in the iron. (Note that the amount of magnetism which can
        be induced is not unlimited because, at a certain level, the iron becomes magnetically
        'saturated'). Figure 8.5. shows the polarity of the magnetism induced in the bar inside
        the solenoid. (If the current flow were reversed the induced magnetic polarity would be
        reversed).

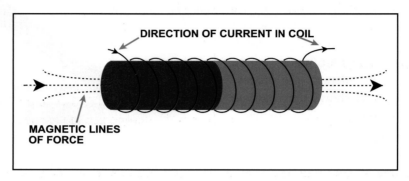

Figure 8.5. Magnetisation by Solenoid.

8.7   METHODS OF DEMAGNETISATION

Three ways of removing most or all of the magnetism from a magnetised item are listed
below.

a)   **Shock**. A magnetised bar of iron can be placed at **right angles** to the earth's
        magnetic field and hammered.

b)   **Heat.** If the specimen is heated to about 900°C, it loses its magnetism and this does
        not return as the specimen cools.

c)   **Electric Current.** The component is placed inside a solenoid carrying alternating
        current, the amplitude of which is gradually reduced to zero. The strong alternating
        magnetic field produced by the alternating current keeps reversing the direction of
        magnetisation (that is the **polarity** of the magnetism) in the specimen.

Decreasing AC current

Not only is the polarity being reversed, but the intensity of magnetisation is being reduced as
the current is reduced. The specimen's magnetism is very quickly reduced to zero or very
nearly zero.

8.10   MAGNETIC AND NON-MAGNETIC MATERIALS

Magnetic materials are 'ferrous' metals iron and steel, steel being iron alloyed with substances such as carbon, cobalt, nickel, chromium, and tungsten. These metals are called 'ferromagnetic' and in an aircraft they may be magnetised and produce deviation in the aircraft's compasses.

Many materials used in aircraft construction are non-magnetic and do not affect the compass.

Examples of such non-ferrous substances are aluminium, duralumin, brass, copper, plastic, and paint.

8.9   HARD IRON AND SOFT IRON

Ferromagnetic material can be broadly divided into two classes, **hard iron** and **soft iron**. The words hard and soft do not refer to the physical properties of the material but to their magnetic characteristics.

A strong magnetising field is required to produce magnetic saturation in hard iron.

Hard iron magnetism is said to be 'permanent', meaning that the material, typically steel containing cobalt or chromium, remains magnetised for an indefinite period after it has been removed from the magnetising field.

Such a substance is suitable for permanent magnets. Soft iron magnetism is called 'temporary' (or 'transient' or 'induced') the substance being easy to saturate magnetically with only a weak magnetising field but retaining little or no magnetism when the field is removed. Nearly pure iron behaves in this way.

Some materials exhibit magnetic characteristics which lie somewhere between those of hard iron and soft iron. These substances can be magnetised but this 'sub-permanent' magnetism is lost partly or wholly over a period of time.

DESCRIPTION	METAL	EASE OF MAGNETISM	RETENTION OF MAGNETISM
HARD IRON	COBALT AND TUNGSTEN STEEL	HARD	CONSIDERABLE LENGTH OF TIME
SOFT IRON	SILICON IRON PURE IRON	EASY	PRACTICALLY NIL

8.10   TERRESTRIAL MAGNETISM

The earth behaves as though a huge permanent magnet were situated near the centre producing a magnetic field over the surface.

Figure 8.6. shows that the poles of this hypothetical earth-magnet do not lie on the earth's spin axis, this lack of symmetry giving rise to magnetic variation. The earth's blue pole lies at present beneath Northern Canada in the area around 70°N 95° W, the red pole being below Antarctica at about 72° S.

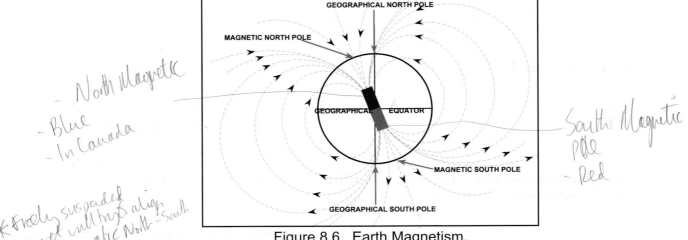

[handwritten: - North Magnetic]
[handwritten: - Blue - In Canada]
[handwritten: South Magnetic Pole - Red]
[handwritten: ★ freely suspended magnet will try to align with Magnetic North - South]

Figure 8.6. Earth Magnetism.

8.11   MAGNETIC VARIATION.

The direction of the earth's field at any given point can be indicated by a freely-suspended magnet. Such a magnet will align itself roughly in a North-South direction with its red pole towards the North magnetic pole.

The longitudinal axis of the magnet defines the direction of the magnet meridian at the point. The **magnetic meridian** is the direction of the horizontal component of the earth's field at a point on the earth's surface.

The angle, measured in the horizontal plane, between the magnetic meridian at a point and the true meridian at the point is known as the magnetic **variation**.

Variation is designated West or East depending on whether the magnetic pole lies to the West or to the East of true North.

Variation can have any value from zero to 180°, the latter occurring on the true meridian linking North geographical with North magnetic pole, similarly in the Southern hemisphere.

[handwritten: Maximum Variation possible is 180°]

[handwritten: - Occurs on Meridian which join (called True Meridian) True North & Magnetic North]
[handwritten: - & also at South]

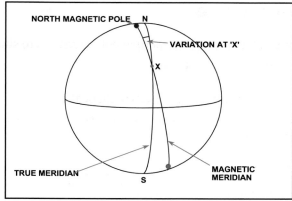

Figure 8.7. Magnetic Variation.

8.12   MAGNETIC DIP

Except near the 'magnetic equator', where the lines of force are parallel to the surface, one end of the freely-suspended magnet will dip below the horizontal, pointing to the nearer pole.

To the North of the magnetic equator, the magnet's red pole will be lower whereas to the South the blue pole will be lower. The angle, measured in the vertical plane, between the axis of the magnet and the horizontal is called the **angle of dip**.

Fairly closely following the geographical equator (in the main 10° of latitude of it) is the 'magnetic equator', which can be represented on a chart by a line joining points on the earth where the angle of dip is zero.

If the freely-suspended magnet is moved either North or South of the magnetic equator the dip gradually increases, reaching about 66° in the United Kingdom. Over the earth's magnetic poles the dip is 90° and the magnet is then vertical.

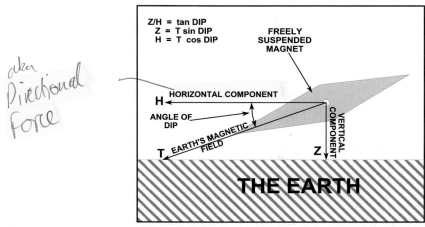

Figure 8.8. Resolution of the Earth's Field.

8.13   FIELD STRENGTH.

The total force T exerted at a point by the earth's field acts in the direction taken up by a freely-suspended magnet influenced **only** by the earth's field. The total force, angle of dip, and magnetic variation at a point are sometimes known as the 'magnetic elements' for that place. It is convenient to resolve this total force T into its horizontal and vertical components H and Z respectively. Figure 8.8. demonstrates this resolution.

8.14   DIRECTIVE FORCE.

The horizontal component H of the earth's field is known as the **directive force** because it is the component which aligns the magnetic compass needle with the magnetic meridian, so providing a directional reference. When either of the earth's magnetic poles is approached, this component approaches zero strength, while the value of Z approaches that of T. Over the pole, with dip 90° and zero directive force H, the magnetic sensor (compass) becomes useless.

In the region of the magnetic equator the strength of the directive force H approaches the value of T, while Z approaches zero as does the angle of dip.

It becomes apparent that the directive force H decreases as the angle of dip increases, and vice versa and Figure 8.9. serves to illustrates this.

In fact, the relationship between H and dip angle is not quite as simple as it appears, because of irregularities in the pattern of the earth's field and variations with position and time of the total magnetic force T.

The strength of the horizontal component H at a latitude about 60°N of the magnetic equator is very roughly half the value of H at the magnetic equator.

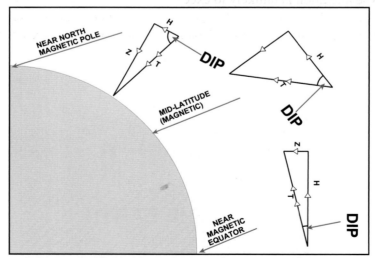

Figure 8.9. The Effect of Latitude on the Components of Dip.

8.15   REGULAR CHANGES IN EARTH MAGNETISM.

Secular Change. The earth's field not only lacks symmetry but is also subject to several known periodic changes.

Of these, the **secular** changes are the most significant and are produced by the slow movement of the magnetic poles about the geographic poles, the period of this cycle being apparently about 960 years.

The North magnetic pole is moving slowly westward, this wander mainly affecting magnetic variation.

In the UK the value of Westerly variation is currently decreasing at a rate of 7 minutes per annum, and the predicted variation in London in the year 2240 is zero.

The annual rate of change of variation is shown on navigation charts so that the variation printed against the isogonals can be readily up-dated.

Other regular changes occur diurnally, annually, and over an eleven-year period, this latter cycle apparently being related to the eleven-year cycle of sunspot activity. These changes, unlike the secular type mentioned earlier, are not of sufficient magnitude to affect normal navigation.

8.16   UNPREDICTABLE CHANGES IN EARTH MAGNETISM.

Magnetic 'storms' of varying intensity and lasting for as long as three days occur at irregular intervals. These phenomena appear to be produced by unusually large sunspots.

The main effect of these magnetic storms is a temporary but significant change in magnetic variation. The alteration is unlikely to exceed 2° in the UK but in the Arctic and Antarctic the change may exceed 5° and last for as long as an hour. The value of the directive force H can also change and in high latitudes may fall below the minimum required for efficient compass operation.

TERRESTRIAL MAGNETISM

1. The red pole of a freely suspended magnet will point towards .... and at latitude 60°N will point .... at an angle known as the angle of ....

    a)   the nose of the aircraft, downwards, deviation.
    b)   the north magnetic pole, downwards, variation.
    c)   the nearest pole, downwards, declination.
    d)   the north magnetic pole, downwards, dip.

2. If the total force of the earth's field at a point is T and the horizontal and vertical components H and Z, the value of H is found by the formula:

    a)   H = T sin dip
    b)   H = Z tan dip
    c)   H = T cos dip
    d)   H = T tan dip

3. In the diagram below, the compass heading of the aircraft is ...., the magnetic heading .... and the true heading ....

    a)   025°   015°   020°
    b)   335°   035°   020°
    c)   335°   340°   035°
    d)   025°   015°   340°

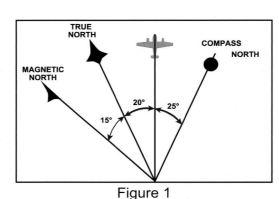

Figure 1

4. The directive force of the earth's magnetic field:

    a)   varies with the heading of the aircraft.
    b)   increases as the magnetic variation increases.
    c)   increases as magnetic latitude increases.
    d)   is greatest at the magnetic equator.

5. The slow change in the earth's magnetic variation is known as the .... change and is caused by ....

    a)   annual, westerly movement of the magnetic pole.
    b)   diurnal, easterly movement of the magnetic pole.
    c)   secular, westerly movement of the magnetic pole.
    d)   annual, sunspot activity.

6.   Soft iron is comparatively .... to magnetise whilst hard iron is .... to demagnetise.

      a)   easy; difficult.
      b)   easy; easy.
      c)   difficult; easy.
      d)   difficult; difficult.

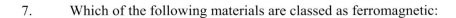

7.   Which of the following materials are classed as ferromagnetic:

      a)   iron, steel, carbon-fibre.
      b)   nickel, iron, steel.
      c)   copper, iron, carbon steel.
      d)   iron, cobalt steel, chromium steel.

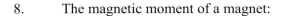

8.   The magnetic moment of a magnet:

      a)   is the product of pole strength and effective length.
      b)   varies inversely as the square of the distance between the poles.
      c)   varies directly as the square of the distance between the poles.
      d)   decreases as the magnet length increases.

CHAPTER NINE - THE DIRECT INDICATING COMPASS

Contents

		Page
9.1	THE MAGNETIC COMPASS	9 - 1
9.2	DIRECT INDICATING MAGNETIC COMPASS	9 - 1
9.3	THE VERTICAL CARD COMPASS	9 - 2
9.4	THE GRID RING COMPASS	9 - 2
9.5	COMPASS REQUIREMENTS	9 - 3
9.6	HORIZONTALITY	9 - 3
9.7	SENSITIVITY	9 - 4
9.8	APERIODICITY	9 - 4
9.9	THE COMPASS LIQUID	9 - 5
9.10	SERVICEABILITY CHECKS	9 - 5
9.11	DAMPING AND PIVOT FRICTION TESTS	9 - 6
9.12	DEVIATION	9 - 6
9.13	ACCELERATION AND TURNING ERRORS	9 - 7
9.14	ERRORS CAUSED BY LINEAR ACCELERATION	9 - 8
9.15	SUMMARY OF ACCELERATION ERRORS	9 - 10
9.16	TURNING ERRORS	9 - 11
9.17	TURNING ERRORS - LIQUID SWIRL	9 - 15
9.18	SUMMARY OF TURNING ERRORS	9 - 15
	DIRECT READING MAGNETIC COMPASSES QUESTIONS	9 - 18

9.1   THE MAGNETIC COMPASS.

A compass is an instrument designed to indicate direction on the surface of the earth, relative to some known datum. The magnetic compass uses the horizontal component of the earth's field as its directional datum. Unfortunately, the earth's field is normally not aligned with the true meridian - the most desirable datum from which to measure direction. The angular difference between true and magnetic meridians is called the **magnetic variation** discussed in the previous chapter.

The purpose of a magnetic 'steering' compass in an aircraft is to indicate heading, the direction in which the aircraft is pointing.

Magnetic influences - iron/steel components, electric currents - distort the earth's field so that the compass magnet assembly deviates from the magnetic meridian. This is called **compass deviation**.

The rules for applying variation and deviation to the compass heading indication in order to determine true heading are detailed in the Navigation notes.

9.2   DIRECT INDICATING MAGNETIC COMPASS.

This chapter deals with the direct indicating or direct reading magnetic compass, where the pilot directly reads his heading in relation to the pivoted magnet assembly.

There are two basic types of direct reading magnetic compasses used in aircraft, **the vertical card** and, less commonly, **the grid ring compass**.

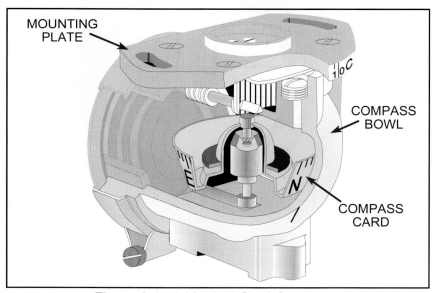

Figure 9.1. A Vertical Card Compass.

© Oxford Aviation Services Limited

9.3   THE VERTICAL CARD COMPASS.

The vertical card compass - which is also known as the B-type or E-type - is the direct reading compass in general use. It is usually the main magnetic heading reference in light aircraft and the standby compass in larger aircraft.

It consists of a circular compass card attached directly to the magnet assembly. This combined unit is suspended in liquid within the compass bowl. A vertical lubber line on the glass window of the bowl, enables the heading to be read off the compass card.

9.4   THE GRID RING COMPASS.

The P-type compass or grid ring compass is found on older aircraft. It is more accurate than the vertical card compass and is more stable.

It is however heavier, bulkier and more expensive. In addition it can only be read in straight and level flight, as the grid ring has to be unclamped and aligned with the north reference before a reading can be taken against the lubber line.

The grid ring compass also differs from the vertical card compass in that it achieves a greater periodicity by the addition of **damping wires** which also rotate through the compass liquid.

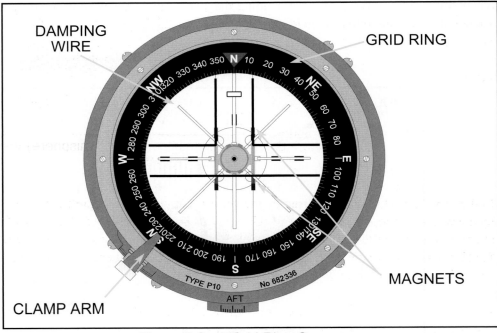

Figure 9.2. A Grid Ring Compass.

9.5   COMPASS REQUIREMENTS.

The direct reading magnetic compass contains a pivoted magnet which must be able to align itself, and remain aligned, with the horizontal component of the earth's magnetic field.   For the compass to succeed, certain requirements must be satisfied. The most important of these are that the magnet system must be:

a)   **Horizontal**
b)   **Sensitive**
c)   **Aperiodic**

9.6   HORIZONTALITY.

In order to measure direction in the horizontal, the magnets must lie as nearly as possible in the horizontal plane during normal straight and level flight. A freely suspended magnet assembly would align itself with the earth's total field so the magnets would only be horizontal at the magnetic equator.

To achieve horizontality, the magnet assembly is **'pendulously suspended'**, the centre of gravity of this assembly being lower than its supporting pivot, as shown in Figure 9.3.

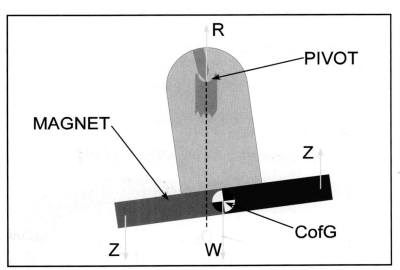

reduce angle of dip

Figure 9.3. Equilibrium (Northern Hemisphere) Viewed From West.

In this way, the tilting effect caused by the vertical component Z of the earth's field is opposed by the weight of the magnet assembly, this equilibrium being achieved at the cost of only a very slight residual tilt of the magnets (North-seeking ends down) - by about 2° in mid-latitudes - in the Northern hemisphere. (South-seeking end down in the Southern hemisphere). Figure 9.3. shows the two turning couples involved.

One is produced by Z which exerts a downward force on the red (North-seeking) end of the compass magnet and an upward force on the blue end.

75°N and above we'd need a longer pendulum

The other couple is produced by the weight W acting downwards through the centre of gravity (displaced because of the tilt) and the reaction R acting upwards through the pivot.

For equilibrium, the magnet takes up the amount of tilt necessary to make the couples balance. (A third - very weak - couple produced by the horizontal component, H, of the earth's field, opposing the tilt has been omitted for simplicity).

9.7   SENSITIVITY.

The magnet system is required to seek the horizontal component H of the earth's field in all areas except near the magnetic poles - where the horizontal component is inadequate.

The notes on magnetism show that the ability of a pivoted magnet to align itself with an external field - its sensitivity - depends on the strength of the external field and on the magnetic moment of the magnet. The weak external field (H) at a place cannot be changed, but the magnetic moment of the magnet can be increased - by increasing the magnet's length and/or pole strength.

It is however undesirable to increase the magnet length (see Paragraph 9.8) so the pole strength is increased by using **two, four or six short magnets** or a circular magnet, made of an alloy which will accept and retain the high degree of magnetism required.

Sensitivity is further increased by reducing friction. This is achieved in three ways:

a)   By using an **iridium-tipped pivot** in a **jewelled** cup

b)   By **lubricating the pivot** with the liquid which fills the compass bowl.

c)   By reducing the **effective weight** of the magnet assembly acting down through the pivot, because the liquid that the magnet assembly is displacing is denser than air .

9.8   APERIODICITY.

The magnetic assembly is required to be aperiodic or **'dead beat'**, which means that it should settle down quickly on a steady indication after being displaced by turbulence or manoeuvres.

Any tendency to oscillate must be quickly 'damped out'. The desired aperiodicity is achieved as follows:

a)   **Several short magnets** are used instead of one longer one. This keeps the mass of the assembly near the centre, so reducing the moment of inertia and consequently making any oscillations easier to damp out. Light alloy is utilised wherever possible in order to minimise the weight of the assembly framework.

9 - 4

b)   The primary purpose of the liquid in the compass bowl is to act as a **damping liquid** on the compass assembly. The grid ring compass dampens oscillations more rapidly than the vertical card compass, due to addition of **damping wires**. These wires are attached to the magnet assembly and also pass through the damping liquid. (See Figure 9.2.)

9.9   THE COMPASS LIQUID

The liquid mentioned earlier is essential to the design of the compass. Two difficulties may arise.

Firstly, the liquid is likely to expand or contract with change of temperature; this is overcome by incorporating an expansion chamber or 'Sylphon tube'.

Secondly, errors occur in sustained turns as a result of 'liquid swirl'. Liquid swirl occurs due to the viscosity of the liquid, because of this the liquid chosen should have a low viscosity to minimise liquid swirl. Liquid swirl is discussed further in Paragraph 9.17.

Various liquids, including alcohol have been used. The main properties required of a compass liquid are:

a)   Low coefficient of expansion

b)   Low viscosity   *(for sensitivity (though Aperodicity needs ↑ viscosity))*

c)   Transparency

d)   Low freezing point

e)   High boiling point

f)   Non-corrosiveness

Dimethyl Siloxane Polymer - meets most of these requirements

9.10   SERVICEABILITY CHECKS.

Compass body. Check that there is no obvious damage such as dents or cracks. Any lighting system should be checked, as should the efficacy of the luminous paint.

Compass Liquid. The compass liquid should be checked and be free from:

a)   Sediment and discolouration - either of which would indicate corrosion which would result in increased pivot friction.

b)   Bubbles - which would probably indicate a leaking seal. Turbulence and manoeuvres would cause any bubbles to move about, creating eddies which could disturb the magnet system.

Accuracy Limits -   BCAR: ± 3°   → *NO-GO Item*
                        JAR: ± 10°

9.11   DAMPING AND PIVOT FRICTION TESTS.

These tests are carried out before a compass is installed or swung, and whenever the accuracy of the instrument is suspect. The exact values quoted in the tests vary with the type, make and mark of compass. Furthermore, the figures are for a specified standard value of the earth's directive force   H. If the tests are to be conducted at latitudes where the value of   H   is significantly different, there may be a need to modify these figures.

Damping Test. This is also known as a 'swing' test designed to check that, after displacement, the magnet assembly returns quickly and without appreciable oscillation to its North alignment.

Using a small magnet, deflect the compass by 90°, holding this deflection for at least 20 seconds to allow the liquid to come to rest. Remove the deflecting magnet; the time taken to swing back through 85° should be 2 to 3 seconds for a standby compass.

Pivot Friction Test. Using a small magnet, deflect the compass by 10° and hold it in this position for at least 10 seconds. Remove the magnet and note the reading when the compass settles. Repeat the procedure, deflecting 10° in the opposite direction, and note the reading when the compass settles again

The two readings should agree within 2½° for a standby compass. It is usual to carry out this test on four headings 90° apart.

9.12   DEVIATION.

Deviation is produced by the iron/steel components in the aircraft. It is the angle between the local magnetic meridian and the direction in which the compass magnets are lying.

Deviation is named Easterly (or plus) if the North-seeking (red) ends of the magnets point to the East of magnetic North. If the North-seeking ends points to the West of magnetic North, deviation is said to be Westerly (or minus).

Deviation varies with heading so it has to be measured on a series of different headings. This is usually done by conducting a **compass swing** (which is fully covered in the chapter on aircraft magnetism). Once deviation has been reduced as far as possible, the residual deviation is recorded on a compass deviation card, which is located in the aircraft.

During the swing, normal flying conditions should be simulated as far as possible, with engines running, electrical / radio services switched on, and the aircraft in a level flight attitude.

It is obviously most important that no ferromagnetic objects such as tools, or watches should be placed near the compass as this would introduce unknown amounts of deviation. Furthermore, ferromagnetic payloads should be stowed as far away from the compass as permissible within the loading limits. With exceptionally large ferromagnetic loads, a compass swing may have to be carried out before flight with the load aboard.

9.13   ACCELERATION AND TURNING ERRORS.

Direct reading compasses are subject to large errors during linear acceleration or deceleration, or during a turn.

Most manoeuvres which cause the centre of gravity of the magnet assembly to move away from its normal position, almost directly below the pivot, will produce an error.

However, if the manoeuvre displaces the centre of gravity North or South of its usual position so that cg and pivot are still in the plane of the magnetic meridian, the magnet assembly merely changes its North-South tilt angle, with no rotation in azimuth and consequently no error.

Note also that turning and acceleration errors only occur where there is a significant vertical component (Z) in the earth's field, so that except for a small liquid swirl effect in turns, the errors are non-existent near the magnetic equator.

The north seeking end of the compass magnet should remain pointing in the same direction (ie Magnetic north) whether the aircraft is moving in a straight line or turning.

Acceleration and turning errors occur however when the north seeking end of the magnet is displaced from Magnetic north and therefore an incorrect heading will be shown on the compass card which is attached to the magnet.

Figure 9.4 shows a pendulously suspended magnet (with residual dip) in the northern hemisphere.

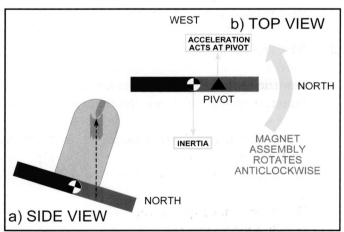

Figure 9.4. A Pendulously Suspended Magnet in the Northern Hemisphere.

Note that the vertical line through the pivot point is now closer to the nearer (north) magnetic pole than the magnet's centre of gravity. Consider an aircraft,(and therefore the magnet assembly) being accelerated towards the west, as shown in Figure 9.4b. The magnet is attached to the aircraft at the pivot point. However while the pivot is being accelerated the magnet's inertia, which acts at the magnet's centre of gravity, will try to maintain its state of uniform motion. The result will be that the magnet will rotate (in this case anticlockwise) and the incorrect heading will be shown.

9.14   ERRORS CAUSED BY LINEAR ACCELERATION.

The size of the acceleration error depends on a number of factors which includes aircraft heading. Acceleration / deceleration errors are **maximum** on **East** and **West** (M) headings and **zero** on **North** and **South** (M) headings.

The error is caused by inertia acting on a magnet which has residual dip due to the effect of the vertical component Z on the magnet.

Acceleration on 270°M (NH)

Figure 9.5 shows an aircraft accelerating on a magnetic heading of 270°M in the Northern hemisphere, such as occurs during take-off on runway 27. Since the magnet assembly is pendulously suspended, its inertia will cause it to swing back behind the pivot point which is offset to the north of the magnet's centre of gravity. This displacement enables a turning couple produced by the earth's vertical component Z to rotate the magnet assembly **anticlockwise** round the pivot.

The angle measured clockwise from the North-seeking end round to the aircraft's nose increases.

The compass reading will therefore **increase**, so indicating an **apparent turn towards North**. Thus, according to the compass, the aircraft is now heading, say, 280° whereas its real heading is in fact still 270°- the compass is **over-reading**.

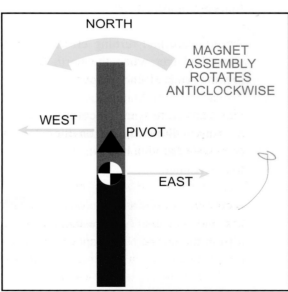

Figure 9.5. Acceleration on 270° M
(Northern Hemisphere)

Acceleration on 090°M (NH)

Figure 9.6 shows an aircraft accelerating on a magnetic heading of 090°M in the Northern hemisphere. Since the magnet assembly is pendulously suspended, its inertia will cause it to swing back behind the pivot point. This displacement enables a turning couple to rotate the magnet assembly **clockwise** round the pivot. The angle measured clockwise from the North-seeking end round to the aircraft's nose reduces. The compass reading will therefore **decrease**, so indicating an **apparent turn towards North**.

Thus, according to the compass, the aircraft is now heading, say, 080° whereas its real heading is in fact still 090°- the compass is **under-reading**.

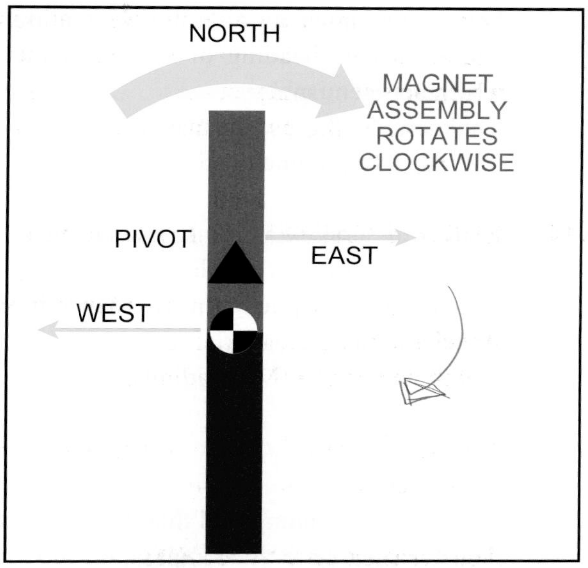

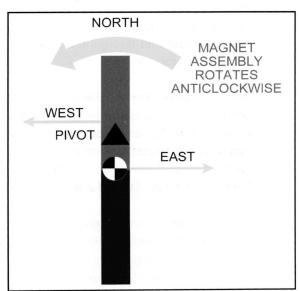

Figure 9.6. Acceleration on 090°M (Northern Hemisphere)

[handwritten: Indicates turn to the North]

[handwritten: due to clockwise rotation → numbers get smaller ∴ Apparent turn to the North]

[handwritten: use back of computer if needed]

Deceleration on 090°M (NH)

Figure 9.7 shows an aircraft decelerating on a magnetic heading of 090°M in the Northern hemisphere.

Since the magnet assembly is pendulously suspended, its inertia will cause it to swing forwards ahead of the pivot point.

This displacement enables a turning couple to rotate the magnet assembly **anti-clockwise** round the pivot.

The compass reading will therefore **increase**, so indicating an **apparent turn towards South**. Thus, according to the compass, the aircraft is now heading, say, 100° whereas its real heading is in fact still 090°- the compass is **over-reading**.

Figure 9.7. Deceleration on 090° M (Northern Hemisphere)

[handwritten: — Deceleration in NH is turn to South]
[handwritten: — Deceleration always causes a turn of compass to furthest pole —]

Acceleration on 270°M (SH)

Figure 9.8 shows an aircraft accelerating on a magnetic heading of 270°M in the Southern Hemisphere.

The inertia will cause the magnet assembly to swing back behind the pivot point which is now offset to the south of the magnet's centre of gravity. This displacement enables a turning couple to rotate the magnet assembly **clockwise** round the pivot.

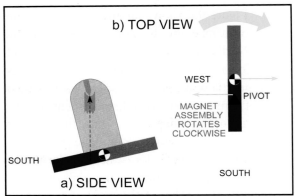

Figure 9.8. Acceleration on 270°M
(Southern Hemisphere)

The compass reading will therefore **decrease**, so indicating an **apparent turn towards South**. Thus, according to the compass, the aircraft is now heading, say, 260° whereas its real heading is in fact still 270°- the compass is **under-reading**.

Acceleration on a northerly heading (NH)

Figure 9.9 shows an acceleration on a northerly heading (northern hemisphere).

The cg lags and the North-South tilt of the magnet assembly changes, but the magnets are tilting in the vertical plane of the magnetic meridian through the pivot - so no error occurs.

With deceleration on North / South headings there is again no error, only a reduced N/S tilt due to the inertial forward swing of the magnet assembly.

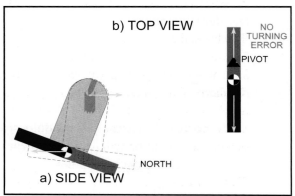

Figure 9.9. Acceleration on 360°M
(Northern Hemisphere)

9.15   SUMMARY OF ACCELERATION ERRORS.

Acceleration errors are **zero** on **N/S magnetic headings** (in both hemispheres), increasing to **maximum** on **headings 090°M and 270°M. Acceleration** causes an **apparent turn** towards the **nearer pole** (apparent turn north in the northern hemisphere, apparent turn south in the southern hemisphere). **Deceleration** causes an **apparent turn** towards the **further pole** (apparent turn south in the northern hemisphere, apparent turn north in the southern hemisphere).

Whenever the **magnet** assembly is displaced **clockwise**, the **readings** will **decrease** and the compass will **under read.**

Whenever the **magnet** assembly is displaced **anti-clockwise**, the **readings** will **increase** and the compass will **over read.**

The size of a linear acceleration error depends on the:

a)   **heading,** ✓

b)   **magnitude of the acceleration,** ✓

c)   **design of the magnet system,** and   *longer pendulum → greater error.*

d)   **magnetic latitude** (which affects the relative strengths of H and Z).

The errors are **maximum** near the magnetic poles, decreasing to **zero** at the **magnetic equator.**

9.16   TURNING ERRORS.

Turning errors are **maximum** when turning through **north** and **south,** and ignoring liquid swirl **zero** when turning through **east** and **west.**

The basic theory of turning errors is much the same as that for linear acceleration errors.

Due to the earth's vertical component of the magnetic field, **Z,** the **compass's cg** will be **displaced** from almost beneath the pivot point away from the nearer pole. In a **turn,** the aircraft accelerates towards the centre of the turn, and therefore an **acceleration force** acts through the **pivot** towards the centre of the turn, while the opposing **centrifugal force** due to **inertia** acts outward through the **cg.**

This results in the **magnet** assembly tending to 'swing out' from the turn, **rotating** the **magnet** assembly around the pivot point and producing a **turning error.**

Turning errors are usually more significant than acceleration errors for the following reasons:-

a)   They are inherently of greater magnitude because greater displacement of the magnet assembly is likely in turns.

b)   Turns occur more often and are likely to be more prolonged than linear accelerations.

✱ *Numbers getting smaller = clockwise rotation*

Turning from 045° to 315° (NH).

Consider an aircraft executing a **left-hand turn** in the Northern hemisphere as it passes through 000°M.

The magnet's cg is displaced from beneath the pivot point away from the north pole due to the vertical component of the earth's magnetic field. Because of inertia the **magnet** assembly will be thrown out of the turn **rotating** the magnet assembly **anti-clockwise**.

If there was no turning error the magnet would remain stationary and the aircraft rotate 90° around it - resulting in the pilot seeing 90° passing beneath the compass's lubber line.

- Overead undershoot

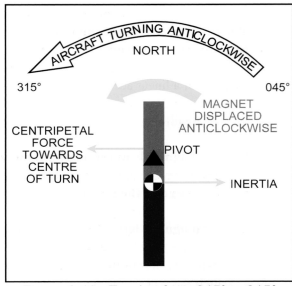

Figure 9.10. Turning from 045° to 315° (Northern Hemisphere)

However the **aircraft** is turning port and the **magnet** assembly **rotates** in the **same (anti-clockwise) direction**.

Although the aircraft has turned 90° around the compass, the magnet has been displaced and rotated in the same direction by a number of degrees (say 20°). The pilot will therefore only see 70° pass beneath the lubber line and the compass is termed **sluggish**. *(a/c & compass going the same way)*

Whenever the magnet rotates anticlockwise it will **overread** .

This means that if the pilot stops the turn at 315° **indicated** the **actual** heading will be numerically smaller such as 295°- therefore the **turn must be stopped early** (such as 335°) to achieve the correct heading.

This can also be described as **undershooting** the required heading (note 'undershoot' is referring to turning through a smaller **angle**, and should not be confused with 'under read' which means that the **numerical** heading indicated is too small).

If the pilot deliberately undershoots, rolling out when the compass reads about 325°, he should observe, when the wings are levelled, the compass 'catch up' and settle on 315°.

Sluggish = Always roll out early

Turning from 315° to 045° (NH).

Consider an aircraft **turning right** through north in the Northern hemisphere as it passes through 000°M, the magnet's cg is displaced from beneath the pivot point away from the north pole due to the vertical component of the earth's magnetic field.

Because of inertia the **magnet** assembly will be thrown out of the turn **rotating** the magnet assembly **clockwise**.

Note that the **aircraft** and the **magnet** assembly are again **rotating** in the **same direction** (but that it is this time clockwise) and therefore the compass will again be **sluggish**.

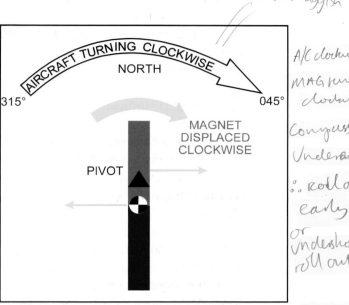

also sluggish

A/C clockwise
MAG ring clockwise
Compass underreads
∴ Roll out early
or undershoot roll out

Figure 9.11. Turning from 315° to 045° (Northern Hemisphere)

★ Error always ~20°

Whenever the magnet rotates clockwise it will **under read** . This means that if the pilot stops the turn at 045° **indicated** the **actual** heading will be numerically larger such as 065°.

Therefore the **turn must be stopped early** (such as 025°), or the pilot should **undershoot the indication**, to achieve the correct heading.

Turning from 135° to 225° (NH).

Now consider an aircraft **turning right** as shown in Figure 9.11 through south in the northern hemisphere as it passes through 180°M, the magnet's cg is displaced from beneath the pivot point away from the nearer pole (the north pole) due to the vertical component of the earth's magnetic field.

Because of inertia the **magnet** assembly will be thrown out of the turn **rotating** the magnet assembly **anticlockwise**.

The **aircraft** is turning **clockwise** (right) but the **magnet** assembly is rotating anticlockwise.

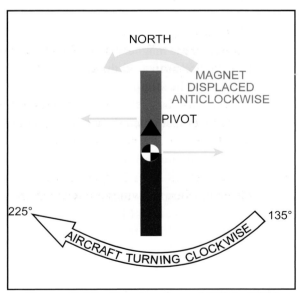

Figure 9.12. Turning from 135° to 225° (Northern Hemisphere)

SAME SECTOR
SAME HEMISPHERE
(SAME DIRECTION)
SLUGGISH
SOONER ROLL-OUT

NO SECTOR (ie 090) = NO ERROR

NO HEMISPHERE = NO ERROR

Therefore the aircraft and the magnet are now **rotating** in **opposite directions**. Although the aircraft has turned 90° around the compass, the magnet has been displaced and rotated in the opposite direction by a number of degrees (say 20°). The pilot will therefore see 110° pass beneath the lubber line and the compass is termed **'lively'**.

Whenever the magnet rotates anticlockwise it will **over read**. This means that if the pilot stops the turn at 225° **indicated** the **actual** heading will be numerically smaller, such as 205°.

Therefore the **turn must be stopped late** (such as 245°), or the pilot should **overshoot**, to achieve the correct heading.

Turning from 135° to 225° (SH).

Now consider an aircraft **turning right** as shown in Figure 9.12 through south in the southern hemisphere as it passes through 180°M, the magnet's cg is displaced from beneath the pivot point away from the nearer pole (the south pole). Because of inertia the **magnet** assembly will be thrown out of the turn **rotating** the magnet assembly **clockwise**.

The **aircraft** and the **magnet** assembly now are **rotating** in the **same direction** (clockwise) and therefore the compass will again be **sluggish**.

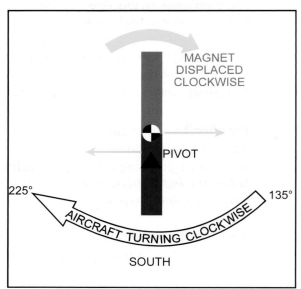

Figure 9.13. Turning from 135° to 225°
(Southern Hemisphere)

Whenever the magnet rotates clockwise it will **under read** . This means that if the pilot stops the turn at 225° **indicated** the **actual** heading will be numerically larger such as 245°. Therefore the **turn must be stopped early** (such as 205°), or **undershoot**, to achieve the correct heading.

Remember that when the wings are levelled, the compass will 'catch up' and settle on 225°.

Turning through East or West

Consider a turning aircraft passing through the magnetic headings of 090° and 270°.
The magnets are not horizontal but their tilt is North-South, that is in the vertical plane of the magnetic meridian through the pivot.

There is no rotational couple acting round the pivot, so there is no turning error.
Turning errors are zero when passing through East or West.

Other notes on turning errors:

It is **easier** to **steer** a **Southerly** rather than a **Northerly** heading, firstly because on South the compass does not indicate the wrong direction of turn as it can on North, and secondly because the 'lively' nature of the indications reduces the risk of over-correcting small steering errors.

Magnitude of Turning Errors:

There are many factors affecting the severity of turning errors.
They are **worst** at **high latitudes** where **Z is strong** and H is weak.
Other relevant variables include **rate** of turn, **duration** of turn, **speed** of the aircraft, the **headings** involved, and the **design of the compass.**

9.17   TURNING ERRORS - LIQUID SWIRL.

[handwritten: Direction always same direction as aircraft turn.]

The effect known as liquid swirl was mentioned in Paragraph 9.13.
During a turn, the liquid in contact with the inside of the bowl tends to be dragged around with the bowl, so producing in the liquid small eddies which drift inwards from the circumference and **deflect the magnet assembly in the direction of turn**. Therefore the liquid tends to swirl - and rotate the magnet assembly with it - in the same direction as the aircraft's turn.

[handwritten left margin: LIVELY = SWIRL WILL REDUCE ERROR AS IT OPPOSES ERROR]

[handwritten right margin: SLUGGISH = SWIRL ACCENTUATES ERROR]

Accordingly, when turning through **north** in the **Northern hemisphere** it will **increase** the magnitude of the **turning error** (in which the assembly turns in the same direction as the aircraft).
The size of the turning error when turning through **south** in the **northern hemisphere** (where the assembly turns in the opposite direction to the aircraft) **will be reduced.**

In the Southern hemisphere the swirl effect will be in the opposite sense.
Note that at the **magnetic equator** where there is no vertical component Z in the earth's field, **liquid swirl is the sole source of turning error**; with most compasses the effect is only slight.

[handwritten right margin: SWIRL ON IT'S OWN = 5° ERROR eg in turn from 060° to 120°]

9.18   SUMMARY OF TURNING ERRORS.

[handwritten left margin: SWIRL always causes]

These are **maximum** when passing through magnetic **North** or **South**, decreasing to **zero** when passing through **East** or **West.**

The **error increases** with **increase** in **magnetic latitude.**
At the magnetic equator the only turning error is due to liquid swirl.

[handwritten: ✱ WATCH OUT FOR WORD 'INDICATE' as underead will 'over' indicate]

[handwritten: 'High Angle of bank' w x 30°]

Whenever the pilot turns through the nearer pole (north in the northern hemisphere, or south in the southern hemisphere):

a)   the aircraft and compass **rotate** in the **same direction,**

b)   the **compass** will be **sluggish,** and

c)   the pilot should **undershoot** the turn / **roll out early.**

d)   **liquid swirl** will **increase** the turning error.

Whenever the pilot turns through the further pole (south in the northern hemisphere, or north in the southern hemisphere):

a)   the aircraft and compass **rotate** in the **opposite direction,**

b)   the **compass** will be **lively,** and

c)   the pilot should **overshoot** the turn / **roll out late.**

d)   **liquid swirl** will **reduce** the turning error.

Table of turning errors

Hemis'	Turning		Aircraft Turns	Magnets' Turn	At the end of the turn compass reads	Stop turn	Effect of liquid swirl	Compass Condition
	From	To						
N	45	315	Anti Clockwise	Anti Clockwise	More than 315 deg	Early	Increases turning error	Sluggish
N	315	45	Clockwise	Clockwise	Less than 045 deg	Early	Increases turning error	Sluggish
N	135	225	Clockwise	Anti Clockwise	More than 225 deg	Late	Reduces turning error	Lively
N	225	135	Anti Clockwise	Clockwise	Less than 135 deg	Late	Reduces turning error	Lively
S	45	315	Anti Clockwise	Clockwise	Less than 315 deg	Late	Reduces turning error	Lively
S	315	45	Clockwise	Anti Clockwise	More than 045 deg	Late	Reduces turning error	Lively
S	135	225	Clockwise	Clockwise	Less than 225 deg	Early	Increases turning error	Sluggish
S	225	135	Anti Clockwise	Anti Clockwise	More than 135 deg	Early	Increases turning error	Sluggish

Table Explained

The term **SLUGGISH** which appears in the right hand column of the table denotes that the compass **HEADING** is **LAGGING BEHIND** the aircraft heading.

Conversely, when the term **LIVELY** is used, the compass **HEADING** is **LEADING** the aircraft around the turn.

The following rules of thumb apply:

a)   During a turn through the pole which is **physically nearer to the aircraft**, the compass will be **SLUGGISH**. It is therefore necessary to **ROLL OUT EARLY** on the indication given by the Direct Reading Compass.

b)   During a turn through the pole which is **physically further from the aircraft**, the compass will be **LIVELY**. It is therefore necessary to **ROLL OUT LATE** on the indication given by the Direct Reading Compass.

From the above statements it can be seen that, at the **MAGNETIC EQUATOR,** there is **NO TURNING ERROR** because there is no "dip".

Remember, that it is a displacement of the **MAGNETS** in a **CLOCKWISE** direction when viewed from above which causes the compass to **UNDERREAD**, and a displacement in an **ANTICLOCKWISE** direction which causes the compass to **OVERREAD**.

DIRECT READING MAGNETIC COMPASSES

1.   In a standby direct reading compass there is:

   a)   a non-pendulously mounted magnet system.
   b)   a single pendulously mounted bar magnet.
   c)   a circular magnet or pair of bar magnets pendulously mounted.
   d)   a low magnetic moment system, either of circular or bar configuration.

2.   The main requirements of a direct reading magnetic compass are that it should be:

   a)   horizontal, sensitive, periodic.
   b)   easily read, floating in a transparent liquid, quick to react to change in aircraft heading.
   c)   positioned directly in front of the pilot, easily corrected for magnetic deviation, aperiodic.
   d)   aperiodic, horizontal, sensitive.

3.   For a position in the southern hemisphere, the effect of acceleration errors are greatest on headings:

   a) $180°(C)$ and $360°(C)$
   b) $045°(C)$ and $225°(C)$
   c) $135°(C)$ and $315°(C)$
   d) $090°(C)$ and $270°(C)$

4.   An aircraft in the southern hemisphere is turning from a heading of $045°(C)$ to $315°(C)$ using a DGI.   At the end of the turn the compass will read .... than $315°$ and liquid swirl will .... this effect.

   a)   more; increase
   b)   less; increase
   c)   more; decrease
   d)   less; decrease

5.   In a standby compass the magnet system is immersed in a transparent liquid. The purpose of this liquid is to:

   a)   increase sensitivity, increase aperiodicity.
   b)   increase sensitivity, decrease aperiodicity.
   c)   increase sensitivity at high latitudes, lubricate bearings.
   d)   increase sensitivity, reduce liquid swirl.

6.   To improve the horizontality of a compass, the magnet assembly is suspended from a point:

       a)   on the centre line of the magnet.
       b)   below the centre of gravity.
       c)   above the centre of gravity.
       d)   varying with magnetic latitude.

7.   The magnitude, and sense, of turning error shown by a direct reading compass varies with:

       1)   the design of the compass.
       2)   the direction of the turn.
       3)   the rate of turn.
       4)   which hemisphere the aircraft is in.
       5)   the heading of the aircraft.
       6)   the amount of dip at the aircraft's latitude.

       Of these statements:

       a)   only 1, 2, 5 and 6 are correct.
       b)   only 1, 3, 5 and 6 are correct.
       c)   only 2, 4 and 5 are correct.
       d)   all are correct.

8.   During a sustained turn .... the nearer magnetic pole, the effect of liquid swirl will .... compass turning error.

       a)   away from; increase.
       b)   towards; not affect.
       c)   away from; not affect.
       d)   towards; increase.

9.   When carrying out a turn at the magnetic equator there will be:

       a)   no turning error.
       b)   a tendency to underread turns through south and overread turns through north.
       c)   a tendency to underread turns due to liquid swirl.
       d)   no turning error when turning through east or west only.

CHAPTER TEN - GYROSCOPES

Contents

Page

10.1 INTRODUCTION. . . . . 10 - 1

10.2 THE GYROSCOPE . . . . 10 - 1

10.3 GIMBAL RINGS. . . . . 10 - 1

10.4 THE FUNDAMENTAL PROPERTIES OF A GYROSCOPE. . . . . 10 - 2

10.5 FACTORS AFFECTING RIGIDITY . . . . 10 - 4

10.6 PRECESSION RATE . . . . 10 - 5

10.7 WANDER . . . . 10 - 5

10.8 TIED GYROS . . . . 10 - 6

10.9 RATE GYROS . . . . 10 - 7

10.10 SUMMARY . . . . 10 - 7

10.11 THE APPLICATION OF THE PROPERTIES OF A GYRO. . . . . 10 - 8

10.12 SUCTION AND ELECTRIC GYROS . . . . 10 - 8

10.13 SUCTION AND ELECTRIC TYPES - COMPARISON . . . . 10 - 9

GYROS QUESTIONS . . . . 10 - 11

10.1   INTRODUCTION.

A knowledge of higher mathematics is required if the subject of gyrodynamics is to be fully comprehended.   However, this is unnecessary for an adequate understanding of the basic principles of the gyroscopic flight instruments.   This chapter aims to provide sufficient background knowledge for the study of the Artificial Horizon, Directional Gyro Indicator, and the Rate of Turn Indicator.

10.2   THE GYROSCOPE

Any rotating body exhibits gyroscopic phenomena. The earth is a gyro, spinning about the axis between the geographic poles. The road wheel of a car is a gyro when it is turning, and so is a child's 'top'. The rotor in an aircraft gyro may be little more than an inch in diameter, spinning at perhaps 25,000 r.p.m.

10.3   GIMBAL RINGS.

These are the supports for the rotor of a gyroscopic instrument. Gimbal rings, are known briefly as gimbals, and sometimes spelled gymbals.

Figure 10.1. shows a spinning rotor mounted in two gimbal rings, the outer one being supported by a fixed frame.
The rotor itself is a metal disc rotating about the axis indicated as X-X and usually called the rotor **spin axis**. The rotor shaft (or spindle) is supported by bearings in a ring called the **inner gimbal**.

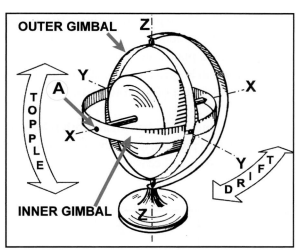

The inner gimbal is in turn supported by bearings mounted inside the **outer gimbal** which can rotate on bearings in the frame (or instrument case).

Figure 10.1. The Rotor and Gimbals.

The arrangement in Figure 10.1. allows
movement of the gyro in three mutually perpendicular planes; this gyro is said to have complete freedom of rotation in three planes at right angles to each other (or freedom of rotation about three axes at right angles to each other).

a)   If the frame is rotated about the XX axis, it is being moved either with or against the direction of the rotor spin, so the position of the XX axis is undisturbed.

b)   If the frame is rotated about the YY axis, the inner and outer gimbals will obviously not remain at 90° to each other, but the XX axis can remain pointing in the same direction.

c)   If the frame is rotated about the ZZ axis (by rotating the base) the alignment of the XX axis will still be unchanged but the frame and the outer gimbal will no longer be at right angles to each other.

It follows from the above, that the gyro in Figure 10.1. has 'three degrees of freedom in rotation', that is to say the frame can be rotated in three mutually perpendicular planes without disturbing the spin axis.

Such a gyro is known as a **space gyro** and its chief virtue is that it allows the spinning rotor to exhibit its fundamental property of rigidity.

Rigidity:
1. Speed ↑
2. Weight/Mass ↑
3. ↑ radius

10.4   THE FUNDAMENTAL PROPERTIES OF A GYROSCOPE.

distance
to move from
where it is

Rigidity.   A spinning rotor maintains its axis pointing in a fixed direction in space, unless subjected to an external force. This property is called **rigidity in space** or **gyroscopic inertia**

ie concentrate mass on periphery of rotor

Proportionality:
– Force (torque)
(force through
an angle)

Precession. If an external force (or more correctly, torque) is applied to change the direction of the rotor axis, the gyro resists angular movement in the plane of the torque applied and instead moves in a plane at right angles to that of the torque, the resulting movement being called **'precession'**. This is the second fundamental property of a gyroscope.

Inversely Proportional
to – Rigidity

With the space gyro, if the instrument case or frame is turned through 90° about its YY axis, that is, in the direction of the broad arrow in Figure 10.2a., so that the inner and outer gimbals lie in the same plane, any movement now imparted about the ZZ axis (in the direction of the broad arrows in Figure 10.2b.) can no longer be taken up by a bearing so any torque applied will change the alignment of the rotor axis.

eg in vertical roll

This condition is known as **gimbal lock**; we have reduced the number of rotational axes, and the gyro will precess, about the YY axis until the rotor axis is aligned with the ZZ axis. At this point precession will cease because the gyro is offering no further resistance to the applied force.

This is the ultimate
Gimballing Error

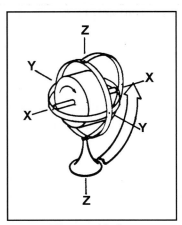

Figure 10.2a.

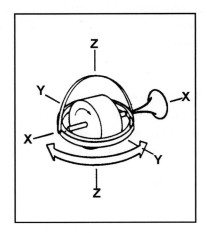

Figure 10.2b.

Rule of Precession. The direction of precessional movement can be found by the following rule:-

The gyro will precess in a direction at 90° to the applied force, measured round the circumference of the rotor in the direction of spin. The force applied appears to have moved 90° in the direction of spin.

Figures 10.3a. and 10.3b. show examples of precession producing Drift and Topple.

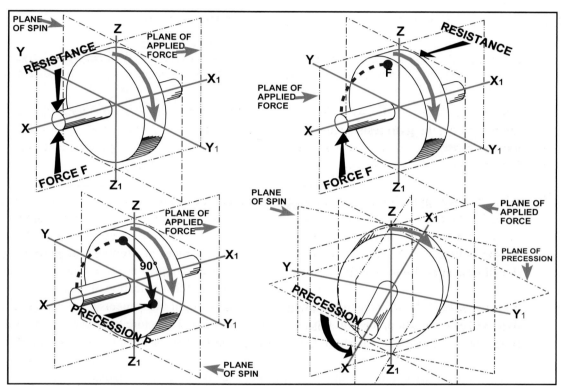

Figure 10.3a Precession Producing Drift

Freedoms

- Degrees of freedom a plane through which we can move a/c around gyroscope

- Max 3

- freedom in Rotation - Max 3°

Freedom in Precession

- Precession ∽ 90 to applied force

- Max 2° = No of gimbals

→ *Precession*
    → Horizontal → Drift
    → Vertical → Topple

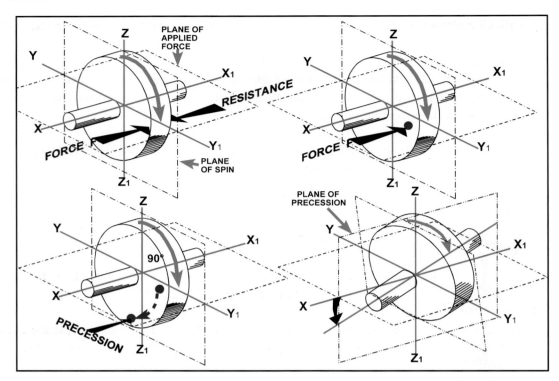

Figure 10.3b. Precession Producing Topple.

As an example, if a weight is hung from the inner gimbal at point A in Figure 10.1, the gyroscope (rotor, inner and outer gimbals) will precess (rotate) in an anticlockwise direction about the axis (viewed from above). Further examples of the application of the rule of precession will be found in the chapters on individual gyroscopic flight instruments.

A gyroscope can not precess in the direction of rotation. Therefore a gyroscope can only have freedom to precess in a maximum of two perpendicular planes. This is referred to as "freedom in precession" - giving a maximum of two degrees of freedom in precession. A gyroscope that is used to measure changes about one, or more, axes is known as a displacement gyroscope.

10.5   FACTORS AFFECTING RIGIDITY

The gyroscopic inertia or rigidity of a gyro rotor can be expressed as $I\omega$ where I is the moment of inertia of the rotor about its spin axis and ω is the angular velocity about that axis. Therefore if we increase the moment of inertia or the rpm, the rigidity will be increased. The moment of inertia (I) can be stated as Mk^2 where M is the mass of the rotor, and k is the radius of gyration (the 'radius at which the mass acts'). Therefore to increase gyroscopic inertia, the moment of inertia would be increased by increasing M and / or k. This is achieved in air-driven gyros by using brass for the rotor and, as far as possible concentrating the metal round the rim, so increasing the effective radius. Summarising, increase of rotor mass, effective radius, or spin rpm will increase the gyroscopic rigidity. At the same time, the rigidity must be considered in terms of the applied force. For example, a kilogram weight hung on the inner gimbal at A (Fig 10.1) will have more effect (producing a greater rate of precession) than a one gramme weight hung in the same position.

10.6 PRECESSION RATE

The formula for the rate of precession (Ω) is:-

$$\Omega = \frac{T}{I\omega}$$

[handwritten right margin: More Torque = More Precession Rate]

where T is the applied torque

I is the moment of inertia of the rotor

[handwritten: (determined by size & weight of gyro & distance of acting weight (ie radius of gyro)]

[handwritten right margin: ∴ Higher 'I' value ∴ ↑ rigidity ∴ less Ω rate]

ω is the angular velocity of the rotor

[handwritten left: ↑ velocity = ↑ rigidity ∴ ↓ Ω rate]

Thus the rate of precession (Ω) is proportional to T, or the greater the applied force (torque) the greater the rate of precession - as stated in the previous paragraph.

The rate of precession is **inversely** proportional to Iω, the rigidity or gyroscopic inertia, so the greater the rigidity the smaller the rate of precession produced by a given applied force.

10.7 WANDER

If the axis of a gyro rotor departs from its chosen direction it is said to **wander**. If the axis of the gyro rotor wanders in the horizontal plane (for instance, as shown by the horizontal arrow in Figure 10.1) it is said to **drift**.

A weight hung on the gimbal at A in Figure 10.1 thus produces drift. If the rotor axis wanders in the vertical plane (as shown by the vertical arrow in Figure 10.1.) it is said to **topple**.

[handwritten left margin: Random Wander]

Real Wander. Manufacturing imperfections in a gyroscope cause small rates of 'random' precession. Other terms given to this precession are 'balance wander' or, if the precession is in the horizontal plane, 'mechanical drift'.

The imperfections concerned are uneven rotor bearing friction, unbalanced gimbals, and friction in gimbal bearings. In-flight turbulence may increase the effect of these imperfections. The precession caused by application of an external force to a gyro is another example of real wander.

Apparent Wander. Consider a space (or 'free') gyro at A in Figure 10.4(a). with the rotor axis horizontal and aligned with the geographic meridian.

The rotor axis is indicating the direction of true North on the earth and is also aligned with a point at an infinite distance in space.

[handwritten left margin: due to earth's rotation | aka Earth rate wander]

[handwritten bottom: numbers will get smaller in N hemisphere @ rate of 360° in 24h ∴ drift rate is ~15°/hour @ North pole | ie 360-270-180-90]

Some time later when point A on the earth has rotated to B in figure 10.4(b), the gyro rotor axis is still aligned with the same fixed point in space (assuming no other disturbing forces) but no longer indicates the direction of North on the earth. It has therefore changed its alignment, **according to the earthbound observer**, by the angle NOX. This is **apparent wander** or **apparent drift,** due only to the rotation of the earth. Further reference is made to wander in the Chapter on the DGI.

No reading error @ equator, or drift

Earth rate drift = 15 Sin (Latitude) — ve in North +ve South

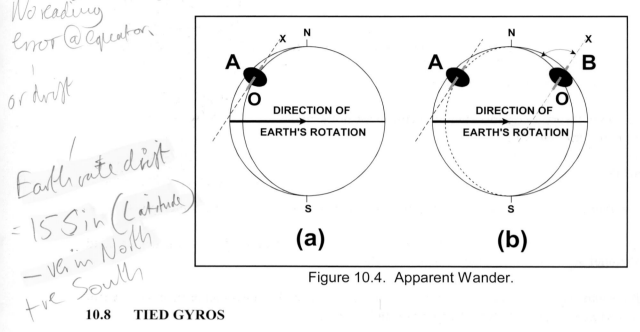

Figure 10.4. Apparent Wander.

10.8   TIED GYROS

Paragraph 10.7. shows that a space gyro, with its rigidity relative to space, is of limited use as an earth reference because the rotating earth's horizontal and vertical references are continually changing relative to space. (Exceptions are the limiting cases of a vertical axis gyro at the pole, or a horizontal axis gyro at the equator with its axis aligned with the meridian.)

A gyro which relates its rigidity to a particular attitude or direction rather than to a space direction has more applications. Such a gyro is called a **tied** gyro.

A tied gyro can be described as one having freedom in three planes mutually at right angles but with the rotor kept (or 'tied') in some desired position by a control system. As an example, the DGI rotor axis is maintained in the yawing plane of the aircraft.

An **earth** gyro (as in the Artificial Horizon) is a tied gyro which utilises the force of gravity to monitor a control system keeping the rotor axis in the earth's vertical.

South Pole

10.9　RATE GYROS

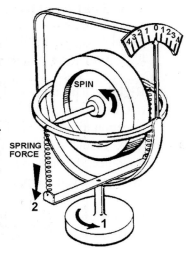

If a gyro has only one gimbal ring, with consequently only two planes of freedom, it can be adapted for use as a **rate** gyro to measure a rate of angular movement. If the gyro frame is rotated in the plane in which the gyro has no freedom, the rotor will precess, unless restrained, until its plane of rotation coincides with the plane in which the frame is being turned. If this precession is restricted by a spring, as shown in Figure 10.5, the resultant tilt of the rotor will be a measure of the rate of angular movement of the instrument.

Rate gyro theory is considered more deeply in the notes on the Rate of Turn Indicator.

Figure 10.5 A Rate Gyro
(A Rate of Turn Indicator)

10.10　SUMMARY

The following brief explanations of terms may help to clarify the foregoing paragraphs:-

Gyroscopic Inertia or **Rigidity in Space** is the property of a spinning body to maintain a fixed direction in space unless acted on by an outside force.

Precession is the movement of a gyro, resulting from the application of an outside force, about an axis perpendicular to both the spin axis and the applied force.

Real Wander is a precession caused by mechanical imperfections (such as uneven bearing friction) or by any applied force.

Apparent Wander is the observed wander of a gyro rotor axis relative to a datum on the earth.

Topple is rotor axis wander - real or apparent - in the vertical plane.

Drift is rotor axis wander - real or apparent - in the horizontal plane.

Space Gyro has complete freedom in three mutually perpendicular planes, and so has gyroscopic inertia relative to a point in space.

A **Tied Gyro** has the rotor axis maintained (tied) in a desired position, so having gyroscopic inertia relative to the reference to which it is tied.

An **Earth Gyro** is a gravity-controlled tied gyro, so having gyroscopic inertia relative to the earth's vertical.

A **Rate Gyro** has freedom in only two planes at 90° to each other and is constructed to measure rate of turn in the third plane at 90° to the other two.

10.11 THE APPLICATION OF THE PROPERTIES OF A GYRO.

The detailed application of the two properties of gyroscopic rigidity and precession are covered in the chapters devoted to the individual flight instruments. A general summary is given below.

Rigidity. This property is used to provide a directional datum. In the Directional Gyro Indicator (DGI), the rotor spin axis is horizontal and so provides a reference for the measurement of direction in azimuth (aircraft heading). The gyro in the DGI is sometimes known as an azimuth gyro. In the Artificial Horizon(AH), gyroscopic rigidity provides a pitch and roll attitude reference, the spin axis defining the earth's vertical. Such a gyro may be called a vertical axis gyro or vertical reference gyro.

Precession. As already explained, the application of an external force to a gyro produces movement of the rotor axis called precession. This property is used:-

a)   In the Rate of Turn Indicator - to measure angular velocities in the yawing plane.

b)   In the DGI control system   -   to maintain the rotor axis in the yawing plane. Additionally, to compensate DGI wander by means of a 'latitude nut'.

c)   In the Artificial Horizon control system - to maintain the rotor axis vertical.

10.12 SUCTION AND ELECTRIC GYROS

Gyroscopic flight instruments may be either air-driven or electric.

With the former, an engine-driven vacuum pump, or venturi tube on some light aircraft, reduces the pressure in the instrument case so that filtered replacement air is sucked in and led through a jet impinging on 'buckets' cut in the periphery of the rotor to make it spin like a water wheel. The air also operates the control systems of tied gyros.

With electric gyros, the rotor is an integral part - comprising the rotor windings - of an AC motor. The control system of an electric tied gyro is operated by limit switches and torque motors.

There are three designs of Gyro currently in use in aviation:

Tuned Rotor Gyro - a mechanical device using a spinning rotor which is engineered to be as balanced and frictionless as possible and which may be found in a number of different instruments.

Laser Gyro - more accurately described as a Rate Sensor this device uses Laser Light set in a rotational pattern to discern movement - it has no moving parts(to be discussed in full later).

Fibre-optic Gyro - an extension of the Ring Laser Gyro but lighter, smaller and less expensive but also less accurate. They may be used in a number of applications, (such as missile initial guidance) that do not require maximum long term accuracy and they may also be employed as a back up to another main system.

10.13   SUCTION AND ELECTRIC TYPES - COMPARISON

The advantages and disadvantages of Electric and Suction gyros:

a)   **Suction Gyros.** These are independent of electric power and so are not vulnerable to the risk of total electric failure. Unfortunately, moisture, dust, oil, and nicotine in the airflow penetrate the filter, reducing bearing life, unbalancing gimbals, and so impairing accuracy. At high altitude, adequate suction cannot be maintained. With a venturi tube, suction is insufficient on the ground and in flight such a tube is subject to icing risk.

b)   **Electric Gyros.** These are a later development than the suction types and in general are more expensive, heavier, and require AC power supplies. They have, however, important advantages over the air-driven types without the latter's disadvantages. The electric rotor can be constructed with higher moment of inertia and spin speed, giving greater rigidity and consequently improved stability. Rotor speed can, at any altitude, be accurately maintained, giving improved accuracy. Operating r.p.m. is more quickly reached when first switching on. The instrument case is sealed, for longer life and greater accuracy.

Note: It is usual to find that the "standby" instruments placed in aircraft are powered by suction if the main gyro instruments are powered by electrical means to allow for an alternate reference system in the event of an electrical power source failure.

Types of Gyro
- Tuned Rotor
- Fibre Optic
- Laser Gyros

(simple type ~ 15,000 rpm) — 10-15°/hr
                                            — 0.1°/hr
(using laser light BUT not real gyro as has   — 0.01°/hr
no mass ∴ no rigidity)

modern
inertial navigation systems

GYROS

1.   Rigidity of a gyroscope depends on:

      a)   weight, disturbing couple and speed of rotation.
      b)   rate of precession and disturbing couple.
      c)   weight, rate of precession and speed of rotation.
      d)   mass, radius of gyration and speed of rotation.

2.   A constant disturbing couple is applied to deflect a gyroscope. If the RPM of the gyro is then doubled the precession rate will:

      a)   remain as before.
      b)   increase.
      c)   decrease.
      d)   cease altogether.

3.   In gyroscopic theory the term 'topple' is defined as:

      a)   real wander only, in the horizontal plane.
      b)   real wander only, in the vertical plane.
      c)   wander, real or apparent, in the vertical plane.
      d)   wander, real or apparent, in the horizontal plane.

4.   A force applied to the spinning axis of a rotor is precessed:

      a)   through 90° in the direction of spin of the rotor.
      b)   through 90° in the direction of spin of the rotor in the northern hemisphere through 90° in the opposite direction in the southern hemisphere.
      c)   through 270° in the direction of spin of the rotor.
      d)   at a rate proportional to the speed of rotation of the gyro.

5.   In gyroscopic theory the term 'drift' is defined as:

      a)   real wander only, in the horizontal plane.
      b)   wander, real or apparent, in the vertical plane.
      c)   apparent wander only, in the horizontal plane.
      d)   wander, real or apparent, in the horizontal plane.

6.   Real wander of a gyro can be caused by:

    a)   asymmetrical friction at the spinning axis.
    b)   rotation of the earth.
    c)   increasing the RPM of the rotor.
    d)   moving the gyro north or south of its present position.

7.   A gyro with only two axes of freedom is known as a:

    a)   tied gyro.
    b)   earth gyro.
    c)   space gyro.
    d)   rate gyro.

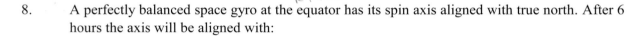

8.   A perfectly balanced space gyro at the equator has its spin axis aligned with true north. After 6 hours the axis will be aligned with:

    a)   true east direction.
    b)   true west direction.
    c)   true north direction.
    d)   true south direction.

9.   The main advantage of electric gyros are:

    a)   light weight, high RPM, constant speed, inexpensive.
    b)   high RPM, only require low voltage DC, constant speed, sealed casing.
    c)   high RPM, high moment of inertia, rapid build-up of speed, constant RPM.
    d)   sealed casing, constant speed, high precession rate, low cost.

10.   Apparent wander of a gyro is caused by:

    a)   rotation of the earth.
    b)   clear air turbulence.
    c)   gymbal friction.
    d)   external torque.

CHAPTER ELEVEN - DIRECTIONAL GYRO INDICATOR

Contents

                                                                                Page

11.1   INTRODUCTION. . . . . 11 - 1

11.2   THE PRINCIPLE AND CONSTRUCTION OF THE DGI. . . . . 11 - 1

11.3   THE CONTROL SYSTEM - SUCTION GYROS. . . . . 11 - 2

11.4   THE CAGING DEVICE. . . . . 11 - 4

11.5   DGI LIMITATIONS. . . . . 11 - 5

11.6   DGI ERRORS. . . . . 11 - 5

11.7   GIMBALLING ERRORS. . . . . 11 - 5

11.8   RANDOM WANDER. . . . . 11 - 6

11.9   APPARENT WANDER (DUE TO ROTATION OF THE EARTH). . . . . 11 - 6

11.10   LATITUDE NUT CORRECTION. . . . . 11 - 10

11.11   ERRORS DUE TO UNSTABLE ROTOR RPM. . . . . 11 - 11

11.12   TRANSPORT WANDER - CHANGE OF LATITUDE. . . . . 11 - 12

11.13   DRIFT RATE CALCULATIONS. . . . . 11 - 13

        DIRECTIONAL GYRO INDICATORS QUESTIONS . . . . 11 - 14

Types of Mounting

- Space Gyro

- Tied Gyro = A/C Axes

               - Earth Field

- Rate gyro

11.1   INTRODUCTION.

The **directional gyro indicator (DGI)**, often called the **'direction indicator' (DI)** provides a **stable directional reference** in azimuth for maintaining accurate headings and for executing precise turns. There is **no magnetic element** in the DI, so it is not North-seeking and must initially be **synchronised** with the **magnetic compass**. The synchronisation must be checked at regular intervals because of real and apparent gyro wander (drift). The **DGI** does not therefore replace the compass; its stable, dead-beat indications are **complementary** to the North-seeking capability of the **compass**. Having no magnetic element, the DGI does not suffer from the compass turning and acceleration errors produced by the vertical component of the earth's magnetic field.

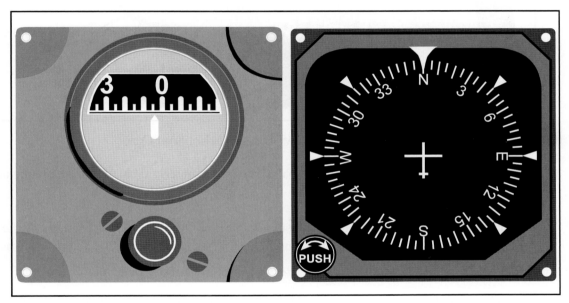

Vertical Display (Old)   Horizontal Display (Modern)
Figure 11.1. Two Directional Gyro Indicators.

11.2   THE PRINCIPLE AND CONSTRUCTION OF THE DGI.

The DI employs a **tied gyro**, that is to say, a gyro having freedom of movement in three planes mutually at right angles but with the **rotor axis** maintained in the **yawing plane** of the aircraft. This means that the rotor axis is horizontal in level flight, and because of gyroscopic rigidity it provides the datum from which heading can be measured.

The rotor is mounted in the inner gimbal (on bearings mounted in the outer gimbal) which has restricted freedom to turn. The outer gimbal can rotate through 360° about the aircraft's vertical axis, on bearings in the case.

© Oxford Aviation Services Limited

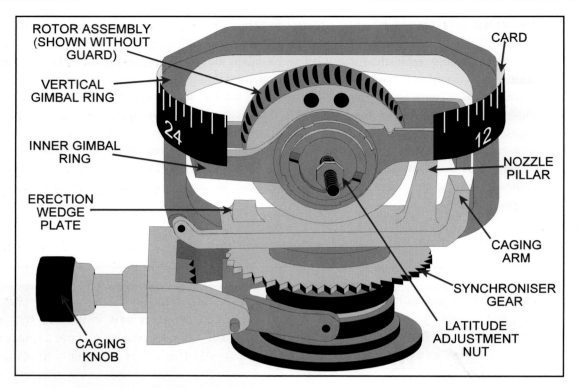

Figure 11.2. An Air Driven Directional Gyro.

Note that the rotor axis, the inner gimbal axis, and the outer gimbal axis are mutually at right angles.

During a turn, the aircraft and instrument case turn on the vertical axis bearings of the outer gimbal whilst the gyro rotor, gimbals and indicating scale all remain fixed in azimuth because of gyroscopic rigidity.

Heading is indicated on the scale by a lubber line painted on a glass window in the instrument case. Some designs have a circular vertical-card indicating scale geared to the outer gimbal, in place of the cylindrical scale fixed to the outer gimbal in the earlier type shown in Figure 11.2.

11.3   THE CONTROL SYSTEM - SUCTION GYROS.

With earlier designs of DGI, the rotor is driven by twin jets of air applied from the outer gimbal ring as shown in Figure 11.3. Suction is applied to the case of the instrument, and replacement air enters the case through a filter and is ducted to the jets on the outer gimbal which act on 'buckets' cut in the rotor.

The **jets** not only **spin** the rotor but also serve to maintain or **tie** the rotor axis in the yawing plane of the aircraft.

The rotor axis is lying in the yawing plane and therefore at right angles to the outer gimbal axis, the full force 'X' of the jets being used to drive the rotor (Figure 11.3). If the aircraft banks, gyroscopic rigidity keeps the rotor axis fixed in space and it is therefore no longer in the yawing plane.

The outer gimbal axis is no longer at right angles to the rotor axis, so the jet driving force 'X' acts at an angle to the plane of the rotor.

This force can now be resolved into two components, component 'Y' in the plane of rotation maintaining the spin of the rotor, and component 'Z' acting at 90° to the plane of rotation (Figure 11.4).

Because this is a gyro, the component 'Z' will precess the rotor as if the force had been applied at a point 90° around the circumference of the rotor in the direction of its spin.

The result will be as though a force 'Q' (Figure 11.4) was operating to re-erect the rotor with its axis in the yawing plane. If the heading is such that the rotor axis is aligned with the longitudinal axis of the aircraft, the application of bank alone (with no turn) will not displace the rotor axis from the yawing plane. This aspect is mentioned again in the paragraph on limitations.

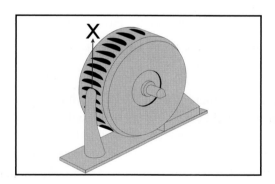

Figure 11.3. Rotor Axis in Yawing Plane.

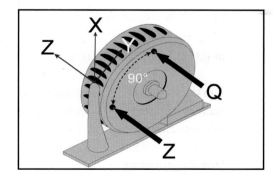

Figure 11.4. Rotor Axis Displaced.

A second control system, which is usually combined with the above system works as follows:

The **jet** of air **spins the rotor** and then flows round the outside of the rotor inside a metal case, as shown in Figure 11.5.

The air leaving the case is directed at a **wedge plate** fixed to the **outer gimbal**. When the gyro is correctly erected, this 'exhaust' jet is divided by the wedge plate into two equal streams producing equal reactions on the outer gimbal (R1 & R2). As soon as the rotor axis is displaced from the yawing plane the streams become unbalanced (Figure 11.6.) and the reactions on the outer gimbal at the wedge plate also become unequal.

The resultant of these reactions applies a torque to the outer gimbal about the vertical axis of the gyro. This torque is instantaneously transmitted by the outer gimbal to the inner gimbal and is represented by force 'F' in Figure 11.6.. This makes the rotor and inner gimbal precess.

Thus an effective force 'P' acts to re-erect the rotor axis back into the yawing plane. If the gyro was displaced so far that the jet was nowhere near the wedge plate, then the first system would restore the gyro to its correct position.

The jet provides coarse adjustment and the wedge plate fine adjustment.

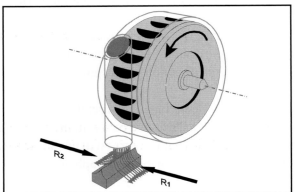

Figure 11.5. Rotor Axis in Yawing Plane

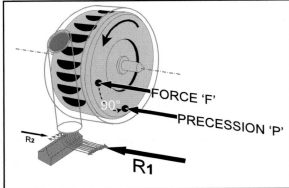

Figure 11.6. Rotor Axis Displaced.

11.4   THE CAGING DEVICE.

On the front of the instrument (see Figure 11.2.) there is a caging knob which, when pushed in, moves a caging arm which locks the inner gimbal at right angles to the outer gimbal so locking the rotor axis in the yawing plane. At the same time a gear engages with the outer gimbal so that by turning the knob the gyro can be rotated and the scale reading synchronised with (usually) the compass reading.

The caging device is designed as described in order that:-

a)   The DGI can be synchronised with the compass and reset as required.

b)   The gyro will not topple during synchronisation.

c)   Toppling and possible damage to the instrument can be prevented by caging before manoeuvres in which pitch and roll limits may be exceeded.

d)   The gyro can be instantly re-erected and re-synchronised if it has toppled.

11.5   DGI LIMITATIONS.

If the aircraft exceeds the pitch or roll limits of 85° (55°in air driven gyro DI's) the gyro will topple as the inner gimbal comes up against the stops, the precession causing the outer gimbal and scale to spin rapidly. Exceptions to this can occur:-

a)   If the rotor axis is athwartships - 360° of aircraft rotation in the looping plane then being possible without toppling the gyro.

b)   If the rotor axis is fore and aft - 360° of roll then being possible without toppling.

The actual indications on the scale at which these two situations can arise depend on the vintage and manufacture of the instrument.

11.6   DGI ERRORS.

There are several reasons why it is virtually impossible for a DGI to remain synchronised with the compass. The most significant errors are listed below and dealt with in subsequent paragraphs.

a)   Gimballing errors.

b)   Random wander.

c)   Apparent wander due to earth's rotation.

d)   Errors resulting from varying rotor rpm.

e)   Apparent wander due to change of aircraft position (transport wander).

11.7   GIMBALLING ERRORS.

These are **errors** in the indications of the DGI which occur when **bank is applied**. If the errors during a 360° turn are plotted, an approximate double sine curve results, with zero error on four headings (90° apart) spaced between alternate positive and negative peaks (two of each). The curve becomes more complex if pitch changes are made during the turn. The actual readings on the DI at which the maximum errors occur depend on its make and mark.

The errors are small, provided deviations in attitude from the level position are only moderate, and they disappear as soon as level flight is resumed. They occur because of the geometry of the gimbal system, in that unless the instrument case (and the aircraft bolted to it) are able to rotate about one of the axes of the gyro, the outer gimbal itself must move - giving an error - if the rotor axis is to maintain its fixed direction.

11.8   RANDOM WANDER.

The gyro rotor axis may change its direction in space (real wander) or appear to change its direction (apparent wander) or suffer from both.

More details of real wander, which is mainly the 'random wander' due to **manufacturing imperfections**, are given in the chapter entitled 'Gyroscopes'. In the case of the DGI, gyroscopic rigidity is high and random wander (or drift) rates are low.

An air-driven type with the rotor spinning at 10,000 rpm has a drift rate of about 16° /hr. A later design with rpm of 20,000 has a quoted drift rate of 12°/hr.

Lower rates of only a few degrees per hour are possible with electrically driven indicators. The random wander rates with gyroscopes used in inertial navigation systems may be less than 0.01°/hr.

11.9   APPARENT WANDER (DUE TO ROTATION OF THE EARTH).

The apparent wander (or drift) of an azimuth gyro has already been mentioned briefly in the chapter on gyroscopes. It is now necessary to consider the magnitude of this wander.

An azimuth gyro (with the axis of the spinning rotor horizontal) is set up in gimbals and frame at the North (or South) pole. The rotor axis will stay rigid in space (assuming zero real wander) while the earth rotates under it through 360° in one day or 360/24 = 15° in one hour.

An observer standing still watching the gyro, will move (with the earth) once round it in 24 hours (See Figure 11.7.)

If the gyro is the DGI, its reading will be **decreasing** (at the **North** pole) at a rate of 15° /hr. At the South pole the reading would **increase** at the same rate. This is the **maximum** rate of apparent wander due to the earth's rotation.

Figure 12.8. shows a gyroscope set up on the ground at the **equator** with the axis horizontal and aligned North/South. In 24 hours, the observer and gyro will move with the earth once round the earth's axis of rotation. There is no change in the direction of the rotor axis relative to the meridian, so there is **zero apparent drift**. The **apparent drift rate** due to the earth's rotation is therefore a **function of latitude**, being maximum at the pole and zero at the equator.

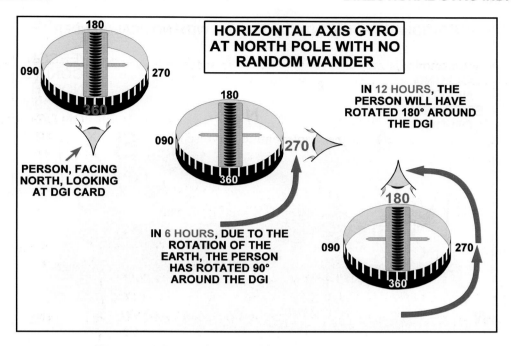

Figure 11.7. Apparent Wander at the North Pole.

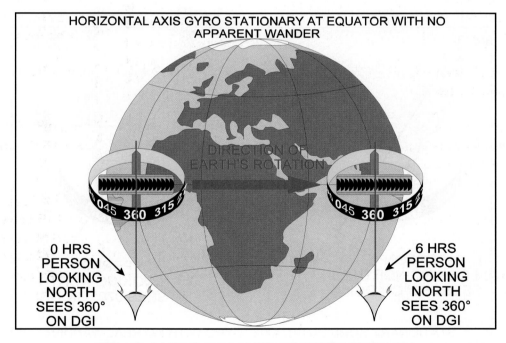

Figure 11.8. Apparent Wander at the Equator.

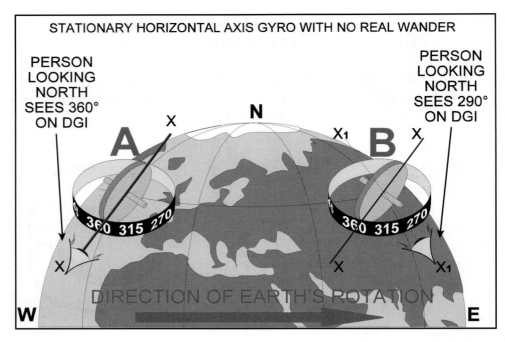

Figure 11.9(a). Apparent Wander at Intermediate Latitudes in the Northern Hemisphere.

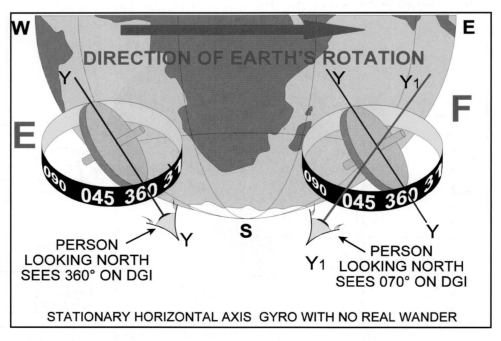

Figure 11.9(b). Apparent Wander at Intermediate Latitudes in the Southern Hemisphere.

Figure 11.9(a). demonstrates how the apparent drift due to the earth's rotation causes the reading of a DI to **decrease in the Northern hemisphere**.

At A, an observer looking North at the DGI reads 360°. When the observer and his gyro have rotated with the earth to B, the observer will see a value some degrees West of North (a DGI reading of less than 360°) because gyroscopic rigidity is keeping the gyro rotor axis aligned with a fixed direction in space.

The rotor axis cannot remain aligned N/S with the meridian because the latter, except at the equator, is continually changing its direction in space - its spatial orientation - as the earth rotates.

As the observer and gyro continue to rotate with the earth, the readings will decrease further. Similarly, it can be seen that if an observer and gyro located in the **Southern hemisphere** rotate with the earth from E, the readings of the DGI will **increase.**

Figure 11.10. shows graphically the variation of apparent drift with latitude. The drift rate is proportional to the sine of the latitude, so that assuming there is zero random drift and no compensation has been made:-

Apparent drift rate = 15 x sin lat (degrees per hour)

Note that this can only be correct if the gyro is 'stationary', meaning that it is not being moved or 'transported' from one place to another.

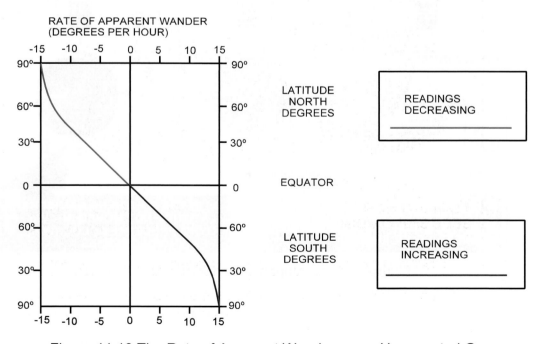

Figure 11.10 The Rate of Apparent Wander on an Uncorrected Gyro.

11.10   LATITUDE NUT CORRECTION.

Compensation for apparent wander (drift) due to the rotation of the earth is by means of an adjustable **latitude rider nut** on a threaded stud fixed horizontally to the **inner gimbal**.

In its central position (Figure 11.11.) the effect of the nut is cancelled by a counter-balance weight on the opposite side of the gimbal.

Screwed out a few turns, the nut applies a downward moment on the gimbal. This force, with the usual precession rule applied, produces (viewed from above) an anticlockwise precession of the gyro, including its scale, in azimuth. This would cause the reading in the window to increase.

Conversely, if the nut is wound in, clockwise precession occurs, making the readings decrease. Apparent drift due to the rotation of the earth can therefore be cancelled for a given latitude by using the latitude nut to produce an equal and opposite real drift. The ability to screw the nut in or out enables compensation to be made for increasing readings (Southern hemisphere) or decreasing readings (Northern hemisphere).

aka pendulous corrector device

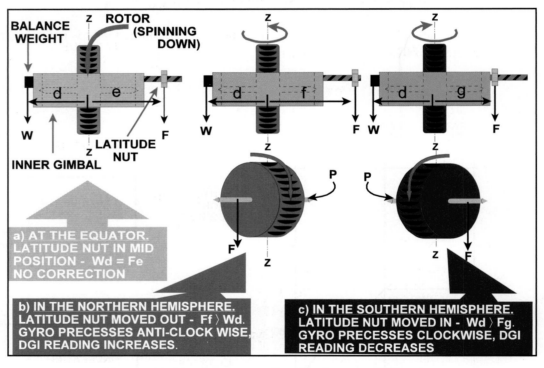

Figure 11.11. Compensation for Apparent Wander.

11 - 10

The setting can only be changed under workshop conditions (not in the aircraft) so that compensation will only be correct for a chosen latitude. However, errors due to latitude changes are usually small compared with random wander errors of the DI.

Should the aircraft be moved to a new operating area involving a latitude change of the order of 60°, a DGI with the appropriate latitude correction would probably be substituted.

Figure 12.12. illustrates graphically the effect of compensating a gyro for the apparent drift of minus 13°/hr at 60°N (15 sin 60°).

The latitude nut introduces a real drift of plus 13°/hr so that the resultant drift (assuming no random error) will be zero at 60°N. It will be realised that the compensation of + 13°/hr applied for 60°N will now be present at all latitudes, and this is represented in the graph by renumbering the drift scale.

The drift in the region of 60°N is negligible after compensation but if the aircraft is now moved to an area South of the equator the drift values will be greater than if no compensation had been made (as a study of Figure 12.12. will show).

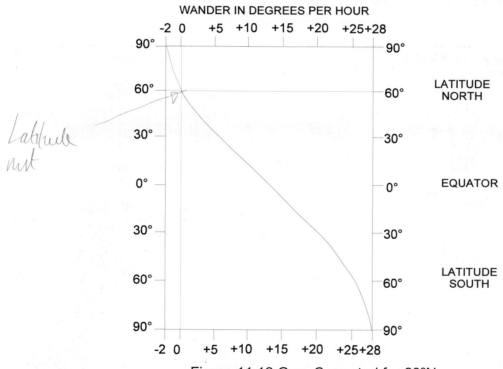

Figure 11.12 Gyro Corrected for 60°N.

11.11   ERRORS DUE TO UNSTABLE ROTOR RPM.

Since the rate of **precession** of a gyro **depends on rotor rpm**, over which no precise control is maintained in a suction-driven DGI, the latitude nut compensation is only approximate.

For instance, at high altitude with **inadequate suction**, the **rotor rpm** will be **lower** than the design value. This results in reduced gyroscopic rigidity and the latitude nut produces **too high a precession rate**, so **over-correcting** the apparent drift. Should rpm exceed the design figure, which is less likely to occur, the rigidity would increase and the latitude nut would produce a lower rate of precession so under-correcting the apparent drift.

11.12 TRANSPORT WANDER - CHANGE OF LATITUDE.

It has already been stated that the apparent drift rate due to the earth's rotation varies with the sine of the latitude (Figure11.10.).

No transport wander @ equator

we have this problem @ latitude ↑ or ↓ equator.

If we consider an aircraft tracking due North, starting from the equator, the initial apparent drift rate of an uncorrected gyro is zero. As the flight progresses, the reading of the DGI decreases. By the time the aircraft reaches 30°N, the DGI reading is decreasing at a rate of 7½°/hr, and at 60°N it is decreasing at 13°/hr. It should be clear that in flight due North or South from the equator at constant ground speed the value of the apparent drift rate will increase from zero to an value of 15 sin lat °/hr at the pole. The rate of increase of drift rate will not be linear - because of the sine function. The same applies if a compensated gyro is transported North or South of its latitude of correction. Summarising:-

Flight North from the **'corrected latitude'** gives a **decreasing reading** (a minus drift rate).

Flight South from the **'corrected latitude'** gives an **increasing reading** (a plus drift rate).

Flight away from the **'corrected latitude'** results in the **drift rate increasing**

Flight towards the **'corrected latitude'** results in the **drift rate decreasing**

11.13 DRIFT RATE CALCULATIONS.

Example 1
An aircraft is stationary at 60°N. Calculate the hourly wander rate, for an uncompensated gyro.

Solution 1

Apparent wander = - 15 x sin 60°(decreasing)°/hr = - 12.99°/hr

Example 2
An aircraft is stationary at 50°N. Assuming the DGI has no random error and is corrected for apparent drift due to the earth's rotation at 50°N, calculate the hourly wander rate.

Solution 2

Random wander	= 0°/hr	0
Latitude nut correction	= + 15 x sin 50°(increasing)°/hr	= +11.49°/hr
Apparent wander	= - 15 x sin 50°(decreasing)°/hr	= - 11.49°/hr
Total observed drift		= zero

Example 3
What is the hourly drift rate of a DGI in an aircraft at 25°S, if the gyro has been corrected for 10°N?

Solution 3

Latitude nut correction	= + 15 x sin 10° (increasing) °/hr	= + 2.60°/hr
Apparent wander	= + 15 x sin 25° (increasing) °/hr	= + 6.34°/hr
Total observed drift		= + 8.94°/hr (Increasing)

DIRECTIONAL GYRO INDICATORS

1.   A directional gyro indicator is basically a:

   a)   horizontal axis earth gyro.
   b)   horizontal axis tied gyro.
   c)   vertical axis earth gyro.
   d)   vertical axis tied gyro.

2.   Apparent wander may be corrected in a DGI by:

   a)   causing the gyro to precess in a clockwise direction (in the northern hemisphere).
   b)   attaching a bias weight to the inner gimbal which makes the gyro precess in azimuth in the same direction as apparent wander.
   c)   correcting wander by means of air jets.
   d)   attaching a bias weight to the inner gimbal which makes the gyro precess in azimuth in the opposite direction to apparent wander.

3.   An air driven DGI is corrected for apparent wander at 56°N. If the aircraft is maintaining constant DGI readings:

   a)   when flying north from 56°N the true heading of the aircraft will decrease.
   b)   when flying east from 56°N the true heading will decrease.
   c)   when flying south from 56°N the true heading will decrease.
   d)   when flying west from 56°N the true heading will increase.

4.   The formula used to calculate apparent wander of a directional gyro in the northern hemisphere is:

   a)   +15 sine latitude in degrees for the time of running.
   b)   +15 sine latitude in degrees per hour.
   c)   -15 sine latitude in degrees per hour.
   d)   15 sine latitude in degrees per hour increasing.

5.   Errors of the directional gyro are:

   a)   acceleration error, turning error, altitude error, transport wander, rotor speed error.
   b)   gimballing error, random wander, apparent wander, rotor speed error, transport wander.
   c)   gimballing error, looping error, rolling error, rotor speed error, transport wander.
   d)   transport wander, apparent wander, latitude error, turning error, acceleration error.

6.   The spin axis of a directional gyro is maintained in .... by means of ...... in an air driven gyro and by means of a .... in an electrically driven gyro:

    a)   the horizontal plane; air jets; wedge plate.
    b)   the vertical plane; air jets; torque motor.
    c)   the yawing plane; air jets; torque motor.
    d)   the yawing plane; air jets; wedge plate.

7.   The purpose of the caging knob is:

    a)   to prevent the gyro toppling.
    b)   to reset the heading.
    c)   to reset the heading and to prevent toppling.
    d)   to prevent apparent wander.

8.   In an air driven directional gyro the air jets are attached to:

    a)   the inner gimbal.
    b)   the outer gimbal.
    c)   the instrument casing.
    d)   the rotor axis.

9.   The limits of pitch and roll for a modern directional gyro are respectively:

    a)   55° and 85°
    b)   85° and 55°
    c)   55° and 55°
    d)   85° and 85°

10.   Gimballing error:

    a)   will disappear after a turn is completed.
    b)   will remain until the gyro is reset.
    c)   will only occur during a 360° turn.
    d)   will be zero on only two headings during a 360° turn.

CHAPTER TWELVE - THE ARTIFICIAL HORIZON

Contents

		Page
12.1	INTRODUCTION.	12 - 1
12.2	CONSTRUCTION	12 - 1
12.3	ARTIFICIAL HORIZON INDICATIONS	12 - 1
12.4	LIMITATIONS	12 - 4
12.5	CONTROL SYSTEMS	12 - 4
12.6	THE AIR DRIVEN ARTIFICIAL HORIZON	12 - 4
12.7	ACCELERATION ERROR IN THE AIR DRIVEN ARTIFICIAL HORIZON.	12 - 6
12.8	TURNING ERRORS IN THE AIR DRIVEN ARTIFICIAL HORIZON.	12 - 8
12.9	RIGIDITY	12 - 8
12.10	SERVICEABILITY CHECKS	12 - 8
12.11	THE ELECTRIC ARTIFICIAL HORIZON	12 - 9
12.12	ELECTRIC ARTIFICIAL HORIZON CONTROL SYSTEM.	12 - 9
12.13	ACCELERATION ERRORS IN THE ELECTRIC HORIZON	12 - 10
12.14	FAST ERECTION SYSTEM.	12 - 10
12.15	ADJUSTABLE AEROPLANE DATUM.	12 - 10
12.16	VERTICAL GYRO UNIT	12 - 11
	ARTIFICIAL HORIZON QUESTIONS	12 - 13

12.1   INTRODUCTION.

The **artificial horizon** (AH) provides the pilot with **information** in terms of the aircraft's attitude both in **pitch** and **roll**. It is a primary instrument, replacing the natural horizon in poor visibility. The attitude display consists of a miniature aircraft shape or 'gull-wing' (tail view) painted or engraved centrally on the inside of the glass face of the instrument, and therefore fixed to the instrument case and the actual aircraft. Behind this representation of the aircraft is the horizon bar, linked to the gyro in such a way that the bar is gyro-stabilised parallel to the true horizon. The artificial horizon may be suction or electrically driven. It is also known as a gyro horizon and attitude indicator.

12.2   CONSTRUCTION

The artificial horizon uses an **Earth gyro** in which the spin axis is maintained in, or tied to, the **vertical** by Earth's gravity. This means that the plane of the rotor rotation is horizontal, so providing the stable lateral and longitudinal references required.

The basis of construction of an artificial horizon is illustrated in Figure 12.1.

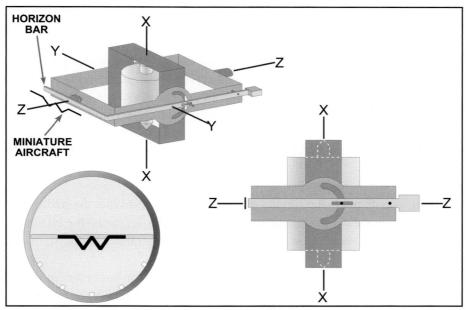

Figure 12.1. Pitch and Artificial Horizon.

12.3   ARTIFICIAL HORIZON INDICATIONS

Figure 12.1. shows the three axes of the gyro; XX, YY and ZZ. Because the gyro is tied to the vertical note that the axis XX (the spin axis) will remain Earth vertical and therefore the axis YY will be Earth horizontal when the aircraft is straight and level.

12 - 1

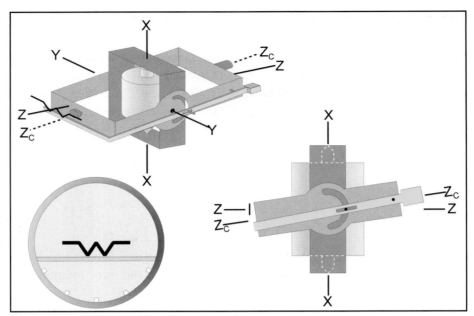

Figure 12.2. A Nose Up Attitude.

Pitch. Figure 12.1. shows the level-flight attitude display and two views of the instrument with the case removed.

In Figure 12.2. a nose-up attitude (of 10 degrees) is shown. The pitch-up movement has rotated the case together with the attached outer gimbal ring about the lateral axis YY. As this occurs, a guide pin protruding from the stabilised inner gimbal forces the horizon bar arm down. The horizon bar is now below the gull-wing producing the nose-up indication. (Figure 12.5. shows the gimbal rings and the pitch-indication linkage in greater detail) The three views in Figure 12.3. relate to a pitch-down situation. Note that the angle of pitch may be selected using the pitch markers shown.

Roll. In roll, as with pitch, the rigidity of the vertical gyro provides the stable attitude reference. As the aircraft rolls (about the longitudinal axis - ZZ in the diagrams) the instrument case and the gull-wing will rotate about the stabilised gyro rotor and gimbal system.

The gyroscopic rigidity of the spinning rotor holds the horizon bar in the rolling plane so that the amount and direction of bank are displayed by the gull-wing relative to the horizon bar. A more accurate indication of the amount of bank is given by a pointer attached to the outer gimbal and showing bank angle on a scale painted on the face of the instrument.

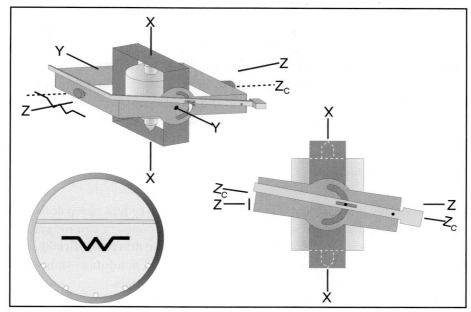

Figure 12.3. A Nose Down Attitude.

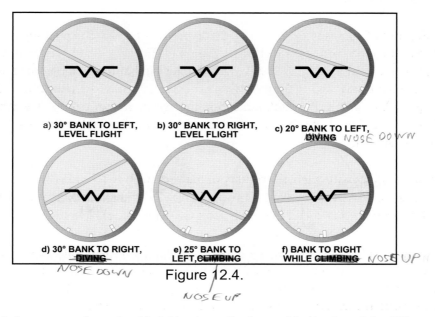

Figure 12.4.

Figure 12.4 shows a number of artificial horizon displays with the aircraft in different attitudes.

12.4 LIMITATIONS

The amount the case can move relative to the gyro is controlled by fixed stops. With **older designs**, typical limits are ± **60° in pitch** and **110° each way in roll**. In **modern** instruments there is **complete freedom in roll** and up to **85° (plus or minus) in pitch**. If the limits are exceeded, the gyro 'topples', giving violent and erratic movements of the horizon bar. Unless a fast erection system is incorporated, accurate indications will not be obtained until the gyro has re-erected itself over a period of 10 to 15 minutes.

12.5 CONTROL SYSTEMS

The rotor assembly is made very slightly bottom-heavy in order to keep down the time taken for initial erection when the gyro is first started up, but a complex control system is required to maintain the rotor axis vertical in flight. A **suction** or **air driven** artificial horizon exhausts air through four **slots** which are normally half covered by four **pendulous vanes**. **Electric** artificial horizons use **levelling / mercury switches** and **torque motors**.

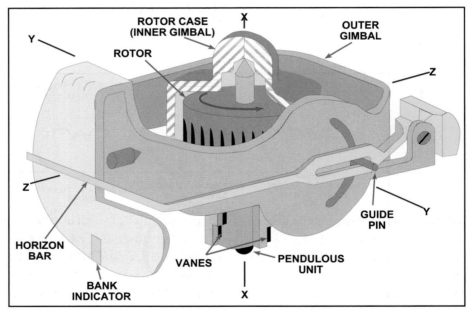

Figure 12.5. The Air Driven Artificial Horizon.

12.6 THE AIR DRIVEN ARTIFICIAL HORIZON

In the air driven artificial horizon an engine-driven suction pump (or venturi tube in some light aircraft) is used to create a suction of about 4 inches of mercury in the instrument case. Replacement air, drawn in by this suction via a filter, is ducted through the outer and inner gimbals to enter the rotor case as a jet which spins the rotor at up to **15,000 rpm**. After driving the rotor, the air passes into the instrument case through slots at the base of the rotor housing.

Control System.

The control system of the air driven artificial horizon consists of four slots and four pendulous (hanging) vanes at the base of the rotor housing. The vanes hang down so that when the rotor axis is vertical each slot is half covered by its vane, and four equal jets of air emerge from the slots, fore an aft and left and right, as in Figure 12.6. Because the four jets are of equal strength but in opposite directions no force is exerted on the gyro and therefore no precession occurs - the gyro rotor remaining vertical.

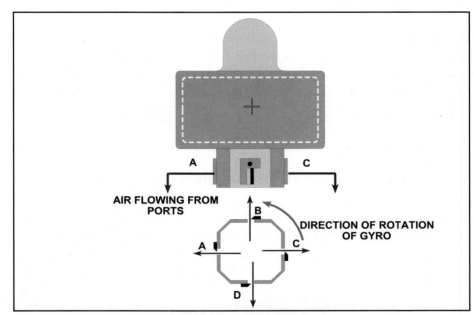

Figure 12.6. Equilibrium.

However the opposing vanes are fixed to a common spindle so that the four vanes operate as two pairs. The positioning of the vanes is such that if the rotor axis wanders from the vertical, one vane will hang clear of its slot, allowing unrestricted airflow, while the opposite slot is completely obstructed by its vane. The resulting unbalanced airflow precesses the gyro and corrects the tilt, returning the gyro axis to the vertical. Exactly how this correction is achieved is shown in Figure 12.7.

The gyro has wandered from the vertical so that vanes A and C are not affected and remain half covering their slots. However, vanes B and D, on a common spindle, hang down so that slot B is now closed and D is wide open. A strong jet exits through D causing an equal and opposite reaction 'R' on the gyro. This reaction is precessed through 90° in the direction of rotor spin (anticlockwise hen viewed from the top) and acts in the direction of 'P' which restores the gyro axis to the vertical.

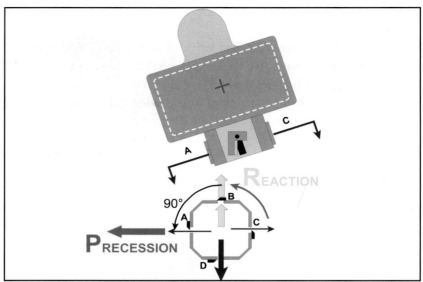

Figure 12.7. Rotor Axis Displaced from Vertical.

12.7   ACCELERATION ERROR IN THE AIR DRIVEN ARTIFICIAL HORIZON.

The control system of the air driven artificial horizon depends on the pendulous vanes being affected by the Earth's gravity. However, the vanes will be affected by any acceleration, not just that due to gravity.

When an aircraft **accelerates** in a level attitude (such as during the take-off run) a false nose up, right wing down, or **climbing right hand turn indication** will result. The **pitch error** is due to the effect of acceleration on the **lateral pendulous vanes**. The **roll error** is due to the inertia of the **bottom-heavy rotor housing**. These effects are now considered in more depth.

a)   **Pitch Error.** During acceleration, the lateral vanes lag, swinging back towards the pilot, opening the starboard slot and closing the port slot. This results in a reaction 'R' which acts to port (see Figure 12.8.) By the rule of precession the effect on the gyro is as if the direction of application of R had been moved 90° in the direction of rotor spin (anticlockwise). The gyro will now be precessed out of vertical with the base moving backwards towards the pilot. As shown in Figure 12.8., this movement is transmitted via the guide pin and horizon bar arm to bring the horizon bar below the gull-wing giving a nose-up indication.

b)   **Roll Error.** Due to inertia, the weighted base of the rotor housing tries to lag during acceleration. However, this force will be precessed, resulting in the base of the rotor housing moving to starboard and the gyro axis precessing out of the vertical (see Figure 12.9.) This rotates the whole rotor / gimbal assembly about the longitudinal axis to give a right wing down indication.

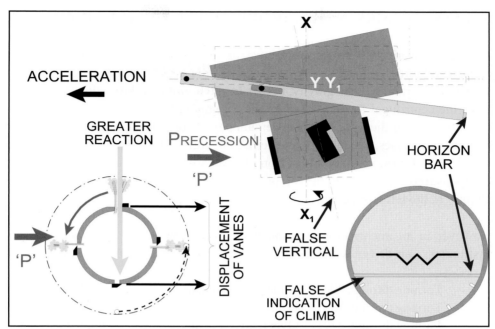

Figure 12.8 Pitch Error Due to Acceleration

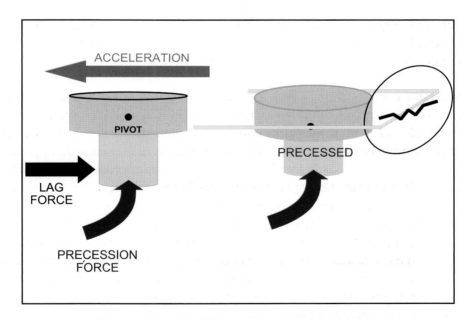

Figure 12.9. Roll Error Due to Acceleration.

Deceleration will cause a nose down, left wing low error, the opposite of the acceleration error indication. These errors assume that the rotor is rotating anticlockwise when viewed from the top, which is the case for British air driven artificial horizons. Most electric horizons and some American air driven horizons have clockwise rotor spin, giving opposite errors.

12.8 TURNING ERRORS IN THE AIR DRIVEN ARTIFICIAL HORIZON.

Whenever an **aircraft turns** there must be an acceleration towards the centre of the turn (centripetal force). Since the pendulous vanes are now affected by a horizontal acceleration as well as acceleration due to gravity, **errors in pitch and roll indications** will occur. During the turns the centrifugal force will act on the fore and aft pendulous vanes ('erection' error) and weighted base of the rotor housing (pendulosity' error). The errors are complex and change as the turn progresses, cancelling out after a 360° turn. The magnitude of the errors varies with speed, rate of turn, and type of horizon. For a chosen speed and rate of turn, the errors can be **compensated** for by **tilting** the top of the **rotor** axis slightly **forward** (for erection error) and slightly to the **left** (for pendulosity error).

However in an uncorrected instrument the following errors will occur. (assume a Classic Instrument - air driven with the gyro rotating anti-clockwise when viewed from above).

Turning through 90⁰ :	Under reads bank angle	Pitch error – indicating a climb
Turning through 180⁰ :	Bank angle correct	Pitch error – indicating a climb
Turning through 270⁰ :	Over reads bank angle	Pitch error – indicating a climb
Turning through 360⁰ :	Bank angle correct	Pitch angle correct

The tilts are of the order of **2°**. The setting of the horizon bar has to be similarly modified to indicate correctly in level flight. Small residual errors occur, particularly if the speed and rate of turn are not those for which compensation has been applied, but the errors are very much smaller than they would be had no compensation been made.

12.9 RIGIDITY

High rotor speeds in suction horizons of up to 15,000 rpm, result in high gyroscopic inertia. With electric horizons, speeds of 22,500 rpm are typical giving even greater rigidity. Because of the high inertia, precession rates are low and therefore once a horizon topples it will take a significant period for re-erection unless a rapid erection device is fitted.

12.10 SERVICEABILITY CHECKS

Before Flight. Check that the horizon bar takes up a laterally level position with the correct pitch indication for the aircraft type, and that this indication is maintained when taxying. If a caging device is fitted, the instrument should be uncaged at least five minutes before take-off to ensure that the rotor axis has had time to reach alignment with the true vertical.

In Flight. The artificial horizon should give an immediate and correct indication of any change in pitch or roll attitude.

12.11   THE ELECTRIC ARTIFICIAL HORIZON

The main advantage of electric artificial horizon over the air driven horizon is its greater rigidity due to its faster spin rate. This greater rigidity results in increased accuracy due to reduced errors. The basic principle of the instrument is the same as the air driven horizon. The vertical gyro is still tied by Earth's gravity, but by **mercury / levelling switches** and **torque motors** rather than the pendulous vanes of the air driven horizon.

12.12   ELECTRIC ARTIFICIAL HORIZON CONTROL SYSTEM.

The gravity-operated control system consists of mercury / levelling switches (which are fixed to the base of the rotor) and electric torque motors. If a levelling switch is not level the mercury liquid ball moves from its central position and closes the circuit to drive its torque motor. The torque motor provides the force which is precessed to return the gyro axis to the vertical. There are **two levelling switches**, one to sense **pitch** and one to sense **roll**.

They activate the pitch and roll torque motors respectively which precess the gyro back to the vertical as soon as it starts to wander.

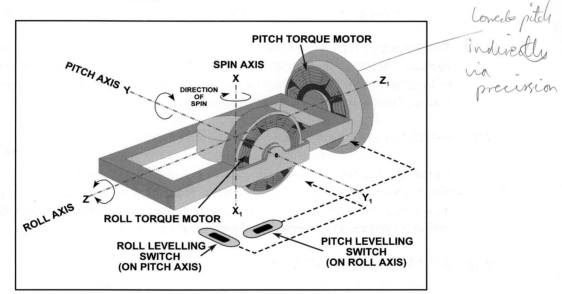

Corrects pitch indirectly via precession

Figure 12.10. The Electric Horizon Control System.

Because of the 90° precession rule, the torque motor on the side of the inner gimbal corrects wander in the rolling plane (applying torque round the lateral axis to produce rotation about the longitudinal axis). Likewise the pitch torque motor is on the outer (longitudinal) gimbal so that the precession is about the lateral axis to correct for pitch.

This control system, like that of the suction horizon, is designed to compensate for turning errors by maintaining the rotor axis slightly tilted away from the true vertical and having the horizon bar compensated by a similar amount. The amount and direction of this tilt depends on the particular model of instrument in use.

12.13   ACCELERATION ERRORS IN THE ELECTRIC HORIZON

Acceleration errors are minimal in the electric artificial horizon for the following reasons;

a)   The **high rotor speed** of an electric artificial horizon, results in very high gyro rigidity and therefore very low precession rates. There is therefore less potential for the gyro to move out of the Earth's vertical.

b)   The **rotor housing** is **less bottom heavy** in the electric artificial horizon and therefore roll error is reduced while accelerating.

c)   **Pitch and roll cut-out switches**. When an aircraft in a level attitude accelerates the pitch levelling switch will falsely complete the circuit as the mercury 'ball' moves back in its tube(due to inertia). As this would then result in the pitch torque motor falsely precessing the gyro out of the vertical, a pitch cut-out switch is included in the circuit which activates when an acceleration of 0.18G or greater is detected.

d)   Similarly in a turn the roll mercury switch would falsely activate the roll torque motor. A cut out is therefore incorporated in the circuit which is activated at 10 degrees angle of bank.

12.14   FAST ERECTION SYSTEM.

In many electric horizons a fast erect system is included to give rapid initial erection and quick re-erection should the instrument have toppled due to exceeding the operating limits. Quoting typical figures, the normal erection rate of 4° per minute is increased to 120° per minute by pushing the fast erection knob on the face of the instrument. This action **increases the voltage** to the erection torque motors. One of the advantages of having a fast erection system is that the pendulosity (bottom-heaviness) of the gyro can be reduced, so decreasing the turning and acceleration errors.

Note: When airborne, the fast erection knob can only be used successfully in level flight with no acceleration. During acceleration or a turn, the liquid level switches would be 'off-centre', and operation of the fast-erection system would align the rotor axis with a false vertical.

12.15   ADJUSTABLE AEROPLANE DATUM.

This is a refinement found on some American artificial horizons. The idea is that if when an aircraft is trimmed out to fly **straight and level** it has a pitch up attitude, the 'aeroplane' datum can be adjusted to lie on the horizon. However, there is a risk that such adjustment in flight could result in a misleading datum for flying approach procedures in IMC conditions. The Aeronautical Information Circular 14/1969 discusses this risk in depth, and strongly recommends that in **light aircraft the datum be set before flight and thereafter left well alone**. The CAA require that such movable datums be removed or otherwise rendered inoperative on aircraft having a maximum all-up weight in excess of 6000 pounds.

12.16 VERTICAL GYRO UNIT

This unit performs the same functions as the Gyro Horizon, i.e. it establishes a stabilised reference about the Pitch and Roll axes of an aircraft.

Instead of providing attitude displays by direct means, it is designed to operate a synchro system which produces, and transmits, attitude related signals to "**a steering computer**" and to an amplifier unit.

After processing and amplification, the signals are then transmitted to servo operated indicator elements within an Attitude Director Indicator (ADI). The synchro system also supplies attitude related signals to the appropriate control channels of an AFCS. The gyroscope and its levelling switch and torque motor system is basically the same as that adopted in electrical gyro horizons.

Whenever a change of aircraft attitude occurs, signals flow from Pitch and Roll synchros disposed about the relevant axes of the **vertical gyroscope** to the corresponding synchros within the indicator. Error signals are therefore induced in the rotors and after amplification are fed to the servo motors, which rotate to position the **pitch** bar and **horizon** disc to indicate the changing attitude of the aircraft.

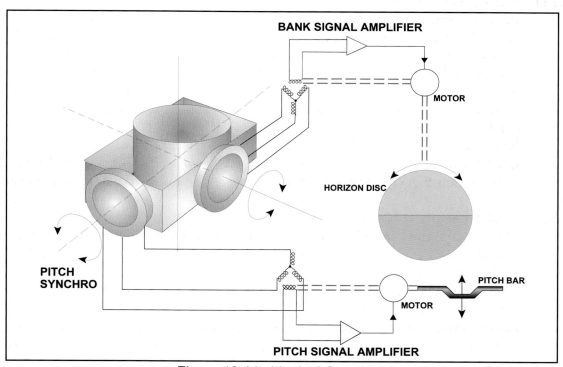

Figure 12.11. Vertical Gyro Unit

✳ VERTICAL DATA GENERATION UNIT
  = VERTICAL GYRO UNIT

The synchro described senses changes in Pitch and Roll attitudes by means of a CX synchro positioned on each corresponding axis of the gyros' gimbal system. The stator of the Roll synchro is secured to the frame of the unit, whilst its rotor is secured to the outer gimbal ring. The Pitch synchro has its stator secured to the outer gimbal ring, and its rotor to the inner gimbal ring. The stators supply attitude error signals to corresponding CT synchros in the ADI, and also to Pitch and Roll circuit modules of the computer.

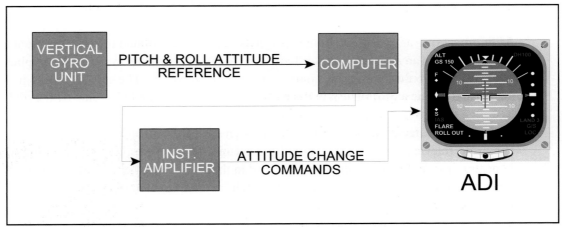

Figure 12.12. Stabilised Reference System.

ARTIFICIAL HORIZON

1.   An artificial horizon utilises (i)............ to show (ii)........ in (iii)....... and (iv).............

  a) (i) an earth gyro (ii) position (iii) latitude (iv) longitude
  b) (i) a space gyro ✗ (ii) attitude ╱ (iii) degrees (iv) minutes
  c) (i) an earth gyro (ii) latitude (iii) pitch (iv) roll
  ⓓ (i) an earth gyro (ii) attitude ╱ (iii) pitch ╱ (iv) roll ╱

2.   During the take-off run an air driven artificial horizon will usually indicate:

  a) nose up and incorrect left bank.
  b) a false descending turn to the right.
  ⓒ increased nose up attitude and right wing low.
  d) a false climbing turn to the left.

3.   The indication at Figure 1 shows:

  a) a climbing turn to the right.
  b) nose-up and left wing down
  c) 30° starboard bank, nose up.
  ⓓ 30° port bank, nose below horizon.

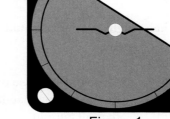

Figure 1

4.   False nose-up attitude displayed on air driven artificial horizon during the take-off run is caused by:

  a) the high pendulosity of the rotor
  ⓑ the lag of the lateral pendulous vanes
  c) the linear acceleration cut out
  d) incorrect rotor speed

5.   The rotor axis of an electrical horizon is tied to the earth's vertical by:

  a) four pendulous vanes
  b) the roll cut out
  c) the low centre of gravity of the rotor housing
  ⓓ two mercury level switches and two torque motors

6.   Items marked in Figure 2. as A, B, C and D respectively are:

      a)   pitch torque motor, rotor housing, roll torque motor, outer ring.

      b)   roll torque motor, pitch torque motor, rotor housing, outer ring.

      c)   pitch torque motor, roll torque motor, rotor housing, outer ring.

      d)   outer ring, pitch torque motor, roll torque motor, rotor housing.

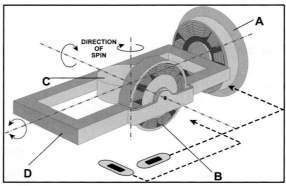

Figure 2

7.   False right wing low attitude shown on an air driven artificial horizon during an acceleration is caused by:

      a)   the lag of the base of the rotor housing

      b)   the logitudinal pendulous vanes

      c)   the roll cut-out

      d)   high rotor speed

8.   Inside an artificial horizon:

      a)   the inner gimbal ring is pivoted laterally inside the outer gimbal ring and the outer gimbal ring is pivoted longitudinally inside the case

      b)   the inner gimbal ring is tied to the vertical by a control system

      c)   the rotor axis is kept level by a calibrated spring attached to the outer gimbal ring and the instrument case

      d)   there is only one gimbal ring

9.   When an adjustable aircraft datum is fitted to an artificial horizon in light aircraft:

      a)   it should be checked at regular intervals

      b)   it should be set to the central position and left there

      c)   it should be rendered inoperative

      d)   it should be set to 15°

10.   An electrically driven artificial horizon has less errors during the take-off run because:

      a)   it is less pendulous, has a higher rotor speed and a linear acceleration cut out

      b)   the mercury level switches are more sensitive than the pendulous vanes fitted to air driven types

      c)   the roll cut-out speed is activated

      d)   it is less aperiodic than the air driven types

CHAPTER THIRTEEN - THE TURN AND SLIP INDICATOR

Contents

		Page
13.1	THE RATE OF TURN INDICATOR.	13 - 1
13.2	THE RATE GYRO.	13 - 1
13.3	OPERATION.	13 - 1
13.4	CONSTRUCTIONAL DETAILS.	13 - 2
13.5	EFFECT OF VARYING ROTOR SPEED.	13 - 3
13.6	ERRORS IN THE LOOPING PLANE.	13 - 3
13.7	THE SLIP INDICATOR	13 - 3
13.8	CONSTRUCTION	13 - 3
13.9	OPERATING PRINCIPLES.	13 - 4
13.10	TURN AND SLIP DISPLAYS.	13 - 6
	RATE OF TURN AND SLIP INDICATOR QUESTIONS	13 - 9

(upto limit of 25° angle of bank)

Rate 1 Turn = 3° / second

$\therefore$ 360° = 120 seconds = 2 minutes

13.1   THE RATE OF TURN INDICATOR.

JAA expert
Measurer
'YAW
AccESS'

This instrument incorporates two measuring devices, both indicating on the same instrument face. One of these, the rate of turn indicator, (commonly shortened to 'turn' indicator), uses a rate gyro to measure rate of turn about a ̋vertical axis. ̋ The other, the slip indicator, is a very simple pendulous device which is used mainly to show whether or not a turn is balanced, (whether the angle of bank is correct for the TAS and rate of turn), and if not, to indicate the extent of slip or skid.

13.2   THE RATE GYRO.

The turn indicator employs a rate gyro which, having only one gimbal, has freedom about only two axes. There is, of course, complete freedom of rotation about one of these - the rotor spin axis - which in level flight lies athwartships (laterally). There is restricted freedom about the fore/aft (longitudinal) gimbal axis. There is no freedom about the aircraft's vertical axis, so any torque applied about this axis - as in a turn - will cause the gyro to precess.

13.3   OPERATION.

Figures 13.1. and 13.2. illustrate the principal of operation. If the aircraft turns, the rotor is subjected to a primary torque acting about the ZZ axis. This produces a primary precession about the YY axis, the direction of this precession being as if the applied force were moved 90° in the direction of rotor spin. As the rotor tilts about the YY axis it causes a spring between gimbal and frame to be extended. The resultant spring tension subjects the rotor to a secondary torque acting about the YY axis. This secondary torque, with the precession will continue until the gimbal has tilted just the right amount to give the spring tension required to generate a rate of secondary precession equal to the rate of turn of the aircraft. This gives equilibrium. It should be emphasised that the chain of events is virtually instantaneous - as the aircraft goes into a turn, the gimbal takes up the appropriate angle of tilt.

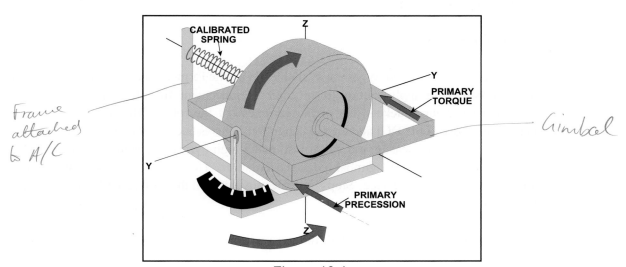

Frame
attached
to A/C

Gimbal

Figure 13.1.

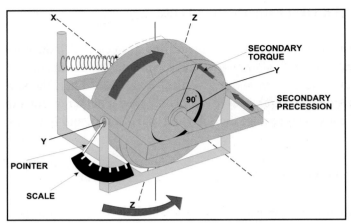

Figure 13.2.

If the rate of turn changes, the tilt of the gimbal will also change, to re-establish the balance of torques on the gyro. The angle of tilt is thus a measure of the rate of turn. A pointer fixed to or linked with the gimbal indicates the tilt on a scale on the face of the instrument. The scale is calibrated to indicate rates of turn either side of the centre zero so that the first graduation corresponds to a Rate 1 turn with the aircraft turning 3° per second. A second mark for Rate 2 corresponds to 6° per second. There may be further graduations for higher rates of turn.

It is desirable that the angle of tilt of the gimbal should equal the angle of bank in a turn, so that the rotor axis remains horizontal and the instrument measures rate of turn about the earth's vertical. By spinning the rotor up and away from the pilot and by having a suitable spring sensitivity, the direction and amount of precessional tilt of the gimbal will keep the rotor axis approximately horizontal in a moderately banked turn. For a given sensitivity, the tilt of the rotor depends on the rate of turn, but the bank angle, even in a balanced turn, depends on rate of turn and TAS. It follows that only at particular TAS, specified in the calibration, will the rotor axis stay horizontal and the rate indications be substantially accurate. In practice the errors produced by TAS deviations are not serious. One manufacturer quotes a maximum error of 5% over a speed range of 85 to 350 knots, the calibration value being 260 knots.

13.4   CONSTRUCTIONAL DETAILS.

Suction and electrically-driven types are available. With the former, an engine-driven pump or venturi tube is used to apply suction to the case. Replacement air enters via a filter and is directed by a jet at the 'buckets' cut in the periphery of the rotor. The rotor rpm are low compared with those of the DGI and artificial horizon. This is because the gyroscopic property of precession is used to measure rate to turn, so that a high gyroscopic rigidity is undesirable. A damping system fitted to the gimbal reduces oscillation. This may be the piston-in-cylinder type or an electro-magnetic device. Stops limit the movement of the gimbal to tilt corresponding to a turn of about 20° per second.

Note: 1) As there is only one gimbal, the gyro will not 'topple' when it comes against the stops.

Calibration of correct rate of turn is optimised for a design TAS. However, only a small amount of error is introduced even it departures from the design TAS are quite large.

2) The warning flag on the face of the TBI indicates that electrical power to the instrument has failed.

13.5   EFFECT OF VARYING ROTOR SPEED.

[handwritten margin: Underspeed ↓ Underread ↓ Under Time. (C less time will be taken for an inducted Rate 1 turn as Rate 1.5 will be occuring when R1 is read)]

If the suction is inadequate (at high altitude, or with a choked filter, or a leaking suction tube) with an air-driven instrument, gyro rigidity will be lowered as the gyro is **"underspeeding"**. Consequently the secondary precession needed to equal the aircraft turn can be generated by a smaller secondary torque. This reduced torque will be produced by a smaller angle of gimbal tilt, and this means that the instrument will **under-read** the turn rate.

Alternatively, if the gyro were to **"overspeed"**, by the same token it will **over-read** the rate of turn that is being achieved by the angle of bank applied.

13.6   ERRORS IN THE LOOPING PLANE.

[handwritten margin: NB Ω will not change]

In a gently banked turn, the aircraft is turning mainly in the yawing plane, but in a steep turn there is more movement in the looping plane. Normally movement in the looping plane means that the aircraft is rotating about the rotor axis, with no effect on the gyro. However, if the gimbal is tilted before movement in the looping plane commences, as happens with a yaw, the movement in the looping plane will cause additional precession of the rotor.

The usual positive movement in the looping plane in a steep turn will increase the gimbal tilt causing the indicator to **over-read**, sometimes coming against the stops.

[handwritten: "STEEP TURNS CAUSE TURN METER TO OVER READ"]

13.7   THE SLIP INDICATOR

*[handwritten margin: * slow gyro is easier to get moving but will move less ∴ underread - fast will be hard to move (∵ rigid) but once moved will precess a lot.]*

It is desirable that turns should be properly balanced, with no side slip or skid. This implies that the angle of bank should be correct for the TAS and rate of turn. The correct bank angle could be accurately calculated, or rules of thumb may be used. For instance, with Rate 1 turns, we can take one tenth of the TAS and add seven to give approximately the required bank angle. For example; Rate 1, TAS 150 knots; bank angle should be 15 + 7 = 22°. This rule gives reasonable accuracy for Rate 1 turns with TAS between 100 and 250 knots. During instrument flight however, the fewer the calculations that have to be made, the better. The slip indicator gives a direct indication of the state of balance of the turn.

[handwritten: $= \dfrac{IAS}{10} + 7°$ @ 100 kts = 17° for rate 1 turn]

13.8   CONSTRUCTION

[handwritten margin right: 180 kts is when rate 1 is 25°]

Early types of slip indicator employed a simple metal pendulum suspended in the instrument case, its oscillations being controlled by a piston-in-cylinder damping device. The modern version is usually a 'ball-in-tube inclinometer'. This comprises a solid ball in a curved tube containing liquid with damps out the unwanted oscillations. It is sketched in Figures 13.3b. and 13.4b. The heavy ball behaves like a pendulum, with the centre of curvature of the tube acting as the effective point of suspension.

[handwritten bottom left: - Turn Indicator only sensitive to Yaw - Turn Co-ordinator is tilted upwards by about 20-30° & is therefore sensitive to roll & yaw.]

[handwritten bottom right: More than 180 kts you limit AOB to 25° Much wont actually be Rate 1.]

13.9   OPERATING PRINCIPLES.

Consider first the aircraft in level flight with lift L balancing weight W viewed in Figure 13.3a. The weight W of the ball in the tube acts downwards and is exactly balanced by the equal and opposite reaction of the base of the tube on the ball, acting upwards towards the centre of curvature of the tube. If the wings are level, the ball will lie just between the two vertical lines etched on the tube, as indicated in Figure 13.3b..

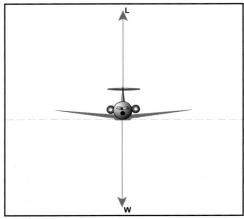

Figure 13.3a.
Aircraft in Level Flight

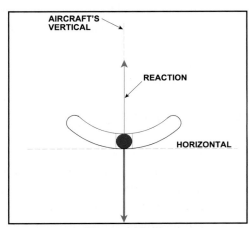

Figure 13.3b.
Ball-in-tube (Level Flight)

Now let us consider a balanced turn to the left. Figure 13.4a. shows the aircraft with lift L equal and opposite to the resultant of aircraft weight W and centrifugal force C, the latter being proportional to TAS and rate of turn.

The ball is also subject to a centrifugal force depending on TAS and rate of turn, so it rolls outwards, taking up a new equilibrium position such that the reaction of the base of the tube on the ball is again exactly balanced, this time by the resultant of ball weight W and centrifugal force C (Figure 13.4b.)

Because both aircraft and the ball are experiencing the same TAS and rate of turn (and so the same acceleration towards the centre of the turn) it can be proved that the resultant weight and centrifugal force for the aircraft will be parallel to the resultant of weight and centrifugal force for the ball. Now if the ball is laterally central in the tube, (between the two etched lines), the resultant and reaction forces of the ball must lie in the aircraft's vertical (see Figure 13.4b.). These forces are parallel, as stated above, to the resultant of aircraft weight and centrifugal force with must therefore also lie in the aircraft's vertical and will thus be in the same line as the lift L (Figure 13.4a.) - which means that the turn is balanced.

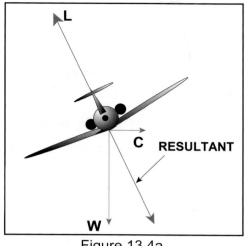

Figure 13.4a.
Balanced Turn To Port

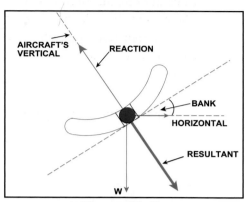

Figure 13.4b.
Ball-in-Tube (Balanced Turn Port)

Unbalanced turns are most simply considered as follows. Let us assume that the TAS and rate of turn are the same as in Figures 13.4a. and 13.4b., so that the ball will not have moved laterally. Now if too much bank is applied, (for the TAS and rate of turn), the tube will have been rotated too far in the rolling plane so that the ball appears as in Figure 13.5., no longer central, but correctly indicating the aircraft to be **'slipping in'** to the turn, the radius of which will be less than it should be. If on the other hand insufficient bank has been applied, the instrument will be indicating that the aircraft is **'skidding out'** of the turn (see Figure 13.6.), the radius of turn this time being greater than it should be.

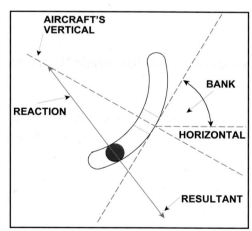

Figure 13.5.
Unbalanced Turn Port (Slipping)

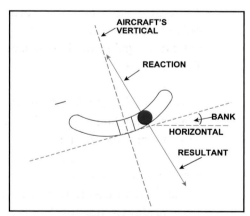

Figure 13.6.
Unbalanced Turn Port (Skidding)

13.10   TURN AND SLIP DISPLAYS.

Several examples of turn and slip indications (needle and ball type) are drawn in Figure 13.7.

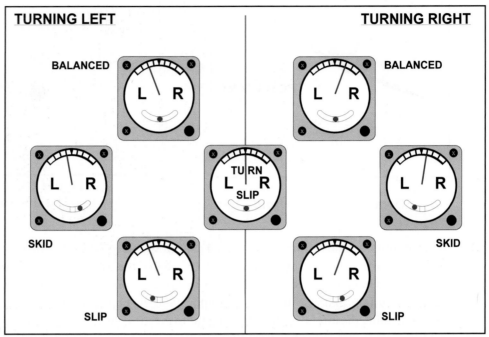

Figure 13.7. Needle and Ball Displays

Example Question - Rate one turn

Flying at 360 kts what is the turn diameter at Rate 1?

120 seconds

1.   A rate 1 turn takes 2 minutes to complete, therefore.........
      Flying at 360 kts each minute I fly 6nmls and so.......... in 2 minutes I will cover 12nmls.

2.   The circumference of a circle = "pi"d (diameter of a circle)

3.   The circumference is 12nmls, therefore

      12 = 22/7 x "d"
              or
      12 x 7 divided by 22 = d
            3.8 = d

4.   To check we can ..... divide 360 by 100 = 3.6 --------- 4 "nmls"
      similarly for   400 =   "4nmls"
      and for   500 =   "5nmls"

∴ Diameter of Rate 1 Turn = $\frac{TAS}{100}$

OR Radius of Rate 1 Turn

$= \frac{TAS}{200}$

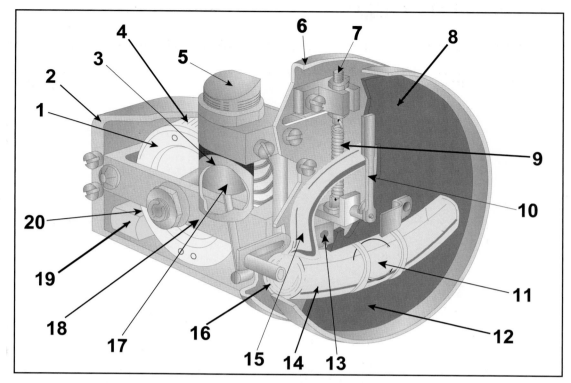

Figure 13.8. Mechanism of an air-driven turn-and-bank indicator.

1. Rotor
2. Instrument frame
3. Damping cylinder
4. Buckets
5. Air bleed
6. Front plate
7. Rate-spring adjusting screw
8. Dial
9. Rate spring
10. Pointer

11. Agate ball
12. Datum arrow
13. Gimbal front pivot
14. Slip indicator
15. Expansion chamber
16. Fluorescent card
17. Piston
18. Gimbal ring
19. Jet block
20. Jet

RATE OF TURN AND SLIP INDICATOR

1.   The rate of turn indicator uses (i) .... which spins (ii).........

	i	ii
a)	space gyroscope	up and away from the pilot
b)	tied gyro	anti-clockwise when viewed from above
c)	rate gyro ✓	up and away from the pilot
d)	earth gyro	Clockwise

2.   The gyro in a rate of turn indicator has (i) ..... operating speed than the gyros used in other instruments because (ii)..........

∴ ∞ precession is required

	i	ii
a)	lower	a higher rigidity is not required
b)	the same	it uses the property of rigidity
c)	a higher	a low precession rate gives a greater operating range
d)	variable	more than one rate of turn is desired

3.   At Figure 1. The TBI shows:

   a)   a rate of turn to the left, slipping in
   b)   an aircraft taxiing and turning starboard
   c)   that the aircraft will complete a turn in one minute
   d)   the aircraft is yawing to the right

Figure 1

4.   When the pointer of a rate of turn indicator shows a steady rate of turn:

   a)   the calibrated spring is exerting a force about the lateral axis equal to the rate of turn
   b)   the force produced by the spring is producing a precession equal to but opposite to the rate of turn is correctly banked
   c)   the spring is providing a force which produces a precession equal to the rate of turn (in the opposite direction).
   d)   the spring is providing a force which produces a precession equal to the rate of turn (in the correct direction)

5.   If the filter of the air driven rate of turn indicator becomes partially blocked:

   a)   the aircraft will turn faster than indicated
   b)   the instrument will overread
   c)   the rate of turn indicated will be unaffected
   d)   the radius of the turn will decrease

6.   The items in Figure 2 labelled A, B, C and D are respectively:

        a)   the rate spring, rotor, gimbal ring, damping cylinder and piston
        b)   the damping ring, expansion chamber, damping cylinder, piston, gimbal ring
        c)   gimbal ring, damping cylinder, rotor, pointer
        d)   piston, rate spring, rotor, gimbal ring

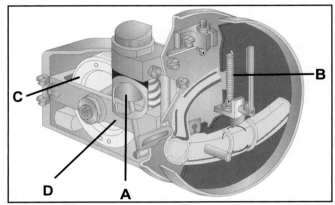

Figure 2

7.   The radius of a turn at rate 1, and TAS 360 kt is:

        a)   10nm
        b)   5nm
        c)   7.5nm
        d)   2nm

CHAPTER FOURTEEN - TURN CO-ORDINATOR

Contents

                                Page

14.1   TURN CO-ORDINATOR . . . . 14 - 1

14.1   TURN CO-ORDINATOR

The **Turn Co-ordinator** is an interesting development of the **Turn** and **Bank** indicators.

The primary difference is in the setting of the precession axis of the rate gyroscope and the method of display.

The gyroscope is spring restrained and is mounted so that the axis is at about 30 degrees with respect to the aircraft longitudinal axis, thus making the gyroscope sensitive to banking of the aircraft as well as to turning.

A turn is normally initiated by banking the aircraft, the gyroscope will precess, and this in turn will move the aircraft symbol in indicate the direction of bank and enable the pilot to anticipate the resulting turn.

The pilot then controls the turn at the required rate by alignment of the aircraft with the graduations on the instrument dial. The rate of turn will depend on the instrument in use either as a rate one turn, 3 degrees per second, or any other rate dependant on instrument design. The ball still has to remain central for a balanced rate of turn.

The annotation "No Pitch Information" on the indicator scale is given to avoid any confusion in pitch control which might result with the similarity with the presentation of the gyro horizon.

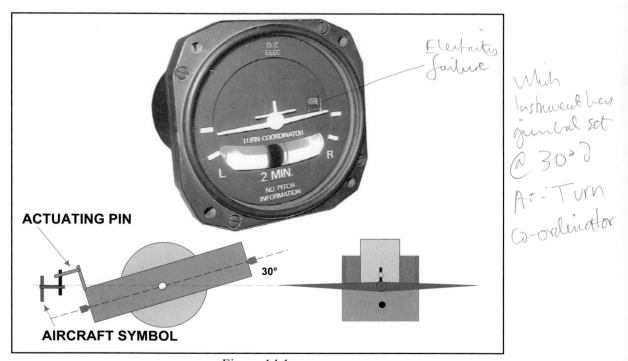

Figure 14.1.

THE TURN CO-ORDINATOR

1.   The gimbal ring of a turn co-ordinator is inclined at about 30° with respect to the aircraft's longitudinal axis in order:

    a)   make the rate of turn more accurate
    b)   make the gyro sensitive to banking of the aircraft as well as to turning
    c)   make the gyro more effective during inverted flight
    d)   have a higher rotor speed which will prolong the life of the instrument

2.   If an aircraft turns as indicated in Figure 1:

    a)   the aircraft will turn through 180° in two minutes
    b)   it will take one minute to turn through 90°
    c)   the aircraft is turning left at less than 3°/ second
    d)   the aircraft is turning left at 3°/ second

Figure 1

3.   A turn co-ordinator has (i) ..... pivoted (ii) .... in the case

	i	ii
a)	two gimbal rings	orthogonally
b)	a single gimbal ring	longitudinally
c)	one gimbal ring	laterally
d)	two gimbal rings	mutually perpendicular

CHAPTER FIFTEEN - AIRCRAFT MAGNETISM

Contents

		Page
15.1	DEVIATION.	15 - 1
15.2	COMPASS SWING.	15 - 1
15.3	HARD IRON MAGNETISM.	15 - 2
15.4	SOFT IRON MAGNETISM.	15 - 3
15.5	CORRECTION OF COEFFICIENTS	15 - 6
15.6	CHANGE OF MAGNETIC LATITUDE	15 - 7
15.7	OCCASIONS FOR SWINGING THE COMPASS.	15 - 7
	AIRCRAFT MAGNETISM QUESTIONS	15 - 9

15.1   DEVIATION

The compass needle would accurately define the magnetic meridian were it not for the aircraft's own internal magnetism deflecting it. Deviation is the angular difference measured between the direction taken up by a Compass Needle and the Magnetic Meridian. Deviation is named Easterly or Westerly depending on whether the North seeking end of the compass needle lies to the East or West of the Magnetic meridian.

	Compass Heading	Deviation	Magnetic Heading
Deviation West Compass Best	095	-5	090
Deviation East Compass Least	090	+5	095

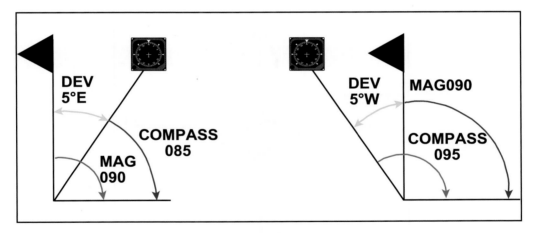

Figure 15.1

15.2   COMPASS SWING

The basic method of determining deviation is to compare the aircraft's heading compass reading with magnetic heading as defined by a high quality 'land or datum' compass. This comparison of aircraft compass and magnetic datum readings is carried out in an area selected specifically for this purpose.

Therefore the aims of a compass swing are as follows:

a)   To observe / determine the deviations / differences between Magnetic North (observed on a Landing Compass) and Compass North (observed in the aircraft) on a series of headings   ~Datum compass 15m away from a/c

b)   To correct / remove as much deviation as possible

c)   To record the residual deviation which is left after the Compass has been adjusted

The magnetic deviation observed during a compass swing can be said to be derived from Hard Iron and Soft Iron magnetism and this total field can in turn, for our purposes, be later resolved into two further combined components (coefficients B and C).   Dev^n = A+B+C

15.3   **HARD IRON MAGNETISM**

The total force at the compass position produced by permanent hard iron magnetism can be resolved into three components. These components will be fixed for a given aircraft and will not change with change of heading.

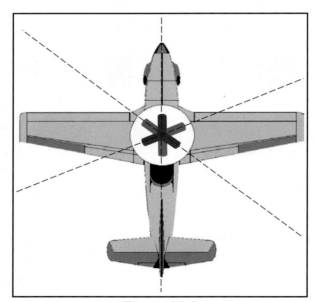

Figure 15.2

15.4   SOFT IRON MAGNETISM

Soft iron magnetism is induced in parts of the aircraft structure by surrounding fields - the most important of these being the earth.   The earth's field has a vertical as well as horizontal component. However, again for our purposes we will within the constraints of the syllabus only consider vertical soft iron (VSI) magnetism (Z is the vertical component of the earths field and H is the horizontal component). The component Z has an increasing affect with latitude as the compass magnets try to follow the earth's flux lines therefore VSI magnetism must also vary with latitude. However, Z is zero at the equator, where the horizontal component H is greatest, so no VSI magnetism is induced there.

When we examine the effective positioning of the imaginary magnets found when completing a compass swing we must remember that we use a real system (the Compass) to give us aircraft heading and that this readout is affected by these magnetic forces which we have gone to some trouble to discover.

We can see from Figure 15.3 that the positioning can vary,(even to the extent of having two imaginary magnets affecting our compass) but the effect will be easily resolved by the compass swing which can cater for any positioning as long as we follow the basic rules.

For example we may examine the case where the effect of the Blue Pole is said to be in the nose or forward of the aircraft compass.

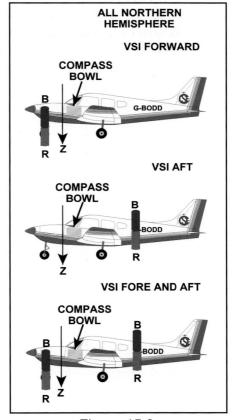

Figure 15.3.

Heading North the isolated Blue pole is in the same horizontal direction as the earths blue pole and so the needle is not deviated. The directive force or alignment of the earths field is being augmented by the blue pole, effectively they are pulling together.

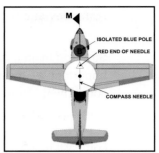

Figure 15.4a. Hdg C 000°

As the aircraft now turns right on to 045° deviation begins to take place and as we can see from the table by 090° this has become maximum and then starts to become less as we approach 180°.

Remember that the blue pole represents a magnetic force which on this heading acts along the same line but in opposition to the stronger earths field.

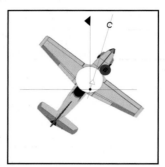

Figure 15.4b. Hdg C 045°.

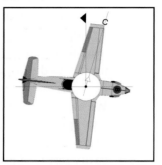

Figure 15.4c. Hdg C 090°.

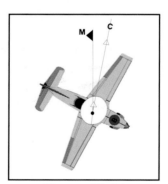

Figure 15.4d

On the remaining headings 180° to 360° the effects of the blue pole in the nose are as expected i.e. the red end of the compass needle is being attracted to the West of Magnetic North giving the maximum westerly deviation on 270°.

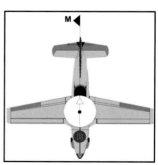

Figure 15.4.e.

If the deviations caused by the blue pole in the nose are plotted against compass heading, a positive sine curve is obtained. Had the blue pole been aft of the compass a negative sine curve would have been obtained. This would mean that on a heading of 090° the deviation would reach a maximum westerly value instead of a maximum easterly value. The changes in directive force would also be revised, the maximum occurring on 180° and the minimum on 360°.

Heading °C	Deviation	Directive Force
000	Zero	Maximum
045	East + some	More than earth's
090	East + max	Earths approximately
135	East + some	Less than earth's
180	Zero	Minimum.
225	West - some	Less than earth's
270	West - max	Earth's approximately
315	West - some	More than earth's
000	Zero	Maximum

What we have examined here is known for compass swinging as Coefficient B which we could view as that component which is resolved along the body of the aircraft. The forces resolved follow a simple Sine Curve which in our case here would be 'positive' although negative curves occur just as frequently.

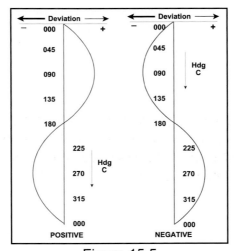

Figure 15.5

Equally we should be able to see that if a further magnetic source is resolved to the right wing we would achieve a positive cosine curve along the same lines and this is more usually described as Coefficient C.

The combination of Coefficients **A (a mechanical function yet to be discussed) + B + C** are resolved during the compass swing and to some extent can be removed by adjustment but other factors are at work here and will probably leave us with some errors at the end.

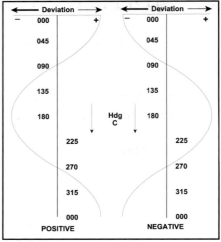

Figure 15.6

15.5   CORRECTION OF COEFFICIENTS

The principle for correcting coefficients is the same for any system and can be summed up as follows:

Coefficient A - a mechanical problem of a displaced Lubber Line corrected by loosening the bolts holding the compass body or in the case of the RIMC the Detector Unit and carefully turning it until the correct heading is in place.

Coefficient B - correction required because of magnetic deviating forces acting upon the DRMC or the detector Unit and giving errors known as deviation. Firstly calculate the error to be removed or more correctly the heading you wish to make the compass read and this will be done on an Easterly or Westerly heading.

Coefficient C - correction required because of magnetic deviating forces acting upon the DRMC or the detector Unit and giving errors known as deviation. Firstly calculate the error to be removed or more correctly the heading you wish to make the compass read and this will be done on a Northerly or Southerly heading.

We can see that the correction for B and C are very similar but that we must remember to apply the sign of the correction properly to ensure an accurate correction to our compass system. When the compass swing is completed we of course have to check our work and this 'check swing' is carried out using eight or perhaps twelve points of the compass to allow us to derive a compass card that will be placed in the aircraft. This compass card indicates to us the residual deviations that we have been unable to resolve within the essentially horizontal procedure. Alternatively, the Residual Deviations affecting the compass after the completion of a compass swing may be shown by the use of a Graphical Table or a Curve constructed from the information obtained. Either set of calculations will allow for the placing of a Compass Deviation Card near to the compass in the aircraft.

Deviation on any heading $\theta = A + B \sin \theta + C \cos \theta$

a/c weight caused by latitudinal sense

total misalignment

coefficient caused by a/c mag' in longitudinal sense

15.6   CHANGE OF MAGNETIC LATITUDE

$$\text{Tan Dip} = \frac{Z}{H}$$

The changes in deviation due to change of magnetic latitude have to be considered firstly with regard to Hard Iron and secondly to Vertical Soft Iron.

Hard Iron.   The hard iron deviating force, remains constant regardless of change of latitude. However, H varies with latitude being maximum at the equator and zero at the poles. Thus the smaller the directive force H the greater the maximum deviation, caused by hard iron deviating force. Hard iron deviating effect increases towards the poles and is minimum at the magnetic equator. The sign of the deviation will be the same in both hemispheres.

To summarise, maximum deviation due to hard iron magnetism, is inversely proportional to the value of H, which changes with change of magnetic latitude.

Vertical Soft Iron.   The directive force at the compass position is H, whilst the magnetising agent of any VSI component is Z. The maximum deviation due to VSI magnetism will vary inversely as H.
The VSI maximum deviation will vary directly as Z. Z has no effect on Hard Iron deviation.
The maximum deviation produced by VSI magnetism increases towards the magnetic poles. *(see over)*

$$\text{Max deviation} = \frac{Z}{H} = \text{Tan Dip}$$

so maximum deviation varies directly with Tan dip.

15.7   OCCASIONS FOR SWINGING THE COMPASS

a)   When compass components are installed or replaced.

b)   Whenever the accuracy of the compass is in doubt.

c)   After a maintenance inspection if required by the schedule.

d)   After a significant aircraft modification, repair or replacement involving magnetic material.

e)   When carrying unusual ferromagnetic payloads!

f)   When the compass has been subjected to significant shock.

g)   If the aircraft has been struck by lightning.

h)   After significant modification to aircraft radio/electrical systems.

i)   After the aircraft has been given a new theatre of operations if the move involves a large change of magnetic latitude.

j)   If the aircraft has been in long term storage standing on one heading.

> JAA

* Limits of Deviations on Compass Swing?

    Standby Compass   Main Compass

> JAR   + 10°   + 1°

Low Magnetic Latitude

Hard Iron

A/C Magnetism

Soft Iron

VSI (function of Z)

High Magnetic Latitude

A/C magnetism

Deviation increases
A/C Mag^n stays Same

Deviation Increases

A/c mag^n Increases

AIRCRAFT MAGNETISM

1.   Joint Airworthiness Requirements (JARs) state that the maximum permissible deviations after compensation are:

   a)   one degree for a remote indicating compass and ten degrees for a direct reading magnetic compass.
   b)   three degrees for a direct reading magnetic compass and one degree for a remote indicating compass.
   c)   ten degrees for a remote indicating compass and one degree for a direct reading magnetic compass.
   d)   one degree for a direct reading magnetic compass and eleven degrees for a slaved compass.

2.   Compass swings should be carried out:

   a)   on the apron.
   b)   only on the compass swinging base or site.
   c)   at the holding point.
   d)   on the active runway.

3.   Aircraft magnetism caused by Vertical Soft Iron:

   a)   varies with magnetic heading but not with magnetic latitude.
   b)   varies with magnetic latitude but not with heading.
   c)   it is not affected magnetic latitude or heading.
   d)   varies as the cosine of the compass heading.

4.   Aircraft magnetism caused by Hard Iron:

   a)   is not usually influenced by the earth's magnetic field.
   b)   varies directly with magnetic latitude.
   c)   varies indirectly with magnetic latitude.
   d)   is maximum on east and west.

5.   The aim of a compass swing is:

      1.   to find deviation on the cardinal headings and to calculate coefficients A, B and C.

      2.   to eliminate or reduce the coefficients found.

      3.   to record any residual deviation and to prepare a compass correction card.

    a)   only answer 1 is correct.
    b)   answers 1 and 3 are correct.
    c)   answers 1, 2 and 3 are all correct.
    d)   none of the above answers are correct.

CHAPTER SIXTEEN - REMOTE INDICATING COMPASS

Contents

		Page
16.1	INTRODUCTION.	16 - 1
16.2	THE DETECTOR UNIT.	16 - 1
16.3	DETECTOR UNIT.	16 - 3
16.4	GYRO UNIT	16 - 4
16.5	AMPLIFIER UNIT.	16 - 6
16.6	CORRECTOR CONTROL BOX.	16 - 6
16.7	MANUAL SYNCHRONISATION.	16 - 6
16.8	REPEATER SYSTEMS.	16 - 6
16.9	ADVANTAGES OF REMOTE INDICATING COMPASSES.	16 - 8
16.10	CORRECTIONS OF COEFFICIENTS (SPERRY CLIA COMPASS).	16 - 9
16.11	PRINCIPLES OF OPERATION.	16 - 10
	REMOTE INDICATING COMPASS QUESTIONS	16 - 13

DISADVANTAGES OF DIRECT READING COMPASS (DRMC)

a) Turning & Acceleration Errors
b) Magnetic sensing element is near source of deviation
c) Stand alone equipment - cannot be used to drive other instruments

COMPONENTS OF HSI

a) Detector Unit (Flux Valve or Flux Gate)
b) HSI Indicator
c) Precession Amplifier
d) Precession Motor
e) Horizontal Gyro (gives basic system)

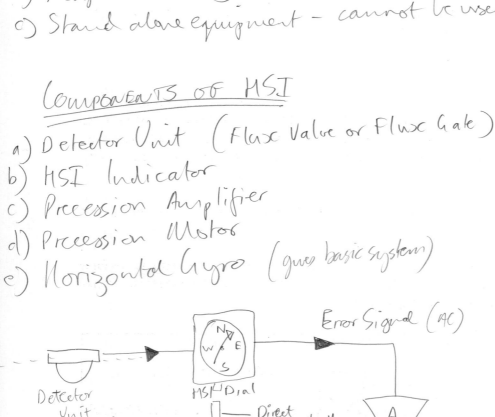

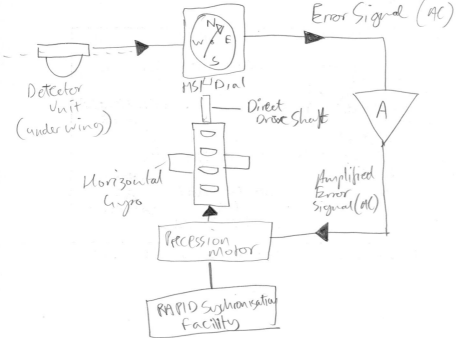

Gyro-Magnetic Compass

Tied

Horizontal Situation Indicator (HSI)

16.1   INTRODUCTION.

The direct reading magnetic compass dealt with in previous notes showed a number of undesirable shortcomings e.g. turning and acceleration errors, deviation produced by electrical instruments and wiring positioned close to the compass and the inability of the compass to feed heading to other navigation instruments. The slaved gyro compass was produced to reduce or eliminate these shortcomings and some notes on the theory of such compasses follow together with a more detailed description of the Sperry Gyro Compass.

16.2   THE DETECTOR UNIT.

The first requirement of a remote reading compass is to position a **detector unit** to sense the direction of the earth's magnetic field in a part of the aircraft least affected by on-board electrical fields and to be free of the turning and acceleration errors found in conventional compasses. Such a unit is the **flux valve**, a 3-spoked device, fixed in azimuth but with some freedom in the vertical to allow alignment with the plane of the earth's magnetic field.

The operation of the flux valve is in accordance with **Faraday's Law of Electromagnetic Induction**:

'If the number of lines of force threading a circuit is changing , an induced electromotive force will be set up in the circuit, the magnitude of the EMF being proportional to the rate of change in the number of lines of force threading the circuit'

A simplified diagram of flux valve leg is shown in Figure 16.1.

Alternating current is fed to the coil wound around the centre post which in turn produces fields of opposite sign in the top and bottom legs of the flux valve.

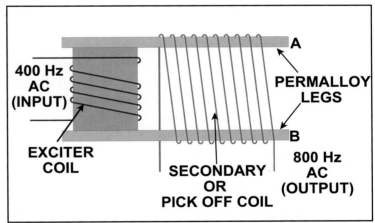

Figure 16.1. A Simplified Diagram of a Flux Valve.

A diagram showing the flux (lines of magnetic force) in legs A and B is shown in Figure 16.2.

At max amplitude the legs are **magnetically saturated**.

However, **total** flux is Zero - no current induced in Pick-Off Coil.

If the flux produced by the earth's magnetic field were to be superimposed on the diagram at Figure 16.2 the total effect would be changed.

As indicated in Figure 16.3 there is now a **change** in the total flux and an EMF will be produced.

If the flux valve leg is **in line** with the earth's field, then the EMF induced will be at a **maximum value.**

If the flux valve leg is at **right angles** to the field, then the EMF induced will be at a **minimum / zero value.**

The effect of the Earth's magnetic flux is to displace the datum. Additionally, upon further investigation, we may note that the voltage induced will actually change as a function(cosine) of the aircraft's magnetic heading as suggested by Figure 16.4.

The ambiguity apparent in this diagram when considering one "leg" in isolation is resolved by using 3 flux valve legs arranged thus:

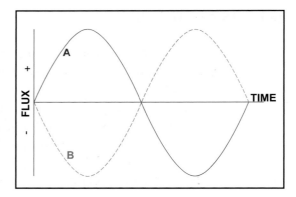

Figure 16.2.

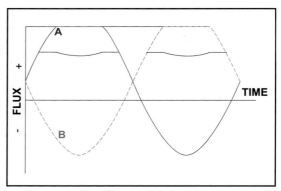

Figure 16.3.

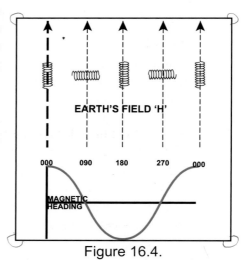

Figure 16.4.

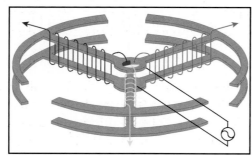

Figure 16.5

16 - 2

16.3   DETECTOR UNIT.

The detector unit contains a pendulous magnetic detecting element mounted on a **Hooke's Joint** which enables the detector to swing within limits of **25 degrees about the pitch and roll axes**, but allows **no rotation in azimuth**. When bank is detected a **cut out switch** is activated which stops erroneous signals being sent to the Selsyn Unit as the Flux Valve starts to pick up excessive values of the Earth's vertical component "Z". The unit itself is contained in a sealed case partially filled with oil to dampen any oscillations created during flight.

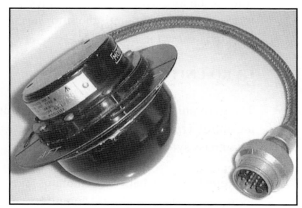

Figure 16.6. A Detector Unit.

The complete unit is usually mounted in the wing tip or tail fin where any aircraft generated magnetic disturbances are at a minimum.

A remotely controlled electromagnetic corrector, utilising corrector coils, is mounted at the top of the detector unit. This is used to compensate for coefficients B and C and enables corrections of up to +/- 15 degrees to be made from the flight deck.

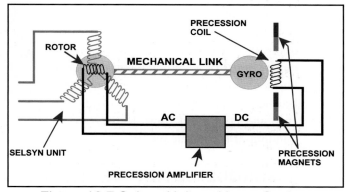

Figure 16.7 Selsyn Unit and Loop System

Currents from the 3 legs of the remote detector unit are passed to the **stator coils** of a receiver unit (control transformer) mounted close to the pilot's position. The field set up by the stator coils reproducing the earth's field is detected by a **rotor coil** and a current is induced if the coil is **not at right angles** to the field. The current is then passed to a motor which will move the rotor until it is once again at right angles to the field when no current will flow and the motor will stop (a null-seeking motor).

If the rotor is driven by a simple electric motor, then any movement of the flux valve caused by aircraft manoeuvre could cause false indications of the earth's field which could in turn result in compass errors. To eliminate the errors, which are likely to be only short term ones, the signal picked up by the rotor is used to precess a horizontal axis gyro in azimuth. The gyro is connected directly to the rotor and used to maintain the rotor's correct alignment.

The rate of precession generated through magnetic monitoring, is kept low at between 2° and 5° per minute so that short term compass errors will not occur. Manual synchronisation enables the rotor to be aligned correctly at a much faster rate. This is achieved by caging the gyro and turning it in azimuth until the rotor lies at right angles to the field. A schematic layout of the system is shown in Figure 16.7.

16.4 GYRO UNIT

The gyro unit, which is the pilot's indicator ("repeater" in some descriptions), contains a gyro, a Control Transformer(CT), a compass card, a heading setting facility, an annunciator unit and a compass synchronizing control.

An erection mechanism maintains the gyro axis horizontal; it comprises a levelling switch and a torque motor. The torque motor is mounted on the top bearing of the vertical ring and has two windings, one of which is permanently energised, the other being controlled by the levelling switch. This levelling switch consists of a commutator which is fixed to the inner gimbal ring and is divided by an insulated strip. Brushes, diametrically opposite to each other, are fixed to the outer gimbal ring. When the gyro axis is horizontal with respect to the airframe, the brushes are in contact with the insulating strip and no current flows to the second winding of the torque motor.

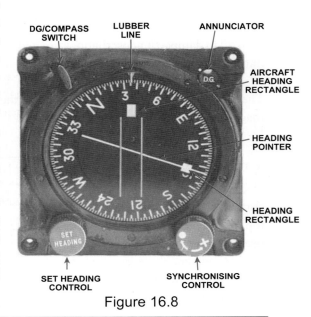

Figure 16.8

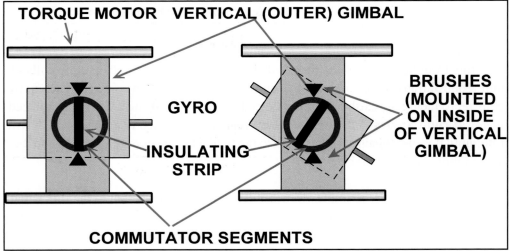

Figure 16.9.

16 - 4

When the gyro axis departs from the horizontal, the brushes make contact with the segments of the commutator and the torque motor is energised. The torque is applied to the inner ring. The normal action of the gyro is to rotate as if the force was applied 90 degrees removed in the direction of rotation (precession), thus returning the rotor axis to the horizontal.

The polarity of the current energizing the torque motor controls the direction of the torque applied to the vertical ring to precess the rotor axis in the correct direction.

Precession in azimuth is achieved by a precession motor mounted on the vertical ring. One of the two coils is permanently magnetized and the other is magnetized when the rotor of the control transformer is not in its null position. Signals are fed via the **Precession Amplifier** to the second precession coil and torque to the inner gimbal which causes the gyro to precess in azimuth.

The DC output of the precession amplifier is also fed through the Annunciator Circuit, which indicates whether or not the compass is synchronized.

The annunciator consists of a pivoted arm, one end of which carries a flag marked with a dot and a cross, and the other a small permanent magnet. The magnet is placed between two annunciator coils and is attracted to one or the other depending on the values of the currents in the two coils. These depend on the amount and direction of the misalignment of the rotor of the CT. The indication, a dot or a cross, being shown in the annunciator window of the indicator. When the compass is synchronised, the flag lies midway between the annunciator coils and a point midway between the dot and cross should be seen. However, owing to aircraft vibration, the synchronised position is generally indicated by a slow oscillation (hunting) between dot and cross.

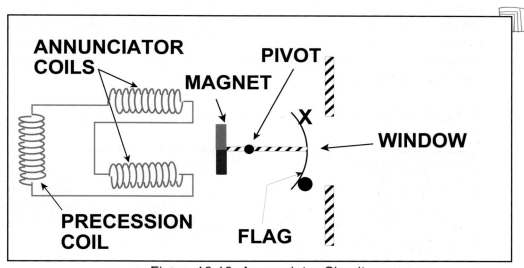

Figure 16.10. Annunciator Circuit.

16.5   AMPLIFIER UNIT.

This unit amplifies and rectifies the signals from the CT before they are applied to the precession circuits of the gyro.

16.6   CORRECTOR CONTROL BOX.

The corrector control box is usually mounted in the cockpit and is electrically connected to Corrector Coils mounted on the Flux Detector Unit. Current to the electromagnetic corrector is varied by means of two controls on the face of the box, one for coefficient B and the other for coefficient C, catering for corrections up to a maximum of ± 15 degrees in either case.

16.7   MANUAL SYNCHRONISATION.

Should the compass become de-synchronised at any time, it should be re-synchronised as follows:

a)   Push in the synchronisation knob and turn in the direction indicated by the symbol in the annunciator window (usually a "dot" or "cross" indication).

b)   Continue turning until a midway or alternating between dot and cross is indication obtained.

c)   Release the knob.

It will not normally be necessary to manually re-synchronise in flight unless the operating limits of the gyro, ± 85 degrees in pitch or roll, have been exceeded, causing the gyro to topple, or the compass has been used in the DG mode.   Pressing in the synchronising knob automatically cages the gyro to enable manual movement of the gyro.

16.8   REPEATER SYSTEMS.

One of the advantages of the gyromagnetic compass is its ability to transmit heading information to other equipment. The diagram at Figure 16.12 shows the arrangement of stators and rotors used to transmit the field generated at the Flux Detector Unit as it is turned within the Earths' magnetic field, it is described as self-synchronous (a Selsyn Unit) because it uses electrical power generated to turn and retain a "null" position. A similar system can be installed to transmit electrical signals around the aircraft for use in other related systems.

The detector unit senses the Earth's magnetic field and sends signals, which vary in amplitude and sign according to the direction of the field, to the stator of the Control Transformer(CT) in the gyro unit.

The compass card is on the same shaft as the rotor of the CT and is aligned during manufacture so that when the rotor is at right angles to the field produced in the stators, the compass card correctly indicates the magnet heading of the aircraft. If the compass card does not indicate the correct heading, the rotor on the same shaft will not be at right angles to the magnetic field set up in the stator by the signals from the detector unit. An error signal proportional to the amount of misalignment will then be induced in the rotor.

This error signal is fed to the precession amplifier where it is phase detected, rectified and amplified and then fed past the Annunciator Unit to the transducer which in the Sperry system converts it back to AC (in some other systems DC is used to power the precession motor device). The AC signals are fed to the precession coils on the vertical gimbal of the gyro. The resultant precession of the gyro in azimuth is translated into a movement of the shaft which carries the compass card and the rotor of the CT.

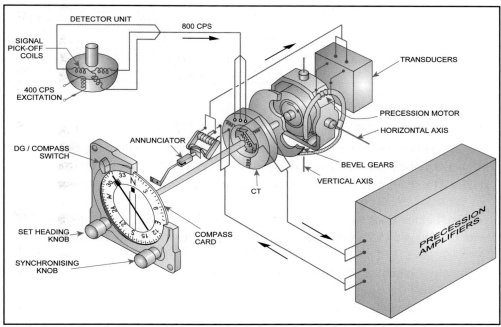

Figure 16.11. The Sperry Gyro Compass.

This rotation moves the rotor of the Control Transformer towards the null position, at which position the precession signal ceases and the system is once again aligned with the magnetic meridian.

When the aircraft alters heading, the gyro axis, and therefore the horizontal bevel gear, remains fixed in space. The gyro unit case turns with the aircraft and the vertical bevel gear turns about the horizontal bevel gear.

The resulting rotation of the shaft of the gyro unit, which carries the compass card, is equivalent to the amount of the aircraft turn. Simultaneously the signals from the detector unit change as the aircraft turns. The amounts of the two changes should be identical and therefore, the compass remains synchronised.

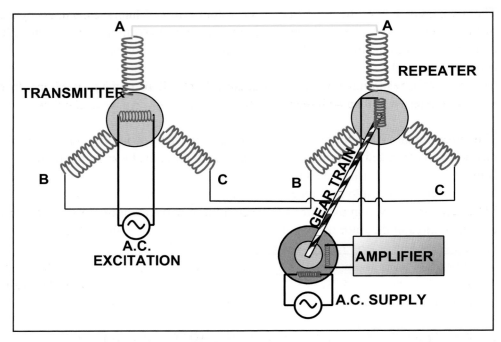

Figure 16.12. Selsyn Unit.

The excitation coil is set in manufacture to generate a current in the Pick-off Coils of the Flux Valve. The field generated in the coils is then modified as the aircraft turns due to the change in angle with relation to the Earths' magnetic field. This field is then transmitted to the Stator Coils of the repeater unit where it is reproduced to, in turn, generate current in a Rotor Coil. Current induced in the rotor will be maximum when aligned with the field and zero when at right angles and is arranged so that the motor will drive the rotor to the null position.

In practice, when in a turn, a false signal may be passed to the precession coils as the flux valve will measure a component of the Earth's field other than the horizontal, and, in a prolonged turn this may cause a slight precession of the gyro resulting in de-synchronisation. However, should this happen, the compass will re-synchronise itself as described above (at a rate of between 2 and 5 degrees per minute), or the operator may re-synchronise manually as described earlier.

16.9   ADVANTAGES OF REMOTE INDICATING COMPASSES.

Remote indicating compasses are designed to overcome the main disadvantages of the direct indicating compass. These disadvantages are:

a)   They must be installed in the aircraft where they can be easily seen by the pilot, and in this position they are usually subject to deviation due to aircraft magnetism.

b)   They are subject to turning and acceleration errors.

c)   They only display compass heading and cannot feed heading information to other equipment or other crew positions.

The first disadvantage is overcome in the Remote Indicating Magnetic Compass by using a small Sensor / Detector Unit(Flux Valve), which can be removed from the greatest aircraft generated magnetic field by placing it at a wing or fin tip.

The turning / acceleration errors are **almost completely** eliminated by combining the directional stability of the gyroscope with the magnetic north sensing property of the detector unit.

The sensing element of a modern compass is subject to errors due to accelerations as the detector swings on its Hooke's Joint, but gives an accurate mean heading over long periods of steady flight.

The aircraft directional gyroscopes on the other hand are unaffected by most aircraft manoeuvres but are subject to long term wander which in a DGI needs correction . However, by combining magnetic sensing and the gyro, the good features of both are retained and by allowing the sensitive element to monitor the gyroscope, the latter is effectively tied to the local magnetic meridian. The resultant steady heading is then transmitted to a vertical display card in front of the pilot and to other equipment (e.g. RMI, Doppler) and crew positions.

16.10   CORRECTIONS OF COEFFICIENTS (SPERRY CL1A COMPASS).

Coefficient 'A' (on any heading).

a)   Calculate heading required after correction

Required heading = Present heading + (Coefficient A)

b)   Plug Centre Reading Voltmeter (CRV) into Corrector Box, with compass synchronised reading will be ZERO.

c)   Push caging knob IN, turn to make compass read required heading. The CRV will deflect from ZERO.

d)   Holding the knob in and with aid of an engineer loosen the bolts holding the detector unit and slowly rotate the unit until CRV reading returns to ZERO.

e)   Tighten bolts holding detector unit and release the caging knob.

Coefficient 'B' (on compass East or West only).

(a) (b) and (c) are as for Coefficient 'A' except:

Required heading = Present heading °(c) EAST + (Coefficient B)
Or = Present heading ° (c) WEST - (Coefficient B)

Place corrector key into 'B' keyway on Corrector Box and turn key in direction indicated on box (towards + for a + Coefficient B or towards - for - Coefficient B) until CRV reading returns to ZERO.

d)   Release caging knob.

Coefficient 'C' (on compass North or South only).

As for Coefficient 'B' except:

Required heading = Present heading °(c) NORTH + (Coefficient C)
Or = Present heading°(c) SOUTH - (Coefficient C)

and, of course, use the 'C' keyway on the Corrector Box.

16.11   PRINCIPLES OF OPERATION.

The following text should be read in conjunction with the signal flow diagram in Figure 16.13. The detector unit senses the Earth's magnetic field and sends signals, which vary in amplitude and sign according to the direction of the field, to the stator of the Control Transformer (CTB).

The heading pointer of the master indicator is mounted on the same shaft as the rotor of CTB, and rotates with it. The position of the heading pointer is aligned during manufacture so that a correct heading indication is given when the rotor lies in the null position, at right angles, to the field created in the stator coils.

If during flight the pointer does not indicate the heading of the aircraft, the rotor on the same shaft will not be at right angles to the magnetic field set up in the stator coils by the signals from the detector unit. An error signal proportional to the amount of misalignment will then be induced in the rotor.

This error signal is fed to the precession amplifier where it is phase detected, rectified and amplified and then fed to a transducer which converts it back to AC. These, now more powerful, AC signals are then fed to the precession coils on the vertical gimbal of the gyro(in the pilots repeater) which will(using precession) turn the gyro in azimuth. (An AC motor is often used because it is lighter, cheaper and creates less heat when operating.)

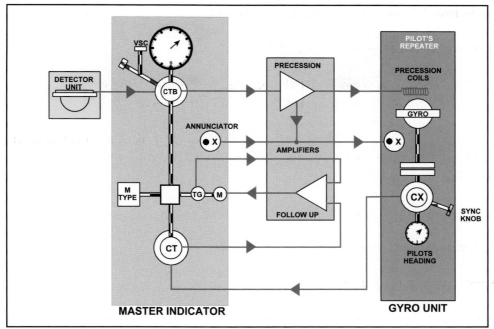

Figure 16.13

The resultant precession of the gyro in azimuth is transferred through bevel gears into a movement of the shaft which carries the **pilot's compass card** and the rotor of a Control Transmitter(CX). This Control Transmitter(CX), a Control Transformer (CT) in the master indicator, the follow-up amplifier and the follow up motor constitute a control synchro transmission system whose function is to rotate the compass pointer in the master indicator and the rotor of CTB, in unison with the precession of the gyro. This rotation moves the rotor of CTB towards the null position, at which position the precession signal ceases because the whole system is aligned with the magnetic meridian. Both compass indicators display magnetic heading and the compass is said to be synchronised.

When the aircraft alters heading, the gyro axis, and therefore the horizontal bevel gear, remain fixed in space. The gyro unit case turns with the aircraft and the vertical bevel gear turns about the horizontal bevel gear. The resulting rotation of the shaft of the gyro unit, which carries the compass card, is equivalent to the amount of aircraft turn. The rotor of the CX is rotated with the shaft and this rotation is transmitted to CT and the follow-up motor. Simultaneously the signals from the detector unit change as the aircraft turns. The amount of the two changes are identical. The rotor of CTB turns, due to the effect of the gyro, at the same rate as the detector unit changes the magnetic field in the stators. The compass, therefore, remains synchronised. In practice a false signal may be passed to the precession coils as the flux valve will measure a component of the Earth's field other than the horizontal and in prolonged turn this may cause a slight precession of the gyro resulting in re-synchronisation. The compass will re-synchronise itself at approximately 2° a minute.

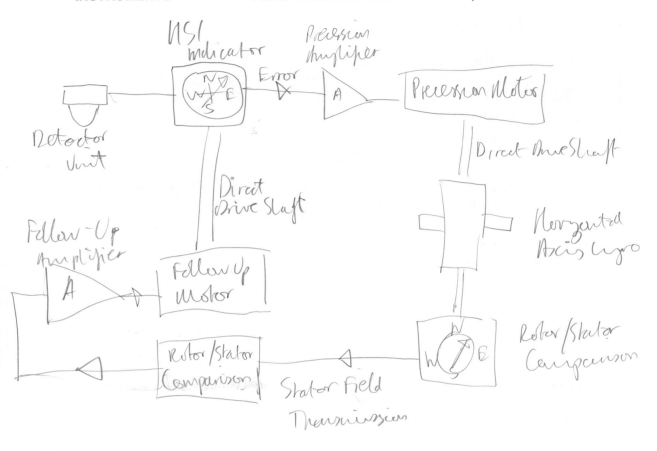

REMOTE INDICATING COMPASS

1.   The detector unit of a remote indicating compass is normally:

        a)   Fixed in the vertical plane only
        b)   Fixed in the azimuth
        c)   Free in the vertical
        d)   Free in the horizontal plane

2.   In a remote indicating compass, the rotor of the slaved gyro is automatically prevented from wandering in the vertical plane by means of:

        a)   A levelling switch and torque motor
        b)   pendulous suspension
        c)   Bevel gears and gimbals
        d)   A torque motor

3.   JARs state that the residual deviation of a remote indicating compass shall not exceed;

        a)   1 degree
        b)   3 degrees
        c)   2 degrees
        d)   5 degrees

4.   What prevents the rotor of the slaved gyro from wandering in the horizontal plane:

        a)   A levelling switch
        b)   An alignment switch
        c)   A precession circuit
        d)   A follow up amplifier

5.   A DG flag appears on the pilots gyro unit. What does it indicate to the pilot?

        a)   Remote indicating compass in unserviceable
        b)   The compass is misaligned
        c)   The gyro is no longer being monitored by the detector unit
        d)   The compass is aligned with the detector unit

6.   The function of the follow up system in a remote indicating compass is to;

        a)   Exercise a low rate if control over the gyro unit
        b)   Maintain the master indicator aligned with the gyro unit
        c)   Ensure the two gyro units are in alignment
        d)   To ensure that the annunciator unit is working

7.   The purpose of the annunciator circuit is to:

   a)   Alternate irregularly
   b)   Alternate regularly
   c)   To indicate that the system is synchronised
   d)   To show by a dot or a cross independently that the system is synchronised

8.   With reference to the flux valve of a remote indicating compass;

   a)   The flux valve is pendulously mounted and is free to turn to remain aligned with the earth magnetic field
   b)   The flux valve is not subject to acceleration errors
   c)   The flux valve is pendulously mounted and so it is not subject to or affected by the earth's magnetic field
   d)   The flux valve is fixed to the aircraft and so turns with the aircraft to measure the angle between the aircraft and the earth's magnetic field

CHAPTER SEVENTEEN - INERTIAL NAVIGATION SYSTEM

Contents

                                                                                   Page

17.1   INTRODUCTION. . . . . 17 - 1

17.2   BASIC PRINCIPLES OF INS. . . . . 17 - 2

17.3   ACCELEROMETER AND INTEGRATORS. . . . . 17 - 2

17.4   ACCELEROMETERS. . . . . 17 - 3

17.5   GRAVITY EFFECTS ON ACCELEROMETER. . . . . 17 - 6

17.6   THE INTEGRATING GYROSCOPE . . . . 17 - 6

17.7   THE PLATFORM. . . . . 17 - 8

17.8   EARTH ORIENTATION. . . . . 17 - 9

17.9   APPARENT WANDER. . . . . 17 - 9

17.10   ALIGNMENT OF THE SYSTEM. . . . . 17 - 11

17.11   SCHULER PERIOD. . . . . 17 - 12

17.12   ERRORS OF INS. . . . . 17 - 13

17.13   BOUNDED ERRORS. . . . . 17 - 13

17.14   UNBOUNDED ERRORS. . . . . 17 - 13

17.15   INHERENT ERRORS. . . . . 17 - 13

17.16   INS CONTROL AND DISPLAY PANELS. . . . . 17 - 14

17.17   LED DISPLAY. . . . . 17 - 17

17.18   MANUAL AND AUTOMATIC SYSTEM CHECKS. . . . . 17 - 22

          INERTIAL NAVIGATIONAL SYSTEMS QUESTIONS . . . . 17 - 23

17.1   INTRODUCTION.

The fundamental element of this complex system is the Inertial Sensor System (ISS). To make up this system we have a stable platform consisting of high quality gyros and accelerometers and a computer.

The purpose of the computer is to integrate the accelerometer outputs with time to give velocity and then integrate velocity with time to give distance travelled. From this is available pitch and roll attitude, true heading, true track, drift, present position in latitude and longitude, groundspeed and wind. To change all this information from ISS to Inertial Navigation System (INS) we have a further computer which allows us to inject and store waypoints and then compute track angle error, distance and time to go to reach them. This information can be used by the autopilot, flight director or for normal manual flying of the aircraft.

The modern INS was the first self contained single-source of all navigation data; now joined by the similar IRS, Laser Gyro System which will be discussed later. The current state-of-the-art engineering has enabled production of INS with performance, size and weight characteristics which far exceed other older navigation systems.

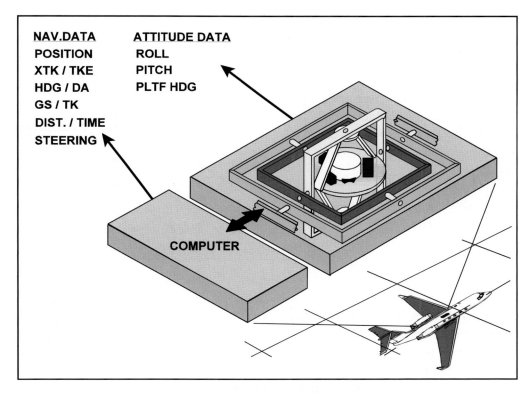

NAV.DATA   **ATTITUDE DATA**
POSITION   ROLL
XTK / TKE   PITCH
HDG / DA   PLTF HDG
GS / TK
DIST. / TIME
STEERING

COMPUTER

Figure 17.1 Basic Principles of INS.

17.2   BASIC PRINCIPLES OF INS.

Newton's laws of motion state:

a)   A body continues in a state of rest, or uniform motion in a straight line, unless it is acted upon by an external force.

b)   The acceleration - rate of change of velocity - of a body is directly proportional to the force acting on the body and is inversely proportional to the mass of the body.

c)   To every action there is an equal and opposite reaction.

Einstein however, in 1905, totally destroyed the premise of absolute motion. The substance of his new theory was that nothing is at rest and that the term at rest meant merely that the object under observation was moving at the same velocity as some other object, its co-ordinate system and the observer.

The primary measuring device in an INS, the accelerometer, demonstrates this theory for it makes no distinction between at rest and any other fixed velocity. It does however, make distinction between truly fixed velocities and those which we may regard as fixed, but are really fixed speeds along curved paths.

17.3   ACCELEROMETER AND INTEGRATORS.

Two accelerometers are mounted at the heart of the inertial system. These acceleration measuring devices sense any change in the aircraft's velocity either as an acceleration or deceleration very accurately.

One of the accelerometers measures the aircraft's acceleration in the North-South direction and the second in the East-West direction.

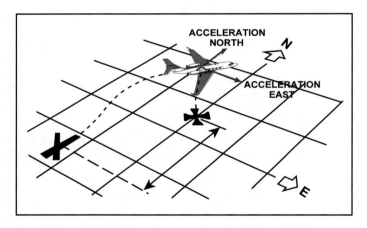

Figure 17.2 Accelerometer and Integrators.

The accelerometer is basically a pendulous device. When the aircraft accelerates, the pendulum, due to inertia, swings off the null position. A signal pick off device tells how far the pendulum is off the null position. The signal from this pick off device is sent to an amplifier and current from the amplifier is sent back into a torque motor located in the accelerometer. A torque is generated which will restore the pendulum to the null position. The amount of current that is going into the torquer is a function of the acceleration which the device is experiencing.

17.4   ACCELEROMETERS.

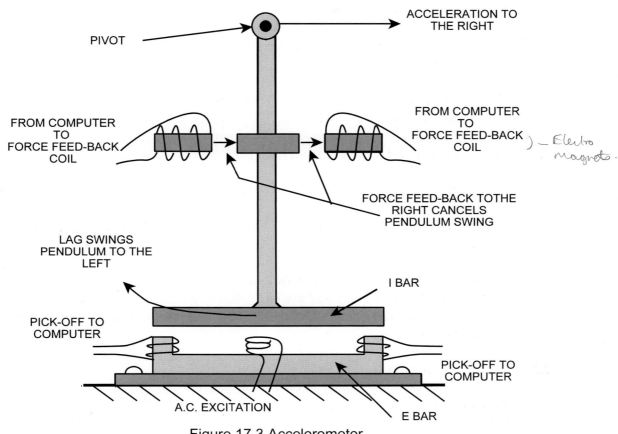

Figure 17.3 Accelerometer

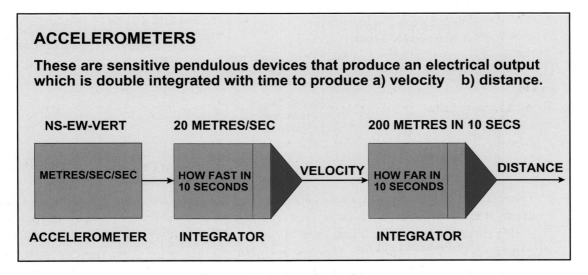

Figure 17.4 Accelerometers.

The acceleration signal from the amplifier is also sent to an integrator which is a time multiplication device. It starts out with acceleration which is in feet per second squared. In the integrator, it is literally multiplied by time and the result is a velocity in feet per second.

N/S
- Northerly Accelerometer measures accelerations along the local meridian
- The 1st stage of Integration N–S measures (ie speed & direction) velocity along the local meridian ie gives us distance
- 2nd Stage of Integration gives change in (ie distance) Latitude (ie N-S location)

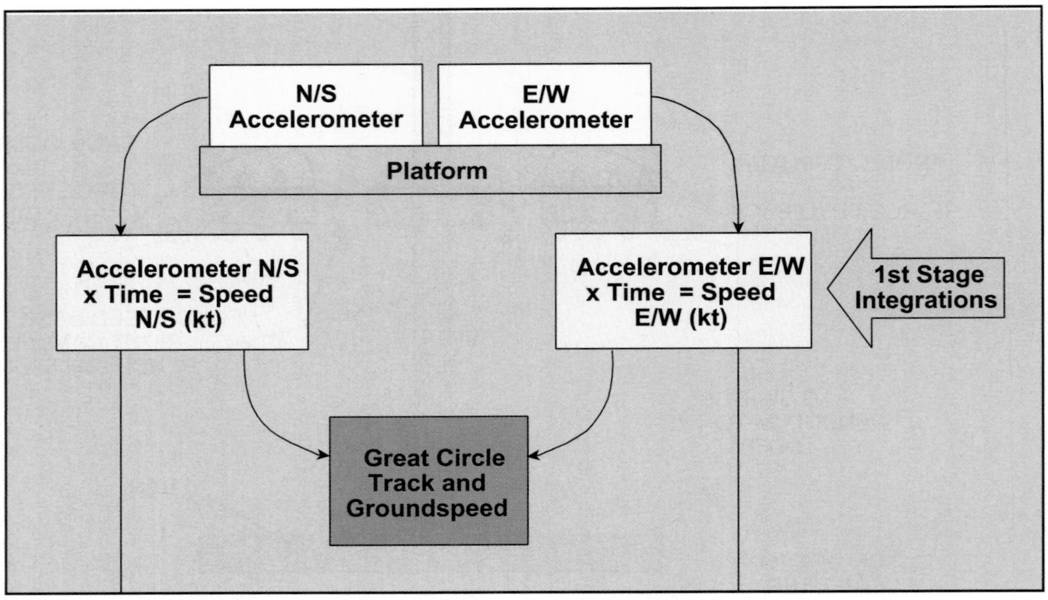

Figure 17.5 Accelerometers and Integrators.

It is then sent through a second integrator, and again, it's just a time multiplier. With an input of feet per second which is multiplied by time, the result is a distance in feet or nautical miles.

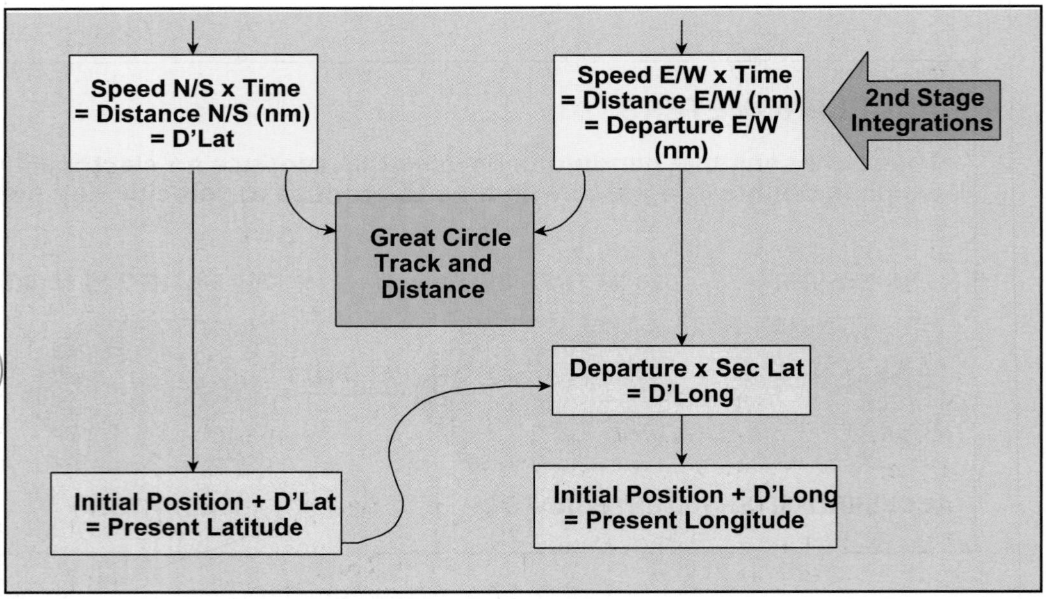

Figure 17.6 Accelerometers and Integrators.

The accelerometers would be mounted on a platform, there would be two, one in the North-South direction, the other in the East-West direction (often a third accelerometer is fitted to measure vertical acceleration).

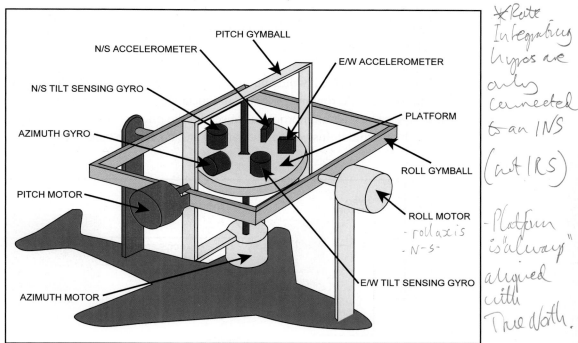

Figure 17.7

The computer associated with the inertial system knows the latitude and longitude of the take-off point and calculates that the aircraft has travelled so far in the North direction and so far in an East direction. The computer can then compute the new position of the aircraft and give a digital read out which we should note is to tenths of a degree.

In like manner using stored velocity, and present positions the system is able to calculate additional navigation data and display it as requested by the operator. The information is chosen for display through the rotary switch at the bottom left of the control unit: the information that may be obtained will be described in full later.

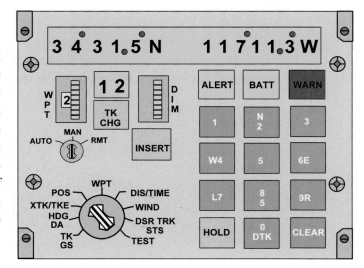

Figure 17.8 POS (Present Position).

17 - 5

17.5   GRAVITY EFFECTS ON ACCELEROMETER.

Normally the accelerometer is part of the gyro stabilised platform, but if it was hard mounted to the aircraft it could suffer problems in the pitch and roll planes.

The fact that the device has been tilted makes the pendulum swing away from the null position through the effects of gravity.

If this were to take place it would obviously output an erroneous acceleration signal which would in turn result in an erroneous velocity and distance travelled. Therefore, if we allow this there will be a false acceleration problem caused by the pitch or roll angle. If the accelerometer was kept earth horizontal this would not happen and no error would occur.

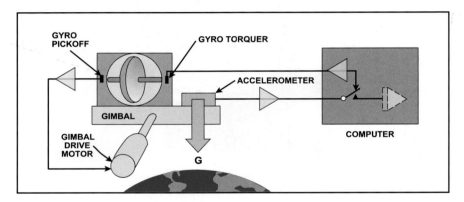

Figure 17.9 Gravity Effects on Accelerometer.

17.6   THE INTEGRATING GYROSCOPE

An integrating gyroscope used in INS's is a two degree of freedom gyro using viscous rather than mechanical (spring) restraint as seen in the more commonly found rate gyroscope

Figure 35.10 shows a simple rate- integrating gyro. It is basically a can within which another can (the inner gimbal) is pivoted about its vertical axis. The outer can (frame) is filled with a viscous fluid which supports the weight of the inner gimbal so reducing bearing torques.

[handwritten notes:]

INS
① STABLE PLATFORM
② GIMBALLED SYSTEM ── CANNOT COPE WITH TRANS POLAR FLIGHT
(a) NORTH ALIGNED
(b) WANDER ANGLE SYSTEM ── DOESN'T CARE ABOUT FLYING OVER POLES
& this is main advantage of
WANDER ANGLE SYSTEM

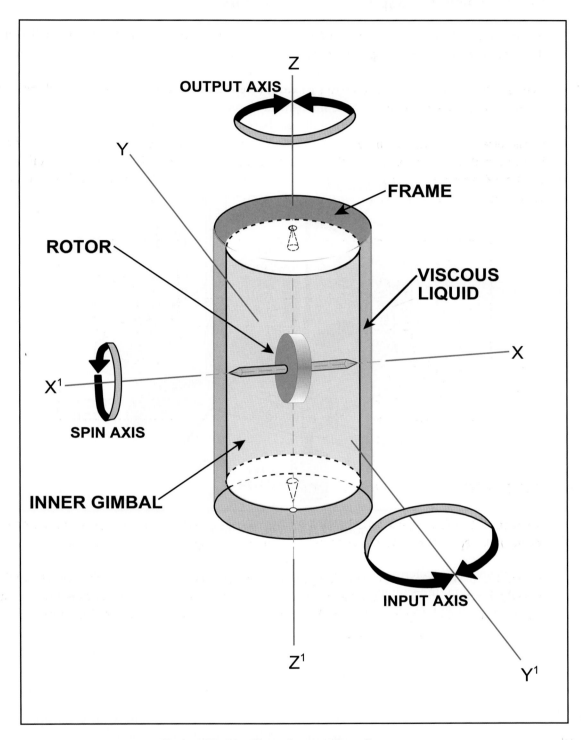

Figure 17.10   Rate-Integrating Gyroscope

* Biggest cause of error in an INS is the 'Real Wander' of the Gyroscopes

17.7   THE PLATFORM.

To keep the accelerometer level, it is mounted on a gimbal assembly, commonly called the platform. The platform is nothing more than a mechanical device which allows the aircraft to go through any attitude change and yet the very inner element of the platform on which the accelerometers are mounted is able to stay earth level. Gyroscopes which are used to stabilise the platform are also mounted on the inner-most element of the platform. They provide inputs to amplifiers and motors which control the gimbals and keep the accelerometers level.

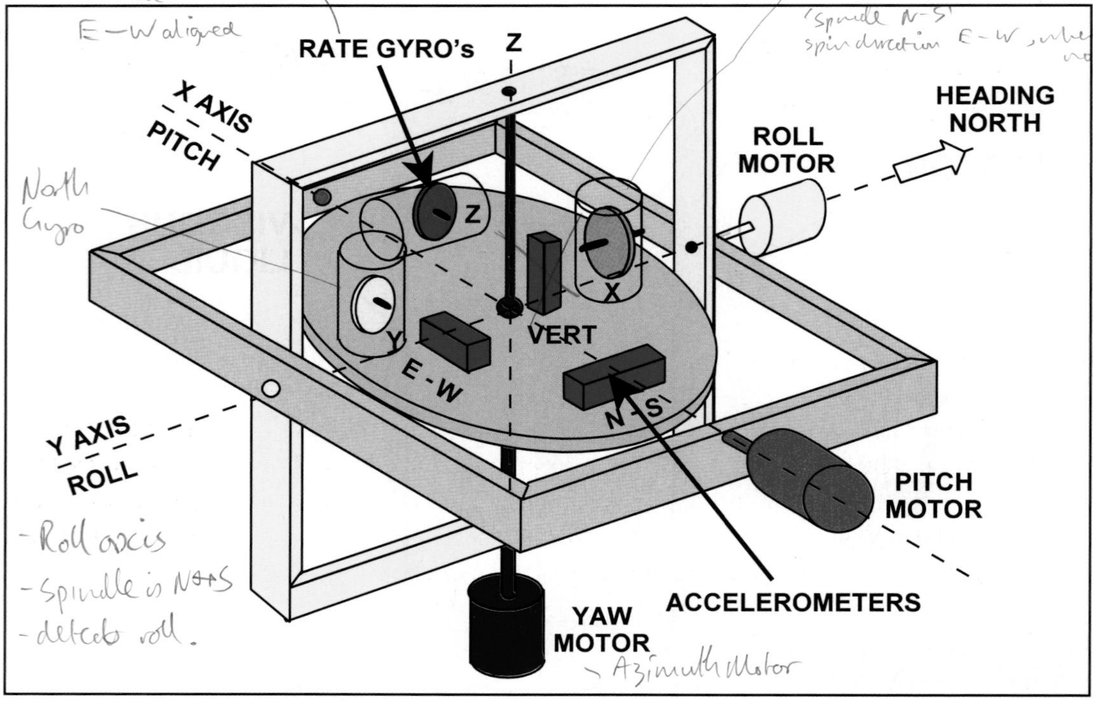

[Handwritten annotations: "Heading" North; 'Spindle' would be – Azimuth Gyro – E–W aligned; RATE GYRO's; North Gyro; East Gyro detects Pitch; 'Spindle N–S' spin direction E–W when facing north; Roll axis; Spindle is N&S; detects roll; Azimuth Motor]

Figure 17.11. The Platform.

The gyro and the accelerometer are mounted on a common gimbal. When this gimbal tips off the level position, the spin axis of the gyro will remain fixed. The case of the gyro, then, is moved off level and the amount that the case is tipped will be detected by the signal pick off in the gyro. That signal is then amplified and sent to a gimbal drive motor which restores the gimbal to the level position again. Since the accelerometer is always kept level, it does not sense a component of gravity and is able to sense only the horizontal accelerations of the aircraft as it travels across the surface of the earth.

In reality, three integrating gyros are mounted on the inertial platform, with their input axis mutually perpendicular. Three gimbal motors drive the platform gimbal rings about the pitch, roll and vertical axes respectively. The gyros sense incipient displacement of the platform and activate the appropriate motors to provide for the relative movement of the gimbal rings, as the aircraft moves about the stable platform.

*[Handwritten margin note: *any manoeuvre in azimuth (yawing plane) will always and only be detected by the azimuth gyro, and will always and only be corrected by the azimuth servo-motor]*

[Handwritten table at bottom:]

Heading	Manoeuvre	Sensing Gyro	Correcting Servo-Motor
North	Yaw	Azimuth	Azimuth
	Pitch	East	Pitch
	Roll	North	Roll

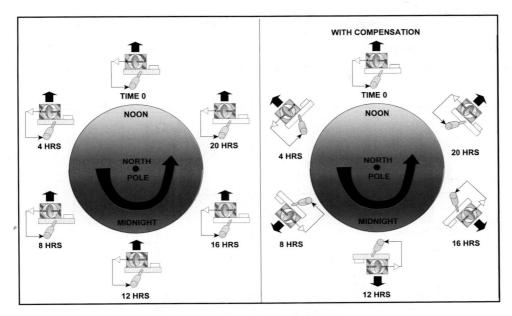

Figure 17.12 Earth Orientation.

17.8   EARTH ORIENTATION.

The previously described gyro stabilised platform would remain fixed in space, but the aircraft is not operating in space. It is operating on an earth which is rotating and an earth which is assumed to be round. In order to keep the accelerometers level with respect to the earth so that they sense acceleration of the aircraft in a horizontal direction only, some compensation must be made for the earth rotating and the earth being assumed to be round.

17.9   APPARENT WANDER.

Corrections must be made to gyroscopically stabilised platforms to allow for apparent wander due to earth rotation and aircraft movement over the earth. The required earth rate compensation is a function of latitude since what is being compensated for is the horizontal component of the earth rate felt by the gyros, and that varies with latitude. At the equator, this value is Zero degs per hour and with travel either further North or South, it increases until it becomes a maximum of +/- 15.04 at the poles.

Transport rate compensation is developed using the velocity signal. The electronics through which it is sent contain a term proportional to the earth's radius. So, in reality, the transport rate signal torquing the gyro is the velocity of the aircraft divided by the earth's radius.

Both the earth rate and transport rate compensations are compensated by torquing the gyro. The following diagrams should be used to follow the system as explained.

Manouvre of the a/c in Pitch & Roll can be detected by either the Pitch or Roll gyros and will always and only be corrected by the appropriate servo motor.

Heading	Manouvre	Sensing Gyro	Correcting Servo motor
East	Yaw Pitch Roll	Azimuth North* East*	Azimuth Pitch Roll

*– Only difference.

There are a number of compensations generated within the system..

Coriolis and Centrifugal effects must be compensated for within the system. Other compensations are necessary because the earth is not a perfect sphere

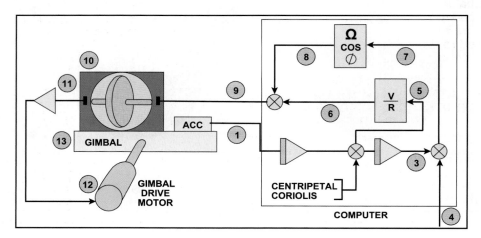

Figure 17.13

a) Centrifugal accelerations caused by platform rotation to maintain the local earth vertical.

b) Coriolis accelerations caused by the aircraft following a curved path in space when flying normal earth referenced flights.

- ● **ACCELEROMETERS MUST BE LEVELED (VELOCITY SET TO ZERO)**

Initial levelling. If the platform is not Earth horizontal one or both of the accelerometers will sense an output which is due solely to gravity (since the aircraft is stationary). These tilt-induced outputs from the accelerometers are used to drive the appropriate torque motors (pitch and / or roll) to level the platform.

- ● **PLATFORM MUST BE ORIENTED TO TRUE NORTH (GYROCOMPASSING) (POSITION VERIFIED)**

Initial alignment (Gyro-Compassing). Once the platform is levelled, the alignment processed is automatically commenced, using a technique which is known as Gyro-Compassing. The platform is now earth horizontal, but will not remain so because of the earth's own rotation about its spin axis.

Figure 17.14 Accelerometers and Integrators.

17.10   ALIGNMENT OF THE SYSTEM.

The stable element in an INS must be accurately aligned in both azimuth and attitude to allow the accelerometers to measure accelerations along their chosen axes.

a)   Warm up period - the first stage in any alignment sequence is to bring the fluid-filled components to the correct operating temperature. This phase normally takes between 3 to 4 minutes.

b)   Coarse alignment - the platform is roughly levelled and aligned in azimuth, this removes gyro alignment errors and cuts the time to a minimum.

   i)   Coarse levelling - pitch and roll driven until they are at 90° to each other. The platform is then roughly levelled using either the aircraft frame as reference, or using the outputs from gravity switches or the horizontal accelerometers.

   ii)   Coarse azimuth alignment - is achieved by turning the platform until the heading output agrees with the aircraft's best known True Heading.

   iii)   Coarse alignment level and aligns the platform within 1° - 2° in a few seconds.

c)   Fine levelling - with zero output from the accelerometers fine levelling is achieved. The process takes anything up to 1 to 1½ minutes, levelling the platform to within 6 seconds of arc.

d) Gyro compassing - the platform can be aligned in azimuth by connecting the gyro normally used to stabilise the platform about an East-West axis, to the azimuth gimbal motor. With the platform correctly aligned in azimuth the East gyro should not be subject to rotation of its input axis due to earth rotation; when the platform is out of alignment the East gyro will detect a component of earth rotation and the resultant output signal can be used to torque the azimuth gyro until the table is aligned.

  i) Accelerometers must be levelled (velocity set to zero).

  ii) Platform must be orientated to True north - gyro compassing (position verified).

17.11 SCHULER PERIOD.

Schuler postulated an earth pendulum with length equal to the radius of the earth, it's bob at the earth's centre and point of suspension at the earth's surface. If the suspension point were accelerated around the earth, the bob would remain vertically below the suspension point because it is at the earth's centre of gravity.

A platform mounted on the suspension point tangential to the earth's surface, ie horizontal would therefore remain horizontal irrespective of the acceleration experienced.

The vertical defined by the normal to the platform is therefore unaffected by acceleration. If, for any reason the bob on the earth pendulum became displaced from the earth's centre, the pendulum would start to oscillate. The oscillation period would be 84.4 minutes.

The INS stable element is maintained normal to the local vertical by feeding back the aircraft's radial velocity as levelling gyro signals, and in this way the North and East accelerometers are prevented from detecting components of the gravity acceleration.

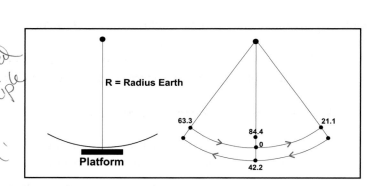

Figure 17.15 The Schuler Period.

The control signals are the $^V/_R$ and $^U/_R$ terms for vehicle movement. By mechanising the platform to remain horizontal, an analogue of the earth pendulum of period 84.4 minutes is produced. Should the platform be displaced from the horizontal it would oscillate with a period of 84.4 minutes, which is known as the Schuler Period.

[handwritten top left margin] Gyro Compassing

[handwritten top] When inserting position into INS @ the stand there must be NO error in latitude but up to 10° error in Longitude

[handwritten left margin] Ellivee (W/s initial position

[handwritten top right] 1 in 60

[handwritten top right] DOT = Distance of track
DG = Distance gone
TE = Track Error (angle)

$$\frac{DOT}{DG} = \frac{TE°}{60}$$

17.12 ERRORS OF INS.

Errors can be conveniently considered under the following headings:

a)   Bounded errors.

b)   Unbounded errors.

c)   Inherent errors.

17.13 BOUNDED ERRORS.

[handwritten] — remains constant with respect to time.
— Schuler Loop ∴ output is in error from true & true but overall value remains accurate

Errors which build up to a maximum and return to zero within 84.4 minutes Schuler cycle, are termed bounded errors. The main cause of these errors are:

[handwritten left margin] Will give a bounded Cross Track error but an unbounded Distance of track

a)   Platform tilt due to initial misalignment.
[handwritten] (Alignment aka Gyro Compassing)

[handwritten right] 1) If there is an error @ the initial levelling of platform the accelerometers will sense gravity. This will give rise to a bounded error in ground speed @ 1st stage & unbounded @ 2nd stage. (error in distance)

b)   Inaccurate measurement of acceleration by accelerometers.

c)   Integrator errors in the first stage of integration.

17.14 UNBOUNDED ERRORS.

[handwritten] ∴ magnitude increases with respect to time.

Unbounded errors - are either cumulative track errors or distance errors:

a)   Initial azimuth misalignment of the platform.

b)   Wander of the azimuth gyro.

[handwritten right] ✱ A bounded error in speed @ the 1st stage of Integration will give rise to an unbounded error in distance @ the 2nd stage.

Errors which give rise to cumulative errors in the recording of distance run:

a)   Wander in the levelling gyros. This causes a Schuler oscillation of the platform but the mean recorded value of distance run is increasingly divergent from the true distance run.

b)   Integrator errors in the second stage of integration.

17.15 INHERENT ERRORS.

The irregular shape and composition of the earth, the movement of the earth through space and other factors provide further possible sources of error. Such errors vary from system to system depending upon the balance achieved between accuracy on one hand and simplicity of design, reliability, ease of construction and cost of production, on the other.

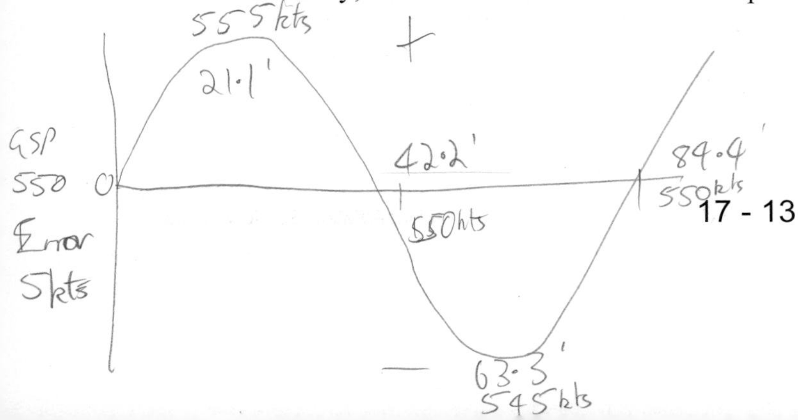

[handwritten left margin] Schuler Principle

[handwritten right] Q: Can you Update position in Flight?
A: NO (only when stationary on ground)

[handwritten bottom left graph labels] 555.5 kts 21.1' 42.2' 550 kts 84.4' 550 kts 63.3' 545 kts
GSP 550 0 Error 5 kts

[handwritten bottom] ✱ Schuler Period = "84.4 mins damped"

17.16   INS CONTROL AND DISPLAY PANELS.

There are many makes and models of INS currently on the market. The "state-of-the-art" trend is towards a single control/display unit with a standard keyboard, but with a single small video screen (rather than the various individual LED windows which are shown in the following illustrations). With the modern video screen presentation, the loading and extraction of information is achieved by selecting a "page number", with each page (which is displayed on the screen) dealing with associated functions. One major advantage of this type of system is that hundreds or even thousands of waypoints can be "stored" in the machine memory. These waypoints (normally airway reporting points such as VORs and intersections) are automatically loaded from a master disc, which is supplied and regularly updated by an agency such as Jeppesen.

Because of the high capital investment which was involved in the last generation of INS systems, and because they are proving to be extremely reliable, you are perhaps more likely to encounter the traditional type of control/display units described below. Another good reason for considering this system, rather than the modern one, is that the JAA examination questions are based on the older type of INS.

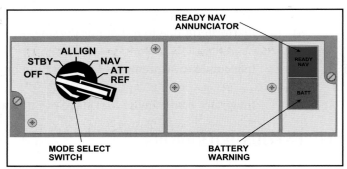

Figure 17.16 Mode Selector Unit.

In any event, please appreciate that the following paragraphs are intended only as a general guide and not as a definitive operating instruction for any particular model of INS.

The traditional INS system employs two panels for control and display. The simpler of the two, the mode selector panel, is shown at Figure 17.16.

The function of the mode selector panel is straightforward:

a)   In the standby mode the power is supplied to all parts of the system. It is normal to insert the start position (the aircraft's ramp position in lat/long to the nearest tenth of a minute of arc) whilst the equipment is in this mode.

b)   In the alignment mode the platform is levelled and aligned (gyro-compassed), and when these processes are complete and **READY NAV** illuminated. The equipment can now be switched into the Nav mode, and the aircraft is free to taxi without degrading the accuracy of the INS.

Should the aircraft electrical supply to the INS cease for any reason the INS will automatically switch to its own battery pack. For as long as a satisfactory level of power is being supplied by the internal battery, the INS Bat light will be illuminated on the Control and Display Unit. As the power from the battery starts to fail, the Bat warning light on the Mode Selector Unit will illuminate, indicating that the INS is about to fail. If you are half way across the Pacific Ocean at this time, this could spoil your whole day, since of course the INS cannot be re-levelled and/or re-aligned in flight (for this the aircraft must be stationary, and the exact position known). The control/display unit (CDU) is shown at Figure 17.17.

The reader who has completed his or her studies of the radio syllabus will undoubtedly notice the similarity between this CDU and the control/display panel of a similar vintage VLF/Omega receiver. Although the inputs for the two equipments are vastly different, the presentation of navigational information to the pilot is more or less identical in both cases.

Cannot carry out Gyro compassing in flight.

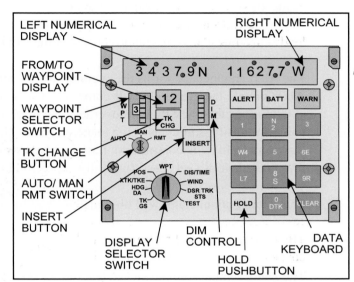

Figure 17.17 Control Display Unit (CDU).

As already mentioned, these notes are not intended as an operator's brief, but rather to help you pass an examination. Please appreciate that, although other INS panels may look dissimilar to the one shown at Figure 17.17 the information given by the system will be basically the same.

Using the panel shown at Figure 17.17 lets start at the top left hand corner and look at the function of each of the displays and controls.

The two large windows at the top of the panel (labelled left and right numerical displays) comprise the principal outputs of the system. Glance now at the function selector (bottom left hand corner), we'll start with the selector in the seven o'clock position (TK/GS) and work anti-clockwise through the functions considering the values shown in the two LED windows as we go.

The waypoint selector switch is thumbed to the appropriate waypoint number (shown in the window to the left of the thumbwheel) when loading the waypoint lat/longs before flight, reloading new waypoints in flight, or checking that waypoints are correctly loaded.

For an INS to provide Wind Speed & Direction we need an input of TAS to Computer

The **FROM/TO** waypoint display shows the two waypoints between which the INS assumes that it is flying. All digital readouts flight director displays and autopilot commands will be based on this information, and so you can imagine the consequences or either giving the equipment the wrong to/from waypoint numbers or feeding the system with the wrong waypoint lat/long to begin with.

The Track change push button enables the operator to tell the system between which two waypoints the aircraft is required to fly (in the event that the system is not set up to fly sequentially through the loaded waypoints).

The Dim control governs the brightness of the LED displays and the panel lighting.

The Alert annunciator warns the operator that the aircraft is approaching the next waypoint. In AUTO mode the alert light will come on, steady, 2 minutes to run to the waypoint, and will extinguish as the track changes overhead the waypoint. In MANUAL mode the alert light will come on, steady, 2 minutes to run to the waypoint; the light will then flash 30 seconds before the waypoint, and will continue to flash until the track is changed. The annunciator will not illuminate below a set speed (typically either 100 kts or 250 kts).

The Battery annunciator will illuminated when the INS is operating on internal power.

The Warning annunciator illuminates when a system malfunction occurs.

The Auto/Manual/Remote switch determines the level of pilot intervention necessary to fly the aircraft. In the automatic mode the INS will automatically switch from one track to the next as each waypoint is overflown. In the manual mode the operator is required to update the waypoint from/to readout as each waypoint is overflown. The exact function of the remote position will depend on the complexity of the INS computer programme, and is outside the scope of this syllabus but in general terms it allows for simultaneous insertion of waypoints into more than one INS from one CDU.

The Insert pushbutton is used in conjunction with the data input keyboard to enter information into the system.

Finally, the Hold pushbutton is used primarily for updating the INS position when overflying a reliable fix, such as a VOR overhead. The **HOLD** button is depressed as the fix is overflown the function switch is placed in the POS (position) mode, the exact lat/long of the radio fix (in this case the lat/long of the VOR) is punched into the machine, and the hold button is then released. Appreciate that if this is done, the radial error rate assessment (discussed shortly) will be invalid, unless the position update vector is accounted for.

SUMMARY INS WARNING LIGHTS

	LIGHT INDICATION	ACTION REQUIRED
READY NAV (MSU)	Green light, indicates alignment complete.	Select 'NAV'
BATT (MSU)	Red light, indicates battery power too low for operation.	Check power supplies
ALERT (CDU)	Amber light, indicates approaching (overflying in a MAN) a waypoint.	None, unless in MAN mode when TK CHG is initiated
BATT (CDU)	Amber light, indicates INS operating on back up power.	Check power supplies.
WARN (CDU)	Flash red light, indicates system malfunction.	Set selector to DSR TK/STS note action code and consult users guide for appropriate action.

17.17   LED DISPLAY.

Please Note: All of the following descriptions are based upon a Desired Track between waypoints of 060⁰.

The INS derived aircraft track (°T) is shown to the nearest tenth of a degree in the LH window.

The INS derived groundspeed is shown to the nearest knot in the RH window.

The track is 040°T and the groundspeed 502 kts at Figure 17.18.

In Fig 17.19 the INS derived true heading (the angle between the north-south axis of the platform and the aircraft fore and aft axis in a north aligned system) is shown to the nearest tenth of a degree in the LH window.

The INS derived drift angle is shown to the nearest tenth of a degree is shown in the RH window, and is preceded by an L(left / port drift) or an R(right / starboard drift).

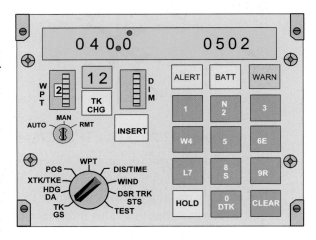

Figure 17.18 TK / GS (Track and Groundspeed).

The heading is 050°T and the drift 10° left at Figure 17.19.

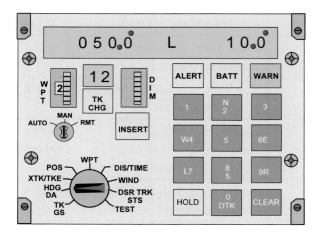

Figure 17.19. HDG / DA (Heading and Drift Angle).

In Fig 17.20 we see **XTK/TKE** (Cross track distance and track error angle). The cross track distance (the displacement of the aircraft perpendicularly from the direct great circle track between the two waypoints selected) is shown to the nearest tenth of a nautical mile in the LH window. This figure is preceded by an L or an R to indicate that the aircraft is left or right of the direct track.

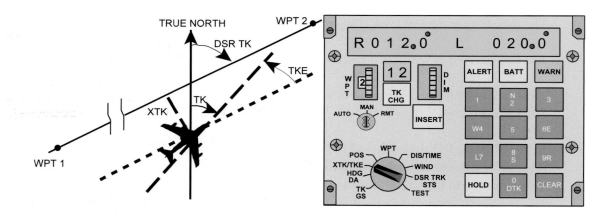

Figure 17.20 XTK / TKE (Cross track distance and track error angle).

The track angle error (the angle between the track which the aircraft would require to make good were it flying along the great circle route between the specified waypoints and the track which it is actually making good) is shown to the nearest tenth of a degree in the RH window. The L or R which precedes this value indicates that the actual track is to the left or right of the required track. In this case, remembering that we desire a track of 060°, we must be "making good" a track of 040° because we have an indication that we are tracking 20° to the left of our desired track between consecutive waypoints.

In summary the cross track error is 12nm to the **R**ight and the track angle error is 20° to the **L**eft in the situation also shown at Figure 17.20

In Fig 17.21 the aircraft's present latitude is shown to the nearest tenth of a minute of arc in the LH window.

The aircraft's present longitude is shown to the nearest tenth of a minute of arc in the RH window.

The aircraft's position is therefore shown as 34°31.5'N 117°11.3'W.

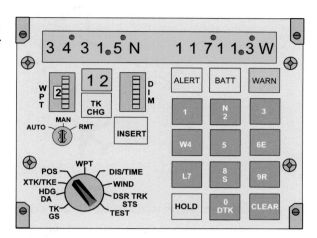

Figure 17.21. POS (Present position).

At Fig 17.22 we see that the waypoint positions are shown in Latitude (LH window) and Longitude (RH window) to the nearest tenth of a minute of arc.

In the system which we are considering there are 10 possible waypoint selections (0 through 9). Waypoints 1 through 9 are simply selected turning points, and are normally placed into the system by the operator before the flight.

Waypoint 0 represents the aircraft's position at the last time a track change from present position to a specified waypoint was selected by the operator.

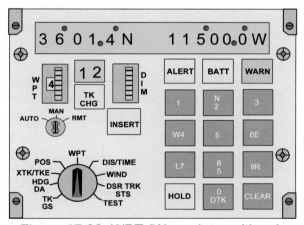

Figure 17.22 WPT (Waypoint positions).

Let us consider briefly how this could be useful.

Suppose that you are half way between, say, waypoints 3 and 4 and air traffic control clear you direct to waypoint 6. By selecting a track change from waypoint 0 (the aircraft's present position) to waypoint 6 and inserting it, the aircraft will fly you to directly to Wpt 6 if coupled to the flight director/autopilot.

The position of waypoint four is shown as 36°01.4'N   115°00.0'W at Figure 17.22.

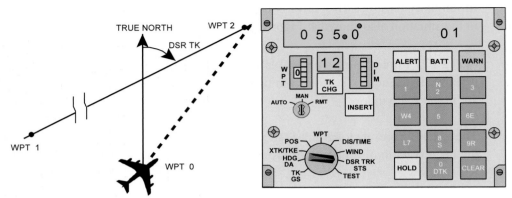

Figure 17.23 Waypoint Zero

Waypoint Zero is reserved for the computer to establish a track from the aircraft's present position and will not accept operator entered waypoint coordinates.

In Figure 17.24 the distance to go from the aircraft's present position direct to the next selected waypoint is shown to the nearest nautical mile in the LH window.

The lapsed time from the aircraft's present position to the next waypoint is shown to the nearest tenth of a minute in the RH window.

The distance to go here is shown as 140nm and the time as 16.7 minutes.

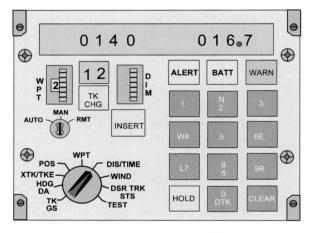

Figure 17.24 DIS / TIME (Distance and time to the next waypoint).

In Figure 17.25. the INS derived wind direction (°T) is shown to the nearest degree in the LH window.

INS derived wind speed is shown to the nearest knot in the RH window.

The W/V is shown as 155°(T)/85 kt.

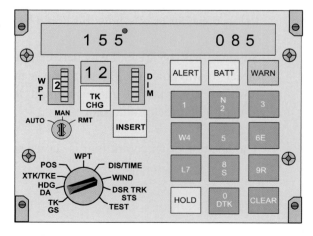

Figure 17.25 WIND (Wind velocity).

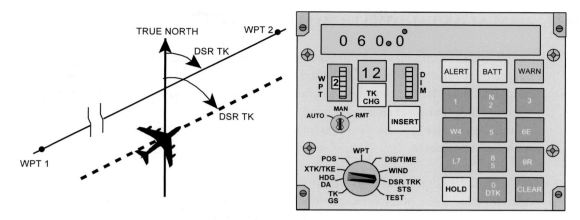

Figure 17.26 DSR TK / STS (Desired track and status).

In Fig 17.26 we see the desired track (assuming that the aircraft is on the direct great circle track between the two selected waypoints) is shown in degrees true to the nearest tenth of a degree in the LH window.

The RH window will normally be blank, since the status check is generally only available with the equipment in the alignment mode.

The desired track is 060.0°(T) which allows us to see the relationship between the aircraft's current position and track and the direct track between the two selected waypoints. You may by now have reached the conclusion that the programme upon which the INS computer operates assumes that the INS will normally operate coupled to the flight director / autopilot, so that across track errors do not occur.

The diagram at Figure 17.27. shows the function switch in the test position resulting in all of the digits on the various displays being illuminated either showing a figure or letters.   This enables the operator to check that all of the functions are operating.

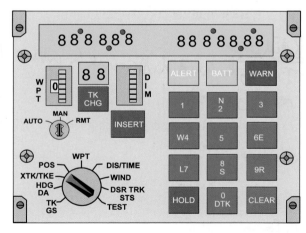

Figure 17.27 TEST (Light emitting diode test)

17.18   MANUAL AND AUTOMATIC SYSTEM CHECKS.

At the initial setting up stage the start position must be fed into the INS computer with a high degree of accuracy. If the initial latitude is slightly in error the platform will not remain Earth horizontal once the equipment is switched into the navigation mode, since the torque motors will be tilting the platform at an inappropriate rate, due to computer calculations based on an incorrect latitude. Likewise, and for the same reasons, the platform will not remain directionally aligned with respect to north.

If the initial latitude setting is grossly in error the system will detect the error and warn the operator (this is one of the principal functions of the warning annunciator on the CDU whilst the equipment is in the align mode). The equipment is able to sense a gross latitude input error since the apparent drift and topple rates sensed by the rate gyros will not correspond to the corrections being applied by the torque motors.

An incorrect operator input of longitude will not affect the stability of the platform, but obviously the track and distance from the departure point to the first waypoint will be incorrectly computed. Furthermore, all subsequent indications of longitude will be in error by the amount of the initial input error.

An incorrect input of the lat / long of any of the waypoints will have serious consequences. The INS will navigate very accurately between waypoints, but it is incapable of detecting operator malfunctions (finger trouble)! In order to check that the waypoints have been correctly inserted they should be recalled from store onto the LED display, and rechecked before flight.

A second check is to call up the initial great circle track(**TK** / GS) and distances(**DIS** / TIME) between consecutive waypoints, and to compare these values against those shown on the flight log/flight progress log/flight plan.

(Handwritten notes:)

Radial Error
- Trying to find difference to where INS tells us we are and where we really are.

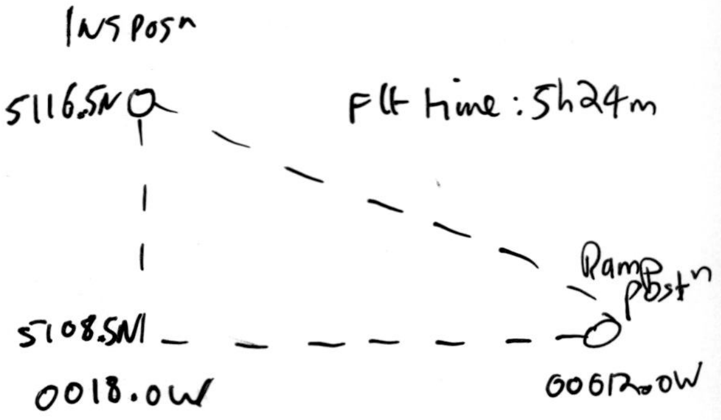

INS posn

5116.5N Q

Flt time : 5h24m

5108.5N
0018.0W

Ramp posn
0061 ... 0W

- ch lat : 0.8'
  = 8 nm

- ch long : 0.6' =
- mid lat : 51° 12.5' N
- Departure =
  ch long × cos (mid lat)
  = 6' × cos (51° 12.5')
  = 3.75 nm

$$x = \sqrt{8^2 + 3.75^2}$$

$$x = 8.8 \text{ nm}$$

∴ Radial Error rate = $\dfrac{8.8}{5h\,24min}$ ⇒ 1.63 nm/hr

INERTIAL NAVIGATIONAL SYSTEMS

1.   INS errors are classified as "Bounded errors" and "Unbounded errors".

     a)   An "Unbounded error" is an error that increases with time, an example being the distance gone error due to a ground speed error.

     b)   An "Unbounded error" is an error that increases with time, an example being an increasing ground speed error due to the platform not being levelled correctly.

     c)   A "Bounded error" is an error that is subject to sudden unpredictable random changes. Most notable during pitching manoeuvres and when raising or lowering flap and U/C.

     d)   A "Bounded error" is an error that is "tied" to the real wander rates of the gyros on the platform.

2.   Two checks that can be carried out to check that two selected sequential waypoints have been entered correctly are:

     a)   select DSR.TK/STS and check that the status is less than 4; select DIS/TIME and check that the time agrees with the flight plan time.

     b)   select DIS/TIME and check that the distance agrees with the distance on the flight plan; then check that the time agrees with the flight plan time for the leg.

     c)   select DIS/TIME and check that the distance agrees with the distance on the flight plan; select DSR.TK/STS and check that the track agrees with the flight plan track for the leg.

     d)   select DIS/TIME and check that the distance agrees with the distance on the flight plan; select HDG/DA and check that the heading agrees with the flight plan heading for the leg.

3.   In an INS the E/W accelerations are converted into an E/W speed (kt) at the first stage of integration and into E/W distance gone (nm) at the second stage of integration. This gives:

     a)   departure which is multiplied by Cosine of the present latitude of obtain d'long (min) which is used to automatically up-date the present longitude.

     b)   d'long (min which is used to automatically up-date the present longitude.

     c)   departure which is multiplied by Secant of the present latitude to obtain d'long (min) which is used to automatically up-date the present longitude.

     d)   departure which is multiplied by Sine of the present latitude to obtain d'long (min) which is used to automatically up-date the present longitude.

4.   At the second stage of integration E/W speed is converted into E/W distance gone. To convert this departure into change of longitude is has to:

     a)   be divided by Secant of the latitude.

     b)   be multiplied by Secant of the latitude.

     c)   be divided by Tangent of the latitude.

     d)   be multiplied by Cosine of the latitude.

5.   The amber ALERT light on an INS control and display unit:

    a)   illuminates steadily 2 minutes, in AUTO mode, before reaching the next waypoint.
    b)   start flashing 2 minutes before reaching the next waypoint and goes out at 30 seconds to run.
    c)   illuminates if power from the aircraft bus bar has been lost and the system is operating on standby battery.
    d)   illuminates steadily after passing a waypoint in manual mode, until the next leg is programmed in.

6.   With reference to Inertial Navigation Systems, the functions of the integrators are:

    i)   at the second stage of integration to suppress unbounded errors (when in the NAV mode).
    ii)   at the first stage of integration to convert acceleration, with respect to time, into speed, (when in NAV mode).
    iii)   at the second stage of integration to convert speed, with respect to time, into distance gone, (when in the NAV mode).
    iv)   to align the platform (when in the level and align modes).

        a)   all the above statements are true.
        b)   only (ii), (iii) and (iv) of the above statements are true.
        c)   only (i), (ii) and (iii) of the above statements are true.
        d)   only (ii) and (iii) of the above statements are true.

7.   The computer of a north referenced Inertial Navigation System (INS) in flight, provides compensation for:

    a)   aircraft manoeuvres, real wander, apparent wander, transport wander.
    b)   coriolis, real wander, apparent wander, transport wander.
    c)   earth rotation, transport wander, coriolis.
    d)   transport wander, apparent wander, coriolis, magnetic variation.

The diagram below shows the situation after an aircraft, equipped with INS, has passed over waypoint 2 and is tracking along the line TK (dashed). Using the information given in the diagram and the fact that with DA/HDG selected on the control and display unit (CDU) of the INS, the display shows 6L/080, answer the following two questions:

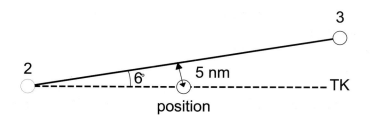

8.   When DSRTK/STS is selected on the CDU, the left window will show:

      a)   074
      b)   086
      c)   068
      d)   080

9.   When XTK/TKE is selected on the CDU, the display will show (to the nearest whole number):

	LEFT DISPLAY	RIGHT DISPLAY
a)	5L	080
b)	5R	6R
c)	5L	6L
d)	6R	5L

10.   During initialisation of an INS the aircraft must not be moved until:

      a)   The ramp position has been inserted and checked.
      b)   The platform is levelled.
      c)   The gyros and accelerometers are in the "null" position.
      d)   The green "ready NAV" light has been illuminated and the mode selector switch has been set to the "NAV" position.

CHAPTER EIGHTEEN - INERTIAL REFERENCE SYSTEM

Contents

		Page
18.1	INERTIAL REFERENCE SYSTEM	18 - 1
18.2	INERTIAL NAVIGATION	18 - 1
18.3	INERTIAL REFERENCE UNIT.	18 - 2
18.4	INERTIAL INFORMATION.	18 - 2
18.5	THE PRIMARY SOURCES OF INFORMATION.	18 - 2
18.6	THE LASER GYRO.	18 - 3
18.7	PRINCIPLES OF LASER GYROS AND IRS.	18 - 3
18.8	CONSTRUCTION AND OPERATION.	18 - 3
18.9	LIMITATIONS AND ACCURACY.	18 - 5
18.10	PLATFORM / STRAP DOWN PRINCIPLES.	18 - 5
18.11	PLATFORM ALIGNMENT.	18 - 6
18.12	ADVANTAGES.	18 - 6

"Strap Down" System / *Exam Q*

//

18.1   INERTIAL REFERENCE SYSTEM

= 3 accelerometers } all physically
3 gyros } bolted to a/c structure

The **laser gyro** has caused a technological revolution in the design of **inertial reference** and **navigation systems**. This solid state high precision ,angular rate sensor is ideally suited for highly reliable strap down system configuration. It eliminates the need for gimbals, bearings, torque motors, and other moving parts, and consequently changes the system operation considerably from conventional **inertial navigation systems**.

Exam Q:
Does an IRS require accurate levelling & aligning?
A: Yes.
↓
1° Lat
1° Long error accepted if entered through IRS

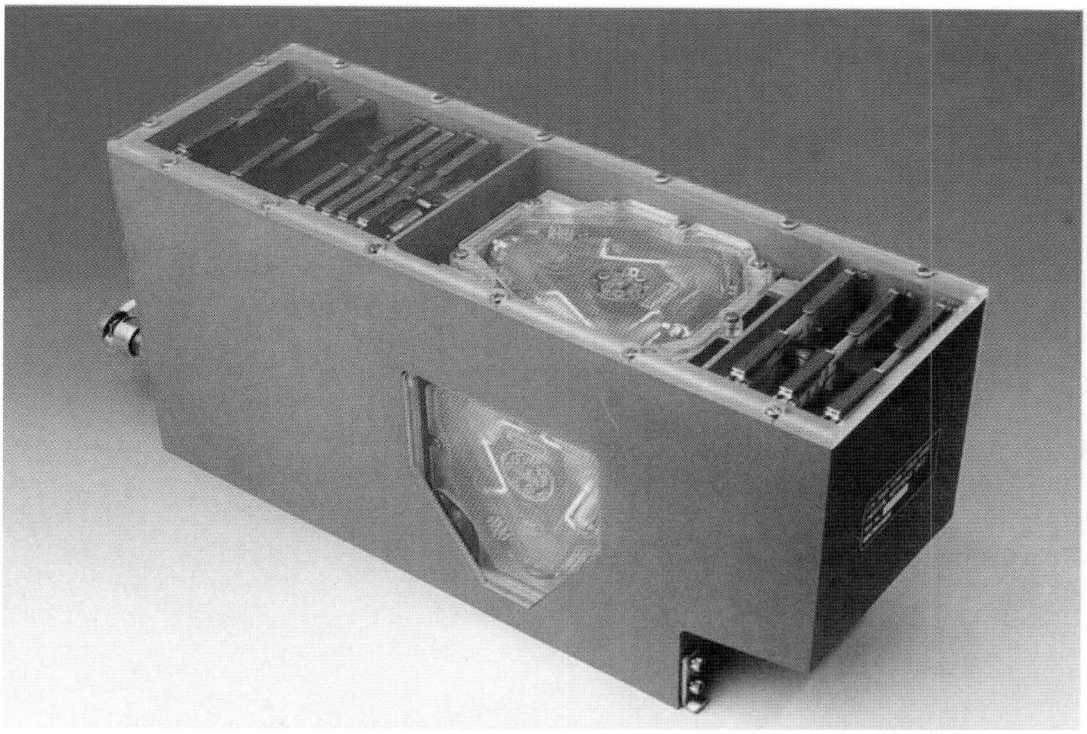

Figure 18.1 GEC-Marconi FIN3060 Commercial Aircraft Inertial Reference

18.2   INERTIAL NAVIGATION

Inertial navigation means the determination of a vehicles location without the aid of external references. **Strap down inertial navigation** goes a step further by enabling navigation without the use of a mechanically stabilised platform. This has been achieved through the advent of **laser gyros / rate sensors** and powerful, high speed microprocessors. The **laser gyros** allow a micro processor to maintain a stable platform mathematically, rather than mechanically.

18.3   INERTIAL REFERENCE UNIT

The **Inertial Reference Unit** (IRU) is the heart of the **Inertial Reference System** (IRS). It provides all required **inertial reference** outputs for the aircraft's avionics.

Outputs are:

Primary attitude	Pitch and roll
Heading	True, Magnetic
Accelerations	Lateral, Longitude, Normal
Angular rates	Pitch, Roll, Yaw
Inertial velocity	N/S, E/W, GS, TA, Vertical rate
Position	Latitude, longitude, inertial altitude
Wind data	Wind speed, wind angle, drift angle
Calculated data	Flight path angle and acceleration
	Along and across track acceleration
	Inertial pitch and roll rate
	Vertical acceleration
	Potential vertical speed.

18.4   INERTIAL INFORMATION.

Inertial information is used by:

Flight management computer
Flight control computer
Thrust management computer
Stability augmentation system
Weather radar
Anti skid auto brake systems
Attitude direction indicator
Horizontal situation indicator
Vertical speed indicator
Radio direction magnetic indicator
Flight data recorder

18.5   THE PRIMARY SOURCES OF INFORMATION.

The primary sources of information for the IRU are its own internal sensors three **laser gyros**, and three **inertial accelerometers**. The only other inputs required are initial position, barometric altitude, and True Air Speed (TAS).

Initial position is required because present position is calculated from the distance and direction travelled from the initial start position entered.

Barometric altitude stabilises the vertical navigation, and thereby stabilises the vertical velocity and inertial altitude outputs.

The TAS input allows the IRU to calculate wind speed and wind direction.

18.6   THE LASER GYRO.

The **laser gyro** is an example of the application that uses the characteristics of light to measure motion. This device operates based on the SAGNAC effect. One beam rotates in one direction and the other beam in the opposite direction. One of the conditions that must be satisfied to maintain **lasing** is that the number of wavelengths in the beams path length must equal a whole number. When the wavelengths change there is a concurrent change in the lights frequency. This means that in a rotating gyro, one laser beam will exhibit an increase in frequency, whereas the other beam will exhibit a frequency decrease. The frequency difference between the two beams is easily and accurately measured along optical paths.

18.7   PRINCIPLES OF LASER GYROS AND IRS.

Laser (Light Amplification and Simulated Emission of Radiation) gyros measure rotation by comparing two laser beams created and directed to rotate in opposite directions within a very narrow tunnel. Photons are emitted within the laser cavity in **all directions** but only the light that radiates backwards and forwards between the mirrors is reinforced by repeated trips through the **gain medium:** continued passage amplification soon reaches saturation and a steady state oscillation ensues, **a laser beam**.

18.8   CONSTRUCTION AND OPERATION.

Construction. The laser gyro contains three mirrors to achieve a **rotational** path for two beams that are generated and sent around in a triangular path in opposite directions. The **lasers** are sent around small tunnels drilled parallel to the perimeter of a triangular block of temperature stable glass with reflecting mirrors placed in each corner.

Lasing is achieved by running high voltages through **helium neon** gas between the anodes and the cathode transforming many of the atoms of the gas into light in the **pinkish orange** part of the visible spectrum (this action is helped by the tuned cavity effect of the tunnel in the glass block).

Operation. The laser beam that is created can be described as a high energy beam of coherent light which is said to be of a **pure frequency**. The light will be reflected by the mirrors but light of **unwanted frequencies** (i.e. not at the design frequency) will be absorbed by the mirrors and their coatings. Because the frequency of the light is known it can be measured and modified by adjustment of the path length i.e. "If the path length is decreased, the light is compressed and the frequency will increase - if the path length is expanded the frequency decreases".

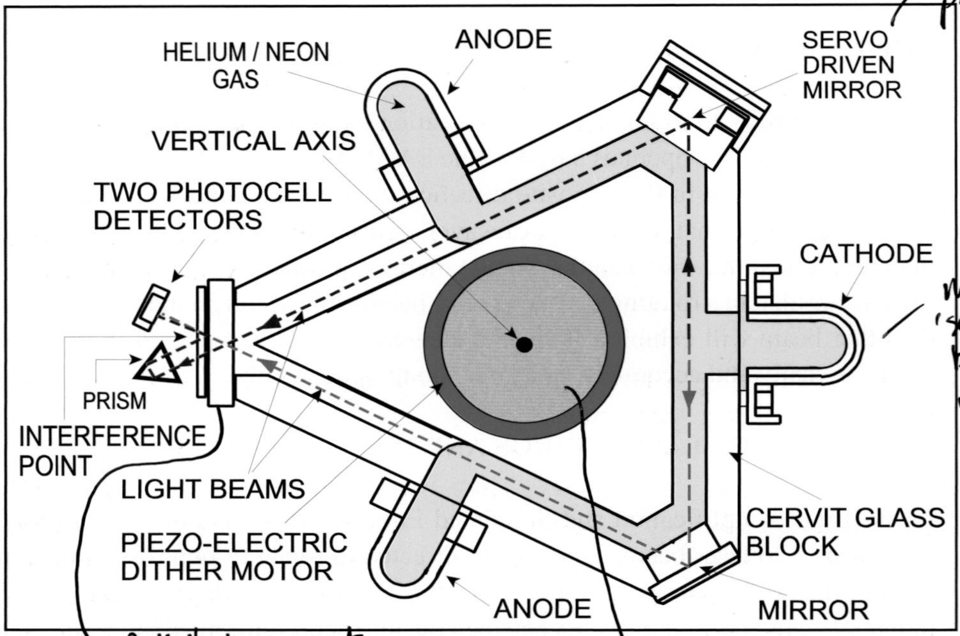

[handwritten: maintain cavity path length]

[handwritten left margin: Gyro is filled with "Helium - Neon" gas]
[handwritten: - Lases into 2 beams of light.]
[handwritten: - One goes clock the other anti-clock wise]
[handwritten: - Both beams are 'orange / pink' in colour]
[handwritten: - Distance around cavity must remain constant ∴ Servo driven motor will move to compensate for expansion]

Labels in figure: HELIUM / NEON GAS, ANODE, SERVO DRIVEN MIRROR, VERTICAL AXIS, TWO PHOTOCELL DETECTORS, CATHODE, PRISM, INTERFERENCE POINT, LIGHT BEAMS, PIEZO-ELECTRIC DITHER MOTOR, ANODE, CERVIT GLASS BLOCK, MIRROR

[handwritten: Partially transparent mirror 'partially silvered']
[handwritten right: made with 'cervitt' block glass which has v. low co-eff of expansion]
[handwritten: Dither Motor]

Figure 18.2

The triangular path of the device does not rotate but the two beams of light are caused to travel in opposite directions and will of course travel at the same speed i.e. **the speed of light**.

If there is no movement of the device the beams cancel each other out but when movement is induced one of the beams will take longer to complete its path and the other, in opposition, a measurably shorter length of time to complete its journey. This whole process is measured by devices known as **gain elements** and the rate of rotation can be calculated.

The three mirrors involved are not identical - one makes micro adjustments to keep the physical light path accurately aligned and another is partially transparent to allow the laser light to be detected on the photo cell detectors.

Included with the second mirror is a prism which **flips / redirects** the light beam around causing it to meet and **interfere** with the light beam that is aimed directly at the photo cell. The beams alternately cancel and reinforce each other (known as interference) **thus generating a fringe pattern**.

[handwritten: ✱ Dither Motor - overcomes laser / phase / frequency lock]

© Oxford Aviation Services Limited

[handwritten: - Biggest cause of errors in IRS area due to Manufacturing errors of Partially Silvered Mirror]

The photo electric cell detects the direction and speed at which the **fringe pattern** moves. The change in the pattern, moving in one direction or other depends upon which way the **laser gyro** is being rotated. The faster the rotation the faster the **fringe pattern** moves across the photo electric cell - this is then converted to signals used within the aircraft systems.

18.9   LIMITATIONS AND ACCURACY.

Drift. The principle source of error with this form of device, as with the conventional **gyro stabilised platform INS** device, is associated with random drift. In a conventional gyro this is caused by imperfections of gyro bearings and mass imbalances but with the **laser** system noise is the cause and this is derived almost entirely from imperfections in the mirrors and their coatings.

Accuracy. The accuracy of the **laser** system is directly influenced by the length of its optical path - the longer the path available the greater the accuracy with a small percentage increase in length leading to a substantial increase in accuracy.

Lock in. The most significant potential problem is **lock in**, also known as **laser lock**, which occurs at very low rotation rates.

At very low rotation rates the output frequency can drop to zero as a result of **back scattering** between the two beams which causes the beams to synchronise, that is, no longer indicate the rotation correctly and indeed introduce undesirable errors. This phenomena is overcome by the introduction of a vibration device known as a **piezo electric dither motor** which breaks the lock in. The motor is mounted in such a way that it vibrates the **laser ring** about its **input axis** through the lock in region, thereby unlocking the beams and enabling the optical sensor to detect the smaller movement of the **fringe pattern**. The motions caused by the dither motor are decoupled from the output of the **ring laser gyro / rate sensor**.

18.10   PLATFORM / STRAP DOWN PRINCIPLES.

Platform. The INS **(platform set in gimbals)** requires three rate integrating gyros and acccelerometers to achieve an output that we can use and this process is started by ensuring that the platform is horizontal at the correct Latitude. **IRS (strap down)** attaches the three laser gyro / rate sensors and accelerometers directly to the aircraft chassis.

High speed micro processors then achieve a stable platform **mathematically** rather than mechanically (as per the INS) - this results in greatly improved accuracy and reliability.

Integration. Integration principles are used as per the older INS system.

SAG - NA C effect.
- In a turn the light takes longer & quicker to get to mirrors
∴ diff in time gives acceleration of a/c
∴ fringe pattern is changed

Gravity. Gravity - the microprocessor subtracts the effect of local gravity from any vertical acceleration to compensate for local effects.

Earth rotation. Earth Rotation Rate - compensated for at the rate of 15.04 degrees as with a gyro (INS) system.

Transport compensation. Transport Rate - **Schuler Tuning** is again required to compensate for oscillation errors as the system is transported over the Earth (this in relation to pendulum theory which results in an 84.4 minute error cycle as described in the older INS.

Calibration. Automatic Calibration - completed automatically by computer to enhance the overall accuracy of the system.

18.11 PLATFORM ALIGNMENT.

True North. The system, as with the INS, requires to find **true north** to achieve an alignment and this is achieved when the aircraft is stationary on the ground and the only rate of change is that associated with the movement of the Earth. True North is then found.

Latitude. Initial Latitude must be put into the system by the operator, the computer then, after assessing the rotational vectors that it is experiencing compares the Latitude it finds with that entered by the operator during initialization. However, it should be noted that with this system the inbuilt memory function remembers its position at landing and will indicate to the crew any errors of initial position input (lat' or long') upon startup.

Alignment. The computer, after confirming the Latitude, completes a full mathematical levelling process - initial Latitude and Longitude must be entered manually as a **present position** to assist this align - **THE AIRCRAFT MUST NOT BE MOVED DURING THIS PROCESS.**

18.12 ADVANTAGES.

Activation. Almost no spin up time, one second activation for the rate sensor.

Manoeuvring. Insensitive to "G" attitude, rolling, pitching manoeuvres.

Construction. Mechanically simple and highly reliable.

Range. Wide dynamic range.

Drift. Very small drift rates - greatest errors induced by the operator.

Example Examination Question.

Dither is used in a laser gyro in order to:

a)   Enhance the accuracy of the gyro at all rotational rates.

b)   Increase the maximum rotational rate that can be sensed by the gyro.

c)   Stabilise the laser frequencies at peak power output.

d)   Break the frequency lock which would prevent small rotational rates from being sensed by the gyro.

CHAPTER NINETEEN - AIR DATA COMPUTER

Contents

		Page
19.1	INTRODUCTION	19 - 1
19.2	PITOT - STATIC SYSTEM.	19 - 1
19.3	AIR DATA COMPUTER.	19 - 1
19.4	SYSTEM REDUNDANCY.	19 - 3
19.5	BUILT IN TEST EQUIPMENT (BIT OR BITE).	19 - 4
19.6	ADVANTAGES OF AN AIR DATA SYSTEM.	19 - 4

Inputs to ADC

- Total Air Temp (TAT)

- Static Pressure

- Pitot Pressure

- A.o.A   (some aircraft)

- Power

dlea
C A D C

(Central

19.1   INTRODUCTION

In many large aircraft currently in service, the conventional pressure instruments which show altitude, airspeed and Mach Number(MNo) are replaced by indicators displaying information generated by a central computer, the Air Data Computer (ADC). The computer unit and displays, together with the sensors of the basic data of pitot pressure, static pressure and air temperature, and a power-pack, form the aircraft's Air Data System (ADS). Whilst such a system is self-contained, its outputs are essential to the operation of the aircraft's Automatic Flight Control System (AFCS). ADS outputs may also be used in the altitude transponder, flight data recorder, navigation computer and more.

A number of different aircraft types may use the same basic Air Data Computer and this device will need to be integrated into the aircraft systems and this is achieved by a **"Configuration Module"**. The module can be calibrated to take into account differences in pressure / temperature gathering efficiencies due to positioning of the gathering probes and this information can then be entered into the computer to obtain the most accurate indications possible.

The standard ADS instruments show altitude, vertical speed, airspeed and MNo. Additional instruments can display Total Air Temperature (TAT), Static Air Temperature (SAT) and TAS. The ADC outputs required for other systems are various and may include TAS, Altitude, Log Mach No, Reciprocal Mach No and Log Vertical Speed. The ADC fitted to Concorde computes Angle of Attack and Side-slip as well as more standard data. A schematic diagram of a conventional ADS is shown in Figure 19.3.

19.2   PITOT - STATIC SYSTEM.

In a typical aircraft, identical sets of air data instruments are provided on the Captain's and First Officer's instrument panels. Each set of instruments is connected to one of two(allowing redundancy) ADC's fed from independent pitot and static sources, which can be cross connected, as shown in Figure 19.2. In addition to the indicators powered by the two ADC's there is a standby barometric altimeter and a standby airspeed indicator, fed direct from pitot and static sources separate from those used for the ADC's. Each of the three independent pitot-static systems makes use of cross coupled static vents located on each side of the fuselage. This arrangement is designed to reduce error due to side-slip or yaw.

19.3   AIR DATA COMPUTER.

The Air Data Computer in current aircraft is a device that uses analogue or digital computing techniques to convert pressure and temperature data into electrical signals which are transmitted to the display instruments and to other systems.

The two types of ADC system found are described as either **Analogue** or **Digital** from the method of assessment and transmission of information used.

The Analog type uses continuous physical variables, such as voltage or pressure, to assess and represent the measurements obtained. The illustration at **Fig 19.1a** shows an Airspeed assessment device from an **Analogue ADC** indicating the inputs of Static and Pitot Pressure. The pressures are joined together mechanically and, using a **Pressure Transducer**, transmitted forward for use through the rotation of a shaft driven by a 2-phase Servo Motor which in turn is connected to a CX Synchro where angular position can be measured and read off as an airspeed.

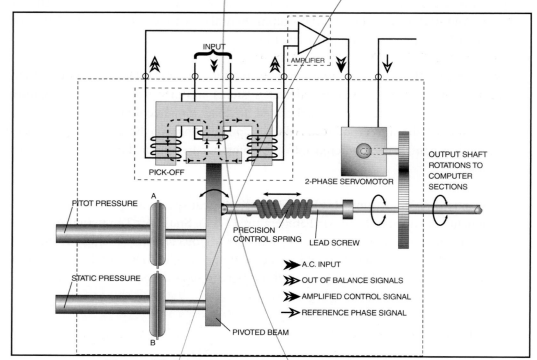

Figure 19.1 Analogue ADC - Airspeed Assessment

An Analogue Air Data Computer may internally be split into the following modules for assessment and onward transmission of data obtained through the Temperature, Static and Pitot Pressure gathering devices - **Altitude, Computed Airspeed, Mach speed, True Air Speed** and using data from the altitude module via a **Rate of Climb** module will give vertical speed.

The relationships between TAS, Mach No, Temperature, Pitot and Static pressures can be expressed as mathematical formulae. The ADC resolves these formulae continuously to produce the required outputs from pressure and temperature inputs in the form of shaft rotations or electrical signals.

The Digital system uses digital data (binary data) in its assessment and transmission of information. The **Analogue to Digital Converters**, at the input side of the ADC, use measurements of Pressure, Temperature and AOA and change them from the Analogue form to Digital form for use within the ADC and onward transmission to the flight deck.

(Both forms of computer system are discussed in the lessons relating to Basic Computers elsewhere in the course.)

19.4   SYSTEM REDUNDANCY.

Provision for blockages and / or failure of an ADC is made through change-over cocks that permit an alternative static source to be connected to the computer or by the use of electrical switching that enables the Captain's instrument to be fed from the First Officer's ADC and vice versa. These arrangements are illustrated in Figures 19.2 and 19.4.

In some aircraft the ADS is designed so that the outputs from each computer are not directed exclusively to instruments on one side of the panel. By mixing the sources of air data to each side, the possibility of an undetected malfunction is reduced.

In the event of total failure of both ADC's due perhaps to loss of power supply, the flight can be continued by reference to the standby instruments.

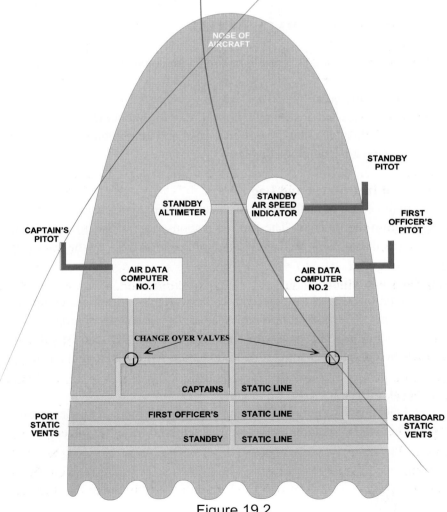

Figure 19.2

Oxford Aviation Services Limited

19.5   BUILT IN TEST EQUIPMENT (BIT OR BITE).

There is no provision made for the manual input of data into the ADC in the event of any failure, but the Built In Test Equipment will give prompt indication of any malfunction that might occur. (See 'Failure Warning' below). In any ADC there will be three types of BITE process:

a)   "Power Up" BITE.   — Takes Place on the Ground
      This functions when power is applied to the ADC on start up or after a break. A check is made on the Microprocessor, the Memory Store and the Air Data functions.

b)   **Continuous BITE.**   — every ½ second to a second — In flight
      This is an automatic check of all stages of input and output carried out throughout the operation of the ADC about once every second.

c)   **Maintenance BITE.**   — can be controlled but by ground engineer
      This enables maintenance crew to carry out checks on the ground using a Test or Test/History switch (current or post failures).

19.6   ADVANTAGES OF AN AIR DATA SYSTEM.

An ADS has certain advantages when compared with conventional mechanical instruments:

a)   **Improved Displays.**
      Electrically-servoed instrumentation allows the manufacturer complete freedom to design new displays that are easier to read and unambiguous. These include digital, moving tape and combined displays.

b)   **Reduced Instrument and Lag Errors.**
      The major cause of instrument error in conventional mechanical instruments is friction loss within the linkage. The limited response rate of such linkages gives rise to lag error. Both problems are largely overcome with ADS's by the use of servomotors.

c)   **Error Correction.**
      Computation of height, airspeed and other variables within one computer permits error corrections to be applied through especially shaped cams appropriate to the particular aircraft. For example, position error correction (PEC) can be calculated within the Mach No computer channel for additional use within the height and airspeed channels.

d)   **Central Source for Other Systems.**
      The ADC provides not only the conventional information displayed on the instrument panel but also air data in many forms as required for other systems.

e)   **Clean Design.**

The use of electrically-driven instruments reduces the amount of pneumatic plumbing

required behind the instrument panel to only those lines connected to the standby airspeed indicator and altimeter. In addition to space saving and easier maintenance, the use of shorter pitot/static line reduces error-producing acoustic effects.

Failure Warning. A comparison monitor can be incorporated to compare the outputs of the ADC's and to give automatic warning to the pilot of malfunction. With a purely mechanical system, comparison between left-hand and right-hand instruments must be carried out visually. A warning flag will appear on the appropriate ADS instrument if there is loss of valid data or if an internal failure occurs. In addition, a light will illuminate either on the instrument warning panel or on the central warning system indicator

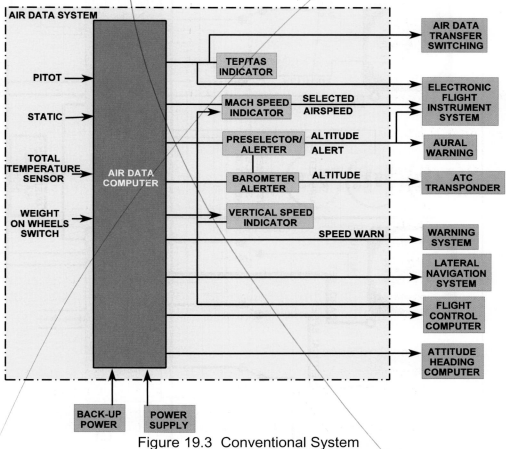

Figure 19.3 Conventional System

Note 1:   The weight on wheels switch decouples the stall warning system when the aircraft is on the ground.

Note 2:   AOA may also be an input to the ADC for use in some aircraft systems.

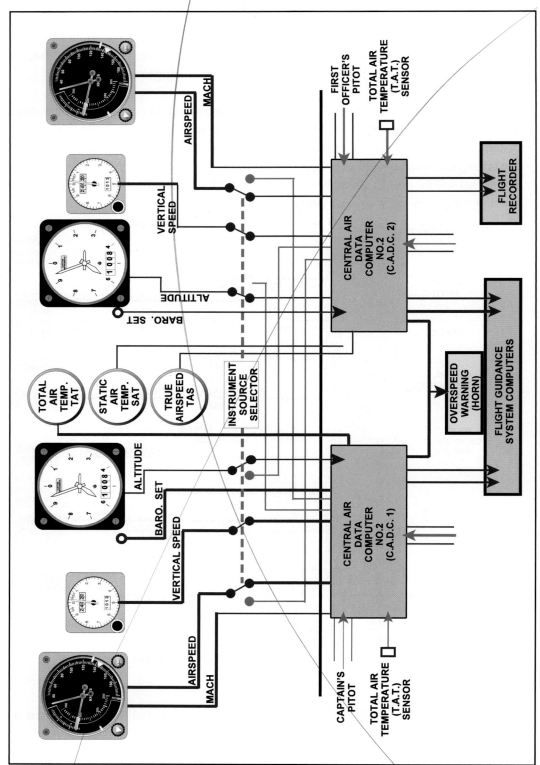

Figure 19.4 - Combined Air Data System

CHAPTER TWENTY - THE RADIO ALTIMETER

Contents

                                                                               Page

20.1   INTRODUCTION .... 20 - 1

20.2   FREQUENCIES. .... 20 - 2

20.3   INDICATOR. .... 20 - 2

20.4   RANGE AND ACCURACY. .... 20 - 5

20.5   AIRCRAFT INSTALLATION DELAY .... 20 - 5

RAD ALT

20.1 INTRODUCTION

Measures true height above the ground.

The Radio Altimeter is a device capable of measuring the height of an aircraft above ground with a high degree of accuracy. Apart from providing a flight deck display of height Above Ground Level(AGL), the radio altimeter has two other important functions. It supplies the automatic flight system with data to affect automatic landings when used in association with the ILS / MLS.

– Pressures are not involved with 'rad alt'

The Radio Altimeter furnishes height information and rate of change of height, to the Ground Proximity Warning System (GPWS), and is a crucial component of this system

The instrument makes use of primary radar principles transmitting a Frequency Modulated Continuous Wave (FMCW) in an elliptical pattern vertically below the aircraft.

The Radio Altimeter determines the time taken for a radio wave to travel from the aircraft to the ground directly beneath the aircraft and back again. During this time the transmitted frequency changes at a known rate from its start level to +50Mhz and back again to complete a "cycle".

The carrier frequency cannot be increased indefinitely and so after half a wavelength the change is reversed, the frequency then being decreased at a constant rate down to a specified value before being increased again. The complete "modulation cycle / frequency sweep" is illustrated in Fig 20.1.

On 737 Rad alt operates from 2,500 ft to ground level.

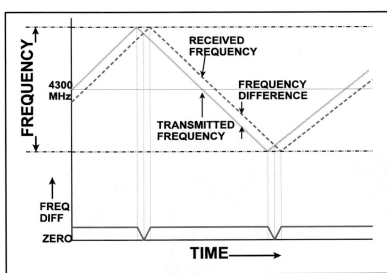

Figure 20.1.

The equipment compares the frequencies of the transmitted and received signals and since the rate of frequency change is known, the frequency difference becomes a measure of the time taken for the radio wave to travel to and from the surface. From the information gained aircraft height may be determined.

The breakdown of frequency difference, which occurs when the transmitter changes the direction of its frequency sweep, is overcome by relating aircraft height to the average beat frequency (the difference between transmitted and received frequency) observed over a short sampling period. The frequency changeover points are thereby ignored.

20.2   FREQUENCIES.

Two frequency bands have been used in the past, but only the SHF band is used at present:

The Rad Act transmits a frequency modulated continuous wave (FMCW) with a low sweep rate in an elliptical beam vertically beneath the a/c

4200 MHz to 4400 MHz - SHF band ✱

1600 MHz to 1660 MHz - UHF band

continuously varied

a 30° fore, 30° aft 60° left, 60° right

The total sweep of the carrier frequency is automatically varied ± 50 MHz 300 times a second. At very low altitude with the reflection returning almost instantaneously, a wide sweep is necessary to give a measurable frequency difference. The signal is transmitted downwards from a flush mounted horn antenna. The conical / elliptical beam generated is wide enough to always allow some portion of the beam to travel vertically even with pitch angles of ±30° and roll angles of ±60°. The height will be determined from the shortest path to the ground which, of course, will always be vertically below the aircraft.

Transmission being continuous, it is necessary to use a separate antenna, similar to the transmitting antenna for reception. The receiver antenna needs to be positioned far enough away to avoid interference with the transmitted signal.

Radiated power generated is of the order of One Watt.

✱ The low sweep rate is to overcome height ambiguity

20.3   INDICATOR.

✱ Rad Act measures the difference in frequency at any instant, between the transmitter and the receiver

Freq 2   *Freq 1*

- difference between frequencies transmitted & received

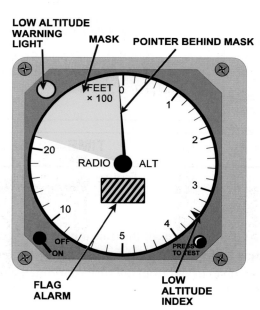

Figure 20.2.

Height Scale   The scale is logarithmic being expanded from zero to 500 feet and at a reduced non-linear scale from 500 to 2500 feet.

Mask   The height pointer disappears behind a mask:

a)   when altitude exceeds 2500 feet

b)   when there is any fault in the transmitted signal

c)   when the altimeter is switched off

Failure Warning Flag The flag appears when there is too much radio noise which will corrupt the returning signal, or if local reflections are received from the airframe itself, or in the event of a loss of power to the equipment.

Press to Test Button When this button is pressed, the height pointer swings round to a known pre-set altitude. This provides a confidence check for the user indicating that the equipment is likely to operate satisfactorily.

Low Height Warning The warning light illuminates if the aircraft is flown below any pre-selected height set by the pilot. The pilot sets his desired height on this instrument by means of the moveable index (DH) control knob on the face of the device. This occurrence is also audibly marked by the sudden cessation of an alert tone which will sound with increasing loudness from approximately 100 feet above the decision height setting

Miscellaneous   A digital read-out, and when below 1,000 feet a pictorial image of an altimeter dial, is drawn on some EFIS displays. The colour of this icon (which also shrinks in size below 1000ft indicating height change) changes from white to flashing amber as decision height is approached. One further function of the radio altimeter is to desensitise the Auto-pilot and Flight Director response to the ILS glidepath in the latter stage of an approach.

   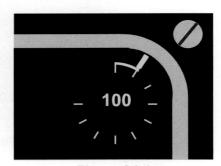

Figure 20.3.   Figure 24.4

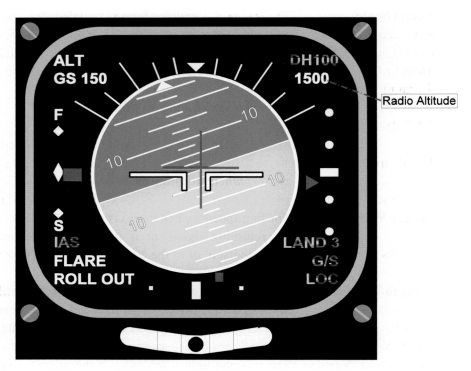

Figure 20.5.

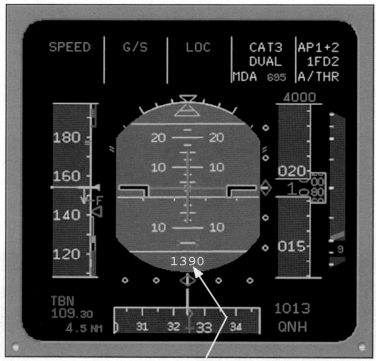

RADIO ALTIMETER -
green above DH, amber below DH and bigger numbers

Figure 20.5a.

Note. On some more modern systems, such as that used by the A300, the indication of height is given at the base of the EADI / PFD attitude display. This height indication changes colour from Green to Amber and the numbers also grow in size as Decision Height is passed. It is also important to note that the Radio Altimeter is a major component of the Ground Proximity Warning System(GPWS).

20.4   RANGE AND ACCURACY.

The instrument can be used between zero and 2500 feet above the surface with an overall expected accuracy of ± 3% of indicated height or ± 1ft whichever is the greater. The figures include various error contributors, principally Doppler Shift, Step Error in the digital counting circuits, and Height Lag.

20.5   AIRCRAFT INSTALLATION DELAY

The Radio Altimeter is required to indicate zero height AGL as the main wheels touch down on the runway, because of this it has to be extremely accurate and in practice is designed to perform to an accuracy of +/- one foot. However, in practice a single manufacturers' product may be found in multiple aircraft types from the very large Boeing 747 to a much smaller corporate commuter jet and this must be catered for. At either extreme the aircraft weight and oleo compression will vary and this leads to the need for compensation to cater for this variable. The height difference between the antennae on the fuselage and the bottom of the trailing wheels on the main landing gear bogeys, on the approach to a touchdown, is known as the Residual Height. In addition, the different physical sizes of the aircraft concerned will create differences in cable run length between the Avionics Bay and the position of the antennae on the underside of the aircraft fuselage. When investigating the larger aircraft this distance may be as much as 100ft or, in the smaller jet, as little as 6ft. If compensation for cable length is not catered for in the larger aircraft an error would be generated and this would be seen as an error of height (perhaps to 100ft in the example above).

The Aircraft installation delay is therefore adjusted to compensate for Residual Height and Cable Length (times two - Tx Antennae/Rx Antennae to Avionics Bay) this is done to ensure that at touchdown with the main bogeys trailing the Rad' Alt' reads zero.

Additionally, it should be noted that when on the ground, the radio altimeter may show a small negative altitude. The reason for this is that the equipment has been adjusted to indicate zero when the main wheels first touch the runway surface on landing and therefore when the aircraft is level on the ground the antenna will be below its calibrated position relative to the aircraft landing attitude. The effect is particularly noticeable with aircraft such as the B747 (which actually indicates -8ft) which have multi-wheel assemblies which are inclined at an upward angle when deployed in flight and thereby create a larger difference between antenna position and wheels at the point of touchdown.

- When installing, the cable length must be considered as it takes time from travelling from transmitter to aerial and vice versa.

- Height @ touchdown should read zero ie height of landing gear must be considered.

   - Residual height is measured from the bottom of the lowest trailing wheels to the antenna

- Accuracy is ± 1 foot or 3% of indicated height.

CHAPTER TWENTY ONE - FLIGHT MANAGEMENT SYSTEM

Contents

		Page
21.1	PRINCIPLE OF OPERATION	21 - 1
21.2	CONTROL AND DISPLAY UNIT (CDU)	21 - 2
21.3	DATA BASE	21 - 3
21.4	OPERATIONAL PROCEDURES - INITIAL ACTIONS	21 - 3
21.5	OPERATIONAL PROCEDURES - CLIMB VERTICAL NAVIGATION (VNAV)	21 - 5
21.6	OPERATIONAL PROCEDURES - CRUISE LATERAL NAVIGATION (LNAV)	21 - 6
21.7	OPERATIONAL PROCEDURES - DESCENT	21 - 6
21.8	OPERATIONAL PROCEDURES - ACCURACY	21 - 6
21.9	OPERATIONAL PROCEDURES - CONTROL AND DISPLAY UNIT	21 - 7

RNAV

RNAV = Area Navigation

= Uses Radio Beacons to create 'Phantom' Waypoints

∴ giving:

- Direct FCE Path
- Shorter Distance, less time, less fuel = Less Cost
- ↑se in capacity
- Reduction in Separation (in time)

Types
- Basic RNAV - ± 5nm
- Precision RNAV = ± 1 nm

Levels
- 2D Horizontal guidance only
- 3D as above + vertical guidance
- 4D as 3D + timing

21.1   PRINCIPLE OF OPERATION

Flight management systems are designed to improve navigation, aid fuel efficiency and to reduce crew workload. Computers are used to fly aircraft along complex routes using Lateral Guidance(**LNAV**).

Vertical Guidance(**VNAV**) enables the system to calculate optimum cruise altitudes and to determine the best combination of auto-throttle control and speed during climb and descent.

At all times when the crew are not actually controlling the aircraft by hand, they use the FMS controls to "fly" the aircraft. The controls of a FMS are, in effect, a miniature flight deck with fingertip control.

[handwritten margin notes: most accurate position for LNAV is "Top of Descent"; Top of Descent]

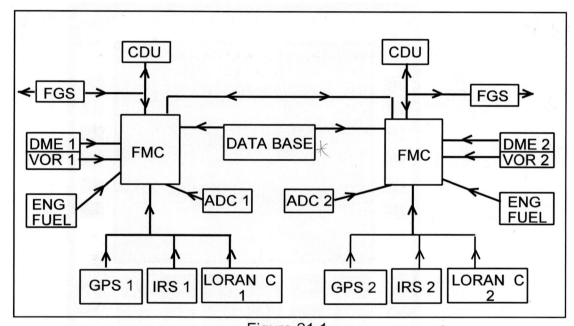

Figure 21.1.

Figure 21.1. shows the schematic lay out of a typical system.

[handwritten margin note: 2 databases: - Nav (cannot change permanently) - Performance]

Legend:

CDU	-	Control and Display Unit
FGS	-	Flight Guidance System
FMC	-	Flight Management Computer
ADC	-	Air Data Computer
IRS	-	Inertial Reference System
GPS	-	Global Positioning System

21.2   CONTROL AND DISPLAY UNIT (CDU)

The primary function of the CDU is to act as the interface between the aircraft and the crew. The CDU can be used to command completely automatic control of the aircraft or semi-automatic with varying degrees of pilot involvement including full manual control.

Two CDUs are usually fitted either side of the centre console with the left CDU normally being the master(in the B747-400 they are joined by a third CDU placed upon the centre console for use primarily by engineering staff). They comprise of a monochrome or coloured cathode ray tube (CRT) display on which different "pages" of selected data can be shown, and a selector key panel. Figure 21.2. shows a typical CDU.

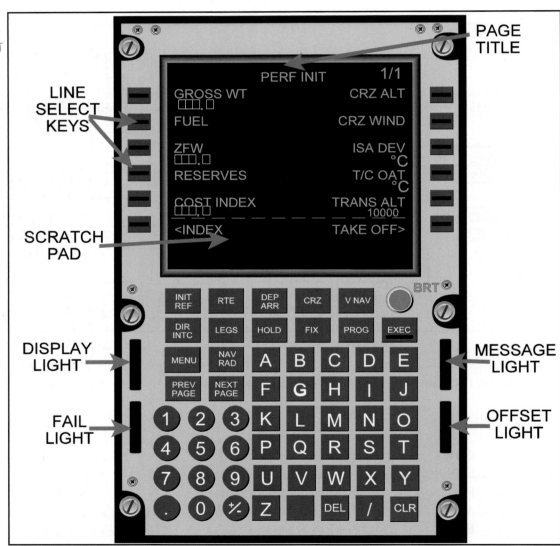

Figure 21.2.

1ᵒⁿᵍ mode

When operating in **Dual Mode** (the norm for ordinary flight profiles) both FMCs independently process pilot entries on both MCDUs and **compare** the results to ensure that crucial information is consistent on both systems.

If there is a failure of an FMC the second system can be expected to operate the aircraft successfully on its own. Each FMC may be selected out of the system to allow independent operation of the "surviving" FMC if required by the crew.

21.3   DATA BASE

The information stored in the FMC is called its data base. The data base is divided into two major sections. One contains **performance** related information and the other contains information dealing with **navigation**.

The purpose of the performance data base is to reduce the need for the flight crew to refer to the Cruise Control Manual during flight and to provide the FMC with information required to calculate pitch and thrust commands. All reference data normally required can be displayed on the FMS-CDU. The data stored in the data base includes aircraft drag and engine characteristics, maximum and minimum speeds. Maintenance can refine the data base for each aircraft by entering factors for drag and fuel flow.

The FMC navigation data base includes most information that would normally be determined by referring to navigation charts. This information may be displayed on the FMS-CDU / AMD and eliminates most of the cockpit chart reading in aircraft without an FMC. The geographic area covered includes all areas where the aircraft is normally flown. The stored information includes the location of navigation aids, airports, runways and other airline selected information such as SIDs, STARs, approaches and company routes.

The FMC contains two sets of navigation data, each valid for 28 days. Each set corresponds to the normal revision cycle for navigation charts. During preflight the flight crew can select which set is active. The FMC uses the active set for navigation calculations. The contents of the navigation data base are **updated by maintenance** every 28 days. When the navigation chart revision date arrives, the new data is already in the FMC and ready for selection.

21.4   OPERATIONAL PROCEDURES - INITIAL ACTIONS

IDENT Page: Upon application of power to the aircraft the FMS immediately executes a self-test procedure and upon its successful self completion the IDENT page of the system is displayed. The IDENT page of the FMC allows the crew to confirm aircraft details on start-up and this in turn initiates a series of prompts to direct the crew through the route procedures that need to be generated for their flight. Importantly on this page we have confirmation of the Navigation Data Base in operation and an indication of the date of changeover to the next programme - if the data base is out of date it will tell us to change to the in date programme.

POS INIT Page: When we have checked the IDENT page we will be directed to the POS INIT page where we must check the FMS clock time against the aircraft clock to ensure synchronisation between the systems: data is saved on the FDR against time and of course ETAs are generated by the FMC and need to be in line with times indicated by the aircraft clock. As we complete this task we must also ensure that the airfield datum or gate position, if available, is entered accurately to allow for IRS alignment (this position will be suitable for alignment but is often updated at the take-off point to obtain the best possible initial position for use in flight).

RTE Page: After completing our tasks upon the POS INIT page we will be directed to the RTE page where we will enter our starting and destination airport ICAO Designators. We may then expect to enter our flight number details and identify a "standard" company route to take us to our destination: if a standard route is not available other actions will have to be taken to input the information into the system.

PERF INIT Page: We may now move on to the PERF INIT page to update the aircraft to its current performance / weight configuration for the route to be flown. On this page we may input details of fuel weight, fuel reserves required, cruise altitude and even, in the case of the B747, if we are carrying a fifth engine to our destination upon its suspension point on the wing. At this stage we may also enter Cost Index requirements related to our flight as discussed later in the chapter.

SUMMARY:

The following is a summary of the initial pages that you may expect to see on the Boeing series of aircraft currently in use but of course this information may vary from company to company as they modify the system for their own use:

IDENT page -

a)   Aeroplane Model / Configuration
b)   Operational Programme Identifier
c)   Drag / Fuel Flow Factors
d)   Navigation Data Base identifier / cycle

POS INIT page -

a)   IRS Position Reference
b)   IRS Heading Reference
c)   GMT / UTC / Time Zone Display

RTE page -

a)   Origin Airport
b)   Destination Airport
c)   Flight Number
d)   Route Activation

PERF INIT page -

a)   Gross Weight
b)   Fuel Quantity
c)   Zero Fuel Weight
d)   Fuel reserves
e)   Cost Index
f)   Cruise altitude
g)   Spare (fifth) engine carriage (B747 specific)
h)   Altitude Step Size

21.5   OPERATIONAL PROCEDURES - CLIMB VERTICAL NAVIGATION (VNAV)

Entering a cost index of "ZERO" provides economy speeds representing a maximum range cruise. The **VNAV** profile that the FMC commands is a climb with climb thrust to remain within all airspeed and altitude constraints that are part of the SID entered into the active route, then climb at economy speed to the entered cruise altitude.

If when flying the climb speed profile it would cause a violation of an altitude constraint the UNABLE NEXT ALT message is displayed. The pilot must then select a different speed on the FMS-CDU that provides a steeper climb angle. Reaching cruise altitude, the FMC commands cruise at economy speed until the top of descent point.

A number of Cost index modifications are allowed until passing Top of Descent point (TOD) for example Long Range Cruise (LRC) and "selected speed" cruise may also be entered.

Note: Time Related Cost is a function of speed selected, the higher the speed in climb, cruise or descent the **higher** the "trip **fuel** cost" but the **lower** the "trip **time** cost".

Note: Economy Cruise Mode will yield the lowest operating cost based on the cost index.

Note: Cost Index is determined by dividing aeroplane operating cost ($ / £ per hour) by fuel cost ($ / £ per pound or litre). A cost index of Zero results in "minimum trip fuel operation" and so will include cruise at "maximum range" cruise and a low speed descent.

21.6   OPERATIONAL PROCEDURES - CRUISE LATERAL NAVIGATION (LNAV)

LNAV guidance outputs from the FMC are normally great circle tracks between the waypoints making up the active route. However, when a procedure stored in the FMS data base is entered into the active route the FMC can supply commands to fly a constant heading, track or follow a DME arc, as required to comply with the procedure.

FMC determines present position by using inputs from the IRS / INS, DME, VOR and other navigation systems fitted. It uses its calculated present position to generate lateral steering commands along the active leg to the active waypoint. To function, the FMC requires position information from at least one IRS / INS. While the aircraft is on the ground, the FMC calculates present position based only on information received from the IRS / INSs.

The FMC present position is normally the combination of all IRS / INS positions and since inertial systems accumulate position errors as a function of time, the position information being used by the FMC is slowly accumulating errors. These position errors can be detected by observing the various positions of the individual IRS / INS s on the CDU. If an extended ground delay occurs and a significant map error is noticed, the IRS / INS should be realigned and present position re-entered.

21.7   OPERATIONAL PROCEDURES - DESCENT

When a programmed "arrival" is entered, the FMC calculates a descent path based on the procedure's airspeed and altitude constraints and the End of Descent (E/D). The E/D is a waypoint with an altitude and airspeed constraint that coincides with a final approach fix or runway threshold.

For VFR and non-precision approaches, the FMC computed path is built to a point that is 50 feet over the approach end of the runway. It is the flight crews' responsibility to not descend below "DH" until adequate visual contact has been achieved. During a missed approach, LNAV guidance is available to the missed approach point and altitude.

21.8   OPERATIONAL PROCEDURES - ACCURACY

Radial error rates of less than 0.05 nm/hour are not uncommon. Introduction of Ground Positioning by Satellite(GPS) as a navigation input will improve overall performance. It must be stressed however that the skill of the operator and the need for constant and careful monitoring will always be a deciding factor.

21.9   OPERATIONAL PROCEDURES - CONTROL AND DISPLAY UNIT

CDU Key Groups. The keys on the lighted switch panel of the CDU perform various functions and may be broken down into three major groups:

a)   Alphanumeric

b)   Function and Mode

c)   Line Select Keys (LSK)

The function of each of the keys is briefly described below:

Alphanumeric Keys -Pressing any alphanumeric key results in that character appearing in the scratch pad.

Function and Mode Keys -Used for initialising the system, access to flight planning functions and status, and modifying the flight plan. Select climb, cruise or descent information for preplanning or modification.

CLB	CLB (climb) - displays current or alternate climb mode for assessment and selection. Cruise altitude is enterable, as is a speed / altitude restriction.
CRZ	CRZ (cruise) - displays current or alternate cruise mode for assessment and selection. Information about optimum altitude, step-climb savings, and turbulence penetration N1 targets is also available.
DES	DES (descent) - displays current or alternate descent mode for assessment and selection. Target speed is enterable, as is a speed / altitude restriction. Flight Path Angle(FPA), Vertical Speed(V/S), and Vertical Bearing(V/B). Information is provided for crew reference.
INIT REF	INIT/REF (initialisation / reference) - allows access to data pages required for start-up of the FMCS and IRS. Also, the operator may select various reference data and maintenance pages.
N1 LIMIT	N1 Limit - permits manual command of the active N1 limit, and selection of any Reduced Climb N1 Limit that may apply. (Allows the crew to select an engine, "LP Turbine", RPM.)

MENU

The N1 Limit key may be shown as a menu key on the master (left hand) CDU and can be used to find data within the system.

DEP ARR

DEP/ARR (departures / arrivals) - used for selection of the procedures and runways at the origin and destination airports.

RTE

RTE (route) - permits flight plan data entries. A primary means for lateral flight plan alteration.

LEGS

LEGS (route legs) - displays and accepts entries of detailed data concerning each leg of the flight plan, for both the lateral and vertical paths.

HOLD

HOLD - permits planning or initiation of holding at a designated waypoint.

DIR INTC

DIR/INTC (direct / intercept) - provides data capability to proceed direct to any point desired, or to intercept any leg presently in the flight plan.

FIX

FIX (fix information) - displays range and bearing data from the present position to an entered fix. Facilitates creation of fixes for use in flight planning.

PROG

PROG (flight progress) - displays current flight status information such as ETA, fuel remaining at waypoint, navigation radio tuning status, wind, and path errors.

========

Line Select Keys (LSK) - entry of data from the scratch pad into the selected line and field is accomplished by using the LSKs. There are twelve LSKs on the CDU panel, six each to the left and right of the CRT display. Data entries are permitted only on lines adjacent to the LSKs. Data can also be duplicated into the blank scratch pad by pressing the LSK adjacent to the desired data line.

+ / -

Change Sign Key - changes data in the scratch pad from positive to negative and back again. May also be used to insert a hyphen for specialised data entries.

EXEC

EXEC (execute) - used to incorporate data displayed on the CDU as part of the active flight plan. The EXEC key is operable when its annunciator bar is illuminated. The key is used for activating the flight plan, changing the active flight plan, changing the active guidance mode, or inserting data which will affect the active flight plan, guidance mode, or data base. Illumination of the white annunciator bar indicates that a valid set of data is on display and may be made active for guidance of the aircraft.

PREV PAGE

NEXT PAGE

Page Select Keys - when multiple-page displays are shown, pressing the NEXT PAGE key advances the display to the next higher page number. Pressing PREV PAGE backs up the display to the next lower page number. Page access wraps around.

CLR

Clear Key - the scratch pad's contents can be edited or cleared by pressing the CLR key. When an entry is present in the scratch pad, a brief depression of the CLR key will clear the last character in the entry. If the CLR key is held down for more than one second, the entire entry in the scratch pad will be cleared. The CLR key is also used to clear advisory and alerting messages from the scratch pad.

DEL

Delete Key - the delete (DEL) key is used to remove data from a display (and thus a flight plan) after it has been line selected and accepted into a data field. If the scratch pad is empty, depression of the DEL key writes ("DELETE") into the scratch pad. The delete process is then completed by line-selecting (LSK) the data item to be removed. If the deletion is a valid one, the data field reverts to its default value (box prompts, dashes, or a system-generated value). The system prevents invalid use of the DEL key.

Illuminated Annunciators. There are four annunciators on the front of the CDU as shown in the illustration:

MSG - Illuminates white in colour; indicates an alerting or advisory message or pending messages.

FAIL - Illuminates amber in colour; lit if FMC failure is detected.

DISPLAY - Illuminates white in colour if the page displayed is not related to the active flight plan leg or to the current operational performance mode.

OFFSET -Illuminates white in colour when a parallel offset is in use (ie. the aeroplane is flying parallel to, but a fixed distance from, the FMS preprogrammed track).

CHAPTER TWENTY TWO - AUTOMATIC FLIGHT 'EFIS'

Contents

                                                     Page

22.1   THE ELECTRONIC FLIGHT INSTRUMENT SYSTEM (EFIS). . . . . 22 - 1

22.2   THE UNITS OF A SYSTEM. . . . . 22 - 1

22.3   SYMBOL GENERATORS (SGs) . . . . 22 - 2

22.4   DISPLAY UNITS. . . . . 22 - 2

22.5   THE COLOUR DISPLAY SYSTEM. . . . . 22 - 3

22.6   THE REMOTE LIGHT SENSOR. . . . . 22 - 3

22.7   THE CONTROL PANEL. . . . . 22 - 3

22.8   THE 'EADI' SECTION OF THE CONTROL PANEL. . . . . 22 - 4

22.9   DECISION HEIGHT (DH). . . . . 22 - 4

22.10 THE 'EADI' DISPLAY PRESENTATION. . . . . 22 - 5

22.11 THE 'EHSI' SECTION OF THE CONTROL PANEL. . . . . 22 - 7

22.12 SYSTEM SYMBOLS. . . . . 22 - 7

22.13 THE 'EHSI' DISPLAY PRESENTATION. . . . . 22 - 8

22.14 FULL VOR MODE . . . . 22 - 9

22.15 EXPANDED VOR . . . . 22 - 10

22.16 FULL ILS MODE . . . . 22 - 11

22.17 EXPANDED ILS . . . . 22 - 12

22.18 MAP MODE . . . . 22 - 13

22.19 PLAN MODE. . . . . 22 - 14

22.20 DATA SOURCE SELECTION. . . . . 22 - 14

22.21 FAILURE ANNUNCIATION. . . . . 22 - 15

22.22 EXAMPLE DISPLAYS . . . . 22 - 19

EFIS QUESTIONS . . . . 22 - 20

22.1   THE ELECTRONIC FLIGHT INSTRUMENT SYSTEM (EFIS).

The Electronic Flight Instrument System presents attitude and navigation information to the pilot on two electronic display units in a format that is easier to read and less likely to be misinterpreted than some older mechanical instruments.

As far as the pure basic functions and number of display units are concerned, this system, (which is generally referred to as 'EFIS'), is fully integrated with digital computer-based navigation systems, and utilises colour Cathode Ray Tube (CRT) or Liquid Crystal Display (LCD) types of **Attitude Director Indicator** (ADI) and **Horizontal Situation Indicator** (HSI).

The system is therefore extremely advanced, not only in terms of physical construction, but also in the extent to which it can present attitude and navigational data to the flight crew of an aircraft.

22.2   THE UNITS OF A SYSTEM.

As in the case of a multi crew conventional flight director system, a complete EFIS installation is made up of left (Captain), and right (First Officer), systems.

Each system in turn is comprised of: _Flight Path_

a)   Electronic Attitude Director Indicator (EADI) or Primary Flight Display (PFD).

b)   Electronic Horizontal Situation Indicator (EHSI) or Navigation Display (ND).

c)   Control Panel.

d)   Symbol Generator (SG).

e)   Remote Light Sensor Unit. — _changes light intensities depending on light level._

737 does not have spare symbol generator

A third (centre) Symbol Generator is also incorporated so that its drive signals may be switched to either the left or right display units in the event of failure of their corresponding Symbol Generators.

The signal switching is accomplished within the left and right Symbol Generators, using electromechanical relays powered from an aircraft's DC power supply, via pilot-controlled switches.

∴ if one is lost must plug into other sides.

The interface between EFIS units, data busses and other systems is shown in Figure 22.1

22.3   SYMBOL GENERATORS (SGs)

Symbol Generators provide the analogue, discrete, and digital signal interfaces between an aircraft's systems, the display units, and the control panel, and they also perform symbol generation monitoring, power control and the main control functions of the 'EFIS' overall.

The interfacing between the card modules of an SG is shown in Figure 22.1.

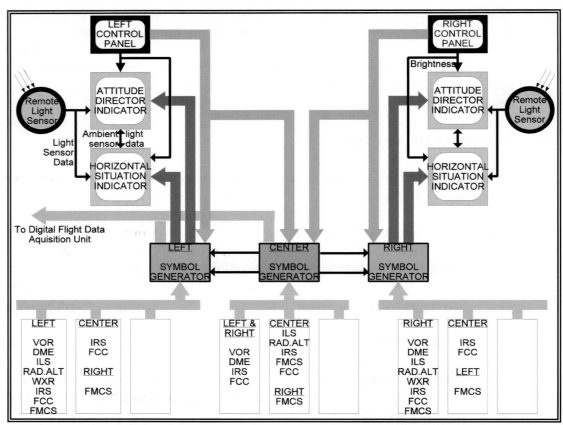

Figure 22.1. Multi-Crew EFIS Units and Signal Interfacing

22.4   DISPLAY UNITS.

The display units may be Cathode Ray Tubes (CRT's) or Liquid Crystal Displays (LCD's). LCD's have the advantage of being smaller and generate less heat therefore need less cooling. The PFD and ND are usually identical units to facilitate spares commonality and are often interchangeable with the systems display units (EICAS or ECAM).

22.5   THE COLOUR DISPLAY SYSTEM.

There is no set colour standard and so colour displays may vary slightly.

In a typical display system, 5 colours are usually assigned for the display of the many symbols, failure annunciators, messages and other alphanumeric information, with a sixth colour (RED) for weather (WXR):

White: Display of present situation information.

Green: Display of present situation information where contrast with white symbols is required, or for data having lower priority than white symbols. Engaged autoflight modes

Magenta: All **'fly to'** information such as flight director commands, deviation pointers, active flight path lines.

Cyan: Sky shading on an EADI and for low-priority information such as non active flight plan map data.

Yellow: Ground shading on an EADI, caution information display such as failure warning flags, limit and alert annunciators and fault messages.

Red: For display of heaviest precipitation levels as detected by the weather radar (WXR).

22.6   THE REMOTE LIGHT SENSOR.

The Remote Light Sensor is a photodiode device which responds to ambient light conditions on the flight deck, and automatically adjusts the brightness of the CRT displays to an acceptable level.

22.7   THE CONTROL PANEL.

A control panel is provided for each system, and are typically, as shown in Figure 22.2, the switches are grouped for the purpose of controlling the displays of their respective **EADI** and **EHSI** units.

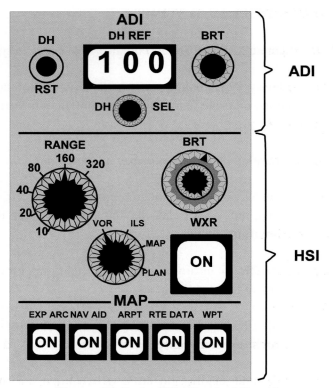

Figure 22.2. An Efis Control Panel

22.8   THE 'EADI' SECTION OF THE CONTROL PANEL.

Brightness Control(**BRT**).	Used to adjust the brightness of the **ADI** display to the desired level.
Decision Height Selector(**DH SEL**).	Used to select desired decision height for **DH** alerting.
Decision Height Reset Switch(**DH RST**).	When pressed it resets a **DH** alert on the associated **ADI**. It changes the **RA** display from yellow to white.
Decision Height Reference Indicator(**DH REF**).	This displays the selected decision height on the controller, and on the **EADI**.

22.9   DECISION HEIGHT (DH).

Decision height is the wheel height above the runway elevation by which a go-around must be initiated unless adequate visual reference has been established and the aircraft position and approach path have been assessed as satisfactory to continue the approach and landing in safety.

22.10   THE 'EADI' DISPLAY PRESENTATION.

The **'EADI'** (Figure 22.3) displays normal pitch and roll attitude indications plus

a)   Attitude data from an Inertial Reference System (**IRS**).

b)   Flight director commands. = Command Bars

c)   Localizer and glide slope deviation.

d)   Ground speed.

e)   Radio Altitude.

f)   Decision height.

g)   Automatic Flight Control System (**AFCS**) and Auto-throttle modes.

h)   Speed error scale (Difference between commanded and actual)

Note: The autoland status, pitch, roll-armed and engage modes are selected on the **AFCS** control panel.

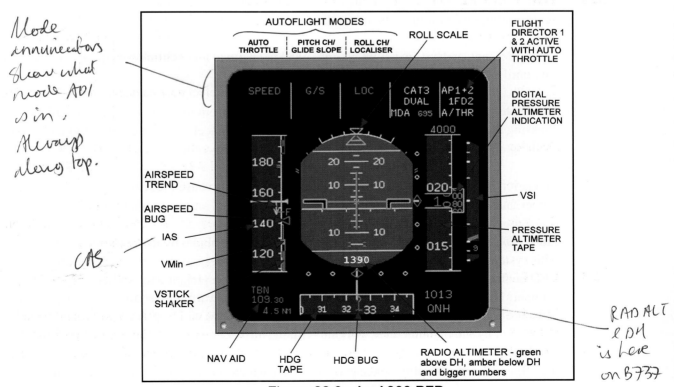

Figure 22.3. An A300 PFD.

© Oxford Aviation Services Limited

Decision height (**DH**) is selected on the **ADI** control panel and shown on both the **ADI** and on the control panel.

Figure 22.4. Decision Height and Radio Altimeter Presentation Below 1,000 Feet.

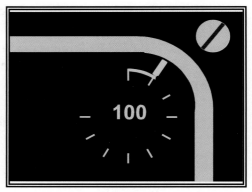

At Decision Height

Radio altitude on some systems is digitally displayed during when the aircraft is between 2,500ft and 1,000 ft above ground level.

Below 1,000 ft the display automatically changes to a white circular scale calibrated in increments of 100 ft, and the selected decision height is then displayed as a magenta-coloured marker on the outer scale. The radio altitude also appears within the scale as a digital readout. As the aircraft descends, segments of the altitude scale are simultaneously erased so that the scale continuously diminishes in length in an anti-clockwise direction.

On the descent, at decision height plus about 50 ft, an **aural alert chime** sounds at an increasing rate until decision height is reached.

On reaching **DH** the marker and scale flash and change from magenta to amber or yellow. Pressing the **EADI** control panel **DH RST** button will cancel the alert chime, stop the marker flashing and change the **DH** displays back to their normal colour.

Deviation beyond normal Localiser and Glide slope limits cause the scales to change colour to amber and the pointer to flash, which ceases if the aircraft returns to within limits.

Note: The **A300** system currently in use differs from the above by using digital readout only. This system, which is also found on some other aircraft types, displays Rad Alt at the base of the PFD centre display using Green numbers above Decision Height and Amber, slightly bigger numbers below. The digital readout is enhanced by a voice warning system which will give aural indications of height passing to the pilot. The aural warnings will be given at significant heights as decided by the manufacturer working with the airline company at time of system build.

The **Speed Error Display** consists of a pointer which moves relative to a deviation scale to show difference between actual speed and commanded speed.

22.11   THE 'EHSI' SECTION OF THE CONTROL PANEL.

Instrument landing System

RANGE.	Selects range for displayed navigation data and WXR.
MODE SELECTOR.	Selects display appropriate to mode required: **VOR, ILS, MAP, PLAN**.

Vhf omni directional range

BRT (BRIGHTNESS).	Outer knob sets main display brightness. Inner knob sets **WXR** display brightness.
MAP switches.	Used in MAP mode. When selected, they cause their placarded data to be displayed on the **EHSI**;- **NAV AID** (NAVIGATION AID), **ARPT** (AIRPORT), **RTE DATA** (ROUTE DATA), **WPT** (WAYPOINTS).
EXP ARC	Selects **VOR** or **ILS** mode to show an **Expanded Arc**
WXR.	When pushed in, **WXR** data is displayed during all modes except **PLAN,** or when the **VOR / ILS** mode is selected to present the **FULL** compass rose.

22.12   SYSTEM SYMBOLS.

Active Waypoint (Magenta), the waypoint the aircraft is currently navigating to.

Downroute

✳ Downpath Waypoint is also white

Inactive Waypoint (White), a navigation point making up the selected active route.

Airports (Cyan).

ie downpath or already past it.

Off Route Waypoint (Cyan)

Tuned Navaids (Green).

Unused Navaid (Cyan)

Shown in all modes except 'PLAN' mode

Wind Direction (White) with respect to map display orientation and compass reference. Symbol shown in white against the black of the screen.

22.13   THE 'EHSI' DISPLAY PRESENTATION.

The **EHSI** presents a selectable, dynamic colour display of flight progress and a plan view orientation. Four principal display modes may be selected on the **EFIS** control panel;-

a)   **VOR**

b)   **ILS**

c)   **MAP**

d)   **PLAN**

Of these VOR and ILS can be displayed as full or expanded compass displays.

Note: Figure 22.5. shows the PFD and ND differing slightly and is an example of the A300 series of aircraft, whereas the previous discussion primarily relates to the Boeing systems as fitted in the B747 series of aircraft.

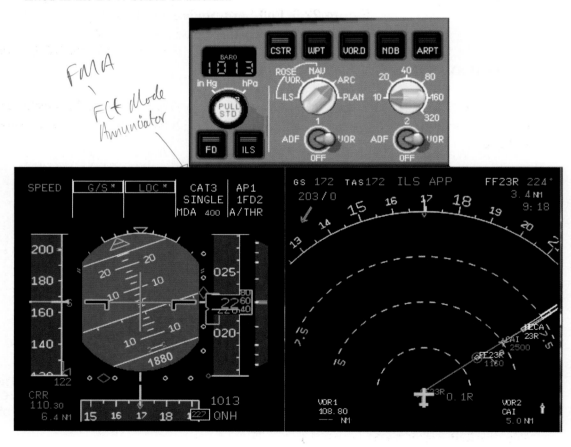

The orientation of the displays may be **Magnetic** or **True, Track** or **Heading** as selected.

22.14 FULL VOR MODE

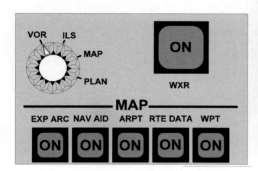

Figure 22.6 Full VOR Mode

With a VOR frequency selected, the EHSI displays a full compass rose with the VOR source in the lower left and the frequency in the lower right.

Course selection is displayed by the magenta course needle the tip pointing to the selected course (150). Course deviation is shown by the traditional deviation bar moving across a two dot left and two dot right scale.

A **TO / FROM** Pointer is shown in addition to the **TO /FROM** annunciation.

DME distance displayed in the top left corner

Current heading is shown in the window and by the lubber line at the top of the compass rose (130), the current selection is Magnetic Heading as shown either side of the window

Current track is shown by the white triangle on the inside edge of the compass rose.

Selected heading shown by the magenta heading "bug" on the outer scale of the compass rose

Wind speed and direction are shown in the lower left corner orientated to the display selection (Heading or Track, Magnetic or True)

Weather Radar displays are not available.

22.15   EXPANDED VOR

With a VOR frequency selected, the EHSI displays about 90^0 of compass rose with the VOR source in the lower left and the frequency in the lower right.

The white triangle at the bottom of the display is the aircraft symbol

Selected course (track) is displayed by the magenta course needle the tip pointing to the selected course (150). The course selectors are usually on either side of the autoflight main control panel (one for the Captain and one for the First Officer). Course deviation is shown by the traditional deviation bar moving across a two dot left and two dot right scale.

A TO /FROM annunciation is shown.

DME distance displayed in the top left corner

Current heading is shown in the window and by the lubber line at the top of the compass rose (130), the current selection is Magnetic Heading as shown either side of the track window Current track is shown by the white line from the tip of the aircraft symbol to the compass arc.

Selected heading shown by the magenta heading "bug" on the outer scale of the compass rose Wind speed and direction are shown in the lower left corner orientated to the display selection (Heading or Track, Magnetic or True).

Weather Radar displays are available, when selected "on" range arcs are also visible. Weather Radar shows three colours green, yellow and red, green being the least turbulence, red being the worst. If turbulence mode is available it is shown as magenta, the area of greatest activity in the cloud. The range of the display can be selected on the control panel, half scale range is displayed (10 Nm) so this display is selected to 20 Nm. The outer arc of the compass rose is the furthest range from the aircraft.

22.16 FULL ILS MODE

With an ILS frequency selected, the EHSI displays a full compass rose with the ILS source in the lower left and the frequency in the lower right.

Course selection (Localiser) is displayed by the magenta course needle the tip pointing to the selected course (150). Localiser deviation is shown by the traditional deviation bar moving across a two dot left and two dot right scale.

Glide slope deviation shown by a magenta coloured triangle moving up and down the traditional scale on the right hand side.

DME distance displayed in the top left corner

Current heading is shown in the window and by the lubber line at the top of the compass rose (130), the current selection is Magnetic Heading as shown either side of the window

Current track is shown by the white triangle on the inside edge of the compass rose.

Selected heading shown by the magenta heading "bug" on the outer scale of the compass rose

Wind speed and direction are shown in the lower left corner orientated to the display selection (Heading or Track, Magnetic or True).

Weather Radar displays are not available.

22.17 EXPANDED ILS

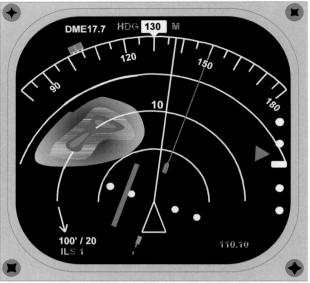

With an ILS frequency selected, the EHSI displays about 90^0 of compass rose with the ILS source in the lower left and the frequency in the lower right.

The white triangle at the bottom of the display is the aircraft symbol.

Selected course (track) is displayed by the magenta course needle the tip pointing to the selected course (150). The course selectors are usually on either side of the autoflight main control panel (one for the Captain and one for the First Officer). Localiser deviation is shown by the traditional deviation bar moving across a two dot left and two dot right scale. Glide slope deviation shown on the right again in the traditional fashion.

DME distance displayed in the top left corner.

Current heading is shown in the window and by the lubber line at the top of the compass rose. In this case is the heading is 130^0 Magnetic, as indicated by markings either side of the window. Current track is shown by the white line from the tip of the aircraft symbol to the inside edge of the compass rose.

Selected heading shown by the magenta heading "bug" on the outer scale of the compass rose. Wind speed and direction are shown in the lower left corner orientated to the display selection (Heading or Track, Magnetic or True).

Weather Radar displays are available, when selected "on" range arcs are also visible. Weather Radar is shown in three colours green, yellow and red, green being the least turbulence, red being the worst. If **TURBULENCE MODE** is available it is shown as magenta, the area of greatest activity in the cloud.

The range of the display can be selected on the control panel, half scale range is displayed (10 Nm) so this display is selected to 20 Nm. The outer arc of the compass rose is the furthest range from the aircraft.

22.18 MAP MODE

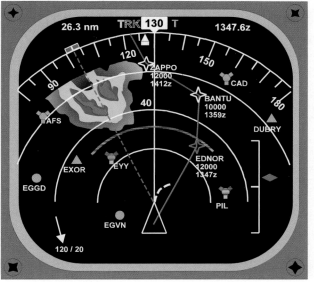

The mode used normally is the **MAP** display, which, in conjunction with the flight plan data programmed into a flight management computer, displays information against a moving map background with all elements to a common scale.

The symbol representing the aircraft is at the lower part of the display, and an arc of the compass scale, or rose, covering 45 degrees on either side of the instantaneous track, is at the upper part of the display.

Heading information is supplied by the appropriate inertial reference system and the compass rose is automatically referenced to magnetic North (via a crew-operated **MAG/TRUE** selector switch) when between latitudes 73°N and 65°S, and to true North when above these latitudes. When the selector switch is set at **TRUE** the compass rose is referenced to true North regardless of latitude.

The aircraft active route as derived from the FMC is shown as a magenta coloured line joining the waypoints. The **active waypoint** (the one the aircraft is currently navigating towards) is shown as a magenta coloured star. The other waypoints making up the active route are called **inactive waypoints** and are shown as a white star. Both identified by name.

Distance to next waypoint and time at next waypoint are shown at the top of the display Weather Radar (WXR) return data and range arcs are displayed when the WXR switch is on. Turbulence mode (+T) may be available as previously described
Indications of other data such as wind speed and direction, lateral and vertical deviations from the selected flight path are also displayed.

The flight management computer (FMC) can predict events by combining current ground speed and lateral acceleration to show a display of either a curved trend vector, white, (during turns) or a range to altitude arc, green, (during climb or descent) . Off route waypoints, Airports , Nav aids can all be shown in their relative position to the aircraft's progress and selected range. Additional waypoint information can be displayed when selected, Altitude, Time etc.

22.19   PLAN MODE.

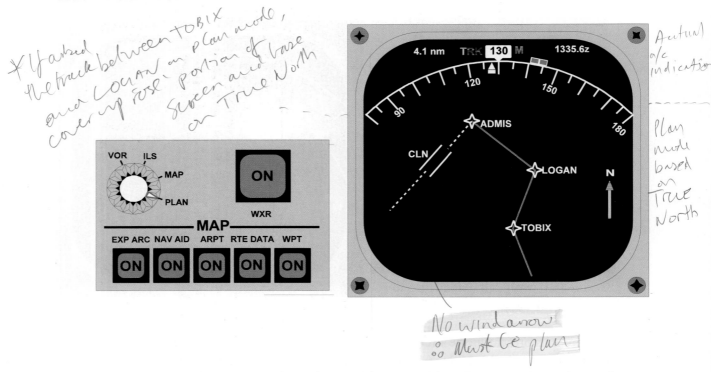

[handwritten note: If asked between TOBIX and LOGAN on Plan mode, cover up "rose" portion of base screen and True North]

[handwritten note: Actual a/c indication]

[handwritten note: Plan mode based on True North]

[handwritten note: No wind arrow ∴ Must be plan]

In **'PLAN'** mode a **static** map background is used with active route data orientated to **true north**. Any changes to the route may be selected at the keyboard of the Flight Management Computer, and the display shown on the **EHSI,** so they can be checked before they are entered into the FMC.

The top portion of the EHSI remains the same as in the map mode.

This mode allows the pilot to review the planned route by using the FMC / CDU LEGS page.

Weather Radar display data is inhibited.

No wind speed or direction information

22.20   DATA SOURCE SELECTION.

In the type of system described earlier, means are provided whereby the pilots can independently of each other, connect their respective display units to alternate sources of input data through a data source switch panel. e.g. the left or right Air Data Computer (ADC), the Flight Management Computers (FMC), the Flight Control Computers (FCC), and the Standby Inertial Reference Systems (IRS).

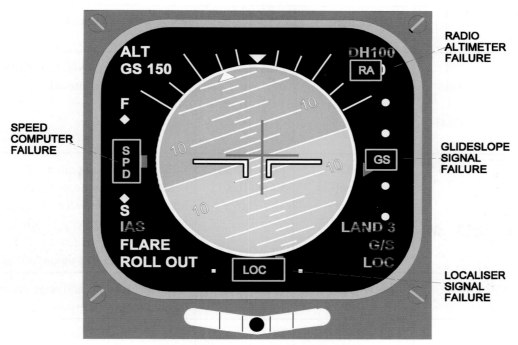

Figure 22.11. Failure Indications.

22.21   FAILURE ANNUNCIATION.

The failure of data signals from such systems as the ILS and radio altimeter is displayed on each EADI and EHSI in the form of yellow flags 'painted' at specific matrix locations on their CRT screens.

In addition, fault messages may also be displayed, for example, if the associated flight management computer and weather radar range disagree with the control panel range data, the discrepancy message 'WXR/MAP RANGE DISAGREE' appears on the EHSI.

Annex A. NAVIGATION DISPLAYS

The following symbols can be displayed on each HSI depending on EFI Control Panel switch selection. Symbols can be displayed with different colours but the general colour presentation is as follows:

GREEN (G)	-	engaged flight mode displays, dynamic conditions.
WHITE (W)	-	present status situation, scales, armed flight mode displays
MAGENTA (M)(pink)	-	command information, pointers, symbols, fly-to condition
CYAN (C)(blue)	-	non-active and background information
RED (R)	-	warning
AMBER (A)	-	cautionary information, faults, flags
BLACK (B)	-	blank areas, display "off"

Symbol	Name	Applicable Modes	Remarks
200nm / 4.4nm or DME 124 / DME 24.6	Distance Display (W)	PLAN, MAP or VOR, ILS	Distance is displayed to next FMC Waypoint(nm) or tuned Navaid(DME).
HDG 263 M	HEADING Orientation(G) Indicator(W) Reference(G)	PLAN, MAP VOR, ILS	Indicates number under pointer is a heading - box indicates actual heading. Referenced to Magnetic North between 60deg South and 73deg North if selected and True North when above those latitudes.
0835.4z	ETA Display (M) & (W)	PLAN, MAP	Indicates ETA at active Waypoint based on current ground speed.
	Selected Heading Marker(M)	PLAN, MAP VOR, ILS	Indicates the heading set in the MCP. A dotted line(M) extends from the marker to the aeroplane symbol for ease in tracking the marker when it is out of view (except plan mode).
	Expanded Compass Rose(W)	PLAN, MAP VOR, ILS	Compass Data is provided by the selected IRS (360deg available but approximately 70deg are displayed)
	Full Compass Rose(W)	Full VOR, Full ILS	Compass Data is provided by the selected IRS.
80	Present Track Line and Range Scale	MAP VOR, ILS	Predicts Ground Track which will result with present heading and winds. Displayed Range Mark is one-half the actual selected range.
	Aeroplane Symbol(W)	MAP VOR, ILS	Represents the aeroplane and indicates its position at the apex of the triangle.

	Aeroplane Symbol(W)	Full VOR, Full ILS	Represents the aeroplane and indicates its position at the centre of the symbol.
AMBOY	Waypoint Active(M) Inactive(W)	MAP, PLAN	Active - Represents the waypoint the aircraft is currently navigating to. Inactive - Represents a navigation point making up the selected active route.
	Altitude Range Arc(G)	MAP	When intersected with the track line, it predicts the point where the reference altitude will be reached.
	Trend Vector	MAP	Predicts aeroplane directional trend at the end of 30, 60 and 90 second intervals. Based on bank angle and ground speed. Three segments are displayed when selected range is greater than 30nm, two on the 20nm and one segment when on the 10nm scale.
AMBOY KILMR PARBY ARO	Active Route(M) Active Route Mod's(W) Inactive Route(C)	MAP, PLAN	The active route is displayed with continuous lines(M) between waypoints. Active route modifications are displayed with short dashes(W) between waypoints. When a change is activated in the FMC, the short dashes are replaced by a continuous line. Inactive routes are displayed with long dashes(C) between waypoints.
	Vertical Pointer(M) and Deviation Scale(W)	MAP	Displays vertical deviation from selected vertical profile(pointer) in MAP mode during descent only. Scale indicates +/- 400ft deviation.

○ ○ ▷ ▭ ○ ○	Glide slope Pointer(M) and deviation Scale(W)	ILS	Displays Glide slope position and deviation in ILS mode.
△	Drift Angle Pointer(W)	Full VOR, Full ILS	Displays difference between FMC track angle and IRS heading.
↑ **120**	Wind Speed and Direction(W)	MAP, VOR, ILS	Indicates wind speed in knots and wind direction with respect to the map display orientation and compass reference.
(offset path symbol)	Offset Path and Identifier(M)	MAP, PLAN	Presents a dot-dash line parallel to and offset from the active route after selection on the FMC CDU.
N ↑	North Pointer(G)	PLAN	Indicates map background is orientated and referenced to true north.
○ **T / D**	Altitude Profile Point and Identifier(G)	MAP	Represents an FMC calculated point and is labelled on the flight plan path as" T/C" (top of climb), "T/D" (top of descent) and "S/C" (step climb).
(weather radar return symbol)	Weather Radar Returns Mapping Radar Returns (both G,A,R)	MAP, VOR, ILS	Multicoloured returns are presented when either "WXR ON" switch is pushed. Most intense regions are displayed in Red, lesser Amber lowest intensity Green.

22.22 EXAMPLE DISPLAYS

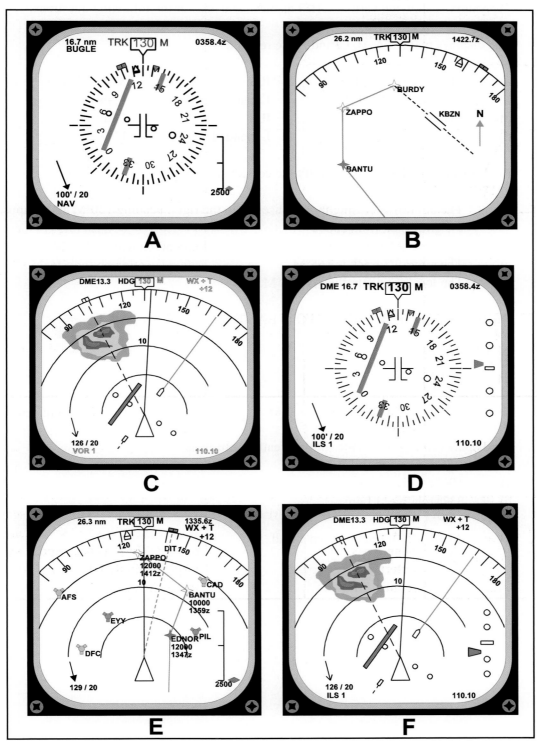

Figure 8.6

EFIS

Refer to Appendix A showing various EHSI displays and answer the following questions:

1.   The displays marked A, B, C, and D are respectively:

a)	Plan	Map	ILS	VOR
b)	VOR	ILS	Expanded ILS	Plan
c)	Map	VOR	ILS	Plan
d)	Map	ILS	Expanded VOR	Plan

2.   Refer display marked E and identify the correct statement:

   a)   The aircraft is closing the localiser from the right, heading 130°M and is approaching the glide path from above
   b)   When established on the localiser the inbound heading will be 165°M.
   c)   The aircraft's track is 165°M
   d)   The localiser centre line is 133°M.

3.   On display D the track from ZAPPO to BANTU is:

   a)   310°M
   b)   130°T
   c)   360°M
   d)   180°T

4.   On display centre C the centre of the weather returns is:

   a)   106° relative, 18 nm
   b)   332° relative, 13 nm
   c)   100°M, 130 nm
   d)   30 nm left of track, 15 nm ahead.

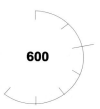

600

5.   The above data shown on the (i)............ is displaying (ii)........... and (iii)............

	(i)	(ii)	(iii)
a)	Primary Flight Display	600 kt TAS	200ft RA
b)	Navigation Display	600ft RA	200ft DH
c)	EADI	600ft Radio Altitude	200ft Decision Height
d)	EHSI	600 kt GS	200ft AGL

6.

This yellow symbol appears in place of the normal radio altitude display when:

a)   the selected radio altitude has been reached
b)   the radio altitude needs re-setting on the EHSI
c)   there is a failure of the radio altimeter
d)   the aircraft descents below 1000ft AGL.

7.

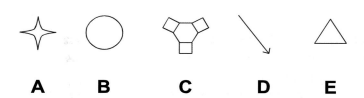

A   B   C   D   E

The above symbols A, C, and E are best described respectively as:

a)   off route waypoint, airport navigation aid.
b)   next waypoint, navigation aid, airport.
c)   off route waypoint, navigation aid, a navigation point making up selected route.
d)   active waypoint aircraft currently navigating to, navigation aid, off route waypoint.

8.   When using EHSI, weather radar may be displayed on following settings:

      a)   map, VOR/ILS.
      b)   VOR/ILS, map, expanded plan.
      c)   expanded map, VOR/ILS, plan.
      d)   map, expanded VOR/ILS.

9.   WXR display is controlled from:

      a)   captains EHSI control only.
      b)   co-pilots EHSI control only.
      c)   a special control panel.
      d)   both captains and co-pilots EHSI control panels.

10.   Decision height is adjusted and set on the:

      a)   flight management computer.
      b)   HSI section of the EFIS control panel.
      c)   ADI section of the EFIS control panel.
      d)   ADI or HSI

11.   WXR display is on:

      a)   the captains CRT only.
      b)   the co-pilots CRT only.
      c)   a special screen.
      d)   on both the captains and co-pilots CRTs.

12.   Airspeed is shown:

      a)   only on the captains EHSI.
      b)   on both EADIs.
      c)   on both EHSIs.
      d)   only on the flight management CRT.

13.   With an EFIS flight director using IRS guidance, reference north can be:

      a)   magnetic north only.
      b)   magnetic north between 73°Nth and 65°Sth and true north above these latitudes.
      c)   magnetic north between 65°Nth and 73°Sth and true north above these latitudes.
      d)   magnetic north between 75°Nth and 75°Sth and true north above these latitudes.

14.   Modes available for (EFIS) HSI on some units are:

        a)   airspeed and Mach.
        b)   MAP and PLAN.
        c)   VOR, ILS, MAP and AUTO TRIM.
        d)   only from manometric sources.

15.   The EFIS symbols for a navaid and enroute waypoint are:

        a)

 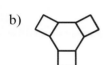

        b)

        c)

        d)

16.   An EFIS as well as having a control panel, symbol generators and a remote light sensor also has:

        a)   EADIS and EHSIs
        b)   EHSIs and altitude indicator
        c)   EADIs and EICAs
        d)   EADI and WXR display tubes.

ANNEX A

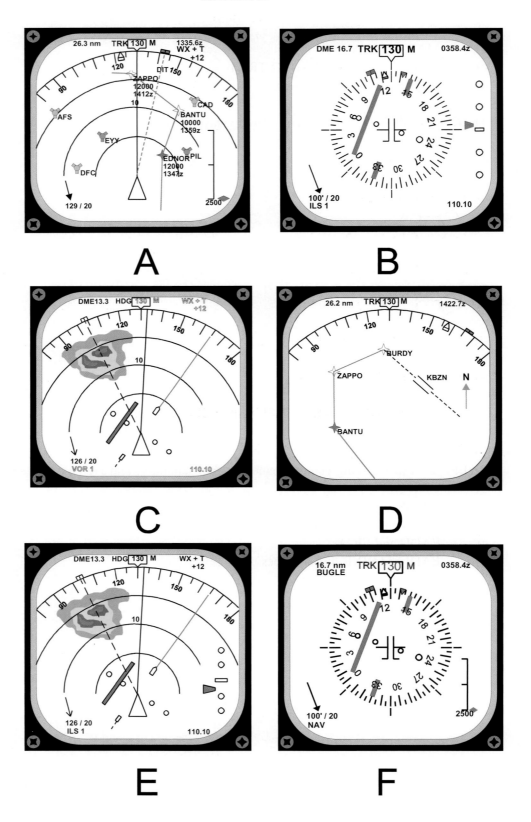

CHAPTER TWENTY THREE - OBJECTIVE REVISION QUESTIONS

Contents

	Page
OBJECTIVE REVISION NO.1	23 - 1
OBJECTIVE REVISION NO 2	23 - 7
OBJECTIVE REVISION NO 3	23 - 13
OBJECTIVE REVISION NO 4	23 - 19
OBJECTIVE REVISION NO 5	23 - 25
OBJECTIVE REVISION NO 6	23 - 31
OBJECTIVE REVISION NO 7	23 - 37
OBJECTIVE REVISION NO 8	23 - 42
ANSWERS TO OBJECTIVE REVISION PAPERS	23 - 51
ANSWERS TO END OF CHAPTER QUESTIONS	23 - 53

OBJECTIVE REVISION

OBJECTIVE REVISION NO.1

1.   A partially blocked air filter will cause the air-driven turn indicator to:

   a)   under read the correct rate of turn.
   b)   over read the correct rate of turn.
   c)   read in the reverse sense.
   d)   indicate zero rate of turn.

2.   An uncorrected gyro is set to read 356° in an aircraft which is stationary on the ground in latitude 50N. The reading after 1 hr 45 mins is:

   a)   339.10
   b)   016.10
   c)   012.90
   d)   335.90

3.   The rotor in an air driven Artificial Horizon rotates anti-clockwise when viewed from above. On the aircraft accelerating, ... will cause the bottom of the rotor axis to lag, resulting in a .... wing .... indication.
   The correct words to complete the above statement are:

   a)   inertia   port   up
   b)   inertia   starboard   up
   c)   precession   port   down
   d)   precession   starboard   down

4.   An aircraft is climbing at a constant Mach No. below the tropopause in ISA conditions. During the climb the CAS will:

   a)   decrease due to decreasing density error.
   b)   increase due to falling temperature.
   c)   decrease due to increasing density error.
   d)   increase due to the LSS decreasing.

5.   An aircraft is flying at FL 390, temperature 207A, at Mach 0.85. The TAS of the aircraft is:

   a)   561
   b)   476
   c)   485
   d)   472

6.   The rate of precession of a gyro varies:

	APPLIED FORCE	ROTOR SPEED	ROTOR MASS
a)	directly	inversely	inversely
b)	directly	inversely	directly
c)	inversely	directly	inversely
d)	inversely	directly	directly

7. An aircraft flying at a constant FL and maintaining a constant TAS flies into an area of warmer air. The air density is .... causing the CAS to ....

   a)   increasing   decrease
   b)   decreasing   increase
   c)   decreasing   decrease
   d)   increasing   increase

8. Referring to the turn and slip indicator shown, the indications are that a 90° turn will be completed in .... secs and there is .... bank for the ....

   a)   more than 15 secs   too much   G factor
   b)   more then 30 secs   too little   radius of turn
   c)   less than 15 secs   too little   TAS
   d)   less than 30 secs   too much   IAS

9. In a climb the pitot line becomes blocked. The vertical speed indicator (VSI) will indicate:

   a)   the original rate of climb.
   b)   too high a rate of climb.
   c)   too low a rate of climb.
   d)   zero.

10. An aircraft accelerates on a westerly heading in the N. hemisphere. The compass needle rotates .... indicating a turn towards ....

    a)   clockwise   north
    b)   anti-clockwise   north
    c)   clockwise   south
    d)   anti-clockwise   south

11. An aircraft is passing 6,500 ft in a descent when the static line becomes blocked. The altimeter then reads:

a)   6,500 ft
b)   less than 6,500 ft
c)   more than 6,500 ft
d)   zero

12.   In high speed flight at high altitude the static source will suffer:

a)   barometric error
b)   lag
c)   temperature error
d)   position error

13.   An increase of 0.15 in Mach number results in an increase of 93 kt in TAS. If the temperature deviation from ISA is +9°C, the FL is:

a)   FL 200
b)   FL 220
c)   FL 170
d)   FL 90

14.   In a stable platform, north referenced INS, the mean groundspeed is 550 kt. After 21.1 mins the indicated groundspeed was over reading by 5 kt. The indicated groundspeed after 63.3 minutes was:

a)   550 kt
b)   545 kt
c)   555 kt
d)   565 kt

15.   A VSI metering unit incorporates a capillary tube to compensate for:

a)   barometric error.
b)   position error.
c)   temperature and pressure changes with height.
d)   viscosity changes.

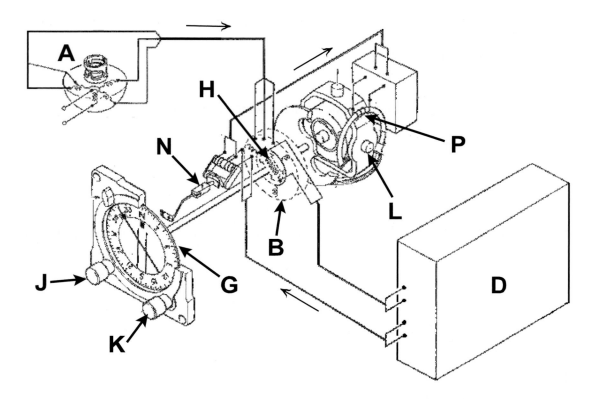

16.   In the above diagram of a gyro magnetic compass, the components labelled B, H and D in order are:

    a)   flux valve   inductive pick-off   servo motor
    b)   signal selsyn   rotor   amplifier
    c)   stators   rotor   two way motor
    d)   servo motor   stator   amplifier

17.   If the pitot line becomes blocked in the descent, the ASI will indicate:

    a)   an increasing CAS
    b)   a decreasing CAS
    c)   a steady CAS
    d)   zero

18.   A gyroscope which utilises gravity to control a vertical reference is termed a:

    a)   tied gyro
    b)   space gyro
    c)   earth gyro
    d)   rate gyro

19.   The product of the first integration of the E/W acceleration sensed by an INS system is:

      a)   departure

      b)   speed along the local parallel

      c)   speed along the local vertical

      d)   distance.

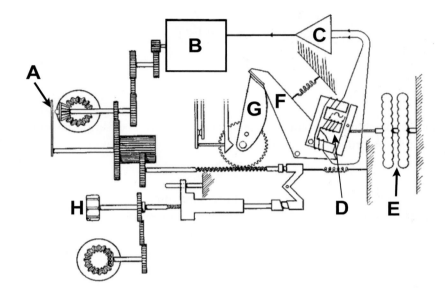

20.   In the above diagram of a servo altimeter the components labelled B, C and D in order are:

	B	C	D
a)	torque motor	inductive pick-off	amplifier
b)	torque motor	amplifier	transducer
c)	two way motor	amplifier	inductive pick-off
d)	two way motor	inductive pick-off	transducer

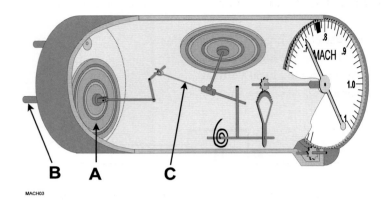

MACH03

21.   With reference to the above diagram of a machmeter, the correct descriptions of the components labelled A, B and C in order are;

	A	B	C
a)	airspeed capsule	pitot pressure entry	ratio arm
b)	airspeed capsule	dynamic pressure entry	ranging arm
c)	altitude capsule	static pressure entry	ranging arm
d)	altitude capsule	static pressure entry	ratio arm

OBJECTIVE REVISION NO 2

1.   Refer to Appendix A. Figure C is a diagram of:

      a)   an altimeter
      b)   a vertical speed indicator
      c)   a machmeter
      d)   an air speed indicator

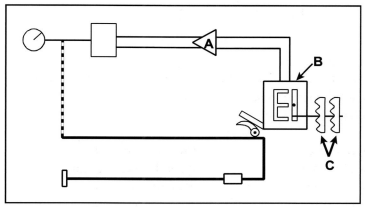

Figure 1.

2.   Figure 1. Is a diagram of a servo-altimeter. The correct description of the components labelled A, B and C in order are:

a)	capsule stack	cam	inductive pick-off
b)	amplifier	cam	inductive pick-off
c)	amplifier	transducer	capsule stack
d)	two-phase motor	transducer	inductive pick-off

3.   The restricted choke in the VSI:

      a)   will prevent the instrument being damaged by high rates of climb and descent.
      b)   compensates for changes in temperature and density only.
      c)   creates a differential pressure between the capsule and the case as its main function.
      d)   compensates for time lag in the instrument.

4.   An aircraft is flying at a constant CAS. If the ambient temperature ...., the TAS will
.... due to .... The words to correctly complete the above statement are:

a)	falls	fall	decreasing density.
b)	rises	rise	increasing density.
c)	rises	rise	decreasing density.
d)	falls	fall	decreasing pressure.

5.   The latitude correcting device of an air driven directional gyro is:

       a)   an adjustable weight attached to the outer gimbal of the DI.
       b)   an adjustable weight attached to the inner gimbal of the DI.
       c)   the air jet which drives the rotor.
       d)   a chamber with four exit slots half covered by pendulous vanes.

6.   Refer to Appendix A (Page 23 - 11). Figure D is a diagram of:

       a)   an altimeter.
       b)   a vertical speed indicator.
       c)   a machmeter.
       d)   an air speed indicator.

7.   An uncorrected gyro is set to read 100°. The gyro reading after 45 minutes when stationary on the ground in latitude 25°S is:

       a)   106.3°
       b)   104.8°
       c)   093.7°
       d)   095.3°

8.   If the static source to an altimeter becomes blocked during a descent, the instrument:

       a)   will over read by a constant amount.
       b)   continues to show the height at which the blockage occurred.
       c)   will progressively under read.
       d)   pointer will return to indicate a height equivalent to the sub-scale setting.

9.   An electrical Artificial Horizon employs .... and .... to maintain its position in relation to ....
       Select the line of phrases given below that would complete the above statement correctly:

       a)   erection chamber   pendulous vanes   space
       b)   fast erect buttons   micro switches   local longitude
       c)   mercury switches   torque motors   the local vertical
       d)   precession circuit   torque motor   azimuth

10.   Refer to the following diagram of a gyro magnetic compass system. The correct description of the components labelled A, B and C in order are:

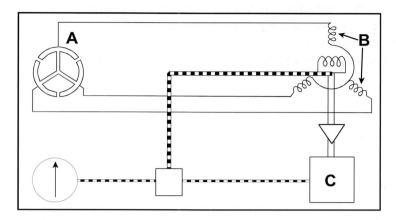

a)	flux valve system	stators	gyro unit
b)	synchronising unit	stators	motor
c)	signal selsyn	stators	follow-up motor
d)	stator system	rotor	gyro unit

11.   Refer to Appendix A (Page 23 - 11). Figure B is a diagram of:

a)   an altimeter
b)   a vertical speed indicator
c)   a machmeter
d)   an air speed indicator

12.   Refer to Appendix A (Page 23 - 11). Figure A is a diagram of:

a)   an altimeter
b)   a vertical speed indicator
c)   a machmeter
d)   an air speed indicator

13.   The product of the first integration of the output from the N/S accelerometer in INS equipment is:

a)   departure
b)   latitude
c)   velocity along the local meridian
d)   distance along the local meridian

14.   The principle of operation of the turn and slip indicator is best described as:

a)   a space gyro which uses the force of precession against a spring to give a reading of the aircraft rate of turn.

b)   a single gimbal gyroscope whose primary precession is opposed by a spring which, in turn, produces a second precession equal and opposite to the aircraft rate of turn.

c)   a single gimbal gyroscope in which a spring, opposing the primary precession, in turn produces a secondary precession equal to the aircraft rate of turn.

d)   an earth gyro in which a calibrated spring ensures the tilt of the gyro is proportional to the aircraft rate of turn.

15.   An aircraft is descending at a constant Mach No. through an isothermal layer. The CAS of the aircraft will:

a)   decrease.

b)   remain the same.

c)   increase.

d)   decrease quickly initially and then remain the same.

16.   With reference to a `north referenced' inertial navigation system (INS), `gyro compassing' is:

a)   the process by which the inertial platform is aligned with magnetic north during the ALIGN phase.

b)   carried out in the STANDBY mode by aligning the platform using the aircraft gyromagnetic compass system to define true north.

c)   the process by which the platform is levelled and aligned with true north using the earths gravity, in the ALIGN mode.

d)   the process by which the platform is maintained in correct alignment with true north during flight.

17.   When accelerating on a westerly heading in the northern hemisphere, the magnet assembly of a direct reading magnetic compass, when viewed from above, will:

a)   turn clockwise indicating an apparent turn towards the north.

b)   turn anti-clockwise indicating an apparent turn towards the north.

c)   turn clockwise indicating an apparent turn towards the south.

d)   turn anti-clockwise indicating an apparent turn towards the south.

APPENDIX 'A'

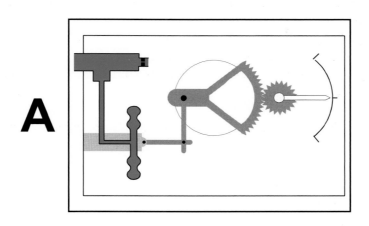

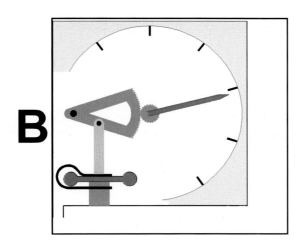

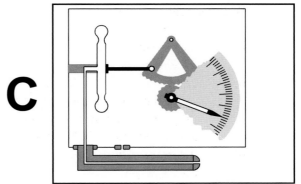

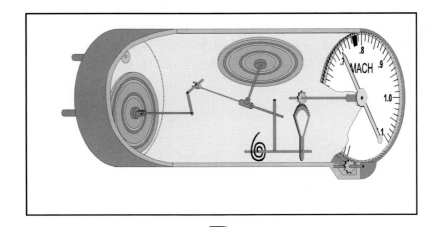

OBJECTIVE REVISION NO 3

1.   An aircraft is flying at mach 0.86, temperature 218 Kelvin. The TAS is:

      a)   494 kt
      b)   477 kt
      c)   607 kt
      d)   575 kt

2.   Compressibility error is caused by a false .... of .... pressure, requiring a ....
correction to the CAS to obtain EAS. The words to correctly complete the sentence above are:

      a)   decrease   pitot   positive
      b)   increase   dynamic   negative
      c)   decrease   dynamic   positive
      d)   increase   static   negative

3.   The subscale of an altimeter is set to 1030 mb and indicates 4500 ft when the QNH is 996 mb.
Assuming 1 mb equals 30 ft, the true height of the aircraft AMSL is:

      a)   3180 ft
      b)   3990 ft
      c)   5520 ft
      d)   3480 ft

4.   An uncorrected DGI is set to read 339° when stationary on the ground in latitude 59N. The
reading after 36 minutes will be:

      a)   346.7°
      b)   331.3°
      c)   326.1°
      d)   351.9°

5.   During the take-off run, the air driven artificial horizon will indicate:

      a)   a climb due to the pendulosity of the inner gimbal.
      b)   a climb due to the action of the pendulous vanes.
      c)   a right turn due to the pendulosity of the outer gimbal.
      d)   a right turn due to the action of the pendulous vanes.

6.   If a simple flux valve lies .... the earths field the current induced in the pick-off coil will
        be .... and the frequency will be .... the input frequency. The words to correctly
        complete the sentence above are:

        a)   in line with   minimum   twice
        b)   at 90° to   minimum   half
        c)   at 90° to   maximum   half
        d)   inline with   maximum   twice

7.   Refer to the diagram below of a servo altimeter. The correct descriptions of the components
        labelled A, B and C in order are:

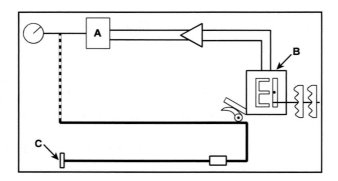

        a)   indicator   transducer   cam
        b)   two-way motor   transducer   sub-scale setting knob
        c)   amplifier   two-way motor   cam and follower
        d)   two-way motor   follower   sub-scale setting knob

8.   In the VSI, viscosity:

        a)   affects the capillary tube in the restricted choke.
        b)   affects the knife edge orifice in the restricted choke.
        c)   affects the bi-metallic strip and compensating spring.
        d)   is compensated for by resetting the VSI to read zero on the ground before take-off.

9.   The precession of a gyroscope varies:

        a)   directly with the applied force and directly with the inertia of the rotor.
        b)   indirectly with the applied force and indirectly with the inertia of the rotor.
        c)   directly with the applied force and indirectly with the inertia of the rotor.
        d)   indirectly with the applied force and directly with the inertia of the rotor.

10.   In Figure 3.2., the turn and slip indicator is showing a turn of:

    a)   6°/sec with too much bank for the TAS.
    b)   3°/sec with too little bank for the TAS.
    c)   3°/sec with too much bank for the TAS.
    d)   6°/sec with too little bank for the TAS.

Figure 3.2.

11.   The air driven artificial horizon uses .... gyroscope which is
       maintained .... by means of ....
       The words which correctly complete the above sentence are:

    a)   a free   horizontal   case levelling
    b)   an earth   vertical   pendulous vanes.
    c)   a space   horizontal   a pitch-bank erection system.
    d)   an earth   vertical   torque motors

12.   The corrections fed to the platform gimbal motors of a north referenced inertial navigation system
       during the ALIGN mode use inputs from:

    a)   the latitude setting, the accelerometers.
    b)   the longitude setting, the latitude setting, the air data computer.
    c)   the latitude setting, the longitude setting, the accelerometers.
    d)   all the factors mentioned in (a), (b) and (c) above.

13.   In the diagram below of a mach meter, the parts labelled A, B and C are in order:

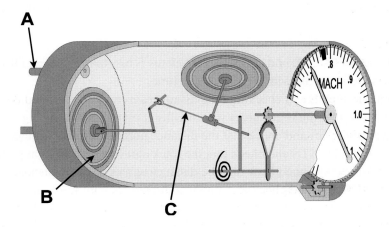

    a)   pitot entry   altimeter capsule   ranging arm
    b)   static entry   altimeter capsule   ratio arm
    c)   static entry   ASI capsule   ratio arm
    d)   pitot entry   ASI capsule   ranging arm

14.   In a turn from 045° to 315° through north in the northern hemisphere, the movement of the magnet system of a direct reading compass, when viewed from above and the effect of liquid swirl on the error caused by the movement are:

	MAGNET SYSTEM	LIQUID SWIRL
a)	anticlockwise	reduce
b)	clockwise	increase
c)	anticlockwise	increase
d)	clockwise	reduce

15.   The rotor of the pitch correction motor of the electrical artificial horizon is on:

a)   the outer gimbal.
b)   the inner gimbal.
c)   the instrument case.
d)   the top of the gyro unit.

16.   An aircraft flying at FL 100 and at a constant CAS, flies from an area of warm air into an area of cold air. Assuming the QNH is the same during the change of temperature, the aircraft height AMSL and the TAS will have:

	Height AMSL	TAS
a)	decreased	increased
b)	increased	increased
c)	decreased	decreased
d)	increased	decreased

17.   Two checks that can be carried out to check that two selected sequential waypoints have been entered correctly are:

a)   select DSR.TK/STS and check that the status is less than 4: select DIS/TIME and check that the time agrees with the flight plan time.

b)   select DIS/TIME and check that the distance agrees with the distance on the flight plan: then check that the time agrees with the flight plan time for the leg.

c)   select DIS/TIME and check that the distance agrees with the distance on the flight plan: select DSR.TK/STS and check that the track agrees with the flight plan track for the leg.

d)   select DIS/TIME and check that the distance agrees with the distance on the flight plan: select HDG/DA and check that the heading agrees with the flight plan heading for the leg.

18. An aircraft is climbing at a constant Mach number. Assuming the temperature is ISA, the CAS will:

    a)   rise due to TAS increasing with falling density.
    b)   fall due to density decreasing due to the increase in local speed of sound.
    c)   rise due to the decreasing pressure.
    d)   fall due to the increasing density error.

19. The main function of the annunciator in a gyro-magnetic compass is:

    a)   to keep the gyro unit aligned with the earths field.
    b)   to maintain the gyro unit horizontal.
    c)   to indicate correct functioning of the compass system.
    d)   to ensure correct alignment with compass north.

OBJECTIVE REVISION NO 4

1. An aircraft is descending at a constant mach number. If the aircraft is descending through an inversion layer, the CAS will:

    a)   remain constant.
    b)   increase.
    c)   decrease.
    d)   decrease then decrease more slowly.

2. Equivalent airspeed (EAS) is:

    a)   IAS corrected for compressibility.
    b)   IAS corrected for instrument error only.
    c)   CAS corrected for compressibility.
    d)   CAS corrected for position error.

3. The computer of a north referenced Inertial Navigation System (INS) in flight, provides compensation for:

    a)   aircraft manoeuvres, real wander, apparent wander, transport wander.
    b)   Coriolis, real wander, apparent wander, transport wander.
    c)   earth rotation, transport wander, Coriolis.
    d)   transport wander, apparent wander, Coriolis, magnetic variation.

4. The DI is set to read 100° in an aircraft stationary on the ground in latitude 45°N. The reading after 45 minutes will be:

    a)   102.50°
    b)   092.05°
    c)   097.78°
    d)   103.75°

5. If during a climb, the static source becomes blocked, the vertical speed indicator (VSI) will show:

    a)   a decreased rate of climb.
    b)   a zero rate of climb.
    c)   an increased rate of climb.
    d)   a normal rate of climb.

6. With reference to the altimeter, pressure fluctuations at the static vent cause:

    a)   Barometric error.
    b)   Temperature error.
    c)   Position error.
    d)   Hysteresis error.

The diagram below shows the situation after an aircraft, equipped with INS, has passed over way point 2 and is tracking along the line TK (dashed). Using the information given in the diagram, and the fact that with DA/HDG selected on the control and display unit (CDU) of the INS, the display shows 6L/080, answer the following two questions:

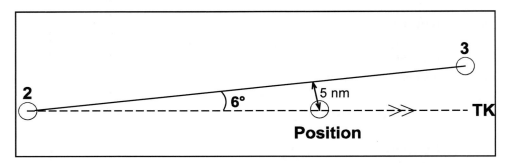

7.   When DSRTK/STS is selected on the CDU, the left window will show:

      a)   074
      b)   086
      c)   068
      d)   080

8.   When XTK/TKE is selected on the CDU, the display will show (to the nearest whole number):

	LEFT DISPLAY	RIGHT DISPLAY
a)	5L	080
b)	5R	6R
c)	5L	6L
d)	6R	5L

9.   Dynamic pressure is:

      a)   static pressure minus pitot pressure.
      b)   pitot pressure plus static pressure.
      c)   density and static pressure.
      d)   pitot pressure minus static pressure.

10.   When accelerating on an easterly heading in the N. Hemisphere, the magnet system of a direct reading magnetic compass will:

      a)   turn clockwise, indicating an apparent turn towards the north.
      b)   turn anti-clockwise, indicating an apparent turn towards the north.
      c)   turn clockwise, indicating an apparent turn towards the south.
      d)   turn anti-clockwise, indicating an apparent turn towards the south.

11.   In the diagram below of a gyromagnetic compass system, the components A, B and C in order are:

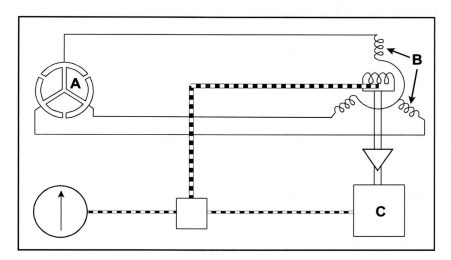

a)	flux valve	rotors	annunciator
b)	signal selsyn	stators	gyroscope unit
c)	flux valve	stators	gyroscope unit
d)	indicator	flux valve	amplifier

12.   The product of the second integration of the E/W accelerometer output in an INS system is:

    a)   longitude.
    b)   departure.
    c)   E/W acceleration.
    d)   E/W ground speed.

13.   Density varies:

    a)   directly with pressure and inversely with temperature.
    b)   directly with temperature and pressure.
    c)   inversely with temperature and pressure.
    d)   inversely with pressure and directly with temperature.

14.   An aircraft is flying at TAS of 1100 kt and FL 650. A change of 0.1 mach causes a change in TAS of 57 kt. The temperature deviation at FL 650 assuming an ISA atmosphere is:

    a)   -6
    b)   +6
    c)   -3
    d)   +3

15.   "The deviating effect of vertical soft iron (VSI) .... with decrease of magnetic latitude, due to the .... of H and the .... of Z".
The line containing the words to correctly complete the above statement is:

    a)   increase   decrease   increase
    b)   decrease   increase   decrease
    c)   decreases   increase   increase
    d)   increases   decrease   decrease.

16.   Angle of attack may be sensed by means of..................mounted..............

    a)   a stick pusher, adjacent to the flying controls.
    b)   an indexer, in the flight director.
    c)   a conical slotted probe, on the wing leading edge.
    d)   a hinged vane sensor, on the wing leading edge.

17.   The speed at the upper end of the Green arc on the ASI is:

    a) V_{RA}
    b) V_{NO}
    c) V_{NE}
    d) V_{MC}

18.   "The rate gyro indicates the correct rate of turn when the .... precession due to the spring is .... to the .... rate of turn".
The line containing the words to correctly complete the above statement is:

    a)   secondary   equal   aircraft
    b)   torqued   opposite   primary
    c)   primary   balanced by and equal   aircraft
    d)   secondary   opposite   aircraft

19.   The servo altimeter is superior to the sensitive altimeter because:

    a)   it reduces barometric error.
    b)   it reduces high altitude error.
    c)   it reduces temperature error.
    d)   all of the above are correct.

20.   An aircraft is flying at FL 290, TAS 500 kt, mach number 0.86. The temperature deviation from ISA is:

    a)   -7
    b)   +7
    c)   -15
    d)   +25

21.   The advantages of the electrical artificial horizon over the air-driven artificial horizon are:

        a)   random wander eliminated - greater rigidity.
        b)   acceleration errors reduced - less rigidity.
        c)   greater rigidity - acceleration errors reduced - tuning errors reduced.
        d)   fast erection button fitted - quicker precession allowing faster indication - cut-out
                switches reduce turning errors.

22.   The rotor of a rate gyroscope is over speeding. The pilot carries out a turn with the rate
        gyroscope indicating Rate 1. The actual rate of turn will be:

        a)   3° per second.
        b)   more than 3° per second.
        c)   less than 3° per second.
        d)   6° per second.

OBJECTIVE REVISION NO 5

1.   The latitude nut of a directional indicator (DI) is on the .... gimbal and causes the gyroscope to precess around its .... axis. The correct words to complete the above sentence are:

> a)   inner   vertical
> b)   outer   vertical
> c)   inner   horizontal
> d)   outer   horizontal

2.   If the rpm of the rotor in a turn and slip indicator is higher than normal, the turn indicator will:

> a)   over read the correct rate of turn.
> b)   under read the correct rate of turn.
> c)   not indicate due to the increased rigidity.
> d)   indicate correctly.

3.   A space gyro has .... gimbal (s) and is .... so as to maintain alignment with ....

> a)   one   gravity   a horizontal earth reference
> b)   two   case levelled   the horizontal
> c)   one   uncontrolled   a fixed space reference
> d)   two   uncontrolled   a fixed space reference

4.   The rigidity (gyroscopic inertia) of a gyroscope may be increased by:

> a)   increasing the number of gimbals and decreasing the number of planes of rotation.
> b)   increasing the speed of rotation and decreasing the mass of the rotor.
> c)   increasing the speed of rotation and increasing the mass of the rotor.
> d)   decreasing the speed of rotation and increasing the mass of the rotor.

5.   An electrically driven artificial horizon considerably reduces the acceleration errors of the air driven variety by:

> a)   being less pendulous and more rigid.
> b)   being more rigid and incorporating erection system cut-out switches.
> c)   using mercury switches and torque motors.
> d)   increased gyro rpm and giving it the opposite rotation direction.

6.   A blockage in the static line to the VSI will subsequently cause the instrument to display:

> a)   a decreased rate of climb.
> b)   an increased rate of climb.
> c)   a zero rate of climb.
> d)   an increased rate of descent.

7.   Machmeter readings are subject to:

   a)   temperature error and pressure error.
   b)   density error and instrument error.
   c)   temperature error and density error.
   d)   instrument error and position error.

8.   In an INS which is Schuler tuned, the largest unbounded errors are:

   a)   due to the output of the first stage integrators.
   b)   due to the real wander of the platform gyroscopes.
   c)   due to accelerometer errors.
   d)   track errors due to initial misalignment.

9.   Temperature error in the altimeter is due to:

   a)   the difference between the actual mean temperature below the aircraft and the mean temperature that would be found in ISA.
   b)   the difference between the actual pressure setting and 1013.2mb.
   c)   inaccurate calibration of the temperature compensating device.
   d)   the ambient temperature at which the aircraft is flying.

10.   An aircraft fitted with a direct-reading compass is turning from 315° through north on to 045° in the southern hemisphere. The direction of turn of the magnet system and the effect of liquid swirl on the error due to the turn are:

	TURN	LIQUID SWIRL
a)	anti-clockwise	reduce
b)	clockwise	reduce
c)	anti-clockwise	increase
d)	clockwise	increase

11.   The inertial platform in a north-referenced inertial navigation system is torqued to perform like a Schuler pendulum, so that when the platform moves over the earth:

   a)   gyro drift errors are cancelled out.
   b)   the platform will always oscillate with respect to true north.
   c)   the platform remains level and aligned regardless of any aircraft accelerations.
   d)   answers b and c are correct.

An INS-equipped aircraft flies from 56° N 20° W (way point 3) to 56°N 30°W (way point 4). Use this information to answer the next two questions.

12.   The initial track at way point 3 is:

        a)   086° T
        b)   082° T
        c)   274° T
        d)   278° T

13.   With constant drift during flight the aircraft's heading will:

        a)   increase by more than 10°.
        b)   decrease by less than 10°.
        c)   increase by less than 10°.
        d)   remain constant.

14.   Refer to Figure 5.1. of a machmeter:

        The correct descriptions of the components labelled A, B and C in order, are:

        a)   pitot pressure entry; airspeed capsule; ratio arm.
        b)   static pressure entry; altimeter capsule; ranging arm.
        c)   dynamic pressure entry; airspeed capsule; ratio arm.
        d)   pitot pressure entry; altimeter capsule; ranging arm.

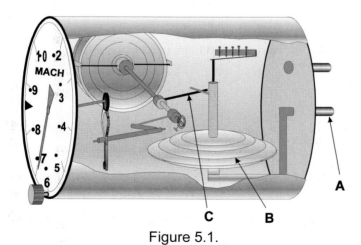

Figure 5.1.

15.   In an inertial-lead VSI the source of the most pronounced error is:

        a)   instrument.
        b)   position.
        c)   steep turn.
        d)   missed approach manoeuvre.

16.   If an aircraft descends from FL 310 at a constant CAS, the Mach No. will:

- a)   increase because the density error is increasing.
- b)   decrease because static pressure is decreasing.
- c)   decrease because density is increasing.
- d)   decrease because static pressure is increasing.

17.   In an inertial reference system the gyros and accelerometers are:

	GYROS	ACCELEROMETERS
a)	non-strap down	non-strap down
b)	strap down	strap down
c)	strap down	non-strap down
d)	non-strap down	strap down

18.   Equivalent Air Speed (EAS) is:

- a)   IAS corrected for compressibility.
- b)   CAS corrected for compressibility.
- c)   TAS corrected for compressibility.
- d)   TAS obtained from indicated Mach No. corrected for pressure and instrument error.

19.   In a turn and slip indicator the largest errors will be induced by:

- a)   yaw
- b)   angle of bank
- c)   primary torque
- d)   reduced spring tension

20.   If the pitot line becomes blocked during a climb the machmeter will:

- a)   be unaffected
- b)   under read
- c)   over read
- d)   under read by an increasingly erroneous amount.

21.   In a direct reading compass the maximum errors will occur when turning through:

- a)   N/S high latitudes
- b)   N/S low latitudes
- c)   E/W low latitudes
- d)   E/W high latitudes

22.   With reference to the flux valve of a gyromagnetic compass:

a)   the flux valve is pendulously mounted and is free to turn so that it remains aligned with the earth magnetic field.
b)   the flux valve is fixed to the aircraft and so turns with the aircraft to measure the angle between the aircraft and the earths magnetic field.
c)   the flux valve is not subject to acceleration errors.
d)   the flux valve is pendulously mounted and so is not affected by the vertical component of the earths magnetic field.

23.   The purpose of the annunciator circuit in a remote indicating compass is:

a)   to align the gyro unit with the aircraft heading suing the output from the rotor of the signal selsyn.
b)   to monitor the signals sent to the precession coil to ensure the gyro is turned the correct way to bring the rotor coil in line with the earths magnetic field.
c)   to indicate the correct way to turn the synchronising knob to initially synchronise the compass system and then to indicate correct operation of the system.
d)   to monitor the signals sent to the precession coil to ensure the gyro is turned the correct way to make its axis line up with the electrical field in the signal selsyn.

24.   If an increase of 0.15 Mach results in an increase of 93 kt TAS of an aircraft, the local speed of sound is:

a)   560 kt
b)   685 kt
c)   620 kt
d)   580 kt

25.   An increase of 0.15 Mach results in an increase of 93 kt TAS of an aircraft. If the temperature deviation from ISA is +5°C, the approximate flight level is:

a)   FL 200
b)   FL 150
c)   FL 220
d)   FL 250

26.   Total air temperature is:

a)   the temperature of air which has suffered the full effect of compression heating.
b)   the ambient air temperature.
c)   static air temperature minus ram air temperature.
d)   true outside air temperature allowing for cooling

27.   In Figure 5.2., a diagram of an electrical A/H gimbal system, the roll torque motor is in position:

a)   A
b)   B
c)   C
d)   D

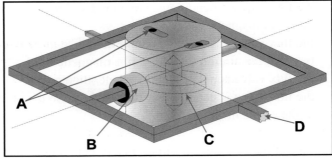

Figure 5.2.

28.   An aircraft is carrying out a rate one turn at a TAS of 480 kt. The diameter of the turn will be:

a)   2.5 nm
b)   15 nm
c)   5 nm
d)   10 nm

OBJECTIVE REVISION NO 6

1.   Total Air Temperature is:

   a)   the maximum temperature attainable by the air when brought to rest, adiabatically.
   b)   the temperature indicated on the air temperature thermometer plus the ram rise.
   c)   the static air temperature minus the recovery factor.
   d)   the recovery factor plus the ram rise.

2.   The difference between static air temperature and total air temperature is known as:

   a)   corrected outside air temperature.
   b)   the ram rise.
   c)   the recovery factor.
   d)   hot ramp radiation.

3.   An Air Data Computer has inputs of:

   a)   dynamic pressure, static pressure and air temperature.
   b)   pitot pressure, static pressure and static air temperature.
   c)   static pressure, pitot pressure and total air temperature.
   d)   dynamic pressure, static pressure and ram air temperature.

4.   The following symbols, A, C and E are best described respectively as:

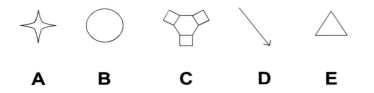

A   B   C   D   E

   a)   off route way point, airport, navigation aid.
   b)   next way point, navigation aid, airport.
   c)   off route way point, navigation aid, a navigation point making up selected route.
   d)   active way point aircraft currently navigating to, navigation aid, off-route way point.

5.   When using EHSI, weather radar may be displayed on following settings:

   a)   MAP, centre map, plan, nav, VOR/ILS.
   b)   VOR/ILS, map, nav, plan.
   c)   nav, map, VOR/ILS, plan.
   d)   expanded nav, map, expanded VOR/ILS.

6.   With reference to an EHSI, the mode in which the following symbols would be displayed is:

        a)   PLAN
        b)   VOR
        c)   MAP
        d)   ILS

7.   On the EHSI the following displays are available:

        a)   ETA to way point and distance to next way point.
        b)   airspeed and altitude.
        c)   way point and real drift.
        d)   pitch and roll attitude.

8.   An IRS with laser gyros should:
        (i)   .... be Schuler tuned, and (ii) .... be strapped down.

                        (i)   (ii)
        a)   always   always
        b)   always   never
        c)   never   always
        d)   never   never

9.   Ring laser gyros utilise a "Dither" motor to:

        a)   prevent "lock-in" of the laser beams.
        b)   to reduce real wander.
        c)   to prevent bounded errors.
        d)   to level and align the gyros.

10.   An INS in the "Align" mode will:

        a)   not accept an error of 10° latitude and 10° longitude of the inserted initial position.
        b)   accept error of 10° latitude and 10° of longitude of the inserted initial position.
        c)   accept an error of 10° latitude but not an error of 10° longitude of the inserted initial position.
        d)   will accept an error of 10° longitude but not 10° error of latitude in the initial inserted position.

11.   During initialisation of an INS the aircraft must not be moved until:

    a)   the ramp position has been inserted and checked.
    b)   the platform is levelled.
    c)   the gyros and the accelerometers are all in the "null" position.
    d)   the green "ready nav" light is illuminated and the mode selector switch has been set to the "nav" position.

12.   Select the correct statement:

    a)   EAS = CAS corrected for compressibility error.
    b)   EAS = IAS corrected for position error.
    c)   CAS = TAS corrected for density error.
    d)   TAS = EAS corrected for compressibility error.

13.   An altimeter is accurate to ± one millibar so at 20,000 feet and 40,000 feet it is accurate to:

	20,000	40,000
a)	± 30 feet	± 50 feet
b)	± 50 feet	± 100 feet
c)	± 100 feet	± 30 feet
d)	± 40 feet	± 75 feet

14.   An aircraft flies an altitude of 3500 feet from A, elevation 700 feet QNH 1015 mb to B, elevation 1120 feet QNH 992 mb. Assuming the altimeter sub-scale is not changed, the aircraft will arrive over B at a height:

    a)   3500 feet
    b)   2810 feet
    c)   1690 feet
    d)   2670 feet

15.   The IVSI reduces (i) .... error by use of (ii) ....

	(i)	(ii)
a)	time lag	dashpots
b)	instrument	jewelled bearings
c)	density	dashpots
d)	compressibility	restricted choke

16.   An aircraft turns left from 045°C to 315°C in the Southern Hemisphere. The magnets turn (i) and liquid swirls (ii) causing the error.

	(i)	(ii)
a)	clockwise	clockwise
b)	clockwise	anti-clockwise
c)	anti-clockwise	clockwise
d)	anti-clockwise	anti-clockwise

17.   During a descent at a constant Mach No. below the tropopause in the ISA:

a)   TAS decreases LSS decreases.

b)   CAS increases TAS increases.

c)   LSS increases CAS decreases.

d)   CAS increases TAS decreases.

18.   The rotational speed of the gyroscope in a turn indicator falls below the correct operational speed. A 90° turn at an indicated `rate one' on this turn indicator will take:

a)   30 seconds.

b)   less than 30 seconds.

c)   more than 30 seconds.

d)   30 seconds ± 10 seconds either way.

19.   In gyroscopic theory the term `Topple' is defined as:

a)   wander, real or apparent, in the horizontal plane.

b)   wander, real or apparent, in the vertical plane.

c)   real wander, only, in the horizontal plane.

d)   real wander, only, in the vertical plane.

20.   An artificial horizon with an air driven gyroscope, (spinning anti-clockwise seen from above), is subjected to acceleration during a take-off run. As a result the instrument indications will falsely show:

a)   the right wing going up and the nose going down.

b)   the right wing going up and the nose going up.

c)   the right wing going down and the nose going up.

d)   the right wing going down and the nose going down.

21.   An uncorrected gyro is set to read 356° in an aircraft which is stationary on the ground in latitude 50N. The reading after 1 hr 45 min is:

a)   339.10

b)   016.10

c)   012.90

d)   335.90

22.   An increase of 0.15 in mach number results in an increase of 93 kt in TAS. If the temperature
        deviation from ISA is +9°C, the FL is:

        a)   FL 200
        b)   FL 220
        c)   FL 250
        d)   FL 90

23.   If a simple flux valve lies .... the earths field the current induced in the pick-off coil will be
        .... and the frequency will be .... the input frequency.
        The words to correctly complete the sentence above are:

        a)   in line with   minimum   twice
        b)   at 90° to   minimum   half
        c)   at 90° to   maximum   half
        d)   in line with   maximum   twice

24.   In Figure 6.1., a diagram of a detector unit and selsyn, the arrowed items are identified as:

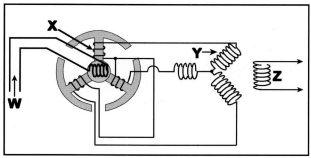

Figure 6.1.

        a)   W = AC excitation, Z = flux valve pick-off coil and Y = stator coil.
        b)   W = AC excitation, X = flux valve pick-off coil and Z = stator coil.
        c)   X = flux valve pick-off coil, Z = rotor pick-off coil and Y = stator coil.
        d)   W = AC excitation, X = stator coil and X = rotor pick-off coil.

25.   The purpose of the Annunciator unit of the Remote Indicating compass is to:

        a)   show whether the compass is operating either in the GYRO or COMPASS mode.
        b)   display the serviceability of the compass.
        c)   indicate that the gyro is synchronised with the detector unit.
        d)   advise if the gyro is subject to excessive wander.

26.   The aerodynamic angle of incidence (angle of attack) is:

      a)   the angle between the longitudinal axis and the relative air flow.
      b)   the angle between the chord line of the wing and the lateral axis.
      c)   the angle between the chord line of the wing of an aircraft and the direction of the relative air flow.
      d)   the angle between the wing and the chord line.

27.   If an alert message is generated by the flight management system:

      a)   it appears in the middle of the CRT screen and a red light flashes.
      b)   it appears at the top of the CRT and an amber light flashes.
      c)   it appears in the scratch pad and the MSG annunciator illuminates.
      d)   it appears in the scratch pad and an amber light flashes

OBJECTIVE REVISION NO 7

1.   Of the four illustrations below, only one is a correct functional diagram of an Airspeed Indicator. The correct diagram is:

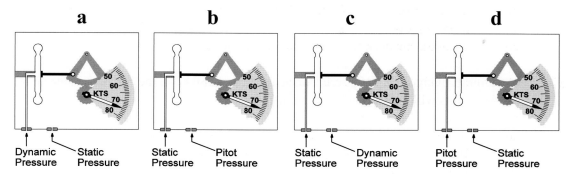

2.   Vertical Speed Indicator indications may be in error for some seconds after starting or finishing a climb or descent. This error is a result of:

a)   a combination of time lag and instrument error.
b)   a combination of position error and time lag.
c)   a combination of time lag and manoeuvre induced error.
d)   manoeuvre induced error only.

3.   The full International Standard Atmosphere (ISA) is assumed in the calibration of:

a)   the pressure altimeter and the airspeed indicator.
b)   the vertical speed indicator and the machmeter.
c)   the pressure altimeter only.
d)   the vertical speed indicator only.

4.   During a steady climb the pitot head becomes totally blocked by ice. As the climb continues the indications of the machmeter will:

a)   increase no matter what the actual Mach number.
b)   progressively under indicate the Mach number.
c)   stick at the Mach number at the time of blockage.
d)   go to zero and stay there.

5.   An aircraft flies from A to B with QNH at A of 1019 mb set on the altimeter subscale throughout the flight. Assuming all other errors are zero and that 1 mb = 30 feet, when overhead B, QNH 1013 mbs, the altimeter will be:

a)   over indicating by 120 feet.
b)   over indicating by 180 feet.
c)   indicating true altitude.
d)   under indicating by 180 feet.

6.   An aircraft maintaining a constant CAS and FL is flying from a warm air mass into a colder air mass. The effect of the change of temperature on the TAS and true altitude will be:

   a)   TAS will decrease and true altitude will decrease.
   b)   TAS will increase and true altitude will increase.
   c)   TAS will decrease and true altitude will increase.
   d)   TAS will increase and true altitude will decrease.

7.   An aircraft flying at FL 310 is cruising at an CAS of 280 kt. If the correct outside air temperature is -48°C, this will give a Mach number of:

   a)   0.76
   b)   0.71
   c)   0.78
   d)   0.805

8.   The reason for the adjustable index on the Machmeter being set at a different Mach number on different aircraft types is:

   a)   to correct for the differing position errors.
   b)   to correct for the differing instrument errors.
   c)   because different aircraft types have different critical Mach numbers.
   d)   to indicate the best cruising Mach number for that aircraft.

9.   The gyroscopic instrument which has its spin axis tied to the earth's vertical is:

   a)   the turn indicator.
   b)   the artificial horizon.
   c)   the INS azimuth gyro.
   d)   the directional gyro indicator.

10.   The rate of precession of a gyroscope varies as:

   a) $\dfrac{\text{rigidity}}{\text{disturbing couple}}$

   b) $\dfrac{1}{\text{rigidity}}$ only

   c) $\dfrac{1}{\text{disturbing couple}}$ only

   d) $\dfrac{\text{disturbing couple}}{\text{rigidity}}$

11.   The turn and slip and artificial horizon shown in Figures 7.1 & 7.2. show the aircraft to be turning left at rate one:

Figure 7.1

Figure 7.2.

a)   with too much bank and nose below the horizon.
b)   with insufficient bank and nose above the horizon.
c)   and skidding out with nose below the horizon.
d)   slipping in with nose below the horizon.

12.   An artificial horizon with an air driven gyroscope (spinning anticlockwise as seen from above), is subject to acceleration during the take-off run. As a result the instrument indications will falsely show:

a)   the right wing going up and the nose going down.
b)   the right wing going down and the nose going up.
c)   the right wing going down and the nose going down.
d)   the right wing going up and the nose going up.

13.   An artificial horizon with an electrical driven gyroscope has greatly reduced take-off errors. This is because:

a)   the gyro has greater rigidity, is less bottom heavy and there is a linear accelerometer cut-out switch fitted.
b)   it is fitted with a roll cut-out switch and a linear cut-out switch.
c)   the gyro has greater rigidity, is less bottom heavy and there is a roll cut-out switch fitted.
d)   the fast erection switch is used to overcome topple by increasing the erection rate to a high value.

14.   The combined Machmeter/ASI is subject to the following errors:

a)   position, density, instrument, compressibility, manoeuvre induced
b)   those of the Machmeter only
c)   instrument, pressure and temperature only
d)   instrument and compressibility only

15.   In Figure 7.3., the diagram of a detector unit and selsyn, the arrowed items are identified as:

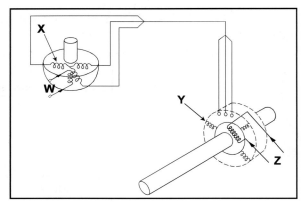

Figure 7.3.

 a) W = AC excitation, Z = flux valve pick-off coil and Y = stator coil.
 b) W = AC excitation, X = flux valve pick-off coil and Z = stator coil.
 c) X = flux valve pick-off coil, Z = rotor pick-off coil and Y = stator coil.
 d) W = AC excitation, X = stator coil and Z = rotor pick-off coil.

16.   According to Joint Aviation requirements, the maximum deviation on any heading after correction of a direct reading magnetic compass is:

 a) 1°
 b) 3°
 c) 5°
 d) 10°

17.   An INS with the accelerometers aligned N/S and E/W is limited to use at latitudes below about 82°. This is because:

 a) it loses horizontal reference as dip becomes large.
 b) at high speed on East or West tracks the rate of convergency is faster than the azimuth motor can correct.
 c) the functions of Secant Latitude and Tangent Latitude used for certain corrections in the computer start to approach infinity and the computer cannot handle the rapid changes involved.
 d) the correction for the Coriolis effect of earth rotation approaches infinity above 82° lat.

18.   At the second state of integration E/W speed is converted into E/W distance gone. To convert this departure into change of longitude it has to:

 a) be divided by Secant of the latitude.
 b) be multiplied by Secant of the latitude.
 c) be divided by Tangent of the latitude.
 d) be multiplied by Cosine of the latitude.

19.   The amber ALERT light on an INS control and display unit:

     a)   illuminates steadily for 2 minutes before reaching the next way point.

     b)   flashes for 2 minutes before reaching the next way point.

     c)   illuminates if power from the aircraft bus bar has been lost and the system is operating on standby battery.

     d)   illuminates steadily after passing a way point in manual mode, until the next leg is programmed in.

20.   With reference to Inertial Navigation Systems, the functions of the integrators are:

     i)   at the second stage of integration to suppress unbounded errors (when in the NAV mode).

     ii)   at the first stage of integration to convert acceleration, with respect to time, into speed, (when in the NAV mode).

     iii)   at the second stage of integration to convert speed, with respect to time, into distance gone, (when in the NAV mode).

     iv)   to align the platform (when in the level and align modes).

     a)   all the above statements are true.

     b)   only (ii), (iii) and (iv) of the above statements are true.

     c)   only (i), (ii) and (iii) of the above statements are true.

     d)   only (ii) and (iii) of the above statements are true.

21.   The correct check for a turn and slip indicator when taxying and turning left is:

     a)   needle left, ball left.

     b)   needle left, ball right.

     c)   needle right, ball left.

     d)   needle right, ball right.

OBJECTIVE REVISION NO 8

1.   The rotor in an electric artificial horizon is tied to the vertical by;

   a)   a jet of air from the rotor impinging on a wedge plate which is on the inner gimbal.
   b)   mercury switches only.
   c)   a jet of air from the outer gimbal striking the rotor buckets.
   d)   torque motors and level switches.

2.   If the alternate static source is selected, the greatest error in the machmeter will be;

   a)   position error
   b)   manoeuvre induced error
   c)   density error
   d)   lag

3.   Which of the following is correct when considering the air data computer?

   a)   A 'constant BIT' automatically checks the performance of equipment continuously through the flight.
   b)   The time date and aircraft position must be entered before it can operate.
   c)   Apart from the maintenance panel there is no adjustment or input possible to the ADC in the cockpit.
   d)   The ADC has its information updated every 28 days.

4.   Compared to the VSI what errors are eliminated by the IVSI?

   a)   lag
   b)   turning
   c)   pressure
   d)   temperature

5.   In the diagram below, a picture of a remote indicating compass, what are the components X, Y and Z?

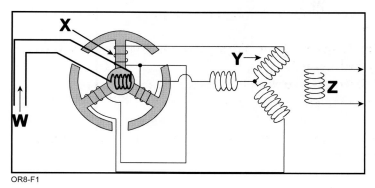

OR8-F1

    a)   ac excitation, pick-off coil and rotor
    b)   pick-off coil, stator and rotor
    c)   pick-off coil, rotor and stator
    d)   stator, ac excitation and pick-off coil.

6.   In an INS the gyros should _____ be strap down. In an IRS the gyros should be strap down.

    a)   always, never.
    b)   always, always.
    c)   never, always.
    d)   never, never.

7.   The airspeed indicator is calibrated to;

    a)   ISA at mean sea level.
    b)   ISA at 36,090 ft.
    c)   ISA at the height the aircraft is flying.
    d)   the full ISA.

8.   Which of the following lists the errors of the machmeter?

    a)   Position, manoeuvre induced, lag, density and instrument.
    b)   Compressibility, position, density, instrument and manoeuvre induced.
    c)   Lag, position, density, compressibility and temperature.
    d)   Position, manoeuvre induced and instrument.

9.   A DGI reads 300°T when the aircraft is stationary at 60°S, what will the DGI read after 40 minutes?

    a)   309°
    b)   287°
    c)   313°
    d)   291°

10.   In the diagram below, a diagram of the machmeter, components C, A and B are:

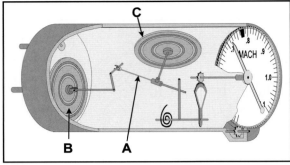

OR*-F2

   a)   ratio arm, airspeed capsule, and altitude capsule
   b)   ranging arm, altitude capsule, and airspeed capsule
   c)   ratio arm, altitude capsule, and airspeed capsule
   d)   main shaft, airspeed capsule, and altitude capsule

11.   Aircraft magnetism;

   a)   varies with aircraft heading and latitude
   b)   varies with latitude but does not vary with aircraft heading
   c)   does not vary with aircraft heading or latitude
   d)   does not vary with aircraft latitude but does vary with aircraft heading

12.   The turn and slip and artificial horizon illustrated in Figure 8.3. show the aircraft to be turning;

Figure 8.3

   a)   right at 30 degrees angle of bank with slip
   b)   right at 30 degrees angle of bank with skid
   c)   right with insufficient bank and the nose above the horizon
   d)   left with skid

13.   An aircraft is flying a rate 1 turn at 480 kt TAS.   What is the diameter of the
        turn?

        a)   3nm
        b)   5nm
        c)   6nm
        d)   2nm

14.   The machmeter measures Mach Number by measuring;

        a) $\dfrac{P + S}{S}$

        b) $\dfrac{D + S}{S}$

        c) $\dfrac{P - S}{S}$

        d) $\dfrac{D - S}{S}$

15.   In gyroscopic theory the term 'Topple' is defined as;

        a)   wander, real or apparent, in the horizontal plane
        b)   real wander only in the vertical plane
        c)   wander, real or apparent, in the vertical plane
        d)   real wander only in the horizontal plane

Referring to the displays in **Appendix A** (Page 23 - 49) answer the following questions:

        16.   Full VOR display is shown in diagram;

                a)   A
                b)   D
                c)   E
                d)   F

        17.   On which of the displays can weather be displayed?

                a)   B, D and E
                b)   A, C and F
                c)   B and D
                d)   C, E and F

18. What would be the display which resulted from the selection shown in Figure 8.4.

    a) B
    b) E
    c) A
    d) D

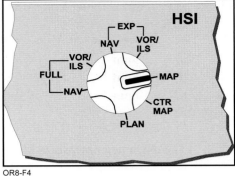

OR8-F4

Figure 8.4

19. Which of the following is the FMS normal operating condition in the cruise?

    a) L NAV only
    b) V NAV only
    c) L NAV or V NAV
    d) L NAV and V NAV

20. Ring laser gyros utilise a 'Dither' motor to;

    a) reduce real wander
    b) prevent unbounded errors
    c) level and align the gyros
    d) prevent lock in of the laser beam

21. Which of the following is true regarding the turn co-ordinator?

    a) It has a tied gyroscope.
    b) Its gyro is offset by 30° to the longitudinal axis of the aircraft.
    c) It gives angle of bank and rate of turn.
    d) It responds to rate of turn only.

22. The product of the first integration of the E/W acceleration sensed by an INS system is;

    a) departure
    b) speed along the local parallel
    c) speed along the local horizontal
    d) distance

23. The altimeter in Figure 8.5. shows;

    a) FL 27
    b) FL 270
    c) a pressure altitude of 20,700ft
    d) a height of 2,700ft

OR8-F5

Figure 8.5.

24.   Compressibility is corrected for when obtaining;

      a)   EAS from CAS and the correction is always subtractive.
      b)   CAS from IAS and the correction can be either additive or subtractive.
      c)   EAS from CAS and the correction is normally subtractive.
      d)   CAS from IAS and the correction is normally subtractive

25.   What are the advantages of an IRS compared to an INS?

      a)   Reduced spin-up time and a dither motor to prevent 'lock-out'.
      b)   Reduced spin-up time and insensitivity to 'g'.
      c)   Increased accuracy and a dither motor to prevent 'lock-out'.
      d)   Insensitivity to 'g' and reduced wander of the gyroscopes.

26.   The colour arcs of an ASI are in ascending speed order?

      a)   green, yellow and red
      b)   blue, yellow and red
      c)   white, yellow and red
      d)   white, green and yellow

27.   An aircraft flying at Mach 0.83 is in air SAT 230 Kelvin. What is the TAS?

      a)   490 kt
      b)   575 kt
      c)   495 kt
      d)   470 kt

28.   An altimeter has an error of 1mb. The error at 20,000ft will be _____, while at 40,000ft the error will be _____.

      a)   30ft,   30ft
      b)   50ft,   100ft
      c)   10ft,   30ft
      d)   50ft,   80ft

Appendix A

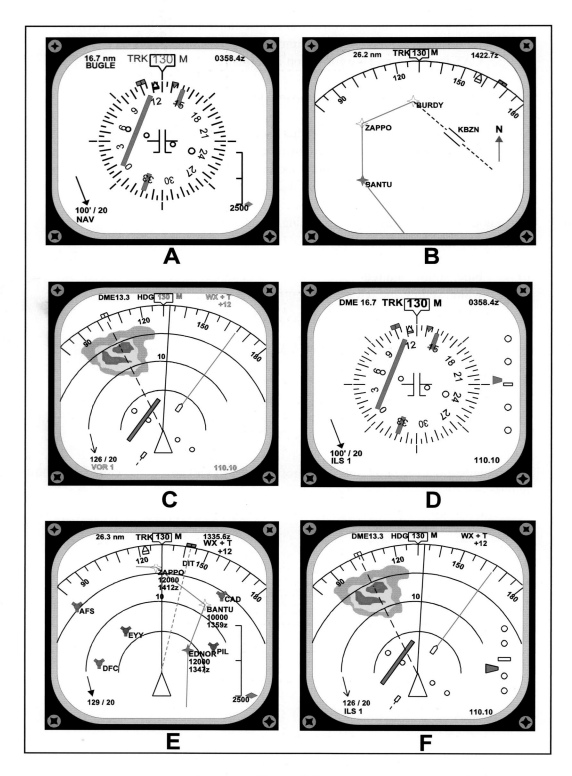

Figure 8.6

Objective Revision Answers

Question Number	Paper number							
	1	**2**	**3**	**4**	**5**	**6**	**7**	**8**
	PH	T	ASI	ACI	VSI	MN		
1	a	d	a	b	a	a	d	d
2	d	c	b	c	a	b	c	a
3	a	c	d	c	d	c	c	c
4	c	c	b	a	c	d	a	a
5	b	b	b	b	b	d	b	b
6	a	c	d	c	c	c	a	c
7	c	b	b	c	d	a	a	a
8	c	b	a	b	b	a	c	d
9	a	c	c	d	a	a	b	a
10	b	a	a	a	a	d	d	a
11	a	a	b	c	c	d	c	b
12	d	b	a	b	c	a	b	a
13	b	c	c	a	b	b	a	b
14	b	c	c	c	a	c	a	c
15	d	c	a	b	c	a	c	c
16	b	c	c	d	c	b	d	a
17	b	b	c	b	b	b	c	d
18	c		d	a	b	b	b	b
19	b		c	b	d	b	a	d
20	c			a	c	c	d	d
21	a			c	a	d	b	b
22				c	b	b		b
23					c	d		b
24					c	c		a
25					a	c		b

Question	P	a	p	e	r		N	o
Number	1	2	3	4	5	6	7	8
26					a	c		d
27					b	c		a
28					c			b

Instrument Annex - Answers.

Chapter 2 - Pressure Heads:

1	2	3	4	5	6	7	8	9	10
B	C	D	D	A	A	C	B	D	C

Chapter 3 - Air Temperature Measurement:

1	2	3	4	5	6	7	8	9	10
B	B	C	A	B	B	A	B	D	B

Chapter 4 - Airspeed Indicator:

1	2	3	4	5	6	7	8	9	10
B	D	A	C	B	B	D	C	B	B

Chapter 5 - Altimeter:

1	2	3	4	5	6	7	8	9	
D	B	A	D	C	A	B	B	B	

Chapter 6 - Vertical Speed Indicator:

1	2	3	4	5	6	7	8	9	10
D	A	A	B	B	B	C	B	B	D

Chapter 7 - Machmeter:

1	2	3	4	5	6	7	8	9	10
B	B	D	C	A	B	B	C	D	B

Chapter 8 - Terrestrial Magnetism:

1	2	3	4	5	6	7	8		
D	C	B	D	C	A	D	A		

Chapter 9 - Direct Reading Magnetic Compass:

1	2	3	4	5	6	7	8	9	
C	D	D	D	A	C	D	D	C	

Chapter 10 - Gyros:

1	2	3	4	5	6	7	8	9	10
D	C	C	A	D	A	D	C	C	A

Chapter 11 - Directional Gyro Indicator:

1	2	3	4	5	6	7	8	9	10
B	D	C	C	B	C	C	B	D	A

Chapter 12- Artificial Horizon:

1	2	3	4	5	6	7	8	9	10
D	C	D	B	D	C	A	A	B	A

Chapter 13 - Rate of Turn and Slip Indicator:

1	2	3	4	5	6	7			
C	A	A	D	A	D	D			

Chapter 14 - Turn Co-ordinator:

1	2	3							
B	D	B							

Chapter 15 - Aircraft Magnetism:

1	2	3	4	5					
A	B	B	A	C					

Chapter 16 - Remote Indicating Compass:

1	2	3	4	5	6	7	8		
B	A	A	C	C	B	C	D		

Chapter 17 - Inertial Navigation Systems:

1	2	3	4	5	6	7	8	9	10					
A	C	C	B	A	D	C	C	B	D					

Chapter 22 - EFIS

1	2	3	4	5	6	7	8	9	10	11	12	13	14	15	16
D	A	D	B	C	C	D	D	D	C	D	B	B	B	C	A

JAAatpl
JOINT AVIATION AUTHORITIES

Theoretical Training Manuals

Revised Edition

AIRCRAFT GENERAL KNOWLEDGE 4

INSTRUMENTATION
WARNING & RECORDING

This learning material has been approved as JAA compliant by the United Kingdom Civil Aviation Authority

CIVIL AVIATION
AUTHORITY

OXFORD
Aviation Training
Succeed through our experience™

CHAPTER ONE -FLIGHT WARNING SYSTEM

Contents

Page

1.1   INTRODUCTION . . . . 1 - 1

1.2   LEVELS OF ALERTS . . . . 1 - 1

1.3   WARNINGS IN GENERAL . . . . 1 - 1

1.4   THE FLIGHT WARNING SYSTEM (FWS) . . . . 1 - 3

1.5   FWS COMPONENTS . . . . 1 - 4

1.1   INTRODUCTION

The purpose of the Flight Warning System (FWS) is to produce cautions and warnings for the crew to increase their situation awareness and to give them suitable indications of the action necessary to avoid impending danger.

The proliferation of various warning systems in today's aircraft poses a severe problem in that the crew could be confused by the multiplicity of warnings. It is therefore necessary to install an integrated flight warning system that will prioritise the warnings. By producing warnings relevant to a particular stage of flight and inhibiting other warnings the system enables the crew to respond to the warning posing the most immediate threat to safety.

1.2   LEVELS OF ALERTS

The alerting and warning system produces the following levels of alerts:

1.1   **Warnings or Level A alerts.** These require immediate crew action. Warnings must attract the pilot's attention in sufficient time for appropriate action to be taken.

1.2   **Cautions or Level B alerts.** These require immediate crew alertness and possible future action.

1.3   **Advisories or Level C alerts.** These require crew alertness.

1.3   WARNINGS IN GENERAL

The alerting and warning messages are presented to the crew in visual, aural and sensory forms.

a)   **VISUAL**. The level of alert is indicated by colours as follows:

3.1   Warnings are presented in **Red**

3.2   Cautions are shown in **Amber** or **yellow**

3.3   Advisories are also shown in **Amber** or **yellow**

These visual indications can be presented in two different forms:

i)   **Electronic Screens.** Alerts and warnings appear in coloured text or symbols on various electronic screens (flight, navigation, engine and aircraft system displays).

ii)   **Lights or Flags**. Red lights or reflective flags signify warnings and require remedial action if flight is to continue. An amber light or flag is used to indicate that a system or equipment is approaching a limit of normal function and that corrective action is necessary to prevent further deterioration and consequent failure.

Additionally, master warning and caution lights are normally provided and are located near the centre of scan in front of each pilot.

b)   **AURAL.** An audible warning is mandatory if the pilot is required to assume control. This can be in a variety of forms depending upon the type of aircraft. The alert can be in the form of sounds or synthetic voice messages or a combination of both.

3.1   **Warnings**
Boeing aircraft produce the following aural warnings:

1)   A bell accompanies Fire messages
2)   A siren accompanies warnings on Cabin Altitude, Configuration and Overspeed
3)   A Wailer accompanies Autopilot disconnect
4)   Synthetic Voice messages for ground proximity, windshear, airborne collision avoidance.

Airbus aircraft produce :

1)   continuous repetitive chimes (red warnings)
2)   cavalry charge (autopilot disconnect)
3)   cricket sound (stall warning)
4)   synthetic voice (GPWS, TCAS warnings)

ii)   **Cautions**
Beepers with various tones or chimes or musical chords are used to caution the crew to potential threats to safety.

c)   **SENSORY.** A vibratory mode on the controls is used to indicate stall approach and demands immediate action to avert loss of control. In some aircraft a stick-pusher provides guidance to prevent a further deterioration of the situation that demanded the vibratory warning.

To rationalize warnings systems, a Master Warning Indicator light is often provided near the centre of scan. In older systems the crew member would then refer to a Master Warnings Panel where warnings were assembled in a rational order and annotated. In the modern Electronic Instrumentation Systems most of the alerts and warnings appear on appropriate electronic screens together with associated aural messages and master warning lights.

Figure 1.1 shows the cockpit displays and warnings of an Airbus A320.

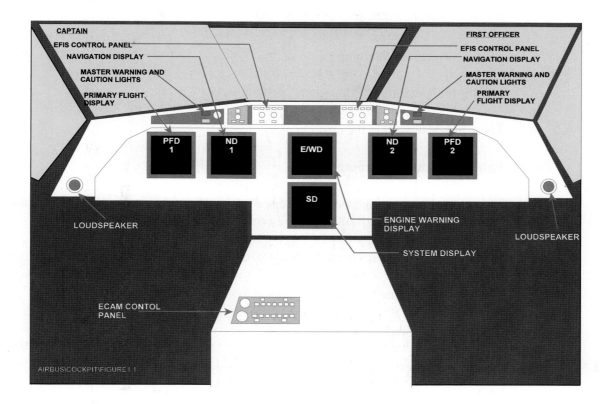

1.4   THE FLIGHT WARNING SYSTEM (FWS)

a)   **General**

The Flight Warning System generates alerts and warnings for the following situations:

i)   Engine and Airframe systems malfunctions

ii)   Aerodynamic limits exceeded

iii)   Presence of external Hazards.

b)   **Engine and Airframe systems malfunctions**

These are dealt with in detail in the Engines and in the Systems sections of the course.

c)   **Aerodynamic limits**

If aerodynamic limits are exceeded the FWS provides the following alerts to the crew:

i)   Altitude Alerting

ii)   Overspeed Warning

iii)   Stall Warning

These are dealt with in the next chapter.

d)   **External Hazard Warning**

The external hazards that constitute a threat to aircraft safety are proximity to terrain and to other aircraft. These hazards can be avoided by the use of:

i)   the Ground Proximity Warning System and

ii)   the Airborne Collision Avoidance System.

These are dealt with in chapters 3 and 4.

1.5   FWS COMPONENTS

The FWS system comprises:

a)   **Inputs.** There are inputs from various sources including hundreds of engine and airframe sensors, air data sensors, GPWS and ACAS systems.

b)   **A processing unit.** This is made up of one or two flight warning computers.

c)   **Outputs**. The outputs are classified either as alerts or as warnings and are generated according to the nature of the malfunction or threat to safety. Alerts can be visual (amber lights or text on VDU's) or aural (chimes or tones). Warnings are given in the form of red lights or by red text on electronic screens (steady or flashing) as well as aural signals (siren, bell, hooter). Additionally there are red and amber lights on the glaresheild in front of the pilots to act as attention getters.

A block diagram of a Boeing 767 warning and alert system is shown at figure 1.2.

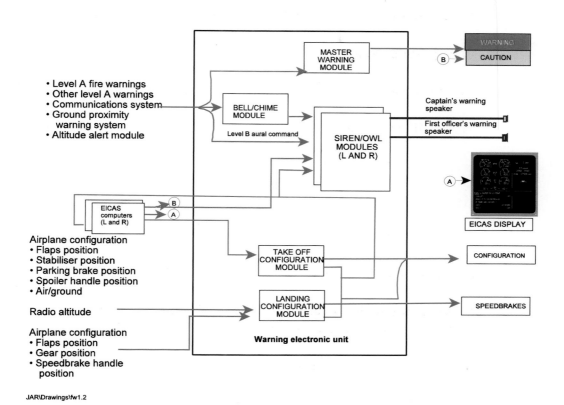

Figure 1.2 Warning and Alerting System (Boeing 767)

CHAPTER TWO -AERODYNAMIC WARNINGS

Contents

Page

2.1   INTRODUCTION . . . . 2 - 1

2.2   ALTITUDE ALERTING SYSTEM . . . . 2 - 1

2.3   OVERSPEED WARNING . . . . 2 - 4

2.4   STALL WARNING SYSTEM . . . . 2 - 6

2.1   INTRODUCTION

The Flight Warning System alerts the crew if there are deviations from certain aerodynamic parameters like altitude, airspeed and angle of attack. The system therefore provides the following alerts and warnings:

a)   Altitude Alerting System

b)   Overspeed Warning

c)   Stall Warning.

2.2   ALTITUDE ALERTING SYSTEM

a)   **Function**
The function of the Altitude Alerting System is to warn the pilots that the aircraft is approaching or deviating from the altitude selected on the Autopilot control panel. It does this in certain height bands above and below the selected altitude.

b)   **Operation**
The height bands within which altitude alerting operates are typically 300 feet to 900 feet for Boeing aircraft and 250 feet to 750 feet for Airbus aircraft. Figure 2.1. shows the operation of altitude alerting on a Boeing 747-400.

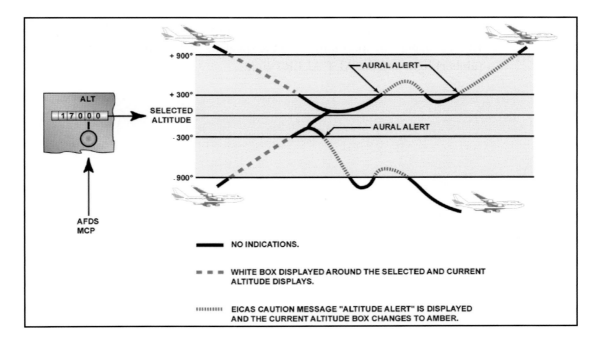

Figure 2.1 Altitude Alert (Boeing 737-400)

i)   **Approaching a selected altitude**
At 900 feet prior to the selected altitude a white box will be displayed around the selected altitude and current altitude displays on the PFD.

At 300 feet prior to the selected altitude the white boxes disappear.

ii)   **Deviation from selected altitude**
At 300 feet from the selected altitude:

1)   master caution lights illuminate
2)   caution beeper sounds
3)   EICAS caution message ALTITUDE ALERT is displayed
4)   current altitude box changes to amber.

At 900 feet from the selected altitude, or on returning to within 300 feet from the selected altitude:

1)   master caution lights extinguish
2)   EICAS caution message disappears
3)   current altitude box changes to white

c)   **Block Diagram**
Figure 2.2 shows a block diagram of a Boeing 767 altitude alerting system. When the aircraft approaches the selected altitude the advisory light on each electric altimeter illuminates. If the aircraft deviates by more than 300 feet from the selected altitude the system generates a level B warning (ie a caution) consisting of a level B message on the EICAS display, an alert tone from the speakers and illumination of the master caution (amber) light and the ALT ALERT light.

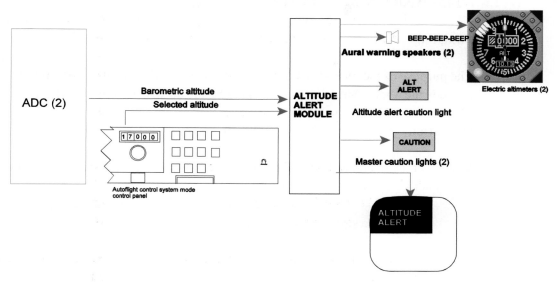

Figure 2.2 Altitude Alerting System (Boeing 767)

d)　　**System inhibition**

Altitude alerting is inhibited in flight whenever glideslope is captured or when landing flaps are selected with the gear down.

e)　　**JAR OPS requirement**

It is a requirement of JAR OPS that an aircraft is equipped with an altitude alerting system if it is :

i)　　a turbine powered aircraft weighing more than 5700 kg **or** has more than 9 seats or

ii)　　a turbojet aircraft

The altitude alerting system must be capable of:

i)　　alerting the crew on approaching the preselected altitude.

ii)　　alerting the crew by at least an aural signal when deviating above or below a preselected altitude.

2.3   OVERSPEED WARNING

a)   **Function**

The purpose of the Overspeed warning system is to alert the flight crew if the airspeed exceeds the Vmo / Mmo limits calculated by the air data computer (ADC).

b)   **Operation**

Whenever an overspeed situation occurs in an aircraft with electronic instrumentation the system:

i)   sounds the siren or horn

ii)   illuminates the red master WARNING lights

iii)   displays the message OVERSPEED on the EICAS upper display in red.

The warning continues while the overspeed situation exists and cannot be cancelled by depressing the red master WARNING light switch.

The system obtains its input from the air data computers (ADC's) via the flight warning system. It can be tested on the ground before flight by pressing a test switch which would then sound the siren or horn as appropriate for that aircraft.

In case of system failure the pilot would receive no warning if Vmo or Mmo is exceeded.

c)   **Displays**

The maximum allowable speed is shown on the airspeed indicator by means of a barber's pole on a conventional meter and on the airspeed tape on the primary flight display or EADI of an EFIS display. These are shown in figures 2.3 and 2.4. The barbers pole indicates the Vmo up until the Mmo (when expressed in terms of an indicated air speed) becomes limiting. The barbers pole will the move counter-clockwise to indicate the maximum allowable speed. As altitude increases when climbing at a constant indicated airspeed the Mmo when expressed as an indicated airspeed will decrease.

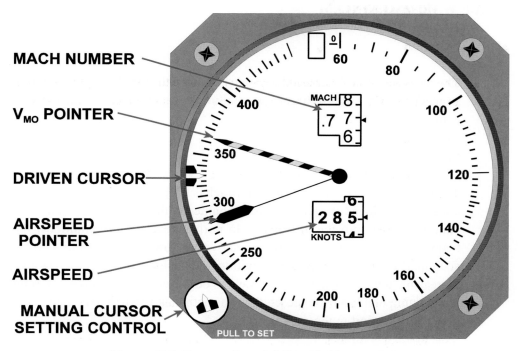

Figure 2.3 Conventional ASI with Vmo pointer

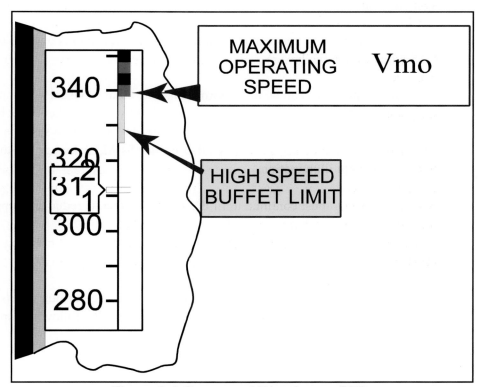

Figure 2.4 Overspeed Warning on PFD

2.4   STALL WARNING SYSTEM

a)   **Function**

The purpose of the stall warning system is to warn the pilot of an impending stall. It does so when the aircraft approaches the stalling angle of attack for the current speed and configuration of the aircraft.

b)   **Stall Warning Systems.**

The simplest form of system, and one which is adopted in several types of small aircraft, consists of a hinged-vane-type sensor mounted in the leading edge of a wing so that the vane protrudes into the airstream. In normal level flight conditions, the airstream maintains the vane in line with the relative air flow. If the aircraft's attitude changes such that α increases, then, by definition, the airflow will meet the leading edge at an increasing angle, and so cause the vane to be deflected. When α reaches that at which the warning unit has been preset, the vane activates a switch to complete a circuit to an aural warning unit in the cockpit.

In larger types of aircraft, stall warning and prevention systems are designed to perform a more active function, such as 'stick-shaker' or 'stick-push or nudger' type.

c)   **The warning**

The regulatory margin between the stall and the stall warning is 5 knots or 5% of the CAS whichever is the greater.

The warning provided can be in the form of tactile, aural or visual or a combination of these signals. Most aircraft have warning provided by stick-shakers which vibrate the control column as well as produce a rattling noise. In fly-by-wire systems the warning consists of a cricket (insect) sound, a synthetic voice STALL message and the red master WARNING light illumination.

The stall warning must continue until the angle of attack is reduced to approximately that at which the stall warning is initiated.

d)   **Operation**

The stall warning module processes the signals from the various inputs to produce appropriate stall warning output signals. The system has the following inputs:

i)   angle of attack

ii)   flap and slat positions

iii)   landing gear weight-on position

iv)   airspeed.

The angle of attack sensors are usually located on either side of the front fuselage. Sensing relays denote the positions of the flaps and slats. Since the pitch attitude of the aircraft is also changed by the extension of flaps or slats the angle of attack signal has to be modified when these are extended. During take-off when the nosewheel lifts off, microswitches operate to make the stall warning system active. The airspeed is usually derived from the ADC.

The output signals from the system can be applied to :

i)   a stick-shaker motor

ii)   an angle of attack indicator

iii)   aural warning

iv)   synthetic voice warning

v)   red master WARNING light

e)   **Components**
A block diagram of the component parts of a stall warning system and an angle of attack sensor are shown at figures 2.5.

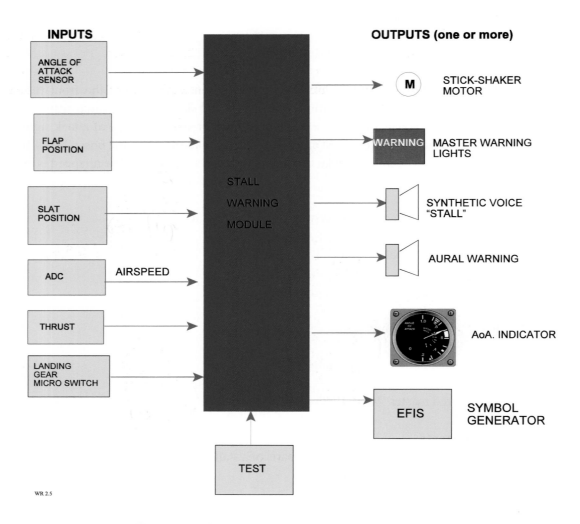

Figure 2.5 Components of a Stall Warning System

i)   **Angle of Attack Sensing.**
        The angle of attack (AoA), or alpha (α) angle, also known as the aerodynamic
        incidence, is the angle between the chord line of the wing of an aircraft and the
        direction of the relative airflow, and is a major factor in determining the
        magnitude of lift generated by a wing. Lift increases as α increases up to some
        critical value at which it begins to decrease due to separation of the slow-
        moving air (the boundary layer) from the upper surface of the wing, which, in
        turn, results in separation and turbulence of the main airflow.   The wing,
        therefore, assumes a stalled condition, and since it occurs at a particular angle
        rather than a particular speed, the critical AoA is also referred to as the stalling
        angle. The angle relates to the design of aerofoil section adopted for the wings
        of any one particular type of aircraft, and so, of course, its value varies
        accordingly; typically it is between 12° and 18° for straight wings but maybe as
        high as 30° or 40° for swept or delta wings.

ii)   **Alpha Probes**

The two types in current use are the conical slotted probe and the vane detector; the conical slotted probe is shown in figure 2.6 and the vane type in figure 2.7. The vane detector is a counter-balanced aerodynamic vane which positions the rotor of a synchro. Both types are protected against ice formation by a heater.

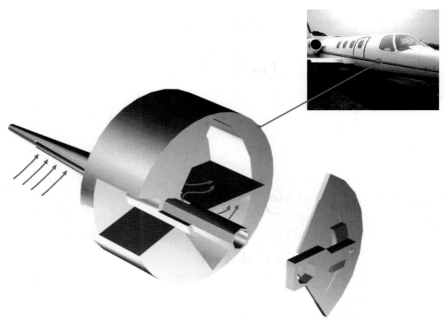

Figure 2.6.

The conical probe extends through the aircraft skin perpendicular to the flow of air. The probe is attached to a paddle inside the transmitter housing. The probe and paddle are free to rotate. Two sets of slots in the probe allow pressure variations, caused by changes in airstream direction, to be transmitted through separate air passages to opposite sides of a paddle chamber. When the pressure acting on one side of a paddle is greater than the pressure on the other side, the paddle and probe rotate until the pressures are equal. The probe thus positions itself to determine the angle of attack of the aircraft. The probe also drives the electrical pick offs such as potentiometers or synchros.

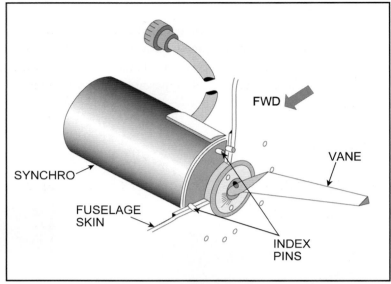

Figure 2.7 Angle of attack sensor

iii)   **Angle of Attack Indicators.**

These may be fitted in addition to the stall warning system. A simple schematic lay-out of the installation is shown in Figure 2.8.

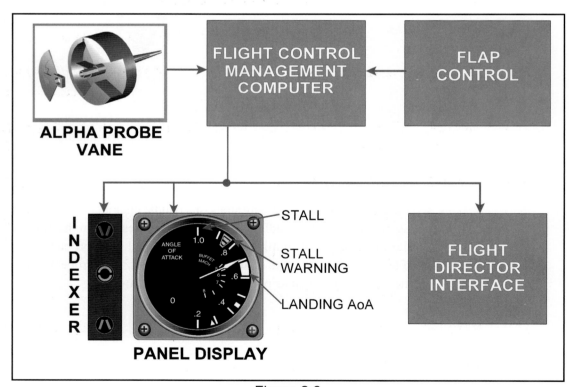

Figure 2.8

CHAPTER THREE - GROUND PROXIMITY WARNING SYSTEM

Contents

		Page
3.1	INTRODUCTION	3 - 1
3.2	DEFINITIONS	3 - 1
3.3	RESPONSE TO ALERTS/WARNINGS	3 - 2
3.4	ACTION TO BE TAKEN ON RECEIVING A WARNING	3 - 3
3.5	EFFECTIVENESS	3 - 3
3.6	INTEGRITY TESTING	3 - 3
3.7	INHIBITION OF EGPWS MODES	3 - 4
3.8	BOEING 737 MARK II GPWS	3 - 5
3.9	MODE 1 - EXCESSIVE DESCENT RATE	3 - 6
3.10	MODE 2 - EXCESSIVE TERRAIN CLOSURE RATE	3 - 8
3.11	MODE 3 - ALTITUDE LOSS AFTER TAKE-OFF OR GO-AROUND	3 - 10
3.12	MODE 4A - UNSAFE TERRAIN CLEARANCE WITH LANDING GEAR NOT DOWN	3 - 12
3.13	MODE 4B - UNSAFE TERRAIN CLEARANCE WITH FLAPS NOT IN LANDING CONFIGURATION	3 - 14
3.14	MODE 5 - BELOW GLIDESLOPE DEVIATION ALERT	3 - 16
3.15	MODE 6 - BELOW SELECTED MINIMUM RADIO ALTITUDE	3 - 18
3.17	DISPLAY OF THREATENING DISPLAY	3 - 20
3.18	"LOOK AHEAD" WARNING	3 - 21
3.19	MODE 6B ALTITUDE CALL-OUTS AND BANK ANGLE ALERT	3 - 22
3.20	MODE 7 WINDSHEAR ALERTING	3 - 23
3.21	TERRAIN CLEARANCE FLOOR	3 - 23

REVISION 5 .... 3 - 24

CHAPTER THREE - GPWS QUESTIONS .... 3 - 25

- GPWS Laws:
    - Descent Rate
    - Aircraft Configuration

- GPWS has mandatory Audio Warnings (at least 1 sound alarm), to which a visual can be added.

- Mandatory to fit GPWS to Turbo Prop a/c & Jet powered a/c.

3.1   INTRODUCTION

The aim of the system is to give **visual and audible warning** signals to a pilot when the aircraft's **proximity to the terrain poses a potential threat to its safety.** Although not a foolproof means of preventing a collision with the earth's surface, **EGPWS enhances flight safety** and can prevent those accidents which could result from crew errors or distraction, malfunction or misinterpretation of navigational equipment, or inappropriate ATC instructions.

Figure 3.1 shows the three elements of a GPWS: inputs, outputs and a central processing unit. The Central Processing Unit will also indicate a computer failure and any failures of the six input signals. The system operates between **50' and 2450' actual height above the surface** and automatically selects the correct mode of operation.

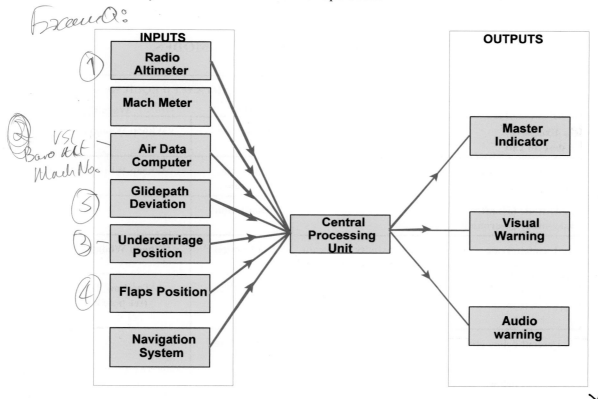

3.2   DEFINITIONS

a)   **ALERT:**   A **caution** generated by the EGPWS equipment.

        WARNING: A **command** generated by the EGPWS equipment.

© Oxford Aviation Services Limited

b)   **Types of Warnings/Alerts**

    i)   **Genuine**

The equipment provides a warning in accordance with its technical specification.

eg triggered by Rad Alt lit above a tall building

    ii)   **Nuisance** *ie unwanted*

The equipment provides a warning in accordance with its technical specification, but the pilot is flying an accepted safe procedure.

    iii)   **False** *- unwanted*

A fault or failure in the system causes the equipment to provide a warning that is not in accordance with its technical specification.

see also Cribb sheet for more info

A TABLE OF THE EGPWS OPERATING MODES.

GPWS MODE		ADVANCED EQUIPMENT	
		Audio Alert	Warning
1. Excessive descent rate		'Sink Rate'	'Whoop Whoop Pull Up'
2. Excessive terrain closure rate		'Terrain Terrain'	'Whoop Whoop Pull Up'
3. Altitude loss after take-off or go-around		'Don't Sink'	-
4. Unsafe terrain clearance while not in the landing configuration	4A. Proximity to terrain - Gear not locked down	'Too Low gear'	'Whoop Whoop Pull Up'
	4B. Proximity to terrain - Flaps not in a landing position	'Too Low Flaps'	'Too Low Terrain' (see note below)
5. Descent below glide-slope		'Glideslope'	-
6. Descent below 'minimums'	6A.	'Minimums'	-
	6B.	'Bank angle'	-
7. Windshear warning		-	'Wind Shear'

NOTE: Although some manufacturers of GPWS equipment may show in their literature 'Too Low Terrain' to be an alert, the view of the CAA is that the response to this should be as for a warning.

Mode 7 overrides everything a pest priority

Priority Order = 7, 2, 4, 6, 1, 3, 5

*Need to know for exam Modes 'Alerts' & Warnings

3.4   ACTION TO BE TAKEN ON RECEIVING A WARNING

The response to all alerts or warnings should be **positive and immediate**: establishing the cause of EGPWS activation should take second place.

There is a risk that repeated experience of unwanted alerts/warnings may reduce confidence in the system. Hence, **flight crews should report ALL alerts/warnings to the operator** thereby ensuring that appropriate analysis and remedial action can be taken. There is a GPWS operation reporting form for this purpose.

GPWS operation
i) Mode 1 if @night.
ii) Mode 4 - any time.

The immediate response must be to **level the wings and to initiate a maximum gradient climb** which should be maintained until the aircraft attains the **minimum safe altitude** for that part of the route being operated. Modification is permissible only in exceptional circumstances such as the necessity to follow a curved path for azimuth terrain avoidance.

When established in the climb every effort shall be made to determine the cause of the warning and to verify the aircraft's position. **The only circumstances when a climb to this altitude may be discontinued are when** :

a)   the cause of the warning has been positively identified and the warning ceases,
     or

b)   the conditions of CAP516 apply ie:

a daylogules! Must continue & get to Safe Alt if Night Time.

    i)   The aircraft is operated by day in meteorological conditions which will enable the aircraft to remain 1nm horizontally and 1000ft vertically away from cloud and an in-flight visibility of at least 5nm;
         and

    ii)   it is immediately obvious to the commander that the aircraft is not in a dangerous situation with regard to terrain, aircraft configuration or the present manoeuvre of the aircraft.

3.5   EFFECTIVENESS

EGPWS does not "look ahead" and **any Mode 2 warning** when flight is towards high ground will be **dependent upon the steepness of the terrain. Hence, a sheer cliff ahead will not generate a mode 2 warning** and any subsequent warning due to rising ground beyond the cliff will be delayed until the aircraft is over that ground. However this limitation has been overcome by **Enhanced GPWS** with the **Terrain Threat Display.** This uses essentially an electronic map of the world (giving ground elevation) and information from the aircraft's navigational system (be that INS/GPS or any combination). Given the location of the aircraft, its course and height (either from the ADC or derived from GPS) a display can be created showing the locations of terrain that could threaten the safety of the aircraft.

Using this system EGPWS can warn of approaching high terrain even when that terrain is not in close enough proximity to initiate a mode 2 warning. This terrain threat display and warning

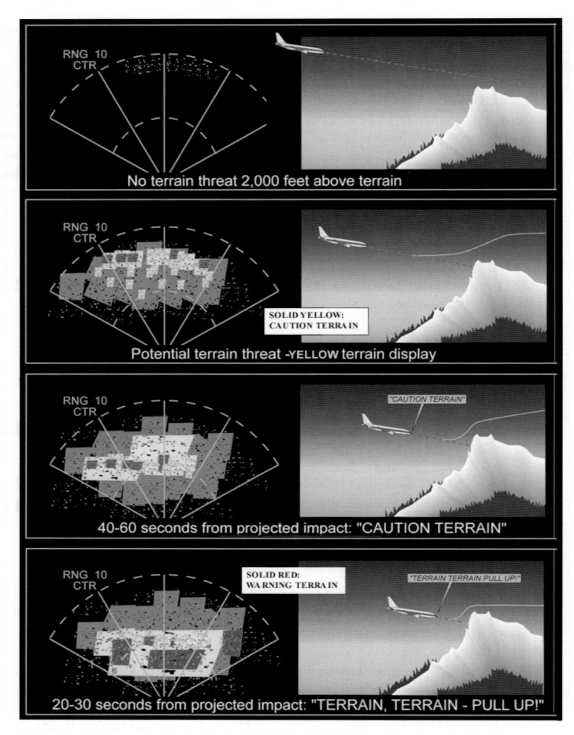

Figure 3.11 Terrain Display

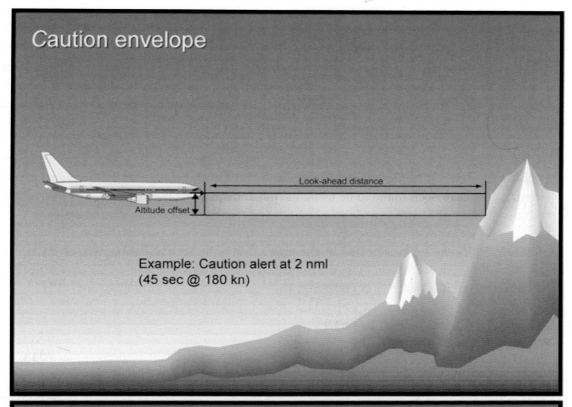

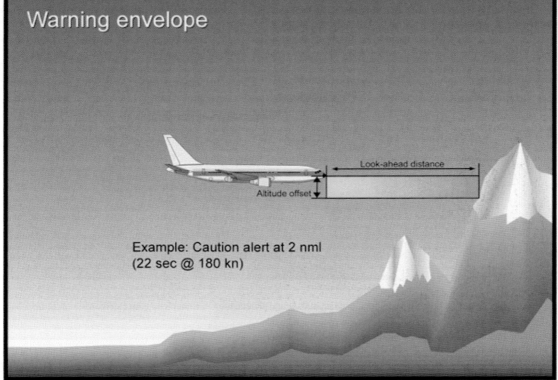

Figure 3.12 "Look Ahead" Warning

will be initiated in sufficient time to comfortably avoid any threat of flight into terrain. The terrain is shown in shades of green, yellow and red and the display indicates terrain not only below the aircraft but also ahead of its flight path. At a certain time before predicted impact the warning will issue a "**Caution Terrain**" message and the threat terrain will turn solid yellow. If the situation is allowed to deteriorate so as to close further with the high ground, the second message **"Whoop Whoop Pull Up"** will sound and the most threatening terrain will turn solid red. This will happen at sufficient spacing to avoid impact with the terrain but this time using more positive control movements.

The accuracy of this display is however linked to the accuracy of the navigational equipment. A poor nav fix or a malfunctioning nav system will result in dangerously inaccurate display. Some pilots have been found to be using the threat display to "thread" their way through high terrain. This is of course a gross misuse of the system and is strongly advised against.

The terrain display can be **selected by the pilot, or may be automatically activated** whenever the terrain becomes a threat. The threat display may be incorporated with the weather radar display, the navigational display or it may have its own Plan Position Indicator (PPI).

3.21   TERRAIN CLEARANCE FLOOR

This alerts the crew to possible premature descent for non-precision approaches regardless of aircraft configuration. It uses the present aircraft position with respect to the runway. It is speculated that in the future the database for this and the EGPWS as a whole will be merged with that for the FMS. This will mean that the EGPWS can work with the latest information and include temporary obstacles normally notified by NOTAM.

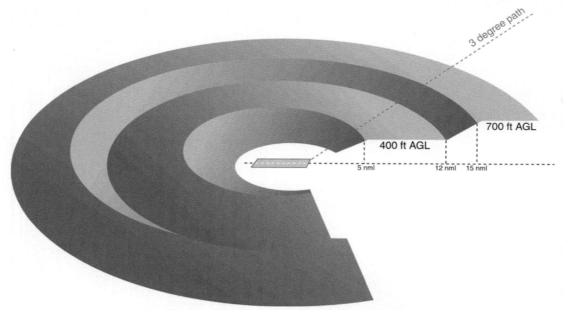

Figure 3.15 Terrain Clearance Floor

3.6   INTEGRITY TESTING

The GPWS is provided with **built-in test equipment (BITE)** which allows **all** its functions and visual/audible warnings to be **tested prior to flight**; the pre-flight BITE is **inhibited in flight**. The test is initiated by the pilot pressing the test switch.

During flight the system is continuously monitored to confirm its serviceability and any in-flight failure is automatically indicated on the flight-deck. **A short confidence check is possible while airborne**, but this is not a full BITE check..

3.7   INHIBITION OF EGPWS MODES

The EGPWS **must not be de-activated** (by pulling the circuit breaker) except for approved procedures. Instructions on inhibition must include a statement that no person may de-activate the EGPWS except in accordance with the procedures stated in the Operations Manual.

Inhibition of the glideslope mode may be desirable when a glideslope signal is present but the aircraft is deliberately being flown without reference to it, e.g. the pilot may have discontinued the ILS, to land on a different runway, or is performing a localiser only approach.

Inhibition may also be required when the **gear or flap position** inputs are known to be non-standard.

3.8   BOEING 737 MARK II EGPWS

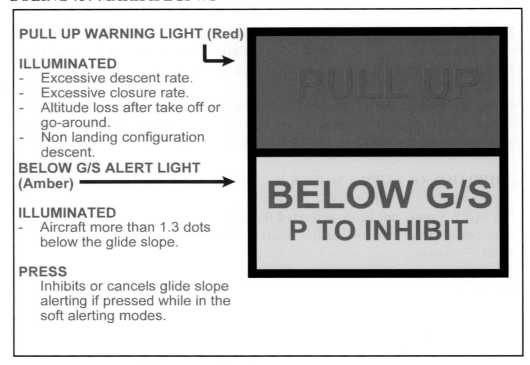

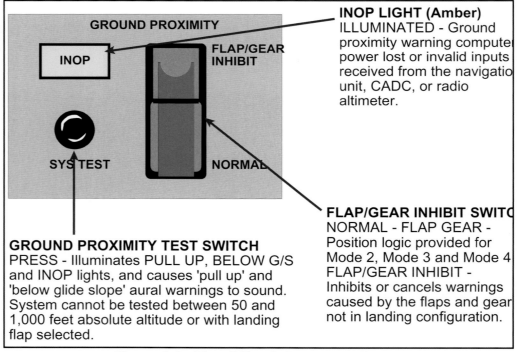

Figure 3.3. First Officer's Instrument Panel.

3.9   MODE 1 - EXCESSIVE BAROMETRIC DESCENT RATE

Mode 1 has two boundaries and is independent of aircraft configuration. Penetration of the **first boundary** generates **an aural alert of "SINK RATE" repeated each 1.5 seconds.**

Penetrating the **second boundary** causes the **repeated warning of "WHOOP, WHOOP PULL UP"**, until the rate of descent has been corrected.

MODE 1

AURAL ALERT - SINK RATE, SINK RATE
AURAL WARNING - 'WHOOP WHOOP PULL UP'

VISUAL -   PULL UP

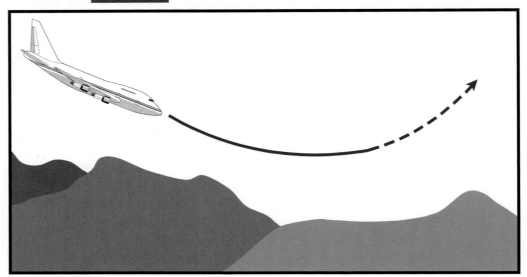

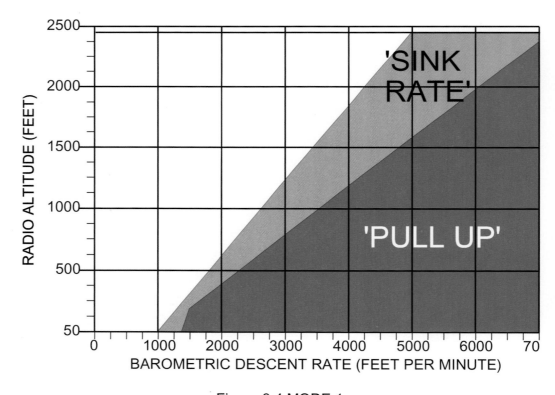

Figure 3.4 MODE 1

3.10   MODE 2 - EXCESSIVE TERRAIN CLOSURE RATE

Mode 2 monitors **Mach number, radio altitude rate of change, barometric altitude and aircraft configuration.**

Mode 2 has two boundaries.   Penetrating the **first boundary** causes an **aural alert** of **"TERRAIN, TERRAIN", followed by the repeated aural warning "WHOOP, WHOOP PULL UP"**. After leaving the PULL UP area, the repeating TERRAIN message will again be heard while in the terrain portion of the envelope. If both boundaries are penetrated while in the landing configuration, only the repeating TERRAIN aural alert will occur. The terrain message is repeated each 1.5 seconds.

As Mach number increases from 0.35 to 0.45 with gear up, the highest radio altitude at which Mode 2 alert warning will occur is increased to 2450 feet. This higher portion of the envelope is inhibited with the flap override switch in the FLAP OVRD position.

MODE 2

AURAL ALERT - 'TERRAIN, TERRAIN'
AURAL WARNING - 'WHOOP WHOOP PULL UP'

VISUAL -   PULL UP

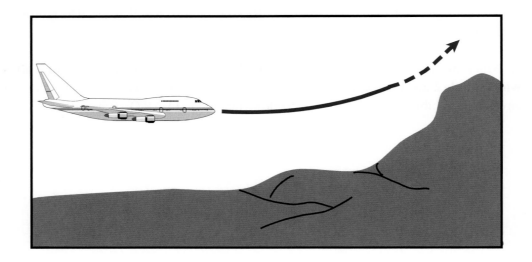

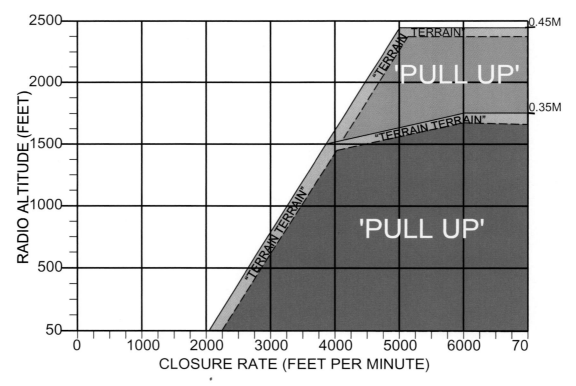

Figure 3.5 MODE 2

3.11   MODE 3 - ALTITUDE LOSS AFTER TAKE-OFF OR GO-AROUND

Mode 3 provides an alert if a descent is made during initial climb or go-around. The aural alert is a voice message of "**DON'T SINK**", repeated each 1.5 seconds until the flight condition is corrected.

Mode 3 is effective between **50 and 700 feet** radio altitude and generates the alert when the accumulated barometric loss equals approximately **10 percent** of the existing radio altitude.

Mode 3 does not **arm during the descent until below 200 feet** radio altitude.

MODE 3

AURAL ALERT - "DON'T SINK"

VISUAL -   PULL UP

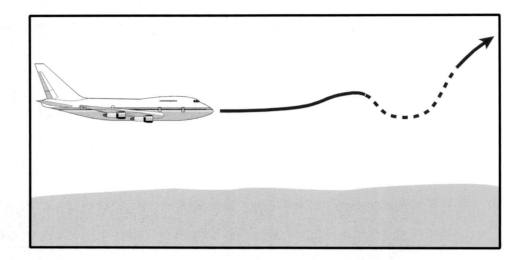

Note Mode 3 arms when the aeroplane descends below 200ft in the landing configuration

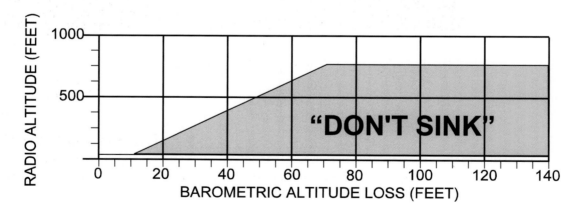

Figure 3.6 MODE 3

3.12   MODE 4A - UNSAFE TERRAIN CLEARANCE WITH LANDING GEAR NOT DOWN

The terrain clearance mode with gear retracted, is **armed after take-off upon climbing through 700 feet radio altitude.**

When this envelope is penetrated **at less than 0.35 Mach**, the aural alert **"TOO LOW GEAR"** is sounded. When the envelope is penetrated **at more than 0.35 Mach**, the aural alert **"TOO LOW TERRAIN"** is sounded and the **upper boundary of the envelope is increased to 1000 feet radio altitude.** The applicable voice message is repeated each 1.5 seconds until the flight condition has been corrected.

MODE 4A

AURAL ALERT - "TOO LOW GEAR"
              "WHOOP WHOOP PULL UP"

VISUAL -   PULL UP

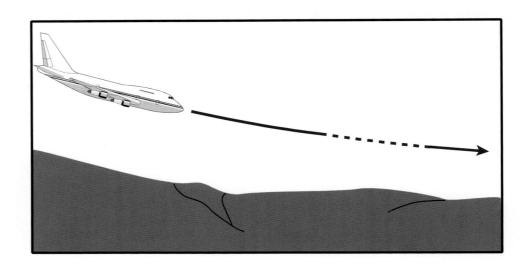

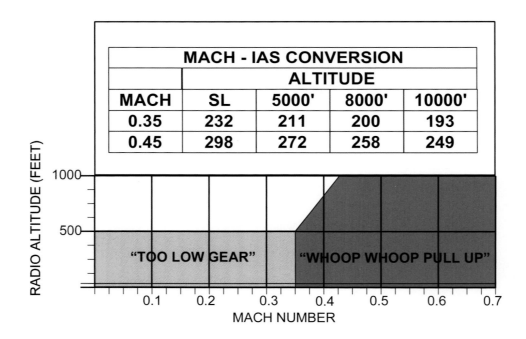

MACH - IAS CONVERSION				
	ALTITUDE			
MACH	SL	5000'	8000'	10000'
0.35	232	211	200	193
0.45	298	272	258	249

Figure 3.7 MODE 4A

3.13   MODE 4B - UNSAFE TERRAIN CLEARANCE WITH FLAPS NOT IN LANDING CONFIGURATION

This mode provides an alert **when the gear is down** and the **flaps are not in the landing position**. If the envelope is penetrated at **less than 0.28 Mach** with the flaps not in the landing position, the aural alert of **"TOO LOW FLAPS"** is sounded.

When the envelope is penetrated **at more than 0.28 Mach,** the aural alert of **"TOO LOW TERRAIN"** is sounded and the upper boundary of the envelope is increased **to 1000 feet radio altitude.**

The applicable voice message is repeated each 1.5 seconds until the flight condition has been corrected. **The "TOO LOW GEAR" alert takes priority over the "TOO LOW FLAPS".** The too low flaps alert and associated too low terrain alert are **inhibited** with the flap inhibit switch in the **FLAP OVRD** position.

MODE 4B

AURAL ALERT -   "TOO LOW FLAPS"
               "WHOOP WHOOP PULL UP"

VISUAL -   PULL UP

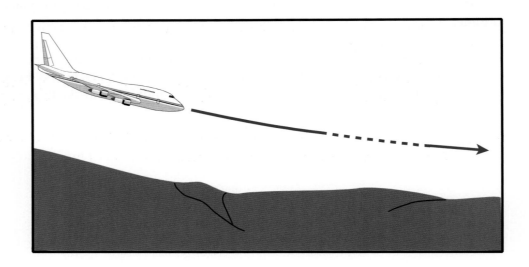

MACH - IAS CONVERSION				
	ALTITUDE			
MACH	**SL**	**5000'**	**8000'**	**10000'**
0.28	185	169	180	154
0.45	298	272	258	249

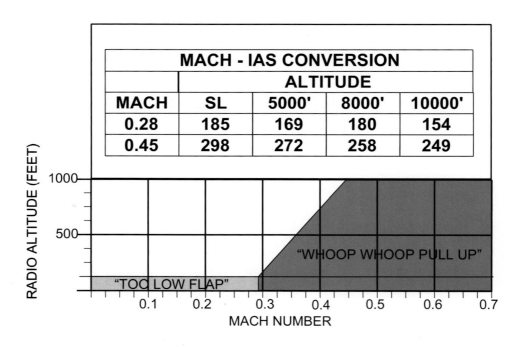

Figure 3.8 MODE 4B

3.14　MODE 5 - BELOW GLIDE SLOPE DEVIATION ALERT

This mode alerts the flight crew of a descent of **more than 1.3 dots below an ILS glide slope.**

The envelope has two areas of alerting, **soft** and **loud.** In both areas, the alert is a repeated voice message of **"GLIDE SLOPE"**, and illumination of both pilots' **BELOW G/S'** lights. The voice message amplitude is increased when entering the loud area. In both areas, the voice message repetition rate is increased as the glide slope deviation increases and the radio altitude decreases.

The mode is armed when a valid signal is being received by the captain's glide slope receiver and the radio altitude is **1000 feet or less**.

The mode may be cancelled or inhibited by pressing either pilot's **below G/S** light while below 1000 feet radio altitude. The mode will re-arm when climbing above 1000 feet radio altitude.

Mode 1 to 4 aural alerts and warnings have priority over mode 5 aural alerts, however both **PULL UP** and **BELOW G/S** lights could be illuminated at the same time.

MODE 5

AURAL ALERT - "GLIDE SLOPE"
"

VISUAL -
```
BELOW G/S
P TO INHIBIT
```

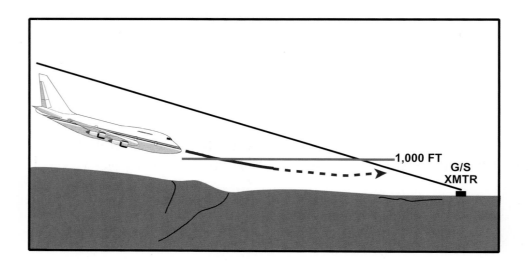

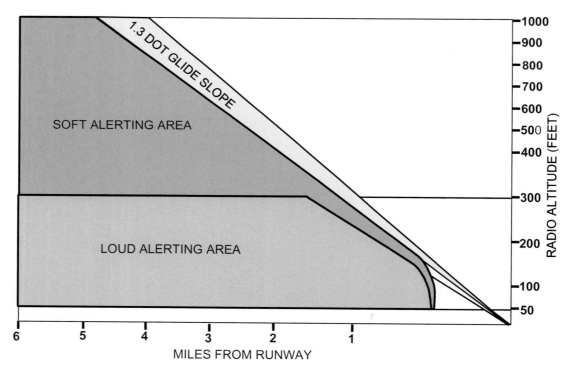

Figure 3.9 MODE 5

3.15   MODE 6A - BELOW SELECTED MINIMUM RADIO ALTITUDE

Mode 6A provides an **aural alert** if a descent is made below the minimum decision altitude cursor in the captain's radio altimeter. This mode operates **between 50 and 1000 feet** of radio altitude.

This alert is aural only and consists of **"MINIMUMS, MINIMUMS" sounded once.**

The mode is rearmed when the radio altitude becomes greater than that selected with the captain's altitude cursor.

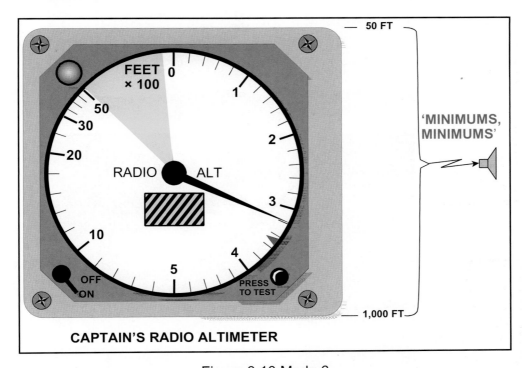

Figure 3.10 Mode 6

3.19   MODE 6B   ALTITUDE CALL-OUTS AND BANK ANGLE ALERT

Call-outs of selected altitudes and minimums is available. The call outs used are a customer option but for example may consist of calls at 200ft and 100ft to decision height, or absolute height call outs from the radio altimeter with respect to the ground.

Figure 3.13 Mode 6B

"**BANK ANGLE**" can be used to alert crews of excessive roll angles. The bank angles will be specific to each aircraft. The bank angle limit reduces with proximity to the ground due to the reduced wing tip clearance to prevent wing tip or engine damage during take off and landing.

3.20   MODE 7   WINDSHEAR ALERTING

Visual and aural windshear warnings are given when several parameters such as ground speed, airspeed, barometric height and rate of descent and radio altitude, indicate the initial conditions of entering an area of windshear. Again as with the terrain threat display there is no scanning beam looking ahead to avoid the condition entirely. Rather the benefit from the system is derived from the fact that it allows the pilot to initiate the windshear go-around procedure earlier, giving the aircraft a greater probability of avoiding an accident.

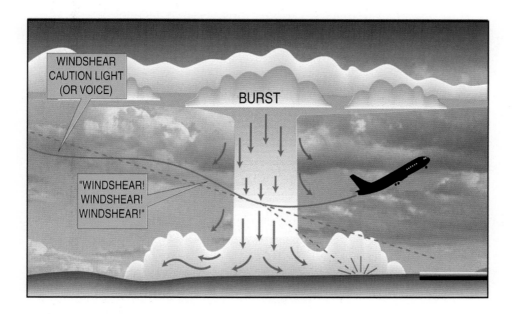

Figure 3.14. Mode 7 Windshear Alerting

CHAPTER THREE - GPWS

1.   The GPWS the alert/warning information is provided by a radio altimeter with:

   a)   a downward transmitting beam whose dimensions are in the order of 60° and 30° in the fore/aft and the athwartship axes.

   b)   a downward transmitting beam whose dimensions are in the order of 30° and 60° in the fore/aft and the athwartship axes.

   c)   a forward transmitting beam.

   d)   a downwards transmitting radio beam

2.   The GPWS would provide visual and audible warning to a pilot if the aircraft descended:

   a)   to below 500' radio altitude with flaps not in the landing position and speed below Mach.28

   b)   to below 500' radio altitude with flaps not in the landing position and speed below Mach.35

   c)   to below 200' barometric altitude with flap not in the landing position and speed below Mach.28

   d)   to below 200' radio altitude with flap not in the landing position and speed below Mach.28.

3.   The Ground Proximity Warning mode 5 provides a visual and audible warning to the pilot if the aircraft:

   a)   descends below 500ft radio altitude with gear retracted.

   b)   is below 1000ft radio altitude and more than 1.3 dots below the ILS glidepath.

   c)   descend below 200ft radio altitude with flaps retracted.

   d)   sinks more than approximately 10% of accumulated altitude.

4.   The GPWS uses inputs from:

   a)   the radio altimeter, the ILS receiver, the Air Data Computers and the landing gear position indicators.

   b)   the radio altimeter, the Air Data Computers, the landing gear position indicators and the flap position indicators.

   c)   the radio altimeter, the Air Data Computers, the Captain's ILS receiver, the landing gear position indicators and the flap position indicators.

   d)   the radio altimeter and the ILS receiver.

WARNING AND RECORDING EQUIPMENT

5.   The Ground Proximity Warning mode 4a provides a visual and audible warning 'Too Low Gear' to the pilot if the aircraft descends below _____ with landing gear retracted.

   a)   200 feet radio altitude with speed below M 0.28.
   b)   200 feet barometric altitude with speed below M 0.28.
   c)   500 feet radio altitude with speed below M 0.35.
   d)   500 feet barometric altitude with speed below M 0.35.

6.   An aircraft 'goes around' after descending to a radio alt of 190 feet. As power is applied a power unit is lost and some height is lost. The GPWS would provide an alert when the aircraft had lost about:

   a)   10 feet
   b)   20 feet
   c)   50 feet
   d)   100 feet

7.   GPWS Mode One gives warning of:

   a)   excessive descent rate.
   b)   height loss after take-off/missed approach.
   c)   unsafe terrain clearance when not in the landing configuration.
   d)   excessive terrain closure rate.

8.   GPWS, Mode Three gives warning of:

   a)   excessive descent rate.
   b)   height loss after take-off/missed approach.
   c)   unsafe terrain clearance when not in the landing configuration.
   d)   excessive terrain closure rate.

9.   GPWS, mode two operates between:

   a)   50ft and 2450ft agl
   b)   50ft and 1800ft agl
   c)   50ft and 700ft agl
   d)   50ft and 500ft agl

10.   With reference to GPWS:

    a)   In all six modes the audible alerts and warnings are accompanied by the red flashing PULL-UP' light.

    b)   Mode 4A activates when the aircraft descends below 500ft radio altitude at a speed less than .35Mach with the landing gear retracted.

    c)   Mode 4A activates when the aircraft descends below 500ft barometric altitude at a speed less than .28Mach with the landing gear retracted.

    d)   Mode 6 re-arms when the aircraft leaves the hard alerting area.

11.   An aircraft 'goes around' after descending to a radio altitude of 190ft. As power is applied a power unit fails and some height is lost. The GPWS would provide an alert when the aircraft had lost about:

    a)   10ft
    b)   20ft
    c)   50ft
    4.   100ft

12.   GPWS mode 3 will operate if altitude loss occurred before you have acquired:

    a)   700 ft barometric altitude gain.
    b)   500 ft terrain clearance.
    c)   200 ft barometric altitude gain.
    d)   700 ft terrain clearance.

13.   With reference to GPWS Mode 4. At or below what radio altimeter altitude is mode 4 activated if not in the landing configuration?

    a)   500 ft
    b)   700 ft
    c)   200 ft
    d)   790 ft

14.   Mode 4 gives warning of:

    a)   excessive descent rate.
    b)   height loss after take-off/missed approach.
    c)   unsafe terrain clearance when not in the landing configuration.
    d)   excessive terrain closure rate.

ANSWERS

QUESTION	ANSWER	QUESTION	ANSWER
01	b	21	
02	d	22	
03	b	23	
04	c	24	
05	c	25	
06	b	26	
07	a	27	
08	b	28	
09	a	29	
10	b	30	
11	b	31	
12	d	32	
13	b	33	
14	c	34	
15		35	
16		36	
17		37	
18		38	
19		39	
20		40	

CHAPTER FOUR AIRBORNE COLLISION AVOIDANCE SYSTEM

Contents

        Page

4.1   INTRODUCTION .... 4 - 1

4.2   TCAS I .... 4 - 1

4.3   TCAS II .... 4 - 1

4.5   PRINCIPLE .... 4 - 1

4.6   AIRCRAFT EQUIPMENT .... 4 - 2

4.7   OPERATION .... 4 - 2

4.8   SYSTEM INTERCONNECTIONS .... 4 - 3

4.4   SYNTHETIC VOICE PRIORITISATION .... 4 - 4

4.9   TRAFFIC ADVISORIES (TAs) RESOLUTION ADVISORIES (RAs)........ 4 - 5

4.10   RESOLUTION ADVISORIES .... 4 - 6

4.11   PROXIMATE TRAFFIC/OTHER TRAFFIC .... 4 - 7

4.12   DATA TAG .... 4 - 7

4.13   OFF SCALE TRAFFIC ADVISORY .... 4 - 7

4.14   TCAS DISPLAYS .... 4 - 8

4.15   COMBINED TCAS AND SSR CONTROL PANEL .... 4 - 11

4.16   TCAS TRAFFIC ADVISORIES ON ELECTRONIC VSI. .... 4 - 12

4.17   TCAS PREVENTATIVE RESOLUTION ADVISORIES ON ELECTRONIC VSI. . . 4 - 12

4.18   TCAS CORRECTIVE RESOLUTION ADVISORY ON ELECTRONIC VSI. . 4 - 13

4.19   TCAS TEST FORMAT ON ELECTRONIC VSI .... 4 - 13

4.20   NO BEARING ADVISORIES. .... 4 - 14

4.21   ACTION TO BE TAKEN ON RECEIVING TA's AND RA's.   . . . . 4 - 14

4.22   STANDARD R/T PHRASEOLOGY   . . . . 4 - 15

4.1   INTRODUCTION

Today's higher traffic densities and greater speed differences have generated a need for an Airborne Collision Avoidance System. Although ICAO named it ACAS it is usually known as **Traffic Alert and Collision Avoidance System (TCAS)**. The system is designed to provide an additional margin of safety and keep commercial aircraft **clear of conflict,** independently of Air Traffic Control. An aircraft must carry a transponder and have the facility to interrogate other aircraft transponders. Of the four proposed systems, TCAS I, II, III and IV, TCAS I and II fulfill present and future requirements. Aircraft built to carry more than 30 passengers must have an approved system for flight in the USA.

4.2   TCAS I

TCAS I is a first generation collision avoidance system and simply warns the crew of other traffic in the vicinity of their aircraft. It will detect and display range and approximate relative bearing. If the TCAS display aircraft and the intruder are carrying Mode C relative altitude will also be displayed. It encourages flight crew to look for the conflicting traffic by generating visual and aural warnings - **TRAFFIC ADVISORIES (TAs):**

> *do not move if receive a 'TA' as it is illegal!*

     " Traffic, Traffic".

It **does not give any resolution advisory** information. i.e a course of action to follow. **The FAA requires smaller aircraft, with 30 or fewer seats, to carry TCAS I.**

> *climb or descend*

4.3   TCAS II

> *Mode 'S' needed*
>
> *Corrective OR Preventive*
>
> *monitor vertical speed - keep out of red*

TCAS II detects intruders in the TCAS aircraft's vicinity, assesses the collision risk and presents warnings to the crew in the form of **TAs** and **Resolution Advisories (RAs)** e.g.:

"Climb" "Increase Climb" Descend" "Increase Descent" Monitor Vertical Speed"

> *Vertical Plane only*

Thus, RAs offer manoeuvring advice **in the vertical plane** to resolve conflict. If the your aircraft and the intruder both have Mode S data-link transponders the system will co-ordinate the RAs to provide complimentary vertical avoidance instructions. The rest of this chapter deals with   TCAS II only and discusses both visual and audible TAs and RAs in detail.

4.5   PRINCIPLE

TCAS II operates on the secondary radar principle using the normal SSR frequencies of 1030MHz and 1090MHz, but in an air to air role. Using this principle the TCAS system creates two protective three dimensional bubbles around the TCAS equipped aircraft (Figure 4.1.)

> *TCAS III — RAs give vertical & horizontal advisory info (still being developed)*

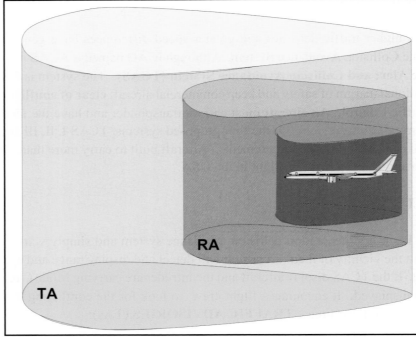

Figure 4.1.

4096 codes are available
0-7 0-7 0-7 0-7
∴4096

4.6   AIRCRAFT EQUIPMENT

For aircraft to be visible to a TCAS equipped aircraft they must have a minimum of A **Mode "A" Transponder.** If the transponder is switched off, or is unserviceable, the intruding aircraft are invisible to the TCAS equipment and a collision risk exists. **Mode A transponders transmit no height information and therefore the information available to the TCAS equipment is two dimensional only** and therefore can only give TAs.

Mode "C" Transponder equipped intruders broadcast height information to the TCAS equipment and the system becomes **three dimensional** and can now give both TAs and RAs.

Mode "S" Transponder TCAS equipped intruders as well as broadcasting height information allow a discrete data link to be established between them.   This data link will allow avoidance manoeuvres to be mutually resolved.

4.7   OPERATION

The **range** of an intruder is determined by measuring the time lapse between transmission of an interrogation and receiving the response. (Radar Principle). The **bearing** of an intruder is determined by a directional antenna (Figure 4.2.). Because of the wavelengths involved and the necessarily small size of the antennas **bearing resolution is the least accurate parameter**. TCAS never offers collision avoidance commands in the horizontal plane; only in the form of climb or descend. .

SSS — Secondary Surveillance Radar

The **relative height** of an intruder is found by comparing it's Mode "C" height with the TCAS equipped aircraft's height.

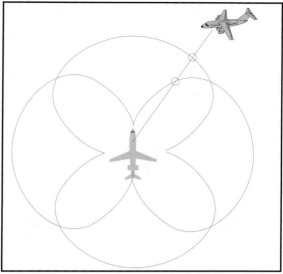

Figure 4.2. TCAS Bearing Determination.

4.8   SYSTEM INTERCONNECTIONS

Figure 4.3. shows a TCAS installation in a Commuter/Feeder airliner. The heart of the system is the TCAS receiver-transmitter-computer unit controlled by a combined ATC/SSR/TCAS control panel. The TCAS displays in this installation are a dedicated TCAS Plan Position Indicator (PPI), and the red and green sectors on the Vertical Speed Tape of the Primary Flight Display (PFD) Electronic Attitude Director Indicator (EADI). A synthetic voice issues TCAS commands over the intercom system.

The TCAS upper and lower antennas are directional while the Mode "S" antennas are omni-directional.

The TCAS also has feeds from the Radio Altimeter to modify the RAs received when in close proximity to the ground i.e. there are no instructions given at all when the aircraft is below 400ft agl, no descent RAs are given below 1000ft agl and no increase rate of descent commands below 1400ft agl. The system will also take aircraft configuration / performance into consideration when deciding an avoiding action. When the aircraft has gear and / or flap deployed its climb performance will be poor so TCAS will avoid giving climbing demands for a RA.

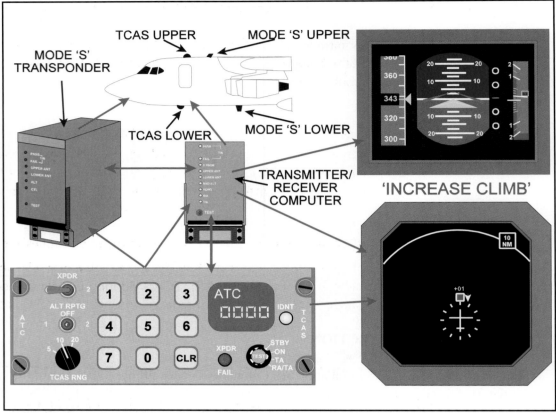

Figure 4.3. TCAS Aircraft Installation.

4.4   SYNTHETIC VOICE PRIORITISATION

Modern aircraft use a synthetic voice to give warning advice to the crew. The voice is used for various systems including Windshear detection, Ground Proximity Warnings, including height call outs, and TCAS. The synthetic voice is prioritised as follows:

a)   **Stall Identification/Stall Prevention.** (Stick Shake/Stick Push). The synthetic voice is inhibited during stick shake/stick push operation.

b)   **Windshear.** The detection of performance decreasing windshear takes first priority with the synthetic voice, inhibiting both GPWS and TCAS warnings.

c)   **Ground Proximity Warning System(GPWS).** Detection of approach to terrain takes priority over TCAS announcements.

4.9   TRAFFIC ADVISORIES (TAs) RESOLUTION ADVISORIES (RAs).

Depending upon the setting of the TCAS function switch on the control panel, the equipment level of intruder aircraft and the phase of flight of the TCAS aircraft, TCAS will generate the following.

α from CPA
(closest point of approach)

a)   **Traffic Advisories (TAs)** exist when an intruder penetrates the outer bubble caution area and is between 45 and 35 seconds from the collision area. TA's appear as **solid amber circles** on the TCAS display and are accompanied by the synthetic voice saying **"Traffic, Traffic"**. This is a potential collision threat.

or yellow

b)   **Resolution Advisories (RAs)** exist when an intruder penetrates the inner bubble warning area and is between 30 and 20 seconds from the collision area. RA's appear as **solid red rectangles** on the TCAS display accompanied by various synthetic voice warnings. RA's indicate a serious collision threat. (See Figure 4.4.)

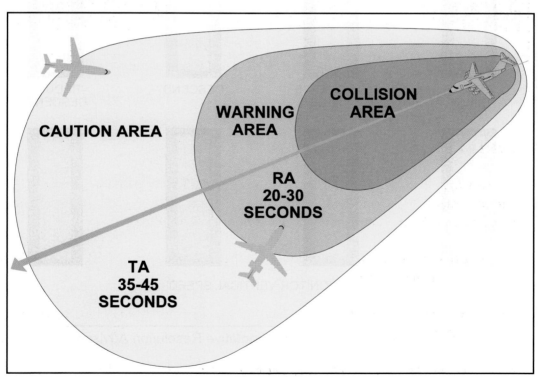

Figure 4.4.

If Intruding a/c has Mode 'A' only selected (α no height)
the most you will get is a 'TA' ∴ cannot manoeuvre

4.10   RESOLUTION ADVISORIES

Resolution Advisories come in two forms:

a)   **Preventative Advisories** are situations where no collision risk exists unless a change of level is initiated by either aircraft. The synthetic voice advisory is **"Monitor Vertical Speed"**

b)   **Corrective Advisories** are situations where a collision risk exists and a manoeuvre is necessary to avert it. The synthetic voice produces the appropriate command.

Figure 4.5. shows examples of Preventative and Corrective RA's displayed on the Vertical Speed tape of the Primary Flight Display.

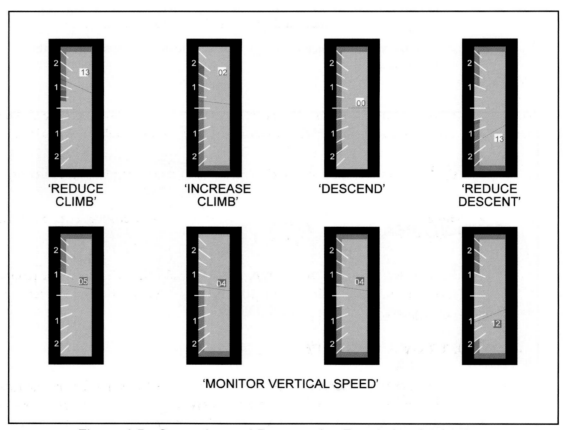

Figure 4.5. Corrective and Preventative Resolution Advisories.

4.11   PROXIMATE TRAFFIC/OTHER TRAFFIC

See Figures 4.6., 4.7. and 4.7a

6 mm

◆   a)   **Proximate Traffic** appears as a solid cyan diamond and represents transponder equipped aircraft within range of the display and within +/- 1200 feet relative height. TCAS does not consider this traffic a threat and displays it to improve crew situational awareness.

1500 ft above

+15

— no audies or manauvr given.

◇   b)   **Other Traffic** appears as **hollow cyan diamonds** which represent transponder equipped aircraft within range of the display and within +/- 2700 feet relative height (+/- 8700 dependant on position of ABOVE and BELOW switch). Again it is displayed to improve situational awareness.

The predicted flight paths of Proximate and Other Traffic do not penetrate the Collision Area of the TCAS aircraft.

4.12   DATA TAG

The traffic symbols may also have an associated altitude TAG which shows relative altitude in hundreds of feet, to indicate whether an intruder is climbing, flying level or descending:

a)   A **+ sign** and number above the symbol means an **intruder is above** the aircraft.

b)   **A trend arrow**   ↑ or   ↓ appears alongside the symbol when the intruder's vertical rate is **500 feet per minute or greater**.

No altitude number or trend arrow will appear beside an intruder that is non altitude reporting. If TCAS II direction finding techniques fail to locate the azimuth of another aircraft a **no bearing** message appears on the screen.

4.13   OFF SCALE TRAFFIC ADVISORY

When TCAS is tracking an intruder that is outside the selected display range, but has entered the caution or warning areas, one-half of the appropriate symbol will appear at the appropriate bearing at the edge of the display area. The symbol will appear in its proper colour and have its data tag displayed providing there is room. See Figure 4.10.

Intruding TA
close TA etc = TA (all the same!)

Q: Where does TCAS get its info from?
— Pressure Alt from mode "S" transponder & Rad Alt
— a/c configuration   *✱ Can disregard*

4.14   TCAS DISPLAYS

TCAS range and bearing information can appear on a variety of displays:

a)   Dedicated Plan Position Indicator. Figure 4.6.

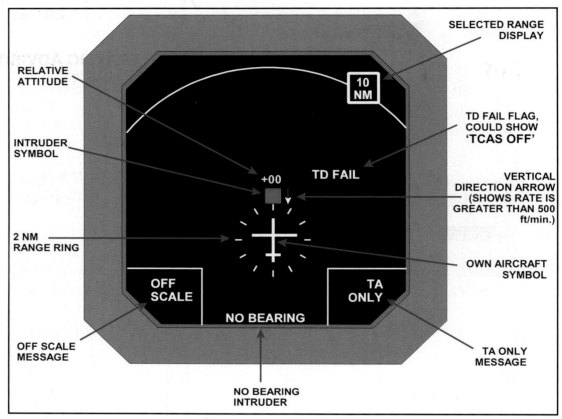

Figure 4.6. TCAS PPI.

*If TCAS & ATC info conflict follow TCAS and tell ATC you are.

If told to climb then get VSI needle into the green segment

b)   **Electronic Vertical Speed Indicator.** Figure 4.7.

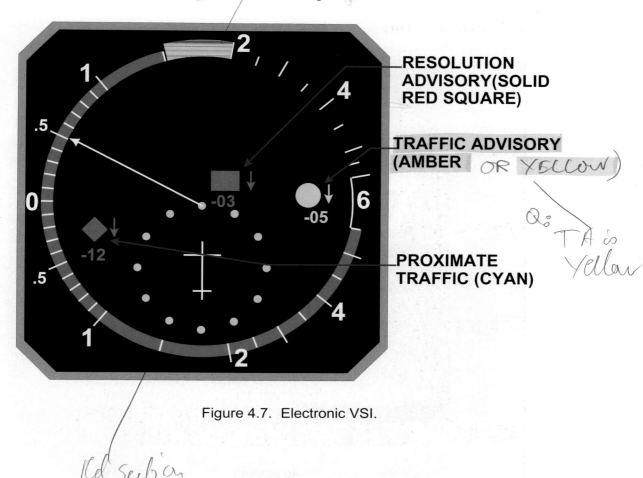

RESOLUTION ADVISORY(SOLID RED SQUARE)

TRAFFIC ADVISORY (AMBER OR YELLOW)

Q: TA is Yellow

PROXIMATE TRAFFIC (CYAN)

Figure 4.7. Electronic VSI.

Red Section

- If told to 'Increase Climb' the green area will move further to a fter climb rate.

- Will not allow a/c to stall

c)   Superimposed on Navigation Display of EFIS equipped aircraft.

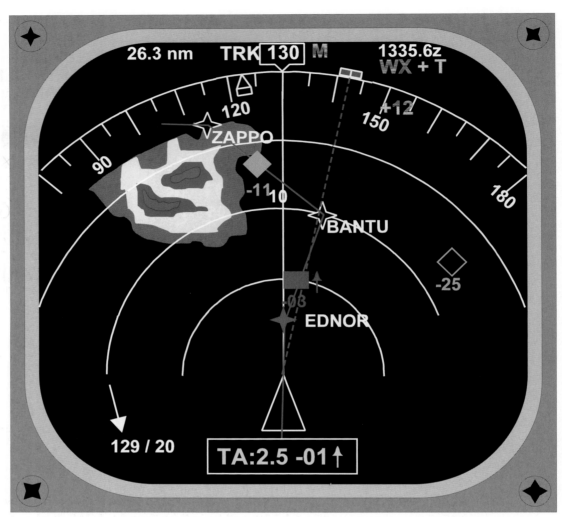

Figure 4.7a. Navigation Display in MAP Mode Showing TCAS.

4.15   COMBINED TCAS AND SSR CONTROL PANEL

The control panel is produced in various forms but all perform the same functions. The TCAS controls are as follows: See Figure 4.8.

Figure 4.8. ATC Transponder/TCAS Control Panel.

a)   **Function Switch**

   i)   Standby - warm-up power is applied to the system, but it is not operational.

   ii)   On - the transponder only is operational.

   iii)   TA - the transponder and TCAS are now operational but only Traffic Advisories are generated.   "TA ONLY" will be indicated on the TCAS display.

   iv)   RA/TA - the transponder and TCAS are operational and both Resolution Advisories and Traffic Advisories are generated.

   v)   TEST - pressing the centre TEST button on the function switch initiates a full Built - in - Test Equipment (BITE) of the system. After completion of a successful test the synthetic voice will respond with "TCAS SYSTEM TEST OK". If the system test is unsuccessful the voice response is "TCAS SYSTEM TEST FAIL".

b.   **TCAS RNG (range)** selects the range of the TCAS display either 5, 10, or 20nm. It does not alter the range at which aircraft are detected or when warnings are given.

4.16   TCAS TRAFFIC ADVISORIES ON ELECTRONIC VSI.

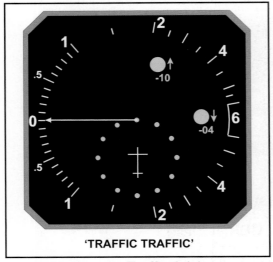

'TRAFFIC TRAFFIC'

Figure 4.9. Traffic Advisory

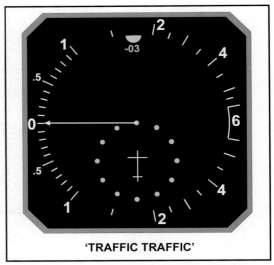

'TRAFFIC TRAFFIC'

Figure 4.10. Off Scale Traffic Advisory.

4.17   TCAS PREVENTATIVE RESOLUTION ADVISORIES ON ELECTRONIC VSI.

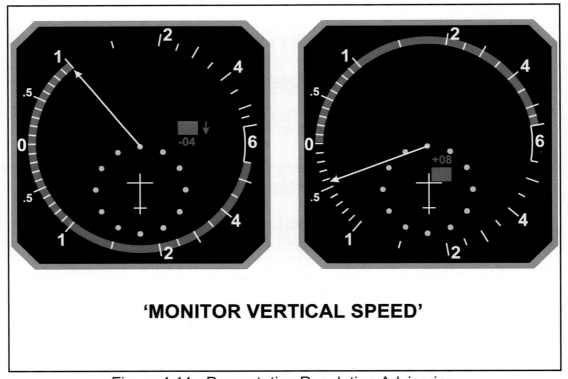

'MONITOR VERTICAL SPEED'

Figure 4.11. Preventative Resolution Advisories.

4.18   TCAS CORRECTIVE RESOLUTION ADVISORY ON ELECTRONIC VSI.

Figure 4.12. Corrective RA.

4.19   TCAS TEST FORMAT ON ELECTRONIC VSI.

Figure 4.13. Test Display.

4.20   NO BEARING ADVISORIES.

If TCAS is unable to track the bearing of an intruder, possibly due to antenna screening, the RA or TA will appear lower centre of the display appropriately colour coded. Up to two lines of information can be displayed. **"TA 2.2- 04"** means the intruder is creating a TA 2.2 nm
away 400 below and the up arrow indicates the intruder is climbing at 500 fpm or greater.

It is important to realise that TCAS' ability to compute a Traffic or Resolution Advisory is not degraded by lack of bearing information.

handwritten annotations: Proximate; "Enhanced RA" as other a/c is getting in the way

Figure 4.14. No Bearing RA and TA.

4.21   ACTION TO BE TAKEN ON RECEIVING TA's AND RA's.
Refer to CAP 579.

a)   **Action on Receiving a TA.** TAs alert flight crews to the possibility that an RA may follow, which could require a flight path change. Flight crews should assimilate the information provided by the TA and commence a visual search of that part of the sky. They should also prepare to respond to an RA if the situation worsens. If the potential threat cannot be seen and continues to give cause for concern flight crews should seek advice from ATC. (para. 6.1.1/2.).

b)   **Action on Receiving an RA.** Pilots are to initiate the required manoeuvre immediately, adjusting flight path, aircraft power and trim accordingly. Crew members not involved in executing this manoeuvre should confirm that the sky ahead is clear of other aircraft and continue the visual search for the established threat. They are to inform ATC as soon as possible of any deviation from an ATC clearance. (Para. 6.2.3.)

c)   **Disregarding RA's.** Manoeuvres should never be made in a direction opposite to that given in an RA; this is because the sense may have been determined following an exchange of data with the established threat. For this reason:

    i)   RA's **may be disregarded only when pilots visually identify the potentially conflicting traffic and decide no deviation from the current flight path is needed.** (para 6.2.4.(a) refers)

    ii)   If pilots receive simultaneously an instruction to manoeuvre from ATC and an RA, **and both conflict, the advice given by TCAS should be followed**. (para. 6.2.4.).

4.22   STANDARD R/T PHRASEOLOGY

a)   **Notification of a manoeuvre in response to an RA.**

Pilot: **TCAS climb** (or TCAS descent).
Controller: **roger**.

b)   **after "clear of conflict".**

Pilot: Returning to xxxxft/flxxx (details of assigned clearance).
Controller: roger; a revised clearance may then be issued.

c)   **inability to comply with atc instruction.**

Controller: climb (descend) flxxx.
Pilot: Unable to comply, TCAS RA..

Further reading: cap 579 airborne collision avoidance systems (ACAS): guidance material.

CHAPTER FOUR - ACAS

1.   On receipt of a TCAS RA your action is to:

   a)   initiate the required manoeuvre immediately.
   b)   make a note of the details.
   c)   request a flight clearance deviation from ATC.
   d)   Do nothing until a TA is received.

2.   Which of the following statements concerning TCAS is correct:

   a)   TCAS 2 provides avoidance instructions in the vertical and horizontal planes.
   b)   TCAS 2 cannot provide information on non-SSR equipped intruders.
   c)   TCAS 2 requires Mode S to be fitted to other aircraft.
   d)   TCAS 2 provides advice on which way to turn.

3.   With reference to Traffic Collision Avoidance Systems. The difference between TCAS I and II is that:

   a)   TCAS II can provide 'Traffic Advisories' and 'Resolution Advisories' whilst TCAS I can only provide 'Traffic Advisories'.
   b)   TCAS II can only be fitted to large aircraft which carry more than 30 passengers. Whilst TCAS I can be fitted to any aircraft.
   c)   TCAS I can be fitted to aircraft which carry transponders with Mode A only whilst TCAS II can only be fitted to aircraft whose transponders include either Mode C or Mode S.
   d)   TCAS II can only be fitted to aircraft which are equipped with EFIS.

4.   The aural messages provided by TCAS II are:

   a)   Threat, Climb; Threat, Descend.
   b)   Climb left; Climb right; Descend left; Descend right.
   c)   Climb; Descend; Increase climb; Increase Descent.
   d)   Turn left, Turn Right, Increase Turn, Decrease Turn

5.   With reference to Traffic Collision Avoidance Systems:

a)   RAs may be disregarded only when the pilot visually identifies the potentially conflicting traffic and decides that no deviation is necessary and has the clearance confirmed by ATC.

b)   RAs may be disregarded only when the pilot visually identifies the potentially conflicting traffic and decides that no deviation is necessary and has advised ATC of the other aircraft's proximity.

c)   RAs must never be disregarded.

d)   RAs may be disregarded only when the pilot visually identifies the potentially conflicting traffic and decides that no deviation is necessary.

ANSWERS

QUESTION	ANSWER	QUESTION	ANSWER
01	a	21	
02	b	22	
03	a	23	
04	c	24	
05	d	25	
06		26	
07		27	
08		28	
09		29	
10		30	
11		31	
12		32	
13		33	
14		34	
15		35	
16		36	
17		37	
18		38	
19		39	
20		40	

CHAPTER FIVE - FLIGHT DATA RECORDER

Contents

		Page
5.1	INTRODUCTION	5 - 1
5.2	FDR DESIGNS	5 - 1
5.3	FDR COMPONENTS	5 - 1
5.4	AIRCRAFT INTEGRATED DATA SYSTEMS (AIDS)	5 - 3
5.5	PARAMETERS RECORDED	5 - 4
5.6	JAR REQUIREMENTS	5 - 5

5.1   INTRODUCTION

Commercial aircraft have a flight recorder which records various aircraft parameters during the entire duration of the flight The main function of the flight data recorder (FDR) is to preserve the aircraft data in order to determine the cause of any aircraft accident. It is also used to gather information for trend analysis and trouble shooting. In smaller aircraft the FDR may be combined with a cockpit voice recorder.

5.2   FDR DESIGNS

The FDR records the last 10 or 25 hours of aircraft data on a digital storage device housed in a fire and shock resistant box. The box that is painted red or orange and located at the rear of the aircraft, normally under the fin . On the front of the unit is an underwater locating device (ULD). The older type of FDR's are of non digital design while the JAR now states that on aircraft registered as of the 1 April 2000, all FDR's must be of the digital type.

5.3   FDR COMPONENTS

The FDR consists of the following components (see figure 5.1):

a)   a recording system

b)   a control unit on the overhead panel

c)   a control unit on the pedestal

The recording system includes a digital flight data recorder (DFDR), a flight data interface unit (FDIU) and a 3-axis linear accelerator (LA).

The control unit on the overhead panel also controls the cockpit voice recorder (CVR). A spring-
loaded switch labelled GND CTL can be selected ON or AUTO as follows:

a)   ON   The CVR and the DFDR are energised and the ON light is lit

b)   AUTO   The CVR and the DFDR are energised:

      i)   on the ground whenever electrical power is applied

      ii)   on the ground with one engine running

      iii)   in flight (with engine running or stopped)

The control on the pedestal consists simply of push button labelled 'EVENT' which sets an event mark on the DFDR recording. This acts as a kind of bookmark to enable the "event" to be found rapidly on the recording at a subsequent analysis.

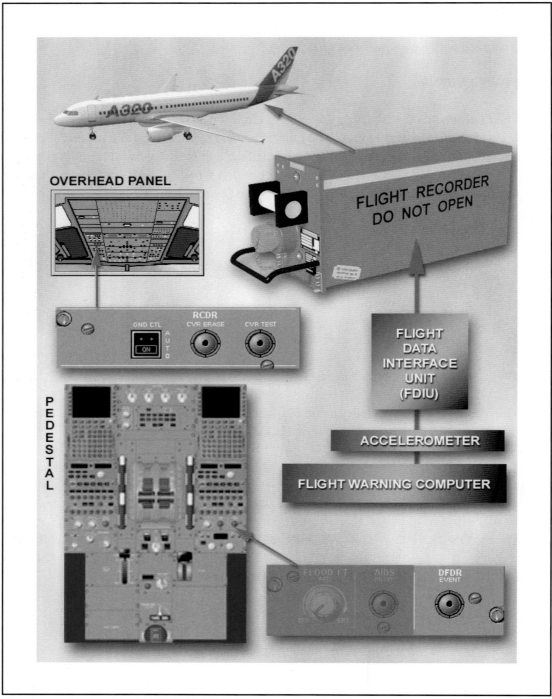

Courtesy of Airbus Industrie

Figure 5.1 Digital Flight Data Recorder

When on the ground the FDR is automatically stopped 5 minutes after the final engine shut-down.

A block diagram of a digital flight data recorder system for a Boeing 767 aircraft is shown in Figure 5.2.

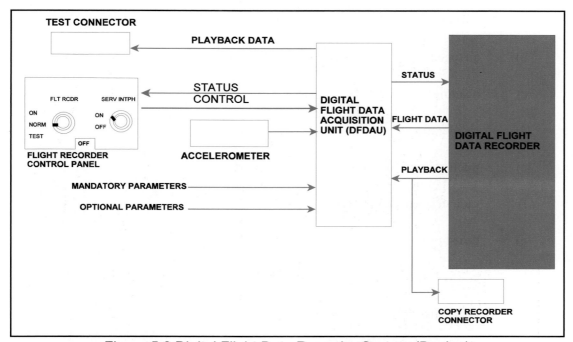

Figure 5.2 Digital Flight Data Recorder System (Boeing)

5.4   AIRCRAFT INTEGRATED DATA SYSTEMS (AIDS)

AIDS processes data for various aircraft systems to ease maintenance tasks. This is done via a data management unit (DMU) that collects and processes data to compile reports for storage and for printing. Some of this information is sent to the FDR via the flight data interface unit (FDIU) for recording mandatory parameters of the flight. The rest of the information is recorded on a separate flight maintenance recorder from which data can be printed out for the purpose of maintenance.

Data stored on the DMU can be printed out both in flight as well as on the ground for the purpose of maintenance.

It is also possible to transmit relevant data from AIDS to ground at certain intervals so that the aircraft performance can be monitored from the ground. This is done via ACARS (Airborne Communications and Reporting System) on a VHF data link.

5.5   PARAMETERS RECORDED

The mandatory aircraft parameters recorded on the FDR depend upon the age and size of the aircraft and are specified in JAR OPS.

The **main parameters** are:

a)   altitude

b)   airspeed

c)   heading

d)   acceleration

e)   pitch and roll attitude

f)   radio transmission keying

g)   thrust or power on each engine

h)   configuration of lift and drag devices

i)   air temperature

j)   use of automatic flight control systems and

k)   angle of attack.

Additional parameters include the following:

a)   positions of primary flight controls and trim

b)   radio altitude and navigation information displayed to the flight crew

c)   cockpit warnings and

d)   landing gear position.

5.6   JAR REQUIREMENTS

Carriage of FDR equipment
Period of Recording

It is a requirement of JAR OPS that aircraft shall be equipped with a flight data recorder capable of recording and storing data as follows:

a)   during at least the last **10 hours** of its operation for an aircraft that is **5700 kg or less** and registered after 1 April 1998

b)   during at least the last **25 hours** of its operation for an aircraft that is:

      i)   over 5700 kg or
      ii)   has more than 9 seats

Parameters Recorded

The main parameters mentioned in para 5.5 must be recorded in all aircraft weighing 27,000 kg or less while the **additional parameters** must also be recorded in all aircraft **over 27,000 kg.**

Method of Recording

All FDR's must use the digital method of recording except that aircraft registered before 1 April 1995 and weighing more than 5700 kg the continued use of non-digital recorders is acceptable until 1 April 2000.

Other Requirements   The other JAR OPS requirements are:

a)   The FDR must start automatically to record the data prior to the aeroplane being capable of moving under its own steam and must stop automatically after the aeroplane is incapable of moving under its own power.

b)   The FDR must have a device to assist in locating that recorder in water.

c)   Aeroplanes of 5700 kg or less may have the FDR combined with the cockpit voice recorder.

d)   An aeroplane may be dispatched with an inoperative FDR provided that:

      i)   it is not reasonably practicable to repair or replace the FDR before flight
      ii)   the aeroplane does not exceed 8 further consecutive flights
      iii)   not more than 72 hours have elapsed since the unserviceability
      iv)   any cockpit voice recorder required to be carried is operative (unless it is combined with the FDR)

CHAPTER SIX - COCKPIT VOICE RECORDER

Contents

		Page
6.1	INTRODUCTION	6 - 1
6.2	THE RECORDING	6 - 1
6.3	THE VOICE RECORDER	6 - 1
6.4	THE CONTROL UNIT	6 - 3
6.5	JAR OPS REQUIREMENTS	6 - 4

6.1   INTRODUCTION

The principle function of a Cockpit Voice Recorder (CVR) system is to preserve, in the event of an air accident, vital information that is recoverable for use by the Accident Investigation Branch (AIB). The CVR automatically records the last 30 minutes of communications and conversations on the flight deck. It becomes operational whenever 115 volts AC power is applied to the aircraft though it can be disabled during aircraft maintenance. The system comprises a tape recorder, a control unit, a monitor display and an area microphone. The units and their locations are shown in figure 6.1.

6.2   THE RECORDING

The voice recorder is a standard magnetic tape recorder using a minimum of four recording heads and a tape that is about 300 feet long in the form of an endless loop. This should give a minimum 30 minutes of 4-channel parallel recording. The recorder should be capable of recording the frequency range 350 Hz to 3000 Hz though this likely to be increased to 6000 Hz in future. The information recorded includes:

a)   communications and interphone audio between the captain's, first officer's and the observer's stations via their boom microphones or oxygen mask microphones (these are applied to channels 1,2 and 3).

b)   conversations and other sounds on the flight deck picked up by a separate area microphone usually mounted on the control unit (applied to channel 4).

a)   on some two-crew aircraft the observer's channel may be used to record public address messages.

6.3   THE VOICE RECORDER

The tape recorder is located inside a crash-proof metal box that is painted red or orange and normally placed at the rear of the aircraft, often adjacent to the flight data recorder. The high impact case should be able to withstand shock, high temperature and fire.

On the front of the unit is fitted an underwater locating device (ULD) that will emit a continuous series of ultrasonic pulses to help locate a submerged CVR. The unit is automatically activated by water and the battery will last several days.

The front panel of the CVR also enables the information recorded on all the tracks to be monitored via a playback head and monitor amplifier.

Courtesy of Airbus Industrie

Figure 6.1 Cockpit Voice Recorder

6.4   THE CONTROL UNIT

This is mounted on the flight deck, usually in the roof panel. It contains monitoring and testing circuitry and also the area microphone to pick up general flight deck conversations and sounds. It has the following controls:

a)   **AUTO / ON**   When the switch is in the AUTO position the CVR will start to record when the first engine is started and will stop 5 mins after the last engine is shutdown. Selection of the ON position starts the CVR recording immediately and latches the switch in the ON posiion until first engine start, when it will click back to AUTO.

b)   **CVR TEST**   Pressing the TEST button activates an extensive set of functional tests which determine the integrity of the system using the BITE (built in test equipment) facility. A successful self-test results in a visual 'good' indication (a status deflection needle or a status LED) and a 600 or 800 Hz audio tone heard via the microphone monitor jack.

a)   **ERASE**   Erasure of the tapes is only possible with the aircraft on the ground, all engines stopped and the parking brake set. Suitable safety interlocks are installed to prevent inadvertent or airborne tape erasure. Additionally the erase button must be held depressed for at least 2 seconds before the circuit activates.

Some CVR control units will incorporate the area microphone as shown in Figure 6.2.

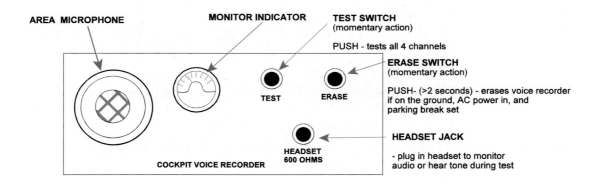

Figure 6.2 CVR Control Unit

6.5   JAR OPS REQUIREMENTS

It is a requirement of JAR OPS that aircraft shall be equipped with a cockpit voice recorder capable of retaining recorded information as follows:

a)   during at least the last **30 minutes** of its operation for an aircraft registered **before 1 April 1998** and is:

      i)   5700 kg or less **and** having more than 9 seats, **or**

      ii)   over 5700 kg

b)   during at least the last **2 hours** of its operation for an aircraft registered on or **after 1 April 1998** and is:

      i)   multi-engine turbine powered with more than 9 seats, **or**

      ii)   over 5700 kg

The other JAR OPS requirements are:

c)   The CVR must be capable of recording:

      i)   voice communications transmitted from or received on the flight deck by radio

      ii)   the aural environment of the flight deck, including where practicable, without interruption, the audio signals received from each boom and mask microphone in use.

      iii)   voice communications of flight crew members on the flight deck using the aeroplanes interphone system.

      iv)   voice or audio signals identifying navigation or approach aids introduced into a headset or speaker and

      v)   voice communications of flight crew members on the flight deck using the public address system, if installed.

d)   The CVR must start to record prior to the aeroplane moving under its own power and continue to record until the termination of the flight when the aeroplane is no longer capable of moving under its own power.

e)   The CVR must have a device to assist in locating the recorder in water.

f)   An aeroplane may be dispatched with an inoperative CVR provided that:

i)   it is not reasonably practicable to repair or replace the CVR before flight

ii)   the aeroplane does not exceed 8 further consecutive flights

iii)   not more than 72 hours have elapsed since the unservicability

iv)   any flight data recorder required to be carried is operative (unless it is combined
        with the CVR)

1.   An altitude alerting system must at least be capable of alerting the crew on:

        1.   Approaching selected altitude
        2.   Abnormal gear/flap combination
        3.   Excessive vertical speed
        4.   Excessive terrain closure
        5.   Excessive deviation from selected altitude
        6.   Failure to set SPS or RPS as required

        a)   1&3
        b)   2&5
        c)   4&6
        d)   1&5

2.   According to JAR OPS subpart K, when must the DFDR on a 12 seat turbo prop a/c begin recording?.

        a)   Switch on until switch off
        b)   From before the aircraft is capable of moving under its own power to after the a/c is no longer capable of moving under its own power
        c)   From lift off until the weight on wheels switch is made on landing
        d)   At commencement of the taxi to turning off the runway

3.   What is the EGPWS mode 3 audible alert?

        a)   "don't sink, don't sink" followed by "whoop, whoop, pull up" if the sink rate exceeds a certain value.
        b)   "don't sink, don't sink" followed immediately by "whoop, whoop, pull up".
        c)   "don't sink, don't sink" continuously.
        d)   "Terrain, don't sink" continuously.

4.   What are the inputs to a modern jet transport aeroplane's stall warning system:

        1.   A.o.A
        2.   Engine RPM
        3.   Configuration
        4.   Pitch and bank information
        5.   Control surface position
        6.   Airspeed vector

        a)   1,2,3&4
        b)   2,4,5&6
        c)   1,2,3&6
        d)   2,3,4&5

5. EGPWS may indicate:

    1. Excessive sink rate after T/O
    2. Excessive descent rate
    3. Excessive closure
    4. Ground proximity, not in the landing configuration
    5. Deviation from glide-slope
    6. Proximity to en-route terrain

    a) 1,4&6
    b) 2,3&5
    c) 1,3&5
    d) 2,4&6

1	2	3	4	5	6	7	8	9	10
d	b	c	c	a					
11	12	13	14	15	16	17	18	19	20
21	22	23	24	25	26	27	28	29	30

JAAatpl
JOINT AVIATION AUTHORITIES

Theoretical Training Manuals

Revised Edition

AIRCRAFT GENERAL KNOWLEDGE 4

INSTRUMENTATION
AUTOMATIC FLIGHT CONTROL

CIVIL AVIATION AUTHORITY

OXFORD
Aviation Training
Succeed through our experience™

CHAPTER ONE -AUTOMATIC FLIGHT CONTROL

Contents

Page

1.1   INTRODUCTION 1-1

1.2   FLIGHT DIRECTOR SYSTEM COMPONENTS 1-2

1.3   FLIGHT DIRECTOR MODES 1-6

1.4   DUAL FDS 1-14

FDS

※ To command an instantanious attitude to achieve,
to maintain or intercept a target value.

1.1   INTRODUCTION

The Flight Director System (FDS) was originally developed as an aid used by the pilot during landing. It gave a pilot the ability to concentrate on fewer instruments and, as it gave instructions as to attitude and steering, it reduced the workload on the pilot. As autopilots became more advanced the signals produced by the FDS could be coupled to the autopilot allowing it to perform more complex tasks.

With a FDS, information about the attitude, heading and flight-path of an aircraft, can be integrated with navigation information to produce either easy to interpret visual instructions for the pilot and / or input to the autopilot, or both.

To bring the terminology of FDS and autopilot together it is usual to describe the FDS as having 2 "channels". The first channel is the **roll channel**, the second is the **pitch channel**. You will learn more about channels in the autopilot section.

Information for the FDS can come from several possible sources:

a)   Pitot-Static system or Air Data Computer (ADC).
b)   VHF Nav receiver allowing input from VOR beacons or ILS.
c)   Flight Management System, Inertial Navigation / Reference System.

The FDS also requires attitude and directional information. On older, electro-mechanical systems this would come from the Gyro Magnetic Compass and a Vertical Gyro System. More modern aircraft use Inertial Navigation/Reference System (INS / IRS) information in place of a vertical gyro and will be able to feed the navigation data from these systems into the FDS / Autopilot combination.

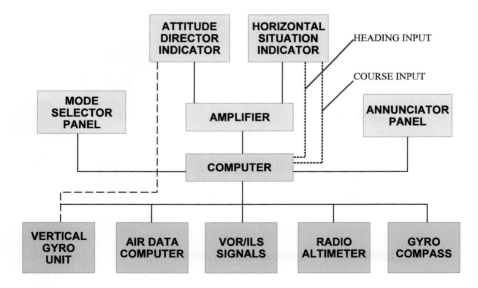

Fig 1.1 A "typical" electro-mechanical Flight Director System

1.2   FLIGHT DIRECTOR SYSTEM COMPONENTS

There follows a description of a "typical modern" FDS:

Electronic Attitude Director Indicator (EADI)

This is a fairly standard artificial horizon providing pitch and roll information and gives the Attitude to the name of the instrument. The Director part comes from the instruments ability to display demand information from the Flight director system using Flight Director Command Bars. These come in 2 main forms as shown below:

Both of the indications for these apparently different displays are intuitive and essentially the same in that the pilot is required to "fly to" either the point where the "wires" cross, or the point between the wedges, in order to satisfy the demand from the FDS.

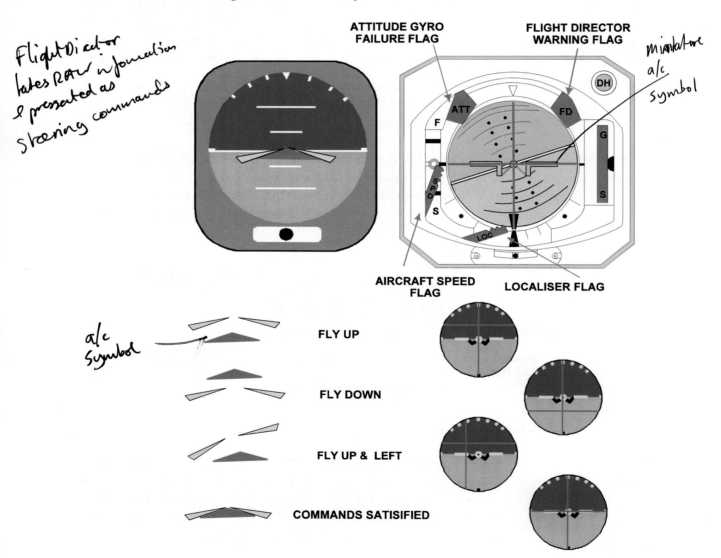

Command Cursor
ADI, EADI, or PFD.

Primary Flight Display (PFD)

The PFD is part of an EFIS (Electronic Flight Instrument System) display and brings all of the information required to fly the aircraft onto one display. It has an EADI normally surrounded by speed, altitude, and vertical speed tapes and often a compass display incorporating some minimal navigation information. It also has an area which is used for annunciating flight director, autopilot and auto-throttle modes and status.

Electronic Horizontal Situation Indicator (EHSI)

You may already be familiar with the Gyro Magnetic Compass. An HSI is a gyro magnetic compass display with a Course Deviation Indicator (CDI bar), a series of dots representing deviation in degrees (the scale varies with the type of display) a from / to pointer, a selected course window and a DME display of range. A heading bug is also included. In older systems the course selection is done directly on the HSI using an attached knob. The system we will refer to uses a remote centralised FD mode control and AP panel called the Autoflight Mode Control Panel (AMCP or simply MCP). The system we will be referring to also uses a Navigational Display (ND). This, like the PFD, is a more flexible display but is able to show "classical" representations of an HSI.

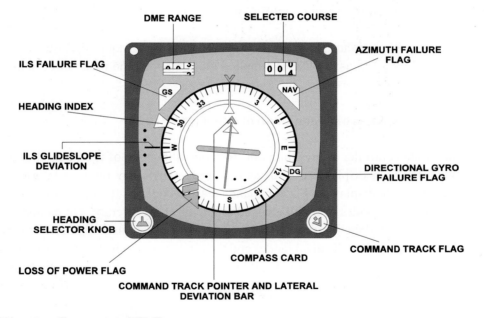

Flight Director Computer (FDC)

This is where all the information is gathered and processed. On older aircraft this information could be in the form of analogue outputs from the ADC and VG. Current systems will be purely digital. Older aircraft that have been refitted may have analogue inputs to a digital converter so that modern displays and autopilot systems can be used. Outputs from here are sent to the symbol generators for the EADI / EHSI and /or the autopilot as required.

Optional Components

FDS use other components depending on what generation they belong to:

Instrument Amplifier or Symbol Generator

Where information is required to be displayed on electro-mechanical instruments the signals require amplification to drive the associated motors. On EFIS fitted aircraft the FDC output can be fed directly to the symbol generators for the Primary Flight Display (PFD) and Navigational Display (ND) units.

Vertical Gyro or INS / IRS

In older or smaller aircraft types, normally without any INS / IRS, reference to the vertical for the Artificial Horizon part of the ADI is provided by a remote Vertical Gyro system. This simply means that the gyro that acts as the artificial horizon is not contained in the instrument in the panel in front of the pilot but can be any where on the aircraft (normally near the C of G). The information derived from it is fed to motors that drive the display of the ADI. The benefits of this system are that the gyro can be near the aircraft's C of G and therefore provide a more accurate display of the attitude of the aircraft, and this data, in electrical form can be fed to any other items requiring attitude information e.g. the Autopilot.

More modern and larger aircraft may use data from their INS or IRS to replace that normally provided by a VG as the INS is simply a more modern and much more sensitive version of a gyro.

Mode Controllers or Mode Control Panel (MCP)

The mode controller allows the pilot to change the mode of the FDS, alter the pitch trim and switch the FDS display on or off as required. Obviously on a visual approach it would be unnecessary to display the FD command bars and could clutter up the display at a critical phase of flight. The modes available depend on the fit of the aircraft. On modern aircraft the MCP, on which most of the information for the autopilot is programmed is used to replace the separate FD mode controller. Typical modes and the pitch trim will be discussed a little later. The MCP will also be described in more detail later.

MODE CONTROL PANEL

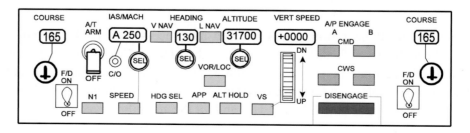

Mode Annunciators / Indicators or PFD Flight Mode Annunciators (FMA)

These are a series of simple lights, magnetic indicators or a small panel of illuminated indicators that **show the pilot what mode or phase of a particular mode that the FDS / Autopilot is in.** In more basic systems the most common indications are during an ILS approach. These panels are usually only powered with the FD switch on.

When the aircraft is awaiting capture of the localiser, the LOC (localiser) light will typically be amber. When the localiser has been captured the light will change to a green LOC light. Approaching the glide-slope the GS light will be Amber and again will change to green to indicate the fact that the FDS has locked on to the GS.

More capable systems will have more functions and consequently more lights, such as those indicating the state of the auto-throttle and flare or Go Around modes.

EFIS equipped aircraft display the appropriate information on the PFD/EADI in an area called the Flight Mode Annunciator. As the same space can be used for all the different messages, it can be kept small. Here all the modes for the FD auto-throttle and autopilot are displayed. Newly changed information is often emphasised on the FMA type display by surrounding it in a box.

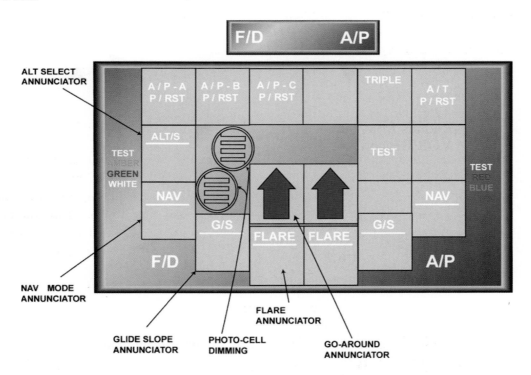

1.3   FLIGHT DIRECTOR MODES

As has been said the modes for each system vary. The modes described now are the most common but not all may be available depending on aircraft fit.

First it must be appreciated that there is a distinction in the way data displayed to the pilot. The glideslope indicator to the side of the ADI and the CDI bar are what is termed **Raw information**. That is the information is not processed in any way and simply indicates that the aircraft is left or right of track / localiser, or above or below the glideslope and knowledge of the system will tell you by how many degrees.

In order to anticipate turns, climbs and descents for smooth flying the FDS can use the raw data, compute and signal commands to either the pilot via the Flight Director bars or directly to the autopilot. This is called **computed information** and is derived from the **rate of change of deviation** of the incoming signal. As the rate of change of deviation from the desired track increases, the FDS computes that in order to intercept the track correctly, rather than fly straight through, it must indicate a turn onto track.

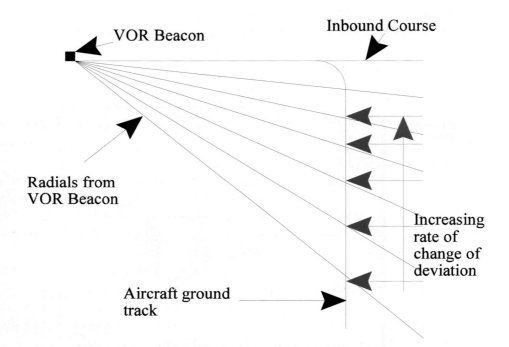

This becomes important if the FDS fails as although the computed information will no longer be reliable / available, the raw information may still be available and used.

Many of the FD modes are common with the autopilot modes. We have detailed the FD modes in the following sections. Where they are similar to the autopilot mode the description is fairly basic with the full description being found in the autopilot chapter. Where the FD mode differs from the autopilot mode the description will detail the differences.

FD Fail indications

Before going on to discuss the modes individually we need to know how the FDS informs us if the information it is giving is reliable. On electro-mechanical displays warning flags are used. If the vertical gyro or other vertical referencing system fails or its power supply fails then a "Gyro" warning flag will pop into view, normally on the ADI. Failures of the FDC, the instrument amplifier, or the ADI itself, are indicated by a flag labelled either "ATT" for attitude or "FD". This will normally again be in the ADI display.

If glideslope information is unreliable, due to poor signal strength or failure of the system, a "GS" flag will appear in front of the raw glideslope scale where it appears, either to the side of the ADI or the HSI.

Poor reception, unreliable or loss of VOR, LNAV or LOC information is indicated by a "NAV" flag, normally located on the HSI.

The HSI will have a power failure flag to indicate loss of power to the instrument or the compass gyro. It will also indicate if the compass system is operating in Directional Gyro (DG) mode i.e. the magnetic reference has been lost and the compass is now essentially a DI.

Command attitude changes

When flying level the pilot selects an attitude that, for the given airspeed, will achieve level flight. With the aircraft at low airspeed the pitch angle will be several degrees nose up to avoid descending. As an aid to keeping a constant pitch angle the FD command bars can be offset vertically to provide an intuitive aiming point for the pilot.

This can also be used for keeping constant pitch angles for climbing and descending. The movement of the bars is achieved by moving the Pitch Trim knob or wheel (dependent on age of design) until the command bars are in the desired position. The pitch trim system is inhibited whenever any other pitch mode is active.

Flight Director Takeoff Mode

Initially both flight director systems should be switched on prior to starting the takeoff roll. The FD takeoff mode is engaged by pressing either of the TO/GA switches on the throttles. The AFDS annunciation is "TO/GA". The initial FD commands are for 10 degrees nose-down pitch and wings level. At 60 kts IAS, the FD command changes to 15 degrees nose-up and wings level.

To engage the FD system during the takeoff even if the FD switches are off press the TO/GA button after 80 kts IAS but before 2000' or 150 seconds after lift-off and the command bars will automatically disappear.

The FD provides pitch commands after lift-off. It continues to command 15 degrees nose-up pitch until sufficient climb rate is achieved. It then commands pitch to maintain the MCP speed plus 20 kts IAS; this speed is calculated and set during the pre-flight. Next, when either autopilot is engaged or when the MCP speed selector is rotated 20 kts IAS is added automatically to the MCP IAS display.

FD roll commands wings level from takeoff mode engagement through to the takeoff climb-out.

To terminate the takeoff mode below 400' RA, both of the FD switches must be turned off. Above 400' RA, the takeoff mode can be terminated by selecting other FD pitch modes or by engaging an autopilot.

Engaging an autopilot after a FD takeoff, automatically engages the autopilot and FD in LVL CHG (level change) for pitch and HDG SEL (heading select) for roll. If the FD mode had been changed from TO/GA to LNAV, HDG SEL or VOR/LOC, the autopilot initially engages in the same roll mode as the FD's. When LVL CHG engages, the MCP IAS/MACH display and airspeed cursors change to $V_2 + 20$ kts.

If an engine fails during takeoff before reaching V_2 speed, the FD pitch commands are referenced to V_2. If the engine failure occurs after reaching V_2, but less than $V_2 + 20$ kts, the reference speed is that at which the engine failure occurred. If the failure occurs at or above $V_2 + 20$ kts, $V_2 + 20$ kts is the commanded speed. Reference speed is never less than V_2 for the current flap setting. Roll control remains the same as for all engines operating.

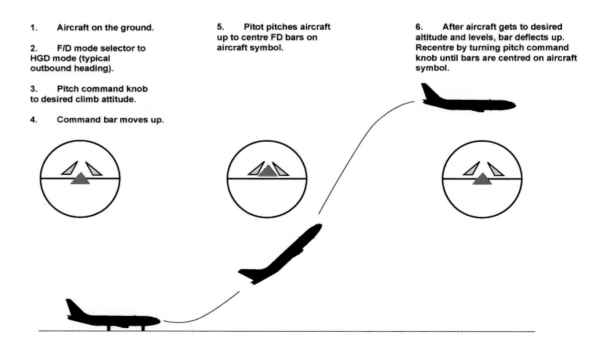

1. Aircraft on the ground.

2. F/D mode selector to HGD mode (typical outbound heading).

3. Pitch command knob to desired climb attitude.

4. Command bar moves up.

5. Pitot pitches aircraft up to centre FD bars on aircraft symbol.

6. After aircraft gets to desired altitude and levels, bar deflects up. Recentre by turning pitch command knob until bars are centred on aircraft symbol.

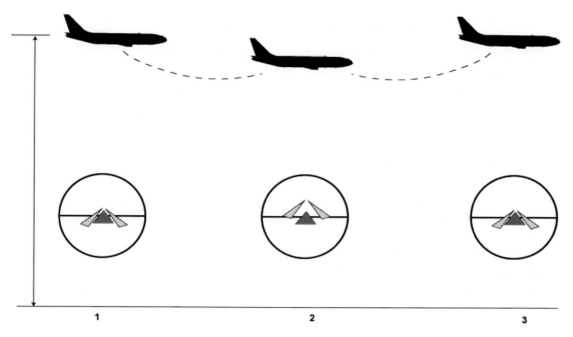

Altitude Acquire / Altitude Hold

In the cruise we require to fly at a constant level. The FDS can be used to help achieve this. Signals from the ADC through the FDS mean that when we are at the selected level, the FD command bars indicate a neutral position. If the aircraft were to deviate above the desired altitude the command bars would indicate a pitch down command and visa versa.

NAVIGATION MODES:

Heading Mode

In this mode VOR beacons and various internal navigation systems can be linked to either display information using the FDS or linked to the autopilot or both.

The simplest nav mode is to have the aircraft keep flying in the direction you select. This is called **Heading Mode**. In this mode the pilot selects a desired heading, either using a knob on the HSI, using the central FDS / autopilot panel or on the MCP. The FDS will now indicate a fly to command to bring the aircraft on to the desired heading.

LOC/ VOR (LNAV)

This selection allows VOR, Localizer or INS/IRS/FMS(GPS) nav information to be fed and displayed on the FDS. In the case of the VOR, after tuning and correctly identifying the station to be used, with VOR / LOC selected on the mode selector and the desired track to (or from) the beacon set in the course selection widow (using either on the HSI, MCP or the CDU) , the FDS will give appropriate steering command to intercept and then maintain track.

© Oxford Aviation Services Limited

Intercepting the LOC is very similar but will be discussed in more detail later.

With aircraft being fitted with more accurate navigation systems it is only logical that this information should be made available to the pilot and autopilot. INS / IRS / FMS / GPS information can be selected for display in very much the same way as the VOR information and is represented in the same way.

Note that because the actual track of the aircraft is being compared with the desired track, and the flight director commands are given to fly the desired track, the flight director system will effectively compensate for drift. There is no need for wind velocity information (although the INS could provide it), it is purely an effect of the flight director giving commands to fly the desired course/track selected.

Flight Director Approaches (FDA)

The ILS frequency is tuned into the VHF nav radios and identified and the QDM for the approach is set up in the course window. The mode selector should be set to AUTO / APP. The annunciator will show that the FDS is looking to capture the LOC. After beam capture, in a similar manner to VOR tracking the FDS will (given enough distance) arrange the intercept to establish on the localizer with a turn demand and the annunciator panel will indicate LOC capture.

The FDS is now looking for the glideslope signal and so the annunciator GS light or MI will indicate such. As soon as the glideslope is captured the annunciator changes again and the FDS will indicate a pitch nose down demand to fly the ILS glideslope.

If the interception of the localiser has been misjudged it is possible to end up established on the localiser past the point of GS intercept i.e. above the glideslope. Modern systems may automatically adjust and capture from above by increasing the rate of descent. On older aircraft it was sometime possible to temporarily switch the FDS mode to MAN / GS. This forces the FDS into accepting a capture from above. It can also be used to establish a fixed intercept angle of the LOC beam and to force a LOC or GS capture condition if it is known that the beam-sensing circuits of the computer are inoperative.

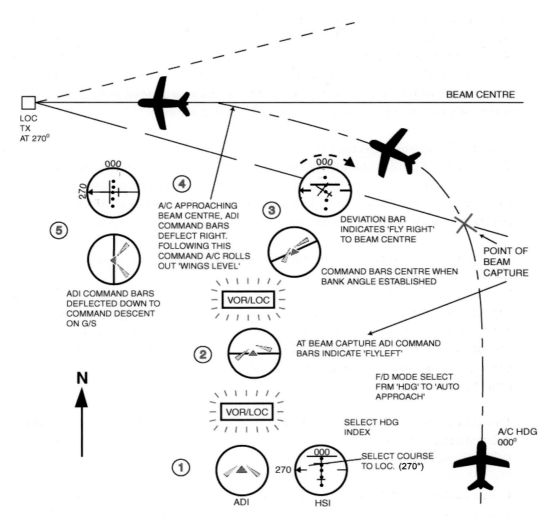

FD Go Around (GA)

For the 737-400 series of a/c 2 criteria must be met before the FD can engage in the GA mode. The FD switches can be either on or off and:

1.   In-flight below 2000' RA and not in the TO mode

2.   TO/GA switch pressed

After engaging in GA, command bars appear for both pilots, TO/GA is annunciated for the FD pitch mode, the MCP IAS/MACH display blanks and the Airspeed Cursors display manoeuvring speed for the existing flap setting.

Below 400' RA, both of the FD switches must be turned from ON to OFF to exit the FD GA mode. Above 400' RA, other pitch and roll modes can be selected. If the roll mode is changed first, the FD pitch mode remains in the GA mode. If the pitch mode is changed first, the FD roll mode automatically changes to HDG SEL.

Engaging an AP following a FD GA automatically engages both the AP and FD in LVL CHG and HDG SEL for pitch and roll respectively.

For a 2 engine GA the FD command a 15 degrees nose-up pitch and roll to hold the approach ground track at the time of engagement. After reaching a programmed rate of climb, pitch commands hold the manoeuvring speed for each flap setting.

During a single engine GA the FD pitch command is initially to 13 degrees nose-up but as climb rate increases, FD pitch commands maintain a target speed. Roll commands are the same as for the 2 engine case. If engine failure occurs prior to GA engagement, then MCP selected speed becomes the target speed. If the engine failure occurs after GA engagement, then FD target speed depends on whether 10 seconds have elapsed since GA engagement:

1.   If prior to 10 seconds, the MCP selected approach speed becomes the target speed.

2.   If after 10 seconds and the airspeed at engine failure is within 5 kts of the GA engagement speed, the airspeed that existed at the GA engagement becomes the target speed.

3.   If after 10 seconds and the airspeed at engine failure is more than 5 kts above GA engagement speed, then the current airspeed becomes the target airspeed.

In all cases, the GA target speed is not less than V_2 speed based on flap position unless in wind-shear conditions.

The FD target speed is displayed on the MCP and by the airspeed cursors. No commanded acceleration can occur until a higher speed is selected on the MCP.

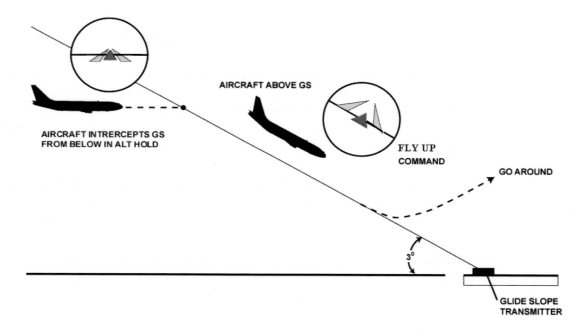

© Oxford Aviation Services Limited

FD Manoeuvre Protection

Because the modern FDC is configured for each particular aircraft type it will have the aircraft performance parameters stored in its memory. As it has inputs from the ADC and other systems it can ensure that it **never commands a manoeuvre which will over-stress the aircraft.** This is the beginning of the systems used for protection in aircraft with fly by wire controls (discussed fully in another chapter).

Flight Director Gain Scheduling   *— Stops over correction when near ground.*

Gain scheduling is the varying of the gain of the pitch and roll demands of the FDC in relation to the task. This has many parallels with autopilot gain scheduling or gain adaption. The FD mode of operation using gain scheduling is the FDA. As the approach progresses the glideslope beam converges with the runway (which is how it works and what we want). The ILS works as a beam set at a certain angle diverging from the runway, normally about 3 degrees. ILS equipment displays that received signal as an error in degrees from the ideal.

At 6nm one degree of error equates to about 608ft of vertical distance. At ½nm that same one degree of error equates to about 54ft of vertical distance. It should be obvious that although the indications on the raw ILS glide-slope will be the same, a less forceful correction is required as the aircraft nears the ILS transmitter. **So the FD computed information must be modified as the approach progresses to reduce the commanded corrections.**

As the aircraft approaches touch-down the magnitude of the pitch changes required to follow GS reduce. Gain scheduling reduces the magnitude of the commands as the aircraft proceeds on the FDA. So initially the FDS can demand manoeuvres almost to the full authority of the system. As the threshold approaches however, the gain is reduced to perhaps a ½ or 1/3 of the original value.

The initiation of this scheduling can come in many forms depending on the age of the system:

a)   Early systems simply used time e.g. 45 seconds after GS capture the gain is reduced.

b)   The next systems used the Marker Beacons to try to actually match the scheduling required to the approach being flown. This system has fallen into disuse however because of the loss of the marker beacon systems at many airfields.

c)   Radio Altimeter. This relies on no ground signals and gives accurate scheduling in relation to actual aircraft height. This also means that the actual scheduling can be phased in gradually as opposed to the stepped method of the timing or marker systems.

Gain scheduling or adaption can made to occur for any change in the flight regime to reduce the demands from the flight director to ensure adequate safety.

1.4   DUAL FDS

When, as on large aircraft 2 FDS are fitted (one for each pilot), each system can be used to monitor the indications of the other. This system is the FD Comparator or Monitor.

The FD Comparator monitors command bar positions. The command bars are removed when a difference is sensed between the 2 FDS of approximately 1 to 4 degrees of pitch and / or 3 to 9 degrees of roll. FD command bars reappear when the difference returns to within limits.

FD comparison is only active during certain modes of FD operation. First, both FD switches must be on and neither autopilot engaged. Second, it only operates in either the TOGA or APP mode below 800 ft RA.

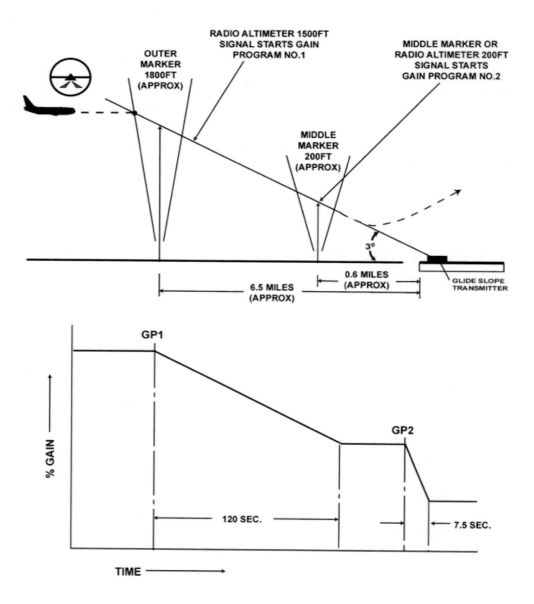

FD comparison is inhibited for several reasons. It is inhibited on the ground or when either FD is affected by electrical bus transfer. Also, it is inhibited by failure of either a FD sensor or an FD itself.

Having 2 FDS also means a certain amount of redundancy in the system. It also means that if one system should fail, as along as the associated display equipment is serviceable, both sets of display can if necessary be run from one FDC. This on electro-mechanical instruments is often simply a switch which when operated, splits the FDC output from the serviceable FDS instrument amplifier and feeds it into both sets of ADIs and HSIs. The flight instrument and FD power (and that of navigational information sources) may also be separate to aid redundancy.

EFIS equipped aircraft have a spare symbol generator also to retain extra redundancy.

With a/p engaged the command bar become an a/p monitor - ie they are not 'commanding' any more.

CHAPTER TWO - AUTOPILOT

Contents

		Page
2.1	INTRODUCTION	2-1
2.2	THE AUTO PILOT	2-1
2.3	CONTROL LOOPS	2-3
2.4	AIRCRAFT INNER LOOP CONTROL SYSTEM	2-4
2.5	TYPES OF AUTOPILOT	2-6
2.6	JAR-OPS REQUIREMENTS	2-8
2.7	TYPES OF ACTUATOR	2-9
2.8	TRIM	2-11
2.9	OUTER LOOP CONTROL (ALSO KNOWN AS FLIGHT PATH MODES).	2-14
2.10	MODE ANNUNCIATOR	2-16
2.11	AIRCRAFT SENSOR INPUTS TO THE AUTOFLIGHT COMPUTER	2-17
2.12	EXAMPLES OF OUTER LOOP INPUTS IN ROLL	2-21
2.13	EXAMPLES OF OUTER LOOP INPUTS IN PITCH	2-22
2.14	AUTOPILOT IN OPERATION	2-25
2.15	OTHER AUTOPILOT FEATURES	2-25
2.16	AUTOPILOT LIMITATIONS AND OPERATIONAL RESTRICTIONS	2-30
2.17	FLIGHT MANAGEMENT SYSTEM	2-33

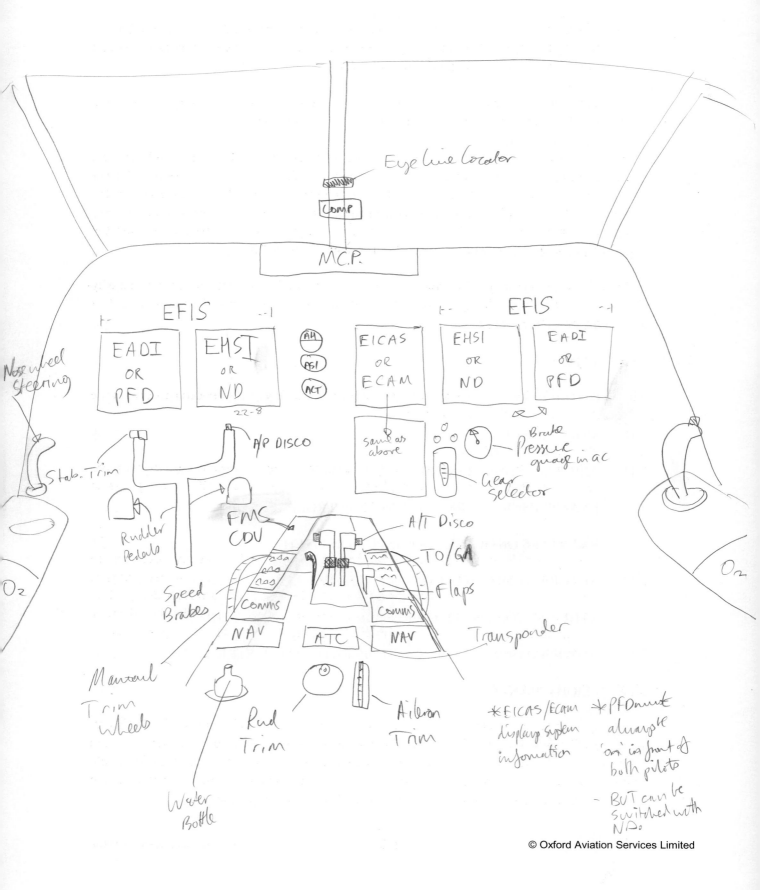

Eye Line Locator

Comp

M.C.P.

EFIS

EADI OR PFD

EHSI OR ND

22-8

AH

ASI

ALT

EICAS OR ECAM

EHSI OR ND

EADI OR PFD

Nose wheel steering

Stab. Trim

A/P DISCO

Rudder Pedals

FMS CDU

same as above

Brake Pressure gauge in ac

Gear Selector

O₂

O₂

Speed Brakes

Comms

NAV

ATT Disco

TO/GA

Flaps

Comms

ATC

NAV

Transponder

Manual Trim wheels

Rud Trim

Aileron Trim

Water Bottle

*EICAS/ECAM
display system
information

*PFD must
always be
'on' in front of
both pilots

- BUT can be
switched with
ND.

AutoPilot
does what pilot
would do manually

2.1   INTRODUCTION

The main purpose of the autopilot is to relieve the pilot of the physical and mental fatigue of flying the aircraft , especially during long flights. This will result in the pilot being more alert during the critical phase of landing the aircraft safely.

Autopilot systems also enable the aircraft to fly a prescribed route accurately due to the autopilots' ability to react quicker than a human pilot to disturbances.

Many different autopilot systems exist offering many different modes of operation and facilities. Generally, however, today's modern airliner, when fitted with an auto-throttle system, will have the facility to fly the aircraft automatically for almost the entire route. In each such system, the autopilot flies the aircraft as it responds to commands from attitude sensors, navigation systems, and pitot-static systems. Power is controlled through the engine throttles moved by auto-throttle servos responding to commands from the thrust management computer.

It should be noted that, as yet, the autopilot does not carry out the take-off which has to done by the pilot. The autopilot, though, can be engaged shortly after take-off at about 400 feet or possibly even a lower height.

2.2   THE AUTO PILOT

The basic autopilot has been in existence for about 50 years. It was introduced as an aid to the pilot flying the aircraft for 2 major reasons:

1.   **Reduction in workload**
        Allowing automatic systems to fly the aircraft means that the crew not only are more rested for the more demanding phases of flight, but it also allows the pilots to concentrate on other tasks such as navigation.

2.   **The response time**
        An autopilot is much quicker than a human and as a result it can fly aircraft more accurately. A human pilot takes approximately 1/5 of a second (200 milliseconds) in detecting a change in the aircraft's attitude and then instigates a further delay while deciding which control to apply to oppose the disturbance. An autopilot will detect a disturbance and put on the required control to correct the disturbance in approximately 50 milliseconds.

FAIL SAFE AUTOPILOT

With any automatic system it is necessary to protect against malfunctions - in particular, runaways. This is achieved either by limiting the authority of the actuator or the rate at which the actuator can travel. In this way the pilot should always be able to override the effects of a malfunction and retain control of the aircraft in the event of autopilot failure. Such a system would be called a fail-safe system and the term applies to any single autopilot.

The Basic Autopilot

The basic autopilot is a very simple system. Understanding of the basic autopilot is essential for understanding and explaining what any autopilot is doing throughout the flight.

Aircraft Stabilisation

This is the key function for an autopilot (and this is all that some basic autopilots may achieve). All the modes such as VOR tracking and altitude hold etc. are "extras".

Consider an early aircraft design. All that was originally required was a system that would keep the aircraft flying in the same attitude once the pilot was happy. He could then concentrate on navigation, disengaging the autopilot as necessary to correct headings and so on. To design such a system we need to consider the sequence of events that must occur to keep the aircraft's attitude constant. Consider yourself flying a light aircraft e.g. a Warrior in slightly turbulent conditions. Now consider that the aircraft experiences a disturbance in pitch:

A human pilot controls the aircraft's stability by sensing a change in aircraft attitude, computing the necessary corrective action required and using his muscles to move the flight controls. He will then sense that corrective action has taken place and move the flight controls back to remove the correcting input.

The Autopilot is capable of producing the same actions as the pilot to maintain aircraft stability in a shorter reaction time. It must detect the disturbance and then work out appropriate corrective action. It must then apply that correction using its "muscles". Finally it must detect that the correction has taken place and re-centre the controls. This is known as inner loop control (or sometimes closed loop or auto-stabilisation). In list form it can:

i)   sense changes in attitude
ii)   compute the amount and direction of control required.
iii)   provide the muscle to move the control surfaces using servo-motors.
iv)   detect that the control has been applied and that the aircraft has responded.
v)   return control surfaces back to the neutral condition when the disturbance has been corrected.

As you will learn in the principles of flight aircraft will naturally tend to be stable in any case so you may wonder why go to the bother of installing this basic autopilot. Yes aircraft are naturally stable but you will learn that there are different type of stability and that stability can change with respect to the ambient conditions. The basic autopilot then augments and fine-tunes this stability to provide enhanced stability over a greater range of ambient conditions.

It must be emphasised that the most basic autopilot available will be of a type that will only provide auto-stabilisation.

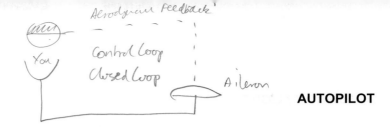

2.3   CONTROL LOOPS

An autopilot is a control system which uses control loops. The inner loop is a classic example of a closed loop control system (hence one of its common titles). Outer loop (which will be described later) is sometimes described as an "open loop". This is not quite correct as there is still feedback in the system. The best name for it is the outer loop because of how it acts on the inner loop to achieve its aims.

The basic elements of a closed loop control system are shown in figure 2.1 and comprise:

1.   Input
2.   error detector
3.   output
4.   control element
5.   feedback

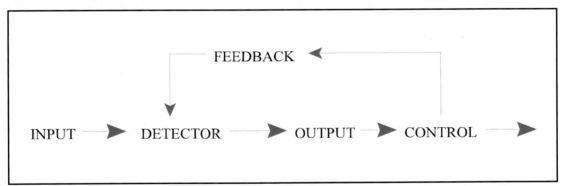

Fig 2.1 Closed Loop Control

Fig 2.2 Open Loop Control

Figure 2.2 shows an open loop control system which does not have feedback. The controller may consist of a pre-determined programme or a human operator. However, if a human operator is used then the system, in effect, becomes a closed-loop system with the human closing the loop and feeding back the output signals.

The difference between open loop and closed loop systems can be illustrated by the domestic central heating system. A system with a timing controller but no thermostat would be an open loop system i.e. the pump would continue to send hot water round the house regardless of the room temperature for the duration of the period set on the timer control. On the other hand, a system with a thermostat would interrupt the circulation when the room temperature reaches the pre-selected level i.e. it has feedback control.

Feedback control systems used for positional control e.g. aircraft flying controls, are usually referred to as servo systems or servomechanisms. An essential feature of such a system is that a low power error signal is used to control the supply of power to the control elements that consist of pneumatic, hydraulic or electrical servo-motors; in other words, there is some form of power amplification in the system.

2.4   AIRCRAFT INNER LOOP CONTROL SYSTEM

The components of an inner (closed) loop control system in an aircraft shown in figure 2.3 are:

Attitude sensor	A rate gyro senses disturbance of the aircraft in one axis only.
Transducer	Converts mechanical movement of the gyro into an electrical signal.
Signal processor	The Error detector. Compares the signals from the transducer with the input signals, determines the required corrective action (the error) and transmits a signal to the servo-motor. Receives and compares position and rate of movement feedback signals from the servo-motor.
Servo-motor	Converts processed signal into movement of the aircraft flight controls proportional to rate and direction of signal. Uses hydraulic, electric or pneumatic power.
Aerodynamic Feedback	The attitude reached by the aircraft is sensed by the rate gyro which gives a measure of the output.

A disturbance to the selected flight path produces an error signal; the autopilot operates to move the aircraft back towards its stabilised condition. This causes the error signal from the transducer to be progressively reduced and therefore removes the control surface deflection after the disturbance has been corrected.

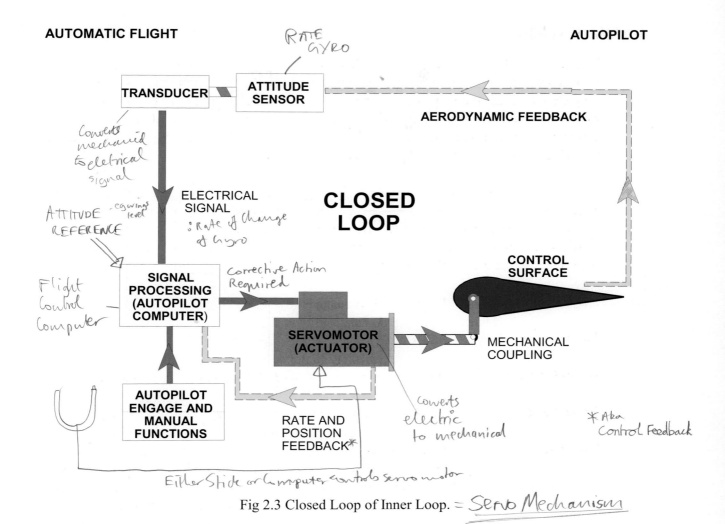

(handwritten annotations on diagram)

RATE GYRO

TRANSDUCER — Converts mechanical to electrical signal

ATTITUDE SENSOR

AERODYNAMIC FEEDBACK

CLOSED LOOP

ELECTRICAL SIGNAL — : Rate of Change of Gyro

ATTITUDE REFERENCE — · cg wings level

SIGNAL PROCESSING (AUTOPILOT COMPUTER) — Flight Control Computer

Corrective Action Required

CONTROL SURFACE

SERVOMOTOR (ACTUATOR) — Converts electric to mechanical

MECHANICAL COUPLING

AUTOPILOT ENGAGE AND MANUAL FUNCTIONS

RATE AND POSITION FEEDBACK* — * Aka Control Feedback

Either Stick or Computer controls servo motor

Fig 2.3 Closed Loop of Inner Loop. = Servo Mechanism

Inner Loop systems

Inner loop systems are those that provide the auto-stability only. It is the Innermost control Loop.

Outer Loop systems

Outer loop systems are those extra facilities offered e.g. Altitude Hold, Heading Hold, LNAV, VNAV. They are still essentially loops (so there is still some confusion occasionally) but they act from an external position on the inner loop and "fool" the inner loop into manoeuvring the aircraft into achieving its aim.

(handwritten note)

JAAQ:

- A "servo mechanism" is a closed loop control system where a small input is converted to a larger output, in a strictly proportionate manner.

- Above is a "servo mechanism" ie all of system.

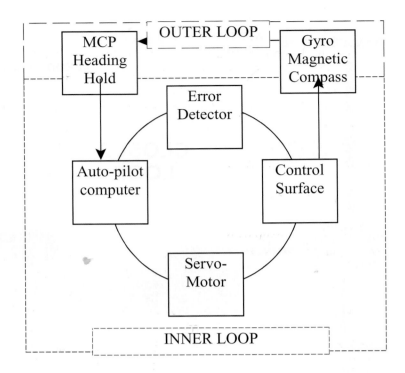

Fig.2.4 Diagram showing the relationship of an outer loop function to the inner loop.

2.5   TYPES OF AUTOPILOT

a)   An aircraft can be subjected to disturbances about its three control axes i.e. longitudinal (roll), lateral (pitch) and vertical or normal (yaw). Stabilisation must therefore be controlled about the same three axes. Autopilot systems are broken down into three basic control channels:

  i)   Roll   to control the Ailerons
  ii)   Pitch   to control the Elevators
  iii) Yaw   to control the Rudder

It is therefore possible to get an autopilot that is classed as single axis, twin axis or triple axis. There will be a separate inner loop for each axis of autopilot control. If an aircraft has more than one autopilot there will be one inner loop for each axis of control for each autopilot.

b)   **A Single Axis System.** — *Roll Only*

A single axis attitude control system would normally be limited to the roll axis only, i.e. a single autopilot channel controlling the ailerons. At its most basic, the single axis system will only give lateral stability or level the wings. The roll axis is known as the primary axis. This system is sometimes simply called a Wing Leveller.

Secondary

c)   **A Two Axis System**.

A two axis control system would control the aircraft attitude about the roll and pitch axes. The pitch axis is known as the secondary axis. There are two autopilot channels which control the ailerons and the elevators. Systems can vary in complexity from the fairly simple set-ups which can be found in smaller aircraft, having only a few basic modes of operation, up to the most intricate integrated systems with full flight profile modes of operation, including auto-land modes. Two axis systems may have an aileron/elevator cross-feed to keep the nose up in a turn.

d)   **A Three Axis System**.

"auto land" a/c must have 3 Axis system

A three axis system would give attitude control about all three axes, namely roll, pitch and yaw. The yaw axis is the third or tertiary axis. The roll and pitch channels are used as the primary control channels. It is these two channels to which outer loop signals (discussed later) are fed to control the various modes. The rudder channel is basically a stability channel. It is common to have interaction between the roll channel and rudder channel to assist in co-ordinated turns and to give faster stability response. On aircraft that require it, a yaw damper will be fitted as a standby rudder channel but would operate independently of the autopilot.

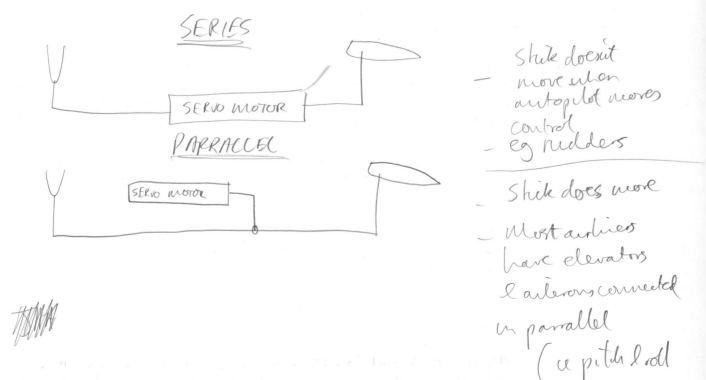

SERIES

SERVO MOTOR

PARRALLEL

SERVO MOTOR

Stick doesn't move when autopilot moves control eg rudders

Stick does move

Most airlines have elevators & ailerons connected in parrallel (ie pitch & roll

2.6   JAR-OPS REQUIREMENTS

Popular JAA Q:

a)   Single pilot operation under IFR   *or at night*

An operator shall not conduct single pilot IFR operations unless the aeroplane is equipped with an autopilot with at least ALTITUDE HOLD and HEADING MODE. This means that the aircraft must have at least a two-axis autopilot.

b)   Installation of automatic pilot system

eg so a fire can be dealt with by single pilot

1.   Each automatic pilot system must be approved and must be designed so that the autopilot can be quickly and positively disengaged to prevent it from interfering with the control of the aeroplane.

2.   Unless there is automatic synchronising, each system must have a means to readily indicate to the pilot the alignment of the actuating device in relation to the control system it operates.

See p 2-30

3.   Each manually operated control for the system must be readily accessible to the pilots.

4.   Quick release (emergency) controls must be on both control wheels, on the side of each wheel opposite the throttles.

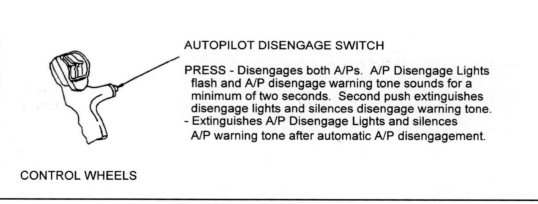

AUTOPILOT DISENGAGE SWITCH

PRESS - Disengages both A/Ps. A/P Disengage Lights
  flash and A/P disengage warning tone sounds for a
  minimum of two seconds. Second push extinguishes
  disengage lights and silences disengage warning tone.
- Extinguishes A/P Disengage Lights and silences
  A/P warning tone after automatic A/P disengagement.

CONTROL WHEELS

Fig 2.5 Instinctive cutout switch

5.   Attitude controls must operate in the plane and sense of motion specified for cockpit controls. The direction of motion must be plainly indicated on, or adjacent to, each control.

6.   The system must be designed and adjusted so that it cannot produce hazardous loads on the aeroplane, or create hazardous deviations in the flight path, either during normal operation or in the event of a malfunction.

7.   If the autopilot integrates signals from auxiliary controls or furnishes signals for operation of other equipment, there must be positive interlocks and sequencing of engagement to prevent improper operation. Protection against adverse interaction of integrated components, is also required.

8.   Means must be provided to indicate to the pilots the current mode of operation and any modes armed by the pilot.

2.7   TYPES OF ACTUATOR

a)   Actuators produce the physical movement of the control surfaces and can be of different types depending on their principle of operation which can be:

1.   **electro-mechanical**.
2.   **electro-hydraulic**.
3.   **pneumatic**.

b)   There are two types of configuration in which actuators are connected to the flying controls:

i)   **Parallel**. The actuator produces the movement of the control surface as well as providing feedback to the control stick i.e. the stick will move when the autopilot is controlling the control surfaces.

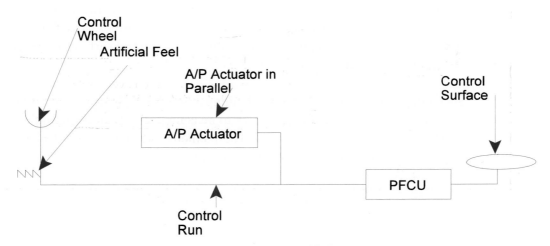

Fig 2.6 A/P Actuator in Parallel

ii)   **Series**. The actuator produces movement of the control surface but not the control stick.

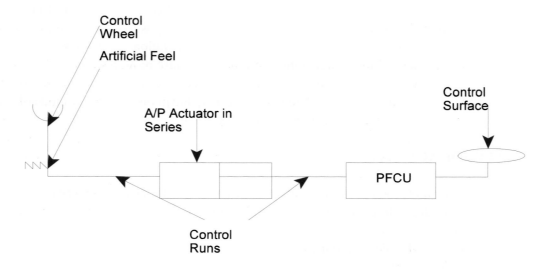

Fig 2.7 A/P Actuator in Series

It is also possible to have a combined series/parallel configuration.

c)   **Torque Limiter**

In flight, particularly where high rates of control are to be produced, the movement of the flight control surfaces can result in loads which may impose excessive stresses on the aircraft structure. It is necessary therefore, under automatically-controlled flight conditions, to safeguard against such stresses, and furthermore to safeguard against a servo-motor 'runaway' condition which would cause control surfaces to be displaced to their maximum hard-over positions.

Such safeguards are implemented by limiting the torque applied to the servo-motors, and also by allowing them either to slip, or to be completely disengaged, in the event that present torque limits are exceeded. The methods adopted usually depend on either mechanical, electrical or electromechanical principles.

2.8   TRIM

a)   **Manual Systems**

The purpose of the trim system is to relieve the pilot of forces on the aircraft controls while maintaining aircraft attitude. In manual control, trim on light aircraft is provided in all three axes through mechanical linkages to trim tabs on the control surfaces. On larger aircraft this is usually achieved by electrical actuators that bias the Powered Flying Control Unit (PFCU), particularly for pitch trim. Trim steering signals would be provided to the trim tab actuators for elevator, aileron and rudder as well as to the horizontal stabiliser.

Manual operation of the pitch trim will, in most systems, automatically disconnect the autopilot as it cannot co-ordinate manual trim movement with movement of the C of G or aerodynamic movements.

b)   **Automatic Trim (Auto-trim)** — *Pitch Channel only*
— *Only when AutoPilot is engaged.*

As the aircraft uses fuel the C of G position will move. If we are flying the aircraft manually we would trim these forces out manually to eliminate stick forces. Currently as our basic autopilot stands if it is flying the aircraft and the C of G changes it will simply hold the stick forces using the brute strength of its servo-motor outputs. This will not pose much of a problem unless the forces overwhelm the servo-motor or until such time as we wish to disconnect the autopilot. Not only does this mean that the aircraft is producing more drag than necessary but if there is a standing load on the controls when we disconnect the autopilot we will not know of its existence or which way the aircraft will pitch. The aircraft will "snatch" or lurch in response to the out of trim condition. This is not a very satisfactory situation so a system of Automatic Pitch Trim was included in most autopilot systems.

When the autopilot is engaged automatic trim is available only in pitch. This is called Automatic Pitch Trim or simply Auto-trim. Auto-trim is active only when the autopilot is engaged (excluding the Airbus series of Fly by Wire aircraft which are a special case). It is typically achieved by a separate trim servo actuator operating either the normal trim tab or, more commonly on modern jet transports, the variable incidence horizontal stabiliser. The latter permits the elevator to always be in neutral position with respect to the horizontal stabiliser, therefore allowing the autopilot full elevator control authority both sides of the trimmed position. Another important consideration is that in the event of autopilot disconnect the aircraft will be in a trimmed condition and thus will not suddenly pitch up or down.

The out of trim condition is sensed most commonly by using one of two methods:

[handwritten margin notes:]

Separate from all manual and electric trim.

— Only works when autopilot engaged.

— Will cause A/P to trip out if it fails

— If a/c is manually trimmed a/p a/p will disengage

JAA Q choice of correct option

Auto-trim:
① Prevents snatch on a/p "disengagement" (ie opposite of synchronisation which sets engagement)
② Removes out trim forces from servomotor (ie not the stick)
③ By reducing elevator hinge moment to zero.
④ Maintains full elevator authority around a trimmed neutral.

i)   A standing load being sensed on an electrical actuator. Due to the out of trim situation the autopilot is having to hold a force against the out of trim condition in exactly the same way as a pilot would have to. The magnitude of the load on the actuator is going to be directly proportional to the force being held, and of course the direction is known from which way the actuator is having to apply that load. That information can be used to move the normal trimming system of the elevators to reduce the standing load to zero. The aircraft is now in trim.

ii)   The actual position of the actuator. If there is an out of trim force to be coped with the actuator will be positioned to input the required control displacement to hold that force. The displacement of the actuator will again give the direction and magnitude of the force. Large modern aircraft tend to use Trim Tails or all moving tail-planes. Both of these systems due to the way they trim reset the control inputs to give full elevator movement up and down from the trimmed position. So now, as the Auto-trim moves the normal elevator trim, the displacement of the normal control input is reset, removing the actuator displacement.

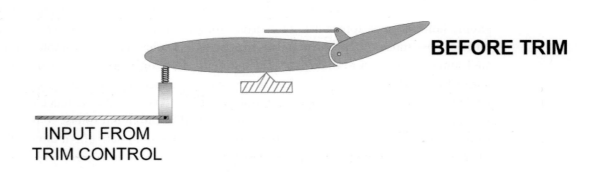

INPUT FROM
TRIM CONTROL

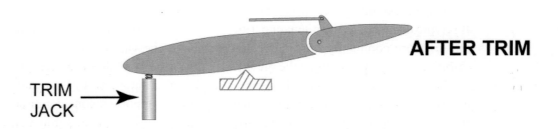

TRIM
JACK

Fig 2.8 Trimming by variable incidence tailplane

The output is applied to the trim tab actuator or the horizontal stabiliser.

In the event of a failure of the trim system the pilots would be alerted by warning lights and/or suitable indications on the electronic display unit. At the same time the autopilot would disengage, giving both visual and aural alerts. The latter can also sound when there is an excessive trim input as, for example , in an actuator runaway situation. If the auto trim system is not available, then the autopilot may become inoperative (will become inoperative for the 737-400). If another autopilot is available it would be common practice to use the fully operative system.

If there is only one autopilot or the aircraft is not fitted with auto-trim, the aircraft must be correctly in trim before the engagement of the autopilot to minimise the control loading expected on disengagement. The standard operating procedure for the aircraft will stipulate a time period after which the autopilot must be disengaged, the aircraft re-trimmed and then the autopilot re-engaged. This will minimise the control snatch on autopilot disengagement.

The pilots may have some indication of the trim controls but in the case of auto-trim there is always a stabiliser trim indicator and a auto-trim failure warning so that the system can be monitored during autopilot operation. The autopilot may not engage if there is too great a standing load i.e out of trim condition already present.

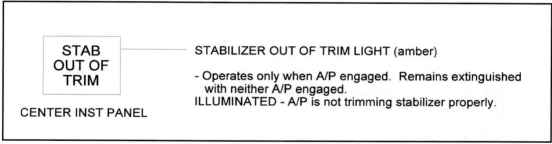

Fig 2.9 Auto-Trim Failure Light

c)   **Independent Systems**

Mach trim (if required) will operate independently of the autopilot. A Mach Trim system is provided in aeroplanes that fly at high subsonic speeds and are susceptible to Mach tuck. At these speeds as the aeroplane approaches it's critical Mach No. the centre of pressure moves aft resulting in a nose down attitude known as Mach tuck. This condition is automatically trimmed out by a mach trim system. The mach trim system will be armed at all stages of flight but will only activate at high subsonic speeds.

Yaw dampers will be covered in detail in another chapter. They are however another example of an inner loop system.

2.9   OUTER LOOP CONTROL (ALSO KNOWN AS FLIGHT PATH MODES).

In addition to performing the primary function of stabilisation, an Automatic Flight Control System (AFCS) can also be developed to control the path of the aircraft horizontally or vertically to predetermined conditions. For example to hold a selected airspeed, altitude, magnetic heading or intercept and track radio beams from ground-based aids, etc. The number of inputs available serve as an indication of the progressive development of automatic flight from the basic single-axis wing-levelling type of autopilot, to the highly sophisticated flight guidance systems now used in many present-day transport aircraft.

The outer loop inputs are applied to the inner loop in such a way as to fool the auto-stability control into believing that the aircraft is being disturbed. The inner-loop systems reaction to the input is calculated to produce the result required, such as altitude holding or turning to follow a heading.

Such data inputs constitute **Outer Loop Control** and can be referred to as **Command Modes** or **Flight Path (Referenced) Modes**. Outer Loop command modes are coupled to the relevant autopilot channel by selection on the Mode Control Panel (MCP) which is located on the glare-shield and provides the pilot's interface with the auto-flight system. A typical example of modern twin jet MCP is shown in figure 2.12. It allows the pilot to engage an autopilot and select any of the pitch and roll outer loop inputs. Incorporated in the selector switches are lights to indicate which autopilot or command modes are engaged.

Only one command mode may be engaged in a single channel at any one time (i.e. one in Roll and one in Pitch). So it is impossible for the autopilot to maintain a speed for example by pitching the aircraft and at the same time hold a height by pitching the aircraft. Do not confuse this with those auto flight control systems that include auto throttle / thrust.

The provision of raw data inputs relevant to a particular flight path is referred to as 'coupling' or as a 'mode of operation'. Other terms commonly used in connection with operating modes are 'hold', 'lock', and 'capture'. For example, an aircraft flying automatically at a selected altitude is said to be in the 'altitude hold' or 'height lock' mode. The term 'capture' relates principally to modes associated with the selection and interception of beams from ground-based radio navigation aids; for example, 'glide slope capture'.

In some cases, mode switching is automatic, thus, to switch from intercepting a beam or a heading, to tracking the beam on reaching it, a **Beam Sensor** is installed. This device senses beam deviation and switches modes automatically when the aircraft flies into the beam. Glide slope capture can also take place automatically, in this case the pitch control channel is switched from 'altitude hold' mode to glide slope track when the aircraft flies into the glide slope beam.

The raw data is supplied from aircraft sensors (attitude, air data, heading, radio etc.) to the relevant auto-flight computer which compares the data with the selected values on the MCP and computes control inputs to achieve those selected values.

In a modern transport aircraft which is using a flight guidance system with an automatic landing capability, the outer loop inputs could comprise some or all of the modes listed in the following table.

Roll Channel	Pitch Channel
Heading hold	Altitude hold
Heading select	Speed hold
VOR intercept and track	Mach hold
LOC intercept and track	Vertical Speed
Inertial Nav or L.NAV	V.NAV

Auto-land

Roll Channel	Pitch Channel	Yaw Channel
Localiser	Glideslope	Runway align
Roll-out	Flare	Roll-out

2.10   MODE ANNUNCIATOR.

The Mode Annunciator will indicate the current auto-flight system status and can be a separate indicator or an integrated part of the EFIS primary flight display (figure 2.10). The electronic display indicates armed and engaged modes of the auto-flight system in different colours. It can also indicate autopilot, autothrottle, auto-land and flight director status.

Fig 2.10 Primary Flight Display.

There will also be an illuminated switches or simply warning lights that will indicate whether an autopilot is engaged, warning of disengagement, warning of auto-throttle disengagement, failure to achieve target speed and of auto-trim failure.

Disengage AP:
- Button on stick
- Disengage button on MCP
- Stab trim
- Brake out force on stick

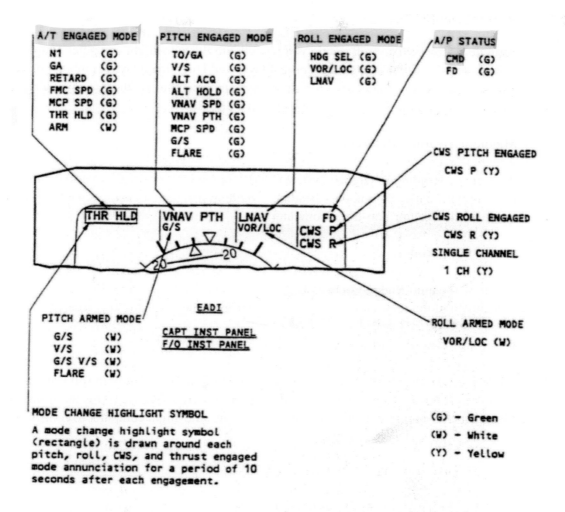

Fig 2.11 Boeing 737-400 Flight Mode Annunciations.

2.11   AIRCRAFT SENSOR INPUTS TO THE AUTOFLIGHT COMPUTER

a)   **Manometric (Or Air) Data**.

Raw data inputs which come under this heading are those associated with altitude, airspeed/mach No, vertical speed. Each of these provides current aircraft status for outer loop control in the pitch channel of the autopilot.

Sensing may be carried out either by independent sensor units, or by a Central Air Data Computer (CADC). The sensors operate on the same fundamental principles as the basic pitot-static instruments, the measuring elements being coupled to appropriate types of electrical transducers instead of instruments.

b)   **Attitude Reference**

Attitude reference data (roll, pitch, yaw) is fed into the auto-flight computer from the primary attitude sensors which could be a Vertical Gyro and Directional Gyro combination, an Inertial Navigation System or an Inertial Reference System depending on the age of the aircraft. These sensors may also transmit data to slave the ADI and HSI.

c)   **Magnetic Heading Reference**

A Magnetic Heading Reference System (MHRS or Gyro Magnetic Compass) combines inertial heading with magnetic compass heading providing magnetic heading signals to the HSI and reference data to the auto-flight computer.

d)   **Radio Navigation**

To allow the auto-flight system to be able to capture and track a radio beam data signals are transmitted to the relevant auto-flight computer from the VOR and ILS receivers.

e)   **Computer Generated Data**

Modern aircraft can follow a computer generated flight profile in both roll (lateral) and pitch (vertical) from a Flight Management System (FMS). Steering signals from the Flight Management Computer (FMC) are connected to the auto-flight computer to control the attitude of the aircraft.

An example of an AFDS (737-400)

For these notes the Boeing 737-400 is used as an example. It is also officially the AFDS that the JAR objectives and exams are currently based around. Therefore a description of the AFDS as fitted to this aircraft is given.

General

The Automatic Flight System (AFS) for the 737-400 consists of the Autopilot Flight Director System (AFDS) and the Auto-Throttle (A/T). The Flight Management Computer (FMC) provides N1 limits and target N1 for the A/T and command airspeeds for the A/T and AFDS.

The AFDS and A/T are operated from the AFDS Mode Control Panel (MCP) and the FMC from the Control Display Unit (CDU).

The AFDS MCP provides co-ordinated control of the autopilot (A/P), Flight Director (FD), A/T and altitude alert functions.

AFS mode status is displayed on the Flight Mode Annunciators (FMA) on each pilot's ADI.

Normally, the AFDS and A/T are used to maintain and or thrust settings calculated by the FMC.

Autopilot Flight Director System (AFDS)

The AFDS is a dual system consisting of 2 individual Flight Control Computers (FCCs) and a single MCP.

The 2 FCCs are identified as A and B. For A/P operation, they send control commands to their respective pitch and roll hydraulic servos, which operate the flight controls through 2 separate hydraulic systems.

For FD operation, each FCC positions the FD command bars on the respective ADI.

MCP Mode Selector Switches

The Mode selector switches are pressed to select desired command modes for the AFDS and A/T. The switch illuminates to indicate mode selection and that the mode can be deselected by pressing the switch again. While a mode is active, de-selection can be automatically inhibited and this is indicated by the switch light being extinguished.

When engagement of a mode would conflict with current AFS operation, pressing the mode selector switch has no effect. All AFDS modes can be disengaged by selecting another command mode or by disengaging the A/P and turning the FDs off.

MODE CONTROL PANEL

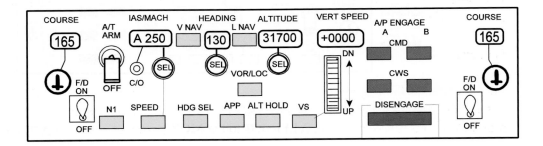

Fig 2.12 Mode Control Panel.

MCP Parameter Selection

The following information is in addition to that contained in the controls and indicators section of this chapter.

Parameter selections common to both FCCs for speed, heading, altitude and vertical speed are made from the MCP.

Two course selectors and course displays are located on the MCP. The Captain's course selector provides selected course information to the A FCC, the No. 1 VHF Nav receiver and to the Captain's HSI course pointer and course deviation bar. The First Officer's course selector provides selected course information to the B FCC, the No. 2 VHF Nav receiver and to the First Officer's HSI course pointer and deviation bar.

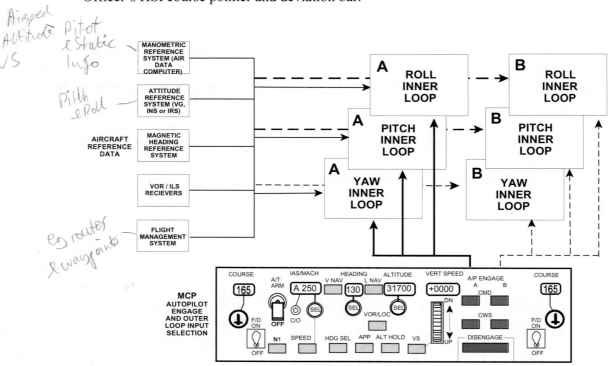

Fig 2.13 Inputs to the MCP.

2.12   Examples of Outer Loop Inputs in ROLL

a)   **Heading Select and Hold**

[handwritten top right: - Heading Hold holds current heading regardless of what is selected in heading selector. - Mode shown in Annunciator]

The Heading Select mode sends roll commands to turn and maintain the heading shown in the MCP Heading Display. After mode engagement, roll commands are given to turn in the same direction as the rotation of the heading selector only. The bank angle limit is established by the Bank Angle Limit Selector on the MCP.

[handwritten left: - Bug stays on display - If selected a/c will turn to the selected heading and hold it.]

Pressing the Heading Select Switch on the MCP engages the heading select mode. HDG SEL is annunciated for the AFDS.

The HDG SEL mode automatically disengages upon capture of the selected radio course in the VOR LOC and APP modes.

b)   **VOR Localiser tracking (VOR LOC) mode**

[handwritten right: VOR is displayed as 'armed' mode in annunciator view. in 'white']

[handwritten left: - Turns the way the bug was moved @ more numbers upwards to turn right.]

The VOR mode gives roll commands to capture and track the selected VOR course.

The LOC mode gives roll commands to capture and track the selected localiser along the inbound front course bearing. Back-course tracking is not available.

[handwritten right: ie the next to engage when conditions are correct]

Pressing the VOR LOC switch selects the VOR mode if a VOR frequency is tuned, or selects a LOC mode if a localiser frequency is tuned. The VOR LOC switch illuminates and VOR LOC armed is annunciated.

The selected course can be intercepted while engaged in L NAV, HDG SEL or CWS ROLL, with an autopilot engaged in CMD. The capture point is variable and depends on intercept angle and closure rate. Localiser capture occurs not later than ½ dot deviation. When within the course capture area, the VOR LOC annunciation changes from armed to captured and roll commands track the VOR or localiser course.

[handwritten right: we are still in heading select mode until VOR is intercepted]

[handwritten left: Faded Error rate is rate at which a/c is crossing radials whilst approaching desired radial]

When a localiser frequency is selected the navigation radios automatically switch from the antenna in the tail to the antenna in the nose when VOR/LOC is annunciated (armed or engaged). If antenna switching does not occur, the localiser and approach modes are inhibited.

Inertial Navigation System (INS)/Inertial Referencing System (IRS)

Older aircraft without a Flight Management System may be able to couple the Inertial Navigation/Reference System to the autopilot to allow the aircraft to be steered sequentially through a series of way points that have been loaded into the INS/IRS before flight.

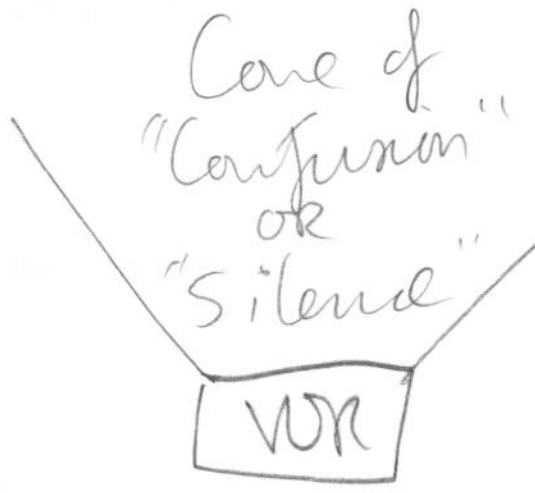

[handwritten left: Once radial is captured the VOR mode in the annunciator will go green]

[handwritten bottom centre diagram: Cone of "Confusion" or "Silence" VOR]

[handwritten bottom right: - When flying over beacon the autopilot will just follow the heading it was on when it entered the zone of confusion - Annunciator stays in VOR mode]

© Oxford Aviation Services Limited

e)   **Lateral Navigation (L NAV)**

In the L NAV mode, the FMC controls AFDS roll to intercept and track the active FMC route. The desired route is activated and modified through the FMC CDUs. In addition to en-route guidance, the active routes can include terminal procedures such as SIDs, STARs and instrument approaches.

Engagement criteria must be met to use L NAV. There must be an active route in the FMC, capture criteria must be satisfied, and the L NAV switch must be pressed.

L NAV capture criteria is divided into 2 categories. First, any aeroplane satisfies capture criteria when within 3nm of the active route segment. Second, outside of 3nm, the aeroplane must be on an intercept course of 90 degrees or less and intercept the active route segment before the active way-point.

L NAV will automatically disconnect for several reasons. It will disconnect upon reaching the end of the active route or upon entering a route discontinuity. Additionally, it will disconnect upon either intercepting or missing the intercept of an approach path inbound track. Finally, either loss of capture criteria or selecting HDG SEL will disconnect L NAV.

2.13   Examples of Outer Loop Inputs in PITCH

a)   **Altitude Hold (ALT HLD)**

The altitude hold mode gives pitch commands to hold the MCP selected altitude or the uncorrected barometric altitude at which the ALT HOLD switch was pressed. ALT HOLD engages in either of 2 conditions

1)   ALT HOLD at the MCP selected altitude. This is indicated by the annunciation of ALT HOLD and the ALT HOLD switch light extinguished.

2)   ALT HOLD not at the MCP selected altitude. This is indicated by the annunciation of ALT HOLD and the ALT HOLD switch light illuminated.

ALT HOLD not at the MCP selected altitude occurs with either of the following:

1)   Pushing the ALT HOLD switch while not at the MCP selected altitude.

2)   Selecting a new MCP altitude while in ALT HOLD at the currently selected altitude.

ALT HOLD is inhibited after glideslope capture. When in ALT HOLD at the selected altitude, LVL CHG, V/S and V NAV climb and descend functions are inhibited until a new altitude is selected.

The altitude selected on the MCP is referenced to the Captain's barometric altimeter setting for the "A" autopilot and FDS, and to the First Officer's barometric setting for the "B" autopilot and FDS. After ALT HOLD engages, changes in the altimeter barometric settings do not change the selected altitude reference.

b)   **Altitude Acquire (ALT ACQ)**

The altitude acquire mode is the transition manoeuvre entered automatically from a V/S, LVL CHG, or V NAV climb or descent to a MPC selected altitude. The altitude acquire mode is also armed while climbing or descending in CWS with an autopilot engaged.

Altitude acquire engagement is annunciated ALT ACQ in pitch when levelling off in either V/S or LVL CHG. However, V NAV remains annunciated throughout the altitude acquire mode when levelling in V NAV.

ALT ACQ engagement is inhibited when the ALT HOLD switch is pressed or while the glideslope is captured.

c)   **IAS/MACH Hold. (SPD)**

This will hold a selected IAS or MACH No. by comparing selected value with actual value from the ADC and pitching the aircraft up or down to decrease or increase speed.

d)   **Vertical Speed (V/S).**   _AP takes priority over A/T so AP will try and alter the V/S so there is a risk of over/under speed._

The V/S mode gives pitch commands to hold the selected vertical speed and engages the auto-throttle in the SPEED mode to hold the selected airspeed. The V/S mode has both an armed and engaged state.

Pressing the V/S switch engages the V/S mode unless the ALT HOLD is engaged or after glideslope capture.

all values displayed on PFD

V/S engaged is annunciated, the Vertical Speed Display changes from blank to present vertical speed and desired vertical speeds can be selected with the vertical spedd thumb-wheel.

Speed/VS/Hdg se/alt
_250   30000_
PFD

The V/S mode becomes armed if, while in the ALT HOLD at the selected altitude, a new MCP altitude is selected which is more than 100 ft different than the previously selected altitude. V/S armed is annunciated and the V/S mode can be engaged by moving the vertical speed thumb-wheel.

automatically

_VS_

AT - SPEED   AT - SPEED
AP - ALT ACQ   AP - ALT HOLD
_30,000_

V/S mode changes to ALT ACQ when getting near required Alt.

A/T - Speed
AP - Vert Speed

VS button will extinguish

JAA Q:
During ALT ACQ mode autothrottle maintains IAS.

A/T - Speed
A/P - Alt
_20,000'_

2-23   © Oxford Aviation Services Limited

*Must select 2 values the a/c can achieve

The V/S mode automatically engages when the altitude acquire mode is engaged and a new altitude is selected which is more than 100 ft different than the previously selected altitude. The V/S mode annunciates engaged and existing vertical speed appears in the vertical speed display. The commanded V/S can be changed with the vertical speed thumb-wheel. Vertical speeds can be selected which command flight toward or away from the selected altitude.

e)   **Level Change Mode (LVL CHG)**

The LVL CHG mode co-ordinates pitch and thrust commands to make automatic climbs and descents to pre-selected altitude at selected airspeeds. A LVL CHG climb or descent is initiated by selecting a new altitude and engaging the LVL CHG mode.

During a LVL CHG climb, the annunciations are MCP SPD for pitch and N1 for the auto-throttle (A/T). During a LVL CHG descent, the annunciations are MCP SPD for pitch and RETARD for the A/T while reducing the thrust toward idle. When at idle thrust, ARM is annunciated for the A/T.

If a speed mode was active prior to engaging LVL CHG, he previous speed is retained as the target speed for the LVL CHG mode. If the LVL CHG mode is engaged with no active speed mode, the IAS/Mach display and airspeed cursors synchronise to existing speed and present speed becomes the LVL CHG target speed. After LVL CHG mode engagement, the target speed can be changed with the MCP speed selector.

f)   **Vertical Navigation Mode (V NAV)**

With the V NAV mode engaged, the FMC commands AFDS pitch and A/T modes to fly the vertical profile selected on the FMC CDUs. The profile includes pre-selected climbs, cruise altitudes, speeds, descents, and can also include altitude constraints at specified way-points. The profile may end with an ILS approach to the destination airfield.

Pressing the V NAV switch selects the V NAV mode provided FMC performance initialisation is complete. The mode selector switch illuminates, the MCP IAS/Mach display becomes blank and the airspeed cursors are positioned at the FMC commanded airspeed. The FMA displays are V NAV SPD or V NAV PTH for the AFDS pitch mode and FMC SPD, N1, RETARD or ARM for the A/T mode.

V NAV climbs and descents are constrained by the selected MCP altitude. V NAV commanded speeds can be changed with the FMC CDUs.

During V NAV path cruise flight, selecting a lower MCP altitude, arms the FMC to automatically begin the descent upon arrival at the FMC calculated top of descent point.

During a V NAV path descent, V NAV remains engaged until:

In descents idle thrust will be used.

1. Glideslope capture, or
2. Another pitch mode is selected, or

3. Flaps are extended beyond 15, or
4. L NAV is disengaged without glideslope capture.

** Speed Intervention
* Alt Intervention
buttons can
be used to massage
FMC speeds & alts.*

Proper MCP altitude selections ensure correct altitude alerting.

2.14   AUTOPILOT IN OPERATION

The modes of operation of the autopilot during the various flight phases can be seen from the following table:

PHASE	ROLL	PITCH	AUTOTHROTTLE
Take-off	TOGA	TOGA	THR REF
Climb	LNAV, HDG or VOR	ALT, SPD, VNAV or V/S	THR REF, or V/S
Cruise	LNAV, HDG or VOR	ALT HOLD, VNAV or SPD	SPD or MACH No
Descent	LNAV, HDG or VOR	FLCH, SPD, VNAV or V/S	SPD or MACH No
Approach	LNAV, HDG or LOC	ALT, G/S, SPD	SPD
Land	LOC, ROLLOUT	G/S, FLARE	SPD, V/S
Go Around	LNAV, HDG or VOR	ALT, SPD or V/S	THR REF

2.15   OTHER AUTOPILOT FEATURES

a)   **Roll and Pitch Modes**

Approach mode (APP) allows Localizer and Glideslope elements of the ILS system to be coupled to the roll and pitch channels of the autopilot to allow automatic control down to decision height, or to effect a fully automatic landing.

b)   **Control Wheel Steering (CWS)** — *some will level the wings if bank angle is <5°.*

A Control Wheel Steering mode (CWS) is provided in some automatic flight control systems(Boeing 737-400), its purpose being to enable the pilot to manoeuvre his aircraft in pitch and/or roll, through the automatic control system without disconnecting the autopilot. The signals for the A/P are produced by transducers in the control column.

*when stick is let go
the a/c maintains the attitude
it was in when the stick was
let go.*

*ie has turned a/c into a fly
by wire a/c!*

*used as we have inner loop stability so we can fly "manually"
retaining advantages of stability*

2-25

© Oxford Aviation Services Limited

Pressing a CWS engage switch, engages the A/P pitch and roll axes in the CWS mode and displays CWS P and CWS R on the FMAs.

With CWS engaged, the A/P manoeuvres the aeroplane in response to control pressures applied by either pilot. The control pressure is similar to that required for manual flight. When control pressure is released, the A/P holds existing attitude.

If aileron pressure is released with 6 degrees or less angle of bank, the A/P rolls the wings level and holds the existing heading. This heading hold feature with bank less than 6 degrees, is inhibited when any of the following conditions exist:

1. Below 1500 ft RA with the landing gear down.
2. After FD VOR capture with TAS 250 kts or less.
3. After FD LOC capture in the APP mode.

Pitch CWS with a CMD Engage switch selected

The pitch axis engages in CWS while the roll axis is in CMD when:

1. A command pitch mode has not been selected or was de-selected
2. A/P pitch has been manually overridden with control column force. The force required for override is greater than normal CWS control column force. This manual pitch override is inhibited in the APP mode with both A/Ps engaged.

CWS P is annunciated on the Flight Mode Annunciators (FMA) while this mode is engaged. Command pitch modes can then be selected.

When approaching a selected altitude in CWS P with a CMD engage switch selected, CWS P changes to ALT ACQ and when at the selected altitude, ALT HOLD engages.

If pitch is manually overridden while in ALT HOLD the annunciator changes to CWS P. If control force is released within 250 ft of the selected altitude, CWS P changes to ALT ACQ and the A/P returns to the selected altitude and ALT HOLD engages. If the elevator force is held until more than 250 ft from the selected altitude, pitch remains in CWS P.

Roll CWS with a CMD engage switch selected

The roll axis engages in CWS while the pitch axis is in CMD when:

1. A command roll mode has not been selected or was de-selected.
2. A/P roll has been manually overridden with control wheel force. The force required for override is greater than the normal CWS control wheel force.

CWS R is annunciated on the FMA while this mode is engaged.

CWS R with a CMD engage switch illuminated, can be used to capture a selected radio course while VOR/LOC or APP mode is armed. Upon intercepting the radial or localiser, the FD and A/P annunciation changes from CWS R to VOL/LOC engaged and the A/P tracks the selected course.

c)   **Touch Control Steering (TCS)**   *only on small a/c not large jet*

Touch Control Steering (TCS) also permits a pilot to manoeuvre his aircraft in pitch or roll, but unlike CWS the appropriate automatic control channels and servo-motors are disengaged while the TCS button is held depressed while the pilot flies the aircraft to the desired attitude using manual control. The autopilot is re-engaged by release of the TCS button and the autopilot continues to again hold the aircraft in the attitude in which it was left.

d)   **Altitude Reference to Autopilot**

The altitude selected in the window on the MCP is referenced to the Captain's barometric altimeter setting when the 'A' autopilot is selected and to the First Officer's when 'B' is selected. After ALT HOLD engages, changes in altimeter barometric settings do not change the selected altitude reference i.e. the autopilot will not change altitude until a new altitude is selected and engaged.

e)   **Automatic Synchronisation**   *— Synchronises autopilot with current attitude & avoids stick being snatched from hands*

In addition to the pre-engage requirements that the autopilot circuits are electrically complete, it must also be ensured that on engagement the 'take-over' is affected smoothly and without 'snatching' of the aircraft's control system. In other words the aircraft must be trimmed for the desired flight attitude before engagement and the automatic control system must be synchronised to maintain that attitude on engagement.

"stick snatch" is prevented (servo unit is always working ↓ JAA Q ↓ Continually working to prevent snatching ↓ maintain attitude

In the majority of autopilot systems synchronisation is effected by specifically designed synchronising circuits which automatically sense any existing 'standing signals' in the pitch and roll channels and automatically reduce or 'wash out' these signals to zero. This stops the servo-actuator in a position which is synchronised with the datum attitude detected by the sensing element, such position being indicated by the return of the trim indicator pointer to its central position.

The basic inner-loop stability as described so far only mentions a gyro as the detector for auto-stability. This is not the whole story. All gyros are short term accuracy items. Rate gyros are only able to detect and respond to changes within their threshold of detection. Very slow rate changes in attitude may not be detected by a gyro. To correct for this and to allow for the detection of these low rates of change various monitors are used. In the pitch and roll axes these are pendulous monitors also fitted with E and I bars which are wired in parallel with the gyros.

For heading monitoring a feed from the Gyro compass can be used although it must be emphasized that the system is only interested in a change in heading over the long term and is not actually trying to fly a particular heading. The auto-stability system will therefore be able to correct for long term changes.

Consider an aircraft taking off. At about 400' the pilot may elect to engage the autopilot. The aircraft however is pitched nose-up for the climb and so the pitch monitor is displaced abaft and a standing signal is present. If the autopilot is engaged now, the pitch monitor sends a signal to pitch the aircraft nose down to regain the level attitude. If this happens then the pitch gyro will detect the nose down pitching movement and send signals to fight it. The net effect is that the aircraft will oscillate following a path which is neither the correct climb out path nor straight and level.

Assume now that we have mounted our gyros on a motorized platform that can tilt in both the pitch and roll axes. The autopilot is powered from before the aircraft begins to move however the signals that would normally go to the servo-motors from the gyros and error detectors go to the platform motors instead while the autopilot is not engaged. As the aircraft rotates the gyros sense the displacement and a signal is produced. This signal is fed to the platform motors essentially leveling the platform. Effectively the platform will remain level no matter the angle of bank and pitch of the aircraft. Now when we come to engage the autopilot the platform and therefore the gyros and monitors are all level so the autopilot engages without incident. The signal that were until recently keeping the platform level are now feeding the servo-motor as before so the autopilot is back to being an auto-stabilization system. This is a basic form of synchronization.

We are now flying with auto-stabilization in the attitude set at autopilot engagement. We would like to be able to maneuver the aircraft using the autopilot systems without having to disconnect the autopilot. If for example we require to climb we could have a switch controlling the motor for pitching the autopilot platform. Using the motor to pitch the platform forward fools the auto-stability system into thinking that the aircraft has pitched nose down. Signals from the gyros to the error detectors move the servos and control surfaces to "correct" for that disturbance an pitches the aircraft up until the platform is level again. The auto stability is not effected by these operations because the difference between a movement of the platform due to the motor and a movement of the platform due to a disturbance of the aircraft. An angle of bank can be established in much the same way by rolling the platform.

Outer loop control is established by setting a desired datum of for example a particular heading. The autopilot compares the desired heading with the actual heading from the compass system and uses the autopilot platform motors to fool the inner loop control into maneuvering the aircraft to achieve the desired result.

Modern aircraft do not require real moving platforms as described above. Accurate sensing of the attitude and accelerations on the aircraft (using IRS type systems) allow the computers to artificially produce signals to counter any synchronization errors and so on. It is however sometimes beneficial to think of a virtual platform to be able to explain the reactions and inputs/outputs of the autopilot system.

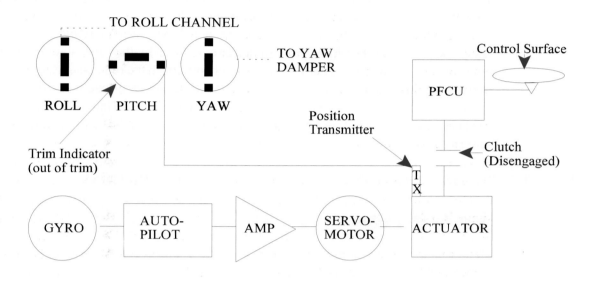

Fig 2.14 The Trim Indicators

Therefore, in aircraft that do not have a self-synchronising autopilot, it is important that the pilot ensures that the aircraft is properly trimmed before engaging the autopilot otherwise 'snatching' could occur at the moment of engagement. This is achieved by use of the **Trim Indicators**. These indicate the current demands on the control surface from the autopilot (not the position of the control surface). So if the aircraft is not in the attitude that the autopilot is set to hold there will be a standing demand from the autopilot even when not engaged. If the autopilot were to be engaged with the standing load, as displayed on the trim indicators, present then all the problems of the unsynchronised autopilot would ensue. To safely engage the autopilot the attitude of the aircraft must be changed to make all the trim indicators read centrally. This is not necessarily the same as the aircraft flying in aerodynamic trim which can be achieved at various attitudes and speeds.

f)   Tracking Through VOR "Cone of Confusion"

The 'cone of confusion' is an area overhead a VOR navigation beacon where the signals are unusable. Thus an aircraft transiting the VOR will receive no usable signals for a period depending upon its ground-speed and altitude.

As the aircraft approaches the VOR the radials are converging and the course deviation indicator becomes more sensitive. At some point , before it enters the cone of confusion the information from the selected inbound radial becomes unusable due to the convergence. At this point the VOR signals are 'cut off' by the 'over station sensing' circuits i.e. the roll channel automatically de-couples from the radio beam and controls the aircraft through the cone of confusion on the drift-corrected heading existing when the radio signals are de-coupled. In other words the autopilot goes into Heading Hold for a set period after which it reverts to the VOR Mode. Note that the autopilot does not go into Heading Mode.

2.16   AUTOPILOT LIMITATIONS AND OPERATIONAL RESTRICTIONS

a)   Autopilot Interlocks.

Before coupling an autopilot with the aircraft's control system the integrity of the Autopilot Inner Loop must be established to ensure that it may safely take control of the aircraft. To monitor the performance of the inner loop components a system of interlocks is provided which close to allow autopilot engagement and hold it engaged if the correct valid signals have been received. The function of the interlocks can be represented by a number of relays in series (see figure 2.9), although in modern aircraft the actual switching is more likely to be accomplished by solid state logic switching. Failure of a circuit monitored by a relay will cause the autopilot to disengage accompanied by the associated aural and visual warning indications. Operation of the disengage switch will have the same effect.

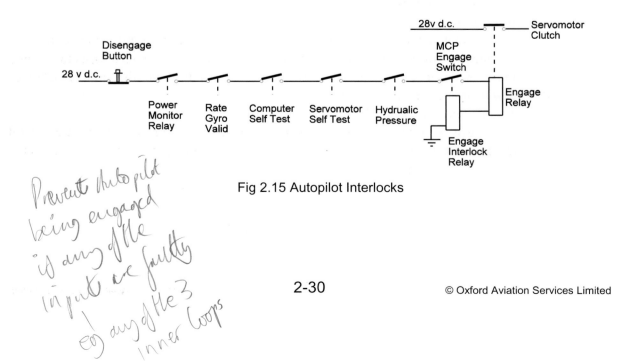

Fig 2.15 Autopilot Interlocks

Prevent Autopilot being engaged if any of the inputs are faulty or any of the 3 inner loops

b)   **Conditions of Engagement**

Before the autopilot can be engaged certain conditions must be met. These conditions vary with aircraft type. For the 737-400 these conditions are as follows.

Each autopilot can be engaged by pressing a separate CMD or CWS engage switch. A/P engagement in CMD or CWS is inhibited unless both of the following pilot-controlled conditions are met:

1.   No force is being applied to the control wheel.
2.   The Stabiliser Trim Autopilot Cut-out Switch is at NORMAL.

Once the above conditions are satisfied and no failures exist, either A/P can be engaged in CMD or CWS by pressing the respective engage switch. Control pressure applied after an A/P is engaged in CMD, overrides the A/P into CWS pitch and/or roll. The light remains illuminated in the CMD engage switch.

The A/P automatically disengages when any of the following occur:

1.   Pressing either A/P disengage switch.
2.   Pressing either TOGA switch with a single A/P engaged in CWS or CMD below 2000 ft RA.
3.   Pressing either TOGA switch after touchdown with both A/Ps engaged in CMD.
4.   Pressing a lighted A/P engage switch.
5.   Pushing the A/P disengage bar down.
6.   Activating either pilot's control wheel trim switch.
7.   Moving the Stabiliser Trim Autopilot Cut-out Switch to CUT-OUT.
8.   Loss of respective hydraulic system pressure.
9.   Repositioning the EFI transfer switch.
10.   Either left or right IRS system failure or FAULT light illuminated.
11.   Loss of electrical power or a sensor input which prevents proper operation of the engaged A/P and mode.

Only one A/P can be engaged at a given time unless the approach (APP) mode is engaged. Pressing an engage switch for the second A/P, while not in the APP mode, engages the second autopilot as selected and disengages the first A/P. The second A/P then operates in CWS or CMD without interrupting CWS or command operation.

If an A/P is engaged with the CMD engage switch during FD only operation while pitch or roll commands are more than ½ scale from centred, the A/P automatically engages in CWS for pitch and/or roll and the FD command bars retract.

Autopilot Disengage Warnings

The "A/P" light flashes red and a tone sounds when an autopilot has disengaged. The warning can be reset by pressing either disengage light or either A/P disengage switch.

The A/P warning light stays at steady red if:

1.   Stabiliser is out of trim below 800ft RA on a dual channel approach.
2.   Altitude Acquire mode is inhibited during an A/P go-around. (stabiliser not trimmed for single A/P operation. See A/P Go-Around).
3.   Disengage light test switch is held in position 2 (red filament test).
4.   Automatic ground system test fail.

The light will illuminate a steady amber when the Disengage Light Test Switch is held in position 1 (amber filament test).

The light will flash amber if A/P automatically reverts to CWS pitch or roll while in CMD. The light will reset when either light is pressed or another mode is engaged.

c)   Maximum Pitch and Bank Angles

During normal autopilot operation the maximum angles are:

1.   Pitch $\pm 10°$
2.   Roll $\pm 30°$

These limits are however not stipulated legally and will vary from aircraft to aircraft.

d)   Gain Adaption

Variations in flight parameters such as altitude, speed, aircraft load, configuration and rate of manoeuvre, will have an effect on the handling characteristics of an aircraft. It is therefore necessary to incorporate 'gearing' elements within flight control systems which will adapt the parameters to the aircraft so that their effect on handling characteristics is reduced. In automatic systems the response is altered by changing the 'gain' of the system to a given level of input signal. This can be likened to changing gear ratios in a mechanical system.

Gain adaptation is particularly important for maintaining handling characteristics with changes in IAS during the different phases of flight and is similar to the gain scheduling in the flight director system.

e)   Approach/Land mode.

During an auto-land sequence the autopilot has to execute many important manoeuvres. These are described in the Auto-land notes.

2.17 FLIGHT MANAGEMENT SYSTEM

The autopilot can form part of the overall Flight Management System (FMS). This is may also be designated the Automatic Flight Control System (AFCS) or the Flight Management and Guidance System (FMGS). It provides manual or automatic modes of control throughout the entire flight envelope from take-off to landing and roll-out. All the subsystems of the FMS are fully integrated and have levels of redundancy to achieve a high level of reliability. Redundancy is accomplished by providing two or more systems of each type so a failure of one system will not affect the operation of the complete system. Figure 2.1 shows the integration of the FMS with other avionics in the aircraft.

The AFCS and FMS will be checked completely during the pre-flight checks. During these checks all the automated systems will be engaged, tested and their various safety devices tested. The FMS will be checked for the correct information and any additional information will be entered.

The following is a list of as yet unanswered objectives:
(Explain the different trim steering signals for elevator, aileron, rudder and elevator trim).
(Define the control law of an autopilot).
(Explain that the position and rate of movement of the flight control surface is fed back to the autopilot computer).

T/0

No A/P

ATT & TOGA

Climb

A/P - Hdg Sel
& V/S
A/T

or LNAV
& VNAV
@ 400ft
or there's
profile in
computer
pnl.

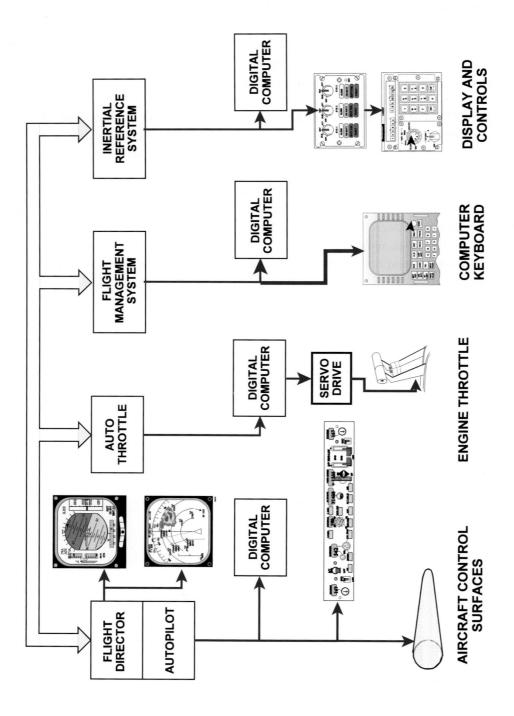

Fig 2.16 Integrated Flight Management System

CHAPTER 3 - AUTOLAND

Page

3.1   INTRODUCTION . . . . 3 - 1

3.2   AUTOLAND SYSTEM. . . . . 3 - 2

3.3   THE AUTOMATIC LANDING SEQUENCE. . . . . 3 - 3

APPENDIX 3A

— Must have 2 autopilots (at least)
— Must have 2 independent NAV radio Receivers
— Must have 2 Rad Alts
— Must have accurate ILS at runway

3.1   INTRODUCTION

The approach and landing manoeuvre is the most difficult one demanded of a pilot in that it entails control of the aircraft in all three axes simultaneously as well as control of airspeed through engine power changes. The pilot has to:

— Must have a/land qualified crew.

1.   Align the aircraft with the runway centre-line
2.   Achieve a sinking rate of about 2 feet per second before touchdown
3.   Reduce the airspeed from 1.3 Vs to about 1.15 Vs by progressive reduction of engine power
4.   Level the wings before actual landing
5.   Yaw the aircraft to remove any drift angle (drift "kick off" or de-crabbing).

An automatic landing system that takes over from a pilot must be able provide guidance and control better than that required of the pilot.

Autopilots have for a long time now been able to fly most of the approach allowing the pilot to concentrate on navigating the approach correctly. The pilot would then take over at decision height and continue to land manually. This is called an auto-approach or a semi-automatic landing. Aircraft that are fitted with all the equipment required for a fully automatic landing may, due to lack of required ground equipment for example or simply for pilot experience requirements, carry out an auto-approach. Essentially all the procedures are carried out as for an auto-land, but when decision height is reached the pilot will take over manually.

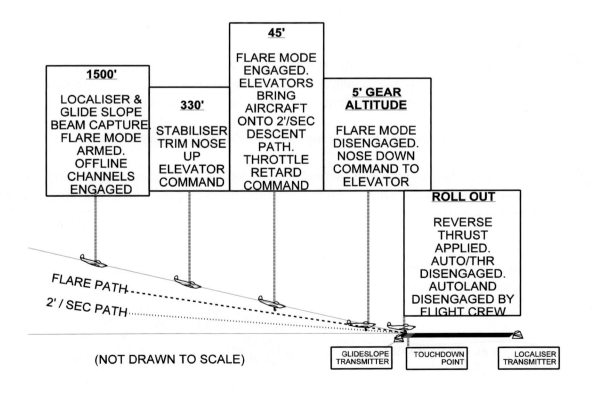

© Oxford Aviation Services Limited

3.2   AUTOLAND SYSTEM

a)   Objective

In order to achieve the objective of automatic landing, the operation of an automatic flight control system must be of such a nature that it will:

1.   Not disturb the flight path as a result of an active malfunction
2.   Have adequate authority for sufficiently accurate control along the required flight path
3.   Warn of a passive failure
4.   Allow the intended flight manoeuvre to be completed following an active or a passive failure.

b)   Requirements

To enable an aeroplane to complete an automatic landing the auto-land system requires

1.   A minimum of **two independent autopilots** capable of following ILS signals
2.   Two independent **Radio Altimeters** to give accurate height from the ground information
3.   **Category 3 ILS** ground installation at the airport.

c)   Auto-land Status

The number of autopilots required also depends upon the auto-land status of the aircraft. These fall into two main categories:

i)   **Fail - passive (Fail-soft).** This is defined as the ability of the system to withstand a failure without endangering passenger safety, and without producing excessive deviations in the flight path but removing its capability to complete an automatic landing.

The minimum number of autopilots required for a fail-passive capability is two.

ii)   **Fail-Operational (Fail - active)** status is defined as the ability of a system to withstand a failure without affecting the overall functioning of the system and without causing degradation of performance beyond the limits required for automatic landing.

The system requires a minimum of three autopilots. However it is possible for an aircraft to have a fail operational category with only two autopilots provided that there is suitable duplicate monitoring for each channel.

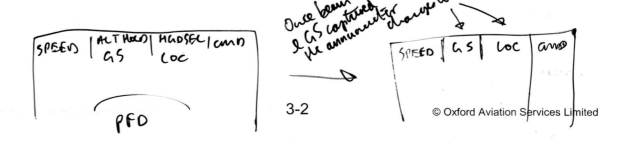

3-2

3.3   THE AUTOMATIC LANDING SEQUENCE.

a)   Profile

During cruise and initial stages of approach to land, the control system operates as a single channel system, controlling the aircraft about its pitch and roll axes, and providing the appropriate flight director commands. The profile of an automatic approach, flare and landing sequence is shown in Figure 3.1 and is based on a system that utilises triple digital flight control computer channels, allowing for redundancy to operate in the fail operational and fail passive conditions already defined.

b)   Status Annunciator

2nd (or 3rd) AP are offline channels. They follow but do not make control adjustments

Depending upon the number of channels that are armed and engaged, the system performs what are termed a **'LAND 2'** status or **'LAND 3'** status auto-land. Thus **'LAND 2'** signifies there is dual redundancy of engaged flight control computers, sensors and servos (**fail passive operation**) while **'LAND 3'** signifies triple redundancy of power sources, engaged flight control computers, sensors and servos (**fail operational**). Each status is displayed on an auto-land status annunciator.

c)   Approach

Since multi-channel operation is required for an automatic landing, at a certain stage of the approach, the remaining two channels are armed by pressing an **'APPR'** switch on the flight control panel. The operation of this switch also arms the localiser and glide slope modes. Both of the 'off-line' channels are continually supplied with the relevant outer loop control signals and operate on a comparative basis the whole time.

d)   Radio Altimeter

Altitude information essential for vertical guidance to touchdown is always provided by signals from a **radio altimeter** which becomes effective as soon as the aircraft's altitude is within the altimeter's operating range (typically 2500 feet).

AFS Radio Altimeter Loss

Two independent radio altimeters provide RA to the respective FCC. The Captain's radio altimeter also provides RA information to the A/T.

With a radio altimeter inoperative, do not use the associated FCC or the A/T, if affected, for approach and landing, i.e. failure of a single radio altimeter causes the auto-land system to fail passive.

— Beam Capture is part at which localizer is captured

© Oxford Aviation Services Limited

e)   **The Sequence**

An example of an auto-land sequence (for a Boeing aircraft) is described below.

Approach (APP) mode

The approach mode arms the AFDS to capture and track the localiser and glideslope. It can be engaged for dual or single pilot operation (auto-land with dual only). Dual autopilot (A/P) approach operation is described first.

Approach mode allows both A/Ps to be engaged at the same time. Dual A/P operation provides fail passive control through landing flare and touch down or an automatic go-around. During fail passive operation, the flight controls respond to the A/P commanding the least control movement.

One VHF Nav receiver must be tuned to an ILS frequency before the approach mode can be selected. For a dual A/P approach, the second VHF Nav receiver must be tuned to the ILS frequency and the corresponding A/P engaged prior to 800 ft RA.

Localiser and glideslope armed.

After setting the localiser frequency and course, pressing the APP switch selects the APP mode. The APP switch illuminates and VOR LOC and G/S armed is annunciated. The APP mode permits selecting the engagement of the second A/P. This arms the second A/P for automatic engagement after LOC and G/S capture and when descent below 1500 ft RA occurs.

The localiser can be intercepted in the HDG SEL, CWS R or L Nav modes. Either the LOC or G/S can be captured first (although it its most common to capture LOC the G/S).

Localiser Capture

The localiser capture point is variable and depends on the intercept angle and rate of closure, but does not occur at less than ½ a dot deviation. Upon LOC capture, VOR LOC annunciates captured, 1 CH is annunciated for the A/P status, the previous roll mode disengages and the aeroplane turns to track the LOC.

Glideslope Capture

The G/S can be captured from above or below (although from below is generally preferred). Capture occurs at 2/5 dot deviation. G/S annunciates captured, the previous pitch mode disengages, the APP switch light extinguishes if the localiser has also been captured, aeroplane pitch tracks the G/S and the annunciated N1 thrust limit for the A/T is GA.

After LOC and G/S are both captured the APP mode can be exited only by pressing the TOGA switch or by disengaging the A/P and turning off both FD switches or re-tuning a VHF Nav receiver.

After Localiser and Glideslope Capture

The A/Ps will disengage and the FD command bars will retract to indicate an invalid ILS signal.

At 1500 feet radio altitude (RA)

White below G.S.

Shortly after capturing both LOC and G/S and descending below 1500 ft RA, the second A/P couples with the flight controls, FLARE mode armed is annunciated and the A/P go-around mode arms but is not annunciated. ROLL OUT mode if available will also now arm. The auto-land status will also now be annunciated as either "**LAND 2**"(or "**LAND 3**" for fail operational aircraft).

& white below Loc

*Learn
↳
1500 to
50ft
sequence*

The pitch and roll axes cannot be manually overridden into CWS. Attempts to do so will result in A/P disengagement.

800 ft RA

The second A/P must have been engaged by 800 ft RA to execute a dual A/P approach. Otherwise, engagement of the second A/P is inhibited on descending through 800 ft RA.

400 - 330 feet RA

The stabiliser is automatically trimmed an additional amount nose-up, with the elevators neutralising and holding the pitching up moment. If the A/Ps subsequently disengage, forward control column force may be required to hold the desired pitch attitude. This biasing aids the flare and in the event of a subsequent fail passive the aircraft will tend to pitch nose up to prevent a hard contact with the ground and aids the initiation of a go around.

If FLARE is not armed by approximately 350 ft RA, both A/Ps automatically disengage.

At 45 feet gear altitude (GA)/ 50 ft RA

The A/P flare manoeuvre starts at approximately 50 ft RA and is completed at touchdown. FLARE engaged is annunciated and the FD command bars retract. Also:

4.   The stabiliser trim is again automatically trimmed an additional amount nose-up.

5.   The **FLARE** mode is automatically engaged (replacing G/S) to give the aircraft a 2 feet/second descent path

*At point of
T/D*

[diagram: LOCE | FLARE]

*Reverse thrust always selected
by pilot*

*as are slats, flaps, landing
gear
_ any config change.*

6.   The A/T begins retarding thrust at approximately 27 ft RA so as to reach idle at touchdown.

The **gear altitude** calculation, which is pre-programmed into the computer, is based upon radio altitude, pitch attitude, and the known distance between the landing gear, the fuselage and the radio altimeter antenna.

nothing else announced

At about 5 feet GA :

1.   the flare mode is disengaged and there is transition to the touchdown
2.   LOC disengages
3.   roll-out mode (if available) will engage.

At about 1 foot GA :

1.   the pitch attitude of the aircraft is decreased to 2°
2.   **at touchdown**, a command signal is supplied to the elevators to lower the aircraft's nose and so bring the nose landing gear wheels in contact with the runway and hold them there during the **roll-out**.
3.   **When reverse thrust is applied** the auto-throttle system is automatically disengaged.
4.   Irrespective of reverse thrust deployment, the A/T automatically disengages approximately 2 seconds after touchdown.

The automatic flight control system remains on until manually disengaged by the flight crew, which is when the auto-land sequence is considered to be completed.

f) Other features of Auto-land

Runway Alignment. Although the yaw channel has not been mentioned any auto-flight system capable of an auto-land must be capable of 'kicking off drift' prior to touchdown. This is known as **runway alignment** mode and will typically be armed at the same time as the flare mode and engaged at less than 100'. During the approach from 1500' the yaw channel will compute the difference between heading and track, when align mode engages the rudder deflects to align the aircraft with the runway centreline before touchdown . This manoeuvre is known as **de-crabbing,** or drift 'kick-off'.

Roll-out. Another function of Cat 3 auto-land systems is **roll-out** which gives steering commands on the ground proportional to localiser deviation along the centreline. These commands can show left/right steering guidance through a rotating 'barbers pole' indicator known as a para-visual display (PVD). Alternatively automatic steering can be achieved by applying deviation signals to the rudder channel and nosewheel steering to keep the aircraft on the centreline throughout the ground roll.

Roll out guidance gives steering guidance via a P.V.D

Q: when is an autoland complete
A: when a/c is on ground after roll-out

A/P selects thrust
A/P selects pitch etc.
Pilot selects gear and flaps up.

A/P Go-around Mode

The A/P go-around (GA) mode require dual A/P operation and becomes armed when FLARE armed is annunciated. The A/P GA mode cannot be engaged before flare arm is annunciated or after the A/P senses touchdown.

Note: if the GA mode is selected after touchdown and prior to A/T disengagement, the A/Ps will disengage and the A/Ts may command GA thrust, with the procedure being flown manually.

Pressing either TOGA switch engages the GA mode and GA engaged is annunciated for the AFDS. The MCP IAS/Mach display becomes blank and the airspeed cursors are positioned at the AFDS commanded speed. Command airspeed is the flap manoeuvring speed.

A/P GA Pitch control

Upon GA engagement, the thrust levers advance toward the reduced GA N1. The A/P initially commands a 15 degree nose-up pitch attitude, and the airspeed cursors display manoeuvring speed for the flap setting. When a programmed rate of climb is established, the A/P controls pitch to hold airspeed based on the normal flap manoeuvring speed.

A/P GA Roll control

With the GA mode engaged, the A/Ps maintain the aeroplane ground track existing at GA engagement.

Leaving A/P GA mode

Below 400 ft RA, the A/Ps must be disengaged to change either pitch or roll modes from GA. Above 400 ft RA, other pitch and roll modes can be selected.

If the roll mode is changed first, the selected mode engages in single A/P roll operation and is controlled by the A/P which was first engaged. Pitch control remains in the dual A/P GA mode.

The pitch mode cannot be changed from GA until sufficient nose-down trim has been input to allow single A/P operation. This nose down trim is automatically added to reset the previous trim inputs that were applied automatically during the Auto-approach. If the pitch mode is the first to be changed from GA, the selected pitch mode engages in single A/P operation and is controlled by the first A/P that was engaged for the approach. The second A/P disengages and the roll mode changes to CWS R.

With pitch engaged in GA, ALT ACQ engages when approaching the selected altitude and ALT HOLD engages at the selected altitude if the stabiliser position is satisfactory for single A/P operation.

The transition from GA to ALT ACQ is normally successful if the selected altitude is at least 1000ft above the GA engagement altitude. A higher selected altitude may be required if full GA thrust is used.

If stabiliser trim is not satisfactory for single A/P operation, ALT ACQ is inhibited and the A/P disengage lights illuminate steady red and pitch remains in GA. To extinguish the A/P disengage lights, a higher altitude can be selected or the A/Ps disengaged.

Approach (APP) Mode / single A/P

A single A/P ILS approach can be executed by engaging only one A/P after pressing the APP switch. Single A/P approach operation is the same as for dual, with the following exceptions:

1.   A/P status of 1 CH is annunciated for the entire approach after localiser capture.
2.   Full automatic flare and touchdown capability is not available. FLARE is not annunciated and stabiliser trim bias is not applied.
3.   An A/P GA is not available.

The following diagram shows an automatic landing, see if you can correctly fill in the pitch and roll armed and engaged modes in the annunciator boxes at each stage of the approach and landing. I've started you off at point A as Approach mode has been selected.

AUTOLAND SEQUENCE

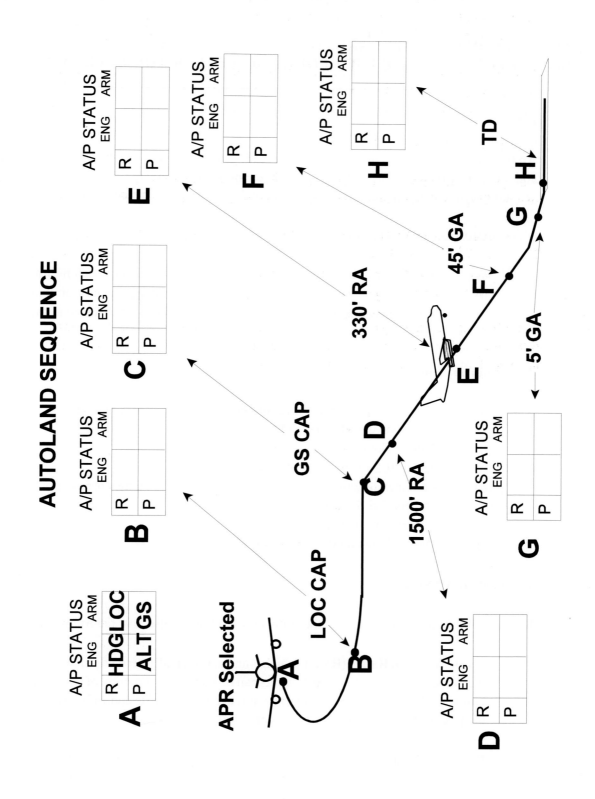

A/P STATUS	
ENG	ARM
R HDG	LOC
P ALT	GS

A

APR Selected

LOC CAP

A/P STATUS	
ENG	ARM
R	
P	

B

GS CAP

A/P STATUS	
ENG	ARM
R	
P	

C

330' RA

A/P STATUS	
ENG	ARM
R	
P	

E

A/P STATUS	
ENG	ARM
R	
P	

F

A/P STATUS	
ENG	ARM
R	
P	

H

1500' RA

A/P STATUS	
ENG	ARM
R	
P	

D

A/P STATUS	
ENG	ARM
R	
P	

G

A B C D E F G H

45' GA 5' GA TD

APPENDIX 3A

THE FOLLOWING NOTES ARE FOR GUIDANCE ONLY AND DO NOT FORM PART OF THE REQUIREMENTS FOR THE JAA EXAM.

ILS.

An Instrument Landing System (ILS) is a short-range navigational aid which provides azimuth and vertical guidance during the approach to an airport runway. The system comprises ground-based transmitting elements and also receiving elements carried on board the aircraft.

The **ground-based** elements are:

a) A localiser transmitter which sends runway azimuth approach information.

b) A glide slope transmitter which provides vertical approach information.

c) Marker beacons which transmit information about the distance to the runway threshold.

The **airborne** elements are:

a) A localiser signal receiving antenna (usually the same antenna as the one used for the VOR).

b) A glide slope signal receiving antenna.

c) A dual ILS receiver installation.

d) An indicator which shows whether the aircraft is on the correct approach path. Loc and GS deviation.

e) A marker beacon antenna and receiver.

f) Marker lights on the main instrument panel.

WEATHER MINIMA.

In low visibility operations, the weather limits for landing are given in the following terms:

a) **Runway Visual Range (RVR)**, which is an instrumentally derived value that represents the range at which high-intensity lights can be seen in the direction of landing **along the runway**. The measurements are transmitted to the air traffic controller who can inform the pilot of the very latest visibility conditions.

b) **Decision Height (DH)**, is the wheel height above the runway elevation at which a go-around must be initiated by the pilot, unless adequate visual reference has been established, and the position and approach path of the aircraft have been visually assessed as satisfactory to safely continue the approach or landing.

Minimum values of DH and RVR are known as 'weather minima' and are specified by the national licensing authorities for various types of aircraft and airports. When the traffic controller advises that the **RVR** is above the specified minimum, the pilot may descend to the specified decision height and if, by then, he has sighted a sufficiently large segment of the ground to enable him to be confident of his judgement, he may carry on an land. He must otherwise overshoot, and either enter the holding pattern pending another approach, or divert to an alternative airport. During the approach, the pilot's line of sight is down the glide-path and not along the runway, and this gives rise to another factor, called **'slant visual range'**, which a pilot must take into account in order to avoid misinterpretation of visual cues.

THE ICAO CATEGORISATION OF LOW VISIBILITY LANDING CAPABILITIES.

All Weather Operations

The term 'all weather operations' is frequently used in connection with automatic landing systems and in describing low weather minima . This is a term which can, and sometimes is, taken to mean that there are no weather conditions that can prevent an aircraft from taking-off and landing successfully. This is not the case, because no automatic system can, for example, perform the landing task in wind conditions in excess of those for which the aircraft has been certified, this being primarily governed by the controllability characteristics and strength factors of the aircraft. Similarly, no automatic system can land an aircraft on a runway which has a surface which is not fit for such an operation because of contamination by water, slush or ice.

Category of Operation

The definitions of the main categories are illustrated in Figure 3.3.

The three categories also serve as an indication of the stages through which automatic approach and automatic landing development progress, and thereby designate the capabilities of individual automatic flight control systems. In addition, they designate the standards of efficiency of the ground guidance equipment available at airports, namely ILS localiser and glide path, and approach, runway and taxi-way lighting.

Not autoland
no have to disco A/P at 200 ft.
- single A/P

Category 1. A precision instrument approach and landing with a decision height no lower than 60 m (200 ft), and with either a visibility not less than 800 m, or a runway visual range not less than 550 m

— Cat 1 can be done with a baro alt.

Category 2. A precision instrument approach and landing with decision height lower than 200 ft but not lower than 100 ft, and a runway visual range not less than 300 m.

— Rad Alt.

ie if we can see outside at 100ft we can continue with the auto land.

2 autopilots
e accurate ILS

e Pilot is the 3rd checker.

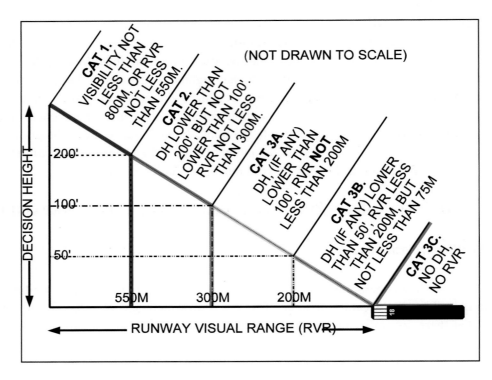

Figure 3.3. Categories of Low Visibility Landing Capabilities.

3 autopilots considered faul safe

Operation

dont need a decision height

Category 3A. A precision instrument approach and landing with a decision height lower than 100 ft and a runway visual range not less than 200 m. *(because pilot has to control a/c down runways)*

Category 3B. A precision instrument approach and landing with a decision height, if any, lower than 50 ft and a runway visual range less than 200 m but not less than 75m.

only 4 in U/K

dependent on accuracy of ILS

Category 3C. To and along the surface of the runway and taxi-ways without external visual reference.

ALERT HEIGHT.

The alert height is a specified radio height, based on the characteristics of the aircraft and its **fail-operational** landing system. In operational use, if a failure occurred **above** the alert height in one of the required redundant operational systems in the aircraft the approach would be discontinued and a **go-around** executed, unless reversion to a higher decision height is possible. If a failure in one of the required redundant operational systems occurred **below** the alert height, it would be ignored and the **approach continued** to compete the auto-land.

CHAPTER FOUR - AUTO-THROTTLE

Contents

4.1   INTRODUCTION 4-1

4.2   AUTO-THROTTLE SYSTEM 4-1

4.3   AUTO-THROTTLE FLIGHT PROFILE 4-10

4.4   THRUST COMPUTATION 4-10

4.5   FADEC 4-11

- MCP speed (ie selected in MCP) as pilot

OR

3 - FMC speed.

(not both)

IAS
or Mach

N₁
or EPR

~~Auto Throttle Controls~~ → ~~Speed or Thrust~~

TOGA
Switches
'on or near'
Throttle

Take off or G/A
A/T will control "Thrust"
target

4.1   INTRODUCTION

An auto-throttle system is a computer controlled, electro-mechanical system which can control the thrust of an aircraft's engines within specific design parameters. The throttle position of each engine is controlled to maintain a specific value of thrust in terms of:

a)   Fan Speed (N1)
b)   Engine Pressure Ratio (EPR) or
c)   Target Airspeed (set by SPD on mode control panel)

Thrust is the **force** generated by the engines. The throttles control the thrust and in some aircraft the preferred name for the throttles is thrust levers. It is worth noting that although there are thrust computation systems there is, as yet, no direct indicator of thrust value in use. Instead N1 and EPR are used to indicate a measure of engine thrust.

Using the above modes the auto-throttle can control aircraft speed from the beginning of the take-off roll until the system is disconnected after an automatic landing.(See figure 4.1).

4.2   AUTO-THROTTLE SYSTEM

a)   **System Components**

The Auto-throttle can also be called the Thrust Management System **(TMS)** that works in conjunction with the autopilot and the FMS**.**

Figure 4.2 shows a basic auto throttle system and signal interfacing between various aircraft systems and sensors.

b)   **Inputs.** These would include:

1.   Mode selection and A/T Arm switch on the MCP
2.   TAS, Mach No and TAT from the ADC
3.   attitude and acceleration from the IRS
4.   N1 speed and/or EPR from engine sensors
5.   angle of attack from AoA sensor
6.   radio altitude from the radio altimeter
7.   air / ground logic from the landing gear switch
8.   reverse thrust requirement from the engine accessory unit
      plus
9.   thrust command from the FMS
      or thrust mode selection from the trust mode select panel
10.   A/T disconnect switch on the throttles
11.   PLA (power lever angle) position from transducers
12.   flap position.

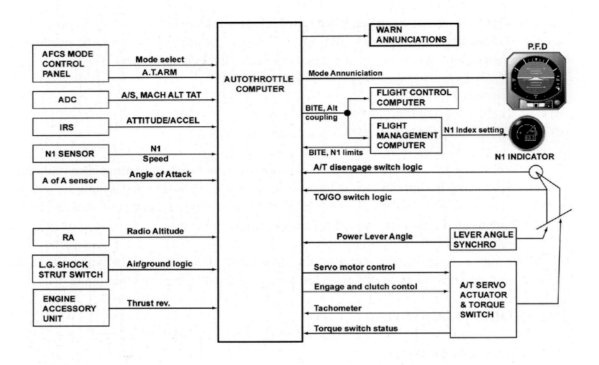

c)   **Outputs.** The main outputs from the system would be signals to:

1.   A/T servo-actuator to move the throttles
2.   A/T disengage circuit
3.   BITE (built in test equipment) circuits in the FCC and the FMC
4.   mode annunciation to the EFIS symbol generator
5.   thrust limits and to the EICAS / ECAM display
6.   failure warnings annunciations (lamp and/or aural, electronic display).

d)   **Feedback**

The auto-throttle system compares the actual values with reference values and passes control signals to the servo-motors of the thrust levers. In order to control the speed at which the thrust levers are moved there is a suitable feedback from the servo actuators to the TMC.

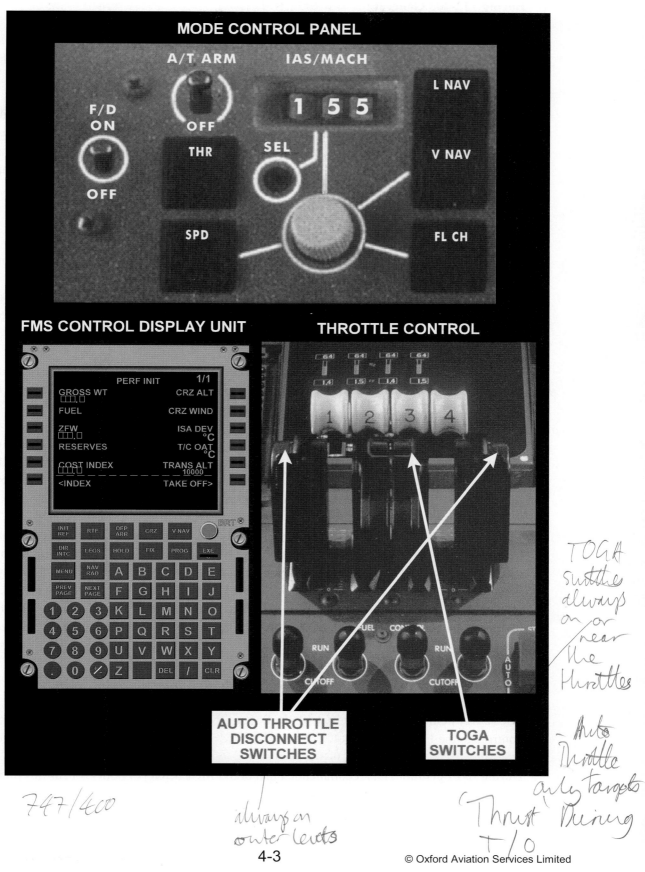

MODE CONTROL PANEL

A/T ARM   IAS/MACH   L NAV

F/D ON   OFF   1 5 5   V NAV

THR   SEL

SPD   FL CH

FMS CONTROL DISPLAY UNIT

PERF INIT   1/1

GROSS WT   CRZ ALT

FUEL   CRZ WIND

ZFW   ISA DEV °C

RESERVES   T/C OAT °C

COST INDEX   TRANS ALT 10000

<INDEX   TAKE OFF>

THROTTLE CONTROL

1   2   3   4

RUN   FUEL   CONTROL   RUN

CUTOFF   CUTOFF   AUTO

AUTO THROTTLE DISCONNECT SWITCHES

TOGA SWITCHES

747/400

always on outer levers

TOGA switches always on or near the throttles

- Auto Throttle only targets 'Thrust' during T/O

not CAS

Boeing 737-400 General

The A/T system provides automatic thrust control from the start of the takeoff through climb, cruise, descent, approach and go-around or landing. In normal operation, The FMC provides the A/T system with N1 limit values.

The A/T moves the thrust levers with a separate servo-motor on each thrust lever. Manually positioning the thrust levers does not cause A/T disengagement unless 10 degrees of thrust lever separation is exceeded during a dual channel approach after FLARE armed is annunciated. Following manual positioning, the A/T may reposition the thrust levers to comply with computed thrust requirements except while in the HOLD and ARM modes.

Power Management Control (PMC)

often incorporated into FMC.

The thrust control system consists of a hydro-mechanical MEC unit and a PMC unit mounted on each engine. The PMC in an electronic system with limited authority over the MEC. The Main Engine Control (MEC) schedules fuel to provide the thrust called for by the Forward Thrust Lever setting on the flight-deck. This fuel flow is further refined electronically by the Power Management Control (PMC) without moving the thrust levers.

The PMC uses MEC power lever angle, N1 speed, inlet temperature and pressure to adjust, or trim, the MEC to obtain the desired N1 speed. The PMC adjusts fuel flow as a function of thrust lever angle.

The PMC provides a constant thrust climb feature once the thrust lever is set at the beginning of climb. Thus, when thrust is set for climb, the PMC automatically maintains that thrust throughout the climb profile with no further thrust lever adjustments. If the thrust lever is repositioned, the PMC maintains the setting corresponding to the new thrust lever angle.

The PMC includes failure detection and annunciation modules which detect PMC failures and provide a signal to the crew. For detectable failure conditions, the PMC schedules a slow N1 drift over approximately 30 seconds and then illuminates the PMC INOP Light, the ENG System Annunciator Light and the MASTER CAUTION Lights. For a PMC failure, the PMC can be selected OFF by a switch on the aft overhead panel. The engine speed is then controlled by the hydro-mechanical MEC only. The PMC INOP light is suppressed below starter cutout engine speed.

A/T - PMC Operation

The A/T system operates properly with the PMCs ON or OFF. In either case, the A/T computer controls to the FMC N1 limits.

During A/T operation, it is recommended that both PMCs be ON or both OFF, as this produces minimum thrust lever separation. A/T takeoffs may be performed with both PMCs OFF.

A/T Engagement and Disengagement

Moving the A/T Arm Switch to ARM, arms the A/T for engagement in the N1, MCP SPD or FMC SPD mode. The A/T Arm Switch is magnetically held at ARM and releases to OFF when the A/T becomes disengaged.

Any of the following conditions or actions disengages the A/T:

9.   Moving the A/T Arm switch to OFF.
10.   Pressing either A/T disengage switch.
11.   An A/T system fault is detected.
12.   2 seconds have elapsed since landing touchdown.

Thrust levers become separated more by than 10 degrees during a dual channel approach after FLARE is annunciated.

A/T disengagement is followed by A/T Arm Switch releasing to OFF and the A/T Disengage Light flashing red.

The A/T Disengage lights can be extinguished by any of the following actions:

1.   Returning the A/T Arm Switch to ARM.
2.   Pressing either A/T Disengage light.
3.   Pressing either A/T Disengage Switch.

The A/T Disengage lights do not illuminate when the A/T automatically disengage after landing.

AUTOTHROTTLE DISENGAGE SWITCHES

PRESS- Disengages A/T. A/T Disengage Lighst flash and A/T ARM Switch trips OFF. Second push extinguishes A/T Disengage Lights.
- Extinguishes A/T Disengage Lights after automatic A/T disengagement.

TAKEOFF/GO-AROUND (TO/GA) SWITCHES
PRESS - Engages AFDS and A/T in takeoff or go-around mode if previously armed.

Take Off Mode.

The Takeoff mode is engaged by pressing either TOGA Switch with the aeroplane on the ground, the A/T armed and the desired takeoff N1 thrust limit selected from a FMC CDU. The A/T annunciation changes from ARM to N1 and the thrust levers advance toward takeoff thrust.

The A/T sets takeoff thrust. THR HLD annunciates at 84 kts (64 kts for aeroplanes with earlier model A/T computers) to indicate that the A/T cannot change thrust level position, but thrust levers can be repositioned manually.

After liftoff, the A/T remains in the THR HLD until 400 ft RA is reached and approximately 18 seconds have elapsed since liftoff. A/T annunciation then changes from THR HLD to ARM. Reduction to climb thrust can now be made by pressing the N1 switch.

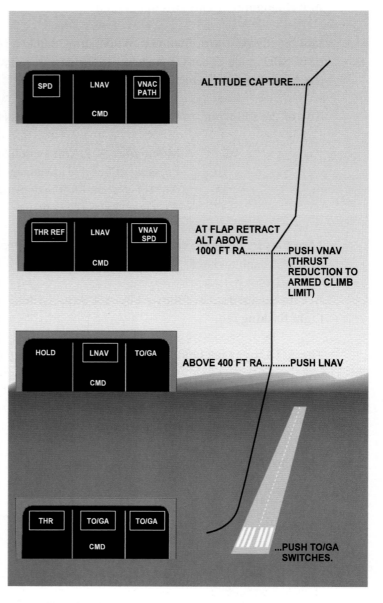

Until 2½ minutes after liftoff, automatic reduction to climb thrust is inhibited when in LVL CHG or V/S mode. If V NAV, ALT ACQ or ALT HOLD is engaged during this 2½ minute period, automatic thrust reduction occurs normally.

N1 Mode

The A/T maintains thrust at the N1 limit selected from a FMC CDU. N1 is annunciated for the A/T and the N1 switch illuminates. Pressing the N1 switch changes the A/T mode from N1 to ARM.

If an engine fails while the A/T is in the N1 mode, the thrust lever of the failed engine will advance forward a few degrees and then return to or below the other thrust lever position.

Speed Mode

The speed mode is available throughout the flight once the takeoff phase is completed. Pressing the MCP Speed Select Switch selects the speed mode if compatible with the engaged AFDS pitch mode. MCP SPD is annunciated for the A/T mode and the Speed Mode Switch illuminates. The speed or Mach shown in the MCP IAS/MACH Display is the target speed. The A/T will not set power above the displayed N1 limit, however, the A/T can exceed an N1 value that has been manually set by the N1 manual set knob. If an engine fails while the A/T is in a speed mode, both thrust levers advance together to maintain the target speed.

When on final approach in landing configuration, it is not recommended to set the A/T command speed to allow for wind or gust corrections. Through airspeed and acceleration sensing, the A/T corrects for normal wind gusts. Higher command speed settings result in excessive approach speeds. The recommended A/T approach speed setting is VREF +5.

Below 400 ft RA, A/T thrust level response rate and engine power levels are sufficient to place the engines in the rapid acceleration range.

FMC Speed Mode

The FMC SPD mode is an A/T mode which is commanded by the FMC during V NAV operation. When engaged, the MCP IAS/Mach display is blank, the airspeed cursors are positioned at the FMC commanded airspeed and the A/T maintains this commanded speed. The A/T is limited to the N1 value shown on the thrust mode annunciators.

N1 Equalization

The A/T attempts to equalize N1 through the dual servo individual thrust lever control. Equalization control is limited to 8 degrees of thrust lever separation.

ARM Mode

The A/T annunciates ARM when the A/T Arm Switch is at ARM and no A/T mode is engaged. The thrust levers can be manually positioned without interference from the A/T system while ARM is annunciated.

The A/T automatically transfers to ARM from the SPEED or N1 mode when the mode is deselected by pressing the respective Mode Selector Switch while the switch light is illuminated.

Descent Retard Mode

The A/T engages and annunciates RETARD during LVL CHG and V NAV descents. RETARD changes to ARM when the thrust levers reach the aft stop or when they are manually prevented from reaching the aft stop.

Landing Flare Retard Mode

During landing, The RETARD mode engages, reduces thrust and annunciates RETARD 2 ½ seconds after FLARE mode engagement or at 27 ft RA, whichever occurs first. During a non-precision or visual approach with flaps extended to 15 or greater and the AFDS not in ALT ACQ or ALT HOLD, the A/T RETARD mode engages at 27 ft RA. The A/T automatically disengages approximately 2 seconds after landing touchdown.

Go-Around Mode

With the A/T Arm Switch at ARM, the A/T go-around mode is armed when descending below 2000 ft RA, with or without the AFDS engaged. Once armed, the A/T go-around mode can be engaged until 2 seconds have elapsed after landing touchdown.

Pressing either TO/GA Switch engages the A/T go-around mode. GA is annunciated for the A/T and the thrust levers advance to the reduced go-around thrust setting. This setting produces a 1000 to 2000 fpm rate of climb. After reaching reduced go-around thrust, pressing either TO/GA Switch the second time signals the A/T to advance thrust to the full go-around N1 limit.

After reaching reduced or full go-around thrust, the A/T GA mode can be terminated by selecting another AFDS pitch mode or when ALT ACQ annunciates engaged.

During a single engine FD go-around, the A/T will increase thrust to the full N1 limit.

Auto-throttle Disengage Switches

Pressing an Auto-throttle Disengage Switch disengages the auto-throttle (A/T). The A/T disengage light flashes and the A/T ARM switch on the MCP trips off. Pressing the Auto-throttle Disengage Switch a second time extinguishes the A/T warning.

After an automatic A/T disengagement pressing the Auto-throttle Disengage Switch will extinguish the A/T warning.

Auto-Throttle Disengage Light

The A/T Disengage Light will flash red if the A/T disengages for any reason.

The A/T Disengage Light will illuminate steady red when the Disengage Light Test Switch is held in position 2 (red filament test position) and steady amber when the Disengage Light Test Switch is held in position 1 (amber filament test position).

The A/T Disengage Light flashing amber indicates an A/T airspeed error if speed is not held within +10 or -5 knots of the commanded speed when all of the following conditions exist:

1. In flight
2. Flaps not up
3. A/T engaged in MCP SPD, or FMC SPD mode

An automatic test of the A/T flashing amber function is performed if the A/T is engaged and the following conditions exist:

1. MCP SPD or FMC SPD is the active A/T mode
2. More than 150 seconds after liftoff
3. Flaps extended

The A/T amber light flashes for 2 seconds, remains extinguished for 2 seconds and then flashes for 2 seconds again.

Thrust Mode Annunciator Panel (TMA)

On the Boeing 737-400 the Thrust Mode Annunciator panel is located on the centre instrument panel, above the N1 RPM indicators. It displays the active N1 limit reference mode for auto-throttle and manual thrust control. N1 limits are also displayed on the N1 RPM indicator cursors with the reference knobs pushed in.

N1 limits are normally calculated by the FMC. When FMC N1 limit calculations become invalid, or if either engine N1 is less than 18%, A/T LIM is annunciated. The auto-throttle computer then calculates a single N1 limit for the affected engine(s).

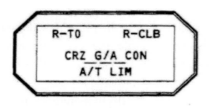

CENTER INSTRUMENT PANEL

R - Reduced. Can appear with TO and CLB.

TO - Takeoff.

CLB - Climb.

CRZ - Cruise.

G/A - Go-around.

CON - Continuous.

——— FMC is not computing thrust limits.

A/T LIM - Autothrottle limit. Indicates that A/T computer is calculating a degraded N1 limit for the affected engine or engines.

Flexible Take-Off

In situations where take-off can be executed without the need for full engine power (such as light weight takeoff from a long runway), then reduced power may be used, thereby reducing engine wear and increasing their life. This is called the Flexible take-off mode (and in the Airbus aircraft there is a detent position for the thrust levers labelled FLEX TO). The most basic way to achieve the reduced thrust is to manually set a lower RPM setting. To achieve a reduced power setting with the auto-throttle we can select a temperature on the control panel that is higher than the ambient airfield temperature. This causes the thrust computation system to calculate a lower limiting EPR or N1, thereby producing reduced power for the take-off.

4.3   AUTO-THROTTLE FLIGHT PROFILE

Figure 4.4 shows the operation of the auto-throttle and autopilot during the different phases of flight.

4.4   THRUST COMPUTATION

a)   **Thrust**

Engine thrust is a **force** which when multiplied by TAS will give us engine **power.**

Thrust = mass x acceleration.

In order to calculate thrust we need to establish the mass of air flow through the engine (M) and the change in velocity between the inlet and outlet of the engine (Vo - Vi). In practice other parameters are measured and the thrust obtained by computation. This process is carried out by the thrust computation system.

b)   **Thrust computation**

The primary thrust parameter is EPR which is the ratio between the pressures at the compressor intake and the turbine outlet or exhaust. If EPR is not available then N1 (fan speed) is used to compute the thrust The thrust lever is therefore used to select a value of EPR or N1.

In the auto-thrust mode (A/THR) the thrust is computed by the flight management and guidance system (FMGC) and is limited to the value corresponding to the thrust lever position. Most modern engines include an electronic control system that manages engine power throughout the flight. This is called FADEC.

c)   **Thrust rating Limit**

The thrust rating limit for the engines for the various phases of flight are determined by a thrust rating limit computer.

JAR - Now we use limit
Limit at T/0
A → Enter a per assumed
temp than actual. — entered
through CDU.

4.5   FADEC

The system example comes from the Airbus series of aircraft.

Function

FADEC stands for full authority digital engine control. It provides complete engine management throughout all phases of flight and performs the following functions:

i)   gas generation control (fuel flow, acceleration/deceleration, variable bleed valve and variable stator vane schedules, turbine clearance control, idle setting)

ii)   engine limit protection (over-speed N1 and N2)

iii)   power management (control of engine thrust rating, computation of thrust parameter limits, auto-thrust system demand, thrust lever position manual demand)

iv)   automatic engine starting sequence (control of start valve, fuel, ignition, monitoring N1, N2, FF, EGT)

v)   manual engine starting sequence (passive monitoring of start valve, fuel, ignition, N1, N2, FF, EGT)

In performing its functions it takes into account such variables as power demanded, air bleed for air conditioning and de-icing, temperature, static pressure and engine accessory selection.

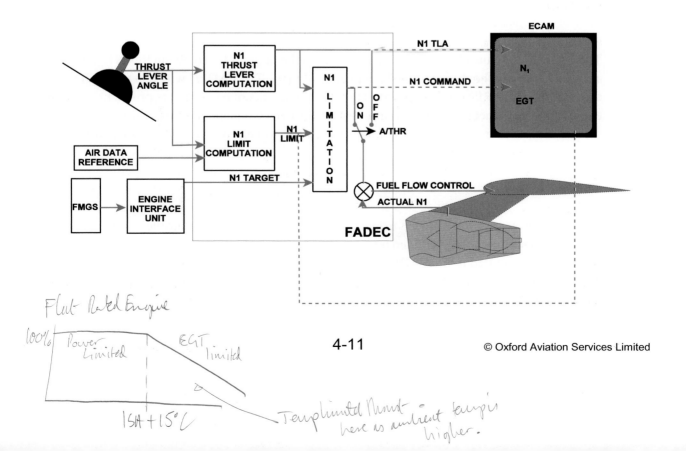

Advantages.

The FADEC system reduces crew workload, provides engine limit protection, improves engine life and saves fuel and maintenance down time.

Components

FADEC consists of an electronic engine control (EEC) plus a fuel metering unit, sensors and peripheral units. There are suitable Interface circuits between the EEC and its peripheral units. There are 2 FADEC channels per engine, oe in control and one in standby for redundancy. Each channel is powered by the aircraft's A/C supply before and during the initial start and then by an individual internal magnetic alternator above 12% engine RPM.

Thrust control is provided by a FADEC dedicated to each engine. Thrust selection is achieved by means of the thrust levers when in manual mode or the Flight Management and Guidance System (FMGS) when in automatic mode. Thrust rating limit is provided by the FADEC according to the thrust lever position both for manual and automatic thrust.

Fuel Control

In addition to the high pressure fuel pumps and shut off system there are again 2 main systems controlling engine performance. The Hydro- Mechanical Unit (HMU) is modulated by the FADEC. It provides control of fuel flow to the combustion chamber, control of fuel hydraulic signals to actuators, and over-speed protection.

The Fuel Metering Valve (FMV) transforms FADEC orders through a torque motor / servo valve into fuel flow to the engine nozzle. The FMV resolver provides an electrical feedback signal proportional to the FMV position. The by-pass valve regulates a constant pressure drop across the FMV to ensure that metered fuel flow is proportional to FMV position.

The FADEC computes fuel flow necessary to hold the target N1. To obtain this N1, the N2 is allowed to vary without exceeding N2 min and N2 max. The FADEC will also vary N2/N1 in order to maintain RPM under varying load conditions, maintain bleed air production, avoid engine stalls or flameout. With the Airbus FADEC it even modulates the cooling airflow around the engine in order to expand or contract the casing to control the compressor and turbine clearances at nominal settings.

Thrust Levers

The thrust levers are only moved manually (unlike many other auto-throttle systems). They move over a sector which is divided into 4 segments defined by 5 detents or stops. Thrust lever position is transmitted to the FADEC which computes and displays the thrust rating limit and the N1 TLA. Note that there is no reverse idle detent. When the idle stop is cleared by pulling up the reverse thrust levers, reverse idle is selected.

Thrust Rating Limit

Thrust rating limit is computed according to the thrust lever position. If the thrust lever is set in a detent the FADEC will select the rating limit corresponding to this detent. If the lever is set between 2 detents the FADEC will select the rating limit corresponding to the higher mode.

Thrust Control:

Manual Mode

The engines are in the manual mode provided that the ATS function is:

1.   Not armed
2.   Armed and not active (thrust lever is not in the ATS operating range and/or no alpha floor condition)

In these conditions, each engine is controlled by the position of the corresponding thrust lever. Thrust modulation is performed by the pilot moving the thrust lever from IDLE to TO/GA position. Each position of the thrust lever within these limits correspond to a N1. When the thrust lever is positioned in a detent, the corresponding N1 is equal to the N1 rating limit computed by the associated FADEC.

When the thrust lever is set in the FLX-MCT detent:

1.   **On the ground**: When the engine is running, the flex TO thrust rating is selected provided a flex TO temperature greater than the current TAT has been selected through the MCDU. Otherwise the MCT thrust is selected.

2.   **After TO**: A change from FLX to MCT is achieved by setting the thrust lever to TO/GA or CL position and then back to MCT. After that FLX rating setting is not possible.

MAX TO power is always available by pushing the thrust lever fully forwards.

Automatic Mode

In the auto-thrust mode (A/THR function active), the thrust is computed by the FMGC and is limited to the value corresponding to the thrust lever position (except if the alpha floor mode is activated).

Inputs

1. Air data parameters from the air data inertial reference system.
2. Operational commands from the engine interface unit (target N1).
3. Thrust lever angle (TLA).
4. Engine Pressure sensors (N1 and N2).
5. Temperature (EGT).
6. Fuel flow.

Outputs

1. Data outputs necessary for the FMGS.
2. Thrust parameters and TLA to the FMGS.
3. Control signals to the fuel metering unit.
4. Command N1 to the ECAM display.

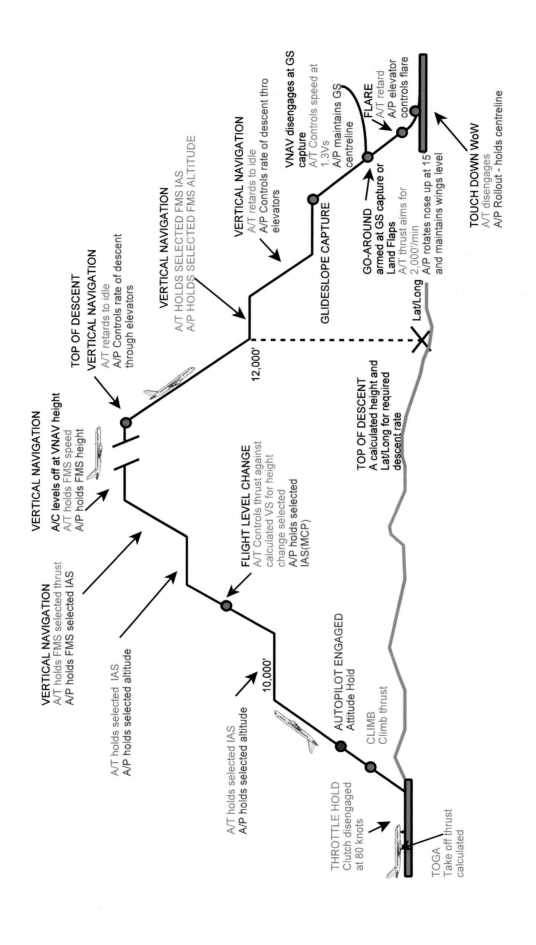

CHAPTER FIVE -YAW DAMPERS

Contents

5.1   DUTCH ROLL 5-1

5.2   FUNCTION OF A YAW DAMPER 5-3

5.3   THE YAW DAMPER 5-3

5.4   DUTCH ROLL FILTER 5-5

5.5   RUDDER CONTROL COMPUTING 5-6

5.6   AUTHORITY 5-7

5.7   THREE AXIS AUTOPILOT WITH SERVO MOTOR 5-7

5.8   RUDDER CONTROL SYSTEM SCHEMATIC (Boeing 727) 5-15

5.9   EXAMPLE OF SEPARATE YAW DAMPER AND MAIN ACTUATOR 5-17

5.10   EXAMPLE OF A DUPLEX YAW DAMPER SYSTEM (SMITH'S-BAE 146) . 5-20

5.1   DUTCH ROLL

Dutch roll is caused by the interplay between lateral stability around the longitudinal axis (roll) and longitudinal stability around the vertical axis (yaw) of an aircraft in flight. An aircraft with an excess of lateral stability will by default have poor directional stability and therefore will be susceptible to dutch roll.

More simply, any disturbance of an aircraft in yaw directly causes a secondary disturbance in roll and visa versa. Stability is determined as the aircraft's natural tendency to resist and counter these disturbances to return to the same conditions as before the perturbation. If the relative stabilities in yaw and roll are in a particular range of proportions to each other, Dutch Roll can be the effect.

Consider an aircraft disturbed by a gust causing it to yaw. As the aircraft yaws one wing will travel slightly faster through the surrounding air and the other wing will travel slightly slower. The fast wing will produce slightly more lift than before and the slower wing will produce slightly less. This obviously will produce a roll.

As lift increases then lift induced drag will increase so the faster, higher wing will produce more drag and the low wing will produce less. This causes a yawing moment in opposition to the initial disturbance and the whole process is reversed.

Swept wing further exasperate the tendency for dutch roll because the forward going wing undergoes a reduction in effective wing sweep, further increasing the lift it produces, while the retreating wing experiences an increase in effective wing sweep, again reducing its lift.

All airline aircraft will be statically stable, in that they will naturally try to return to the undisturbed condition. Whether or not they are dynamically stable depends on the amount of damping force available. This is produced by the stabilizing aerodynamic surfaces in the main. As an aircraft climbs however its true air speed must increase to maintain the lift pressure. This increase in TAS means that the relative angle of attack for the aerodynamic surfaces is reduced for the same given disturbance, and so the corrective force supplied by that surface is reduced, so the damping effectiveness is reduced at high altitude.

- Moves rudder in proportion to rate of angular velocity

- Limited authority of rudder (1-2°)

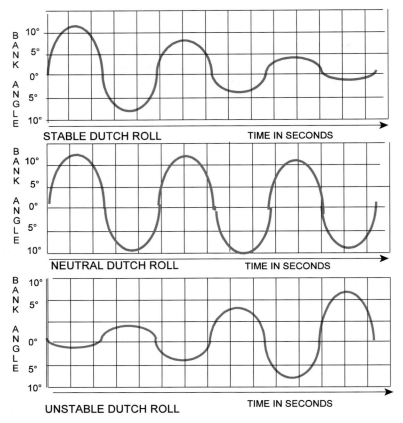

DUTCH ROLL STABILITY - Figure 5.1

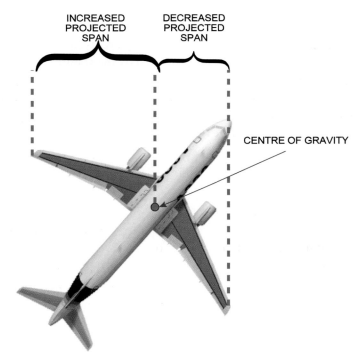

CHANGE IN EFFECT ASPECT RATIO WITH YAW - Figure 5.2

5.2   FUNCTION OF A YAW DAMPER

To increase the damping forces at altitude could mean an increase in the overall size of the stabilizing surfaces but this would also increase drag. Another option is to produce an aircraft that is dynamically stable at lower and middle altitudes and have a system to automatically counter dutch roll which can detect the start of the oscillations at levels below the threshold of the pilots ability to detect and with rapid, effective rudder deflections, stopping the dutch roll almost before it starts. This system we call a **Yaw Damper**.

The number of yaw dampers fitted depends on how stable the aircraft is. If the dutch roll is easy for the pilot to control (it is not diverging quickly and the frequency of oscillation is reasonably large) then only one yaw damper may be required. Large, modern, airliners generally have poor dutch roll characteristics and so tend to have 2 and even 3 yaw damper systems, because a failure of all the systems may well limit the altitude at which the aircraft can operate to one suitably low to increase the damping forces available and reduce the tendency for dutch roll to start.

5.3   THE YAW DAMPER

Typical Yaw Damping Signal Processing

Sensing

Sensing of a disturbance in yaw is usually by a rate gyro, though some systems may employ an accelerometer. The objective being to sense the yawning motion as quickly as possible and produce a correcting signal / demand to the servo/actuator which then feeds signals to the rudder control system to apply rudder in opposition to that yaw.

Phase Advance

Is means of applying the damping application as soon as possible. The reason for this is that damping must be applied when the **rate of disturbance** is at its greatest, not when the disturbance as moved to the point where the natural stability of the fin has arrested the disturbance. If a rudder application is applied at the same instant the fin starts to return the aircraft, both the combined forces will over correct and cause the aircraft to overshoot. Figure 5.3 tries to explain the ideal damping required.

Figure 5.3 shows a typical phase advance of the signal by **90°.** It can be seen that it is nothing more than a capacitor and resistor connected to form a differentiator. The output of a differentiator is a rate signal. Therefore, if the input to the phase advance is a yaw rate, the output must be rate/rate, which is acceleration. The circuit has effectively accelerated the yaw signal to provide the rapid damping the system requires.

Rudder is moved 90° out of phase with plane of oscillation, as rate of movement is greatest as swing through middle of sine wave, thus trying to prevent movement at all.

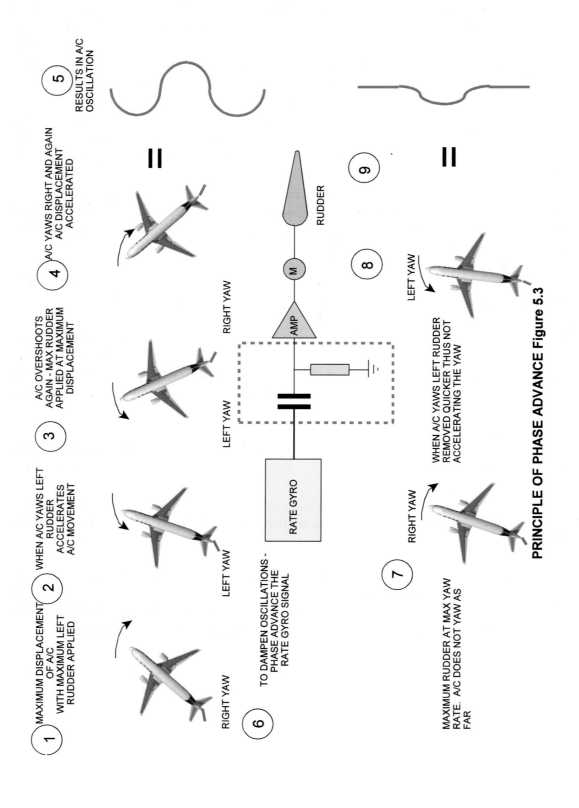

PRINCIPLE OF PHASE ADVANCE Figure 5.3

1. MAXIMUM DISPLACEMENT OF A/C WITH MAXIMUM LEFT RUDDER APPLIED

2. WHEN A/C YAWS LEFT RUDDER ACCELERATES A/C MOVEMENT

3. A/C OVERSHOOTS AGAIN - MAX RUDDER APPLIED AT MAXIMUM DISPLACEMENT

4. A/C YAWS RIGHT AND AGAIN A/C DISPLACEMENT ACCELERATED

5. RESULTS IN A/C OSCILLATION

6. TO DAMPEN OSCILLATIONS - PHASE ADVANCE THE RATE GYRO SIGNAL

7. MAXIMUM RUDDER AT MAX YAW RATE. A/C DOES NOT YAW AS FAR

8. WHEN A/C YAWS LEFT RUDDER REMOVED QUICKER THUS NOT ACCELERATING THE YAW

RIGHT YAW

LEFT YAW

RIGHT YAW

LEFT YAW

RUDDER

M

AMP

RATE GYRO

RIGHT YAW

LEFT YAW

5.4   DUTCH ROLL FILTER

The system as described, however, would also interpret a normally commanded turn as a yaw and act in opposition to produce an uncoordinated turn (in fact the rudder would be exacerbating the coordination problem by introducing the full amount of its rudder authority in the opposite direction to that required).   So the Yaw Damper system needs to be able to distinguish commanded turn inputs from yaw due to a disturbance or apparent dutch roll.

When an aircraft is turned, the aircraft rolls about the longitudinal axis in the direction of the turn and also YAWS about the vertical axis. A yaw damper is provide to dampen dutch roll, not to prevent the aircraft following a turn command. Therefore only the dutch roll frequency must be acted upon by the yaw damper.

The dutch roll frequency is based on the natural yawing frequency of the aircraft. The frequency is relatively LOW and will differ slightly with aircraft type. Typical valued being 0.2hz - Bae 1-11, 0.4Hz - Boeing 747.

Yaw dampers must be designed to allow the dutch rollfrequency to control the rudder but block other frequencies. Figure 5.5 illustrates a typical dutch roll filter and circuit action.

Initially, while the rate of turn is building up to the constant rate, the dutch roll filter output also builds, then falls off to nothing when the rate of turn becomes constant. The reverse, with opposite polarity as the filter capacitor discharges, occurs as the aircraft levels out on completion of the turn. Therefore, whilst the turn is constant the filter output is zero. This results in no rudder demand.

Figure 5.4 shows an aircraft yawing at the dutch roll frequency. Since the rate of turn is the constantly changing, the output from the rate gyro is constantly changing. The D.C. graph at the bottom of Figure 5.4. is the dutch roll filter output.

The D.C. polarities are the greatest when the rate of turn is the greatest and reverse when the direction of turn (rate of gyro signal) reverses.

Figure 5.5 is s super simplified yaw damper, illustrating mainly dutch roll filter. The dutch roll filter is a NARROW BAND PASS FILTER designed to pass only signals which change the frequency of the dutch roll. The rate gyro produces outputs for all turns, but only those related to dutch roll will appear at the input to the servo amplifier driving the rudder servo motor.

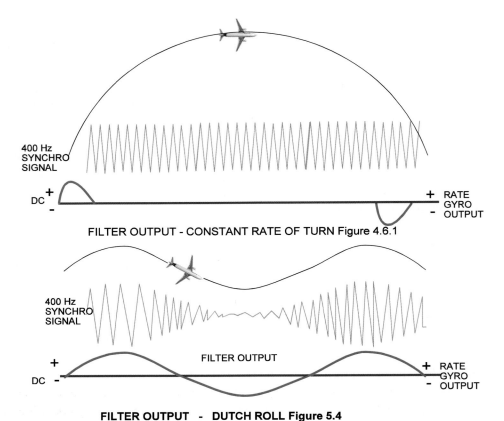

FILTER OUTPUT - CONSTANT RATE OF TURN Figure 4.6.1

FILTER OUTPUT - DUTCH ROLL Figure 5.4

5.5   RUDDER CONTROL COMPUTING

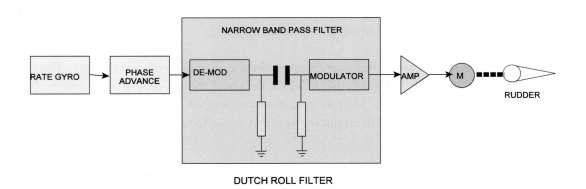

BASIC YAW DAMPER SHOWING DUTCH ROLL FILTER
Figure 5.5

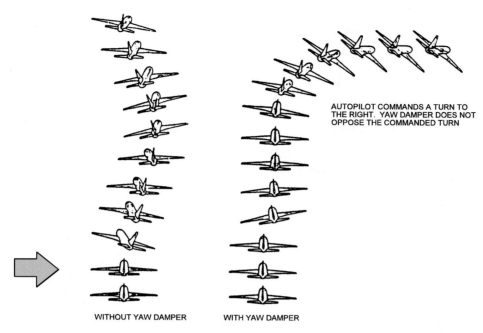

AUTOPILOT COMMANDS A TURN TO
THE RIGHT. YAW DAMPER DOES NOT
OPPOSE THE COMMANDED TURN

WITHOUT YAW DAMPER   WITH YAW DAMPER

YAW DAMPER - EFFEFT IN A COMMANDED TURN

5.6   AUTHORITY

As removal of oscillations does not require a large rudder movement and to reduce the hazard posed by a yaw damper runaway, yaw damper authority is normally only about 3-6 degrees left and right of centre. If 2 yaw damper systems are operating on a single span rudder their authority is accumulative, i.e. singly each system could move the rudder by 3 degrees, together they can move it by 6 degrees.

On aircraft with a split rudder surface, if one yaw damper system fails then the aircraft has only ½ the yaw damper protection that it originally had. This is allowed for in the design and operation of the aircraft. As even this small input may cause over-stress in certain flying conditions, some aircraft have an input to the yaw damper computer from the CADC to schedule the gain of the yaw damper inputs for the ambient flying conditions. At high speed therefore the yaw damper authority may be even further reduced to avoid an over-stress condition.

5.7   THREE AXIS AUTOPILOT WITH SERVO MOTOR

Engagement

Prior to engagement, the rudder signal chain is earthed and the rudder servo, which is disconnected from the rudder control runs, synchronises to the null position. Refer to Figure 5.6 for circuit description. On engagement, 29.5V AC is connected to the rudder servo clutch. At the same time, a rudder engage thermal relay operates and energises a rudder engage relay to connect filtered bank demand signal from the aileron channel to the rudder servo loop. The half second delay between energising the rudder servo clutch and operating the rudder engage relay permits a transient free engagement. Any yaw rate which then develops, produce a rudder deflection which tends to oppose the yaw rate.

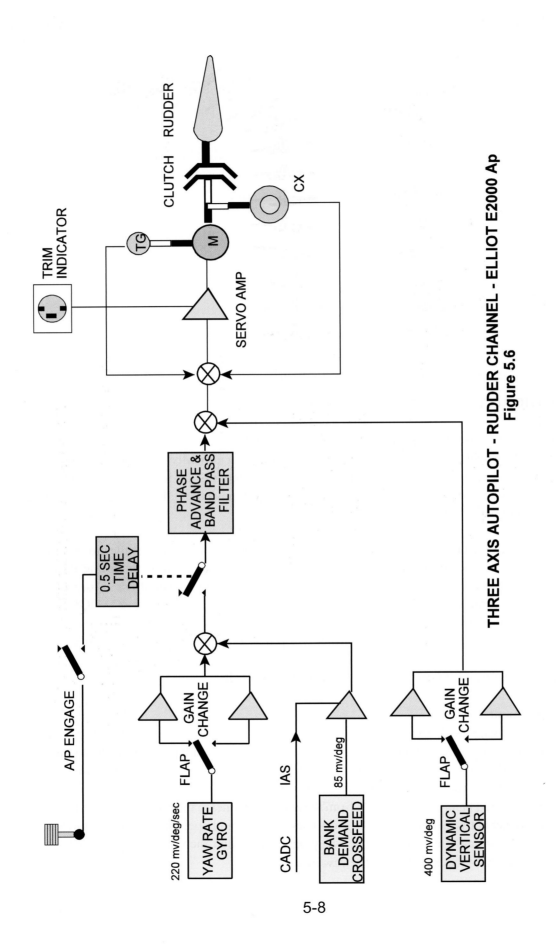

THREE AXIS AUTOPILOT - RUDDER CHANNEL - ELLIOT E2000 Ap

Figure 5.6

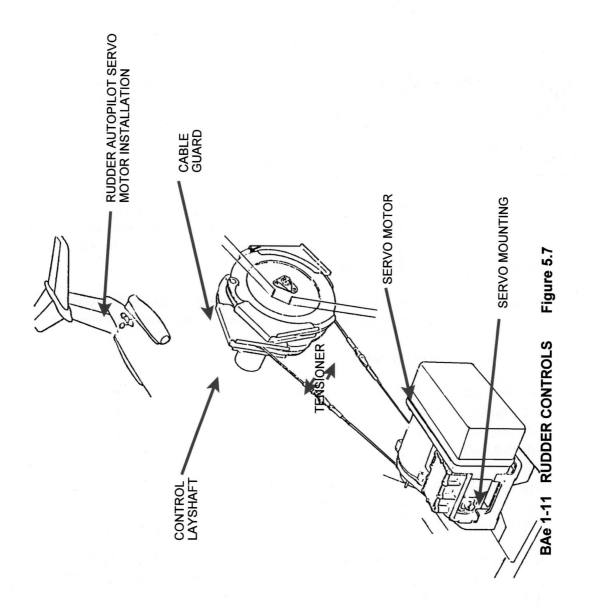

RUDDER AUTOPILOT SERVO MOTOR INSTALLATION

CABLE GUARD

CONTROL LAYSHAFT

TENSIONER

SERVO MOTOR

SERVO MOUNTING

BAe 1-11   RUDDER CONTROLS   Figure 5.7

Yaw Rate Signal

The yaw rate signal is derived from a synchro attached to the yaw rate gyro which forms part of the Three-Axis rate transmitter. The Band Pass Filter has a peak frequency of 0.2Hz, which is the natural yawing frequency of the aircraft. It attenuates steady and slowly changing yaw rate signals which are present during a steady turn to prevent unwanted rudder deflection which would mis-coordinate the manoeuvre.

Bank Demand Crossfeed

To improve co-ordination in autopilot control, the rudder correction is applied during the manoeuvres. the demand signal is modified by a function of IAS from the CADC. This is because a smaller rudder deflection is needed at high speed than at low speed for a given bank angle.

Dynamic Vertical Sensor

Dynamic Vertical Sensor, which consists of a damped pendulum, provides a signal which is proportional to the difference between the aircraft vertical and the dynamic vertical. In the long term, yawing movement caused by an un-coordinated turn or engine failure is thus opposed by a sustained rudder deflection instead of a side slip.

When the flap selector lever is moved to give more than 26° of flap, the flap relays the increase the gain of the dynamic vertical sensor signal, and decrease the gain of the yaw rate signal.

Series Yaw Damper Operation

The yaw damper provides damping of the aircraft's yaw axis movement by shaping, amplifying and coupling rate gyro and yaw damper actuator position signals to control the rudder through the hydraulic actuator. The yaw damper operation is confined to **synchronisation mode and engaged mode.**

Operating Modes

Synchronisation

Is to prevent yaw axis engagement transients by cancelling servo motor outputs by an inverting integrator. RL1 is energised prior to yaw damper engagement. Any amplifier output is fed back through the integrator, the inversion through the integrator cancels any transients present. On engagement of the yaw damper, RL1 is de-energised.

Engaged Mode

Providing the interlock logic is good, the engage solenoid engages allowing the yaw damper elements of the Power Control Unit (PCU) to pressurise. The rate gyro signal is phase advanced and applied to the de-modulator. The demodulator converts the signal to a DC signal where the output polarity will represent the AC signal input phase. The yaw damper frequency is passed by the bandpass filter which blocks all other frequencies. Consequently, the yaw damper does not oppose normal turn manoeuvres and does not respond to aircraft vibration and bending. The modulator restores the AC signal maintaining the appropriate phase. The servo amplifies the signal and applies it to the transfer valve which in turn drives the yaw damper actuator which drives the main actuator. The maximum deflection of the rudder is 3° - 4° in either direction.

The LVDT position feedback is applied to SP2 to cancel the processed rate gyro signal when the corresponding change in rudder position is appropriate for the rate of yaw change. Position feedback is also applied through the energised relays of RL2 which is fed back to SP2. The purpose of this is to ensure that the rudder will always return back to the neutral position. The rudder can be effected by crosswinds. If the crosswind is strong, the position feedback voltage may not be large enough to drive the rudder to the central position. The position feedback voltage now causes INT 2 to ramp up, increasing the voltage at SP2. This increase in position feedback starts to drive the rudder back to the neutral position. As the rudder returns the position feedback voltage decreases allowing the integrator to run down.

Yaw Damper Testing

Actuation of the yaw damper test switch to either the right or the left applies a voltage to the yaw damper rate gyro torquing coil which torques the rate gyro and simulates aircraft movement. The rudder position indicator responds to this action of an output from the position transducer. If the switch is moved to the left the indication will first move to the left and then back to the centre, on release of the switch the indication will move to the right and back to the centre. The reverse will happen if the switch is first moved to the right.

Yaw Damper Indications

Yaw damper controls and indications are fairly simple. On a typical aircraft (fitted with 2 yaw dampers), the main indications will be a panel or part thereof that contains an on/off switch, a test switch or button and a failure light for each of the yaw dampers. The failure light indicates many faults in the system; loss of hydraulic or electrical power, logic failure in the yaw damper computation system, loss of input from the rate gyro. The switch can then be used to isolate the inoperative yaw damper to avoid spurious rudder inputs.

Also involved with the monitoring of the yaw dampers is a small rudder trim indicator, one for each yaw damper system fitted. It indicates the demands on the rudder by moving left and right of centre. It is mainly used during the testing of the yaw dampers during pre-flight checks. If the yaw damper test switch is operated for one of the yaw dampers a test signal operates a small torquing coil on the yaw damper rate gyro. This moves the gyro and fools the yaw damper system into thinking that an yaw condition exists. A pass at test is indicated by the position moving in the direction tested and back to centre. Moving the switch to the left simulates a yaw in one direction and the position indicator should move to left also. If the switch is operated to the right then the rudder should move to the right.

Other aircraft use a test system where an artificial signal representing an oscillatory yaw is used causing the rudder to move left and right at approximately 0.5 Hz. The yaw damper is switched on and the oscillations should stop.

Common to all these tests is the fact that if the yaw damper is engaged the rudder itself may be being moved and as with moving any surface or service on the ground there are safety considerations.

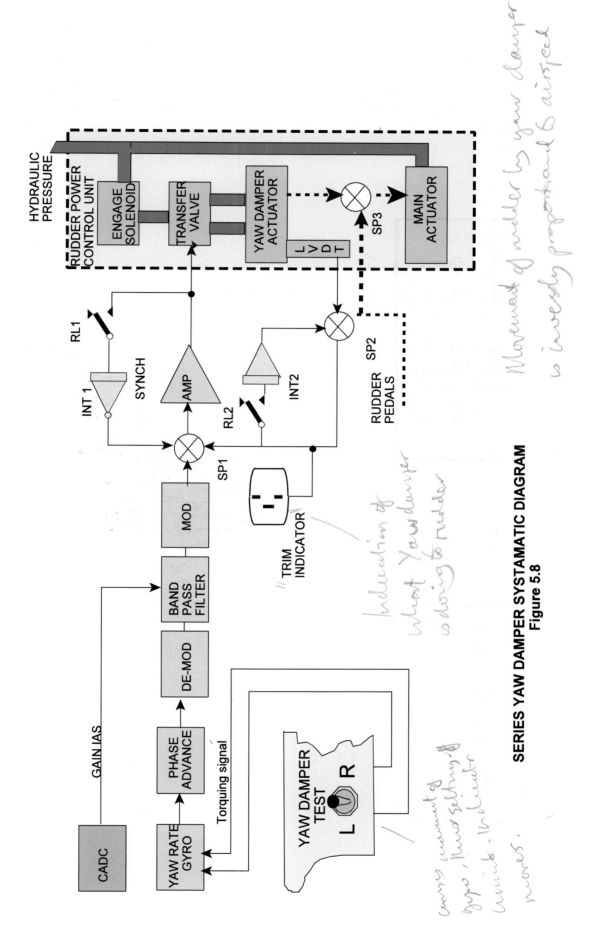

SERIES YAW DAMPER SYSTAMATIC DIAGRAM
Figure 5.8

Movement of rudder by yaw damper is inversely proportional to airspeed

Indication of what Yaw damper is doing to rudder

Any movement of gyro, trim setting if during initial movements.

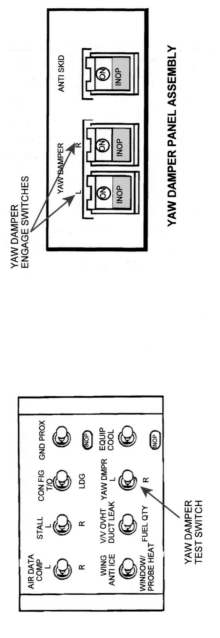

YAW DAMPER
ENGAGE SWITCHES

ANTI SKID

YAW DAMPER

L   R

YAW DAMPER PANEL ASSEMBLY

AIR DATA
COMP   STALL   CON FIG   GND PROX
L   L   T/O
R   R   LDG

WING   V/V OVHT   YAW DMPR   EQUIP
ANTI ICE   DUCT LEAK   L   COOL
WINDOW/   FUEL QTY   R
PROBE HEAT

YAW DAMPER
TEST SWITCH

TEST PANEL

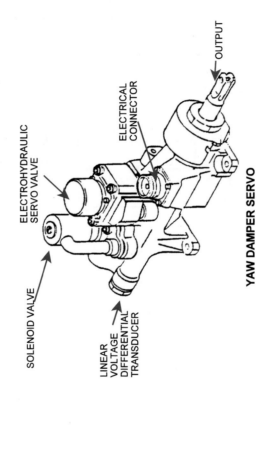

ELECTROHYDRAULIC
SERVO VALVE

ELECTRICAL
CONNECTOR

OUTPUT

SOLENOID VALVE

LINEAR
VOLTAGE
DIFFERENTIAL
TRANSDUCER

YAW DAMPER SERVO

BOEING 757 YAW DAMPER PANELS AND YAW DAMPER SERVO
Figure 5.9

5.8   RUDDER CONTROL SYSTEM SCHEMATIC (Boeing 727)

Manual inputs from the rudder pedals to the rudder power unit is by cables through the rudder feel and centring unit. The feel is accomplished by a feel and centring spring. The input crank positions the control valve through the summing assembly. The hydraulic pressure is ported to move the main actuator. The main actuator to the external summing lever returns the control valve to neutral, stopping further movement. A right rudder command is demonstrated by the solid arrows and the dashed line indicates feedback.

When the yaw damper is engaged, the yaw damper actuator solenoid will energise allowing hydraulic pressure into the transfer valve. When a signal is received from the yaw damper the transfer valve converts the signal from an electrical signal into a hydraulic signal. The output of the transfer valve displaces the yaw damper actuator which is pivoted about "A" displacing the control valve. The hydraulic output moves the main actuator, the feedback will move the external summing lever as the rudder is moved. This will stop the rudder movement. The rudder is recentered by a feedback signal from the LVDT to the yaw damper coupler. Command is limited to $\pm 5°$.

The Boeing 727 yaw damper is a series system. Therefore, yaw damper inputs will not be fed back to the rudder pedals. This is achieved through the external summing lever. This unit allows the main rudder power control unit to move the rudder but the swinging function about the input shaft pivot does not transfer the movement back to the rudder pedals.

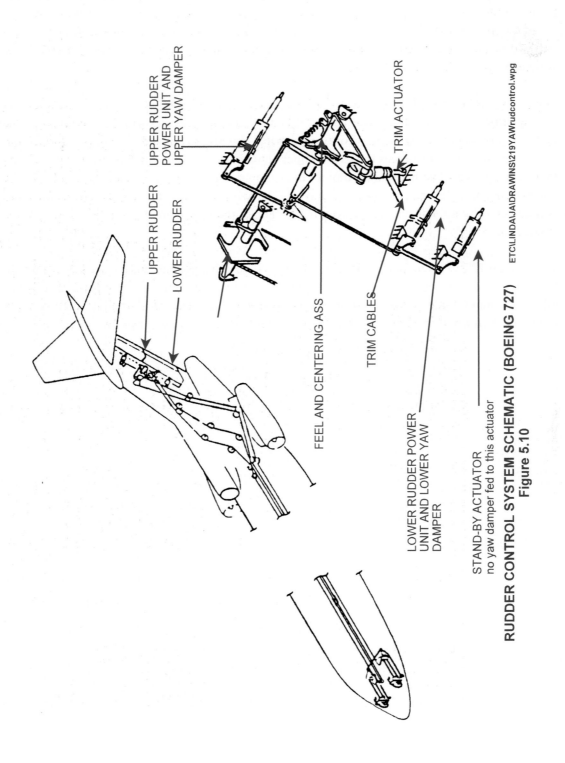

UPPER RUDDER POWER UNIT AND UPPER YAW DAMPER

TRIM ACTUATOR

UPPER RUDDER

LOWER RUDDER

FEEL AND CENTERING ASS

TRIM CABLES

LOWER RUDDER POWER UNIT AND LOWER YAW DAMPER

STAND-BY ACTUATOR
no yaw damper fed to this actuator

ETCILINDAIJAIDRAWINSI219YAWrudcontrol.wpg

RUDDER CONTROL SYSTEM SCHEMATIC (BOEING 727)
Figure 5.10

5.9 **EXAMPLE OF SEPARATE YAW DAMPER AND MAIN ACTUATOR** (BOEING 757/767)

The input from the servo amplifier to the actuator is converted from an electrical signal to a hydraulic demand by a conventional **transfer valve.** The yaw damper usually has its own actuator with a LVDT for position feedback. A main actuator controls the rudder. The two individual actuator systems allows easy separation between manual inputs and autopilot inputs in a **series** connected yaw damper.

Figure 4.12 shows practical connection of the two actuator systems. The diagram is based on a Boeing 757. Two yaw dampers are fitted, the left and right system. Each yaw damper can be selected individually from the yaw damper control panel, both systems are operating together.

Each system feeds its own servo actuator, supplied by a different hydraulic system. A mechanical linkage connects both outputs into the main rudder actuators. With all three hydraulic systems and all three actuators serviceable, the three actuators will operate simultaneously to control the rudder.

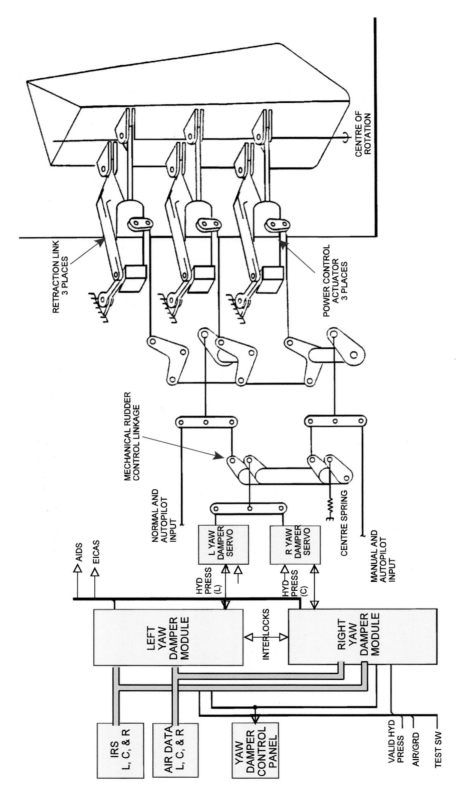

SIMPLIFIED SCHEMATIC OF A BOEING 757 YAW DAMPER ACTUATORS
Figure 5.11

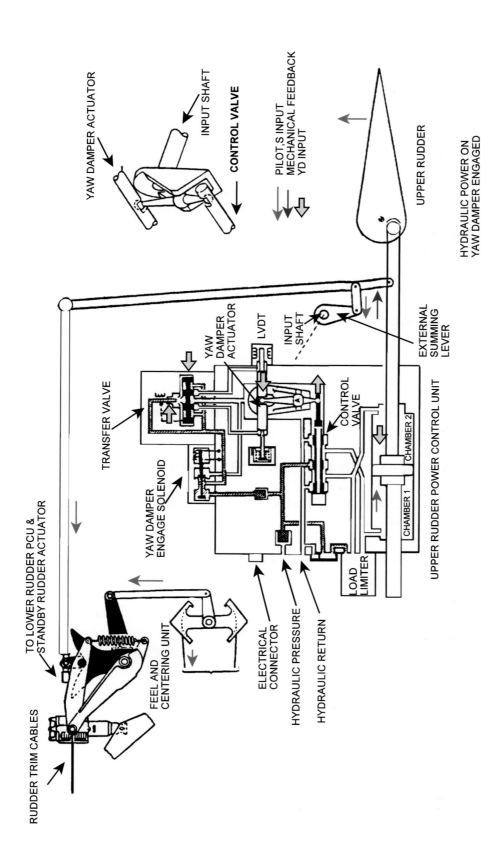

RUDDER CONTROL SYSTEM SCHEMATIC
Figure 5.12

YAW DAMPER ACTUATOR

INPUT SHAFT

CONTROL VALVE

PILOT,S INPUT

MECHANICAL FEEDBACK

YD INPUT

UPPER RUDDER

HYDRAULIC POWER ON
YAW DAMPER ENGAGED

YAW DAMPER
ACTUATOR

LVDT

INPUT
SHAFT

TRANSFER VALVE

EXTERNAL
SUMMING
LEVER

CONTROL
VALVE

YAW DAMPER
ENGAGE SOLENOID

UPPER RUDDER POWER CONTROL UNIT

CHAMBER 2

CHAMBER 1

LOAD
LIMITER

TO LOWER RUDDER PCU &
STANDBY RUDDER ACTUATOR

ELECTRICAL
CONNECTOR

HYDRAULIC PRESSURE

HYDRAULIC RETURN

FEEL AND
CENTERING UNIT

RUDDER TRIM CABLES

Series interfacing with rudder

The inputs to the rudder system are in series with the pilots rudder input. This means that although the rudder is being moved by the yaw dampers and some of the rudder authority that pilot would normally have is being lost, the pilot will not feel the operation of the yaw damper through the pedals.

Power Sources for movement (s/m/l)

Small aircraft without a substantial hydraulic system that still require yaw damping may use electrical actuation to achieve rudder movement. Large aircraft will invariably use hydraulic actuation through the normal rudder power system. Some more obscure types may use pneumatic actuation.

Monitoring

As has been stated previously a yaw damper runaway can be guarded against by reducing the amount of control input it can achieve in the event of a fault occurring. With 2 yaw damper systems running side by side however, they can be used to monitor each other. This is called Duplexing.

This comparison can be carried out electrically or mechanically. The example shown is of the latter type from a BAe 146 RJ.

5.10   EXAMPLE OF A DUPLEX YAW DAMPER SYSTEM (SMITH'S - Bae 146)

Some yaw damper systems operate in a **duplex** mode (**duplex monitoring**), providing lateral stabilisation through all phases of flight.

A duplex system provides the monitoring necessary to prevent large fast movements of the rudder in the event of a runaway fault condition. The two channels are identical and independent, their outputs being fed to a comparator. Misalignment between them will cause automatic disengagement of both channels. Figure 4.15 shows a block diagram of the system.

As the channels are identical, only one single channel will be considered:

Any unwanted lateral movement generates a yaw rate gyro 400 Hz signal. The phase of the signal will determine the direction of the rudder and the amplitude will determine the rate of movement of the rudder. The signal is reduced at 30° of flap to compensate for the effects of increased airflow over the control surface.

The vertical gyro input is differentiated to produce a roll rate signal to assist in rudder application when a roll is sensed. If the roll is a commanded turn , the roll rate signal decays quickly to prevent the rudder opposing the turn.

The roll rate and yaw rate signals are fed through a 90° phase advance differentiating capacitor to accelerate the signal to ensure that damping is applied at the correct time. The signal is then summed with the Lateral Accelerometer. The accelerometer applies rudder to compensate for slip and skid during a turn.

The summed yaw rate, roll and lateral signal is fed to the input of a servo amplifier where it is summed with the rate and position feedback. The resultant of this summation is used to control the actuator motor drive circuit and hence the actuator motor. This is mechanically linked to a tacho-generator to provide rate feedback and an LVDT to provide position feedback.

Each actuator motor drives two rams which drive one side of a 'T' bar onto the rudder drive mechanism. The right angles at the top of this 'T' bar are checked by the comparator switches, misalignment causes **both** yaw dampers to be disengaged.

Different sources of 115V 400Hz and 28VDC are provided to both channels. The initial switch on is made by two master yaw damper switches. This provides initial power to the system and allows the gyros to run up. The actuator brake will still be on at this time and the power held off the servo amp. Engaging the yaw dampers on the autopilot controller starts interlock and monitor circuit operation. A one second timer starts, which allows the actuators to align. The actuator brakes are released and engagement is complete.

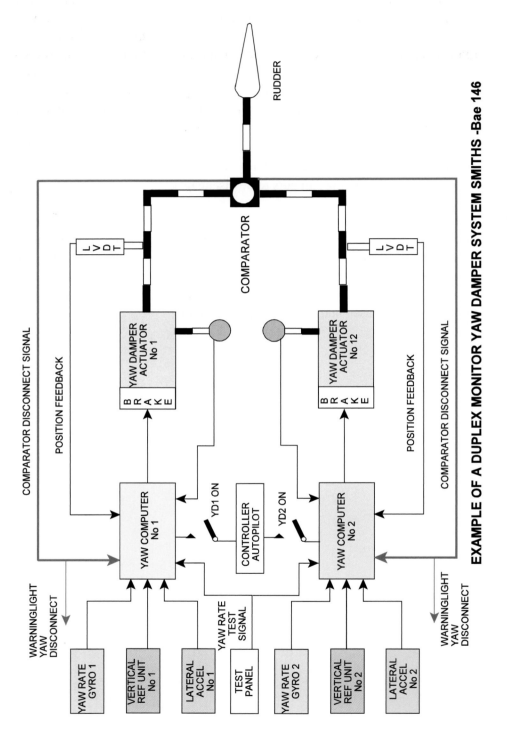

EXAMPLE OF A DUPLEX MONITOR YAW DAMPER SYSTEM SMITHS -Bae 146

Figure 5.13

Vibration

All structures have frequencies at which they oscillate or resonate. The vibrations can be caused by the engines, pumps, generators, aerodynamic loads etc. These vibrations cause flexing of the structure which leads to fatigue and eventually failure of the structure. The vibrations can also cause passenger discomfort in the form of fatigue due to excess noise and motion sickness. The very latest yaw damper systems (767 era) have between 2 and 4 Modal Accelerometers fitted fore and aft. These are fed in parallel with the gyro input and allow the yaw damper system to utilize the rudder to damp out these vibrations. This increases both passenger comfort and decreases fatigue of the airframe thus increasing its life.

Yaw damper can also counteract unwanted vibrations / bending of fuselage (dampen out)

Primary function is to prevent dutch roll

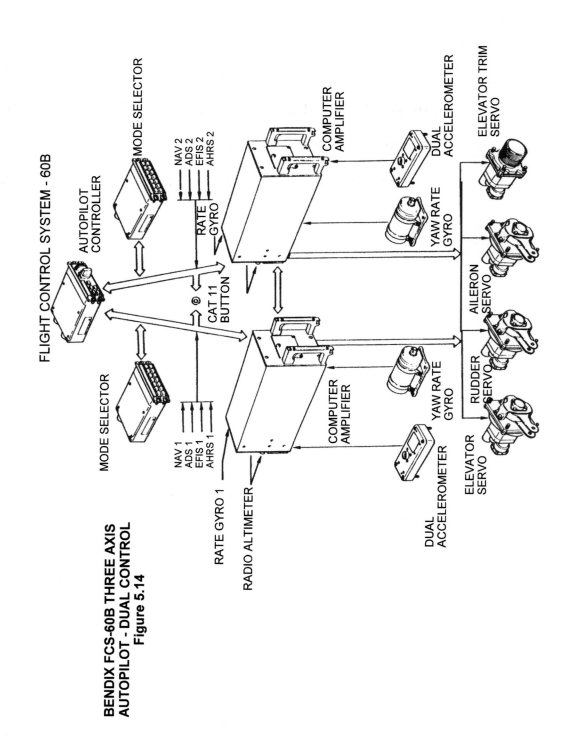

FLIGHT CONTROL SYSTEM - 60B

BENDIX FCS-60B THREE AXIS
AUTOPILOT - DUAL CONTROL
Figure 5.14

MODE SELECTOR

AUTOPILOT
CONTROLLER

NAV 2
ADS 2
EFIS 2
AHRS 2

RATE
GYRO

COMPUTER
AMPLIFIER

DUAL
ACCELEROMETER

YAW RATE
GYRO

ELEVATOR TRIM
SERVO

AILERON
SERVO

RUDDER
SERVO

ELEVATOR
SERVO

DUAL
ACCELEROMETER

YAW RATE
GYRO

COMPUTER
AMPLIFIER

RADIO ALTIMETER

RATE GYRO 1

NAV 1
ADS 1
EFIS 1
AHRS 1

MODE SELECTOR

CAT 11
BUTTON

5-24

CHAPTER SIX - CONTROL LAWS

Contents

		Page
6.1	INTRODUCTION	6-1
6.2	BOEING 737-400 AUTO PILOT LIMITING AND REVERSION MODES	6-1
6.3	FLIGHT ENVELOPE PROTECTION	6-3
6.4	AUTOPILOT GAIN ADAPTION / GAIN SCHEDULING	6-5

Fly by Wire

- Direct Law — Stick movement proportional to control surface movement. (downgrades to this if only 1 comp is available)

- Alternate Law — When some of computers are not working ∴ not providing full protection.

- Normal Law — When all computers are working correctly providing full flight envelope protection

∝ Relationship between input from pilot & flt control surface movement.

Fly by wire — input signal is electrical but control surface movement is by hydraulics

- Point of it is - Direct Weight Saving (cables etc..)
  - Indirect Weight Saving (by fact that airframe cannot be overstressed ∴ less strength needed)

  - Improves Pilot technique

- Stabilizer & rudder are manually Controlled
- Elevator trim tabs " " "
- 777 has physically controlled spoilers.

- "Alpha Floor" is A320's way of preventing stall.

6.1 INTRODUCTION

The autopilot must be able to manouevre the aircraft logically and safely in a similar manner to the way a human pilot should. This means ensuring the autopilot does not break aircraft limitations in terms of speed, load factor, pitch and bank limits etc. However the autopilot should be able to use a satisfactory amount of the performance of the aircraft otherwise the manoeuvres would take too long to execute.

For example consider a light aircraft on a VFR navigational exercise. Overhead the next way-point the pilot requires an 80° left turn to proceed to the next point. The bank angle used will be determined by that turn. The pilot will not generally choose under normal circumstances to turn with 5° of bank as that would mean the turn taking an inordinate amount of time. Conversely the pilot would not normally choose a 90° banked turn as that would be excessively hard, possibly breaking load factor limitations as well as probably causing a loss of height. A turn using 30° - 45° angle of bank would be the most sensible. If the turn required was about 10° instead of 80° then banking to 30° would generally be considered to be too harsh.

The autopilot needs to be able to apply similar logic to all its actions. Whenever the autopilot is required to make a correction either for stability or when referring to a particular flight path the control response will always be in proportion to deviation or corrective action required but only up to a limit that prevents the autopilot attempting a manouevre that would cause an excursion from the safe flight envelope.

6.2 BOEING 737-400 AUTO PILOT LIMITING AND REVERSION MODES

Command Speed Limiting and Reversion Modes

To prevent the AFS from causing a flight envelope excursion there is a system of command speed limiting and reversion modes. AFS command limiting and reversion is independent of the stall warning and airspeed/Mach warning systems.

Command Speed Limiting

The AFS provides speed, pitch and thrust commands to avoid exceeding the following limit speeds:

1. $V_{MO} / M_{MO.}$
2. Wing flap limiting speeds.
3. Landing gear speeds.
4. Minimum speeds

The commanded speed can be equal to, but will not exceed a limit speed.

Speeds greater than V_{MO} / M_{MO} cannot be selected from the MCP. Speeds can be selected which exceed flap and gear limiting speeds or that are less than the minimum flight speed.

Minimum speed is based on an angle of attack and is approximately $1.3V_S$ for the current flap configuration. It is sensed by the angle of attack vanes, one on either side of the forward fuselage.

If a speed greater than a placard speed, or less than the minimum speed is selected, the AFS allows acceleration or deceleration to slightly short of the limit, then commands the limit speed. The over-speed or under-speed limiting symbol appears in the MCP IAS/Mach display when the commanded speed cannot be reached.

Either pitch or thrust, whichever is engaged in a speed mode, attempts to hold the limit speed. The commanded limit speed and MCP speed condition symbol remain until another speed is selected which does not exceed the limit. A speed 15 kts greater than the minimum speed must be selected to remove the under-speed symbol.

Reversion Modes

During some flight situations, speed control by the AFDS or A/T alone could be insufficient to prevent exceeding a limit speed. If this occurs, AFDS and A/T mode automatically revert to a more effective combination. The reversion modes are:

1.   Placard Limit reversion.
2.   Minimum airspeed reversion.

Mode reversion occurs slightly before reaching the limit speed. Both the AFDS and the A/T have reversion modes which activate according to the condition causing the reversion.

Placard Limit Reversion

When one of the placard limits (gear, flap or V_{MO} / M_{MO}) is reached, the over-speed limiting symbol appears in the MCP IAS/Mach display and the following occurs:

1.   If not in AFDS or A/T speed control and the A/T is armed, the A/T reverts to SPEED mode and controls speed to the placard limit.

2.   If in AFDS or A/T speed control, no reversion is necessary. The AFDS or A/T, whichever is controlling speed, holds speed slightly below the placard limit.

3.   If the A/T is not available, no reversion response to gear or flap placard speeds is available. The AFDS reverts to speed control for V_{MO} / M_{MO} speed limiting.

Minimum Speed Reversion

The AFDS and A/T do not control speed to a speed which is less than the minimum speed for the current flap configuration. This speed is approximately 1.3 V_S. Minimum speed, FMC speed or selected speed, whichever is higher, becomes the AFS commanded speed. If actual speed becomes equal to or slightly less than the minimum speed, the under speed limiting symbol appears in the MCP IAS/Mach display and if operating in the V/S mode, the AFDS reverts to LVL CHG.

The AFS commands a speed 5 kts greater than the minimum speed. Selecting a speed 15 kts greater than the minimum speed reactivates normal MCP speed selection control. The AFDS commands nose down pitch to increase airspeed if the thrust levers are not advanced. When actual speed becomes 15 kts greater than minimum speed, the under speed limiting symbol disappears.

The A/P disengages and the FD command bars retract when in LVL CHG climb with a command speed equal to minimum speed and a minimum rate of climb cannot be maintained without decelerating.

No minimum speed reversion is available when the A/T is OFF and the AFDS is in ALT HOLD, ALT ACQ or after G/S capture.

6.3   FLIGHT ENVELOPE PROTECTION

a.   INTRODUCTION

Flight envelope protection is taken to the extreme by fly-by-wire aircraft with the aim of ensuring that the aircraft remains **within** the normal flight envelope in all phases of flight. The system prevents the envelope being violated during **extreme situations**, such as:

- windshear
- very high turbulence
- midair collision avoidance
- GPWS or TCAS activation
- mismanagement by the crew.

The purpose of the flight envelope protection is to:

- give **full authority** to the pilot in order to consistently achieve the **best possible aircraft performance** in those extreme conditions.
- **reduce the risks** of over controlling / overstressing the aircraft
- provide the pilot with an easy, instinctive and immediate procedure to achieve the best possible performance when required.

b.   THE PROTECTION

The system provides protection in all phases of flight to prevent the aircraft exceeding the limits for the following parameters:

1.   angle of attack
2.   speed
3.   pitch attitude
4.   bank angle
5.   load factor.

c.   HIGH ANGLE OF ATTACK

The protection enables the pilot to execute a rapid pull-up manoeuvre in an emergency situation (as in a midair collision avoidance situation) at **maximum angle of attack,** α max, without over-controlling the aircraft. The technique requires simply that the pilot "snatch stick fully back". If the aircraft exceeds the normal flight envelope for any reason , the pilot is immediately made aware of the situation by the pitch auto-trim stop and the aft pressure required on the stick to keep the flight path. The high angle of attack protection is an aerodynamic protection but thrust is required to maintain the flight path and the auto-thrust function would automatically provide TOGA thrust when the aircraft reaches a certain value (called α floor) before it gets to α max. The input to the circuit is the angle of attack and the output is applied to the elevators and the auto-thrust.

d.   HIGH SPEED

High speed protection circuits prevent the aircraft from reaching Vd / Md by adding a positive nose-up G demand to the pilot demand on the stick; this **demand is proportional to the amount of speed overshoot beyond Vmo / Mmo.** This enables a pilot to enter a steep dive rapidly by pushing the stick forward,- safe in the knowledge that the high speed protection will prevent the aircraft from exceeding the design speed limits.

The inputs to the unit would be airspeed/mach no. from the air data computer and the output is applied to the elevators.

e.   PITCH ATTITUDE

The pitch attitude protection enhances the high angle of attack protection and the high speed protection. The circuit reduces the pitch demand of the stick when the aircraft reaches the pre-defined maximum pitch attitude values which are:

30° nose-up and 15° nose-down.

The input is the pitch angle from the attitude gyros and the output is applied to the elevators.

f.   BANK ANGLE

On a commercial aircraft the bank angle does not normally exceed 30°. However in certain circumstances higher bank angles might be required. Bank angle protection allows the pilot to achieve any roll manoeuvre efficiently and prevents the aircraft entering into an uncontrollable state. For example, the limits of bank angle for an Airbus aircraft are:

1.   67° in the normal flight envelope
2.   45° when high A.o.A is triggered
3.   40° when high speed protection is triggered.

After a roll manoeuvre if the pilot releases the stick the aircraft would return to a bank angle of 33°. The bank angle limit is achieved by **reducing the roll rate demand progressively** as the bank angle increases.

g.   LOAD FACTOR

A commercial aircraft is designed to withstand a maximum load factor, beyond which structural damage is likely to occur. In aircraft where no protection is provided the pilot has to assess the instantaneous G load and could overstress the aircraft in an urgent situation.

Load factor protection is provided by sensing the G load on the aircraft with accelerometers. The G load limiter protects the aircraft against overstress by maintaining it within its structural limitations while allowing the pilot to react immediately to an evasive manoeuvre. The load factor protection is linked to the high angle of attack protection.

6.4   AUTOPILOT GAIN ADAPTION / GAIN SCHEDULING

In the same way as the Flight Director System uses gain scheduling to reduce demands when in close proximity with the ground in order to ensure that the FD system does not demand a manouevre that would endanger the aircraft, the autopilot has a comparable system. This ensures that for example, during an auto-land the autopilots pitch and roll authority is significantly reduced as the aircraft nears the ground. An example of this may be an aircraft that has an autopilot which when used in the manual mode may have bank angle limited to 45°. During VOR or Localiser tracking this may be reduced to 30° as that is deemed all that is necessary. However during the final phase of an automatic approach or an auto-land this may be reduced to 15°.

Gain adaption may also be used to alter the autopilots limits to allow for differing aircraft performance at different altitudes and speeds. Although artificial feel is provided to give pilots awareness of control forces, autopilots could easily ignore artificial feel inputs and overstress the aircraft. So an input from the ADC to the autopilot may be used to reduce the autopilots authority in proportion to Q.

CHAPTER SEVEN - QUESTION PAPERS

Contents

Page

QUESTION PAPER 1 . . . . 7 - 1

QUESTION PAPER 1 - ANSWERS . . . . 7 - 8

QUESTION PAPER 2 . . . . 7 - 9

QUESTION PAPER 2 - ANSWERS . . . . 7 - 12

PAPER 1

1.   A single axis autopilot system:

   a.   Provides stabilisation about the normal axis
   b.   Provides control about the pitch axis
   c.   Is unsuitable for use in powered aircraft
   d.   Provides control about the roll axis

2.   A single axis autopilot may also be called:

   a.   Altitude hold
   b.   Wing leveller
   c.   Pitch control loop
   d.   Auto stabilisation loop

3.   An auto pilot:

   a.   is a system which will maintain a preselected altitude
   b.   is a system which will maintain a preselected airspeed
   c.   is an auto stabilisation system
   d.   is an outer loop control system

4.   The fundamental components of an autopilot control loop are:

   a.   Rate gyro, servomotor, error signal generator
   b.   Rate gyro, servo motor, torque limiter
   c.   Torque limiter, error signal generator, servomotor
   d.   Servo motor, rate gyro, torque limiter, error signal generator

5.   A device in a closed loop control system in which a small power input controls a much larger power output in a strictly proportionate manner is:

   a.   An amplifier
   b.   A servomechanism
   c.   A powered flying control unit
   d.   A rate gyro

6.   An automatic flight control system:

   a.   Is another name for an autopilot system
   b.   Applies flight data to the auto pilot system
   c.   Is automatically disengaged by a GPWS alert
   d.   Can only be used in EFIS equipped aircraft

7.   An aircraft has yaw damping included in its auto stabilisation system. An essential requirement of such a system is:

        a.   A three axis autopilot system
        b.   Parallel connected servo motors
        c.   Automatic maintenance of c of g position
        d.   INS inputs to the CADC

8.   Automatic flight systems may be capable of controlling the aircraft flight in:

        a.   Azimuth, elevation and velocity
        b.   Azimuth and velocity only
        c.   Azimuth only
        d.   Azimuth and elevation only

9.   An automatic flight control system is fitted with control wheel steering (CWS)

        a.   The autopilot must be disengaged before the pilot can input manoeuvring commands
        b.   Manoeuvring commands may be input by applying normal forces to the control yoke without first disengaging the autopilot
        c.   Manoeuvring commands may be input using pitch and turn controls on the automatic flight system control panel, without first disengaging the autopilot
        d.   The CWS is only there for steering on the ground

10.   During an approach to an autoland at 1500 feet:

        a.   Off line channels are manually engaged, flare mode is armed
        b.   Localiser is controlling the roll channel, off line channels are automatically engaged and flare mode is armed
        c.   Localiser is controlling the roll channel, stabiliser is trimmed nose up and roll out is armed
        d.   Provided both localiser and glideslope signals are valid LAND 3 will illuminate

11.   What type of autoland system would be required for the landing to continue following a single failure below alert height:

        a.   Fail soft
        b.   Fail passive
        c.   Fail operational or fail active
        d.   Land 2 system

12.   Inputs to the rudder channels initially originate from:

        a.   Servomotors
        b.   Compass gyro and gyro for AH
        c.   Compass gyro and turn and slip gyro
        d.   AH gyro and turn and slip gyro

13.   An automatic flight system which can safely continue with an automatic landing after a
        system failure is a:

        a.   Fail redundant system
        b.   Fail passive system
        c.   Three axis system
        d.   Fail operational system

14.   Altitude Select and Altitude Hold are examples of:

        a.   inner loop functions in pitch
        b.   manometric functions from the ADC
        c.   interlocking functions
        d.   outer loop functions in roll

15.   During an autoland the caption LAND 2 is illuminated. The system is:

        a.   Fail active or fail operational
        b.   Fail passive
        c.   Approaching decision height
        d.   Requiring a crew input

16.   For an autoland system to meet FAIL PASSIVE criteria it must:

        a.   Have suitable system redundancy
        b.   Withstand a system failure without excessive deviations from flight path
        c.   Can continue with an autoland below alert height
        d.   Can continue with an autoland above alert height

17.   During an autoland at 50 ft AGL (45' GA) the pitch control of the autopilot is .... and
        the roll control is ....

        a.   glideslope   localiser
        b.   glideslope   roll out
        c.   flare   roll out
        d.   flare   localiser

18.   During an autoland approach:

        a.   flare is engaged at 1500'agl
        b.   localiser roll control is disengaged just prior to touchdown
        c.   flare is disengaged prior to touchdown at 5'GA
        d.   glideslope is the engaged pitch mode until 5'GA

19.   In an autoland at 1000' AGL with two autopilots engaged:

     a.   the armed roll mode would be LOCALISER
     b.   the engaged roll mode would be GLIDESLOPE
     c.   the engaged pitch mode would be FLARE
     d.   the engaged roll mode would be LOCALISER.

20.   An automatic flight control system in which the application of normal forces on the control column allows the pilot to input demands to the autopilot is a:

     a.   control wheel steering
     b.   touch control steering
     c.   series connected system
     d.   parallel connected system.

21.   If a fault develops in a Triplex auto-pilot system during an approach, the system will revert to;-

     a.   fail passive and the landing may continue.
     b.   fail control wheel mode.
     c.   fail operational.
     d.   a manual disconnect.

22.   Central Air Data Computers (CADC's) transmit data concerning;-

     a.   airspeed, altitude and decision height.
     b.   airspeed, altitude and Mach Number.
     c.   airspeed, attitude and Mach Number.
     d.   airspeed and altitude only.

23.   Inner loop stability is obtained by;-

     a.   inputs from the Air Data Computer.
     b.   manometric locks.
     c.   'I' bar displacement.
     d.   raw data feed to the data control bus bar.

24.   The auto-throttle is used to control some factors during the three primary control modes, they are:-

     a.   EPR, Mach and Speed.
     b.   EPR, wheel and speed
     c.   EPR, Mach and altitude.
     d.   EPR, wheel and altitude.

25.   The mode that enables the pilot to manoeuvre his aircraft in pitch and roll by use of the automatic control system is called the;-

        a.   control wheel steering (CWS)mode that allows the pilot to control the aircraft, and when the wheel is released, the aircraft holds the newly established attitude.
        b.   touch control steering that will permit the pilot to control the aircraft via the air data computer.
        c.   control wheel steering mode which will disengage the servomotors.
        d.   the touch control steering mode which will prevent the flaps retracting.

26.   Touch control steering;-

        a.   prevents aerodynamic feedback.
        b.   will only operate while the flaps are down.
        c.   allows the pilot to control the aircraft with the servomotors disengaged.
        d.   engages the servomotors during manual operation in pitch and roll.

27.   A system which can still function without degradation of performance after a failure has;-

        a.   fail passive ability.
        b.   fail soft ability.
        c.   fail operational ability.
        d.   fail symbol ability.

28.   During a CAT 2 ILS automatic approach, the source for altitude information is the:-

        a.   basic altitude capsule stack.
        b.   radar altimeter which becomes effective below about 2,500 feet.
        c.   radio altimeter which becomes effective below about 2,500 feet.
        d.   mode comparator sensor.

29.   Heading hold mode relates to control in ;-

        a.   the height lock via the CADC.
        b.   the pitch channel via the inner loop.
        c.   the roll channel via the outer loop control source.
        d.   the manometer mode of the CADC.

30.   The system which allows the pilot to control the aircraft with the servomotors engaged is called;-

        a.   touch control steering.
        b.   control wheel steering.
        c.   the electronic inner / outer axis loop.
        d.   the outer loop control.

31.   The type of automatic landing system which would necessitate a manual landing after a
        system failure during an automatic approach is;-

        a.   fail passive.
        b.   fail safe.
        c.   fail active.
        d.   fail operational.

32.   After a failure of one of the necessary redundant systems below alert height you would;-

        a.   continue the descent but revert to a higher D.H.
        b.   carry out a missed approach.
        c.   disengage autoland and take over manually.
        d.   continue descent and land automatically.

33.   When localiser and glide slope are captured at 1,500 feet during an automatic landing
        sequence, two other functions will be activated at the same time, they are;-

        a.   touch down mode and roll out mode.
        b.   flare mode arm and touch down mode.
        c.   flare mode engage and roll out mode.
        d.   flare mode arm and off line channels engaged.

34.   A fundamental requirement of a closed loop servo-mechanism is;-

        a.   a stable reference device.
        b.   an interlock control.
        c.   a tacho-generator.
        d.   feedback.

35.   ALT HOLD is an example of :-

        a.   Inner loop control in the roll axis
        b.   Outer loop input to the pitch channel
        c.   Outer loop control about the longitudinal axis
        d.   Inner loop control in the pitch axis

36.   A rate gyro:-

        a.   Has three degrees of freedom, two gimbals and a transducer
        b.   Senses rate of turn and positions an indicator on the EHSI
        c.   Supplies rate and displacement information to the computer
        d.   Controls the outer loop inputs

37.   To prevent servo motor runaway from producing excessive demands to the control surface :-

    a.   A gyro damper is fitted
    b.   A torque limiter is fitted
    c.   A gyro limiter is fitted
    d.   A torque converter is fitted

38.   Autotrim is functional :-

    a.   In the pitch and roll channel with the autopilot engaged
    b.   In the pitch channel only with the autopilot engaged
    c.   In the pitch channel only with the autopilot disengaged
    d.   In the pitch and roll channel with the autopilot disengaged

39.   L.NAV is an............. input to the ....channel using data from the...........

    a.   outer loop, pitch, FMC
    b.   inner loop, pitch, ADC
    c.   outer loop, roll, FMC
    d.   inner loop, roll, ADC

40.   In an aircraft which requires a mach trim system it will apply inputs to the horizontal stabilizer:-

    a.   All the time
    b.   At high mach numbers with the autopilot engaged
    c.   At mach one with the autopilot engaged or not
    d.   At high subsonic speeds with the autopilot engaged or not.

PAPER 1 - ANSWERS

QUESTION	ANSWER	QUESTION	ANSWER
01	d	21	a
02	b	22	b
03	c	23	c
04	a	24	a
05	b	25	a
06	a	26	c
07	a	27	c
08	a	28	c
09	b	29	c
10	b	30	b
11	c	31	a
12	c	32	d
13	d	33	d
14	b	34	d
15	b	35	b
16	b	36	c
17	d	37	b
18	c	38	b
19	d	39	c
20	a	40	d

QUESTION PAPER 2

1.   With the Autopilot engaged in the Alt mode the Captain alters the barometric setting. The aircraft:

        a.   maintains its altitude
        b.   changes its altitude in accordance with the change in pressure setting
        c.   switches barometric input over to the 1ˢᵗ Pilot setting
        d..   trips out of altitude hold.

2.   Control wheel steering enables a pilot to:

        a.   taxy the aircraft on the ground
        b.   manoeuvre the aircraft in the air while the autopilot is engaged
        c.   alter the flight path while the autopilot is engaged by applying a breakout force
        d.   manoeuvre the aircraft with the autopilot disengaged.

3.   Autopilot synchronisation in an aircraft:

        a.   requires that the interlocks are made before the autopilot will engage
        b.   ensures that, when the autopilot is engaged, the take-over is effected smoothly and without snatching on the control system
        c.   requires that the aircraft is trimmed out before the autopilot can be engaged
        d.   needs at least two alternators running in parallel.

4.   The rules for the use of Autotrim are that it:

        a.   can be engaged without the autopilot
        b.   usually operates on all three axes
        c.   is not needed if the autopilot is engaged
        d.   operates only in conjunction with the autopilot.

5.   The JAR OPS requirements for single pilot operation under IFR state that the aircraft must be fitted with:

        a.   a single axis autopilot
        b.   a two axis autopilot
        c.   a three axis autopilot
        d.   a two axis autopilot with autothrottle

6.   JAR 25 operational requirements for the installation of automatic pilot state that the system must have:

   A.   automatic synchronisation
   B   quick release controls on both control wheels.

       a.   Only statement A is correct
       b.   Only statement B is correct
       c.   Both statements are correct
       d.   Neither statement is correct.

7.   Consider the following statements regarding flight envelope protection:
   A   High speed protection prevents the airspeed from exceeding Vmo/Mmo
   B   High angle of attack protection comes in when the aircraft reaches the stalling AoA

       a.   Only statement A is correct
       b.   Only statement B is correct
       c.   Both statements are correct
       d.   Neither statement is correct.

8.   In an Autothrottle system the effect of temperature increase on cruise altitude is to cause the aircraft to:

       a.   lose altitude
       b.   gain altitude
       c.   remain at its cruise altitude at the same airspeed
       d.   gain airspeed at the same altitude.

9.   The control laws for an autopilot are known as:

       a.   normal law and emergency law
       b.   alternate law and direct law
       c.   normal, alternate and emergency laws
       d.   normal, alternate and direct laws.

10.   An autoland system that, in the event of an autopilot failure, continues to function without degradation of performance beyond the limits required automatic, would be one with the status:
       a.   fail passive
       b.   fail safe
       c.   fail operational
       d.   duplex.

11.   The Autoland. sequence is considered to be complete when:

       a.   reverse thrust is engaged
       b.   the autopilot is manually disengaged by the pilot
       c.   the aircraft touches down
       d.   the aircraft reaches the end of the runway.

12.   The Autothrottle will come on automatically even with the A/T switch OFF when:

        a.   in a FBW aircraft the AoA reaches a critical value called α floor
        b.   the AoA reaches the stalling angle
        c.   TOGA button is pressed
        d.   reverse thrust is selected in flight.

13.   An aircraft on Autopilot is engaged in the VOR mode and loses the VOR signals as it flies through the VOR cone of silence. The autopilot:

        a.   automatically switches to Heading mode
        b.   decouples from the VOR and disconnects
        c.   tunes to the next VOR on the route
        d.   decouples from the VOR and flies the last heading for a fixed period.

14.   For an aircraft with a non-synchronised autopilot system, 'snatching' of the controls by the autopilot when engaging or disengaging can be prevented by:

        a.   the pilot ensuring that the aircraft is trimmed out before selecting or disengaging the autopilot
        b.   being in a straight and level position
        c.   disengaging the autotrim
        d.   switching on the yaw dampers.

15.   With the autopilot in CWS the pilot manoeuvres the aircraft and releases control. The aircraft will maintain :

        a.   heading and altitude
        b.   heading, speed and attitude
        c.   altitude and attitude
        d.   attitude at the time of release.

16.   Autopilot corrections affecting Pitch are carried out by:

        a.   autotrim only
        b.   autotrim and elevators
        c.   elevators only
        d.   autothrottle.

17.   For a commercial aircraft operating with a single pilot in IFR the minimum requirement is that the autopilot should have control in:

        a.   three axes
        b.   Heading mode
        c.   Altitude Hold and Heading mode
        d.   Altitude Hold, Heading mode and Speed.

PAPER 2 ANSWERS

QUESTION	ANSWER	QUESTION	ANSWER
01	a	21	
02	b	22	
03	b	23	
04	d	24	
05	b	25	
06	b	26	
07	d	27	
08	a	28	
09	d	29	
10	c	30	
11	b	31	
12	a	32	
13	d	33	
14	a	34	
15	d	35	
16	b	36	
17	c	37	
18		38	
19		39	
20		40	

A/P	Autopilot
A/T	Auto-Throttle
A/L	Auto-Land
ADC	Air Data Computer (sometimes CADC (Central Air Data Computer))
ADI (EADI)	Attitude and Direction Indicator (Electronic)
AFCP	Auto-Flight Control Panel (see also MCP)
AFCS	Auto-Flight Control System
AFDS	Auto-Flight Director System
AFS	Auto-Flight System
ALT ACQ	Altitude Acquire (mode)
AoA	Angle Of Attack
APP	Approach (mode)
CDI (bar)	Course Deviation Indicator (bar)
CDU	Control and Display Unit
CMD	Command (or Autopilot Engage)
CWS	Control Wheel Steering
DG / DI	Directional Gyro / Direction Indicator
ECAM	Electronic Centralised Aircraft Monitoring *✳ AIRBUS*
EFIS	Electronic Flight Instrumentation System
EICAS	Engine Instruments and Crew Alerting System
EPR	Engine Pressure Ratio
FADEC	Full Authority Digital Engine Control
FCC	Flight Control Computer
FD	Flight Director
FDC	Flight Director Computer
FDS	Flight Director System
FMA	Flight Mode Annunciator
FMC	Flight Management Computer
FMGS	Flight Management and Guidance System
G/S	Glideslope or groundspeed dependant on context
GA	Go Around or Gear Altitude dependant on context

HDG	Heading (mode)
HSI (EHSI)	Horizontal Situation Indicator (Electronic)
INS	Inertial Navigation System
IRS	Inertial Reference System
LAND 2	Fail Passive
LAND 3	Fail Active
LNAV	Lateral NAVigation (mode)
LOC	Localiser (mode)
LVL CHG	Level Change (mode)
MCP	Mode Control Panel (see also AFCP)
MI	Magnetic Indicator
N1	RPM of the first stage of compression (normally the fan in a high bypass engine) expressed as a percentage
ND	Navigational Display
PFCU	Powered Flying Control Unit
PFD	Primary Flight Display (EADI including speed, altitude, VSI tapes and commonly a compass and annunciator panel)
PMC	Power Management Computer
QDM	"Q" code for a magnetic heading to fly assuming zero wind
RA	Radio Altitude
SPD	Speed (mode)
TCS	Touch Control Steering
TLA	Thrust
TMA	Thrust Mode Annunciator
TMS	Thrust Management System
TO/GA	Take Off / Go Around
TRK	Track
V/S	Vertical Speed (mode)
VG	Vertical Gyro
VNAV (SPD/PTH)	Vertical NAVigation /Path or Speed (mode)
VOR	VOR tracking (mode) or a VHF omni-range beacon dependant on context

JAAatpl
JOINT AVIATION AUTHORITIES

Theoretical Training Manuals

Revised Edition

AIRCRAFT GENERAL KNOWLEDGE 4

INSTRUMENTATION
POWER PLANT & SYSTEM MONITORING INSTRUMENTS

CIVIL AVIATION AUTHORITY

OXFORD
Aviation Training
Succeed through our experience™

CHAPTER ONE - ENGINE INSTRUMENTATION

Contents

Page

1.1   AN INTRODUCTION TO THE ENGINE INSTRUMENTS . . . . 1 - 1

1.2   TYPES OF DISPLAY . . . . 1 - 2

1.3   THRUST MEASURING INSTRUMENTS . . . . 1 - 2

1.4   ENGINE TORQUE . . . . 1 - 4

1.5   ENGINE R.P.M . . . . 1 - 7

1.6   TEMPERATURE SENSING EQUIPMENT . . . . 1 - 12

1.7   PRESSURE GAUGES . . . . 1 - 16

1.8   ENGINE VIBRATION . . . . 1 - 19

1.9   FUEL GAUGE . . . . 1 - 20

1.10   REMOTE (SIGNAL) TRANSMISSION SYSTEM . . . . 1 - 26

1.11   FLIGHT HOUR METER . . . . 1 - 28

1.1   AN INTRODUCTION TO THE ENGINE INSTRUMENTS.

Just as it would be impossible to fly a large modern aircraft safely without the flight instruments, so would it also be impossible to fly it safely without the engine and aircraft systems instruments.

The engine instruments are divided basically into two categories, **Performance Indicators** or **Engine Condition Indicators**.

Performance Indicators are thrust indicating instruments such as the Engine Pressure Ratio (E.P.R.) gauge or the Fan Speed (N1) gauge.

Engine Condition Indicators include the Exhaust Gas Temperature (E.G.T.) gauge, Compressor Speed, Oil Pressure and Oil Temperature gauges. We will be discussing these and others in the following text.

Figure 1.1 shows some of the parameters previously mentioned and the position of the sensors that are required to measure them.

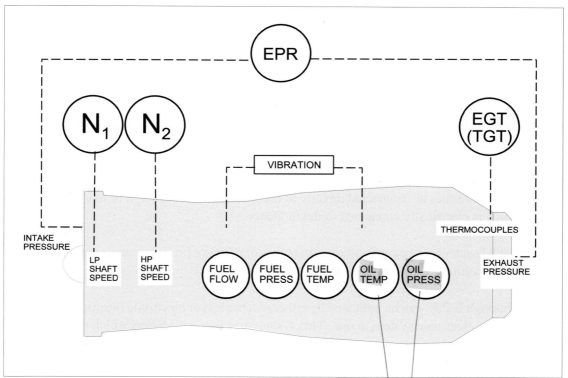

Figure 1.1 Some of the Parameters Required to be Displayed.

Main Indications

1.2   TYPES OF DISPLAY

There are two types of cockpit display, the analogue display (clockwork cockpit), or the electronic display (glass cockpit). This is covered in Chap 18

In the former, there are a multitude of gauges displaying information, in the latter the display is shown on cathode ray tubes (C.R.T.s) or liquid crystal display panels (L.C.D.s) with light emitting diodes (L.E.D.s) for digital displays. A small number of conventional gauges are retained in case of failure of the electronic displays.

Both types of display convey essentially the same information to the pilot, but the flexibility of the Glass Cockpit system means that it is now taking over as the preferred means of showing both flight and engine instrumentation.

1.3   THRUST AND POWER MEASURING INSTRUMENTS.

EICAS ECAM

Thrust measuring instruments are of two basic types:-

a)   the type that measures the jet pipe pressure, the **P7 gauge**. *(act on most modern a/c)*

b)   the type that measures the ratio of two parameters, the jet pipe pressure and the engine air intake pressure, the **E.P.R. gauge**. (fig 1.2) *Engine Pressure Ratio*

c)   propeller driven aircraft measurer and indicate **Torque**. This is an indication of engine power. The propeller converts power into thrust.

On some large turbo-fan engines the integrated turbine discharge pressure and fan outlet pressure is compared to the compressor inlet pressure to produce what is called 'integrated' E.P.R..

Pitot tubes, suitably positioned, sense the pressures which are required to work the system, the tubes can either be connected directly to the indicator in the cockpit or to a pressure transmitter which is electrically connected to the indicator.

The P7 system gauge can be marked in inches of mercury (in Hg), pounds per square inch (p.s.i.), or a percentage of the engine's maximum thrust.

Although E.P.R. can be indicated by either mechanical or electronic means, it is more normal to find the electronic system in use. This system uses two transducers which sense the relevant air pressures and vibrate at frequencies proportional to these pressures. A computer works out the electrical signal appropriate to the pressures and that signal is sent to the E.P.R. gauge in the cockpit and to the engine management system.

Thrust is maximum when a/c is stationary

EPR will go down as we accelerate.

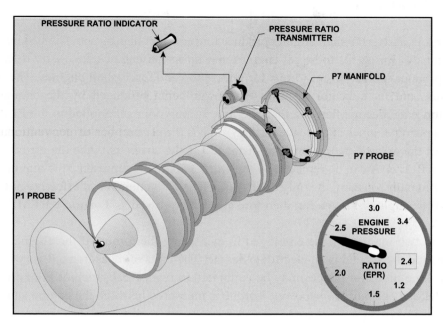

Figure 1.2 The Engine Pressure Ratio (E.P.R.) Indicating System.

The engine intake pressure will vary with changing ambient pressure and also with changing airspeed. An increase in forward airspeed during take off will cause a drop in the reading on the E.P.R. gauge. This is only an 'apparent drop' because it is only the ratio of two pressures, engine intake pressure and the jet pipe pressure, which is changing.

This apparent change is caused by a relative increase of the engine intake pressure with forward airspeed during take off. The jet pipe pressure being unaffected at low airspeeds, which causes the ratio between the two pressures to fall.

This will be seen as a reduction in E.P.R. on the gauge, which might cause the inexperienced engine operator to open the throttles further in an attempt to restore the loss, having eyes for only the one parameter, while the other parameters, (N1, N2, N3 & E.G.T.) are in danger of exceeding their limits without his knowledge.

In an attempt to prevent this happening, most operators require that E.P.R. is set before the aircraft has reached approximately 60 knots, no increase in engine power being allowed unless in emergency after this speed.

After take off, as the airspeed increases beyond V_2, the increase in engine intake pressure is passed through the engine to the jet pipe, so changing the ratio back to that set on take-off.

1-3

1.4   ENGINE TORQUE.

Turbo-props and turbo-shaft engines produce torque rather than thrust. The systems that produce indications of thrust for turbo-jet engines and turbo-fan engines are vastly different to those which produce indications of torque for turbo-prop and turbo-shaft engines. The Torque meter measures, and its indicator displays the power being produced by the engine. Torque by definition is a force applied at a distance to a turning point. If applied to the **PLANE** formula given in piston engines chap 1, the turning force is the product of the mean effective pressure **P** acting on the area of the piston **A** at distance **L** (the stroke is twice the throw of the crank) Therefor **P, L & A** can be replaced by the word **Torque. N** represents the number of cylinders and will remain constant, the only other variable is **E** the number of effective power strokes or RPM of the engine. **Power** can therefore also be expressed as **Torque x RPM.**

There are two main methods employed in measuring the torque of the engine. One uses oil pressure and the second is an electronic device. The units of measurement vary from system to system. The indicator gauges may be calibrated to read, P.S.I., Inch or Foot pounds, Newton metres, Brake or Shaft Horsepower. Torque is measured between the engine and the reduction gearbox.

The oil torque meter system makes use of a phenomenon that axial thrust (movement) is generated when **helically cut gears** are used to transfer power from one shaft to another. Figure 1.3 shows how this end thrust can be utilised to provide an indication of the torque output of a turbo-prop or turbo-shaft engine.

As the gears in the propeller reduction gearbox rotate to drive the propeller, the amount of torque that they are transmitting attempts to move them axially, this axial force is proportional to the torque that is producing it.

The gears cannot be allowed to move axially because this would cause the teeth to no longer mesh with each other and the drive would fail, the axial force has to be counteracted to maintain the gears in alignment. The force comes from passing engine oil through a filter and then to a torquemeter pump which enables its pressure to be boosted to (in some cases) as much as 800 p.s.i.. This high pressure is allowed into cylinders which form the bearings within which the helical gear shafts rotate.

A small bleed hole in the wall of the cylinder will be covered by the gear shaft if it moves into the cylinder under increasing axial load, this will cause the oil pressure within the cylinder to build up until it can move the gear shaft back to its original position. Conversely, if the load on the helical gear shaft decreases, the existing oil pressure will force its shaft slightly out of the cylinder. This uncovers the bleed hole allowing the balancing oil pressure to be reduced and so the gear shaft moves back into correct position within the cylinder.

If the oil pressure balancing the axial force is measured, it can be compared with reference figures which take into account the ambient pressure and temperature and the performance of the engine, its power output, can be judged.

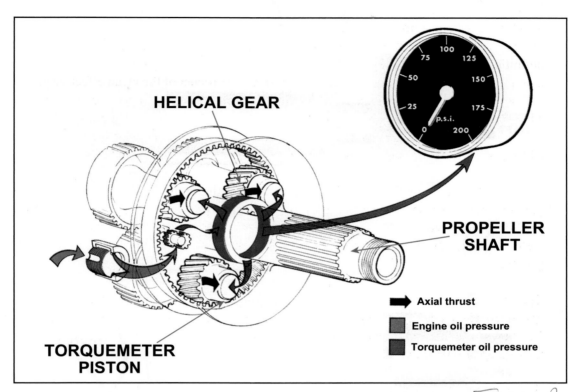

Figure 1.3. The Torquemeter System.   ~ Turbo Props

Oil pressure proportional to torque

The Electronic system comprises of two concentric shafts. One, the **Torque Shaft,** is connected to both the engine and the **propeller's reduction gear box.** The second shaft, the **Reference Shaft,** is connected only to the engine. An exciter wheel (toothed gear)is formed at the forward end of each shaft. The exciter wheels rotate past an electro magnetic pick-up and produce an AC voltage. The exciter wheels are aligned at assembly, but as power is increased the torque shaft twists, this displaces the phase relationship of the voltages produced. The displacement is proportional to the change in power, and is used to drive an indicator. This system is simple, and lighter than other systems and has proven to be very reliable in service. (fig 1.4)

The torque indicator may indicate negative (windmilling propeller) as well as positive torque. The torque limits are colour coded and shown on the gauge. A red coloured band or marker indicating maximum limits. On a FADEC system these limits may be adjusted and set by the crew, the indication can be presented in a digital readout.

Full Authority Digital Engine Control System

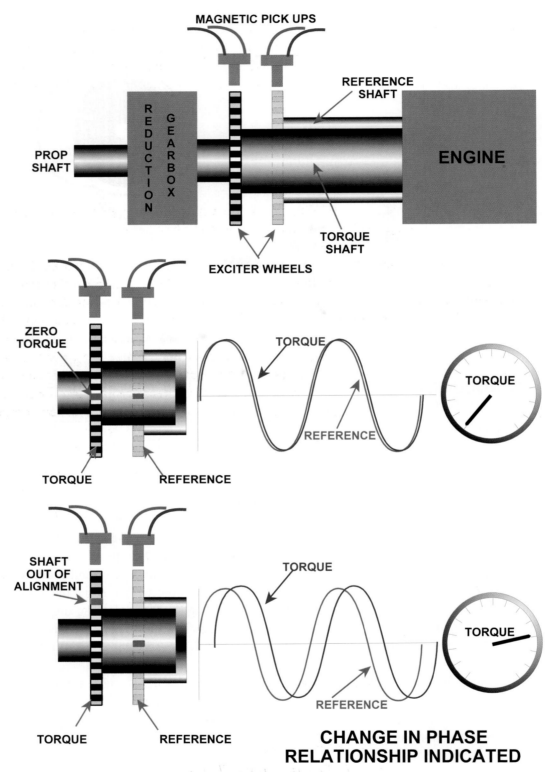

Figure 1.4 ELECTRONIC TORQUEMETER

1.5   ENGINE R.P.M.

The measurement of engine speed is of vital importance, since together with other parameters accurate control, and monitoring of the engine can be achieved. On piston engines it is crankshaft speed that is measured, whilst on gas turbine engines it is the speed of the compressor. The RPM indicator is called a **Tachometer (Tacho).** There are three basic methods of measuring engine rotational speeds:-

1. Mechanical (Magnetic) Tachometer.
2. Electrical Generator System. (Tacho Genny)
3. Inductive Probe System.

There are no firm guidelines as to the application of each of the tachometer system, although engine and aircraft design will dictate which system can be best utilised.

The **Mechanical Tachometer (** fig 1.5 **)** is now only found on older piston aircraft. It consists of a **Flexible Drive Shaft** that is connected to the flight deck **Tacho Indicator.** The input drive causes a magnet in the indicator to rotate. The magnet rotates inside a copper or aluminium drag-cup, this induces **Eddy Currents** in the drag-cup which opposes the magnetic field of the magnet. A torque is established which turns the drag -cup in the same direction as the permanent magnet. A shaft extends from the drag-cup and is connected to a pointer. The turning motion of the pointer is against the tension of a **Hairspring** which controls the drag cup position and hence the position of the pointer. The flexible drive is driven at reduced speed, but true speed will be shown on the indicator.   The indicator incorporates compensation devices for change in temperature.

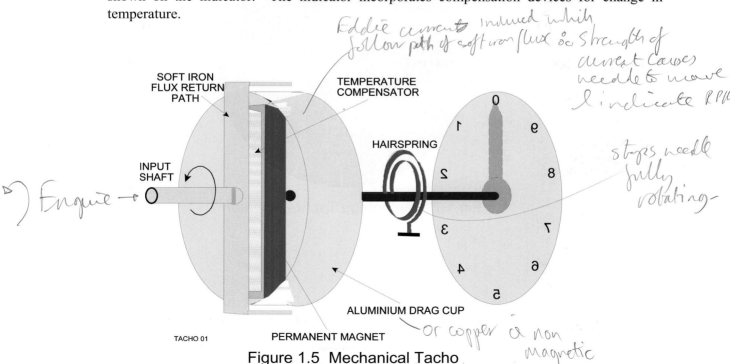

Figure 1.5 Mechanical Tacho

The **Electrical Generator System** (fig 1.6) is possibly the oldest form of engine speed measurement still in use on large aircraft. It utilises a small three phase (tacho) generator, driven by the engine. The output of this generator is then taken to an indicator which consists of a synchronous motor turning a drag cup assembly which moves a pointer over a scale as in the mechanical system.

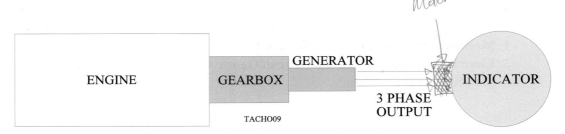

Figure 1.6 Tacho-Genny

The indicator (fig 1.7) can either show the actual revolutions per minute (not too common), or the speed as a percentage of maximum engine speed.

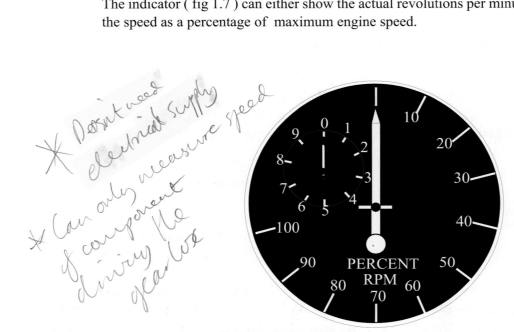

Fig 1.7 Percentage Tacho-Indicator.

On twin or triple spool engines the speed of rotation of the high , intermediate and low pressure compressors can be displayed. These would be termed N3, N2 and N1. N being the SI symbol for rotational speed.

An overspeed pointer (Trailing or Limit pointer) can also be fitted concentrically with the main pointer, and is initially positioned at the appropriate max RPM graduation. If the main pointer exceeds this position, the limit pointer is carried with it. When speed is reduced the limit pointer will remain at the maximum speed reached. It can be reset by applying a separate 28V DC supply to a solenoid in the indicator.

Although there would always be provision on the H.P. compressor spool for driving a tacho-generator through the high speed gear box. Facilities may not always be available for driving tacho-generators from the intermediate and low pressure compressor shafts. If this is the case, a **Speed Probe**, shown in Figures 1.8 and 1.9, can be used to very good effect.

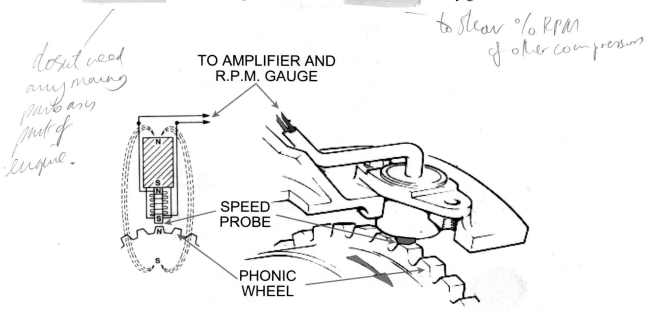

Figure 1.8 Measuring Engine Speed With a Phonic Wheel and a
Speed Probe.

The speed probe is positioned on the compressor casing in line with either a phonic wheel (Figure 1.8), or the actual fan blades (Figure 1.9). As the spool rotates, the magnetic flux in the probe or sensor head is altered. This changes the current flowing in the coil fitted inside the probe and the frequency with which it changes is directly related to the spool speed. This frequency is fed to an indicator in the cockpit to show the spool rotational speed.

In addition to providing an indication of spool speed, the tacho-generator or speed probe can both be used to provide a signal which will illuminate a warning lamp on the engine start control panel. This can tell the pilot not only that the engine is turning, but also whether the engine is turning in the correct direction. This is particularly important during engine start as it is used to inform the pilot when to open the H.P. Fuel Cock. This lamp is only illuminated during the start cycle.

An advantage of this system is the reduction in moving parts required in the engine, and that a number of separate electrical outputs additional to those required for speed indications can be provided, e.g. automatic power control and flight data acquisition systems.

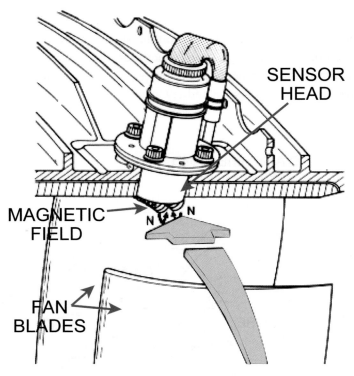

Figure 1.9 The Use of a Speed Probe to Measure Fan
Speed.

The Tacho indicators mentioned in the text above receive their speed signals directly from speed sensors or via servo operated systems. These indicators require a power source from the aircraft airborne power supply. In the event of power supply or signal failure, the indicator is returned to an **Off Scale** position, and a **Power Off Flag** may be displayed.

As previously stated, presentation of speed is now usually displayed as a percentage figure. It is only piston engine aircraft where the actual speed of rotation is displayed. Gas turbine engines have dial displays which show percentage speed, with 100% corresponding to the optimum turbine speed. Two scales are displayed, a main scale calibrated 0 to 100% in 10% increments. A second pointer or digital counter displays speed in 1% increments. As well as digital read out vertical ribbon displays are used.

In line with other instruments, coloured arcs or indicators lines are used to show ranges and limits of engine speed. Green representing normal operating range, with Amber denoting caution. Red arcs show maximum or minimum speed, and ranges that are restricted because of excessive vibration.. On a piston engine the reference RPM should also be placarded.

On multi-engine aircraft, to reduce structural vibration and noise the speed of all engines must be synchronised. It is impractical to have the pilot adjust the throttle of each engine manually to synchronise the speed, and individual indicators may vary in accuracy. In order to facilitate manual adjustment of speed an additional instrument known as a **Synchroscope** (fig 1.10) is used. The instrument was designed at the outset for operation from the AC generated by the tachometer system. The instrument provides qualitative indication of the difference in speeds between two or more engines. One engine is selected as a master, the others are slaves to it. The instrument shows clearly whether a slave engine is running faster or slower than the master. An example of the dial presentation for synchroscopes for a Twin and Four-engine aircraft, and Combined tacho and Synchroscope are shown.

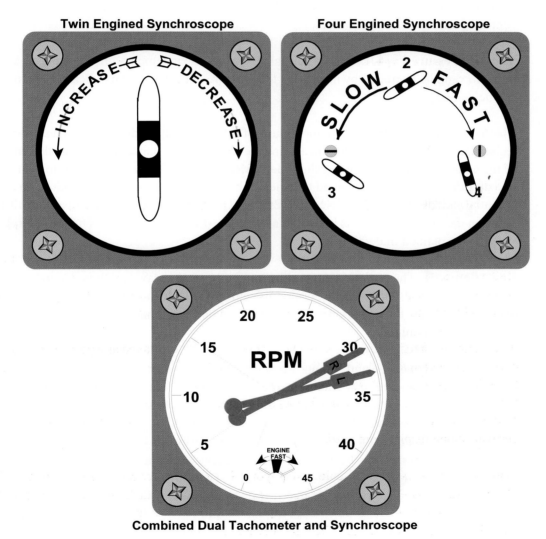

Figure 1.10 Synchroscopes

1.6   TEMPERATURE SENSING EQUIPMENT.

Piston and gas turbine aero engines are heat engines. The power they produce is directly proportional to the heat released during combustion of fuel. Engine components and systems are designed to withstand certain temperatures. If their limits are exceeded they may fail. To allow safe operation the engine temperatures must be monitored. The effect of ambient temperatures as well as combustion must be considered. The following temperatures are monitored on piston and gas turbine engines: Air Inlet, Piston Cylinder Heads, Piston Exhaust Gas, Gas Turbine Compressor outlets, Turbines Oil and Fuel systems and Internal Air system.

The temperatures monitored may range from -56°c to +1200°c. Different sensors are used depending on the temperature range to be monitored. They fall broadly into two categories, High temperatures and low temperatures. There are four major types of measuring devices. They are:

Expansion Type. This relies on the principle that most solids, liquids and gases expand and contract with temperature changes. e.g. The mercury Thermometer and Bi-metallic strip

Vapour Pressure Type. Liquids when subjected to a rise in temperature change their state from liquid to vapour. Therefore by measuring the pressure of the vapour an indication of temperature can be gained.

Electrical Type. A change in temperature of an electrical conductor can cause a change in resistance of the conductor. Thus measuring the change in resistance can indicate the temperature of the conductor. This sensor is called the **Resistance Type** (Temperature Bulb). In addition, two dissimilar metals when joined together at their ends (a junction) can produce an electrical potential called a thermo EMF(Seebeck Effect). This is dependant on the temperature difference between the junctions. This is known as a '**Thermo-Electric Type**' or '**Thermo-couple**'. This system is explained in detail later.

Radiation type. The radiation emitted by any body at any wavelength is dependant upon the temperature of that body. This is termed its 'emissivity'. If the radiation is measured and the emissivity is know the temperature of the body can be determined. Such a measuring technique is known as **Pyrometry.**

Generally the Expansion and Vapour Pressure sensors are used to indicate lower temperatures. They are direct reading. e.g Thermometer. The Electrical and Radiation sensors are used to measure higher temperatures and can be direct reading to a moving coil Indicator. e.g. Piston Engine Exhaust Gas Temperature. However most systems today use remote sensors that feed to servo-operated indicators after the signal from the sensor has been amplified. A **Ratiometer-Type** indicating system can be used to obtain the greater accuracy required when indicating the temperature of critical component (Turbines).

The temperature of the gas passing through the turbine in a gas turbine engine is the most important parameter of those displayed on the engine instruments. Operation of the engine beyond the limits of turbine temperature, even for only a moment, is liable to cause excessive turbine blade creep which can be catastrophic if the rotating blades touch the casing of the engine.

The gas temperature must be monitored closely and automatic temperature limiting equipment is fitted to most gas turbine engines operating today. To enable this monitoring to be achieved temperature probes are inserted in the gas stream.

Temperature probes are formed from the junction of two dissimilar metals, when heated the junction generates a small voltage which is proportional to the actual temperature which produced it. The voltage can be measured on a milli-voltmeter and displayed in the cockpit as the temperature at the rear of the engine. A **Galvanometer** is a very sensitive instrument used to indicate these low voltages. The galvanometer uses a basic **Wheatstone Bridge Balancing** circuit that alters the magnetic field in a coil, this change produces a torque to drive an indicator.

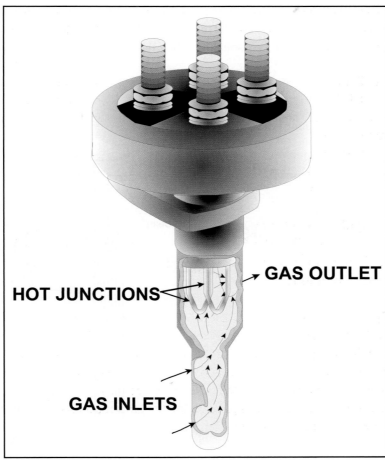

Figure 1.11 The Gas Flow Over the Probes and Their
Electrical Connections.

Figure 1.11 shows how the probes, the hot junctions, are connected and also how the gas flows over them. The output from the probes is sent to the cockpit engine instrument, which is the cold junction, where the e.m.f. is measured on a very sensitive milli-voltmeter to display the engine gas temperature.

Just one probe would obviously not supply enough information to accurately tell the pilot what was going on in the whole turbine, it could only inform him about the small part of the turbine that it was monitoring. It is therefore necessary to place a number of probes, **electrically connected in parallel**, all around the periphery of the engine or the exhaust system, this means that the gas stream is sampled in many more places and that the output is the average of all of the probes. This has an added advantage that **if one probe is damaged, the temperature reading on the gauge is virtually unaffected.**

The actual position of the probes depends upon two things, the anticipated maximum temperature of the gas, and the ability of the probe material to withstand that temperature

The industry standard for the material used in the temperature probes in gas turbine engines is chromel (nickel chromium), and alumel (nickel aluminium). These two materials may not have the highest milli-voltage output of the materials available, but their ability to withstand very high temperatures coupled with a reasonable volts / degree ratio makes them ideal for the job.

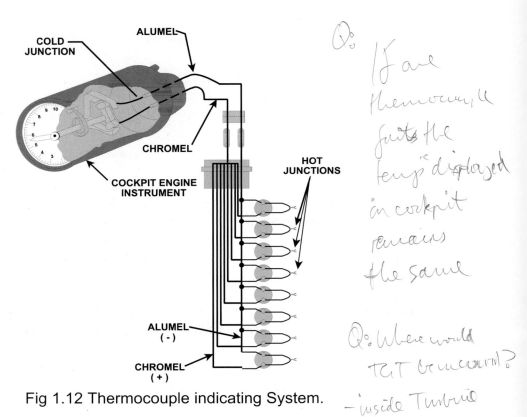

Fig 1.12 Thermocouple indicating System.

Note:- The system requires no power supply to indicate temperature.

However if the signal is to be used to supply a temperature limiting system the voltage will need to be amplified. This will be supplied by the aircraft's electrical system.

In the case of a system that supplies both a temperature limiting system (top temperature control) and a temperature indicating system, the probes will contain two hot junctions, one to feed the limiter and one to feed the indicator. As illustrated in fig 1.11

The positioning of the probes within the engine depends on the temperature of the gas and the ability of the metal they are made of to withstand it. On engines where the temperature of the gas within the turbine is too high for the metal of the probes to stand it, they may be positioned after the turbine and the gauge calibrated to read 'exhaust gas temperature' (E.G.T). On other engines, it may be found convenient to combine the temperature probes with the pitot probes which measure exhaust gas pressure (P7), in this case the gauges will read 'jet pipe temperature' (J.P.T.).

Obviously it would be ideal if the temperature could be sampled either before the turbine, called either 'turbine inlet temperature' (T.I.T.), or 'turbine entry temperature' (T.E.T.), or inside the turbine, called 'turbine gas temperature' (T.G.T.), in every case the position of the probes is dependent upon their ability to withstand the temperatures they encounter.

Actual blade temperature can be measured by the radiation method, with the use of a **Optical of Pyrometer.**

Air temperature is one of the basic parameters used to establish data vital to the performance monitoring of aircraft engines. e.g thrust settings, fuel/air ratios settings etc. The temperature ideally required is that sensed at static conditions at various flight levels. This is called **Static Air Temperature (SAT)**. However this is not possible for all types of aircraft or, in many instances, for one type of aircraft, for the measurements can be effected by the adiabatic compression with increase speed. Below 0.2 Mach the temperature is very close to SAT, but at higher Mach Nos an increase in skin friction will raise the air temperature. This increase is commonly referred to as **'Ram Rise',** and the temperature indicated called **Ram Air Temperature (RAT)** i.e. SAT plus the ram rise. The ram rise can be calculated mathematically as a function of Mach No, and for each type of aircraft tables or graphs can be included in flight manuals, or computed by air data computers to correct the indicators to SAT. The proportion of ram rise dependant on the ability of the sensor to sense or recover the temperature rise. The sensitivity in this case being expressed as a percentage and termed **Recovery Factor.** If for example , a sensor has a recovery factor of 0.80, it will measure SAT plus 80% of the ram rise.

For use at high Mach Nos **Total Air Temperature (TAT)** is measured. The air is brought to rest (or nearly so) without addition or removal of heat. The temperature probes used have a high recovery factor (approximately 100%). TAT is equal to SAT+Ram Rise.

Temperature indicators use coloured arcs to show their operating range. Green for normal, Amber for caution and Red upper or lower limits.

1.7   PRESSURE GAUGES

In many of the systems associated with the operation of the aircraft and its engines, liquids and gases are used the pressures of which must be measured and indicated. The gauges and indicating systems fall into two categories: **Direct Reading** and **Remote Indicating**. Remote indicating is where a separate sensing element is connected to a pressure source at some remote point.

Pressure, is defined as force per unit area. It is normally indicated either as **Pounds Per Square Inch (PSI)** or **Inches of Mercury (in Hg)**. In connection with pressure measurement we are concerned with the following terms: **Absolute Pressure** and **Gauge Pressure.** Most pressure gauges measure the difference between absolute pressure and the atmospheric pressure . This is gauge pressure.

To actually measure pressure in a system **Elastic Pressure Sensing Elements** are used in which forces can be produced by applied pressures and converted to mechanical movement. The movement can then operate a direct reading gauge or electrical transmitter. The sensing elements commonly used are **Diaphragms, Capsules, Bellows and Bourdon tubes.**

Diaphragms (fig 1.13) consist of corrugated circular metal discs which are secured at their edge, and when pressure is applied they are deflected. Diaphragms are used to measure low pressures.

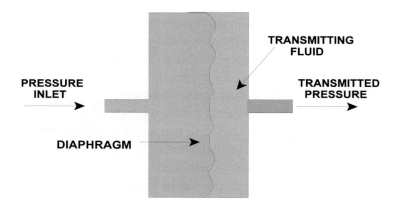

Figure 1.13 A Diaphragm Pressure Sensor

Capsules (fig 1.14) are made up of two diaphragms placed together and joined at their edges to form a chamber which may be sealed, called an **Aneroid,** or open to a pressure source and called a **Pressure** capsule. Like diaphragms they are used to measure low pressure, but they are more sensitive to small pressure changes.

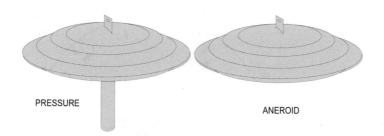

Figure 1.14 Pressure and Aneroid Capsules

The bellows (fig 1.15) type element can be considered as an extension of the corrugated diaphragm principle. It may be used for High, Low or differential pressure measurement. It is typically used to measure pressures like the aircraft's LP Booster pump output.

The Manifold Absolute Pressure Gauge or **MAP** (fig 1 .17) of a piston engine measures both pressure and differential pressure. Note this gauge measures **Absolute Pressure** and indicates inches of mercury (in Hg.). When the engine is running this gauge can indicate less than atmospheric pressure. Earlier versions of this gauge were calibrated to read **Boost** in **PSI** and called **Boost Gauges**. Under standard conditions the Boost Gauge will read 'Zero' and the MAP gauge will read 30 in Hg. This indication is called **Static Boost**.

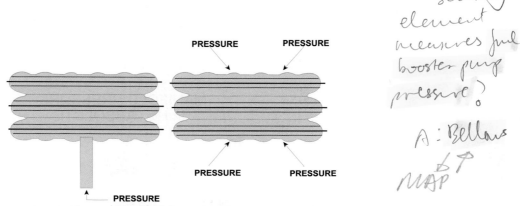

Figure 1.15 Bellows Sensors.

The Bourdon tube (fig 1.16) is about the oldest of the pressure-sensing element. The element is essentially a length of metal tube with an elliptical cross section, and shaped into a letter C. One end of the tube is sealed, and called the free end. The other end is connected to the pressure source and fixed. When pressure is applied the tube tries to straighten, this movement is magnified to drive and indicator pointer. The Bourdon tube can be manufactured to indicate high or low pressures, but is normally associated with higher pressures such as engine oil pressure.

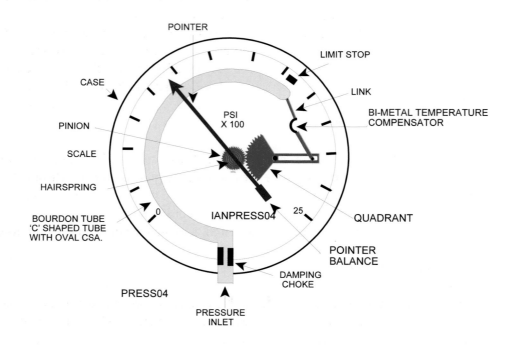

Figure 1.16 The Bourdon Tube

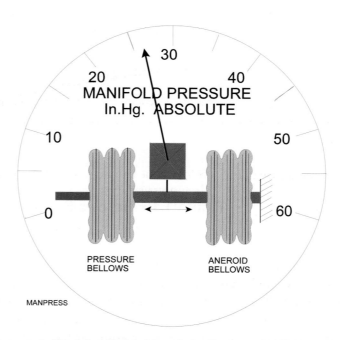

Figure 1.17 Manifold Absolute Pressure Gauge.

It would be impractical to run an oil feed pipe from the outer engine of a Boing 747 to a flight deck pressure indicator of the Bourdon tube type. To overcome this problem remote- indicating systems are used. They consist of two main components, a transmitter unit located at the pressure source, and an indicator mounted on the appropriate panel. They have distinct advantages over direct-reading gauges; for example, the pressure of hazardous fluids can be measured at their source and not brought into the cockpit. Also weight can be saved by reducing the length of pipelines. The transmitters feed varying current to an indicator and can be AC or DC in operation. These systems are covered in Para 1.10 .

As well as indicating actual pressures, warnings can be displayed to the pilot by pressure operated switches. These switches can operate for Low, High or incorrect Differential pressures. A differential Switch or gauge is subjected to pressure on both sides of its sensor

Coloured arcs of Green, Amber or Red are used to indicate the range and limits of the system.

1.8   ENGINE VIBRATION.

Vibration monitoring equipment (V.M.E.) is fitted to almost all commercial jet engined aircraft. Although gas turbine engines have an extremely low vibration level, any change in that level is usually indicative of damage which may lead to failure.

Warnings will be given in the cockpit if the vibration levels are exceeded and some systems have a continuous readout of vibration levels.

The latest engines have the facility whereby the vibration level of each rotating assembly is monitored so that the source of the vibration can be pin pointed.

The principle upon which V.M.E. works requires either an input from a **Piezo** electric crystal mounted strategically on the engine, or an input from a coil which will be affected by the movement of a **Magnet** mounted loosely within it. In either case, the frequency of the incoming vibrations will be filtered so that only those frequencies that are indicative of damage occurring will affect the output.

These systems utilise the principle that the magnet and piezo crystal which are suspended within a fixed coil carrying 115 volts at 400 Hertz, will move in sympathy with any vibration suffered by the engine. This will affect the current flowing through the coil into the amplifier and filter. The filter will erase any output which is normal to the engine, and allow through to the amplifier any frequency that is considered to be harmful to the engine.

The result of this amplification is sent to the instrument via the rectifier and warning circuit. The needle will show the appropriate deflection for the amount of vibration being suffered by the engine at that time. If the level of vibration exceeds a predetermined amount, a warning light on the instrument illuminates. Vibration is measured and displayed in **'Relative Amplitude'** (Rel Ampl)

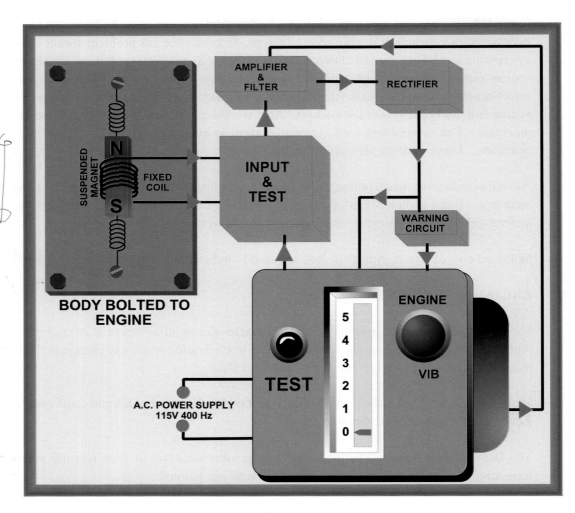

Figure 1.18 The Circuitry of a Vibration Monitoring System.

1.9   FUEL GAUGE

The measurement of the quantity of fuel in the tanks of an aircraft fuel system is an essential requirement, and in conjunction with measurements of the rate at which the fuel flows to the engine or engines permits an aircraft to be flown at maximum efficiency.

There are two principle methods of indicating the quantity of fuel carried. Either the **Volume (e.g. Gallons)** or **Mass (kg or lbs)** are measured. The former is now only used on light aircraft as the **Mass** of the fuel is of more interest to the pilot. This assists the pilot in calculating the aircraft's 'all-up-weight ' and also gives a better indication of the energy that can be released by the fuel. One pound of fuel has the same number of energy molecules regardless of temperature and volume.

The simplest form of volume indication is a float system. Early aircraft had a float which sat on the level of fuel. Attached to the float was a piece of wire that protruded out the top of the fuel tank. As the fuel level reduced so the wire disappeared from view. There have been many variations of this system. The most common of these is where the float moves to reposition a wiper on a variable resistor which alters the current to an indicator moving a pointer over a scale calibrated in volume. This is a DC powered system. (fig 1 .19)

The disadvantage of this system is that the indication is not linear, and there is no provision for making adjustments for system accuracy. The gauge is set to be accurate at the low and empty positions. The system is also subject to errors whenever the aircraft manoeuvres and the attitude changes.

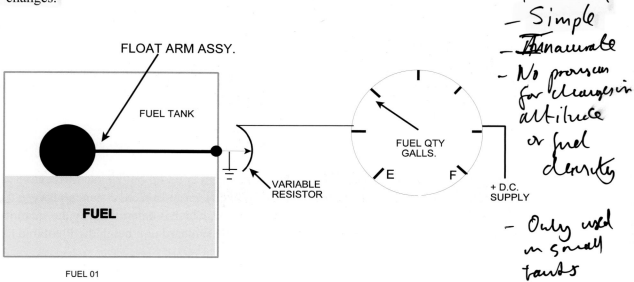

- 'Simple'
- Inaccurate
- No provision for changes in attitude or fuel density

- Only used on small tanks

figure 1.19 DC Float Type System

Capacitance Type Fuel Gauge System. In its basic form a capacitance system (fig 1.20) consists of a variable AC capacitor located in the fuel tank **(Tank Unit** fig 1.21 **)** an amplifier and a indicator. This system will indicate volume without the errors of the float system. If a correction voltage due to change in volume or temperature change is fed to the circuit, **Mass** of fuel will be indicated. A tank unit consists of two concentric aluminium alloy tubes which are held apart by pairs of insulating pins. The electrical connections are insulated and the unit is insulated from the tank. Co-axial connectors are used throughout.

Incorporated in the system are **Reference units,** which improve indication errors that would occur if the permittivity of the fuel changes from its normal value. The reference unit is located on the lower end of a tank unit and is always totally submerged in the unusable fuel level in the tank.

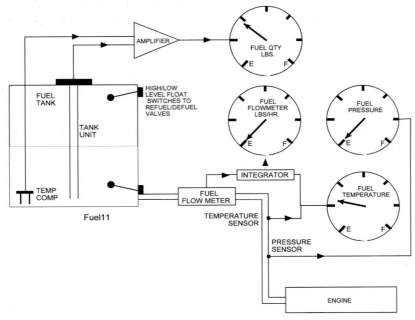

Figure 1.20

The principle of operation of the capacitance system is based on the use of fuel and air as the dielectric between parallel- plate capacitors of fixed area and a fixed distance between the plates. The only variable then being the ratio of fuel and air, which is determined by the quantity of fuel in the tank. Capacitance is measured in Farads, the standard unit being the Picofarad (10^{-12} F). The capacitance depends on the following .

$$\text{Capacitance} = \text{Relative Permittivity } \text{x } \frac{\text{Area of plates}}{\text{Distance between Plates.}} \quad \text{ or } \quad C = Er \text{ x } \frac{A}{D}$$

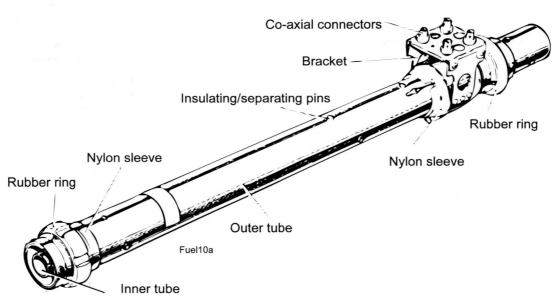

Figure 1.21 Capacitance Tank Unit

The **Relative Permittivity (Er)** is a number given as a ratio of the capacitance of a capacitor having a certain material as a dielectric to the capacitance of the same capacitor with a vacuum (or air) as its dielectric.

In a aircraft fuel system, the area of the plates and their distance apart remain constant, but the capacitance of the tank units will vary depending upon the level of fuel within the tanks.

The value of capacitance of a tank can be considered as two components. Ca (air) and Cf (fuel) and at any instance Tank Capacitance (Ct) =Ca + Cf. (fig 1 22).

presence of will drive indicators to full.

Typical Dielectric Values	
Material	**Relative Permittivity**
Impure water	0
Vacuum	1.0
Air	1.0006
Gasolene	1.95
Kerosene	2.10
Distilled Water	81.00

density Up = Er

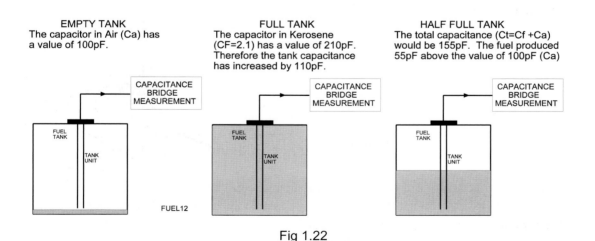

EMPTY TANK
The capacitor in Air (Ca) has a value of 100pF.

FULL TANK
The capacitor in Kerosene (CF=2.1) has a value of 210pF. Therefore the tank capacitance has increased by 110pF.

HALF FULL TANK
The total capacitance (Ct=Cf +Ca) would be 155pF. The fuel produced 55pF above the value of 100pF (Ca)

Fig 1.22

The pointer in the fuel quantity system measuring fuel by volume is directly related to:

1.   The change in fuel level.
2.   the ER- 1 value.

fuel contents indicated stay the same if there is an Ψ8 or ↑ in density due to tempre.

In an A. C. Capacitance circuit the Current is equal to the voltage over the capacitive reactance.

$$\mathbf{I} \text{ (current)} = \frac{\mathbf{V}}{\mathbf{Xc}} \quad \begin{array}{l} \text{(Voltage)} \\ \text{(Capacitive Reactance)} \end{array}$$

The capacitive reactance Xc is equal to $1/(2\pi\, f\, c)$. Since the voltage, frequency and 2π are constants, as the fuel level and capacitance change current in the circuit changes.

Changes in temperature of the fuel will effect its **density, volume and dielectric value (Er)**. A decrease in temperature would cause a decrease in volume , increase in density and increase in Er. The circuit is compensated for changes in temperature and can now indicate **Mass** of fuel which is of more value to the pilot.

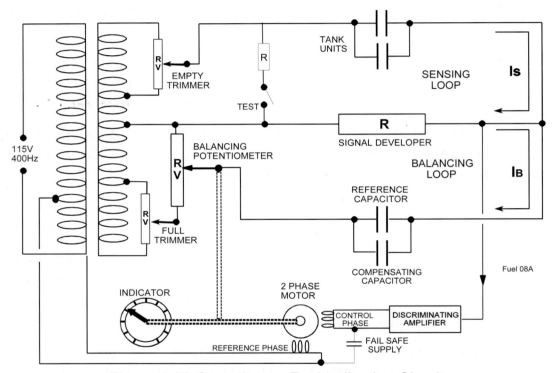

Figure 1.23 Capacitance Fuel Indicating Circuit

The system consists of a sensing and balancing loop circuit connected together by a signal developing resistor. When the fuel quantity is stable the current in the two loops are equal but anti-phase. No signal voltage is produced. As the fuel is consumed the capacitance and therefore the current in the sensing loop will decrease. The current in the balancing loop will then be greater and a signal voltage is produced across the signal developing resistor. The voltage is phase detected and amplified to drive an indicator. The system can be calibrated by the addition of trimming resistors.

As previously stated a more useful way of indicating fuel quantity is measurement by weight. For the calibration of gauges in terms of mass, an assumption is made that there is a constant relationship **Er** value and density (ρ) for a given sample of fuel at a given temperature.. Temperature of course is not a constant and a **Compensating Capacitor** circuit is incorporated in the system . This is fitted to the reference unit . The system will now sense changes in **Specific Gravity (SG)** of the fuel and so indicate mass.

The indicating system can incorporate an additional indicator know as the **'Fuel Totaliser'** which will indicate the sum of all the tank gauges. In the event of failure, the system will fail safe and drive the indicator slowly to the zero position. A test circuit is incorporated that when selected will simulate the emptying of the tank. When the switch is released the pointer should return to its original position. *ie full indication*

If water is present in the tanks it will cause errors with the indicating system. The capacitors in the sensing units are effectively shorted, and the indicator is driven beyond the full scale.

If the unusable fuel supply for any tank exceeds one gallon, or 5% of the tank capacity, whichever is greater, a **Red Arc** must be marked on its indicator extending from the calibrated zero reading to the lowest reading obtainable in flight. *ie fuel that cannot be used .*

As well as the quantity of fuel measured, the rate of fuel consumed and the instantaneous rate of fuel flow can be shown. The **Fuel Flowmeter** can display volume flow or mass flow. Flow is proportional to the square root of pressure drop across an orifice. A simple flowmeter can be a adaption of a pressure gauge. This is used on many light piston engine injection systems. Most modern engines use an electrical sensor, which utilise the change in torque or speed of a turbine (impeller). Typical construction consists of a light alloy casting with guide vanes and an electrical 'pick off 'coil. Inside the casting there is a helical vane impeller which has a magnet embedded in it. When the impeller rotates due to fuel flow, the pick off coils will have a sinusoidal signal induced in it, at a frequency proportional to the speed of the rotor, which is proportional to the rate of volume flow. To measure mass flow the signal is corrected for temperature. (fig 1.24)

The total consumption is obtained by integrating the rate of fuel consumption over time, this time is one hour. Units used for volume flow are **Gallons** and for mass flow **Pounds** or **Kilogrammes.** A flow meter that displays fuel consumed as well as fuel flow is broadly defined as a **Integrated** Flowmeter. The flow meter is located in the **High Pressure** fuel line to the fuel spray nozzles (burners).

✳ Having a capacitors means that the reading remains the same if altitude is change

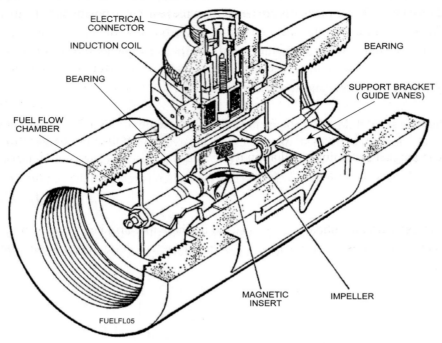

Figure 1.24 A typical Fuel Flowmeter

1.10   REMOTE (SIGNAL) TRANSMISSION SYSTEM.

To control an aircraft system may require the movement of a valve, flap or lever on the engine, the pilot may need to know the position of the control. Early systems had **Mechanical Feedback** to a position indicator in the flight deck. Most of the aircraft flying today employ remote indicating systems that can be either D.C or A.C operated. Whichever system is used each data transmission system employs a **Transmitter** located at the source to be measured and a **Receiver,** which acts on the information received.

The D.C. systems are called **Desynn** indicators. The desynn system is available in 24 or 12v aircraft systems. The indicating accuracy is approximately 2.5%, which is not good by modern standards. The desynn is an old British design and will only be found on British built aircraft. This system may take one of three forms, namely; **Rotary Motion, Linear Motion** and **Slab - Desynn.** The rotary motion arrangement may be considered as the basic system from which the others have been developed. These transmitter's can be used to indicate contents, pressures or movement. The system consists of a Transmitter, Transmission Leads and a Receiver.

Volumetric Flow meter = Volume

Mass Flow meter = Mass

The transmitter consist of a wiper arm which is supplied with D.C. and is positioned on a toroidal resistance. Three pick-offs are taken from the resistance positioned at 120 degrees apart. The current which flows from each pick-off is proportional to the relative position of the wiper arm on the toroidal resistance. The receiver consist of a magnetised pointer and three coils positioned 120 degrees to each other. Each coil is in series with one of the pick-offs on the toroidal resistance in the transmitter. The flow of current through each coil is therefore relative to the position of the wiper arm on the toroidal resistance. Each coil will produce a magnetic field, the strength and polarity of the field is dependant upon the amount and direction of the current flowing through the coil. The three magnetic fields will combine to form one resultant field. The magnetised pointer will align itself with this resultant field and thus the receiver can be calibrated to remotely reproduce the position of the wiper arm on the toroidal resistance. See fig 1.25

The desynn system has inherent errors caused by the wiper arm being in physical contact with the resistor, this causes inaccuracies due to friction and carbon contamination. The scale is also non-linear.

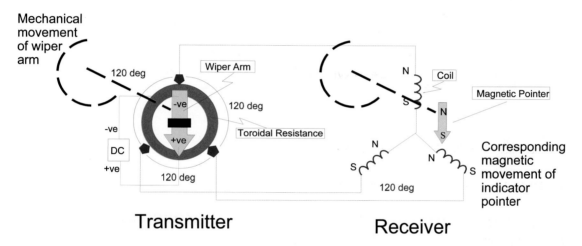

Figure 1.25 Desynn Data Transmission System

The A.C. systems are collectively called **Synchros** , and work on the principle of a variable transformer. The A.C. voltage used is 26 volt. In the illustration below (fig 1.26), as the input shaft is rotated the induce signal in the secondary winding can be varied in two ways.

a.   The magnitude of the induced signal will vary in direct relationship to the angle between the primary and secondary windings.

b.   The phasing of the induced signal will vary twice for one complete rotation of the primary winding.

The synchro device works on the principle described above, but to obtain more precise information it is necessary to modify the transformer design so that we have one rotor coil (primary), and three stator coils to produce the output (secondaries). It is much more accurate than the desynn system. For this reason it is used when precise position information is required.

The transmitter consist of three secondary coils positioned at 120 degrees to each other and a fourth primary coil placed within them. An A.C. current is passed through the primary coil which produces an alternating magnetic field. This alternating magnetic field causes an EMF to be induced in the three secondary coils. The value of the EMF induced in any one of the secondary coil is dependant upon its relative position to the primary coil.

The receiver also consists of three secondary coils positioned at 120 degrees to each other and a fourth primary coil placed within them. The receiver secondary coils are in series with the secondary coils of the transmitter. This closed circuit causes a current to flow through the coils.

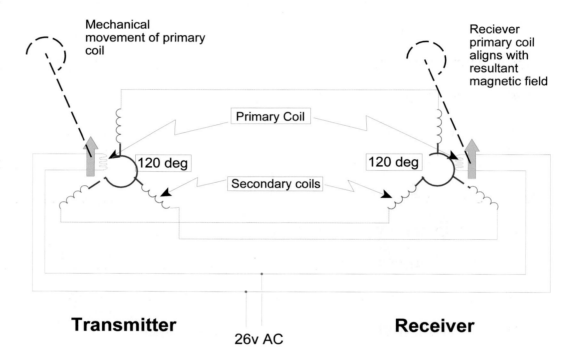

Figure 1.26 AC Synchro System

The value of the current is proportional to the value of the induced EMF in the associated transmitter secondary coil. The three magnetic fields produced by the secondary coils combine to produce a resultant field. The receiver primary coil is in series with the transmitter primary coil. This causes the receiver primary coil to align itself in the resultant magnetic field produced by the receiver secondary coils and thus remotely reproduce the position of the input.

1.11   FLIGHT HOUR METER.

Some aircraft indicate and record usage of the engines in flight. This information is used to determine engine condition. The flight hour meter can be coupled to an airborne sensor which becomes active at certain speeds.

CHAPTER TWO - ELECTRONIC INSTRUMENTATION

Contents   **Page**

2.1   ELECTRONIC INSTRUMENTS, ENG & A/FRAME SYSTEMS CONTROL . 2 - 1

2.2   EICAS . . . . 2 - 2

2.3   DISPLAY UNITS . . . . 2 - 3

2.4   DISPLAY MODES . . . . 2 - 4

2.5   OPERATIONAL MODE . . . . 2 - 4

2.6   STATUS MODE . . . . 2 - 4

2.7   MAINTENANCE MODE . . . . 2 - 5

2.8   DISPLAY SELECT PANEL . . . . 2 - 5

2.9   ALERT MESSAGES . . . . 2 - 7

2.10   DISPLAY UNIT FAILURE . . . . 2 - 9

2.11   DISPLAY SELECT PANEL FAILURE . . . . 2 - 10

2.12   STANDBY ENGINE INDICATOR . . . . 2 - 10

2.13   MAINTENANCE CONTROL PANEL . . . . 2 - 11

2.14   ELECTRONIC CENTRALIZED AIRCRAFT MONITORING (ECAM) . . . . . 2 - 13

2.15   DISPLAY UNITS . . . . 2 - 14

2.16   DISPLAY MODES . . . . 2 - 14

2.17   THE FLIGHT PHASE-RELATED MODE . . . . 2 - 15

2.18   ADVISORY (MODE AND STATUS) . . . . 2 - 15

2.19   FAILURE-RELATED MODE . . . . 2 - 16

2.20   THE FOURTH MODE (MANUAL),
       THE AIRCRAFT SYSTEM DISPLAY MODE . . . . 2 - 17

2.21   THE 'ECAM' CONTROL PANEL . . . . 2 -18

2.22   SYSTEM TESTING . . . . 2 - 20

       ECAM AND EICAS QUESTIONS . . . . 2 -21

Primary Engine
Indications:

- EPR
- N1
- EGT

2.1   ELECTRONIC INSTRUMENTS FOR ENGINE AND AIRFRAME SYSTEMS CONTROL.

The display of the parameters associated with engine performance and airframe systems control by means of Cathode Ray Tube type display units has, like those of flight instrument systems, become a standard feature of many types of aircraft.

The display units form part of two principal systems designated as Engine Indicating and Crew Alerting System (**EICAS**), and Electronic Centralized Aircraft Monitoring (**ECAM**) system. These systems were first introduced in Boeing 757 and 767 aircraft and the Airbus A310 respectively.

EICAS

At the time of their introduction there were differing views on the approach to such operating factors as flight deck layouts and crews' controlling functions, the extent to which normal, alerting and warning information should be displayed, and in particular, whether engine operating data was required to be displayed for the whole of a flight, or only at various phases.

In respect of **EICAS**, engine operating data is displayed on its CRT units, thereby eliminating the need for traditional instruments.

This data, as well as that relevant to other systems, is not necessarily always on display but in the event of malfunctions occurring at any time, the flight crew's attention is drawn to them by an automatic display of messages in the appropriate colours.

The **ECAM** system, on the other hand, displays systems' operation in checklist and schematic form, and as this was a concept based on the view that engine data needed to be displayed during the whole of a flight, traditional instruments were retained in the Airbus A310.
It is of interest to note, however, that in subsequent types produced by this manufacturer, e.g. A320, the ECAM system is developed to include the display of engine data in one of its display units.

2.2   EICAS.

The basic **EICAS** system comprises two display units, a control panel, and two computers supplied with analog and digital signals from engine and system sensors as shown in the schematic functional diagram of Figure2.1.

The computers are designated 'Left' and 'Right', and only one is in control at a time; the other is on 'standby', and in the event of failure it may be switched in either manually or automatically. Operating in conjunction with the EICAS system are discrete caution and warning lights, standby engine indicators and a remotely-located panel for selecting maintenance data displays.

The system provides the flight crew with information on primary engine parameters (full-time), with secondary engine parameters and advisory / caution / warning alert messages displayed as required.

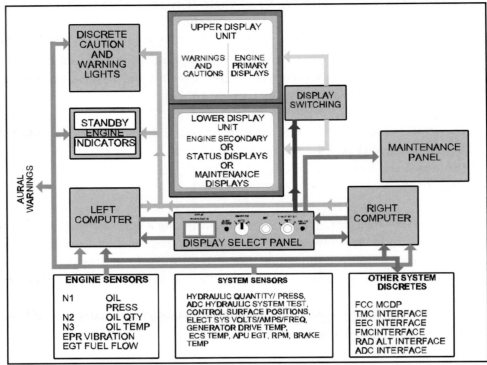

Figure 2.1. The EICAS Functional Diagram.

2.3   DISPLAY UNITS

The display units provide a wide variety of information relevant to engine operation, and operation of other automated systems, and they utilize colour shadow mask CRTs and associated card modules whose functions are identical to those of the EFIS units. The units are mounted one above the other as shown in Figure 2.2.

The **upper unit** displays the primary engine parameters, N_1 speed, EGT, and warning and caution messages.

In some cases this unit can also display EPR, depending on the type of engines installed and on the methods used to process data by the thrust management control system.

The **lower unit** displays secondary engine parameters, i.e. N_2 speed, fuel flow, oil quantity, pressure and temperature, and engine vibration. In addition, the status of non-engine systems, e.g. flight control surface positions, hydraulic system, APU, etc., can also be displayed together with aircraft configuration and maintenance data.

The rows of 'V's shown on the upper display unit only appear when secondary information is being displayed on the lower unit.

Seven colours are produced by the CRTs and they are used as follows:

White
All scales, normal operating range of pointers, digital readouts.

Red
Warning messages, maximum operating limit marks on scales, and digital readouts.

Green
Thrust mode readout and selected EPR / N_1 speed marks or target cursors.

Blue
Testing of system only.

Yellow
Caution and advisory messages, caution limit marks on scales, digital readouts.

Magenta
During in-flight engine starting, and for cross-bleed messages.

Cyan
Names of all parameters being measured (e.g. N_1 oil pressure, TAT etc) and status marks or cues.

The displays are selected according to an appropriate display selection mode.

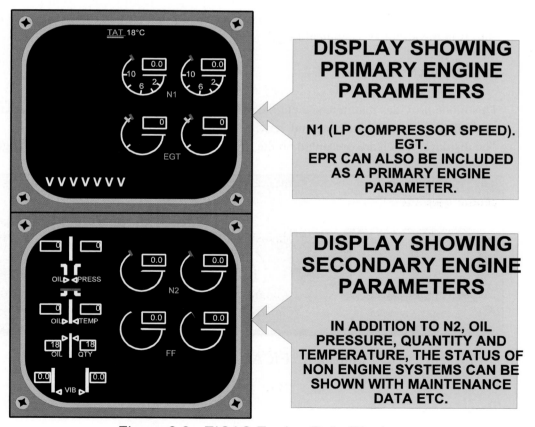

Figure 2.2. EICAS Engine Data Displays.

2.4   DISPLAY MODES

EICAS is designed to categorize displays and alerts according to function and usage, and for this purpose there are three modes of displaying information: (i) **operational**, (ii) **status** and (iii) **maintenance**.

Modes (i) and (ii) are selected by the flight crew on the display select panel, while mode (iii) is selected on the maintenance panel which is for the use of ground engineering staff only.

2.5   OPERATIONAL MODE.

The **operational mode** displays the engine operating information and any alerts required to be actioned by the crew in flight.

Normally only the upper display unit presents information, the lower one remains blank and can be selected to display secondary information as and when required.

2.6   STATUS MODE.

When selected, the **status mode** displays data to determine the dispatch readiness of an aircraft, and is closely associated with details contained in an aircraft's Minimum Equipment List.

The display shows positions of the flight control surfaces in the form of pointers registered against vertical scales, selected sub-system parameters, and equipment status messages on the lower display unit. Selection is normally done on the ground either as part of pre-flight checks of dispatch items, or prior to shut-down of electrical power to aid the flight crew in making entries in the aircraft's Technical Log.

2.7   MAINTENANCE MODE.

This mode provides maintenance engineers with information in five different display formats to aid them in trouble-shooting and verification testing of the major sub-systems.

The displays, which are presented on the lower display unit, are not available in flight.

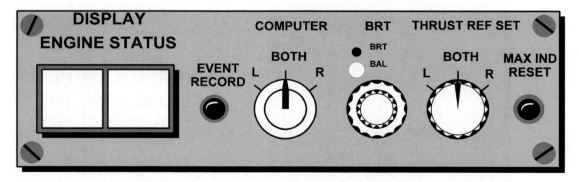

Figure 2.3. EICAS Display Select Panel.

2.8   DISPLAY SELECT PANEL.

This panel, as indicated in Figure 2.3, permits control of EICAS functions and displays and can be used both in flight and on the ground. It is normally located on the centre pedestal of an aircraft's flight deck, and its controls are as follows:

a)   **Engine Display Switch**. This is of the momentary-push type for removing or presenting the display of secondary information on the lower display unit.

b)   **Status Display Switch.** Also of the momentary-push type, this is used to display the status mode information referred to earlier, on the lower display unit. The display is known as a 'status page', an example of which is shown in Figure 2.4.

c)   **Event Record Switch.** This is of the momentary-push type and is used in the air or on the ground, to activate the recording of fault data relevant to the environment control system, electrical power, hydraulic system, performance and APU. Normally if any malfunction occurs in a system, it is recorded automatically (called an 'auto event') and stored in a non-volatile memory of the EICAS computer. The push switch also enables the flight crew to record a suspected malfunction for storage, and this is called a 'manual event'. The relevant data can only be retrieved from memory and displayed when the aircraft is on the ground and by operating switches on the maintenance control panel.

Figure 2.4. Status Mode Display.

d) **Computer Select Switch.** In the 'AUTO' position it selects the left, or primary, computer and automatically switches to the other computer in the event of failure. The other positions are for the manual selection of left or right computers.

e) **Displays Brightness Control.** The inner knob controls the intensity of the displays, and the outer knob controls brightness balance between displays.

f) **Thrust Reference Set Switch.** Pulling and rotating the inner knob positions the reference cursor on the thrust indicator display (either EPR or N_1) for the engine(s) selected by the outer knob.

g) **Maximum Indicator Reset Switch.** If any one of the measured parameters e.g. oil pressure, EGT, should exceed normal operating limits, this will be automatically alerted on the display units. The purpose of the reset switch is to clear the alerts from the display when the excess limits no longer exist.

2.9 ALERT MESSAGES.

The system continuously monitors a large number of inputs (typically over 400) from engine and airframe systems' sensors and will detect any malfunctioning of systems.
If this should occur, then appropriate messages are generated and displayed on the upper display unit in a sequence corresponding to the level of urgency of action to be taken.
Up to 11 messages can be displayed, and at the following levels:

Level A - Warning requiring immediate corrective action. They are displayed in red. Master warning lights are also illuminated, and aural warnings (eg fire bell) from a central warning system are given.

Level B - Cautions requiring immediate crew awareness and possible action. They are displayed in amber, and also by message caution lights. An aural tone is also repeated twice. _yellow._

Level C - Advisories requiring crew awareness. Also displayed in amber. No caution lights or aural tones are associated with this level.

The messages appear on the top line at the left of the display screen as shown in Figure 2.5.

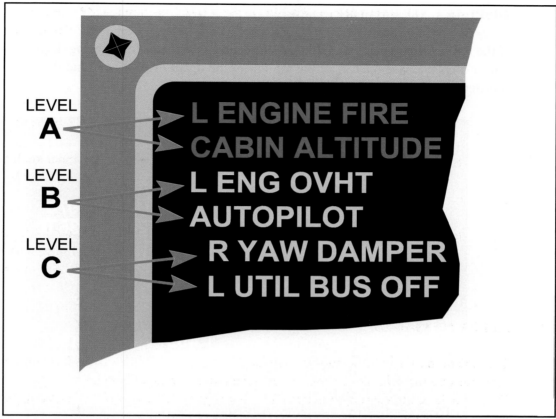

Figure 2.5. Alert Message Levels.

In order to differentiate between a caution and an advisory, the latter is always indented one space to the right.

The master warning and caution lights are located adjacent to the display units together with a 'CANCEL' switch and a 'RECALL' switch. Pushing the 'CANCEL' switch removes only the caution and advisory messages from the display; the warning messages cannot be cancelled.

The 'RECALL' switch is used to bring back the caution and advisory messages into the display. At the same time, the word '**RECALL**' appears at the bottom of the display.

A message is automatically removed from the display when the associated condition no longer exists. In this case, messages which appear below the deleted one each move up a line.

When a new fault occurs, its associated message is inserted on the appropriate line of the display.

This may cause older messages to move down one line. For example, a new caution message would cause all existing caution and advisory messages to move down one line.

If there are more messages than can be displayed at one time, the whole list forms what is termed a 'page', and the lowest message is removed and a page number appears in white on the lower right side of the list.

If there is an additional page of messages it can be displayed by pushing the 'Cancel' switch. Warning messages are carried over from the previous page.

2.10   DISPLAY UNIT FAILURE.

If the lower display unit should fail when secondary information is being displayed on it, an amber alert message appears at the top left of the upper display unit, and the information is transferred to it as shown in Figure 2.6.

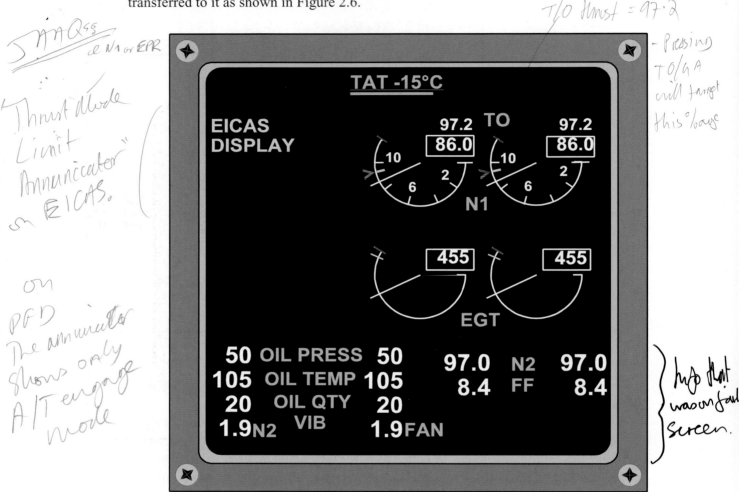

Figure 2.6. The 'Compact Format' Display.

The format of this display is referred to as 'compact', and it may be removed by pressing the 'ENGINE' switch on the display select panel. Failure of a display unit causes the function of the panel 'STATUS' switch to be inhibited so that the status page format cannot be displayed.

2.11   DISPLAY SELECT PANEL FAILURE.

If this panel fails the advisory message 'EICAS CONTROL PANEL' appears at the top left of the upper display unit together with the primary information, and the secondary information automatically appears on the lower display unit. The 'CANCEL / RECALL' switches do not operate in this failure condition.

Used if EICAS system or display fails

2.12   STANDBY ENGINE INDICATOR.

This indicator provides primary engine information in the event that a total loss of EICAS displays occurs.

As shown in Figure 2.7, the information relates to N_1 and N_2 speeds and EGT and the displays are of the LCD type. Operating limit values are also displayed.

On old EICAS system.

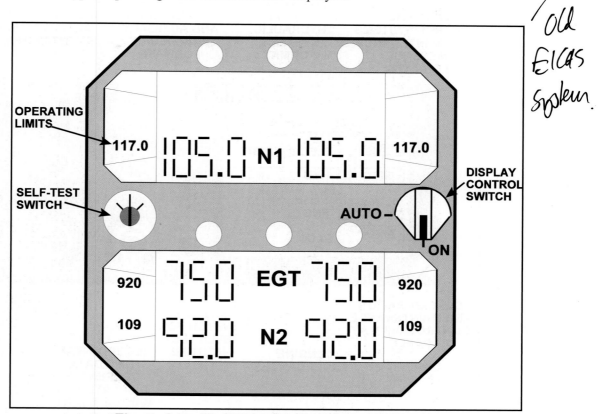

Figure 2.7. The Standby Engine Indicator.

The display control switch has two positions, 'ON' and 'AUTO'.

In the 'ON' position the displays are permanently on. In the 'AUTO' position the internal circuits are functional, but the displays will be automatically presented when the EICAS displays are lost due to failure of both display units or both computers.

The test switch has three positions, and is spring-loaded to a centre off position. It is screwdriver-operated and when turned to the left or right, it changes over power supply units within the indicator to ensure that they each provide power for the displays. The test can be performed with the display control switch in any position.

2.13   MAINTENANCE CONTROL PANEL.

The maintenance control panel is for use by maintenance engineers for the purpose of displaying maintenance data stored in system computer memories during flight or ground operations. The layout of the panel and the principal functions of each of the controls are shown in Figure 2.8.

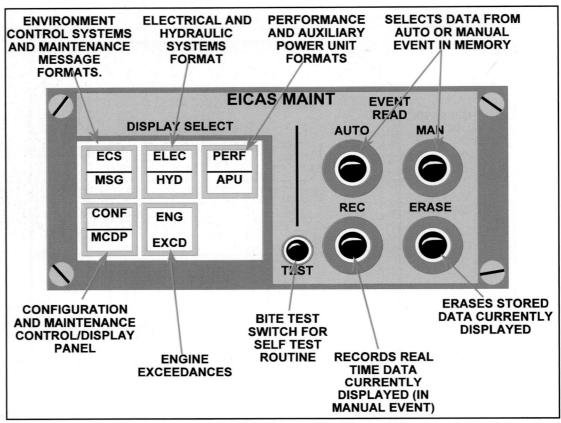

Figure 2.8. The Maintenance Control Panel.

The five display select switches are of the momentary-push type, and as each one is activated, a corresponding maintenance display page appears on the lower display unit screen. The pages are listed together with two example displays in Figure 2.9.

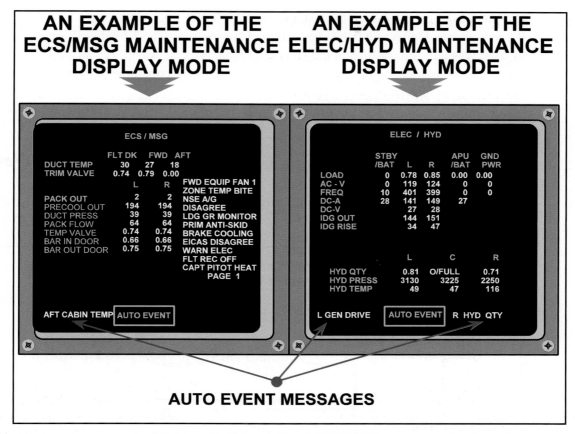

Figure 2.9. Examples of Maintenance Mode Displays.

The upper display unit displays data in the 'compact' format (see Figure 2.6.) with the message 'PARKING BRAKE' in the top left of the screen.

System failures which have occurred in flight and have been automatically recorded ('auto event') in computer memory, and also data entered as a 'manual event', can be retrieved for display by means of the 'event record' switch on the panel. A self-test of the whole system, which can only be activated when an aircraft is on the ground and the parking brake set, is performed by means of the 'TEST' switch on the maintenance control panel.

When the switch is momentarily pressed, a complete test routine of the system, including interface and all signal-processing circuits, and power supplies, is automatically performed. For this purpose an initial test pattern is displayed on both display units with a message in white to indicate the system being tested i.e. 'L or R EICAS' depending on the setting of the selector switch on the display select panel.

During the test, the master caution and warning lights and aural devices are activated, and the standby engine indicator is turned on if its display control switch is at 'AUTO'.

The message 'TEST IN PROGRESS' appears at the top left of display unit screens and remains in view while testing is in progress.

On satisfactory completion of the test, the message 'TEST OK' will appear.

If a computer or display unit failure has occurred, the message 'TEST FAIL' will appear followed by messages indicating which of the units has failed.

A test may be terminated by pressing the 'TEST' switch a second time or, if it is safe to do so, by releasing an aircraft's parking brake.

Test termination will allow the display units to revert to showing their normal primary and secondary information displays.

2.14 ELECTRONIC CENTRALIZED AIRCRAFT MONITORING (ECAM). *A300 also*

The units comprising this system, and as originally developed for the Airbus A310, are shown in the functional diagram of Figure 2.10.

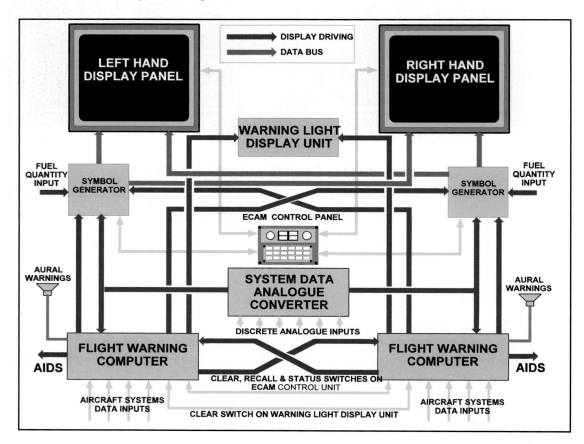

Figure 2.10. ECAM System Functional Diagram.

As far as the processing and display of information are concerned, the ECAM system differs significantly from EICAS in that data relates essentially to the primary systems of the aircraft, and is displayed in check-list and pictorial or synoptic format.

Engine operating data is displayed by conventional types of instruments as noted in the introduction to this chapter. Other differences relate to display locations and selection of system operating modes.

Different from EICAS

2.15   DISPLAY UNITS.

These units may be mounted side-by-side; the left-hand unit is dedicated to information on the status of systems, warnings and corrective action in a sequenced check-list format, while the right-hand unit is dedicated to associated information in pictorial or synoptic format.

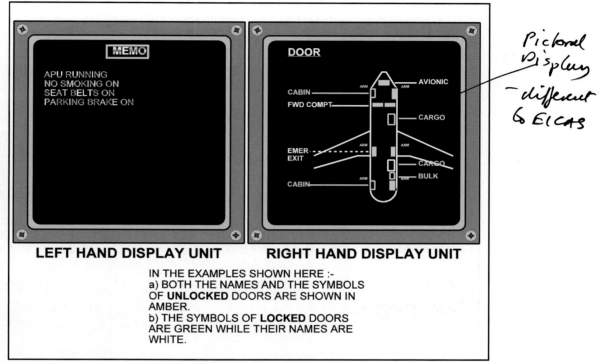

Pictorial Display — different to EICAS

IN THE EXAMPLES SHOWN HERE :-
a) BOTH THE NAMES AND THE SYMBOLS OF **UNLOCKED** DOORS ARE SHOWN IN AMBER.
b) THE SYMBOLS OF **LOCKED** DOORS ARE GREEN WHILE THEIR NAMES ARE WHITE.

Figure 2.11. Pre-Flight Phase-Related Mode Display.

2.16   DISPLAY MODES.

There are four display modes, three of which are automatically selected and referred to as:-

      a)   Flight Phase-related
      b)   Advisory (mode and status)
      c)   Failure-related modes.

The fourth mode is manual

      d)   Aircraft System Display.

2.17   THE FLIGHT PHASE-RELATED MODE.

In normal operation the automatic 'flight phase-related mode' is used, and in this case the displays are appropriate to the current phase of aircraft operation, i.e. pre-flight, take-off, climb, cruise, descent, approach, and after landing.

An example of a pre-flight phase is shown in Figure 2.11, the left-hand display unit displays an advisory memo mode, and the right-hand unit displays a diagram of the aircraft's fuselage, doors, and arming of the escape slides deployment system.

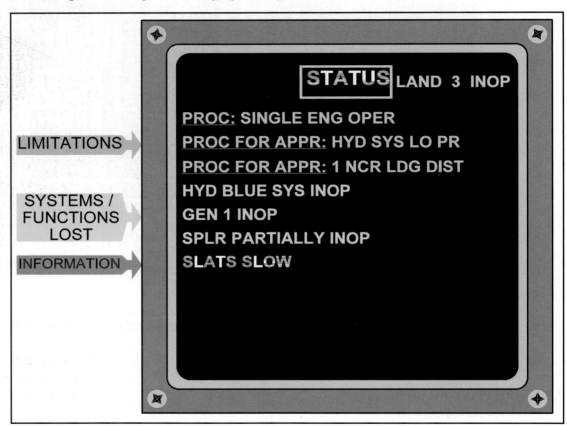

Figure 2.12. An Example of the Status Display.

2.18   ADVISORY (MODE AND STATUS).

Status messages, which are also displayed on the left-hand display unit, provide the flight crew with an operational summary of the aircraft's condition, possible downgrading of autoland capability, and as far as possible, indications of the aircraft status following all failures except those that do not affect the flight. The contents of an example display are shown in Figure 2.12.

2.19   FAILURE-RELATED MODE.

The failure-related mode takes precedence over the other two automatic modes and the manual mode.

An example of a display associated with this mode is shown in Figure 2.13.

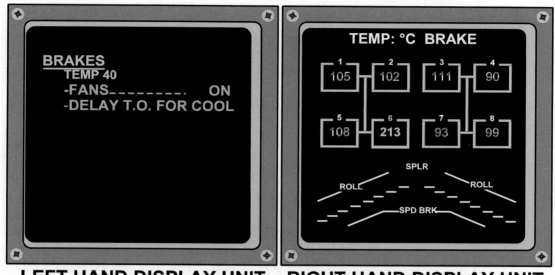

LEFT HAND DISPLAY UNIT   RIGHT HAND DISPLAY UNIT

Figure 2.13. The Failure-Related Mode Display.

In this case, while taxying out for take-off, the temperature of the brake unit on the rear right wheel of the left main landing gear bogie has become excessive.

A diagram of the wheel brake system is immediately displayed on the right-hand display unit, and simultaneously the left-hand unit displays corrective action to be taken by the flight crew. In addition, an aural warning is sounded, and a light (placarded 'L/G WHEEL') on a central warning light display panel is illuminated.

As the corrective action is carried out, the instructions on the left-hand display are replaced by a message in white confirming the result of the action. The diagram on the right-hand display unit is appropriately 'redrawn'.In the example above, the 'failure related mode' displaces warning relates to a single system, and by convention such warnings are signified by underlining the system title displayed.

In cases where a failure can affect other sub-systems, the title of the sub-system is shown 'boxed', as for instance in the display shown in Figure 2.14.

Warnings and the associated lights are cleared by means of 'CLEAR' push-button switches on either the ECAM control panel or a warning light display panel.

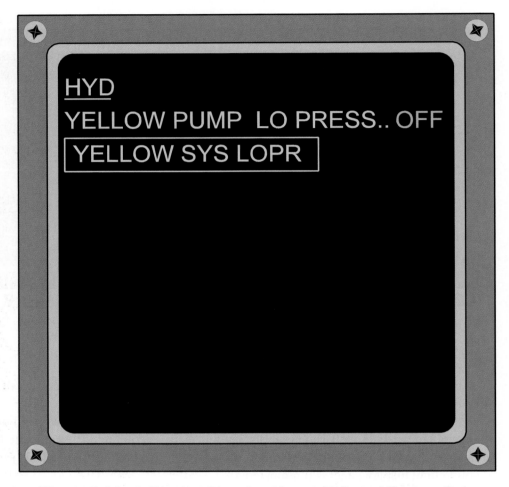

Figure 2.14. A Display Showing How a Failure Affects a Sub-System.

2.20 THE FOURTH MODE (MANUAL), THE AIRCRAFT SYSTEM DISPLAY MODE.

This mode permits the selection of diagrams related to any one of 12 of the aircraft's systems for routine checking, and also the selection of status messages provided no warnings have been 'triggered' for display. The selections are made by means of illuminated push-button switches on the system control panel.

2.21   THE 'ECAM' CONTROL PANEL.

The layout of the 'ECAM' control panel is shown in Figure 2.15., all switches, with the exception of those for display control, are of the push-button, illuminated caption type.

- **SGU Selector Switches**. These control the respective symbol generator units, and the lights are off in normal operation of the system. The 'FAULT' caption is illuminated amber if a failure is detected by an SGU's internal self-test circuit. Releasing a switch isolates the corresponding SGU, and causes the 'FAULT' caption to extinguish, and the 'OFF' caption to illuminate white.

- **Synoptic Display Switches**. These permit individual selection of synoptic diagrams corresponding to each of 12 systems, and illuminate white when pressed. A display is automatically cancelled whenever a warning or advisory occurs.

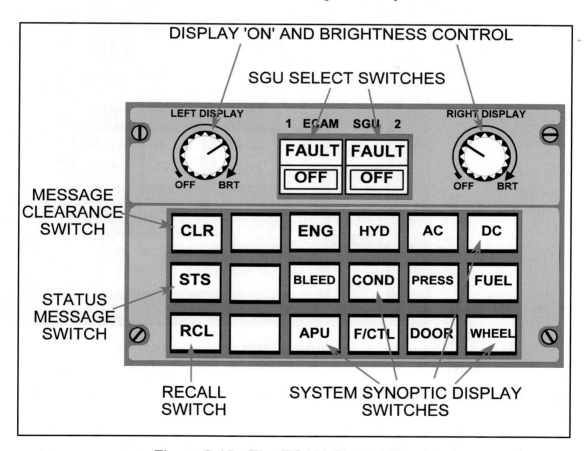

Figure 2.15. The ECAM Control Panel.

- **CLR Switch**. The light in the switch is illuminated white whenever a warning or status message is displayed on the left-hand display unit. The Switch is pressed to clear messages.

- **STS Switch**. The Status Switch permits manual selection of an aircraft status message if no warning is displayed; illuminated white. Pressing the switch also causes the 'CLR' switch to illuminate. A status message is suppressed if a warning occurs or if the 'CLR' switch is pressed.

- **RCL Switch**. The Recall Switch enables previously cleared warning messages to be recalled provided the failure conditions which initiated them still exist. Pressing the switch also causes the CLR switch light to illuminate. If a failure no longer exists the message 'NO WARNING PRESENT' is displayed on the left-hand display unit.

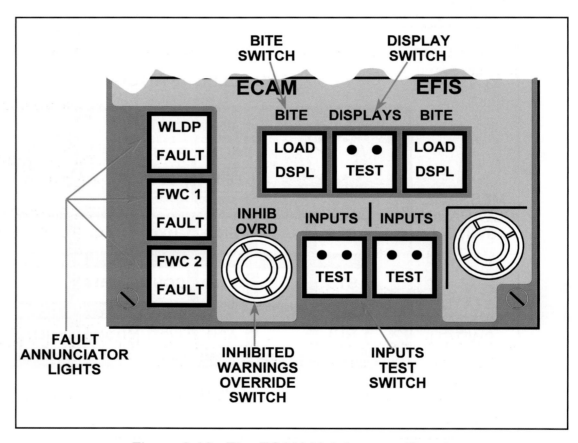

Figure 2.16. The ECAM Maintenance Panel.

Not needed in detail

Built in Test Capability

2.22   SYSTEM TESTING.

Each flight warning computer of the system is equipped with a monitoring module which automatically checks data acquisition and processing modules, memories, and the internal power supplies as soon as the aircraft's main power supply is applied to the system.
A power-on test routine is also carried out for correct operation of the symbol generator units. During this test the display units remain blank.

In the event of failure of the data acquisition and processing modules, or of the warning light display panel, a 'failure warning system' light on the panel is illuminated.
Failure of a computer causes a corresponding annunciator light on the maintenance panel, captioned '**FWC FAULT**', to illuminate.

A symbol generator unit failure causes a '**FAULT**' caption on the appropriate push-button switch on the system control panel to illuminate.

Manual self-test checks for inputs and displays are carried out from a maintenance panel shown in Figure 2.16.

When the '**INPUTS**' switch is pressed, a '**TEST**' caption is illuminated white and most of the inputs to each computer are checked for continuity.

Any incorrect inputs appear in coded form on the left-hand display unit. The right-hand display unit presents a list of defective parameters at the system's date analog converter.

The diagrams of systems appear on the right-hand display unit with the caption 'TEST' beside the system title, as each corresponding push-button switch is pressed. Calibrated outputs from the data analog converter are also displayed.

Any defective parameters are identified by a flag display.

A '**DISPLAY**' push-button switch is provided on the maintenance panel. When pressed it initiates a check for correct operation of the Symbol Generator Units (SGU's), and the optical qualities of the display units by means of a test pattern display.

The '**LOAD**' caption is illuminated each time a failure is memorized in the relevant test circuits of the SGUs.

The annunciator lights on the maintenance panel illuminate white simultaneously with a failure warning system light on the central warning light display panel when a corresponding computer fails.

The '**INHIB OVRD**' switch enables inhibited warnings to be displayed.

ECAM and EICAS

1.   With an Engine Indicating and Crew Alerting System:

   a)   the secondary display will show continuously the engine primary instruments.
   b)   the primary display unit will continuously show the engine primary instruments such as N1 N2 N3 and maybe oil pressure.
   c)   the primary engine display will continuously show the engine primary instruments such as N1 EGT and maybe EPR.
   d)   the primary engine instruments are N1 EGT and EPR and are on the primary and secondary display units.

2.   The electronic engine display system with three automatic modes is:

   a)   the Electronic Centralised Aircraft Monitor, with the fourth mode manual.
   b)   the Electronic Centralised Aircraft Monitor, with the fourth mode flight phase related or manual.
   c)   the Engine Indicating and Crew Alerting System, with the fourth mode manual
   d)   the Engine Indicating and Crew Alerting System, with the fourth mode a manual cross over from the Electronic Centralised Aircraft Monitor System.

3.   The display modes for the Engine Indicating and Crew Alerting System are:

   a)   operational, status and maintenance of which status and maintenance are automatic.
   b)   flight phase related, advisory and failure related.
   c)   operational, status and maintenance.
   d)   operational, flight phase related and status.

4.   With an Engine Indicating and Crew Alerting System lower display unit failure:

   a)   a compact message will only appear on the upper display unit.
   b)   a compact message will only appear on the central display unit.
   c)   a compact message will appear both on the upper display unit and the captains Electronic Flight Instrument System.
   d)   a compact message will appear on the upper display unit when the status button is pressed on the control panel.

5.   With an Electronic Centralised Aircraft Monitoring type of system:

   a)   the display units have two control panels and with any system failure the control will be from the port control box only.
   b)   the left display unit shows warning and corrective action in a check list format.
   c)   the two display units are only fitted side by side.
   d)   the left display unit shows the synoptic format and the right or lower unit shows the corrective format.

6.   The Engine Indicating and Crew Alerting System alert messages are shown on the upper display unit in three forms:

   a)   Level 'C' are warnings that require immediate corrective action.
   b)   Level 'A' are cautions that require immediate crew awareness and possible action.
   c)   Level 'B' are advisories requiring crew awareness.
   d)   and these messages appear on the top left of the upper display unit.

7.   The electronic engine display system will have:

   a)   one primary and one secondary display unit for an EICAS and a change over selector to change to the ECAM mode if necessary.
   b)   two display units for ECAM and three display units for EICAS.
   c)   either EICAS or ECAM but not both.
   d)   an interconnect to the EFIS symbol generators in an emergency.

8.   In an Engine Indicating and Crew Alerting System if both displays fail then the following information is displayed on the standby engine indicator:

   a)   N1, EGT, N2.
   b)   N1, EGT, EPR.
   c)   N2, EGT, EPR.
   d)   N4, EGT, EPR.

9.   The Electronic Centralised Aircraft Monitor (ECAM) type of system shows a:

   a)   checklist format on the left display panel and schematic form always automatically on the right display unit.
   b)   checklist format on the left display unit and the right, or lower display unit , a diagram or synoptic format.
   c)   synoptic format on the left display unit and a warning and corrective action display on the right or lower display unit.
   d)   continuous primary engine display on the primary display unit.

10.   The electronic display system that has three automatic modes plus one manual is the:

   a)   Electronic Management and Control Section.
   b)   Electronic Indication and Fail Safe system.
   c)   Electronic Indication and Crew Alert system.
   d)   Electronic Centralised Aircraft Monitor.

11.   A boxed message shown as an electronic engine display system fault is one that:

   a)   affects other sub-systems and is used in the Engine Indicating and Crew Alerting System.
   b)   does not affect any other system.
   c)   does not affect any other system and is used in the Engine Indicating and Aircraft Monitor system.
   d)   affects other sub-systems and is used in the Electronic Centralised Aircraft Monitor type of system.

12.   An engine fire indication on an electronic engine display is shown:

   a)   on the primary display panel in red.
   b)   on the secondary display panel in amber.
   c)   on both the Electronic Flight Instrument System and Engine Indicating and Crew Alerting System secondary panels.
   d)   only on the Flight Management Computer primary panel.

13.   An engine electronic system which in normal conditions of flight shows only the primary engine instruments is:

   a)   An EICAS system with EPR, EGT and N2 shown on the primary instruments.
   b)   An ECAM system with the primary engine instruments displayed on the lower screen.
   c)   An EICAS system with the primary engine instruments displayed on the primary screen, the secondary screen being blank.
   d)   An ECAM system with the primary engine instruments displayed on the primary screen, the left screen being blank.

ECAM & EICAS

QUE	1	2	3	4	5	6	7	8	9	10
ANS	C	A	C	A	B	D	C	A	B	D
REF										

QUE	11	12	13							
ANS	D	A	C							
REF										

JAAatpl
JOINT AVIATION AUTHORITIES

Theoretical Training Manuals

Revised Edition

AIRCRAFT GENERAL KNOWLEDGE 4

INSTRUMENTATION
SPECIMEN QUESTIONS & EXAMINATION PAPER

This learning material has been approved as JAA compliant by the United Kingdom Civil Aviation Authority

CIVIL AVIATION AUTHORITY

OXFORD
Aviation Training
Succeed through our experience™

SECTION FIVE – SPECIMEN QUESTIONS

Contents

Page

SPECIMEN QUESTIONS – FLIGHT INSTRUMENTS……………..……………….. 1

ANSWERS TO SPECIMEN QUESTIONS...……………………..…………. …27

SPECIMEN QUESTIONS – AUTOMATIC FLIGHT………………..……………….29

ANSWERS TO SPECIMEN QUESTIONS...……………………..…………. …39

SPECIMEN QUESTIONS – WARNING & RECORDING……………..……………41

ANSWERS TO SPECIMEN QUESTIONS...……………………..…………. …47

SPECIMEN QUESTIONS – ENGINE INSTRUMENTS……………..……………49

ANSWERS TO SPECIMEN QUESTIONS...……………………..…………. …59

SPECIMEN EXAM PAPER...……………………………………..……………….61

ANSWERS TO SPECIMEN EXAM PAPER...……………….……………. …73

EXPLANATIONS TO SPECIMEN EXAM PAPER...……….…………….. …75

SPECIMEN QUESTIONS

1   A 2 axis gyro, measuring vertical changes will have:

   a   one degree of freedom, vertical axis
   b   two degrees of freedom, vertical axis
   c   one degree of freedom, horizontal axis
   d   two degrees of freedom, horizontal axis

2   The properties of a gyro are:

        1.   mass
        2.   rigidity
        3.   inertia
        4.   precession
        5.   rotational speed

   a.   1,2, & 3
   b.   2 & 4
   c.   2 & 3
   d.   1 & 3

3   An aircraft fitted with a DRMC upon landing in a northerly direction will indicate:

   a   no change
   b   oscillation about north
   c   a turn towards east
   d   a turn towards west

4   Which of the following will effect a direct reading compass?

        1.   ferrous metals
        2.   non-ferrous metals
        3.   electrical equipment

   a.   1 only
   b.   1 & 3
   c.   1 & 2
   d.   all 3

5   A vibrator may be fitted to an altimeter to overcome:

   a   friction
   b   hysterysis
   c   lag
   d   pressure error

6   An aircraft is flying at constant indicated altitude, over a warm airmass. The altimeter reading
     will be:

   a   correct
   b   greater than the real altitude
   c   less than the real altitude
   d   oscillating around the correct altitude

1

7   The machmeter consists of:

        a   an airspeed indicator with mach scale
        b   an airspeed indicator with an altimeter capsule
        c   an altimeter corrected for density
        d   a VSI and altimeter combined

8   CAS is IAS corrected for:

        a   position and instrument error
        b   instrument, pressure and density error
        c   relative density only
        d   compressibility

9   A DGI has;

        a   one degree of freedom & a horizontal spin axis
        b   two degrees of freedom & a vertical spin axis
        c   two degrees of freedom & a horizontal spin axis
        d   one degree of freedom & a vertical spin axis

10   An aircraft is flying at an indicated altitude of 16,000ft. The outside air temperature is -30^0 C
        What is the true altitude of the aircraft?

        a   16,200 ft
        b   15,200 ft
        c   18,600 ft
        d   13,500 ft

11   The main cause of error in a DRMC is:

        a   parallax in the rose
        b   turning
        c   magnetic deviation
        d   latitude

12   QNH is:

        a   the airfield barometric pressure
        b   the setting that will give zero indication on the airfield
        c   the equivalent sea level pressure at the airfield
        d   the setting that will indicate airfield height

13   What is the Schuler period?

        a   21 minutes
        b   84 minutes
        c   1 oscillation in azimuth
        d   63 minutes

14   The vertical reference of a data generation unit is:

      a   horizontal axis with 1 degree of freedom
      b   vertical axis with 1 degree of freedom
      c   horizontal axis with 2 degree of freedom
      d   vertical axis with 2 degree of freedom

15   The torque motor of a gyro stabilised magnetic compass:

      a   precesses the directional gyro
      b   takes its input from the flux valve
      c   moves the heading pointer
      d   moves the Selsyn stator

16   A factor giving an error on a direct indicating compass would be:

      a   crosswinds – particularly on east/west headings
      b   parallax due to oscillations of the compass rose
      c   acceleration on east/west headings
      d   turning through east/west headings

17   A rate integrating gyro is used in:

      1.   inertial attitude unit
      2.   autopilot system
      3.   stabiliser servo mechanism system
      4.   inertial navigation unit
      5.   rate of turn indicator

      a   1, 2, 3, 4, & 5
      b   1 & 4
      c   2, 3, & 5
      d   2, 3, & 4

18   The errors of a DGI are:

      1.   earth rate
      2.   transport wander
      3.   banking when pitched up
      4.   annual movement of poles
      5.   mechanical problems

      a   2, 3, & 5
      b   3, 4, & 5
      c   1, 2, 3, & 5
      d   all 5

19   An Air Data Computer (ADC) obtains altitude from:

      a.   outside air temperature
      b.   barometric data from static source
      c.   time elapsed for signal to travel to and return from the earth
      d.   difference between absolute and dynamic pressure

20   If the needle and the ball of a Turn & Slip indicator both show right, what does it indicate:

    a.   turn to left & too much bank
    b.   turn to right & too much bank
    c.   turn to left & too little bank
    d.   turn to right & too little bank

21   What formula gives the total temperature (T_T) from the static temperature (T_S):

    a $T_T = T_S (1 + 0.2 \, M^2)$
    b $T_T = T_S (1 + 0.2 \, KrM^2)$
    c $T_T = T_S / (1 + 0.2 \, KrM^2)$
    d $T_T = T_S (1 - 0.2 \, M^2)$

22   The Inertial Strapdown Unit of an IRS is programmed with co-ordinates during alignment in order to:

    a   establish the trihedron with reference to the earth
    b   establish true or magnetic heading
    c   check the function of the laser gyros
    d   compensate for aircraft movement

23   When descending through an isothermal layer at constant CAS, what does the TAS do?

    a   increase at a linear rate
    b   increase at an exponential rate
    c   remain the same
    d   decrease

24   What is V_{MO} calculated from:

    a.   CAS
    b.   TAS
    c.   COAS
    d.   EAS

25   Descending from FL390 at maximum groundspeed, what will the pilot be limited by:

    a. V_{MO} initially then M_{MO} at a specified altitude
    b. M_{MO} initially then V_{MO} at a specified altitude
    c. V_{NE} initially then M_{MO} at a specified altitude
    d. V_{NO} initially then V_{NE} at a specified altitude

26   At constant weight, regardless of altitude, an aircraft always lifts off at a constant:

    a   EAS
    b   TAS
    c   ground speed
    d   CAS

27 V_{FE} is the maximum speed that:

 a. the flaps can be operated
 b. the flaps may be extended in the take-off configuration
 c. the flaps may be extended in the landing configuration
 d. the flaps may be extended in a specified configuration

28 The white arc on the ASI indicates:

 a. V_{S1} at the lower end and V_{LE} at the upper end
 b. V_{S0} at the lower end and V_{LE} at the upper end
 c. V_{S0} at the lower end and V_{FE} at the upper end
 d. V_{S1} at the lower end and V_{FE} at the upper end

29 An ASI circuit consists of pressure sensors. The Pitot Probe measures:

 a total pressure & static pressure
 b dynamic pressure
 c static pressure
 d total pressure

30 Mach number is defined as the ratio of:

 a IAS to LSS
 b TAS to LSS
 c CAS to LSS
 d EAS to LSS

31 If a pitot source is blocked in an ASI, and the drain hole is blocked, but the static source is open, what will happen?

 a ASI reading goes to zero
 b ASI under reads
 c ASI over reads
 d ASI behaves like an altimeter

32. In a turn at constant angle of bank ... the rate of turn is:

 a. independent of weight and proportional a to TAS
 b. dependant on weight and inversely proportional to TAS
 c. independent of weight and inversely proportional a to TAS
 d. dependant on weight and proportional to TAS

33. The Turn Indicator is a useful gyroscopic instrument. When used in association with an attitude indicator will show:

 1. angular velocity about the yaw axis
 2. direction of turn
 3. angular velocity about true vertical axis
 4. speed of turn

 a 1, & 3
 b 2, & 3
 c 3, & 4
 d 1, & 2

34   If an aircraft, fitted with a DRMC, takes off on a westerly heading, in the northern
      hemisphere, the DRMC will indicate:

      a   a turn to the north
      b   oscillates about west
      c   no turn
      d   a turn to south

35   When turning through 90^0 at constant attitude and bank, a classic Artificial Horizon indicates:

      a   nose up and correct angle of bank
      b   attitude and bank angle are correct
      c   nose up and bank angle too low
      d   nose up and bank angle too high

36   The factors which will affect a Turn Indicator are:

            1.   angle of bank
            2.   aircraft speed
            3.   aircraft weight

      a.   all 3
      b.   1 & 2
      c.   1 & 3
      d.   2 & 3

37   To obtain heading information from a Gyro Stabilised platform, the gyros should have:

      a   1 degree of freedom and a horizontal axis
      b   1 degree of freedom and a vertical axis
      c   2 degrees of freedom and a horizontal axis
      d   2 degrees of freedom and a vertical axis

38   What are the inputs to the ADC?

            1.   OAT
            2.   dynamic pressure
            3.   TAT
            4.   static pressure
            5.   electric power
            6.   pitot pressure
            7.   AOA

      a.   1, 2, 5 & 6
      b.   all 7
      c.   3, 4 & 6
      d.   3, 4, 5, 6, & 7

39   The properties of a Turn Indicator are:

        1.   One degree of freedom
        2.   two degrees of freedom
        3.   two springs connected to the aircraft frame
        4.   spin axis in the longitudinal plane
        5.   spin axis parallel to the yaw axis
        6.   spin axis horizontal

    a   1, & 6
    b   2, & 5
    c   1, & 4
    d   2, & 6

40   A gravity erector system corrects errors on a:

    a.   DGI
    b.   artificial horizon
    c.   turn indicator
    d.   RIMC

41   In a Gyro magnetic Compass the flux gate transmits information to the:

    a   heading indicator
    b   amplifier
    c   error detector
    d   erecting system

42   V_{NO} is the max. speed which:

    a   the pilot can fully deflect the controls.
    b   should only be exceeded in still air and with caution.
    c   should never be exceeded.
    d   must not be exceeded for flap/gear extension

43   If while level at FL 270, at a constant CAS, temperature falls, what happens to the Mach No.

    a   decreases.
    b   increases.
    c   remains constant.
    d   increases depending on whether temp >ISA or < ISA.

44   If the static vent becomes blocked on an unpressurised a/c, what could you do?:

    a   open the window.
    b   break the VSI glass.
    c   compute altitude mathematically.
    d   Select standby pitot source

45   What does the "barbers pole" on an ASI indicate?:

    a V_{MO} & altitude.
    b V_{MO} & temperature.
    c V_{NO}
    d V_{NE}

46   On board a/c, true altitude shown from:

      a   standard atmosphere.
      b   pressure altitude.
      c   density altitude.
      d   temperature altitude.

47   On a turn and slip indicator, needle to the left and ball to the right indicates:

      a   turn to the right, not enough bank.
      b   turn to the left, too much bank.
      c   turn to the left, not enough bank.
      d   turn to the right, too much bank.

48   What is density altitude:

      a   altitude in the standard atmosphere at which the prevailing density is equal to the density in the standard atmosphere
      b   pressure altitude corrected for prevailing temp.
      c   temperature altitude.
      d   pressure corrected

49   A radio altimeter is:

      a   ground based and measures true altitude.
      b   ground based and measures true height.
      c   a/c based and measures true altitude.
      d   a/c based and measures true height.

50   An a/c is travelling at 120 kts, what angle of bank would be required for a rate 1(one) turn:

      a. 30^0
      b. 12^0
      c. 18^0
      d. 35^0

51   An a/c is travelling at 100 kts forward speed on a 3^0 glideslope. What is its rate of descent?:

      a   500 ft/min.
      b   300 ft/min.
      c   250 ft/min.
      d   600 ft/min.

52   If the pitot tube is leaking (and the pitot drain is blocked) in a non-pressurised a/c, the ASI will:

      a   under-read.
      b   over-read.
      c   over-read in the climb, under-read in the descent.
      d   under-read in the climb, over-read in the descent.

53   An RMI rose is mechanically stuck on 090 degrees. The ADF pointer indicates 225 degrees.
        What is the relative bearing to the beacon?

        a   225 degrees.
        b   135 degrees.
        c   Cannot be determined.
        d   000 degrees.

54   Using a classic Artificial Horizon, the a/c performs a right turn through 270 degrees at a
        constant angle of bank and rate of turn. The indication is:

        a   Nose up, too much bank.
        b   Nose up, not enough bank.
        c   Nose up, wings level.
        d   Bank and pitch correct.

55   In a DGI what error is caused by the gyro movement relative to the earth?

        a.   Earth Rate
        b.   Transport Wander
        c.   real wander
        d.   latitude error

56   In a right turn while taxiing, the correct indications are:

        a   Needle left, ball right.
        b   Needle left, ball left.
        c   Needle right, ball right.
        d   Needle right, ball left.

57   An aircraft is taking of on a runway heading 045^0, in still air, with a compass having 0^0
        deviation. The runway is on an agonic line. What are the northerly turning errors (northern
        hemisphere)?

        a.   compass moves to less than 045^0
        b.   compass moves to more than 045^0
        c.   compass stays on 045^0 if wings are kept level
        d.   compass remains on 045^0

58   True heading can be converted into magnetic heading using a compass and:

        a   A map with isogonal lines.
        b   A map with isoclinal lines.
        c   A deviation card.
        d   A deviation curve

59   At sea level ISA, TAS:

        a   Equals CAS
        b   Is greater than CAS
        c   Is less than CAS

60   What will the altimeter read if the layers beneath the aircraft are all colder than standard?

      a   read lower than the real altitude
      b   read higher then the real altitude
      c   read the correct altitude
      d   readings will fluctuate

61   The flux valve in a RIMC

      a   is supplied with AC current (usually 487.5 Hz).
      b   is fed with DC.
      c   is made of perm-alloy magnetic steel.
      d   has its own self exciter unit.

62   The indications of a machmeter are independent of:

      a   Temperature (OAT)
      b   Static Pressure
      c   Differential static and dynamic Pressure
      d   Dynamic Pressure

63   An artificial horizon has:

      a   1 degree of freedom and an horizontal axis.
      b   2 degree of freedom and an horizontal axis.
      c   1 degree of freedom and a vertical axis.
      d   2 degree of freedom and a vertical axis.

64   The rigidity of a gyro is improved by:

      a   Increasing RPM and concentrating the mass on the periphery of the rotor.
      b   Increasing RPM and concentrating the mass at the hub of the rotor.
      c   Decreasing RPM and concentrating the mass on the periphery of the rotor.
      d   Decreasing RPM and concentrating the mass at the hub of the rotor.

65   What is the speed of sound at sea level ISA

      a   644kts.
      b   661kts.
      c   1059 kts
      d   583kts.

66   What is the speed of sound at 25,000 ft and -28 degrees C.

      a   624kts.
      b   618kts.
      c   601kts
      d   610kts.

67   What is the speed of sound at 30,000 ft and -40 degrees C.

      a   562kts.
      b   595kts.
      c   590kts.
      d   661kts.

68   If a constant CAS is maintained in a climb, what happens to the mach number

     a.   remains constant
     b.   increases
     c.   decreases

69   A compass swing is used to:

     a   align compass north with magnetic north.
     b   align compass north with true north.
     c   align magnetic north with true north.
     d   get true north and lubber line aligned.

70   The TAT probe measures TAT by:

     a   TAT = SAT + kinetic heating.
     b   TAT = SAT - heating due to compressibility.
     c   TAT = SAT - kinetic heating.
     d   TAT = SAT + heating due to compressibility.

71   If a pitot tube and drains are blocked at altitude by icing, during a descent the ASI will:

     a   read constant airspeed.
     b   under read.
     c   over read.
     d   show zero.

72   An IRS is aligned when turned on so as to:

     a   calculate the computed trihedron.
     b   establish true and magnetic north.
     c   establish position relative to true north and magnetic north.
     d   establish magnetic north.

73   The advantages of an ADC over a traditional pitot - static system (list)

     1.   Position and compressibility correction.
     2.   reduced lag
     3.   ability to supply many instruments
     4.   ability to act as an altimeter following failure.
     5.   (apparently all the answer bar one had 4 as a correct answer)

     a.   1, 2 & 3
     b.   1, 2 & 4
     c.   2, 3 & 4
     d.   1, 3 & 4

74.   The frequency band used for a Radio Altimeter is:

     a.   SHF
     b.   VHF
     c.   UHF
     d.   LF

75   What is the purpose of the latitude nut in a DGI?

      a.   to correct for latitude error
      b.   to correct for transport wander
      c.   to correct for earth rate
      d.   to correct for coriolis error

76   Total Air Temp is always _____ than Static Air Temp and the difference varies with _____.

      a   warmer, altitude.
      b   colder, altitude.
      c   warmer, CAS.
      d   colder, CAS.

77   In a slightly banked turn, the turn needle will indicate:

      a   roll rate.
      b   rate of yaw.
      c   angular velocity about the vertical axis.
      d   rate of pitch.

78   The Primary Flying Display (PFD) displays information dedicated to:

      a.   engine data and alarms
      b.   flight path
      c.   weather radar
      d.   aircraft systems

79   What are the inputs to the FMS?

      1.   Radio Aids
      2.   Engine Parameters
      3.   Air Data
      4.   Route Data
      5.   Terminal Data
      6.   Operating Data

      a.   1, 3, 4 & 6
      b.   2, 3, 4, & 5
      c.   All of the above
      d.   1, 2, 3 & 6

80.   What are the upper and lower limits of the yellow arc on an ASI?

      a.   lower limit V_{LO} and upper limit V_{NE}
      b.   lower limit V_{LE} and upper limit V_{NE}
      c.   lower limit V_{NO} and upper limit V_{NE}
      d.   lower limit V_{LO} and upper limit V_{LE}

81.   What does the blue line on an ASI of a twin propeller engined aircraft indicate?

     a. V_{YSE}

     b. V_{NO}

     c. V_{FE}

     d. V_{MCA}

82.   The gravity erecting device on a vertical gyro is used on which instrument;

     a.   directional gyro unit

     b.   turn indicator

     c.   artificial horizon

     d.   gyromagnetic device

83.   In a VSI lag error is improved by:

     a.   bi-metalic strip

     b.   two

     c.   use of an accelerometer system

     d.   return spring

84.   An aircraft fitted with a DRMC is landing in a southerly direction, in the Southern Hemisphere. What indications will be seen on the DRMC?

     a. 180^0 turn to east

     b.   no apparent turn

     c.   turn to west

85.   What is the maximum drift of a gyro, due to earth rate:

     a. 90^0 per hour

     b. 180^0 per hour

     c. 15^0 per hour

     d. 5^0 per hour

86.   An aircraft is flying a true track of 360^0 from 5^0 south to 5^0 north. What is the change in apparent wander rate:

     a. 0^0 per hour

     b. $+5^0$ per hour

     c. -5^0 per hour

     d.   depends upon groundspeed

87.   When turning through 180^0 at constant attitude and bank, a classic Artificial Horizon indicates:

     a   nose up and correct angle of bank

     b   attitude and bank angle are correct

     c   nose up and bank angle too low

     d   nose up and bank angle too high

88.   What is the Schuler period?

        a.   48 minutes
        b.   84 seconds
        c.   48 seconds
        d.   84 minutes

89.   Mach number is defined as:

        a.   The ratio of pitot pressure to dynamic pressure
        b.   The ratio of static pressure to dynamic pressure
        c.   The ratio of dynamic pressure to static pressure
        d.   The ratio of static pressure to pitot pressure

90.   You are flying at a constant FL 290 and constant mach number. The total temperature increases by 5^0. The CAS will:

        a.   remain approximately constant
        b.   increase by 10 kts
        c.   decrease by 10 kts
        d.   will increase or decrease depending on whether you are above or below ISA.

91.   An aircraft turns from south-west to south-east when situated at 45^0N, what heading should you roll out on if using a DRMC?

        a. 130^0
        b. 115^0
        c. 140^0
        d. 155^0

92.   What is SAT?

        a.   relative temperature measured in K
        b.   differential temperature measured in K
        c.   relative temperature measured in ^{0}C
        d.   ambient temperature measured in ^{0}C

93.   If an aircraft climbs, at constant mach No, in ISA conditions what happens to the TAS and the CAS?

        a.   TAS increases and CAS increases
        b.   TAS remains constant and CAS decreases
        c.   TAS decreases and CAS increases
        d.   TAS decreases and CAS decreases

94.   Where is the earth rate wander, and the transport wander of a gyro equal to zero?

        a.   North Pole
        b.   Equator
        c. 45^0 N
        d. 45^0 S

95.   What happens when the static pressure supply, to an altimeter, becomes blocked during a descent?

     a.   reduces to zero
     b.   over reads
     c.   under reads
     d.   indicates altitude at which blockage occurred

96.   What happens when the static vent supplying an ASI is blocked, and the ram air inlet remains clear?

     a.   ASI acts opposite to an altimeter
     b.   ASI always over reads / reads a higher value
     c.   ASI always under reads / reads a lower value
     d.   ASI acts like an altimeter

97.   In a left turn while taxiing, the correct indications are:

     a   Needle left, ball right.
     b   Needle left, ball left.
     c   Needle right, ball right.
     d.   Needle right, ball left.

98. V_{LO} is defined as:

     a.   the maximum speed at which to fly with the landing gear retracted
     b.   the maximum speed at which the landing gear may be retracted or extended
     c.   the maximum speed at which to fly with the landing gear extended
     d.   the minimum speed at which to fly with the landing gear extended

99. V_{NE} is defined as:

     a.   the speed which must not be exceeded in still air, or without caution
     b.   the speed above which the landing gear may not be extended
     c.   the speed which must never be exceeded
     d.   the maximum speed for normal flap extension to be selected

100.   In a left turn, the ball of the turn co-ordinator is out to the right, what corrective action is required?

     a.   more right rudder
     b.   less right bank
     c.   more left bank
     d.   more left rudder

101.   In a gyro magnetic compass, where does the torque motor get its information from?

     a.   the flux gate
     b.   error detector
     c.   the rotor gimbal
     d.   amplifier

102.   If an aircraft is descending at constant mach number, and the total air temperature remains constant, what happens to the CAS?

a.   remains constant
b.   decreases
c.   increases
d.   increases if the temperature is below standard, and decreases if the temperature is above standard

103.   What are the advantages of a laser gyro compared to a conventional gyro?

a.   has a longer cycle life
b.   takes longer to set up/ spin up
c.   uses more power
d.   takes longer to align

104.   A machmeter measures the ratio of;

a.   pitot pressure to static pressure
b.   (pitot pressure minus static pressure) to static pressure
c.   pitot pressure times static pressure
d.   pitot pressure to (static pressure times pitot pressure)

105.   Which instrument has a 2° rotation in the horizontal axis?

a.   artificial horizon
b.   flux detector
c.   directional gyro indicator
d.   turn indicator

106.   The maximum drift error sensed by an uncompensated DGI will be:

a. 15° per hour
b. 30° per hour
c. 45° per hour
d. 60° per hour

107.   The green arc on the ASI is used to identify which speed range:

a. V_{SO} to V_{NO}
b. V_{S1} to V_{FE}
c. V_{S1} to V_{NO}
d. V_{S1} to V_{LO}

108.   Pressure altitude may be defined as:

a.   lowest forecast regional pressure
b.   pressure measured in the standard atmosphere
c.   altitude indicated with QFE set on the altimeter
d.   altitude indicated with QNH set on the altimeter

109.   What is the effect on an altimeter reading if variations in static pressure occur near to the pressure source?

    a.   a change in hysterysis error
    b.   a change in the instrument error
    c.   a change in the position error
    d.   a change in the compressibility error

110.   What is the value of the angle of magnetic dip at the South Pole?

    a. 0^0
    b. 45^0
    c. 90^0
    d. 60^0

111.   A standby artificial horizon must have the following properties:

            1.   a remote gyro
            2.   its own power supply
            3.   only to be used in emergency
            4.   its own gyro
            5.   one for each certified pilot

    a.   all the above
    b.   1,3, & 5
    c.   2, 3, & 4
    d.   2 & 4

112.   During a descent at constant CAS and total temperature, the mach no:

    a.   increases
    b.   remains constant
    c.   increases if SAT is greater than standard temperature and decreases if it is lower
    d.   decreases

113.   The single most significant item which makes a servo altimeter more accurate is:

    a.   electromagnetic pick-off
    b.   logarithmic scale
    c.   temperature compensated spring
    d.   multiple pointers

114.   Which of the following gyro instruments has one degree of freedom?

    a.   artificial horizon
    b.   turn indicator
    c.   directional gyro
    d.   slaved gyro compass

115.   If a large aircraft is slide slipped to starboard, and the port static vent is blocked, what will the altimeter read?

    a.   under read
    b.   read correctly
    c.   Over read
    d.   fluctuate

116.   Mach number is determined from: (P_T = total pressure, P_S = static pressure)

    a. $(P_T + P_S) \times P_T$
    b. $(P_T - P_S) \times P_S$
    c. $(P_T \times P_S) \times P_T$
    d. $(P_T - P_S) / P_S$

117   The right static vent is blocked, when the aircraft yaws to the right. Does the altimeter:

    a.   Over read
    b.   under read
    c.   unaffected
    d

118   If the radio altimeter fails:

    a.   height information disappears
    b.   aural warning given
    c.   radio alt flag, red lamp, and aural warning given
    d.   radio alt flag and red lamp activates.

119   During a descent at a constant mach number, there is an increase of total temperature by 5^0. What effect does this have on CAS?

    a.   remains almost constant
    b.   increases if SAT is more than standard and decreases if SAT is less than standard
    c.   increases by 10 kts
    d   decreases by 10 kts

120   V_{NO} is defined as:

    a.   maximum structural cruising speed
    b.   never exceed speed
    c.   manoeuvring speed
    d.   maximum operating speed

121   If the left static vent is blocked, and the right static vent is clear. What will the altimeter read if the aircraft maintains constant level?

    a.   read correctly whatever the situation
    b.   under read
    c.   if side slipping to the left, altimeter will over read.
    d.   if side slipping to the right, altimeter will over read.

122   An aircraft is flying at constant indicated altitude, over a cold airmass. The altimeter reading will be:

     a.   greater than the real altitude
     b   standard altitude
     c   same as the real altitude
     d.   less than the real altitude

123.   The machmeter compares: (P_T = total pressure, P_S = static pressure)

     a. $(P_T - P_S)$ to P_T
     b. $(P_T + P_S)$ to P_S
     c. $(P_T - P_S)$ to P_S
     d. P_T to P_S

124.   From where does the air data computer (ADC) obtain aircraft altitude?

     a.   OAT probe
     b.   dynamic – absolute ambient pressure
     c.   absolute barometric sensor on aircraft fuselage
     d.

125.   An aircraft is accelerating to take-off on a runway with a QDM of 045^0. Which way does the DRMC move, if the aircraft is in the Northern Hemisphere?

     a.   less than 45^0
     b.   more than 45^0
     c.   correct if wings are level
     d.   correct

126.   When turning right onto north, through 90^0, what heading on your DIC should you roll out on, if the aircraft is in the Northern Hemisphere?

     a. 020^0
     b. 360^0
     c. 340^0
     d. 320^0

127.   What does a radio altimeter, for an aircraft in the landing configuration, measure:

     a.   height of aircraft wheels above the ground
     b.   height of the aircraft above the ground
     c.   altitude of the aircraft
     d.   altitude of the aircraft wheels

128   Why is a servo altimeter better than a sensitive altimeter/

     a.   it has a pick-off coil
     b.   it is more accurate at low level
     c.   it has ambient pressure in the capsule
     d.   it is fitted with a knocking device

129.   In an altimeter what is fed to: the capsule (i) and to the case (ii)?

      a.   (i) vacuum   (ii) static input
      b.   (i) static input   (ii) vacuum
      c.   (i) pitot input   (ii) static input
      d.   (i) total input   (ii) ambient input

130.   What principle does the radio altimeter work on?

      a.   pulse modulation
      b.   amplitude modulation
      c.   pulse modulation and carrier wave
      d.   frequency modulation and carrier wave

131.   What is indicated on the ASI when the static vent blocks during a descent?

      a.   under reads
      b.   reads correctly
      c.   over reads
      d.   reads zero

132.   A rate integrating gyro is used in:

      a.   inertial attitude unit
      b.   autopilot system
      c.   inertial navigation system
      d.   a rate of turn indicator

133.   The error in a Directional Gyro due to the earth's rotation, at a mean latitude of 45^0 N, will cause the spin axis to move by:

      a. 10.6^0 Clockwise
      b. 10.6^0 Anti-clockwise
      c. 7.6^0 Clockwise
      d. 7.6^0 Anti-clockwise

134.   What are the components of a Ring Laser Gyro?

      a.   mirrors and 2 cavities
      b.   2 anodes and 2 cathodes
      c.   2 beams of laser light
      d.   horizontal gryo axis and 1 degree of freedom

135   Where on the earth's surface is the earth rate drift of a DGI equal to 15.04^0 per hour?

      a. 15^0
      b. 30^0
      c. 0^0
      d. 90^0

136.   If you maintain the same CAS and Altitude (FL270), and the temperature increases, what happens to the Mach No?

     a.   increases at an exponential rate
     b.   decreases at an exponential rate
     c.   remains the same
     d.   increases

137.   If CAS is kept constant, what happens to the Mach No?

     a.   as the altitude increases the mach No will increase
     b.   as the altitude increases the mach No will decrease
     c.   as the temperature increases the mach No will increase
     d.   as the temperature decreases the mach No will decrease

138.   The pendulous type correction detector fitted to the DGI provides:

     a.   torque on the sensitive axis
     b.   two torque motors on the horizontal axis
     c.   pendulous internal nozzle on the outer gimbal
     d.   one torque motor

139.   An aircraft is fitted with two altimeters. One is corrected for position error, the other is not corrected for position error.

     a.   ATC will receive erroneous information of flight level
     b.   at high speed the non-compensated altimeter will show a lower altitude
     c.   provided that the ADC is working normally, there will be no error to either altimeter
     d.   at high speed the non-compensated altimeter will show a higher altitude

140.   Density altitude is defined as:

     a.   the altitude of the airfield elevation corrected for Lapse Rate
     b.   the altitude reading on the altimeter which has QNH set on it
     c.   the altitude corresponding to the standard atmosphere compensated for ambient density
     d.   the altitude showing on the altimeter with the lowest regional QNH set

141.   The pitot tube of an ASI gives a direct reading of:

     a.   static pressure
     b.   total & static pressure
     c.   total pressure
     d.   dynamic pressure

142.   When descending from FL230 to FL50 at maximum speed, the limitations which apply are:

     a. V_{MO}
     b. V_{MO} then M_{MO}
     c. M_{MO} then V_{MO}
     d. M_{MO}

143.   The pressure measured at the forward face of the Pitot probe is:

      a.   dynamic pressure
      b.   static pressure
      c.   total pressure
      d.   total pressure + static pressure

144.   What has inputs from the flux valve;

      a.   error detector
      b.   heading indicator
      c.   amplifier
      d.   precession motor

145.   Machmeter readings are subject to which of the following errors;

      a.   density error
      b.   setting error
      c.   temperature error
      d.   position/pressure error

146.   Sound propagates at a speed which depends only on;

      a.   density
      b.   temperature
      c.   temperature & pressure
      d.   pressure

147.   What aircraft system uses a frequency of 4,400 MHz?

      a.   SSR
      b.   radio altimeter
      c.   weather radar
      d.   ATC radar

148.   A low altitude Radio Altimeter, used in precision approaches, has the following characteristics:

      1.   1540MHz to 1660 MHz range
      2.   pulse transmissions
      3.   frequency modulation
      4.   height range between 0 and 5,000ft
      5.   an accuracy of +/- 2ft between 0 and 500ft

      a.   1, 4 and 5
      b.   3 and 4
      c.   3 and 5
      d.   2, 3 and 5

149.   A modern low altitude Radio Altimeter uses the principle of:

   a.   pulse modulated waves, with the difference between the transmitted and received waves
        displayed on a circular screen.
   b.   Frequency modulated waves, where the difference between the transmitted wave and the
        received wave is measured.
   c.   Wave modulation, with frequency shift due to Doppler effect of the ground reflected
        wave being measured
   d.   Triangular wave, with the frequency shift of the ground reflected wave being measured

150.   The frequencies used in a low altitude Radio Altimeter are:

   a.   5 GHz to 6 GHz
   b.   5400 MHz and 9400 MHz
   c.   4200 MHz to 4400 MHz
   d.   2700 MHz to 2900 MHz

151.   The difference between Magnetic North and True North can be derived by:

   a.   deviation curve
   b.   deviation card
   c.   map with isoclinic lines
   d.   map with isogonal lines

152.   A direction gyro gets its directional information from:

   a.   air data computer
   b.   direct reading magnetic compass
   c.   flight director
   d.   flux valve

153.   What is the principle of operation of a VSI:

   a.   differential pressure across a capsule
   b.   total pressure in a capsule
   c.   static pressure in a capsule
   d.   dynamic pressure in a capsule

154.   In a Remote Indicating Compass, what component feeds the Amplifier?

   a.   gyro precession signal
   b.   flux valve
   c.   annunciator
   d.   error detector

155.   An aircraft turns right, through 90^0, onto North, at 48N, using a direct indicating compass.
        The aircraft is turning at rate 2. What heading should the aircraft roll out on?

   a. 010^0
   b. 030^0
   c. 330^0
   d. 350^0

156.   What is the normal operating range of a low altitude Radio Altimeter?

   a.   0 to 2,500ft
   b.   50ft to 2500ft
   c.   0 to 10,000ft
   d.   0 to 7,500ft

157.   What is a radio altimeter used for?

   a.   to determine aircraft height above mean sea level
   b.   to determine aircraft height above ground level
   c.   to determine pressure altitude
   d.   to determine aircraft altitude

158.   Why must Latitude and Longitude be inserted into an IRS?

   a.   to determine the aircraft position relative to the earth
   b.   to check the IRS position with the Flight Management System
   c.   to enable the levelling procedure to commence
   d.   to determine the accuracy of the alignment

159.   An aircraft is flying a true track of 360^0 from 5^0 south to 5^0 north. What is the average apparent wander rate:

   a. 0^0 per hour
   b. $+5^0$ per hour
   c. -5^0 per hour
   d.   depends upon groundspeed

160   You commence a rate 2 turn from south-east to south-west, in the Northern Hemisphere. On what heading do you stop the turn?

   a. 240^0
   b. 255^0
   c. 235^0
   d. 205^0

161   A directional gyro is valid only for a short period of time. The causes of this inaccuracy are;

         1.   earth rotation
         2.   longitudinal accelerations
         3.   a/c motion over the earth
         4.   mechanical defects
         5.   gyro mass

   a.   1, 3 & 5
   b.   1, 3 & 4
   c.   1, 2 & 3
   d.   all of the above

162   A V_{MO} / M_{MO} alarm system, on an airline aircraft, is fitted with an aneroid capsule which is:

    a.   subjected to static pressure and an anemometer subjected to dynamic pressure
    b.   subjected to dynamic pressure and an anemometer subjected to static pressure
    c   subjected to static pressure and an anemometer subjected to static pressure
    d   subjected to dynamic pressure and an anemometer subjected to dynamic pressure

163   An aircraft, in the southern hemisphere, is decelerating to land on a westerly heading. The direct reading magnetic compass will indicate:

    a.   an apparent turn to north
    b.   an apparent turn to south
    c.   correctly
    d.   an oscillation about west

164.   What is the input to a VSI?

    a.   static pressure
    b.   differential pressure
    c.   total pressure
    d.   dynamic pressure

165.   The component(s) used to align an inertial strap-down unit in the horizontal plane is/are:

    a.   Accelerometers and gyroscopes
    b.   Accelerometers
    c.   Flow inductors
    d.   Gyroscopes

166.   A ring laser gyro consists of;

    a.   A gyro with 2 degrees of freedom
    b.   Two moving cavities using mirrors
    c.   A laser split into two beams
    d.   Two electrodes (anodes and cathodes)

167.   The Directional Gyro Indicator (DGI) can:

    a.   not align itself with magnetic north
    b   can automatically align itself with magnetic north
    c   have 1^0 of freedom
    d.   have 2^0 of freedom

168.   The Pitot tube comprises a mast to position it below the skin of the aircraft for:

    a.   avoid disturbance from aerodynamic flow about the aircraft
    b.   position it outside the boundary layer
    c.   anti-ice protection
    d.   easy access for maintenance

169. Using a classic Artificial Horizon, the a/c performs a right turn through 360 degrees at a
      constant angle of bank and rate of turn. The indication is:

      a.   Nose up, too much bank.
      b.   Nose up, not enough bank.
      c.   Nose up, wings level.
      d.   Bank and pitch correct.

ANSWERS

1	B	**31**	D	**61**	A	**91**	B	**121**	C	**151**	D
2	B	**32**	C	**62**	A	**92**	D	**122**	A	**152**	B
3	A	**33**	D	**63**	D	**93**	D	**123**	C	**153**	A
4	B	**34**	A	**64**	A	**94**	B	**124**	C	**154**	D
5	A	**35**	C	**65**	B	**95**	D	**125**	A	**155**	C
6	C	**36**	B	**66**	D	**96**	A	**126**	C	**156**	A
7	B	**37**	A	**67**	B	**97**	A	**127**	A	**157**	B
8	A	**38**	D	**68**	B	**98**	B	**128**	A	**158**	A
9	C	**39**	A	**69**	A	**99**	C	**129**	A	**159**	A
10	B	**40**	B	**70**	D	**100**	C	**130**	D	**160**	B
11	B	**41**	C	**71**	B	**101**	D	**131**	C	**161**	B
12	C	**42**	B	**72**	A	**102**	C	**132**	C	**162**	A
13	B	**43**	C	**73**	A	**103**	A	**133**	A	**163**	A
14	D	**44**	B	**74**	A	**104**	B	**134**	C	**164**	A
15	A	**45**	A	**75**	C	**105**	A	**135**	D	**165**	A
16	C	**46**	B	**76**	C	**106**	A	**136**	C	**166**	C
17	B	**47**	C	**77**	C	**107**	C	**137**	A	**167**	D
18	C	**48**	A	**78**	B	**108**	B	**138**	A	**168**	A
19	B	**49**	D	**79**	C	**109**	C	**139**	D	**169**	D
20	B	**50**	C	**80**	C	**110**	C	**140**	C		
21	B	**51**	A	**81**	A	**111**	D	**141**	C		
22	A	**52**	A	**82**	C	**112**	D	**142**	C		
23	D	**53**	B	**83**	C	**113**	A	**143**	C		
24	D	**54**	A	**84**	B	**114**	B	**144**	A		
25	B	**55**	B	**85**	C	**115**	A	**145**	D		
26	D	**56**	D	**86**	C	**116**	D	**146**	B		
27	A	**57**	A	**87**	A	**117**	B	**147**	B		
28	C	**58**	A	**88**	D	**118**	A	**148**	B		
29	D	**59**	A	**89**	C	**119**	C	**149**	B		
30	B	**60**	B	**90**	A	**120**	A	**150**	C		

SPECIMEN QUESTIONS – AUTOMATIC FLIGHT

1   The flight director command bars on the display
        shown are commanding

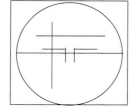

        a   fly up and left
        b   fly down and right
        c   fly down and left
        d   fly up and right

2   Where are the flight director modes displayed?

        a   PFD
        b   ND
        c   EICAM
        d   FD control panel

3   The autopilot is in heading select mode, and the aircraft is flying on a heading of 270^0. If you
        change heading to 360^0, the flight director command bars will;

        a.   roll command bar goes full deflection right and then doesn't move until the aircraft
                heading is within 30^0 of the selected heading
        b.   roll command bar moves to right and centres when AFDS angle of bank to intercept
                has been achieved
        c.   the heading command bar will disappear and the heading hold will disengage
        d.   roll command bar moves to the right and then progressively returns to the centre as
                the deviation from the selected heading reduces

4   What are the basic functions of an autopilot?

                1.   Maintain pitch attitude
                2.   Maintain wings level
                3.   Altitude hold
                4.   Heading hold
                5.   Speed hold

        a.   all 5
        b.   1 & 2
        c.   1, 2 & 3
        d.   1, 2, 3, & 4

5   At 50 feet agl during an autoland, what happens to the glideslope signal?

        a   continues to be actioned
        b   is disconnected
        c   is factored for range
        d   is used to flare the aircraft

6   What is the wavelength of an ILS signal

        a..   Centimetric
        b.   Hectometric
        c.   Metric
        d.   Decimetric

7   A Yaw damper indicator will indicate to the pilot:

        a   yaw damper movement of rudder position
        b   rudder position
        c   rudder position due to pedal displacement
        d   yaw damper movement on ground only

8   The Autothrottle is set to climb at a constant mach number. If the temperature does not change, what happens to the CAS?

        a   Increases
        b   Decreases
        c   Increases, but only if the outside air temperature decreases
        d   Stays the same

9   Autothrottle engaged mode can be checked by the pilot, using:

        a   primary flight display
        b   thrust control computer
        c   position of throttles
        d   navigation display

10   The interception of the localiser beam by the autopilot is:

        a   on a constant magnetic course
        b   a mode using an interception verses range computation
        c   a mode using an interception verses radio deviation law
        d   on a constant heading

11   Engagement of the autopilot is not possible when:

                1.   electrical supply is faulty
                2.   the turn control knob is not set to centre off
                3.   there is a synchronisation fault
                4.   there is a fault in the attitude reference unit

        a   1, 2, 3, & 4
        b   1, & 4 only
        c   1, 3, & 4
        d   2 & 4 only

12.   On which instrument are the flight director bars normally present?

        a.   Primary EICAS
        b.   ADI
        c   ND
        d.   EHSI

13.   What happens at 50ft whilst carrying out an autolanding?

        a.   glideslope and localiser disconnect and aircraft continues to land
        b.   radio altimeter controls the rate of descent
        c.   radio altimeter controls the angle of attack
        d.   glideslope disconnects and aircraft continues descent

14.   If you have selected a heading of 180^0 and are flying aircraft on heading of 160° to intercept the correct course, the ADI vertical bar be central when?

    a.   only if aircraft is subject to 20^0 port drift
    b.   only if aircraft is subject to 20^0 starboard drift
    c.   cannot be centralised
    d.   will only be central when flying correct attitude to intercept desired heading

15.   If the autopilot is selected to VOR mode, what happens if the aircraft flies over the cone of confusion?

    a.   Temporarily follows current heading until exiting the cone of confusion
    b.   VOR disengages and Heading hold engages
    c.   The pilot must select an alternate roll mode
    d.   The pilot manually flies the aircraft following flight director roll commands.

16.   The autopilot disconnects (or the autoland is completed) at:

    a.   100 ft
    b.   decision height
    b.   flare
    d.   roll out

17.   The control law in a fly-by-wire system is a relationship between:

    a.   how the pilot's control demands are translated into control surface movements.
    b.   input and output at the amplifier level respectively control the deviation data
    c.   computer input deviation data and flap position modification
    d.   the versine signal between the ailerons and elevators

18.   What are the autopilot minimum requirements in order to fly single pilot operations in IFR conditions or at night?

    a   Two axis autopilot with altitude hold and heading hold.
    b   Two axis autopilot with altitude hold, heading hold, VOR tracking and Alt acquire
    c   Single axis autopilot with Altitude hold only
    d.   Single axis autopilot with Heading select and VS

19.   When flying level in the cruise the ……….…….. holds height and the …………… holds the speed:

    a   Autopilot,   Autopilot
    b   Auto-throttle,   Auto-throttle
    c   Auto-throttle,   Autopilot
    d   Autopilot,   Auto-throttle

20.   At what height during a semi-automatic landing is the autopilot disengaged:

    a   100 ft
    b   45 ft
    c   Decision height
    d   14 ft

21.   At the missed approach point the TOGA switch on the throttles is depressed. Which of the
        following statements are correct:

            1.   Autopilot selects max. power
            2.   GA power selected
            3.   Aircraft automatically cleans up
            4.   Autopilot fly's the GA manoeuvre
            5.   Pilot manually fly's manoeuvre

        a   2 & 5
        b   1 & 5
        c   1 & 4
        d   2 & 4

22   If a Go-Around is initiated from an auto-approach:

            1.   the autothrottle selects maximum power as soon as the TOGA switch is
                    pressed
            2.   the auotpilot monitors the climb
            3.   the autopilot retracts flap and landing gear to reduce drag
            4.   the pilot performs the climb
            5.   the pilot retracts the flap and landing gear to reduce drag

        a.   1, 2 & 4
        b.   1, 4 & 5
        c.   1, 3 & 4
        d.   1, 2 & 3

23.   An auto-land system which can continue to automatically land the aircraft after a single
        failure is called:

        a.   Fail passive
        b.   Fail Soft
        c.   Fail Safe
        d.   Fail active

24.   Where can the pilot look to see the autothrottle mode?

        a.   PFD
        b.   overhead panel
        c.   throttle control panel
        a   EICAS

25.   Where can the pilot look to see the thrust limit mode?

        a.   PFD
        b.   Overhead panel
        c.   Throttle control panel
        d.   Primary EICAS

26   The autopilot is engaged with no modes selected. What is the autopilot providing:

    a.   wing leveling
    b.   altitude hold
    c.   Auto-stability with auto-trim
    d.   LNAV and VNAV

27   When is an Autoland procedure complete

    a.   At the markers
    b.   At the beginning of the ground roll
    c.   At decision height
    d.   At the flare

28   During a CAT2 approach, what is providing the height information

    a.   Capsule stack
    b.   Radio Altimeter
    c.   Captain's barometric altimeter
    d.   Central Air Data Computer

29   Autoland Flare is initiated at

    a.   1500 ft
    b.   330 ft
    c.   50 ft
    d.   5 ft

30   An autopilot capable of altitude hold and heading hold is a minimum requirement for:

    a.   Single pilot operation in VMC and IMC.
    b.   Single pilot operation under IFR and at night.
    c.   Aircraft over 5700kg.
    d.   Dual pilot operation (in IFR).

31   During a fully automatic landing the autopilot:

    a.   and the auto-throttle control the approach at least until the flare.
    b.   and the auto-throttle control the approach at least until the roll-out.
    c.   and the auto-throttle control the approach at least until decision height.
    d.   controls the approach (at least) until the roll-out, the pilot controls the power.

32   A landing is considered to be Automatic when:

    1   autopilot flies the ILS to Decision Height, and then disengages
    2   autothrottle maintains speed until Decision Height, and then disengages
    3   autothrottle disengages thrust at 50ft
    4   autopilot flies the ILS until the flare
    5   the flare is automatic

    a.   2, 3 & 5
    b.   1 & 2
    c.   4 & 5
    d.   1 & 4

33   In an autopilot system, modes for stabilising the a/c include which of the following:

        1   Yaw damper.
        2   Pitch attitude holding.
        3   VOR axis holding.
        4   ASI & Mach hold.
        5   Horizontal wing holding.
        6   Altitude holding.

   a.   1, 2 & 4
   b.   1, 2 & 5
   c.   1, 5 & 6
   d.   2, 4 & 6

34   In an autopilot system, a/c flight path modes include which of the following:

        1   Pitch attitude holding.
        2   Horizontal wing holding.
        3   VOR axis holding.
        4   Inertial heading holding.
        5   ASI & Mach hold.
        6   Yaw damper.

   a.   1, 2 & 4
   b.   1, 2 & 5
   c.   2, 4 & 6
   d.   3, 4 & 5

35   Auto-throttle can hold which of the following:

        1   Speed.
        2   Mach No.
        3   Altitude.
        4   N_1/EPR.
        5   VOR capture.
        6   Vertical profile.

   a.   1, 2 & 3
   b.   1, 2 & 4
   c.   1, 2 & 6
   d.   1, 3 & 5

36   An autopilot system whereby if one A/P fails cannot carry out an auto-land is called
      fail_____:

   a.   passive.
   b.   safe.
   c.   operational.
   d.   redundant.

37   In a yaw damper:

    a.   ailerons are moved in proportion to Mach No.
    b.   ailerons are moved in proportion to rate of angular velocity.
    c.   rudder is moved in proportion to Mach No.
    d.   rudder is moved in proportion to rate of angular velocity.

38   "LOC ARMED" lights up on the annunciator, this means:

    a.   localiser beam captured.
    b.   localiser armed and awaiting capture.
    c.   localiser alarm is on.
    d.   ILS is captured

39   What is the most basic function of an autopilot?

    a.   altitude hold
    b.   heading hold
    c.   wing leveller
    d.   altitude and heading hold

40   What does the autopilot pitch / rotate around?

    a.   centre of gravity
    b.   manoeuvre point
    c.   centre of pressure
    d.   neutral point

41   During a semi-automatic landing

    a.   the A/P is disengaged at DH having followed the ILS.
    b.   the A/T flies airspeed down to approximately 30 ft and automatically disengages.
    c.   the A/P flies the approach and flare and roll-out.
    d.   the A/T flies approach speed and disengages automatically at DH

42   If only a single A/P is used to climb, cruise and approach; following a failure:

    a.   it is fail passive with redundancy.
    b.   it is fail operational and will not disconnect.
    c.   it is fail soft and will not disconnect.
    d.   it is fail safe and will disconnect.

43   In heading select the autopilot delivers roll commands to the controls to bank the aircraft:

    1   proportional to TAS, but not beyond a specified maximum.
    2   Set bank of 27 degrees.
    3   Set bank of 15 degrees.
    4   Proportional to the deviation from the selected heading.

    a.   1&2
    b.   2&3
    c.   3&4
    d.   4&1

44   Regarding autopilot and auto-throttle:

    1   A/P holds IAS/MACH when climbing in LVL CHG and A/T controls thrust.
    2   A/P holds altitude in cruise with ALT HOLD, A/T controls IAS/Mach.
    3   A/P holds pitch in descent in V/S mode, A/T controls thrust.
    4   A/P holds alt in climb mode, A/T controls IAS/Mach in speed.

    a.   1 & 2
    b.   3 & 4
    c.   1, 2 & 3
    d.   2, 3 & 4

45   Auto-trim is fitted to an autopilot:

    a.   To provide control about lateral axis.
    b.   To prevent snatching on disengaging A/P.
    c.   To prevent snatching on engaging A/P
    d.   To correct for Mach tuck

46   Auto throttle can hold

    1.   speed
    2.   flight path
    3.   altitude
    4.   Mach
    5.   EPR / N_1
    6.   attitude

    a.   1,2,6
    b.   1,4,5
    c.   1,2,3,4
    d.   3,4,5

47.   What is the purpose of the synchronisation in an autopilot.(list)

    1.   Prevents snatch on disengagement.
    2.   Pevents snatch on engagement.
    3.   Cancels rudder control inputs.
    4.   May not allow the autopilot to engage if unserviceable.

    a.   1 & 2
    b.   1 & 3
    c.   2 & 4
    d.   3 & 4

48.   When operating with the autopilot in ALT hold mode what happens if the Captain's barometric altimeter pressure setting is increased.

    a.   ALT hold disengages
    b.   Nothing
    c.   The aeroplane will climb
    d.   The aeroplane will descend

49.   TO/GA is engaged

        a.   automatically at GS capture
        b.   automatically when an autopilot fails
        c.   by the pilot pressing a button on or near the throttles
        d.   by the pilot selecting flare

50.   On crossing the cone of confusion of a VOR when in VOR mode of the autopilot what will
        happen to the roll channel.

        a.   Always coupled to the selected VOR radial
        b.   Temporarily disconnected
        c.   Damped by a trim input from the lateral trim system
        d.   Temporarily switches to heading mode

51.   The function of autotrim is

        a.   to synchronise the longitudinal loop
        b.   to relieve forces on the autopilot servomotor prior to hand over
        c.   to react to altitude changes in ALT HOLD mode
        d.   to relieve forces on the control column before hand over

52.   The Mach Trim system

        a   compensates for the rearward movement of the CP due to shockwave formation
        b   compensates for the forward movement of the CP due to shockwave formation
        c   controls the aircraft in roll
        d   is operational at low subsonic speeds

53   The Flight Director horizontal and vertical bars are up and left of aircraft symbol on the ADI,
        these indications are directing the pilot to:

        a.   Increase pitch angle, turn left
        b.   Decrease pitch angle, turn left
        c.   Increase pitch angle, turn right

54   What does FADEC do?

        1.   engine limitation protection
        2.   automatic engine starting sequence
        3.   manual engine starting sequence
        4.   power management

        a   1& 2
        b   4 only
        c   1& 4
        d   1, 2,3&4

55   What does the Mach trim system use to prevent 'Mach Tuck'?

        a   elevator
        b   elevator/rudder
        c   rudder
        d   elevator/aileron/rudder

56   The autosynchronisation system does which of the following?

        1.   prevents snatching on engagement
        2   prevents snatching on disengagement
        3   cancels rudder input
        4   works in climb, cruise and descent

    a   1&2
    b   2&3
    c   1&4
    d   3& 4

57   When turning into a desired radial, FD bars indicate:

    a   a 45° angle of bank
    b   a 30° angle of bank
    c   a 15° angle of bank
    d   correct attitude to intercept radial

58   If a pilot was to carry out a roll maneuver, on release of CWS what does the AP do?

    a   Roll wing level and maintain heading only
    b   Maintain attitude only
    c   Maintain track and attitude only
    d   Roll wing level and maintain MCP selected roll

ANSWERS

1	A	21	D	41	A
2	A	22	B	42	D
3	B	23	D	43	D
4	B	24	A	44	A
5	B	25	D	45	B
6	C	26	C	46	B
7	A	27	B	47	C
8	B	28	B	48	B
9	A	29	C	49	C
10	C	30	B	50	D
11	A	31	B	51	B
12	B	32	C	52	A
13	D	33	B	53	A
14	D	34	D	54	D
15	A	35	B	55	A
16	D	36	A	56	C
17	A	37	D	57	D
18	A	38	B	58	B
19	D	39	C		
20	C	40	A		

SPECIMEN QUESTIONS – WARNING & RECORDING

1   The input to a basic stall warning system are:

     a   Angle of attack
     b   IAS
     c   Slat/flap position
     d M_{no}

2   Where in the aircraft does JAR require the FDR to be fitted:

     a   At the back
     b   At the front
     c   In the wings
     d   In the undercarriage bay

3   An FDR fitted to an aircraft of over 5700kgs after Apr 98 must record for:

     a   10 hours
     b   25 hours
     c   30 minutes
     d   60 minutes

4   Where is TCAS displayed?

     1.   On its own screen
     2.   On the EFIS
     3.   Weather Radar
     4.   On VSI

     a.   All 4
     b.   1 ,2 & 4
     c.   2 & 3
     d.   1 & 4

5   The principle that TCAS uses is:

     a.   Primary radar
     b.   ATC radar
     c.   RT communications
     d.   Transponders in the aircraft

6.   When an intruder aircraft has no Altitude Reporting facility, i.e. Mode equipped with 'A' transponder only, TCAS can only give:

     a.   Corrective RA only
     b.   TA followed by a Preventative RA
     c.   TA only
     d.   Preventative RA only

7.   What does a FDR record when combined with a CVR?

        1.   Cockpit voice
        2.   Radio
        3.   Public addresses from the cockpit
        4.   Cabin voice

    a.   1, 2 & 3
    b.   1 & 2
    c.   All 4
    d.   2 & 4

8.   A GPWS system requires:

    a   Light & bell
    b   Aural signals only
    c   Aural signals which may be supplemented by visual signals
    d   Aural, tactile and visual signals or a combination thereof

9.   The Altitude Alert system alerts the pilot:

    a   At decision height
    b   At the selected altitude
    c   When reference altitude equals the selected altitude
    d   When deviating from the selected altitude

10   The Altitude Alert system :

    a.   May alert by visual signals when approaching the selected altitude
    b.   Activates a warning light on reaching selected altitude
    c.   Engages autotrim on reaching selected altitude
    d.   Disengages autotrim on reaching selected altitude

11   TCAS II obtains information from:

        1   Pressure encoding from mode S transponder
        2   Radio altimeter
        3   Aircraft specific configurations
        4   Inertial reference unit (IRU)

    a   1, & 2
    a.   1, 2, & 4
    b.   1, 2, 3, & 4
    c.   1, 2, & 3

12   What does a CVR record?

    a.   Cabin crew conversations
    b.   Cabin crew conversation on intercom
    c.   PA announcements even when not selected on flight deck
    d.   Radio conversations

13   A stall warning system fitted to a large aircraft will always include:

    a   Various inputs including speed brake position, a warning module and a visual or aural warning

    b   Various inputs including landing gear micro switch, a warning module and an aural warning

    c   Various inputs including EGT, a warning module and an aural warning

    d   Stick shakers and/or stick push

14   GPWS is active between what heights:

    a.   0ft and 2500ft

    b.   50ft and 2450 ft

    c.   0 ft and 2450 ft

    d.   50 ft and 5000 ft

15   What is the correct response to a TCAS RA?

    a.   Smoothly and immediately follow the climb or descent commands

    b.   Request permission to manoeuvre from ATC

    c.   Follow ATC instructions as these override TCAS RAs

    d.   Turn 90^0 and smoothly and immediately follow the climb or descent commands

16   What symbol is used to represent a RA on a TCAS PPI?

    a.   Yellow circle

    b.   Red lozenge

    c.   Red square

    d.   Red circle

17   Which of the following is a preventative RA?

    a.   Monitor vertical speed

    b.   Turn left

    c.   Traffic, traffic

    d.   Climb, climb now

18   What input is there to TCAS 2?

    a   Mode 'A' transponder which gives TA and RAs

    b   Mode 'C' transponder which co-ordinates avoidance manoeuvres

    c   Mode 'C' and 'S' transponders which co-ordinate avoidance manoeuvres

    d   Mode 'S' transponder which co-ordinates avoidance manoeuvres

19   An aircraft registered after the 1 April 1998 requires a CVR which:

    a.   Records the last 2 hours of flight

    b.   Records the last 72 hours of flight

    c.   Records the last 30 minutes of flight

    d.   Records the last 8 hours of flight

20   What are the JAR OPS requirements for the CVR to start and stop recording?

    a.   From the time when the aircraft is first able to move under its own power until it is no longer able to do so.

    b.   From the time the first engine is started and stops 5 minutes after the last engine is shutdown.

    c.   From the time when the first engine is started and stops 5 minutes after the APU is shutdown.

    d.   From the time when the aircraft is first able to move under its own power until 5 minutes after it is no longer able to do so.

21   An altitude alerting system must at least be capable of alerting the crew on:

    1   Approaching selected altitude.
    2   Excessive deviation from selected altitude.
    3   Excessive vertical speed.
    4   Excessive terrain closure.
    5   Abnormal gear/flap combination.

    a.   1&2.
    b.   1,2,3&4.
    c.   1,2,3,4&5.
    d.   1,2&3.

22   An aircraft that weights more than 5,700 kg and was registered after 1 April 1998, the FDR and CVR must record respectively:

    a.   25 hr. and 1 hr.
    b.   25 hr. and 2 hr.
    c.   10 hr. and 2 hr.
    d.   10 hr. and 1hr.

23   "Other traffic" which is assessed as not being a threat will be indicated by a TCAS system as:

    a.   A solid red square.
    b.   A solid white or cyan diamond.
    c.   A hollow cyan diamond.
    d.   A hollow cyan square.

24   Which of the following are modes of the GPWS?

    1   Excessive sink rate.
    2   Altitude loss after T/O or go-around.
    3   Excessive Glideslope deviation.
    4   High climb rate.
    5   Flaps in incorrect position.
    6   High altitude descent.
    7   Stall.

    a.   All 7
    b.   1, 2, 3, & 5
    c.   1, 2 & 3
    d.   1, 3, 5 & 7

25.   What corrective action is given by TCAS?

         a   Turn left or right.
         b   Climb or descend.
         c   Contact ATC
         d   Turn then climb or descend.

26.   The Flight Data Recorder actually starts running:

         a   At the beginning of the T/O run.
         b   Before the a/c starts moving under its own power
         c   When the gear is retracted.
         d   When a/c lines up on runway.

27.   GPWS may indicate (list):

                 1.   Excessive sink rate after T/O.
                 2.   Excessive descent rate.
                 3.   Excessive closure with terrain.
                 4.   Ground proximity not in the landing configuration.
                 5.   Excessive glide-slope deviation.
                 6.   Altitude call-outs.
                 7.   Bank Angle alerting.

         a   1, 4, 5 & 7
         b   All 7
         c   1, 2 & 3
         b   1, 3, 6 & 7

28.   TCAS 2 when fitted with mode C transponder may give:

         a   TA only.
         b   TA and RA in horizontal plane.
         c   TA and RA in vertical plane.
         d   RA only.

29.   According to JAR OPS when must the CVR on a 50 seat turbo prop a/c begin recording?

         a   Switch on to switch off.
         b   From lift off to when the weight on wheels switch is made on landing.
         c   From before the a/c is capable of moving under its own power to after the a/c is no
                 longer capable of moving under its own power.
         d   At commencement of the taxy to turning off the runway.

30.   What is the GPWS Mode 3 audible alert?

         a   DON'T SINK, DON'T SINK followed by WHOOP WHOOP, PULL UP if the sink
                 rate exceeds a certain value.
         b   DON'T SINK, DON'T SINK continuously.
         c   DON'T SINK, DON'T SINK followed immediately by WHOOP WHOOP, PULL
                 UP.
         d   SINK RATE repeated each 1.5 seconds. Penetrating the second boundary generates
                 an aural alert of WHOOP, WHOOP PULL UP.

31.   CVR components consist of:

      1   Microphone
      2   Crash/Fire resistant construction
      3   Independent battery
      4   A Flight data recorder

a   1 & 2
b   1 & 4
c   1, 2, 3 & 4
d   1, 2 & 4

32   If an aircraft GPWS detects an excessive rate of descent with gear and flaps up, the alert and warning will be :

a   DON'T SINK, DON'T SINK
b   TOO LOW TERRAIN, TOO LOW TERRAIN followed by TOO LOW GEAR TOO, LOW GEAR
c   SINK RATE followed by 'WHOOP WHOOP PULL UP
d   TERRAIN TERRAIN followed by 'WHOOP WHOOP PULL UP

33   The requirement to carry a GPWS concerns aircraft which are, depending on their age, weight and passenger capacity

1. Turbo prop   2. Piston   3. Jet

a   1, 2 & 3
b   1, 3
c   3
d   1

ANSWERS

1	A	21	A
2	A	22	B
3	B	23	C
4	A	24	B
5	D	25	B
6	C	26	B
7	A	27	B
8	C	28	C
9	D	29	C
10	A	30	B
11	C	31	A
12	D	32	C
13	B	33	B
14	B		
15	A		
16	C		
17	A		
18	D		
19	A		
20	A		

SPECIMEN QUESTIONS – ENGINE INSTRUMENTS

1.   What type of sensor is used to measure the output of a low pressure booster pump

        a)   bourdon tube
        b)   aneroid capsule
        c)   bellows
        d)   differential capsule

2.   A vibration meter measures

        a)   frequency in Hz
        b)   amplitude at a given frequency
        c)   period in seconds
        d)   acceleration in g

3.   Which of the following are used to measure temperature

                1.   thermocouple
                2.   resistance
                3.   reactance
                4.   mercury

        a)   1,2,3,4
        b)   1,2, & 4
        c)   2,3, & 4
        d)   1,3,& 4

4.   A millivoltmeter measuring electromotive force between a hot and a cold junction of a
        thermocouple can be graduated to read temperature if: -

        a)   the hot junction is kept at a constant temperature
        b)   the cold junction is maintained at 15 degrees C.
        c)   the hot junction is maintained at 15 degrees C.
        d)   the cold junction is maintained at a constant temperature

5.   If both displays of an EICAS system fail what information will be displayed on the standby
        engine indicator

        a)   N1,EPR,N2
        b)   N1,EPR, EGT
        c)   N2,EPR, EGT
        d)   EGT,N1, FF

6.   A capacitive type gauging system may measure mass due to:

        a)   fuel dielectric constant being equal to that of air and proportional to density
        b)   fuel dielectric constant being equal to that of air and proportional to1/density
        c)   fuel dielectric constant being twice that of air and proportional to density
        d)   fuel dielectric constant being twice that of air and proportional to 1/density

7.　　　If the intake probe of an EPR system becomes blocked with ice this will cause the EPR gauge to

　　　a)　　　under-read during take off
　　　b)　　　over-read during take off
　　　c)　　　be unaffected
　　　d)　　　read zero

8.　　　The power output of a turbo-propeller aircraft is measured by the amount of torque being produced. The indication can be in which of the following units.

　　　　　　1.　　　Newton metres
　　　　　　2.　　　PSI
　　　　　　3.　　　Percentage
　　　　　　4.　　　Pounds feet
　　　　　　5.　　　EPR

　　　a)　　　1,2,3,4,5
　　　b)　　　1,2,3,5
　　　c)　　　2,3,4,5
　　　d)　　　1,2,3,4

9.　　　If one probe of a multi-sensor T.G.T. system failed , the reading would:

　　　a)　　　increase by 20 – 30 degrees C
　　　b)　　　decrease by 20 – 30 degrees C
　　　c)　　　be practically unaffected
　　　d)　　　fall to zero.

10.　　　During the take-off run , the effect of increasing airspeed is to cause the EPR indication to :

　　　a)　　　remain constant
　　　b)　　　increase
　　　c)　　　decrease
　　　d)　　　increase and subsequently decrease

11.　　　An advisory message on the EICAS system screen would be:

　　　a)　　　displayed in amber on the lower screen with associated caution lights and aural tones
　　　b)　　　displayed in red, normally on the upper screen , and requiring immediate corrective action
　　　c)　　　displayed in amber, normally on the upper screen with aural warnings .
　　　d)　　　displayed in amber, normally on the upper screen, indented one space to the right.

12.　　　A supercharged aircraft is climbing at its maximum permitted boost of 8 psi (16in.Hg) from sea level to its full throttle height of 10,000 feet. If sea level pressure is 29.92in.Hg , when the aircraft reaches 5000 feet, where the pressure is 24.72in.Hg, what will be the approximate indication on the MAP gauge.

　　　a)　　　18 in Hg
　　　b)　　　33 in Hg
　　　c)　　　41 in Hg
　　　d)　　　46 in Hg

13   An aircraft has a compensated capacitance fuel contents gauging system and is refuelled so
      that the total fuel contents are 76000kg at a temperature of 18 degrees C and an S.G. of 0.81.
      Whilst the aircraft is parked the temperature increases to 26 degrees C and the S.G. becomes
      0.80. The indicated fuel contents have:

      a)   increased by 5%
      b)   increased by 10%
      c)   decreased by 5%
      d)   remained the same

14   The working principle of a capacitive fuel contents gauging system is based upon

      a)   volume of fuel
      b)   changes in capacitance
      c)   height of fuel
      d)   dielectric value

15   A volumetric fuel flow meter is different to a mass flow meter because the mass flow meter
      compensates for:

      a)   dielectric
      b)   density
      c)   volume
      d)   pressure

16.   Cylinder head temperature measurement works on the principle of

      a)   differential expansion
      b)   wheatstone bridge
      c)   ratiometer
      d)   thermocouple

17.   The electrical tacho generator system uses

      a)   single phase a.c. whose frequency varies with the speed of the engine delivered to a
              single phase synchronous motor and drag cup.
      b)   three phase a.c. whose frequency varies with the speed of the engine delivered to a
              three phase synchronous motor (squirrel cage) and drag cup.
      c)   A tacho probe and phonic wheel measuring speed and sending information to a
              squirrel cage motor and drag cup
      d)   Single phase d.c. whose frequency varies with speed of the engine converted to a
              square wave pulse delivered to a servo driven instrument

18.   Where very accurate temperature indication is required the indicator used will be:

      a)   galvanometer
      b)   direct reading
      c)   moving coil
      d)   ratiometer

19   Total Air Temperature (TAT) is equal to:

a)   SAT + ram rise
b)   RAT + friction rise
c)   SAT – RAT
d)   RAT + ram rise

20.   The principle of the fuel-monitoring device giving the fuel burnt is:

a)   multiplying flight time by fuel consumption
b)   capacitance variation of a capacitor
c)   difference of indication according to departure value
d)   integration of instantaneous flow

21.   To measure the fuel quantity on a heavy aircraft we use:

1   capacitor gauges
2   electric gauges with round floats
3   the indication can directly be indicated as a mass
4   the indication can not be indicated as a mass

The combination of all correct statements is:

a)   1,4
b)   2,3
c)   2,4
d)   1,3

22.   For a capacitor gauge:

1   the fuel dielectric value is half that of air
2   the fuel dielectric value varies proportionally to the temperature of the fuel
3   the probes are connected in parallel
4   fuel dielectric value varies inversely with the fuel level
5   the gauge accuracy is within 2%

The correct statements are:

a)   3,5
b)   2,3
c)   3,4
d)   1,2

23.   The capacitor gauge principle is based on:

a)   variation of capacitance of a capacitor with the nature of the dielectric
b)   variation of capacitance by volume measure at the probe
c)   variation of the EMF in a wheastone bridge
d)   variation of outflow and couple in the system

24.   Among the following parameters:

        EGT
        EPR
        FF
        N1
        N2
        Oil pressure
        Fuel pressure

        The ones that can be used to monitor a gas turbine thrust setting are:

        a)   EGT, N1, N2, oil pressure
        b)   EGT, N1, FF, EPR
        c)   EGT, EPR, FF, High-pressure fuel
        d)   fuel pressure, N1, N2, oil pressure

25.   The most significant parameters and the most important that express the thrust of a gas
        turbine engine are;

        a)   EGT or N2
        b)   N2 and FF
        c)   FF and EGT
        d) N_1 and EPR

26.   On a modern twin spool turbofan, the main handling parameter is:

        a)   the temperature upstream the turbine or EGT
        b)   a rotational speed and a temperature
        c)   the rotational speed of the high-pressure compressor
        d)   the rotational speed of the low-pressure compressor

27.   Two main indications used to evaluate a turbojet thrust are:

        a)   rotational speed of the fan (N_1) or the total pressure at the outlet of the low-pressure
                turbine
        b)   fan rotational speed (N_1) or total pressure at the high-pressure compressor outlet
        c)   fan rotational speed (N_1) or EPR
        e)   high pressure turbine rotational speed or EPR

28.   The measure of a torque can be made by measuring:

        a)   oil pressure at a fixed crown of an epicyclical reduction gear of the transmission box
        b)   the amount of light through a gear linked to a transmission shaft
        c)   the frequency of a phonic wheel linked to a transmission shaft
        d)   the frequency difference between two phonic wheels linked to a transmission shaft

29.   Among these instruments, which one uses aneroid capsules?

        a)   oil thermometer
        b)   air intake pressure sensor
        c)   oil pressure sensor
        d)   fuel pressure sensor

30.   In a three phase tachometer installation:

        1   the transmitter is a DC generator
        2   we measure an EMF proportional to the driving speed of the transmitter
        3   we measure a frequency proportional to the driving speed of the transmitter
        4   the receiver is a galvometer
        5   the receiver is an synchronised motor driving a magnetic tachometer

        The correct statements are:

        a)   1,2
        b)   2,5
        c)   1,4
        d)   3,5

31.   The working principle of mass flow meters mostly used now days, is to measure in their system:

        a)   the volume and viscosity of the fuel
        b)   the temperature and pressure of the fuel
        c)   volume mass and dielectric value of fuel
        d)   kinetic energy transmitted

32.   The advantage of a ratiometer is

        a)   doesn't require an electrical supply
        b)   does not suffer from errors due to variations of supply voltage
        c)   is calibrated at sea level and will be inaccurate at high altitudes
        d)   it requires an ac voltage and therefore has no commutator.

33.   What is a synchroscope used for

        a)   reducing vibration
        b)   putting the propellers in phase
        c)   allowing the pilot to adjust several engines to the same RPM
        d)   viewing the underside of the aircraft during flight

34.   On an EICAS display what does the yellow arc on the temperature gauge signify,

        a)   Forbidden operating range
        b)   Exceptional operating range
        c)   Normal operating range
        d)   Frequent operating range

35.   An RPM gauge has a red line at the upper end of the green arc, in the middle of the green arc is a smaller red arc. What is the significance of this smaller red arc

        a)   it indicates an RPM that must not be used continuously because of the increased vibration level from the engine/propeller
        b)   it is maximum continuous RPM
        c)   it is the RPM at which there is an increased likelihood of oil leakage
        d)   it indicates an RPM that must not be used continuously because there is insufficient cooling air for the engine

36.   In an ECAM system if a caution message appears the system will

a)   illuminate the page number that requires to be selected
b)   display a diagrammatic view of the affected system
c)   will alert the pilot by an audible warning only
d)   will cause the relevant buttons to light up

37.   A cylinder head temperature measuring system in a piston engine has a sensor

a)   One in each cylinder head to average the temperature
b)   One in the coolest running cylinder
c)   One in the hottest running cylinder
d)   One in each of the two banks of cylinders in a horizontally opposed engine.

38.   The principles used in an electrical RPM indicating system are:-

1.   Tacho probe and phonic wheel
2.   DC generator producing AC
3.   3 phase AC generator driving a 3 phase AC motor
4.   Single phase AC generator driving a single phase AC motor

a)   1 and 4
b)   1 and 3
c)   2 and 3
d)   2 and 4

39.   What does the yellow band on an EICAS generated engine gauge indicate?

a)   Precautionary operating range
b)   Maximum operating range
c)   Warning limit
d)   Normal range

40. Advantage of a ratiometer type measuring circuit is

a)   Very Accurate
b)   Simple
c)   Changes indication if voltage changes
d)   No external power supply is required

41.   In a Turbojet thrust is measured by

a)   Fan Speed (N1) and Turbine Inlet Pressure
b)   N1 and EPR
c)   Compressor outlet pressure and jet pipe pressure
d)   Compressor inlet pressure and combustion chamber pressure

42.   How will a system failure warning be shown to the pilot in the ECAM system

a)   The failure will appear as a wording on the screen
b)   The master warning caption will illuminate and the pilot will manually select failure
        mode
c)   The master warning will illuminate and the ▢▢▢▢ screen will display a check list
        while the secondary shows a graphica▢
d)   The Engine parameter displays will b▢   Mode screen.

43.   What is used to measure gas turbine inlet pressure

        a)   Bourdon Tube
        b)   Differential capsule
        c)   Aneroid capsule
        d)   Bellows

44.   What does a bourdon tube measure

        a)   Temperature
        b)   Quantity
        c)   Capacitance
        d)   Pressure

45.   What are the disadvantages of an electrical float fuel quantity measuring system

                1   Attitude
                2   Acceleration
                3   Temperature
                4   Ambient pressure
                5   Needs an AC power supply

        a.   1,2,3,4,5
        b.   1,2,3
        c.   1,2,5
        d.   2,3,4,5

46   How can temperature be measured

                1.   Resistance
                2.   Mercury
                3.   Thermocouple
                4.   Reactance

        a.   1,2,3,4
        b.   1,2,4
        c.   1,2,3
        d.   1,3,4

47   A Thermocouple would normally be used to measure the temperature of the:

        a.   Turbine
        b.   Exterior
        c.   Cabin
        d.   Oil

48   The Bourdon Tube is used in:

        a.   Temperature probes in front of the engine
        b.   Smoke detectors
        c.   Pressure measurement
        d.   Vibration detectors

49   The principle upon which flowmeters (mass flow) most commonly used today work, is to measure:

      a.   The Volume and Viscosity of the fuel
      b.   The Pressure and Temperature of the fuel
      c.   Density and Dielectric constant of the fuel
      d.   The Kinetic energy transferred

A primary example of this is in fact the FF meter on the C130. The flow of fuel through the meter has swirl imparted into it by a constant speed impeller. This swirling fuel is then allowed to impinge on a turbine, which can rotate against a spring. The rotation of the turbine will depend on the speed of flow and the density of the fuel.

50   A small turbine placed in the flow of fuel to the burners of a Gas Turbine engine measures:

      a.   Volume of flow by the measurement of magnetic impulses
      b.   Mass flow by the measurement of magnetic impulses
      c.   Mass flow by the measurement of frequency
      d.   Volume flow by the measurement of reactance

51   The torquemeter is an instrument:

      a.   Allowing automatic synchronisation of the engines
      b.   Giving the power available by the engine
      c.   Giving the power from the propeller by direct reading
      d.   Allowing the determination of the power from the propeller by using a formula which is a function of the RPM

52   Torque can be calculated in a torquemeter system by the measurement:

      a.   Of the oil pressure resisting lateral movement of the gearing in an epicyclic reduction gearbox
      b.   Of the amount of light through a gear wheel connected to the transmission
      c.   Of the frequency of a phonic wheel connected to the planet gears of an epicyclic gearbox
      d.   Of the difference between 2 phonic wheels connected to the transmission

ANSWERS

1	C	19	A	37	C
2	B	20	D	38	B
3	B	21	D	39	A
4	D	22	A	40	A
5	B	23	A	41	B
6	C	24	B	42	C
7	B	25	D	43	D
8	D	26	D	44	D
9	C	27	C	45	B
10	C	28	A	46	C
11	D	29	B	47	A
12	D	30	D	48	C
13	D	31	D	49	D
14	B	32	B	50	A
15	B	33	C	51	D
16	D	34	B	52	A
17	B	35	A		
18	D	36	B		

SPECIMEN QUESTIONS, WITH EXPLANATIONS

1   A modern Radio Altimeter uses the frequency band:

    a   VHF   30 - 300 Mhz
    b   SHF   3000 Mhz - 30 Ghz
    c   UHF   300 Mhz - 3 Ghz
    d   HF   3 Mhz - 30 Mhz

2   An aircraft that is assessed as not being a threat would be indicated on a TCAS system as:

    a   a solid red square
    b   a solid white or cyan diamond
    c   a hollow white or cyan diamond
    d   a solid yellow circle

3   During descent through a block of airspace of constant temperature and while flying at a constant mach no will cause the CAS to:

    a   increase
    b   decrease
    c   remain constant
    d   increase at a rate of 1·98º/1000 ft

4   The true altitude of an aircraft in flight is shown from:

    a   the standard atmosphere
    b   pressure altitude
    c   density altitude
    d   temperature altitude

5   On a Turn and Slip indicator, needle to the left and ball to the right indicates:

    a   right turn   not enough bank
    b   left turn   too much bank
    c   left turn   not enough bank
    d   right turn   too much bank

6   What is Density Altitude?

    a   temperature altitude
    b   pressure altitude corrected for the prevailing temperature
    c   the altitude in the International Standard Atmosphere at which the prevailing density would be found
    d   pressure altitude corrected for Total Air Temperature

7   A Radio Altimeter is:

    a   ground based and measures true altitude
    b   ground based and measures true height
    c   aircraft based and measures true altitude
    d   aircraft based and measures true height

61

8   Which of the following are modes of the GPWS?

         i   excessive sink rate
         ii   altitude loss after take-off or go-around
         iii   excessive glideslope deviation
         iv   high climb rate
         v   flaps in the incorrect position
         vi   high altitude descent
         vii   stall

         a   i ii iii v
         b   ii iii v vii
         c   i ii iii vii
         d   iii iv v vi

9   An aircraft is travelling at 120 kt, what angle of bank would be required for a rate one turn?

         a   30°
         b   12°
         c   19°
         d   35°

10   An aircraft is travelling at 100 kt forward speed on a 3° glideslope. What is its rate of descent?

         a   500 ft/min
         b   300 ft/min
         c   250 ft/min
         d   500 ft/sec

11   What correction is given by TCAS?

         a   turn left or right
         b   climb or descend
         c   contact ATC on receipt of a Resolution Advisory
         d   climb or descend at 500 ft/min

12   If the Total Pressure sensor supply line leaks, and with the drain element blocked, in a non-pressurised aircraft this will cause the ASI to:

         a   under - read
         b   over - read
         c   over - read in the climb and under - read in the descent
         d   under - read in the climb and over - read in the descent

13   Using a Classic Attitude Indicator, an aircraft performs a turn through 270° at a constant angle of bank and rate of turn. The indication is:

         a   nose up   bank right
         b   nose up   bank left
         c   nose up   wings level
         d   bank and pitch correct

14   The needle and ball of a Turn Indicator are both to the left of the datum. This indicates:

      a   a left turn with too much bank
      b   a left turn with too little bank
      c   a right turn with too little bank
      d   a right turn with too much bank

15   Under conditions determined by the International Standard Atmosphere, at MSL True Air
      Speed is:

      a   greater than CAS
      b   less than CAS
      c   equals CAS
      d   is indeterminate due to the variation in temperature

16   In what range is GPWS operative?

      a   2450 - 0 ft
      b   3000 - 50 ft
      c   2450 - 50 ft
      d   3000 - 0 ft

17   Which of the following are inputs to the central processing unit of the GPWS?

                  i   flaps
                  ii   landing gear
                  iii   glideslope
                  iv   unusual attitudes
                  v   radio altimeter
                  vi   VOR

      a   i   ii   vi
      b   i   ii   iii   v
      c   i   ii   iv   v
      d   i   ii   iii   v   vi

18   What is another name for fail active?

      a   fail soft
      b   fail operational
      c   fail safe
      d   fail passive

19   Why must an autopilot be synchronised when you wish to disconnect?

      a   to ensure fail operational landings can continue safely
      b   to allow automatic pitch trimming to reset
      c   to secure against abrupt changes in aircraft attitude
      d   to allow for FD coupling

20   What is used for EGT measurement?

        a   helical bi-metallic strips
        b   thermistors
        c   radiation pyrometry
        d   thermo emf thermocouples

21   When accelerating on a northerly heading what does the Direct Reading Magnetic Compass indicate?

        a   no change
        b   north
        c   a turn to the west
        d   a turn to the east

22   Why is there a vibration device in a pressure altimeter?

                i   to prevent hysteresis
                ii   to prevent lag in a mechanical system
                iii   to keep pilots happy during long flights
                iv   to prevent icing
                v   to overcome dither

        a   i   ii   iv
        b   i   ii
        c   ii iii v
        d   i   ii   iii

23   What does the white arc on a temperature scale indicate?

        a   never exceed
        b   maximum start and acceleration temperature
        c   normal operating temperature
        d   minimum temperature

24   The rate of turn indicator is a very useful gyroscopic instrument. When used in conjunction with the Attitude Indicator it provides:

        a   angle of bank
        b   rate of turn about the yaw axis
        c   rate of climb
        d   rate of turn athwartships

25   With the aircraft weight constant but variations in airfield altitude, take-off will always be at a constant:

        a   equivalent airspeed
        b   calibrated airspeed
        c   groundspeed
        d   true air speed

26   An inertial reference system is aligned when turned on so as to:

      a   calculate the computed trihedron with reference to the earth
      b   establish true and magnetic north
      c   establish position relative to true and magnetic north
      d   establish magnetic north

27   Total Air Temperature is _____ than static air temperature and the difference varies with _____

      a   warmer   altitude
      b   colder   altitude
      c   warmer   CAS
      d   colder   CAS

28   True heading can be converted into magnetic heading using a compass and:

      a   a map with isogonal lines
      b   a map with isoclinal lines
      c   a map with isobars
      d   a deviation card

29   An aircraft flies into a colder airmass. This will cause the altimeter to:

      a   over-read
      b   under-read
      c   read the correct altitude
      d   the indication will depend on the hemisphere of operation

30   A gravity-erecting device is utilised in:

      a   an artificial horizon
      b   a directional gyroscopic indicator
      c   vertical speed indicator
      d   a turn and slip

31   The rigidity of a gyroscope can be improved by:

      a   increasing the angular momentum and concentrating the mass on the periphery of the rotor
      b   increasing the angular momentum and concentrating the mass at the hub of the rotor
      c   decreasing the angular momentum and concentrating the mass on the periphery of the rotor
      d   decreasing the angular momentum and concentrating the mass at the hub of the rotor

32   The outputs of a flux valve are initially sent to:

      a   an amplifier
      b   an error detector
      c   a compass card
      d   a feedback loop

33   The period of validity of an FMS data base is:

        a   56 days
        b   one week
        c   28 days
        d   varies depending on the area of operational cover

34   An IRS differs from an INS in that it:

        a   has a longer spin-up (is not affected by vertical accelerations due to gravity)
        b   has a shorter spin-up time and suffers from laser lock.
        c   does not need to correct for coriolis and central acceleration)
        d   does not experience Schuler errors as accelerometers are strapped down and not
                rotated by a feedback loop

35   In a solid state gyroscope the purpose of the dither motor is to:

        a   enhance the acceleration of the gyro at all rotational rates
        b   overcome laser lock
        c   compensate for transport wander
        d   stabilise the laser frequencies

36   In an IRS:

        a   the accelerometers are strapped down but the platform is gyro-stabilised
        b   the platform is strapped down but the accelerometers are gyro-stabilised
        c   accelerometers and gyros are both gyro-stabilised
        d   accelerometers and gyros are both strapped down

37   Which of the following correctly describes the gyroscope of a Rate of Turn Indicator?

                i   1 degree of freedom
                ii   2 degrees of freedom
                iii   its frame is held by two springs
                iv   its spin axis is parallel to the pitch axis
                v   the spin axis is parallel to the yaw axis
                vi   the spin axis is horizontal

        a   i ii
        b   i iv v
        c   i iii v
        d   i iii vi

38   A blockage occurs in the ram air source and the drain-hole. The ASI in a non-pressurised
        aircraft will:

        a   read a little low
        b   read a little high
        c   act like an altimeter
        d   freeze at zero

39   The errors associated with the Directional Indicator are:

        i   earth rate
        ii   transport wander
        iii   banking when pitched up
        iv   annual movement of the poles
        v   mechanical problems

        a   i ii iii
        b   i ii iv v
        c   i ii iii iv v
        d   i ii iii v

40   A rate integrating gyroscope is used in:

        i   inertial attitude system
        ii   automatic flight control systems
        iii   inertial navigation systems
        iv   rate of turn indicators

        a   i ii
        b   i iii
        c   i iii iv
        d   i ii iii

41   Rate of turn is affected by:

        i   aircraft speed
        ii   angle of bank
        iii   aircraft weight

        a   i ii
        b   i iii
        c   ii iii
        d   none of the above

42   The ability of a gyroscope to indicate aircraft heading is based on it having:

        a   one degree of freedom in the vertical axis
        b   two degrees of freedom in the vertical axis
        c   two degrees of freedom in the horizontal
        d   one degree of freedom in the horizontal

43   A Vmo/Mmo alerting system contains a barometric aneroid capsule:

        a   which is subjected to dynamic pressure and an airspeed capsule which is subjected
                to static pressure
        b   and an airspeed capsule subjected to static pressure
        c   and an airspeed capsule subjected to dynamic pressure
        d   which is subjected to static pressure and an airspeed capsule which is subjected to
                dynamic pressure

44   When measuring different pressures (low/med/high) which of the following has the three
        types of sensing devices in ascending order of pressure measurement?

                i   bourdon tube
                ii   bellows type
                iii   aneroid capsule

        a   i   ii   iii
        b   iii ii   i
        c   i   iii ii
        d   ii iii i

45   Sound is propagated at a velocity which is dependent upon:
        a   barometric pressure
        b   density
        c   static pressure
        d   temperature

46   The local speed of sound at mean sea level at ISA -10°C is:

        a   661 kt
        b   650 kt
        c   673 kt
        d   680 kt

47   What would the compass heading be given a true heading of 247° in an area where the
        variation is 8°W and a compass deviation of 11°E?

        a   255°
        b   244°
        c   247°
        d   266°

48   An aircraft is flying at flight level 350 at a CAS of 290 kt and a temperature deviation of
        ISA -10°C. The TAS and MN will be:

        a   TAS   498 kt   Mach   0·885
        b   TAS   520 kt   Mach   0·882
        c   TAS   481 kt   Mach   0·855
        d   TAS   507 kt   Mach   0·86

49   An aircraft in the northern hemisphere lands and decelerates on a westerly heading. The
        compass will indicate:

        a   a turn north
        b   no turn will be indicated
        c   an oscillation
        d   a turn south

50   A compass swing is used to:

        a   align compass north with magnetic north
        b   align compass north with true north
        c   align magnetic north with true north
        d   get true north and the lubber line aligned

51   The angle formed between the directive force and the total magnetic force is called:

a   variation
b   deviation
c   dip
d   isoclinal

52   What is the speed of sound at 30,000 ft and -40°C?

a   562 kt
b   595 kt
c   590 kt
d   661 kt

53   If a constant CAS is maintained under normal conditions in the climb what happens to the Mach No?

a   it will decrease
b   it will remain constant
c   it will decrease in an isothermal layer
d   it will increase

54   Regarding magnetism; which of the following statements is correct?

i   lines of flux run from blue pole to red pole
ii   like poles repel
iii   unlike poles repel
iv   like poles attract
v   unlike poles attract

a   i   ii   v
b   i   iii v
c   ii v
d   i   iii iv

55   The output of a double integration N/S is:

a   velocity
b   departure
c   distance
d   longitude

56   A solid state gyro is:

a   a rate gyro
b   a rate sensor
c   an earth gyro
d   a tied gyro

57   The magnetic heading reference unit has a precession rate of:

a   1°/min
b   2°/min
c   5°/min
d   3°/min

58   If the TAS at 40,000 ft is 450 kt the Mach No is:

    a   0·815
    b   0·783
    c   0·76
    d   0·825

59   The EADI and the EHSI of an EFIS installation are also referred to by the manufacturers as:

    a   primary display and navigation display respectively
    b   navigation display and primary display respectively
    c   EICAS and ECAM respectively
    d   ECAM and EICAS respectively

60   In which of the following modes may information from the AWR be displayed?

    i   plan
    ii   expanded ILS
    iii   map
    iv   full nav
    v   full ILS
    vi   expanded nav
    vii   full VOR
    viii   expanded VOR
    ix   centre map

    a   i ii iv vii
    b   i iii vii viii ix
    c   ii iii vi viii ix
    d   ii iii v vii ix

61   Wind information can be displayed in an EFIS system in which of the following modes?

    a   plan   map   expanded ILS   full VOR
    b   map   centre map   plan   full ILS
    c   full nav   full ILS   map   centre map
    d   full ILS   full VOR   map   plan

62   On an EADI radio altitude is displayed:

    a   digitally between 2500 ft and 100 ft
    b   on an analogue scale below 2500 ft
    c   digitally between 2500 ft and 1000 ft and thereafter as an analogue/digital display
    d   as an analogue display between 2500 ft and 1000 ft and thereafter as a digital
    display

63   In FMS fitted aircraft the main interface between pilot and system will be provided by:

    a   the automatic flight control system
    b   the multi-purpose control and display unit
    c   the flight control unit
    d   the flight management source selector

64   In the ILS mode, one dot on the lateral deviation scale on the EHSI indicates:

     a   1 nm
     b   2nm
     c   1°
     d   2°

65   On a standard 2-dot EHSI in the en-route mode each dot represents:

     a   1 nm
     b   2 nm
     c   5 nm
     d   10 nm

66   Given the following information calculate the instrument error of a pre-flight altimeter check.

     i   aerodrome elevation: 235 ft
     ii   apron elevation: 225 ft
     iii   height of altimeter above apron: 20 ft
     iv   altimeter reading with QFE set: 40 ft

     a   +20 ft
     b   +30 ft
     c   +40 ft
     d   +10 ft

EXPLNATIONS TO SPECIMEN QUESTIONS

1   A modern radio altimeter operates on the principle of a frequency modulated continuous
        wave in the   frequency band 4200 - 4400 MHz. This is the SHF band also referred to as
        the centimetric (microwave) band of 3 - 30 GHz

        <u>Answer B</u>

2   The symbols in the answers represent the following:

        a   solid red square - Resolution Advisory
        b   solid white or cyan diamond (lozenge) - Proximate traffic
        c   hollow white or cyan diamond (lozenge) - Other traffic
        d   solid yellow circle - Traffic Advisory

        <u>Answer C</u>

3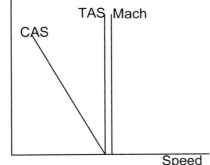

        <u>Answer A</u>

4   True altitude is the exact vertical distance above mean sea level (AMSL). This differs from
        the indicated   pressure if ambient conditions vary from ISA. True altitude may be
        calculated from pressure altitude using   the navigation computer.

        <u>CRP 5 Method.</u>
        Given:
        i   indicated pressure altitude - 25,000 ft
        ii   ambient temperature - -50°C

        Method:

        i   in the altitude window set pressure altitude of 25,000 ft against the
                temperature of -50°C.
        ii   Against indicated altitude on the inner logarithmic circular scale read off
                the true altitude of 23,400 ft.

        <u>Answer B</u>

5   In the answers the needle and ball indicate the following:

        a   right turn with skid (insufficient aileron, too much rudder)
        b   left turn with slip (too much aileron, insufficient rudder
        c   left turn with skid (insufficient aileron, too much rudder
        d   right turn with slip (too much aileron, insufficient rudder)

        <u>Answer B</u>

6   Density altitude is defined as "The altitude in the ISA at which the prevailing density would be found".

Density Altitude may be calculated using the navigation computer or by formula.

Example:

i   pressure altitude - 3000 ft
ii   ambient temperature - +20°C

CRP 5 Method

i   in the airspeed window set the pressure altitude of 3000 ft against the temperature of +20ºC.
ii   read the density altitude over the arrow in the density altitude window. (4000 ft)

Formula Method

i   density altitude = pressure altitude x (± ISA deviation x 120)
therefore: 3 x (+11 x 120)
= 3960 ft

NB.   If the ambient temperature is lower than ISA then density altitude will be lower than pressure altitude and vice versa.

Answer C

7   Answer D

8   Answer A

9   The formula to calculate angle of bank for a rate one turn is:
A of B = true airspeed/10 + 7°
therefore: 120/10 + 7° = 19°

Answer C

10   To calculate the rate of descent of an aircraft in feet per minute the Rule of Thumb is:
          5 x aircraft groundspeed
          therefore: 5 x 100 = 500 ft/min rate of descent

Answer A

11   TCAS I will issue a Traffic Advisory only. Manoeuvre of the aircraft is prohibited.
TCAS II will issue a Corrective Resolution Advisory instructing the pilot to take corrective action in the vertical plane only.
TCAS III will issue a Corrective Resolution Advisory instructing the pilot to take corrective action in the vertical and/or horizontal planes.

NB: Do not confuse a "Corrective Resolution Advisory" with a "Preventative Resolution Advisory" which only provides limitations on aircraft manoeuvres as opposed to a "Corrective Resolution Advisory" which issues corrective aircraft manoeuvres.

Answer B

12   A leak in the total (pitot) pressure line will exhaust a percentage of that pressure to atmosphere causing both the ASI and the mach meter to under read. The loss of pressure will cause the airspeed capsules in both instruments to under - expand.

      Answer A

13   A Classic Attitude Indicator is referring to an Air Driven Artificial Horizon. During a standard 360° the following indications will be apparent:

		PITCH	ROLL
Roll in:	360°	normal	normal
	90°	high (nose up)	too low
	180°	high (nose up)	normal
	270°	high (nose up)	too high
Roll out:	360°	normal	normal

      This error is used by the application of compensation tilt.

      Answer A

14   See answers to question 6

      Answer A

15   This can be proved on the navigation computer. Set all parameters for ISA at mean sea level. Read off CAS   on the inner scale against TAS on the outer scale. They are the same.

      Answer C

16   This is based on radio altimeter height above terrain.

      Answer C

17   inputs to GPWS are as follows:

              i   radio altimeter
              ii   vertical speed
              iii   ILS glideslope deviation
              iv   undercarriage position
              v   flap position
              vi   mach number

      Answer B

18   A system that can withstand at least one failure but leaves the system capable of completing the landing and roll is described as 'fail operational'. An alternative term is 'fail active'.

      Answer B

19   The auto-pilot synchronisation system prevents 'snatching' of the flying controls on engagement of the auto-pilot. The auto-trim system adjusts the trim of the aircraft during automatic flight to prevent 'snatching' of the controls on disengagement of the auto-pilot.

      Answer C

20   EGT is measured using a number of thermocouples connected in parallel to minimize the effect of failure of one of them.

        <u>Answer D</u>

21   Newton' third law: 'to every action there is an equal and opposite reaction'.
        In this case the forces cancel out and the compass will continue to indicate North.

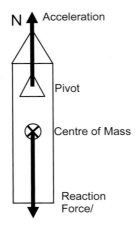

        <u>Answer B</u>

22   <u>Answer B</u>

23   <u>Answer C</u>

24   <u>Answer B</u>

25   <u>Answer B</u>

26   A trihedron is defined as figure having three sides. Additionally, the IRS establishes True North. Magnetic indications are obtained by the application of variation, which, in the case of the Boeing 737-400 is stored in each IRS memory. The range covered for variation is from 73° North to 60° South latitude.

        <u>Answer A</u>

27   Total Air Temperature (TAT) is warmer than Static Air Temperature due to the effect of compressibility. The faster the aeroplane flies the greater the TAT.

        <u>Answer C</u>

28   Isoclinal lines refer to magnetic dip, isobars refer to atmospheric pressure lines on a meteorological chart and a 'deviation card' is a compass correction card positioned along side the compass in the aircraft.

        <u>Answer A</u>

29   If the actual temperature of the column of air in which the aircraft is flying is COLDER than ISA then the True Altitude of the aircraft above mean sea level will be LOWER than the Indicated Altitude. If the actual temperature is WARMER than ISA the True Altitude will be higher.

        <u>Answer A</u>

30   The air driven artificial horizon is also known as the 'classic attitude indicator'.

      Answer A

31   Angular momentum means speed of rotation (RPM).

      Answer A

32   The error detector is also known as a signal selsyn.

      Answer B

33   Answer C

34   The question refers to a ring laser gyro.

      Answer B

35   Answer B

36   Answer D

37   Answer C

38   Answer C

39   Answer D

40   Answer B

41   Answer A

42   Vertical axis means horizontal plane. The two are at 90° to each other. It follows, therefore, that heading information only requires one degree of freedom in the horizontal plane about the vertical axis of the gyroscope.

      Answer A

43   Answer D

44   Answer B

45   LSS = 38.94 x √temp in °K.
      Or, on the CRP 5

      Answer D

46   The first thing to remember is that the local speed of sound is dependent on AMBIENT
        temperature not ISA. In this case, applying the temperature deviation to the ISA
        temperature at mean sea level gives an ambient temperature of +5°C. There are two
        methods of calculating the local speed of sound.
        The first is to use the formula in question 51 as follows:

$$LSS = 38.94 \times \sqrt{278°K}$$
$$LSS = 649.26 \text{ kt}$$

        The second method is to use the CRP 5 navigation computer as follows:

        i   in the airspeed window set the ambient temperature of +5°C against the
                mach number index.
        ii   against 10 on the inner (CAS/Mach number) scale read off the LSS on the
                outer (TAS) scale. 650 kt

        Answer B

47   C   ±   D   =   M   ±   V   =   T
                244° +   11° =   255°   -   8° = 247°

        Answer B

48   On the CRP 5 first calculate the TAS from the information given. Don't forget
        compressibility! This will give a TAS of 481 kt. Now in the airspeed window set the
        ambient temperature of -65°C against the mach number index. Against the TAS of 481 on
        the outer scale read off the mach number on the inner scale, in this case 0.855M.

        Answer C

49   During a deceleration the direct reading compass will indicate an apparent turn towards the
        further pole. In the northern hemisphere it will give an apparent turn towards the south
        whereas in the southern hemisphere it   will indicate an apparent turn towards the north.
        Accelerations are exactly opposite indicating apparent turns towards the nearer pole.

        Answer D

50   Answer A

51   Variation is the angular difference between True North and Magnetic North
        Deviation is the angular difference between Magnetic North and Compass North
        'Dip' is the angle formed between the horizontal component (H or Directive Force) of the
        earth's magnetic field and the Total Magnetic Force (Intensity) of the earth's magnetic field.
        An isoclinal is a line joining lines on a chart of equal 'dip'. The aclinic line is a line
        indicating zero 'dip' and is also referred to as the Magnetic Equator.

        Answer C

52   In this question the altitude is of no consequence. Use the same techniques as shown in
        question 52

        Answer B

53   Owing to density error the TAS will increase dramatically in the climb even at a constant CAS. The LSS, being controlled by temperature, will also reduce. It can be seen from the formula that where Mach No = TAS ÷ LSS an increase in TAS and a decrease in LSS must result in a marked increase in Mach No. A descent would mean a reversal of the speed changes seen in the climb.

Answer D

54   This question refers to the basic rules of magnetism; like poles repel, unlike poles attract and the lines of flux run from the red north seeking pole to the blue south seeking pole.

Answer C

55   Double integration means the second stage of integration, in this case distance along the local meridian.

Answer C

56   A solid state gyro refers to the ring laser gyro as used in Inertial Reference ('Strapdown') systems. It is also referred to as a rate sensor.

Answer B

57   Answer B

58   The ISA temperature at 40,000 ft is -56.5°C. Using the airspeed window of the CRP 5 set the temperature of   -56.5° against the Mach number index. Now against the TAS of 450 kt on the outer scale read off the Mach number on the inner, 0.783.

Answer B

59   Answer A

60   Answer C

61   In an EFIS system wind information can be displayed in every mode except PLAN.

Answer C

62   Answer C

63   Answer B

64   In the NAV mode 1 dot = 2 nm, in the VOR mode 1 dot = 5° and in the ILS mode 1 dot = 1°

Answer C

65   Answer B

66   The apron is 10 ft below the stated aerodrome elevation, so assuming the QFE to be for the aerodrome level, an altimeter on the apron should read (–10) ft. However, the instrument is positioned in the aircraft 20 ft above the apron so it should show (–10) + 20 = +10 ft. Its actual reading is +40 ft so it is over-reading by 30 ft, an instrument error of +30 ft.

Answer B

SPECIMEN EXAMINTION PAPER

55 QUESTIONS   TIME 1hr 30mins

1   An aircraft maintaining a constant CAS and altitude is flying from a cold airmass into warmer air. The effect of the change of temperature on the speed will be:

1 Mark   a. CAS will increase
             b. EAS will decrease
             c. TAS will increase
             d. TAS will decrease

2   Select the correct statement:

1 Mark   a. EAS = CAS corrected for compressibility error
             b. EAS = IAS corrected for position error
             c. CAS = TAS corrected for density error
             d. TAS = EAS corrected for compressibility error

3   V_{LO} is defined as:

1 Mark   a. the maximum speed at which to fly with the landing gear retracted
             b. the maximum speed at which the landing gear may be retracted or extended
             c. the maximum speed at which to fly with the landing gear extended
             d. the minimum speed at which to fly with the landing gear extended

4   An aircraft taking off from an airfield with QNH set in the altimeter has both static vents blocked by ice. As the aircraft climbs away the altimeter will:

1 Mark   a. Read the airfield elevation
             b. Indicate the aircraft height amsl
             c. Read the height of the aircraft above the airfield
             d. Show only a very small increase in height

5   In an inertial-lead VSI the source of the most pronounced error is:

1 Mark   a. Instrument
             b. Position
             c. Steep turn
             d. Missed approach manoeuver

6   An aircraft is descending at a constant mach number. If the aircraft is descending through an inversion layer, the CAS will:

1 Mark   a. Remain constant
             b. Increase
             c. Decrease
             d. Decrease then decrease more slowly

7   The combined Machmeter/ASI is subject to the following errors:

1 Mark   a. Position, density, instrument, compressibility, manoeuvre induced
             b. Those of the Machmeter only
             c. Instrument, pressure and temperature only
             d. Instrument and compressibility only

© Oxford Aviation Services Limited

8   You are flying at a constant FL 290 and constant mach number. The total
        temperature increases by 5°. The CAS will:

1 Mark   a. remain approximately constant
            b. increase by 10 kts
            c. decrease by 10 kts
            d. will increase or decrease depending on whether you are above or below ISA.

9   A factor giving an error on a direct indicating compass would be:

1 Mark   a. crosswinds - particularly on east/west headings
            b. parallax due to oscillations of the compass rose
            c. acceleration on east/west headings
            d. turning through east/west headings

10   If an aircraft, fitted with a DRMC, takes off on a westerly heading, in the northern
        hemisphere, the DRMC will indicate:

1 Mark   a. a turn to the north
            b. oscillates about west
            c. no turn
            d. a turn to south

11   To improve the horizontality of a compass, the magnet assembly is suspended
        from a point:

1 Mark   a. On the centre line of the magnet
            b. Below the centre of gravity
            c. Above the centre of gravity
            d. Varying with magnetic latitude

12   Which of the following will effect a direct reading compass?

            1.   ferrous metals
            2.   non-ferrous metals
            3.   electrical equipment

2 Marks   a. 1 only
            b. 1 & 3
            c. 1 & 2
            d. all 3

13   The rigidity (gyroscopic interia) of a gyroscope may be increased by:

1 Mark   a. Increasing the number of gimbals and decreasing the number of planes of
               rotation
            b. Increasing the speed of rotation and decreasing the mass of the rotor
            c. Increasing the speed of rotation and increasing the mass of the rotor
            d. Decreasing the speed of rotation and increasing the speed of the rotor.

14   The gravity erecting device on a vertical gyro is used on which instrument;

1 Mark   a. directional gyro unit
            b. turn indicator
            c. artificial horizon
            d. gyromagnetic device

15   If the rpm of the rotor in a turn and slip indicator is higher than normal, the turn indicator will:

1 Mark   a. Overread the correct rate of turn
            b. Underread the correct rate of turn
            c. Not indicate due to the increased rigidity
            d. Indicate correctly

16   When the pointer of a rate of turn indicator shows a steady rate of turn:

2 Marks   a. The calibrated spring is exerting a force about the lateral axis equal to the rate of turn
            b. The force produced by the spring is producing a precession equal to but
            c. The spring is providing a force which produces a precession equal to the rate of turn (in the opposite direction to the turn)
            d. The spring is providing a force which produces a precession equal to the rate of turn (in the same direction as the turn)

17   With reference to the flux valve of a remote indicating compass:

1 Mark   a. The flux valve is pendulously mounted and is free to turn to remain aligned with the earth magnetic field
            b. The flux valve is not subject to acceleration errors
            c. The flux valve is pendulously mounted and so it is not subject to or affected by the earth's magnetic field
            d. The flux valve is fixed to the aircraft and so turns with the aircraft to measure the angle between the aircraft and the earth's magnetic field

18   In a Schuler tuned INS, the largest unbounded errors are:

1 Mark   a. Due to acceleration errors
            b. Track errors due to initial misalignment
            c. Due to real wander of the platform gyroscopes
            d. Created at the first stage of integration

19   The amber ALERT sign is on an INS control and display unit:

1 Mark   a. Illuminates steadily for 2 minutes before reaching the next waypoint
            b. Start flashing 2 minutes before reaching the next waypoint and goes out at 30 seconds to run
            c. Illuminates if power from the aircraft bus bar has been lost and the system is operating on standby battery
            d. Illuminates steadily after passing a waypoint in manual mode, until the next leg is programmed in

20   To obtain heading information from a Gyro Stabilised platform, the gyros should
        have:

1 Mark   a. 1 degree of freedom and a horizontal axis
            b. 1 degree of freedom and a vertical axis
            c. 2 degrees of freedom and a horizontal axis
            d. 2 degrees of freedom and a vertical axis

21   What are the advantages of an IRS compared to an INS?

2 Marks   a. Reduce spin-up time and a dither motor to prevent "lock-out".
            b. Reduce spin-up time and accuracy not adversely affect by "g"
            c. Increase accuracy and a dither motor to prevent "lock-out".
            d. Insensitively to "g" and reduced wander of the gyroscope.

22   What errors can the Air Data Computer correct for?

            1.   instrument error & ram rise
            2.   compressibility & density error
            3.   lag & density error
            4.   position & temperature error
            5.   temperature & instrument error
            6.   manoeuvre error & ram rise
            7.   manoeuvre & position errors

2 Marks   a. 2 & 4
            b. 1 & 6
            c. 3 & 7
            d. 3 & 5

23   Which of the following is the FMS normal operating condition in the cruise?

1 Mark   a. L NAV only
            b. V NAV only
            c. L NAV or V NAV
            d. L NAV and V NAV

24   Weather Radar returns can be displayed in which of the following EFIS Modes:

3 Marks   a. Plan   Exp ILS   Exp VOR
            b. Plan   Exp ILS   Map
            c. Map   Exp ILS   Exp VOR
            d. Map   ILS   VOR

25   What are the colours used on an EFIS display to show a tuned navigation aid and an
        airport?

2 Marks   a. green & white
            b. white & magenta
            c. green & cyan
            d. white & yellow

26   WXR display is on :

1 Mark   a. The captains CRT only
            b. The co-pilots CRT only
            c. A special screen
            d. On both the captains and co-pilots CRTs

27   Altitude select and altitude hold are examples of:

1 Mark   a. Inner loop functions in pitch
            b. Manometric functions from the ADC
            c. Interlocking functions
            d. Outer loop functions in roll

28   An autopilot delivers roll commands to the ailerons to achieve a bank angle:

1 Mark   a. proportional to TAS, but below a specified maximum
            b. set bank of 25 degrees
            c. set bank of 30 degrees
            d. proportional to the deviation from the desired heading, but not exceeding a
               specified maximum

29   At 200ft on an auto-land:

1 Mark   a. The LOC mode is engaged in the roll channel and the G/S mode is engaged in
               pitch.
            b. The LOC mode is engaged in the roll channel and the FLARE mode is
               engaged in the pitch channel
            c. The ROLL OUT mode is engaged in the Roll channel and the G/S mode is
               engaged in pitch.
            d. The auto-throttle is maintaining the speed and the pitch channel is maintaining
               the height.

30   During a CAT 1 ILS approach, height is indicated by:

1 Mark   a. GPS
            b. Radio Altimeter
            c. Marker
            d. Barometric

31   During an approach to autoland at 1500feet;

2 Marks   a. Off line channels are manually engaged, flare mode is armed
            b. Localiser is controlling the roll channel, off line channels are automatically
               engaged and flare mode is armed
            c. Localiser is controlling the roll channel, stabiliser is trimmed nose up and roll
               out is armed
            d. Provided both localiser and glideslope signals are valid LAND 3 will

32   During an autoland the caption LAND 2 is illuminated. The system is:

1 Mark   a. Fail active or fail operational
            b. Fail passive
            c. Approaching decision height
            d. Requiring a crew input

33   If only a single A/P is used to climb, cruise and approach; following a failure:

1 Mark   a. it is fail passive with redundancy
          b. it is fail operational and will not disconnect
          c. it is fail soft and will not disconnect
          d. it is fail safe and will disconnect

34   "LOC ARMED" lights up on the FMA part of the PFD, this means:

1 Mark   a. localiser beam captured
          b. localiser beam armed and awaiting capture
          c. localiser alarm is on
          d. a/c is on localiser centerline

35   What is the purpose of the auto-synchronisation system in an A/P:

          1.   Prevents snatching on disengagement
          2.   Prevents snatching on engagement
          3.   Cross feeds rudder and aileron inputs for co-ordination
          4.   May not allow the A/P to engage if unserviceable
          5.   Displays the control positions
          6.   Removes standing demands from the autopilot system prior to the CMD
                button being selected

1 Mark   a. 2,4&6
          b. 1,3&5
          c. 2,3&5
          d. 1,4&6

36   What type of autoland system would be required for the landing to continue
      following a single failure below alert height?

1 Mark   a. Fail soft
          b. Fail passive
          c. Fail operation or fail active
          d. Land 2 system

37   Which of the following apply to the a Yaw damper :

          1.   May aid the pilot in the event of asymmetric thrust after engine failure
          2.   Applies measured amounts of aileron to counter dutch roll
          3.   Increases lateral stability to stop dutch roll
          4.   Is required at high altitude
          5.   Can automatically help in turn co-ordination
          6.   May deflect the rudder to counteract the natural oscillating frequency of
                the aircraft.

1 Mark   a. 1, 4 & 6
          b. 2, 3 & 6
          c. 2, 3 & 4
          d. 1, 4 & 5

38   A stall warning system fitted to a large aircraft will always include:

1 Mark a. Various inputs including speed brake position, a warning module and a visual
           or aural warning
        b. Various inputs including landing gear micro switch, a warning module and an
           aural warning
        c. Various inputs including EGT, a warning module and an aural warning
        d. Stick shakers and/or stick push

39   TCAS 2 when fitted with mode C transponder may give:

1 Mark a. TA only.
        b. TA and RA in horizontal plane.
        c. TA and RA in vertical plane.
        d. RA only.

40   The Altitude Alert system alerts the pilot:

1 Mark a. At decision height
        b. At the selected altitude
        c. When reference altitude equals the selected altitude
        d. When deviating from the selected altitude

41   The GPWS uses inputs from;
1 Mark a. The radio altimeter, static pressure monitor, ILS receiver and the landing gear
           and flap position monitors
        b. The radio altimeter and the ILS receiver only
        c. The radio altimeter, ILS receiver, static pressure monitor, and the landing gear
           position monitor only
        d. The radio altimeter, static pressure monitor, landing gear position monitor,
           and the flap position monitor only

42   What are the components of a CVR

        1   Microphone
        2   Crash/Fire resistant construction
        3   Independent battery
        4   A Flight data recorder

2 Marks a. 1 & 2
        b. 1 & 4
        c. 1, 2, 3 & 4
        d. 1, 2 & 4

43   What corrective action is given by TCAS?

1 Mark a. Turn left or right.
        b. Climb or descend.
        c. Contact ATC
        d. Turn then climb or descend.

44   What input is there to TCAS 2?

1 Mark   a. Mode 'A' transponder which gives TA and RAs
          b. Mode 'C' transponder which co-ordinates avoidance manoeuvres
          c. Mode 'C' and 'S' transponders which co-ordinate avoidance manoeuvres
          d. Mode 'S' transponder which co-ordinates avoidance manoeuvres

45   When an intruder aircraft has no Altitude Reporting facility, i.e. Mode equipped
      with 'A' transponder only, TCAS can only give:

1 Mark   a. Corrective RA only
          b. TA followed by a Preventative RA
          c. TA only
          d. Preventative RA only

46   Which of the following are modes of the GPWS?

          1.   Excessive sink rate.
          2.   Altitude loss after T/O or go-around.
          3.   Excessive Glideslope deviation.
          4.   High climb rate.
          5.   Flaps in incorrect position.
          6.   High altitude descent.
          7.   Stall.

2 Marks   a. All 7
          b. 1, 2, 3, & 5
          c. 1, 2 & 3
          d. 1, 3, 5 & 7

47   A warning message on the EICAS system screen would be:
1 Mark   a. displayed in amber on the lower screen with associated caution lights and
             aural tones
          b. displayed in amber, normally on the upper screen with aural warnings .
          c. displayed in red, normally on the upper screen , and requiring immediate
             corrective action
          d. displayed in amber, normally on the upper screen, indented one space to the
             right.

48   An aircraft equipped with digital avionics includes an ECAM system.
      This centralised system, if a failure in one of the monitored systems is displayed,
      the crew must:

2 Marks   a. cancel the warning
          b. analyse initially the failure and only respond to a level 1 warning
          c. reset the warning display after noting the failure on the left screen
          d. apply the immediate actions as directed by the checklist on the left of the two
             screens

49   An aircraft has a compensated capacitance fuel contents gauging system and is refuelled so that the total fuel contents are 76000kg at a temperature of 18°C and an S.G. of 0.81. Whilst the aircraft is parked the temperature increases to 26°C and the S.G. becomes 0.80. The indicated fuel contents have:

1 Mark   a. increased by 10%
          b. remained the same
          c. increased by 5%
          d. decreased by 5%

50   EPR is the ratio of;

1 Mark   a. The compressor outlet pressure to the compressor inlet pressure
          b. Jet pipe pressure to compressor inlet pressure on a turbo-prop engine only
          c. Jet pipe pressure to the compressor inlet pressure on a gas turbine engine
          d. Jet pipe pressure to the compressor outlet pressure on a gas turbine engine

51   If one probe of a multi-sensor EGT system became disconnected, the reading would:

1 Mark   a. Increase by between 20°C to 30°C
          b. Decrease by between 20°C to 30°C
          c. Fall to zero
          d. Be largely unaffected

52   The principle of the fuel-monitoring device giving an indication of the total fuel burnt is:

1 Mark   a. multiplying flight time by fuel consumption
          b. capacitance variation of a capacitor
          c. difference of indication according to departure value
          d. integration of instantaneous flow

53   The red arc in the middle of the green band of a piston engine RPM indicator signifies:

1 Mark   a. Maximum RPM
          b. Minimum RPM
          c. RPM at which a greater level of vibration is encountered
          d. RPM that must never be exceeded in the cruise

54   Torque meters provide a reliable measure of power output from:

1 Mark   a. A turbo-jet engine
          b. A noise suppression unit
          c. A turbo-propeller engine
          d. An APU

55   Which of the following types of pressure gauge would be best suited to a high pressure input?

1 Mark   a. aneroid capsule
          b. bourdon tube
          c. bellows
          d. dynamic probe

ANSWERS TO SPECIMEN EXAMINATION PAPER

(w = weighting/marks allocated for the question)

1 .	C	w 1	35 .	A	w 1
2	A	w 1	36 .	C	w 1
3 .	B	w 1	37 .	A	w 1
4	A	w 1	38 .	B	w 1
5	C	w 1	39 .	C	w 1
6 .	B	w 1	40 .	D	w 1
7	A	w 1	41 .	A	w 1
8 .	A	w 1	42 .	A	w 2
9	C	w 1	43 .	B	w 1
10 .	A	w 1	44 .	D	w 1
11 .	C	w 1	45 .	C	w 1
12 .	B	w 2	46 .	B	w 2
13 .	C	w 1	47 .	C	w 1
14 .	C	w 1	48 .	D	w 2
15 .	A	w 1	49 .	B	w 1
16 .	D	w 2	50 .	C	w 1
17 .	D	w 1	51 .	D	w 1
18 .	C	w 1	52 .	D	w 1
19 .	A	w 1	53 .	C	w 1
20 .	A	w 1	54 .	C	w 1
21 .	B	w 2	55 .	B	w 1
22 .	A	w 2			
23 .	D	w 1			
24 .	C	w 3			
25 .	C	w 2			
26 .	D	w 1			
27 .	B	w 1			
28 .	D	w 1			
29 .	A	w 1			
30 .	B	w 1			
31 .	B	w 2			
32 .	B	w 1			
33 .	D	w 1			
34 .	B	w 1			